Lauren Groveman's Kitchen

NURTURING FOOD
FOR FAMILY & FRIENDS

ILLUSTRATIONS BY JUDITH REED
TECHNIQUE ILLUSTRATIONS BY JAN PIETROBONO

CHRONICLE BOOKS
SAN FRANCISCO

Book and cover design: Robin Weiss
Cover calligraphy by: Georgia Deaver

Library of Congress Cataloging-in-Publication Data:

Groveman, Lauren.
    Lauren Groveman's kitchen : nurturing food for family and
friends / illustrations by Judith Reed.
        p. cm.
    Includes bibliographical references and index.
    ISBN 0-8118-0609-X
    1. Cookery.   I. Title
TX652.G775   1994
641.5—dc20   94-13263
                                                         CIP

Printed in the United States of America.

Distributed in Canada by Raincoast Books,
112 East 3rd Ave., Vancouver, B.C. V5T 1C8

10 9 8 7 6 5 4 3 2 1

Chronicle Books
275 Fifth Street
San Francisco, CA 94103

DEDICATION

To my dearest children Benjamin, Julie and Jessica.

Take this book with you, my darlings, when you've grown into independent adults. Use it to comfort you when you're in need of nurturing. Let these pages fill your homes with the sights and scents of your childhood.

Benjamin . . .
On mornings when you're tired and find it hard to rise and shine, remember the aromas that greeted you in bed when you were little. Toasted slices of raisin bread swirled with cinnamon sugar, buttermilk pancakes, banana bread, English muffins and fresh bagels. Remember the chocolate chip cookies and the brownies with a peanut butter pocket. (Then get up and make them yourself . . . sweetheart.)

Julie . . .
When it's cold outside and you want to feel all cozy inside, assemble the dish that has always made you happy—spinach penne noodles bathed in a soothing cheese sauce embellished with bits of fresh broccoli. And never be embarrassed to order extra chopped onions and anchovies on your salad. Try to find the time to take your children blueberry picking in the heat of summer and then use those gorgeous berries to make all of your favorites—blueberry muffins, blueberry pancakes and preserves (and don't forget your sunscreen, bug repellent and a wide-brimmed hat).

Jessie . . .
Always have a supply of olives and capers on your pantry shelf and keep a jar of peeled garlic ready and waiting in your refrigerator. When you want to feel close to me and my love for you, prepare a platter of honey-roast chicken or the perfect roast chicken and then relive through your own sense memory, how happy these meals made you and your siblings.

It's my love for the three of you and your father that has fueled and sustained me through all these years of hard work. Thank you for sharing me with this book, for consistently encouraging me to express my creativity and for always being proud of me. I love you all.

ACKNOWLEDGMENTS

Writing a book requires an incredible amount of focus and dedication—not easy while you are also raising three young children. I could not have accomplished even half the work without the unyielding support from my husband, Jonathan Groveman. He not only nurtured our children, but me as well, and he did it in such a loving way that I was able to do my work with a full heart. Thank you, Jon, for being a truly special, caring and giving person. I will always be grateful to you for this, as for so many things. I love you.

I have been extremely fortunate to be represented by Heide Lange, my literary agent. Thank you, Heide, for being a dynamic agent, for trusting and believing in me and for enriching my life with your friendship.

In today's highly competitive market, it is not easy for a first-time author to find a publisher. For this, my deep heartfelt gratitude goes to Bill LeBlond, my editor at Chronicle Books. Thank you, Bill, for your courage to take a chance with someone new. You have made this entire experience a wonderful one and your friendship is of great value to me.

And it was my lucky day when Jacqueline Killeen was assigned to edit my manuscript. Jackie, you are not only an incredibly talented editor, but also a kind and sensitive person. You understood my difficulty in "parting with my darlings" (making cuts) and you always did so with the utmost respect and forethought. Thank you for imparting your acquired wisdom and clarity.

I want to thank Jerry Ruotolo, who epitomizes the word "friend." Jerry, your constant support has meant more to me than I can say. To Kathy Braddock, the sister that I never had, thank you for everything. I also want to thank my parents and two brothers for always loving me. To Sue McNeley, Kelly Anchrum, Chris Lansing, Ann Jenemann-Smith, and Mitch Wecop, thank you from the bottom of my heart for you generous support and faith in me.

I'd also like to thank all those who work at the Larchmont Meateria in Larchmont, New York, for their fine quality meat and poultry. A special acknowledgment goes to Alfred Gentil (my favorite butcher). Thank you, Al, for being so generous with your vast knowledge and so patient as a teacher. To my friends at the Apple Tree Market in Larchmont, New York, thanks, for having the cleanest, most beautiful vegetables in town. And I am forever grateful to the people who work at the Imperial Seafood Market in Mamaroneck, New York, for their dedication to quality and for their patience in guiding me as I split my first live lobster (I almost died).

Contents

INTRODUCTION

GOOD FOOD FOR
THE FAMILY TABLE

My passion is cooking. My joy is creating soothing, comforting food to nurture my family and friends. My mission is to teach others that making a meal is not drudgery, but a source of deep satisfaction—to spread the word that no one is too busy to cook; they simply haven't made it a priority.

Does this sound crazy coming from a "liberated" woman of the nineties? No, because I've come full circle.

Like so many of my generation, growing up in the sixties and seventies, I never smelled the aroma of baking cookies on my return from school and I never tasted freshly baked bread until I made it for my own children. My mother was—and still is—a creative, successful career woman who instilled in me a sense of self worth and encouraged me to excel professionally. She was a wonderful role model, but unfortunately she didn't know how to cook. My only childhood contact with the culinary arts came from religiously watching Julia Child on TV.

In those days, when so many women were burning their bras and fighting for professional equality, the family table for many Americans consisted of takeout pizza and TV dinners. I believe that this disregard for the concept of homemaking and the lack of shared family meals are responsible for many of society's current ailments.

Many of my contemporaries (male and female) and my students (of all ages) share this view, and they no longer view cooking and baking as a step back to a time when women felt unfulfilled and unappreciated. In this era of life-threatening conflicts, we all believe that the spiritual strength derived from the family table is needed more than ever. Although highly educated and professionally skilled, many of my generation are kitchen illiterate. They lack the knowledge—or think they're too busy in their chosen professions—to nurture their families and friends with a comforting meal at the end of the day.

But the technology of cooking and baking in this decade, in both food and appliances, has advanced to such a degree that no one can truly say that she—or he—is too busy to cook. Although I was trained in the classics at some fine cooking schools in New York, I have spent many years adapting these Old World techniques to today's technology.

So this is a cookbook for the nineties. My goal is to teach you, as I teach my students, how to cook comforting meals, mostly from scratch, while maintaining an active—even hectic—schedule. But first you must learn to think of cooking as fun, not work. Most busy people find time for a movie, a concert, a ball game, a set of tennis, or just a good book. Well, cooking is recreation, too, as creative as any art form or as challenging as any sport.

This book is meant to inspire you to take that time off for recreation and spend a few rewarding and fulfilling hours in your kitchen. I'll show you how to make a succulent stew or a soothing pot of soup that you can enjoy with your family and then freeze the remainder for those busy days ahead. I'll teach you how to prepare batters for cookies and muffins and doughs for crusty loaves of bread to be baked days later, if necessary, filling your house with wafts of that heavenly fresh-from-the-oven scent. Just like at that illusory grandma's house—except that you've been gone all day and the real-life grandma was probably too busy to cook.

But in this book, I've also included quick and easy recipes for those days when the fridge or freezer is bare and you actually were too busy to cook: fast and simple, but absolutely delectable salads, sautés and grills. And I'll instruct you on making homemade noodles, using an inexpensive hand-cranked pasta machine, along with complex make-ahead sauces and quick pasta dishes that can be thrown together in the time it takes to boil a pot of water.

Most of my recipes include Time Management Tips that explain in detail what can be done days or hours in advance to eliminate as much last-minute preparation as possible. The purpose of the family table is best served if the cook is relaxed, not harassed. And the "family," by the way, does not mean just relatives. Everyone who shares a meal at my table is regarded as my family.

Although I firmly believe that most foods taste better (and are better for you) when made from scratch, I'm not a food snob. I have discovered a number of commercial products that not only save time, but even enhance a dish. Many of my sauces, for example, are based upon the classic *mirepoix* of minced aromatic vegetables, yet my favorite "homemade" steak sauce is based on a bottle of store-bought ketchup! The trick is knowing which brands to buy.

I've discussed these bottled and canned goods in my introductory chapter on Kitchen Management. Here you will also find a compendium of equipment—tools, cookware and appliances—that will do the best job for you (so you can do more). No, I don't advocate always beating egg whites with a wire whisk in a copper bowl, when an electric mixer will work just fine. But I do advise you on the best equipment to do it either way. I adore my food processor for many jobs, but for others my blender works better. And I say "no thank you" to those so-called bread machines. They not only make an inferior loaf but rob the cook of one of the greatest joys in the kitchen—making yeast breads.

Scattered throughout my book are Tips from a Teacher on a variety of subjects from detailed instructions on cutting up a chicken or making a never-fail caramelized syrup to chopping an onion. (A friend says the latter tip is worth the price of the book!) These explain in depth various techniques for both the novice and the experienced cook who may be venturing into a new culinary arena, such as yeast breads. But in general, I have endeavored to include all the vital information in each recipe so you won't waste your time and money on a dish that turns into a disaster due to inadequate instructions. And I don't just tell you what to do and how to do it, but *why* certain reactions take place in the cooking process. I also warn you of potential pitfalls based upon many years of experience—not only with my students, but also as one who learned to cook as an adult, not at my mother's knee.

Glancing at my recipes, you may wonder why—in these fat-conscious days—I use a lot of butter and eggs. It's because they enormously enhance the flavor and texture of the dish. But wherever appropriate, I also provide low-fat "skinny" variations. Let your conscience be your guide and remember that moderation is the key to good health. Limiting the fat and cholesterol in your daily diet is important, but (barring a serious medical problem) if you indulge in a favorite "full" food at one meal, balance your meals with lighter foods for the rest of the day accordingly. Skip the cream in your morning coffee and put a dab of sweet créme fraîche on your dessert.

Finally, please don't think you have to be a working wife and mother to appreciate this book. I am addressing busy men and women of all ages and all lifestyles—both novice and experienced cooks—who care to enrich their own lives and to nurture their loved ones with good food at a convivial table for their friends and family.

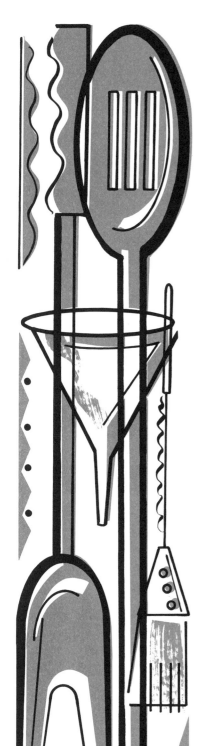

KITCHEN MANAGEMENT

Equipment, Staples and Jargon

Without the proper tools and ingredients, even the best of cooks can falter. And knowing how to use and care for food and equipment properly is just as important as knowing what to buy and where to find it. In this foundation chapter, I will help the novice cook to set up a kitchen and I will expose the more seasoned cook to the tools and ingredients needed to delve into unfamiliar culinary territory, along with notes on new products. Most of the recipes in this book have a "special equipment" list. Whenever an unfamiliar implement is requested, please refer to the following equipment section before making a purchase.

This chapter also includes a staples section, to provide more information and tips about the most commonly called-for ingredients. I have also included (when deemed appropriate) specific brand names of products that have satisfied my family, friends and students over the years. In addition, a kitchen jargon section explains culinary terminology as well as various procedures that are commonly referred to in my recipes. Finally, since the best meal in the world will taste even better in beautiful surroundings, I've included a section on "Tips for the Table" to help you entertain with grace and ease.

KITCHEN EQUIPMENT

On the following pages I've listed the basic essentials to accomplish a multitude of tasks for various cuisines, plus many implements that are so helpful, I've come to regard them as essentials in my kitchen. You'll also find some tools and cookware that are nice to have, but not necessary—I've refrained from mentioning useless gadgets that just take up space in your cabinets. Then for each recipe, I've included a list of special equipment (aside from the bare basics) that is either essential to that recipe or gets the job done more efficiently. The following listings are arranged under the headings of kitchen tools, knives, stovetop and oven cookware for general purposes and equipment primarily for baking. There is also a section on small hand or electric appliances.

Kitchen Tools

From apple corers to whisks, here are all the tools to make cooking as fun, easy and efficient as possible. Unless otherwise mentioned, I recommend stainless steel for its durability and resistance to rust. Those tools that I consider essential and use most often in my recipes are marked with an asterisk. All of these items should be available in your local hardware store for a modest price. If not, check the housewares section of a department store or specialty kitchen shop. Also see Mail Order Sources.

Apple corer: Although a melon scoop can be used to remove seeds from halved fruit, the only way to remove the core without cutting the fruit in pieces is to use a corer. I prefer the larger corer that comes as one long cylinder with a circular blade, which is particularly suited to larger baking apples, pineapple or citrus fruit.

Bean frencher: Slices mature green beans lengthwise into thin strips. (This takes time and patience.)

Bowls (glass): Although I prefer stainless steel for its durability, glass is the perfect material to use to reheat foods in the microwave and then serve straight from the oven.

Bowls (stainless steel): These lightweight, heatproof, nonreactive, nested bowls are invaluable to any kitchen for mixing, storage and even heating. They come in a variety of sizes and I recommend having at least one of each size.

Bowl (unlined copper): For beating egg whites by hand. (Some electric mixers like KitchenAid have a copper insert bowl, which can be purchased separately.)

Brushes (feather): Soft feather brushes are used before baking to apply glaze gently to very delicate pastries that might be pierced or scratched by stiffer bristles. Also used for applying a fruit glaze to a tart before serving.

*Brushes (pastry): An essential tool for basting meat, poultry and fish with marinades, as well as for applying an egg glaze to yeast breads or a fruit glaze to sweet tarts. Buy two brushes and tag one handle for sweet and the other for savory purposes with a piece of adhesive tape. Wash bristles meticulously with warm soapy water and rinse thoroughly in several changes of water to remove any trace of soap.

TIPS
FROM A TEACHER

Protecting Your Hands

Your most valuable kitchen tool is your hands. Take care to protect them from knives, heat and irritants—even those contained within foods like fiery hot chili peppers. Following are some safeguards.

Oven mitts: You should own two pairs in mint condition. Purchase mitts preferably made from heavy terry cloth that reach up to your elbows for maximum protection to your arms. (Gloves that are very stiff make it hard to manipulate your fingers to gain maximum control.) Don't quibble with price; cheaply made mitts won't last long and you'll end up spending more money by constantly having to replace them. Read the manufacturer's instructions before washing so you can maintain them in good condition. *Never* use oven mitts when they are even slightly wet; the dampness will allow heat to penetrate the glove immediately. And frequently inspect the gloves for small holes, especially in the spot where the thumb meets the body of the mitt.

Rubber covers for heatproof handles: If you've ever touched one when hot, you know what I mean.

Rubber gloves: Buy a thick pair to help keep your hands soft and the thin disposable variety (available in most pharmacies) for working with hot chili peppers and the like. And don't forget to keep a jar of hand lotion next to your kitchen sink. My favorite product — and I think I've tried them all— is the new Vaseline Petroleum Jelly Cream by Chesebrough-Ponds (available in many supermarkets).

Brushes (vegetable): You need a stiff brush (to scrub potatoes, carrots and the like) and a small soft brush with plastic bristles (frequently made in the shapes of fruits and vegetables) to scrub debris out of the thin crevices on young and delicate root vegetables. A soft brush is also a quick and efficient way to scrub scraps of dough off your hands after kneading a yeast dough.

Bulb baster: A long tube, topped with a hollow rubber bulb to suck up hot drippings for basting a roast during cooking. Preferably, the tube should be stainless steel or tempered glass.

Can opener: I prefer the hand-held openers to the electric ones, since some electric machines can't hold heavy cans. I suggest owning two hand-operated openers, since you never know when a can opener will decide not to work right in the middle of a cooking procedure.

Can opener (pointed/bottle-cap opener): The pointed end is used to punch two triangular openings on the top of a can for easy pouring. The other side is used to bend off metal bottle caps.

Carving board: Purchase a large wooden board with a groove or "valley" that goes all around the edge to catch the juice from your roast as you carve.

Caviar spoon: These smooth wood or mother-of-pearl spoons with a flat bowl are specifically made to scoop caviar without leaving the metallic taste left by a metal spoon.

Colander: Large, sturdy and preferably stainless steel. To rinse large amounts of fruits, vegetables and shellfish as well as to strain large amounts of heavy solids from liquid after cooking.

Comb (decorating): This triangular tool (usually in stainless steel or plastic) with three degrees of a zigzag edge, is used to comb decoratively the top of soft mixtures, such as frostings, mashed potatoes, thick dips and savory spreads. Use a serrated knife as a substitute.

Citrus juicer: I prefer a wooden reamer. After each use, clean out the deep crevices on a reamer thoroughly by hand and let dry before storing.

Corkscrew: Strong and preferably with wing handles.

Fork (long two-pronged): Used for carving, this is also called a "roast fork" and is available in three different degrees of "curve." The straightest ones are the most desirable for carving and those with the most severe curve are preferred for moving large roasts from the roasting rack to the carving surface. The third and most versatile is only slightly curved and is the one I suggest for a "bare essentials" list since it can be used for all of the above purposes as well as for stirring pasta strands during cooking.

Fork (wide blending or mashing): A large serving fork can be substituted. This wide fork with just four large prongs is used to mash bananas, avocados or gently combine a meatloaf mixture. It also helps to combine wet and dry ingredients with few strokes, reducing the risk of toughening a delicate mixture (especially helpful with biscuit dough and muffin batter).

Fruit wedge cutter: This cuts apples or pears into eight uniform wedges while removing the central core. Make sure it's sturdy. This tool gets a lot of action in a home with young children and it's perfect for making apple pies and applesauce.

*Funnels: One standard-size funnel, preferably heatproof, is essential. A wide-mouth funnel is also very helpful when transferring dry and thick liquid mixtures to jars before storing foods.

Garlic press: For pulverizing peeled garlic cloves. The self-cleaning type has a small pronged disk to push out any remaining garlic left from the holes. Although many cooks frown on using a garlic press, I find it particularly efficient to make a base for a garlic paste to season meat before roasting.

*Grater (hand-held four-sided): For grating citrus zest, shredding or slicing cheese, potatoes and the like.

Grater (nutmeg): Once you smell and taste freshly grated nutmeg, you'll think this tool should be on the "essentials" list.

Ice cream scoops: Buy several sizes of round scoops. Not only do these make perfectly shaped balls of ice cream, but they can be used to shape dumpling batter (like matzo balls) or to fill a stuffed tomato with a salad. I highly recommend "cookie scoopers" to produce cookies of uniform size. Oval scoopers are also available.

*Ladles (stainless steel): Buy one small ladle for gravy and sauces and one standard-sized ladle for soups. A 2-cup ladle is also very handy for ladling large amounts of food, but not essential.

*Measuring cups (dry): One set with capacities of ⅛, ¼, ⅓, ½, 1 and 2 cups. These spoutless cups are essential to obtaining an accurate dry measurement (see page 421).

*Measuring cups (liquid): With capacities of 1, 2 and 4 cups. Although these are available in plastic, glass is preferable for withstanding hot liquids.

Also, after the plastic ones have been washed several times, the measurement lines seem to disappear.

*Measuring spoons: Although these sets come nested and attached by a piece of wire, they usually come apart after time and easily can be misplaced. I suggest having two sets for this reason. And I strongly recommend stainless steel instead of plastic.

Melon ball scoop: This tool is ideal for making uniform rounds of fruit and also various types of hors d'oeuvres. Choose one with two scoops of different sizes, on opposite ends of the stem.

Microwave turntable: If you use a microwave, this wind-up turntable will turn a dish of food continually during cooking. It is especially helpful for defrosting frozen foods.

Mortar and pestle: Commonly made of marble, used to grind seeds and spices to a powder or to make pesto by hand. The Japanese version of a mortar, called a *suribachi,* comes in several sizes made out of ceramic; it's available at Japanese import stores. The Mexican version, made out of rough stone, is called a *molcajete* and is traditionally used to grind chilies and make guacamole.

*Nutcracker: You need one, but consider buying extras for guests to use for cracking Dungeness crab or lobsters.

*Peeler (vegetable): Use the old-fashioned swivel-blade peeler. When well made, this tool also eliminates the need for a zester, to remove thin outer strips of citrus rind.

*Peppermill: Quality and strength is vital here. The Peppermate peppermill (by East Hampton Industries) is *the best* peppermill, and I can't recommend it highly enough! Made of heavy-duty plastic, it has a see-through plastic cup underneath the grinding element to catch the freshly ground pepper for easy measuring. Although it's not as pretty to look at as the beautifully curved and sculptured wooden ones (which often don't work properly), you can easily grind some pepper before being seated at the table and pass it in a small salt-cellar with a tiny spoon. And just for the record, I've used my Peppermate for the past fifteen years, and it's still grinding strong! Also, consider buying a second grinder for white peppercorns.

Pitter: Used to remove pits from cherries and olives.

*Potato Masher: The best potato masher is the old-fashioned type with a

Q AND A

Q. I don't have enough room for all my equipment—and I hate the clanging and banging sound of utensils when searching for a tool at the bottom of the drawer. Any tips?

A. If you have any bare wall space in your kitchen or on the back-splash between your cupboards and counter or even in the laundry room, line the walls with peg board or stainless steel grids. Using heavy-duty hooks, hang as many saucepans, skillets, whisks, large ladles and strainers as possible on the wall. You won't believe how quiet your kitchen will become!

flat perforated disc that sits at the end of a long sturdy handle. The newer version has a squiggled bottom and is a suitable substitute.

Scale: Since many cookbooks have recipes that call for a bulk measurement of meat or vegetables after trimming or flour after sifting, a kitchen scale will alleviate any guesswork when measuring. The most useful scale comes with a large bowl and registers between six and ten pounds.

Skewers: Should be strong, unbendable and stainless steel. Used to roast peppers over an open flame or to grill marinated cubes of meat, fish, poultry and vegetables.

Skimmers: This large, round and usually perforated spoonlike disc sits at the end of a long thin handle and is essential for skimming the foam off stock as it simmers. A fine-mesh skimmer is a nonessential but handy tool for skimming fat from simmering stock as well as clarifying butter.

Spatter shields: The spattering that occurs when searing chicken or meat pieces in hot oil can be quite dangerous. I suggest owning two of these circular wire mesh screens for use in a pot that's larger than the shield (overlap them so they completely cover the top of the pot while browning). For protection while turning meat, rotate the handle so the side of the screen that's farthest from you tilts up. Stick your turning spatula or tongs into the pot from behind. And if the handle of the screen is plastic, make sure it doesn't touch the rim of the pot or it will melt.

Spatulas (metal): Thin stainless steel spatulas for turning food should be perforated to allow fat to drip through when removing fried or sautéed food from a skillet. Two spatulas are necessary to turn safely large pieces of food when panfrying—one underneath the food and the other on top. If you have a nonstick skillet, a nonabrasive turning spatula is essential, since the sharp edges of a stainless steel spatula can easily scratch and cut into the finish of some nonstick pans (even if they say it won't happen, it does). Nice but not necessary is an extra-long perforated spatula for turning large fish fillets or butterflied trout when panfrying to keep the fish from breaking apart.

Spatulas (rubber): I recommend buying two, preferably with wooden handles since the plastic handles break easily when folding stiff mixtures. Spatulas with heatproof rubber are wonderful to fold hot mixtures as well as to transfer hot food from a pot to a serving bowl. Additionally, the new spoon-shaped spatulas (while not heat resistant) are helpful to scoop and transfer large amounts of ingredients when assembling a dish.

Spatula (wooden): The flat, nonabrasive edge on this tool makes it perfect for scraping up caramelized bits of meat or vegetables when deglazing a skillet as well as for helping to force the pulp out of a fine-mesh sieve when straining puréed berries. Wash by hand as you would a wooden spoon.

*Spoons (metal): You should have at least two large stainless steel spoons: a solid one for stirring and transfering ingredients and a slotted spoon for transfering solids out of pans containing liquids.

*Spoons (wooden): Since wood is warm in the hand and nonabrasive to the vast variety of interiors found in today's pots and pans, these are invaluable and essential tools in the kitchen. But since wood is also porous, it retains the scent of flavors from aromatic vegetables, herbs and spices. Thus, it's not recommended to use the same spoon (even after cleaning) for both sweet and savory mixtures. Purchase four spoons of varying lengths and save two for sweet mixtures and two for savory. (Identify which is which with white adhesive tape on the handles.) Make sure you have at least one spoon with an extra-long handle to stir deep liquid mixtures like soup and stock. Wash wooden spoons by hand as they will splinter after several cycles in the dishwasher.

*Storage containers: High on my list of essentials are heavy-duty freezer containers of various sizes with tight-fitting lids. You should also have an assortment of large and small airtight tins for storing at room temperature certain cookies and other baked goods. Also handy for tea bags, clipped coupons, receipts and so forth.

*Strainers (or sieves): Three types are essential: a small wire strainer to strain egg glaze or fruit glaze before applying it to breads and certain pastries as well as to strain fresh citrus juice before measuring; a large fine-mesh strainer to strain seeds out of fruit purées as well as to clarify homemade stock; and a large triple-mesh strainer with a sturdy handle to sift dry mixtures as well as to strain solids from liquids.

Strawberry huller: This small inexpensive tool resembles an oversized tweezer. It is used to remove the white, firm and tasteless hull (core) from a fresh strawberry. Some are flimsier than others; only purchase one that's made of strong stainless steel.

Sugar shaker: I recommend a small aluminum or stainless steel shaker with a lid that has a wire mesh insert instead of holes. This gives a very delicate application of confectioner's sugar on pastries just before serving. If unavailable, use a triple-mesh wire sieve.

Thermometer (deep-fat): This is essential to certain cooking procedures (making candy and some syrups as well as deep-frying) and should be cared for properly in order to keep it in reliable working order. Make sure that you don't store this thermometer where things can clang around on top of the delicate glass stem. It's best to store it alone on a shelf, in an "out of traffic" cupboard wrapped in a cushioned type of paper towel.

Thermometer (for meat, instant): Although some cooks swear by this tool, the thought of continually poking holes in my roast during cooking to check the internal temperature really bothers me. I never do it because when you remove the stem of the thermometer, valuable flavor-packed juices pour out and ultimately the doneness of the roast is inconsistent. However, this thermometer is helpful to gauge quickly the temperature of stuffing that's baking inside poultry since it must reach 160°F before being consumed. Purchase one with a skinny stem and a large dial that registers from 100°F to 200°F.

*Thermometer (for meat, not instant): Make sure your meat thermometer has a large dial and registers as low as 120°F. Many thermometers start to register at 140°F, which is far too late for timing rare, medium-rare and even medium roast beef since the roast continues to cook after being removed from the oven. Purchase a thermometer that can withstand long exposure to heat. To use, insert the thermometer deeply into the thickest part of the meat without allowing the stem to touch bone. For rare beef, remove your roast just as the temperature is approaching 120°F; for medium rare, between 120°F and 125°F; and for medium, 125°F. Leave the thermometer in place and tent the roast loosely with aluminum foil for 15 to 20 minutes so the internal temperature can rise sufficiently and the juices can centralize before carving.

*Thermometer (oven): It's best to keep an eye on your oven temperature since ovens tend to become either overly hot or too slow over time. But for best results when cooking and baking, it's not wise to compensate for an off oven by continually raising or lowering the temperature. As soon as you notice a problem, call a repair service and have the thermostat adjusted.

*Timers: It's best to own two timers for occasions when you are timing more than one dish at the same time—and make sure they both work!

Tomato shark: Relatively new, this tool is used to scoop out the stem end of a tomato. It has a thin short stainless steel handle and a round, concave bowl with spiked tips.

Tongs (with and without teeth): Tongs without teeth are used to serve asparagus and those with teeth are used to grab and serve hot pasta. Both can be used to remove freshly cooked ears of corn from boiling water and to turn certain foods while shallow panfrying.

Trussing needle: This long needle with a large hole is used to sew up the cavity of a turkey. Regardless of whether or not I stuff my turkey, I usually truss the bird to maintain the best appearance through roasting; trussing also makes it easier to turn the bird during roasting.

Whisk (all-purpose): Although whisks come in many sizes to accomplish different procedures, the basic all-purpose whisk (called a "sauce whisk") measures 8 to 14 inches in length. It's the perfect whisk to combine and lighten dry mixtures as well as to make simple custards and complex sauces. The following nonessential whisks will help you accomplish more specific cooking procedures.

Whisk (balloon whip): Primarily used to whip egg whites or heavy cream manually, this whisk forms an oversized bulb shape at the top allowing each stroke to incorporate more air into a given mixture.

Whisk (batter): A thin piece of coil, wound into an irregular circular shape, sits at the end of a long tapered wooden handle. This silly-looking stirring device does allow you to mix delicate mixtures more thoroughly without increasing the risk of toughening your batter.

Knives and Other Cutlery

Always purchase the best quality knives that you can afford and store them properly encased in a wooden block to protect the blades—and your fingers. It's best to purchase only a few all-purpose blades instead of buying an entire set of knives of a lesser quality, which ultimately will need far more mainte-nance and won't last as long as the better made ones. Generally, the German and French are the most renowned for producing top quality knives with blades that are meticulously Forged out of long, thick pieces of high carbon stainless steel. This painstaking process, which takes numerous steps to accomplish, is blatantly reflected in the knife's inflated price. But without good knives, basic cooking chores take much longer to accomplish, and using a dull or poorly made knife is one of the largest causes of accidents in the kitchen.

Before buying a knife, lift it and caress the handle. It's important to be comfortable with the weight of it. The knife should feel "weighty" but not heavy and clumsy. The handle should feel smooth with the rivets (visible bolts) flush with the surface. Avoid knives with a space between the handle and the blade since it's a perfect spot for food to lodge and get stuck while chopping.

If you do opt for a set of knives, however, I recommend those made by Wusthof-Trident, Inc., the offshoot of a well-respected German company that manufacturers fine, dependable knives. They also have just come out with a new line of knives (with reverse serrations) specifically designed for left-handed people. But whether you buy a set or individual knives, you should have one of each of the following asterisked knives or accessories.

Wooden block to store knives safely.

Long steel rod or other good quality device for sharpening.

8- to 10-inch chef's knife: The most versatile knife of all, this is used for general cutting and chopping and is essential to even a barely stocked kitchen. If you have a large family or frequently cook big and freeze, I suggest the longer knife since it chops larger amounts more efficiently.

4-inch paring knife: Light and basic, this knife is used for many kitchen jobs, such as cutting, trimming, slicing and peeling.

2-inch "clip point" paring knife: This small knife, with an angular tip and a very sharp point enables you to have close control when trimming vegetables, when removing hard-to-reach pockets of fat from meat and when picking out any blemishes from fruit.

8- to 10-inch serrated knife: This long knife with a ragged edge, most commonly called a "bread knife," should also be used to slice tomatoes, which will dull the blade of a chef's knife when done repeatedly.

10-inch carving knife: This long thin blade is perfect to slice roasts with a single stroke. Although carving knives come shorter for other cutting chores, the longer one is more practical for the basic kitchen.

4- to 6-inch boning knife: This thin sharp knife comes either with a rigid or flexible blade and is the best knife for separating flesh from bone on poultry, meat, pork or fish. When choosing, select the more versatile knife with the rigid blade.

Sharp kitchen shears: It's preferable to purchase a strong pair of kitchen

The Cutting-Surface Controversy: Wood or Plastic?

For many years it's been said that cutting raw meat or poultry (which could harbor parasites) on wood (which is a porous material) could be potentially dangerous to one's health. The fear has always been that these parasites would become absorbed into the wood beneath the surface where even vigorous washing couldn't reach; they would then multiply and spread into other cut foods that, when eaten raw, might cause food poisoning. So, plastic (supposedly nonporous) cutting surfaces became very popular.

To the surprise of many, however, recent studies have shown that wood is preferable to plastic for cutting both pork and poultry. It's now believed that the atmosphere within wood is not favorable for bacteria to multiply. But plastic (when cut into with a sharp blade) is said to become a perfect breeding ground for the spread of such bacteria. A researcher from the Centers for Disease Control and Prevention (in Atlanta) advised me to use wood for a cutting surface but to keep a homemade cleaning solution available to clean the surface thoroughly after each use. The solution should be made from 1 part chlorine (liquid bleach) to 10 parts water. Keep this in a container, such as an empty bleach bottle, and each time you cut meat or poultry on your wooden surface, rinse thoroughly and then wash the board down with this solution. Afterwards, rinse thoroughly with plain water, and then rub a cut lemon over the surface. Always dry the board well. Store this solution away from children and pets.

But there's still a lot to be said in favor of plastic boards. Since wood is porous, it does retain odors from aromatic vegetables and herbs. Boards made of either semirigid polyethylene or clear acrylic plastic are great for chopping aromatics. Boards with small rubber feet are particularly helpful to keep the board stationary when chopping vegetables. If your board has no feet, place a dampened cloth underneath the cutting board to help secure its position. These boards are dishwasher safe.

scissors made by a reputable knife company. This is an essential tool to accomplish many basic kitchen chores and, when well made, eliminates the need for poultry shears.

Clam knife: Not essential—unless you are opening clams.

Meat cleaver: Not essential but useful to cut through stubborn spots when separating the ribs on a roast or to hack up large beef bones for stock.

Meat mallet: A heavy flat 2- to 3-inch disc with a short handle extending upward. Used to flatten butterflied chicken breasts and lean cuts of meat such as lamb and veal

Meat tenderizer: A wooden hammerlike tool used to hit a tough cut of thinly sliced raw meat in order to break down any connective tissue and render it more tender.

Stovetop and Oven Cookware

I truly empathize with the person who enters the housewares section of any up-to-date department store with the goal of outfitting a kitchen with the right pots and pans. There are *so many* to choose from! Please, don't buy a "set" just because they look great or have an attractive price tag. It's better to collect only a few wonderful pieces than to have loads of something that you won't ever use.

When selecting cookware, you should know that certain materials definitely lend themselves better to specific cooking procedures. Although copper is thought of as the crème de la crème of cookware because of its superior heat-conduction qualities, copper cookware is also delicate, extraordinarily expensive and hard to maintain. For these reasons I don't recommend purchasing copper pots in quantity. However, if possible, I do suggest buying one 2½-quart copper saucepan with a tight-fitting lid, just so you can experience its unique character. I've chosen this size because it's one of the most frequently used pots in most kitchens.

But for durability, ability to conduct heat evenly, price and especially versatility, I recommend that most of your pots and pans be made from stainless steel with a thick bottom layer of copper and/or aluminum. This combination of materials gives you the best of all worlds: the heat-conduction ability of copper and aluminum and the nonreactive surface of stainless steel. Aluminum, unlined copper and cast iron by themselves react poorly with acidic ingredients (such as tomatoes, citrus juice, wine and vinegar) by imparting a metallic taste and an off color, thus it is extremely important to use a nonreactive pan when cooking acidic foods. The stainless cookware that I prefer for its ability to distribute heat efficiently (as well as for its effortless maintenance) is made by All-Clad Metalcrafters, Inc. They also have a great (and durable) line of nonstick cookware. Enamel-coated cast iron (although heavy) is a wonderful choice when making delicate sauces because the bottom is so heavy that the mixture has less chance of scorching and the enamel coating is nonreactive.

In the following list, I have asterisked those items that I feel are essential to successful cooking with minimal frustration. I have also listed some of my favorite extras that I use in my recipes. You'll find more about specialized cookware for baking in the following section.

Baking dishes (oven-to-table): Made from heatproof glass, ceramic or porcelain in assorted sizes, with and without heatproof covers. A 2½-quart dish with cover and a shallow 9x13-inch uncovered glass roasting pan (Pyrex) are very useful sizes. The latter is particularly good for making one-dish meals like lasagna.

Baking sheets (cookie sheets or half-sheet pans): For all-purpose use, you should have two shallow heavy metal sheets with one-inch sides and as wide and long as your oven can accommodate. (In most double ovens, one oven is larger than the other so purchase accordingly.) These pans are sometimes called cookie sheets but I don't use them to bake cookies, because their sides shield the cookies from full heat during baking. (See the following section on baking.) Nevertheless, these baking sheets (preferably made from heavy aluminum) are indispensable in even the most basic kitchen. Those sheets made from black steel are perfect for baking crusty sheet breads on hot quarry tiles, but I don't recommend them for everyday use. Also their darker color makes them extra heat retentive and therefore not suitable for all cooking or baking purposes. (See following section on baking.)

Blanching pot (with built-in strainer): See stockpot.

Broiler pan: Purchase a two-part pan with a shallow rectangular bottom and a top covered with open slots to enable fat to drain away from meat being broiled.

Butter pot with spout: A small saucepan, just right for melting butter for basting, greasing pans and so forth.

Double boiler: Preferably heatproof glass to enable you to view the behavior of the water beneath the delicate mixture in the upper pan.

Dutch oven with a tight-fitting lid: I recommend the 10- or 12-quart size for making large batches of braised dishes like osso buco where the meat should lay flat to maintain its shape through cooking. Another option is a 6- or 8-quart Dutch oven. But since most braised foods are so freezer friendly, I suggest owning the larger pot.

Fish poacher: These are 18 to 24 inches long, but the shorter one is better suited for stovetops in most homes.

Griddle: Choose a nonstick stovetop model for making pancakes and cooking English muffins, fresh tortillas and so forth. (Owning two is a substantial time-saver when making a large batch of pancakes on weekend mornings.)

Grill: For indoor grilling, there are cast iron, stovetop grills; Le Crueset makes a very efficient and durable product. But be forewarned that proper ventilation is imperative when grilling indoors (see page 224).

TIPS
FROM A TEACHER

Making the Most of Your Stove

If you're in a position to choose your heating elements, the decision is simple. Choose a gas stovetop and an electric oven. The reasons are just as simple. When cooking on a gas stove, you have total control of the size of your flame and thus, the amount of heat generated to the food being cooked. Conversely, electric heat usually takes a number of minutes to go from high to low or vice versa.

Although most of us aren't able to redesign our kitchens, there is one way to get more control over an electric range. When cooking a mixture that's heat sensitive (like egg-based mixtures), heat two adjacent burners to two different heat settings (low and medium) so that you can quickly rotate the pot from one burner to the other (as well as occasionally removing the pot entirely from the heat source).

Electric wall ovens are superior for their ability to maintain consistently the desired temperature until you manually change it. Gas ovens are known to fluctuate frequently up and down to maintain the correct temperature. Also, many gas ovens are lower to the floor, making it more difficult and dangerous to lift in and out heavy roasts and hot Dutch ovens. To help assure that your oven is consistently maintaining an accurate temperature while cooking, don't open the door unnecessarily and use a reliable oven thermometer during baking or roasting. One good feature, however, of an

Omelet pan: A small 6-inch nonstick pan with sloping sides is perfect for making an individual omelet using 2 extra-large eggs. These pans are readily available in many supermarkets.

Potato "bird's nest" maker: To make individual fried-potato baskets for housing another vegetable (like green peas) or perhaps your favorite dip.

Ramekins: Small individual baking cups with a ¾ cup capacity, made out of heatproof ceramic or glass.

**Roasting pan:* Rectangular uncovered pan usually 2 to 4 inches deep and available in a variety of sizes. Purchase a heavy stainless steel pan for its durability and nonreactive qualities, preferably with a layer of aluminum on the bottom underside for best heat conduction. I suggest owning at least one that is as large as your oven rack will accommodate. These pans are used to roast large heavy cuts of beef, pork or turkey and to make gravy over direct heat after roasting. They may also be used for a hot-water bath when baking delicate egg-based mixtures.

---

older type of gas oven is that the cooking space is generally larger than the newer wall ovens.

Convection ovens are fabulous and are available in countertop models that simply plug in to a regular wall outlet. Hot air is blown at the food from all directions, producing a roast with a browner, crisper exterior while keeping the interior tender and juicy. Convection ovens also cook in one-third less time than conventional ovens. These countertop models can comfortably accommodate a 16-pound turkey and some models also double as a microwave eliminating the need for two separate appliances. Although professional convection ovens are wonderful for baking, I don't bake bread or cookies in the countertop version since they tend to produce baked goods with both inconsistent color and texture. But, if you have the space, having this extra oven is a true comfort when entertaining and you find yourself searching for a way to bake just one more casserole.

A microwave oven (whether countertop or incorporated into a conventional oven) is a lifesaver when a frozen block of stew awaits you after a long work day. Other than thawing, the major benefit of a microwave is to reheat foods delicately without recooking them. (See page 288 for instructions to defrost and reheat prepared foods in a microwave.)

Roasting rack: Raises meat or poultry off the bottom of a roasting pan to allow for total heat exposure during roasting. If using a large roasting pan, be sure your rack is strong enough to support large cuts of meat or poultry.

Saucepans: For a basic kitchen, I recommend three stainless steel saucepans with a layer of aluminum or copper on the bottom underside for best heat conduction. You should purchase 1-quart, 2½-quart and 4-quart sizes, all with tight-fitting lids.

Saucepan (2-quart heavy-bottomed enamel-coated cast iron saucepan): Preferably with a spout. Le Crueset makes the perfect pot for making delicate custards or caramel syrup and enabling you to pour hot liquids into an electric mixer without spilling. This nonreactive pan not only has a heavy bottom for even heat distribution, but because of its light-colored interior, you will be much less likely to burn sugar when making a caramel syrup due to misjudging the stage of caramelization. Take care not to use abrasive tools or the enamel will chip. Also, don't overheat this type of pan while empty; doing so can cause the interior to crack.

Skillets and sauté pans: These terms are really interchangeable, although the shape is somewhat different. (Technically sauté pans have straight sides and can be deeper than skillets which have sloped sides.) I have used only the term "skillet" in my recipes, but have specified when a "deep-sided" pan is preferable. In a basic kitchen, start with a 12- to 14-inch deep-sided nonreactive skillet with lid, a 10- to 12-inch nonstick skillet and an 8- to 10-inch sauté pan. And because of the unique results from cooking with properly seasoned cast iron, I highly suggest owning a 10½-inch cast iron skillet (see page 29 for more information).

Soufflé dishes: With 4-cup and 8- or 9-cup capacities, these round, straight-sided bowls make excellent oven-to-table serving dishes as well as baking dishes.

Stockpot (8-quart preferably with built-in strainer): Called a blanching pot or spaghetti pot, this is ideal for blanching successive batches of vegetables without draining the water or for easily draining hot pasta. This is my favorite pot and I use it every day. Whether or not you purchase one with the strainer, you'll need a pot with this capacity. Stockpots are tall rather than wide to inhibit excess evaporation during long exposure to gentle heat when making stock. If you have a large family or like to cook big and freeze, owning a 16-quart stockpot is very useful (also available with a built-in strainer).

Cast iron cookware is great for some jobs and not at all good for others. Pure cast iron is the wrong material for cooking liquids since the surface is flavor retentive and will pass along the flavors from previously cooked mixtures. Cast iron is also a reactive material and can't be used with acidic foods (like vinegar or wine) since it will impart both a metallic taste and an "off" color to the mixture. And if you should rinse cast iron and not dry it meticulously, it will surely rust. However, cast iron is proclaimed superior for frying because of its ability to endure and retain high temperatures for long periods of time (with no negative side affects). Cast iron also distributes heat extremely efficiently and evenly and produces food with a crisper, more golden exterior. And if seasoned and cared for properly, the interior will develop a blackish non-stick finish that will last from generation to generation.

To season your cast iron skillet:
Before using skillet for the first time, wipe the entire surface (inside, outside, bottom and handle) generously with a flavorless vegetable oil or mild peanut oil. (The oil must be able to withstand high temperatures without smoking.) Place skillet into a preheated 375°F oven and "bake the surface" for 1 hour. Turn off heat and leave pan in oven for an additional hour. Remove skillet and use a paper towel to remove any excess oil, allowing only a thin layer to remain. Your pan is now seasoned and ready to use.

To clean your cast iron skillet:
After each use, don't wash your skillet, just give the interior a thorough wiping. If any pieces of food stick to the pan, sprinkle the surface with coarse (kosher) salt and use a clean kitchen towel to rub away the food. Once clean, apply another thin layer of oil (again, to the entire surface) and wipe off any excess. Occasionally, give the pan an additional "greased baking" at 375°F. But, if you do choose to wash your cast iron cookware, only use water so no soapy taste will linger. Thoroughly dry every exposed spot and then bake as directed for seasoning the skillet.

To store seasoned cast iron: It's best not to hang your cast iron skillet out in the open since this encourages dust, flying pet hairs and other airborne debris to cling to the seasoned surface. Instead, wrap your skillet in a medium-sized plastic trash bag or an old pillowcase and store in a cupboard.

TIPS
FROM A TEACHER

Cast Iron Cookware

Vegetable steamer (stainless steel): Purchase the collapsible type for its ability to fit within pots of different sizes.

Wok with lid: Fun and efficient when making authentic Asian stir-fry or deep-fry dishes, woks come in a variety of sizes. Originally made to be used over direct flame, woks are now available with a flat bottom for use on an electric stovetop. When made out of ordinary (nonstainless) steel, woks must be cared for properly in order not to rust. Do not wash these pans; instead, only wipe out thoroughly, sprinkle some coarse salt on the interior and use a paper towel to rub around the salt until completely clean. Then rub both the interior and exterior with vegetable oil, wipe out excess and store. Don't allow a seasoned wok to hang in the open or the seasoned finish will attract airborne dust and debris. Do not use salt or other abrasives when cooking in a wok with a nonstick finish.

Primarily for Baking

The following equipment is used primarily for baking breads, pastries, cookies and the like. As in the previous sections, items that are essential for basic baking are marked with an asterisk.

Baker's peel: This large, smooth, wooden board with a long handle is used to transfer free-form loaves and rolls to and from hot baking tiles. It's also used to remove a hot and crusty pizza from the oven. A flat cookie sheet usually can be used as a substitute except when lifting weighty assembled pizzas out of the oven.

Baking sheets (black or blue steel): The dark color makes these pans extremely heat retentive and encourages dough to sear quickly on the outside, producing a thicker, crisper and more deeply colored crust on ethnic sheet breads. However, these pans will rust easily if scratched or if not dried thoroughly after being washed. Also acidic or overly salted foods can ruin the surface of these pans. (See also cookie sheets, jelly-roll pans and the section on cookware for other baking pans.)

Biscuit cutters: Nested and fluted, either round or square. Make sure to dry cutters thoroughly after cleaning or they will rust.

Brioche mold: These fluted round metal pans come in a large size (about 9½ inches in diameter) or in individual sizes (about 3½ inches). For best results, purchase molds without seams. In addition to being used for brioche, these pans can be used to bake cake batter and to mold salads. The capacity of these pans ranges from about 2 to 8 cups.

Cake cover: A 6-inch high domed cover is handy for storing high cakes with soft frostings.

Cake discs (cardboard): These are placed underneath cakes to lend support when cakes are stored or transported in a box. They're also a great help when separating thin cake layers before frosting or filling.

*Cake pans: These round pans are made from heavy aluminum with straight sides for baking layer cakes. I recommend starting with two 9-inch pans (2 inches deep) and one 10x2-inch pan. You should also have a 9-inch flat (not fluted) springform pan; these have detachable rims. I prefer one with a non-stick finish for making cheesecake and unmolding ice cream cake. Do not use springform pans to bake mixtures in a water bath unless you wrap the bottom seams securely with aluminum foil.

Cake stand: A swivel turntable is helpful when decorating cakes or cutting thin cake layers.

*Canisters: It's essential that your flour and sugar canisters be wide enough to allow easy access for a loaded 2-cup dry measuring cup. For the basic kitchen I suggest two airtight canisters, but you will need more if you choose to make your own pancake mix and/or hot cocoa mix in bulk. If you decide to become an active baker, you will need even more to store different types of flour and meal.

*Cookie cutters: Collect assorted shapes and sizes with tight seams and strong stainless steel sides. Flimsy cutters lose their shapes quickly and need to be replaced frequently.

*Cookie sheets: These baking sheets have no sides. Buy two each of the flat type and the newer cushioned variety; each is better suited for different types of cookies. The thin, perfectly flat sheets facilitate immediate heat penetration to baked goods like biscuits, encouraging a fast generous rise. The newer cushioned cookies sheets are made from double sheets of aluminum or stainless steel with an air pocket between them. This protects certain heat-sensitive cookies that might otherwise burn on the bottom before cooking sufficiently throughout. If you only have the thinner sheets, improvise by baking the cookies on the bottom underside of a heavier baking sheet (with 1-inch sides). This way delicate cookies are elevated from the hot oven rack and will bake more gently.

TIPS

FROM A TEACHER

The Baker's Work Surface

A bread baker and a pastry maker have vastly different needs. When baking yeast breads, a wooden surface is essential for proper traction when kneading the dough. On the other hand, a proficient pastry maker will settle for nothing less than a marble slab. A cold work surface is imperative when rolling out a pastry dough that's high in butter (croissant, Danish pastry and many pie crusts). If your work surface is made of a warm material such as wood, it's probable that your dough will warm up while rolling, causing the butter to ooze out and adversely affect the ultimate texture in your pastry. A marble pastry slab (although heavy and cumbersome) provides a cold work surface for such procedures. Corian (artificial marble) and stainless steel countertops also work well, whereas Formica becomes quite warm when used as a work surface.

Cooling racks: You should have at least two (and preferably four) wire racks for cooling breads and other baked goods. Having four racks is especially helpful at holiday time when baking large batches of cookies.

Cornmeal sweeper: When baking successive batches of bagels, rolls, or free-form loaves on quarry tiles, this small, short-handled broom will quickly sweep any cornmeal or seeds off the tiles before preheating for your next batch.

Docker: This intimidating baking tool is a long wheel with large spikes protruding outward. It's used (mostly by professionals) to make many small holes in thin sheets of dough to prevent it from bubbling and puffing up in a hot oven. A docker is also used when preparing napoleons to prick thin sheets of puff pastry before baking to keep the pastry thin and crisp. This tool is not essential but very efficient. Use the prongs of a large serving fork as a substitute.

Icing spatula (long): This has an elbow bend at the end of a long thin strip of stainless steel for easy spreading of icing on cakes.

Jelly-roll pan: This 12x18x1-inch pan may be used for any recipe calling for a baking sheet with sides.

Loaf pans: Buy two to four each of both 9x5-inch and 8x4-inch pans, either in heatproof glass or metal coated with a nonstick finish. Remember to reduce the oven temperature by 25°F when using glass.

Muffin tins: Preferably nonstick. For starters, buy one standard-sized 6-muffin tin and one 12-muffin tin. It's fun to have mini and maxi muffin tins as well.

Muffin tin liners: Made of nonstick paper, these eliminate the need to grease the interior of the tins (but be sure to grease the tops of the tins). Although not essential, these do help muffins to stay fresher longer.

Pastry bag with an assortment of tips: If not using a disposable bag, it's important to clean and dry the bag thoroughly after each use. For complete information on how to clean and use pastry bags, see page 505.

Pastry blender: A hand-held implement used to cut butter and/or solid shortening into a dry mixture before adding liquid. Be sure to buy a sturdy blender with rigid blades, not flimsy wires.

Pastry cloth with rolling pin bootie: This strong, canvas cloth is made specifically to prevent pastry dough from sticking when rolling it out. The

bootie pulls down over the rolling pin so dough will not stick to the pin. Always rub flour evenly into both the cloth and bootie before rolling out pastry. Purchase the largest cloth that you can find; avoid those smaller than 18x18 inches.

Pastry scraper: Although this tool is not vital to every kitchen, it is an essential aid when working with a yeast dough. The rectangular metal blade that stems from a sturdy handle enables you to scrape right down to the bare surface of your wooden board while working to build texture in your yeast dough. A pastry scraper is also ideal to scrape up chopped vegetables from your cutting board, eliminating unnecessary wear and tear on your knives. Some scrapers have flexible blades that are not as versatile as the rigid ones.

Pastry wheel (fluted): This tool is used to cut strips or shapes decoratively from pastry dough.

Pie plates: These come in metal and glass with sloping sides; I prefer glass. Buy one 10-inch plate and one 9-inch plate. (See also tart pans.)

Pie weights: Commercial weights are available in kitchen shops and some hardware stores. Dried beans or rice may be substituted and reused for this purpose; do not eat rice or beans after using them for weights.

Pizza pans: For cooking pizza, I prefer perforated pans for the crispest crusts. But you should also have some solid pizza pans to serve your pizza directly from the oven. (Slicing pizza on a perforated pan makes a mess of your tablecloth!)

Pizza wheel: For cutting pizza into slices. The larger the wheel, the better.

Quarry tiles or a large pizza stone: The best way to simulate the intense dry heat of the brick ovens used to create breads with a tender and chewy interior along with a thick, very crisp crust. For a complete discussion of the tiles and stone, see page 400. If either of these is unavailable, use shallow dark steel baking sheets.

*Rolling pin: For best control when rolling out pie crust or other types of dough, use a long smooth wooden pin with tapered ends, *without ball bearings.*

Spray bottle (plastic): Spraying bread dough with a light mist of ice water at the beginning of baking is an optional step to help assure a crisp crust. A spray bottle also helps to keep the leaves of fresh cut herbs lightly moistened so they stay supple longer.

Springform pans: See cake pans.

Tart pans with removable bottoms: I suggest both a 9-inch and 10-inch fluted pan—the darker in color, the better. You might also consider a 10-inch deep-dish fluted tart pan and individual tart pans, also dark in color to obtain a deep golden color in your pastry.

Small Kitchen Appliances

Not too long ago, a hand-cranked meat grinder was a common sight in most kitchens (along with egg beaters and ice boxes). If you're too young to remember those days, you probably wonder how our mothers (or grand-mothers) got along without a food processor—or even a blender or an electric mixer. They did just fine, but there's no need for today's busy cook to spend a lot of time chopping, grinding, whipping and the like, when a machine will do the work—often more proficiently—in minutes. My recommendations follow. Although you can get by without any of them, owning these appliances has been a true source of comfort for me. These items surely will help you make the most of the time spent in your kitchen.

Blender: Although technically the food processor does many of the same jobs as a blender (purée, liquify and blend), the results are frequently different. Use a blender when puréeing bananas or when a thicker, more emulsified texture is desired in mixtures that don't contain eggs or an acidic ingredient (such as vinegar or mustard). The food processor tends to leave these types of mixtures with a thinner, more watery consistency. The blender made by Oster (the company that started it all) is heavy, efficient and durable. Steer clear of blenders that have loads of buttons. The most reliable blenders have only an on/off switch along with a pulsing switch for more control.

Deep-fat fryer: A thermostatically controlled electric fryer is the safest, most efficient way to fry in deep fat, especially if your stove is electric and it's more difficult to regulate the heating element quickly.

Food mill: This mechanical sieve—a survivor of the past—has a long crank-type handle on top. Just above the perforated bottom is a blade that rotates when the handle is cranked. As the blade turns, it will purée cooked foods and also separate the pulp from the skin and/or seeds. This device allows a soft mixture to retain a bit more texture than a food processor. This tool has no emulsifying capability.

Food processor: Although some still refer to this as a luxury piece of equipment, over the past decade a good basic food processor has become much more readily available at a more affordable price. Pie crust dough, home-made butter, fresh mayonnaise are all made so quickly and efficiently in the food processor that this is one machine I'd rather not do without. Although there are many different companies that now manufacture food processors, Cuisinart is the one I've always trusted to perform and it has never let me down.

Ice cream maker: Either hand-cranked or electric. Although very pricey, if you plan on making homemade ice cream often, the electric model by Gaggia comes with built-in refrigeration and allows you to churn successive batches of ice cream without having to wait twenty-four hours between each batch for the canister to chill properly. A less expensive alternative is to choose a simpler model that will allow you to purchase extra canisters that can chill simultaneously.

Meat grinder: Certain electric mixing machines (such as KitchenAid) have grinding attachments available.

Mini chopper (electric): The Mouli Mincer, by Moulinex is my favorite for mincing garlic, puréeing small roasted peppers, grinding hard seeds into fine powder and also does a fine job of finely mincing citris zest. However, you will need to purchase two choppers since, after being used for garlic, the cup will forever retain the scent. Label one "garlic only" to avoid mixups.

Mixer (electric hand-held): For those who only dabble in baking, KitchenAid makes a great hand-held appliance with surprising power.

Mixer (electric heavy-duty): The durable machine by KitchenAid, with its many attachments, is my pick. Among machines made by other companies, the best and most reliable have one central paddle and separate whisk attachment instead of two separate rotating beaters. The bowl capacity should be at least 4 quarts. When making certain cakes, a heavy, good-quality mixing machine will do a superb job of creaming butter and sugar. It then enables you to incorporate eggs slowly while continuously beating in air to achieve greatest volume, and thus the lightest texture. A heavy-duty mixer is also very helpful when making brioche dough or cream cheese pastry and whipping egg whites. It's wise to purchase an extra bowl for mixtures that are made in stages.

Pasta rolling machine (hand-cranked): The Atlas pasta machine is very efficient and durable. For more information, see Making Homemade Noodles (page 180).

Pasta rack (wooden): For hanging fresh pasta strands to dry.

Spice grinder (electric): An electric spice grinder is the most efficient way to grind hard seeds, whole spices or beans to a fine powder. Use a mortar and pestle as an adequate—and muscle building—substitute.

Toaster: A toaster oven is more versatile than the regular push-down-the-slice type. Great for open-faced grilled cheese sandwiches, baking potatoes and even warming small plates or serving dishes!

STAPLES

Following are lists of products that are used in my recipes and require further
comment as to what they are, where to buy them, or how to store and use
them properly. To prevent your wasting time and money on an inferior product, I have (where appropriate) recommended some of my favorite tried-
and-true brands that have consistently satisfied me and my family over the
years. In addition, I have pointed out some of the newer products that I find
particularly good. If you can't locate these brands or items, ask your shopkeeper to order them for you. I haven't provided a specific brand name when
I find little difference between the brands available.

I have organized this list of products like the layout of a supermarket—
from the herb and spice aisle and the shelves of baking needs to the sections
of dried foods and bottled or canned goods, winding up at the dairy case.
In this chapter, we don't visit the produce departments or the butcher's
counter, because scattered throughout my recipes you will find Tips from
a Teacher on buying, storing and preparing various types of fresh produce,
meat, poultry and seafood.

Although personal recommendations are subjective in nature, you can be
sure that when it comes to feeding my family, friends and students, I'm very
particular; if it's not "just right," I won't buy it.

Dried Herbs and Spices, Seeds and Extracts

When purchasing dried herbs and spices, think small. Spices don't stay fragrant forever and it's best to purchase small amounts of those that you use
often. Keep jars of spices and dried herbs in a cool dark place since both light
and heat will encourage flavor loss. (Even under the best conditions, the shelf
life of dried herbs won't be much more than 6 months.) Most spices and
dried herbs are available in the supermarket and are usually of good quality;
I don't find much difference between the brands available there. Spices by
Wagner's, found in many gourmet shops, are of excellent quality. But when
buying dried herbs or spices, try to discern their age and condition through
the glass bottles, which might have been sitting on the shelf for many months.
Generally, if dried herbs look overly white, dry or brittle, don't buy them.
Dried leaves should be as large and as green as possible. The color of ground
spices should be vibrant and the aroma potent. If not, these need to be

replaced. Space does not permit me to comment on each of the myriad spices, herbs and seeds available to today's cook. But I have annotated some general rules about them and listed a few specific seasonings that require more information regarding their purchase and use.

Dried Herbs: When I request the use of dried herbs, I am referring to dried leaves, not the powdered form which I rarely use. To release the dormant flavor of dried herb leaves, always crumble them between your fingers as you add them to a mixture. (Or grind them in a mortar and pestle when making an herb blend.) Because dried herbs have a more concentrated flavor than fresh, use this general rule when using dried as a substitute.

> 1 teaspoon crumbled aromatic dried leaves equals 1 tablespoon chopped fresh leaves.

Ground spices: When a recipe calls for ground spices, you are ensured of the fullest flavor if you buy the spices whole and grind them in an electric spice grinder (or a small hand-held grater in the case of nutmeg). This applies to allspice, cardamom, cloves, cumin, and white and black peppercorns.

Seeds: If desired, finely grind whole seeds (such as anise, fennel and caraway) using an electric spice grinder, coffee grinder or a mortar and pestle. Grinding seeds disperses them better throughout your mixture, resulting in a more intense and distinctive flavor. I usually use both—some whole seeds for texture and ground seeds for flavor. Store seeds on a cool, dark pantry shelf for six months, unless otherwise specified. The flavor of many seeds, such as sesame, is enhanced greatly by toasting them (see page 76).

Extracts: Whenever possible, purchase pure (not imitation) extracts and keep the bottles tightly shut on a cool, dark pantry shelf. If stored correctly, extracts should keep indefinitely. With the exception of vanilla, use extracts sparingly for the most delicate flavor. Wagner's puts out an excellent assortment of pure extracts. But my favorite vanilla extract is Royal Tahitian blend (Tahitian Import/Export Inc.) which combines the distinctive flavor of Tahitian beans and Bourbon beans. In addition to vanilla, extracts commonly found in most supermarkets include almond, banana, lemon, maple, mint (including peppermint and spearmint) and orange. Unfortunately, supermarkets don't always carry pure extracts so be prepared to go to a specialty gourmet shop or see Mail Order Sources.

Basil: Although I adore this herb fresh and use an abundance of it, I don't care for its overly sweet taste when dried and rarely use it in this form. When fresh basil isn't available, substitute only a tiny amount of dried basil (or try oregano) and use chopped flat-leaf Italian parsley for its green color and fresh taste.

Bay leaves: Turkish leaves lend a smoother, less pronounced flavor than the California leaves and are almost as readily available. Remove bay leaves from a soup or sauce before serving as they can cause choking.

Cardamom seeds (in their pods): This spice that's most renowned for lending a distinctive flavor to Danish pastries is also used as a staple spice in India, where it originated. Because cardamom is not as frequently used in America as other spices, it's likely that the bottled seeds or preground cardamom will lose its potency before being used. Thus, it's best to purchase the seeds still encased in their pods and crack them to extract the seeds yourself. Grind the seeds and use as directed in your recipe.

Cayenne: Ground hot red chilies, now synonymous with mixtures labeled "ground red pepper." Crushed red chili pepper flakes can be ground to a powder and used in place of cayenne.

Chili powder: Not only ground chiles but a blend of several spices, including coriander, cloves, cumin, garlic and oregano. Some blends are hotter than others.

Cinnamon sticks: They must be steeped in hot liquid in order to release their sweet, peppery flavor. Ground cinnamon is simply finely ground cinnamon sticks. By the way, sticks are curls of the dried inner bark from a tropical evergreen tree.

Cloves (whole or ground): Use this pungent spice very sparingly when ground since the flavor can easily overwhelm a dish whether sweet or savory. Whole cloves must be steeped in hot liquid in order to release their flavor.

Coriander: Tiny dried coriander seeds are used to add flavor to mulled wine and some pickled mixtures. A light pinch of ground seeds is used to add a distinctive taste to Danish pastries. Fresh coriander (better known as cilantro or Chinese parsley) looks like feathery flat-leaf Italian parsley, and has no resemblance to the dried herb. Many people passionately dislike cilantro, but eventually grow to love it (as I do) after being exposed to its flavor a number of times. The fresh herb is great in marinades, Mexican foods, spreads and salad dressings.

Curry powder: This East Indian spice mixture (invented by Brits doing service in colonial India) is a blend of coriander, cumin, turmeric, fenugreek, ginger, fennel, chiles, garlic, cinnamon and salt. Blends vary greatly by brand; my favorite is Madras by Sun Brand. It's delicious in rice, soups, lamb or poultry stews and fish dishes and particularly terrific in chicken salad.

Dill: Since fresh dill weed is usually available and doesn't even vaguely resemble dried dill, I only use this herb fresh. (For best flavor, add these chopped feathery leaves toward the end of cooking.) Dill seeds have a stronger flavor than dill weed and are commonly used for pickling brine.

Garlic powder and flakes: Although I use a ton of fresh garlic, I also use ground dehydrated garlic flakes (garlic powder—not garlic salt) to create my own spice blends to flavor other foods. Garlic flakes, when softened in a little warm water, can be used to top homemade breads before baking.

Ginger: This powdered form should not be used as a substitute for fresh ginger root, but it does add a distinctive sweet and peppery taste to confections as well as to certain savory sweet-and-sour dishes.

Kosher salt and sea salt: Since these coarse salts are not as readily absorbed into foods as plain table salt, they are particularly good sprinkled onto the outside of crisp foods just before serving. I prefer the taste and texture of kosher salt to the more expensive sea salt.

Mint: Although fresh mint is far superior to dried, the latter will do in a pinch.

Mustard (dried and seeds): You can't beat Coleman's. Use when the flavor of ground mustard seeds is desired without the added moisture and seasonings of prepared mustard. Mustard seeds come in four colors: white, yellow, brown and black. The white and yellow seeds have the mildest flavor and are predominantly used in American prepared mustards and to make pickles. The brown ones (although smaller) are far more pungent and spicy and are used to make strong Chinese mustard. Some European mustards are made from brown seeds alone, while others are made from a blend of various colored seeds.

Nutmeg: A nugget of fresh nutmeg must be rubbed vigorously against a small hand-held grater to release the powdered spice. Freshly grated nutmeg is far superior in flavor to the preground spice.

Onion powder and flakes: (Not onion salt.) I use this as I do garlic powder or flakes.

Oregano: Use the dried leaves, not powder, to add a distinctive zip to many mixtures. Actually, this is the only dried herb that I prefer over fresh. Sweet marjoram is similar to oregano, only more delicate.

Paprika: Made from both sweet and hot red capsicum pepper pods, without their seeds and veins. Hungarian paprika is the most renowned. The sweet variety usually is used to give added color to a dish and the hot paprika adds pungent flavor.

Peppercorns (black and white): Black peppercorns and white peppercorns actually come from the same plant—a tropical vine. The black peppercorns are picked before they ripen and dry; white peppercorns are picked ripe and their skins are removed before drying. Always freshly grind black pepper for best and fullest flavor. And by using this spice generously, you'll be less likely to use—or misuse—table salt in order to give your savory foods an intensely satisfying flavor. Ground white pepper has a powerful and distinctive flavor all its own and (although some might disagree with me) the two are not interchangeable. Ground white pepper is particularly delicious when added to either potato mixtures or cream soups.

Seasoned salt: I prefer Lawry's. When used sparingly, this blend of spices and flavorings is particularly complementary to poultry. Sprinkle on the bird before roasting or broiling or use to season flour before dredging the chicken for frying.

Sesame seeds: These seeds come in a variety of shades ranging from ivory to beige, brown, red and black. But the lightest, ivory seeds are used most often to add a rich and delicious flavor to many baked goods, both sweet and savory. Particularly complementary to dried bread crumbs and as a topping for fresh breads. Store these oily seeds in the freezer in a doubled heavy-duty plastic bag (securely sealed) for up to one year. Usually, sesame seeds can be purchased in bulk from a health food store. To toast, see page 76.

Vanilla beans: Store plump vanilla beans on a cool, dry pantry shelf or refrigerate in a plastic bag within a tightly closed glass jar. If they should become brittle, place the beans on a steamer rack over (not touching) simmering water. Cover the pot and steam the beans for 2 minutes or until supple.

Flours and Other Baking Needs

For a more detailed discourse on the properties of various flours and leaveners, see Notes on Baking Yeast Breads (page 373).

Flour (all-purpose unbleached): For the most basic kitchen, this is all you need. I prefer Heckers, Pillsbury, Gold Medal and King Arthur. On all other brands, check the package for its protein (gluten) content. All-purpose flour should contain 12 to 15 percent protein.

Flour (bread, high-gluten, high protein): Pillsbury, Gold Medal or King Arthur are my favorite brands. On all others, check the package for its protein (gluten) content. Bread flour should have a minimum of 20 percent protein to create a sufficiently elastic network in your dough.

Flour (cake): I prefer Swans Down. A soft, highly refined white flour, used to give cakes, certain muffins and quick breads a velvety texture. Do not confuse this with self-rising flour which has added salt and leavening.

Flour (coarse specialty): For specialty flours such as stone-ground wheat and medium rye, I prefer King Arthur. This rapidly growing company has expanded its nationwide distribution, but you can also order their hard-to-find flours by direct mail (see Mail Order Sources). Since these flours are more perishable than white flour, store opened bag in a doubled, well-sealed heavy-duty plastic bag and refrigerate or freeze for longer storage. If you use these flours often, store in an airtight canister at room temperature.

Flour (instant dissolving): I sprinkle Wondra (by Gold Medal) directly into hot or cold mixtures to correct consistency instantly without lumps. Also can be used to coat foods before frying for an unusually crisp exterior.

Flour (100 percent pure gluten): This will give a light texture to breads made (almost) exclusively with a coarse, whole grain flour (available in specialty bakers' catalogs; see Mail Order Sources).

Flour (pastry): Softer than all-purpose flour but stronger than cake flour, this can be used to make pastry dough and cookies. Since this is not an ingredient that's commonly used, it's smarter to make your own pastry flour as needed by simply whisking together 1 part cake flour to 2 parts all-purpose flour.

Flour (semolina for pasta): Essential for making certain pastas, preferably a fine grind. (See page 178 for further information.)

Baking Powder (double-acting): This leavening agent enables you to assemble a mixture now and bake it later without affecting its rising capability. And although this type of baking powder does have salt and other additives, the benefits of the double action outweigh the negatives. You can buy single-acting baking powder in health food stores, but, when using, the batter must be baked immediately after mixing. To check if your baking powder is active and functioning, stir 1 teaspoon baking powder into ¼ cup hot water; if the mixture quickly bubbles, it's fine.

Baking soda (bicarbonate of soda): This leavening agent works with acid ingredients (like buttermilk, yogurt or mixtures with molasses) to form bubbles filled with carbon dioxide which cause the batter to rise—even before it enters the oven. For best results, it's best to bake a batter or dough leavened exclusively with baking soda as soon as the mixture is assembled. However, when a batter contains both double-acting baking powder and baking soda (for certain muffins and pancakes), the mixture will leaven long after being assembled.

Coconut: Shredded sweetened coconut is available in cans or plastic bags. I buy the Baker's brand of the latter. Desiccated coconut is dried, untreated coconut meat and is available in bulk at health food stores. Place bags of either variety (unopened or not) in another heavy-duty plastic bag and refrigerate to preserve freshness.

Coconut cream and milk: The liquid inside a fresh coconut makes a refreshing drink, but it is not the coconut milk used in cooking. That is made by processing freshly grated coconut meat with boiling water; coconut cream is the thick liquid that rises to the top of the milk after it's processed and strained. There is also a commercial product called cream of coconut which is used to add flavor and a velvety texture to flans and ice creams. Coco López brand of cream of coconut is my favorite, although it must be emulsified in a blender before using.

Cornmeal: I use nongerminated (water-ground) cornmeal (available in health food stores) because it's higher in nutrients. Although cornmeal comes in blue, white and yellow (and are interchangeable), the latter has the most vitamin A. When I request cornmeal in this book, I am referring to medium-ground meal. Store as you would specialty flours and be aware that the nongerminated cornmeal is much more perishable than the newer highly refined meal and therefore will have a shelf life of only four months under refrigeration and six when frozen.

Cornstarch (corn flour): Flour made from corn, this thickening agent is used when a smooth, shiny finish is desired in a sauce. Puddings and custards made from cornstarch tend to be less "pasty" than those made exclusively with wheat flour. Also, foods dredged in cornstarch and then fried will have a harder, crisper exterior than foods fried in regular wheat flour. To avoid lumps, cornstarch must first be dissolved in a cold liquid before being stirred into a hot mixture. If cooked too long (after becoming thick), the mixture will return to being thin. Cornstarch also can be used in combination with white wheat flour to add a different, slightly smoother texture to cakes and a "melt-away" texture to cookies.

Cream of tartar: Most commonly used to help strengthen and stabilize egg whites while whipping them to almost triple their original volume. Cream of tartar is also used to give certain candies and frostings a creamier, less granular texture. A by-product of winemaking, this white powder is made from the residue that accumulates on the inside of wine barrels.

Nuts and dried fruits: See page 463.

Wheat bran and wheat germ: Pure wheat bran is the outer layer of bran that's removed from the wheat berry during milling. This layer is loaded with fiber and can be added to both sweet and savory mixtures without being detected since it's flavorless. I find all brands of pure wheat bran the same. Wheat germ, which is at the center of the wheat berry, is loaded with nutrients and has a distinctively crunchy texture and nutty flavor that adds dimension (as well as nutrition) to breakfast cereal and yogurt. I prefer the toasted variety made by Kretschmer. Once opened, wheat germ and wheat bran must be kept in a tightly closed jar in the refrigerator.

Yeast (active dry): Comes in ¼-ounce packets or small blocks of compressed cake yeast. Refrigerate both types to preserve freshness. My brand is Fleischmann's. I do not use, nor do I recommend, any brand of "fast-rising" yeast.

Sugars and Other Sweeteners

Store on a cool, dry pantry shelf, unless otherwise specified.

Brown sugar (light and dark): The color depends on the amount of added molasses. Once a bag is opened, insert the bag into another heavy-duty plastic bag and seal. If brown sugar becomes hard, wrap a piece of raw apple loosely in a piece of perforated plastic wrap and place in the bag of sugar for up to two days. The moisture in the apple will keep the sugar supple; replace the apple as needed. "Brownulated" sugar is a crystallized form of brown sugar that pours like granulated sugar. Brown sugar will create a moister texture in your baked goods than brownulated sugar and therefore the two products are not interchangeable.

Confectioner's sugar (powdered): Granulated white sugar that has been ground to a powder with cornstarch to help prevent clumping. (If clumping does occur, sift before measuring.)

Superfine granulated white (castor) sugar: Since superfine sugar only comes in small boxes, I fine it more economical and convenient to make my own (see granulated sugar). If you do buy a commercial brand, however, "instant dissolving sugar" by Domino is excellent.

Raw (turbinado) sugar: A homey yet sophisticated touch for your sugar bowl. Although raw sugar doesn't dissolve quickly, the flavor is nicely reminiscent of molasses.

White granulated cane or beet sugar: This is what most recipes mean when they just list "sugar." Highly refined, it's the most commonly used sugar for both baking and table use. Purchase the brand that has the finest granules. (This seems to vary with each bag that I purchase.) If your sugar has undesirably large crystals or many lumps, process the sugar in small batches in a food processor fitted with the steel blade to create a finer consistency; this can also be used as substitute for superfine (instant dissolving) sugar.

Corn syrup: Although this comes in both light and dark varieties, light corn syrup is most versatile. My choice is Karo.

Honey: A good mild-flavored, clover honey for cooking or spreading is Golden Blossom. For spreading, I also like the thick and delicious honey by Langnese.

Q AND A

Q. What's "brownulated" sugar and is it interchangeable with white granulated sugar or softer brown sugar in bags?

A. Brownulated sugar is crystalized brown sugar. It dissolves much like white granulated sugar but has the added molasseslike flavor and the deeper color inherent in brown sugar. Although some feel that brownulated sugar is an adequate substitute for the softer brown sugar, I disagree. Brownulated sugar should be used when you want to lend the taste and color of brown sugar to a baked product but you desire the crispness that white granulated sugar provides. This type of sugar will not yield the same degree of moistness in a baked product as the nongranulated brown sugar and, therefore, the two are not interchangeable.

Maple syrup (honey-maple blend): Honeyup by Maple Grove Farms is a mixture of corn syrup, cane syrup, maple syrup and honey. It's less expensive than "pure" maple syrup and has a slightly thicker consistency, making it great for pancakes.

Maple syrup (pure): From Vermont, this pure syrup is graded (going from mild to robust): AA, A, B and C. This is expensive and must be refrigerated once opened to preserve freshness. Generally, a lighter colored syrup has the most delicate flavor and is considered to be higher in quality than the darker varieties.

Molasses (unsulphured): Molasses is derived from the early phases of refining cane or beet sugar. Unsulphured molasses, which is processed without sulphur dioxide, has a milder, more soothing flavor than sulphured molasses. I like Grandma's Molasses to add moistness, color and rich flavor to baked goods and some savory mixtures.

Chocolate

A product sold as "real chocolate" legally must have a minimum of 35 percent cocoa butter (vegetable fat) and 27 percent chocolate liquor (the brown, thick pastelike substance left after grinding the "nibs" [the inside of a cocoa bean that's first been fermented, dried and roasted]). The rest is a mixture of varying degrees of sugar, vanilla and lecithin (an emulsifier). Although many fine chocolates are imported from Switzerland, France, Belgium, England and Holland, I've had very good results with chocolates that are manufactured here in America. Following are some brands (both domestic and imported) that I've had success with for specific procedures. When dark sweet, bittersweet or semisweet chocolate is well wrapped in pliable plastic and stored on a cool, dry (well ventilated) pantry shelf, chocolate should last for up to 1 year. Milk chocolate and white chocolate will only have half the shelf life since their increased milk content makes them more perishable.

Baking chocolate (unsweetened): This is pure hardened chocolate liquor. Baker's and Hershey's sell it in a box with eight 1-ounce squares. San Francisco's Ghirardelli produces baking chocolate in 4-ounce bars and Callebaut provides unsweetened chocolate in large 11-pound slabs.

Bar chocolate (bittersweet, semisweet, milk): Domestic brands I like include Baker's, Peter's (by Nestlé) and Ghirardelli. Imported brands are Lindt Excellence, Callebaut, Valrhona and Tobler Tradition. Peter's chocolate is also sold in 10-pound slabs.

Chocolate morsels (semisweet and milk chocolate): For chocolate morsels (chips, bits or chunks) to retain their shape after being exposed to heat, the type of fat used should be cocoa butter and not palm oil. And the higher the fat content, the more stable the morsel will be. Baker's, Nestlé, Ghirardelli, Hershey's and Guittard are all brands to trust. (For all other brands, check the label since it should say "real chocolate.")

Cocoa powder: This is made from pure chocolate liquor that is dried and then hydraulically ground to a powder to separate and remove as much as 75 percent of the cocoa butter. The remaining solids are then pressed into a hard cake (to remove more fat) and ground into a fine powder called pure cocoa powder.

Cocoa powder (unsweetened Dutch): My preference for cocoa powder is Dutch-processed by Droste. Treated with an alkali to neutralize the acid in chocolate liquor, the resulting cocoa has a smoother flavor than regular cocoa powder. When using nonalkalized cocoa powder in baking, you must neutralize the mixture with the addition of baking soda in order for the mixture to leaven properly.

White chocolate (not real chocolate): Although white chocolate has cocoa butter, it lacks chocolate liquor and is therefore not "real chocolate." When looking for white chocolate, Lindt Blancor (Swiss Confectionery Bar) is a wonderful choice. Since this is more perishable than real chocolate, purchase only when needed. (And stay away from white compound chocolate—called white morsels—which taste awful.)

Grains, Dried Beans and Pasta

You're likely to find all of these in the same section of your supermarket. After opening the packages, store the contents in airtight containers in a cool, dry pantry, unless otherwise specified. Dried beans and pasta will keep almost indefinitely (although the older they become, the more cooking they will require to render them tender). Rice can be stored indefinitely without affecting cooking time.

Barley: Medium-sized pearl barley is an easy and substantial addition to soups and stews. Rinse well before using. Scotch barley (available in health food stores) is less processed and more nutritious than pearl barley, but will also take longer to cook.

Many times throughout this book, I suggest long-grain white rice as the preferred accompaniment to various entrées or soups and for good reason. Not only is converted white rice relatively quick to prepare and easy to embellish but, contrary to popular belief, it's also nutritious. Although white rice has, during milling, lost its fiber-rich bran layer, converted white rice is enriched before being milled with a generous dose of niacin, thiamin and iron. So much so that white rice actually exceeds brown rice in these nutrients. Although all domestic white rice is now enriched, converted rice ranks highest nutritionally among them.

Beans and legumes (dried): Dried beans are preferable to the canned versions and, except for split peas and lentils, are usually soaked overnight or precooked before adding to a recipe. Don't cook newly purchased dried beans with older stored ones since the older ones will require longer cooking to become tender. Even packaged beans must be thoroughly rinsed and picked over carefully to remove small stones before using.

Buckwheat groats (kasha): These come in whole kernels or coarsely ground. For more information, see This Mama's Kasha Varnishkes (page 368).

Oats (rolled): You can buy both quick-cooking and regular old-fashioned rolled oats; my brand of choice is Quaker. After oats have been cleaned and toasted, they are hulled and then cleaned again. At this point, they are technically no longer oats, but "oat groats" and are still very nutritious. Regular rolled oat groats, which have been rolled and flattened into flakes, will cook in 15 minutes. The quicker-cooking oats have been first cut into smaller pieces and then briefly steamed and softened before being rolled; they will only require 5 minutes to cook. Most often, regular and quick-cooking oat groats are interchangeable in recipes. But "instant oats" are not interchangeable with either; they have been precooked and softened to such an extent that, once moistened, their mushy (almost gluey) texture is not desirable in baked goods. Also, instant oats contain additives that could interfere with other ingredients when used in baking.

Pasta (dried): For dried spaghetti, linguine, fettuccine, angel hair, rigatoni, penne, orzo, parpardelle and farfalle (bow-ties), I prefer the pasta imported from Italy. Although there are now many wonderful imports, my favorite is De Cecco, a fine and well-respected brand, available in many supermarkets.

Rice (brown): Because the oily and fiber-rich brown bran layer is left intact, brown rice is very nutritious, but unlike white rice, it's much more likely to become rancid. Store brown rice in the refrigerator in a sealed screw-top jar. When stored on a cool pantry shelf, brown rice will remain fresh for only six months; when refrigerated, you can double the shelf life. Brown rice takes longer to cook than white rice, but a partially cooked version is also available.

Rice (white): Store an opened bag or box of white rice within a sealed heavy-duty plastic bag. I use converted (enriched) long-grain white rice in most of my recipes and recommend Uncle Ben's as the best around (see page 363 for a full description). I also frequently use aromatic rice, such as basmati, Texmati, jasmine, Wehani and Popcorn rice (see page 363). White rice also comes in a medium-grain variety (mostly produced in California for

Japanese cooking) and in a short-grain variety. The most notable of these available in America is the stubby arborio rice, which is imported from Italy and used primarily for making risotto.

Wild rice: Actually, this is not rice but long-grain marsh grass. When these dark needlelike kernels are cooked they have an earthy, nutty flavor and a chewy texture. Before cooking, soak wild rice in cold water for 10 minutes and then drain thoroughly to remove debris. Wild rice will take from 45 minutes to 1 hour to cook when simmered in a tightly covered saucepan. Use 1 part rice to 3 parts slightly salted water.

Cooking and Salad Oils

Most oils can be stored at room temperature, away from light for six months, unless otherwise specified, but you will double the shelf life of many oils if you refrigerate them after opening. (Most refrigerated oil must be brought to room temperature in order to become fluid and pourable.) All oils made from vegetables and nuts contain no cholesterol and most are low in saturated fats. They fall into three groups: Monounsaturated oils (made from olives and nuts) are now said to be the healthiest. But they are more perishable than polyunsaturated oils so it's always best to refrigerate them after opening. Polyunsaturated oils (made mostly from vegetables) may be stored at room temperature tightly sealed. Coconut and palm oils do contain high levels of saturated fats, which are thought to increase the buildup of cholesterol.

Cooking spray: Used to spray oil onto a cooking surface *before* heating, a spray is a good way to reduce substantially the amount of fat in your diet. Originally all vegetable sprays were made from corn oil or safflower oil, but now Bertolli offers a spray using olive oil. Pam and Baker's Joy make a baking spray that combines oil and flour to eliminate the additional step of dusting a pan with flour after greasing. Check the label since this type is not suitable for sautéing. Store all sprays at room temperature away from heat and never spray directly into a hot oven or into a skillet over direct heat.

Olive oil (extra-virgin): Made from the first press of green olives after crushing, this oil has a deeper green color and a more distinctive olive flavor. But due to its pronounced flavor and low smoke point, extra-virgin oil is not suitable for deep-frying. It's best suited for marinades, salad dressings, shallow panfrying, sautéing vegetables and for using "straight" on bread. My choices of brands are Loriva, Bertolli, Colavita or Colle Monacesco; the latter is pricey but very delicious.

Olive oil (pure): Lighter than extra-virgin, this bright yellow oil is from the second press of the olives and has no additives. I like Bertolli. It's great for salad dressings and shallow panfrying. Because this oil has a low smoke point, it's not suitable for deep-frying.

Olive oil (light): This pale yellow filtered oil is just right when you want the benefits of a monounsaturated oil but you don't want to taste the flavor of the olives. And you can use it to deep-fry since it has a higher smoke point. Again my choice is Bertolli.

Peanut oil (aromatic): Loriva manufactures the most delicious and aromatic peanut oil I've had yet. It smells and tastes like fresh peanuts. Use this cold-pressed oil for sautéing vegetables, shallow panfrying or in marinades. Look for this oil in gourmet shops, health food stores and Asian markets.

Peanut oil (light): Planters makes a peanut oil that is perfect for deep-frying since it has a very high smoke point. About 50 percent monounsaturated, peanut oil takes on a rancid scent soon after opening so use it promptly.

Toasted sesame oil: This is a very flavorful concentrate used extensively as a seasoning in Asian cooking. I've never tasted a "brand" that I didn't like. Use sparingly to season—*never* for cooking.

Walnut oil and hazelnut oil: These fatty oils turns rancid quickly. Purchase small amounts and, once opened, store in the refrigerator. Use these (pricey) oils sparingly in salads or to drizzle over freshly sautéed vegetables. Heating these oils will ruin their flavor.

Vegetable oils: Safflower, soybean, corn and light sesame oils are all polyunsaturated. All are suitable for shallow panfrying, sautéing vegetables and for salad dressings, as is canola, a bland-tasting oil, but very high in monounsaturates. Corn oil, sesame oil (light, not toasted), soybean oil and safflower oil have a high smoke point, making them all a good choice for deep-frying. Safflower oil (although bland) is a perfect choice when making vinaigrettes in advance since the oil won't solidify when chilled. My choice for all of these oils is Loriva. When I purchase large quantities of oil to deep-fry, I buy Crisco, Puritan oil or Planters peanut oil.

Vegetable shortening: Unsaturated oil that's been hydrogenated (hardened to a semisolid state). An essential tenderizing ingredient in certain baked goods, it can also be melted and used to fry—but be aware that once it's hydrogenated it is considered a saturated fat and therefore loses the healthful benefits of the liquid vegetable oils. My preference is Crisco. Does not require refrigeration.

Canned, Jarred and Bottled Items

Once opened, all canned items should be emptied into a glass jar or heavy-duty plastic container (along with any packing liquid) and closed securely. The containers should be labeled with the date opened and then stored in the refrigerator. After opening, most bottled items (except vinegars, honey and certain syrups) should be stored in the refrigerator.

Anchovy fillets: I usually purchase anchovies packed in glass jars; I've found these fillets to be larger and firmer than those packed in tins.

Apple juice (bottled): My favorite is natural and unfiltered by Red Cheek.

Bovril: This meat-flavored extract, when used sparingly, will enhance sauces and gravy (especially if you're not using homemade stock).

Broth (canned chicken and beef): I'll always feel that using canned broth instead of homemade stock is a compromise. But for emergencies, Campbell's Healthy Request (with no MSG) is the best broth from the super-market. College Inn makes a good beef broth, although a bit salty; you might want to dilute it with a little water. And to "doctor" canned chicken broth so it tastes more like fresh, see page 140 or 143. Some specialty food shops carry Perfect Addition, a line of high-quality, commercially prepared frozen stocks that are salt-free; they come in 8-ounce containers of beef, veal, chicken and fish varieties.

Capers: Although the tiny capers from southern France are considered non-pareil, my favorite caper is the larger Italian bud that's packed in balsamic vinegar by Dal Raccolto. When using either of these types in a sauce or as a garnish, rinse and drain them first. If using them to spice up a salad, dip or spread, rinsing isn't necessary, since the vinegar will usually only add flavor to the mixture. On the other hand, salt-packed capers should always be rinsed and drained thoroughly before using.

Chili sauce: By Heinz, of course.

Chutney: Major Grey's is not a brand name, only a type of chutney made by a number of companies with varying degrees of success. Cross & Blackwell, however, makes the best. This spicy melange of peaches or mangoes is the perfect condiment for curried dishes. It also adds dimension to rice, to savory sauces and to a simple wedge of cheese. The chutneys made by Cross & Blackwell have a chunky texture and a full-bodied flavor.

Clam juice: Only purchase bottled clam juice, never canned which tastes metallic. Refrigerate once opened and use within a couple of days.

Coconut: See Flours and Other Baking Needs.

Dijon mustard: I like both regular and country-style whole grain made by Grey Poupon and Maille.

Fermented black beans: These tiny fermented soybeans are preserved in salt and once rinsed, dried and chopped, add a wonderful dimension to Asian sauces (see Whole Red Snapper, page 229, for more information). Although I've purchased small jars of fermented black beans by Ka-me in Asian produce markets in large cities, you might not find them in smaller suburban areas. See Mail Order Sources.

Espresso powder (instant): I recommend the brands Medaglia d'Oro or Ferrara.

Jalapeño peppers (whole and sliced): These peppers come jarred and canned, sliced or whole, pickled or packed in salt water and from hot to very hot. I find little difference between the brands available but I do prefer jarred peppers to canned so I can view their appearance through the glass.

Kalamata olives: These small meaty brownish-black Greek olives are tree ripened and oil cured. The tiny French Niçoise olives may be substituted but they don't have the same robust flavor as kalamata olives.

Ketchup: By Heinz, again.

Kitchen Bouquet: When this vegetable extract is rubbed into certain cuts of meat (such as brisket) before searing, it gives the meat an extra savory flavor. Usually found with gravy enhancers.

Lumpfish caviar: Make sure the jar says "lumpfish" eggs, and not "whitefish" eggs, which are overly fishy. I like the Romanoff brand of lumpfish.

Mayonnaise: Although I love my Homemade Mayonnaise (page 86), I always have a jar of Hellmann's in the refrigerator. (It's known as Best Foods in the West.)

Roasted peppers (and pimentos): When time is scarce, these will quickly add color and flavor to a salad. Peloponnese (a product of Greece) makes a great product. Drain and pat dry before adding to a dish.

Tabasco sauce: Any other hot pepper sauce may be substituted, but Tabasco is the brand that started it all.

Tamari: More intensely flavored than regular soy sauce, smooth, rich-tasting wheat-free tamari by San-J is my preference as a table condiment and for most cooking purposes. It's available in some supermarkets, as well as health food stores and most Asian vegetable markets.

Tomatoes: Progresso (Italian style) or Red Pack are my choices for canned tomatoes—whole and peeled, puréed, crushed, and in a thick concentrated tomato paste. Tomato paste also comes in tubes—the perfect solution when you only need a tablespoon or so; store an opened tube in the refrigerator. The tubes can be found in most Italian delicatessens or gourmet food shops (see Mail Order Sources).

Tomatoes (dried/marinated): Instead of buying those expensive bottles of marinated sun-dried tomatoes from Italy, I buy plain dried tomatoes and marinate them at home (or sometimes even dry them myself), see page 124.

Tuna: For use in a dip, I like Progresso's Italian solid light tuna, packed in olive oil; it's meaty without an overly fishy taste. For sandwiches and salads, Bumble Bee's solid white tuna packed in water has a light, mild taste.

Vinegars: Only purchase a bottle of vinegar with a tight-fitting cork or a screw- top lid. Avoid bottles with a plastic lid, which rarely fits right once the bottle is opened. My choices for various types of vinegar are: red wine by Heinz "Gourmet," or Monari Federzoni; white wine by Monari Federzoni; chianti wine by Mazzetti; apple cider and white distilled by Heinz; and bal-samic by Fini, Cavalli, Monari Federzoni or Giuseppe Giusti.

Worcestershire sauce: Lea & Perrins, the granddaddy of them all.

From the Dairy Case

Make your choices of dairy products according to the needs of the week. When in the market, make the dairy section your last stop and store these perishables in the coldest part (bottom shelf) of your refrigerator as soon as you reach home. When cultured products such as sour cream, yogurt or cottage cheese show even the slightest signs of mold, throw them away since this means that mold might be growing throughout the mixture.

Butter: For general cooking and baking purposes, I use regular unsalted sticks made by Land O Lakes or Calbot.

Buttermilk: This cultured product comes both salted and unsalted. The salted buttermilk will have a longer shelf life, but if you frequently use buttermilk, the added salt is not necessary.

TIPS
FROM A TEACHER

How to Hard-Cook Eggs

Although hard-cooked eggs are commonly referred to as "hard-boiled" eggs, they should not be boiled aggressively. Gentle cooking is the secret to perfectly cooked hard-cooked eggs. And you'll know if you've done it correctly when you view the inside of the peeled egg after cooking: The yolk should be bright-bright yellow (almost orange) and the white should be tender and very white. Overcooked whites are rubbery with a grayish cast, and overcooked yolks have a greenish outer film and a pungent odor.

To hard-cook eggs: Place eggs into a 2-quart saucepan. Run enough cold water into the pot to cover eggs by 2 inches. (Don't run water directly over eggs as the pressure from the tap can cause the eggs to crack.) Place pan, uncovered, over medium heat. As soon as the water begins to bubble, sprinkle in a generous teaspoon of salt. (The salt cushions the eggs from each other as the water begins to move more aggressively.) Bring water to a full boil, cover pan and remove from heat. Let pan sit undisturbed for 15 minutes. Drain and immediately run eggs under cold water until just cool enough to handle. One at a time, tap each egg with the back of a spoon all over to crack the shell. Gently roll the egg between your hands to loosen the shell. Peel off shells and discard.

Cheese: Store wedges of freshly cut cheese wrapped well in a double layer of pliable plastic wrap and keep well chilled. But for best flavor, cheese (even hard cheese) should never be served cold. And creamy cheese (like Brie or Camembert) should be removed from the refrigerator hours before serving (unless the room is excessively warm) and served at room temperature. Or (if the outer rind is uncut) warm these soft cheeses and then allow to firm slightly so the cheese won't run out after being cut.

Cheese (Cheddar): Use aged Cheddar to crumble into salads and on top of baked potatoes and choose a young Cheddar to slice and use for grilled cheese.

Cheese (cream): Temp Tee's whipped texture gives the best consistency to dips and I use Fleur-de-Lait for baking. Fleur-de-Lait comes in 8-ounce blocks and is made without guar gum (a thickening agent). This brand has a shorter shelf life and a more crumbly texture than the ubiquitous Philadelphia brand; it also has a fresher taste. Philadelphia brand is a good substitute and it comes in both 8-ounce blocks and 3-ounce squares.

Cheese (farmer): This moist, crumbly cheese is a form of cottage cheese with most of the excess moisture pressed out. It makes a delicious low-fat cream cheese when blended until smooth with a small amount of plain yogurt in a food processor. (See Low-Fat Cream Cheese, page 82.)

Cheese (Jarlsberg): Sliced or in a wedge, this has a deeper more buttery flavor than regular Swiss cheese and is great for both cooking and snacking (also comes in a low-salt variety which tastes very good).

Cheese (mozzarella): Whenever possible, use fresh mozzarella since the creamy texture and fresh flavor is so much better than those rubbery blocks of so-called mozzarella sold in most supermarkets. Fortunately, Polly-O now supplies many supermarkets with fresh mozzarella in 8-ounce, 4-ounce and 1-ounce balls (the smaller balls requested in some of my recipes are called *bocconcini*). Keep fresh mozzarella covered in water to prevent a crust from forming on its surface.

Cheese (Parmigiano-Reggiano): This, the very best of Parmesan cheese, is quite pricey but holds up well if stored correctly. Only those wheels stenciled with this name are authentic. All others are a more economical substitute. If possible, purchase a wedge from a newly opened wheel and, once home, tightly double-wrap the wedge in pliable plastic wrap. Grate only as needed for best flavor.

Cream products: Whenever possible, purchase only pasteurized cream products, not ultrapasteurized. Although the ultrapasteurization process (intended to prevent the growth of bacteria by heating the cream to 300°F) gives cream an extended shelf life, neither the flavor nor the whipping qualities are as good as in the more perishable pasteurized cream. Purchase small amounts when needed and keep cream in the coldest part of your refrigerator. If you're watching your fat intake, note that heavy whipping cream contains three to four times more butterfat than half-and-half. The contents are: half-and-half, 10 to 12 percent butterfat; light cream, 18 to 30 percent butterfat; light whipping cream, 30 to 36 percent butterfat; heavy whipping cream, 36 to 40 percent butterfat; and sour cream, 18 to 20 percent butterfat (this "cultured" cream will have an extended shelf life and the percentage of butterfat is lower in reduced-fat sour cream).

Eggs: All recipes in this book refer to extra-large eggs (unless otherwise specified). To best preserve freshness, store eggs in their original carton (not in the provided "egg trays") on the lowest shelf, the coldest place in your refrigerator.

Margarine: Although margarine is made with all vegetable oils and no animal fat, this is still 80 percent fat and fat *is* fat! (The remaining 20 percent is made up of flavorings, color and other additives.) Margarines that are made with either pure safflower oil or corn oil are considered to be the lowest in saturated fat. Most companies that produce margarine have recently reduced the level of fat to between 60 and 70 percent, and these are now called "spreads." I feel Fleischmann's makes the best-tasting spread. Sometimes sticks of unsalted margarine (not spreads) can be substituted for sticks of unsalted butter in baking recipes where the flavor of real butter is not essential. I don't care for any of the brands of reduced-calorie margarines or spreads.

Yogurt: Colombo makes a rich, smooth flavored yogurt with no aftertaste. Dannon makes a fine (and natural) plain yogurt and a refreshingly tart, distinctively cultured fruit-flavored product. Always use plain yogurt in cooking unless otherwise specified.

Kitchen Helpers

A staple does not have to be edible. I could not be nearly as proficient in my kitchen without a good supply of the following.

Aluminum foil: Although Reynolds Wrap seems thicker and more sturdy than most generic brands, any foil will do an adequate job.

Freezer bags: Keep on hand a selection of heavy-duty plastic bags in assorted sizes. Although most brands are very similar, Glad-Lock bags have the added feature of a color-coded top to indicate whether or not the bag is sealed correctly. I also use Ziploc jumbo storage bags, the only ones that come in a 2-gallon capacity; these larger bags are perfect to store hefty loaves of homemade bread in the freezer.

Paper toweling: For me it's Bounty by Procter & Gamble. Hands down, Bounty is unquestionably the most absorbant paper towel—and their new quilted version is even stronger! Since Bounty is the strongest paper towel, it's also the most economical since you would need twice as much to accomplish the same job with a weaker brand. Bounty also makes a Select-a-Size variety where you can, if desired, tear off only half a sheet for smaller jobs.

Parchment paper: Purchasing a roll of parchment paper is more economical than precut sheets. Papier Cuisson by SCI: Cuisine Internationale is a French rolled baking paper that's thin and crisp with an opaque sheen. It's superior to those in the supermarkets, but can only be purchased from specialty kitchen shops (see Mail-Order Sources). Parchment paper is used to line baking sheets and even to bake individual packets of food *en papillote*.

Plastic wrap: When choosing plastic wrap, don't purchase a brand that's made with polyethylene since these plastic wraps are not very pliable and they also allow air and moisture to pass through to foods; thus encouraging the moist texture of baked products to become dry and other foods to lose flavor and aroma. The best, most pliable wrap that will cling to foods (and not get tangled up in the process) is Reynolds Plastic Wrap which is made with polyvinyl chloride. This brand is also microwave safe.

Wax paper: Ever since I was a child I've used Reynolds Cut-Rite wax paper.

KITCHEN JARGON

Although most cookbooks place the glossary in the back of the book, I've always felt strongly that the front of a cookbook should provide a solid foundation of information—not only about tools and ingredients, but also about unfamiliar culinary terms that shroud the fun of cooking and baking with an unnecessary mystique. In this section, you'll find the clarification of terms frequently used in this book. Please read this section before delving into the recipes to increase your understanding of the methods and techniques I mention. And I suggest that you insert a bookmark here so you can refer to these pages whenever necessary.

Acidulated: Water to which an acidic ingredient has been added (such as citrus juice or vinegar) to prevent certain fruits or vegetables (such as peaches, apples, pears and artichokes) from discoloring after being peeled or trimmed. Often, citrus juice alone can be used to treat these fruits; peeled bananas should not be submerged in acidulated water, but only tossed with a small amount of strained lemon juice.

Al dente: Literally "to the tooth" in Italian, this term describes properly cooked pasta. This is also used to describe the texture of certain types of rice and vegetables.

Baguette: A long thin loaf of French bread, sometimes also used to describe a long loaf of Italian bread.

Baste: To brush with liquid (usually melted fat or drippings) during roasting to keep foods from becoming dry.

Bind: To hold together a mixture or to thicken it with various substances such as flour or bread crumbs.

Blanch: To cook fruits or vegetables partially by boiling or steaming. Blanched nuts are briefly boiled or steamed just long enough to release and remove their outer skins, as are tomatoes and other fruits.

Boil: When a liquid reaches 212°F, bubbles appear vigorously at the surface. As these bubbles burst, a constant stream of new bubbles appears. When the bubbles won't cease (even while stirring), that's a "rolling boil."

Braise: To cook foods slowly (securely covered) in a small to moderate amount of liquid. A stew is the perfect example of a braised dish that needs long, slow exposure to moist heat in order to break down and dissolve the tough, connective tissue within certain cuts of meat. For best results, always use a well-made, heavy-bottomed Dutch oven or casserole to promote even heat distribution and prevent scorching on the bottom. A similar technique is used with whole or chopped vegetables (see Sweat).

Bruise: To hit a whole firm or semifirm ingredient so that the flesh releases the food's flavor but remains intact. This technique frequently is used with peeled cloves of fresh garlic before browning them in hot fat to infuse the fat with garlic flavor.

Caramelize: To cook a sugar syrup until it reaches a deep amber color. This begins at around 295°F and is completed at 300°F to 310°F.

Chiffonade: Ribbonlike strands of fresh leafy greens or herbs. They first are trimmed, stacked and rolled widthwise into a thin tube, which is thinly sliced; when each slice is unraveled, the strands resemble ribbons. Commonly, this is done to fresh basil, spinach and lettuce, either to give dimension to the overall look and texture of a finished dish or to act as a bed for other ingredients.

Chop: To reduce a whole food into small (but not tiny) irregular pieces.

Clarify: To remove cloudy sediment from a liquid.

Coddle: To cook briefly a food (such as an egg) in liquid that's just below the simmering point.

Condensation: Water droplets that form from the rising steam that emanates from a hot mixture within a closed environment, such as a covered pan.

Core: To remove the central core of seeds from fruit.

Cream: To beat softened butter until smooth and light. In baking, this process is frequently done in combination with sugar and eggs to achieve a light texture in baked goods.

Crudités: Uniformly cut-up raw vegetables (and sometimes fruit), usually served as "finger food" with a savory dip or sweet sauce.

Curdle: A usually undesirable chemical reaction that occurs when dairy products (milk, cream, sour cream or eggs) are combined with an acid ingredient (wine, vinegar, tomatoes or citrus juice) or when dairy products are overheated or heated too quickly. The smooth substance breaks and forms small granular (coagulated) pieces of protein within the product.

Cut in: To incorporate a solid fat (butter, shortening or margarine) into a combination of dry ingredients until the mixture resembles coarse "mealy" flakes.

Deglaze: A process used after browning meat or poultry. The fat is poured out and stock, wine, vinegar or juice is added and briskly simmered to release any caramelized bits of meat or poultry from the bottom of the pan. This liquid is usually reduced further to concentrate its flavor and added directly to a stew or strained through a fine sieve to create a smooth sauce.

Desiccated: Dried and untreated. (In this book, this term refers to dried coconut, found in health food stores.)

Dice: To cut a whole food into small uniform cubes.

Dissolve: When an ingredient (solid or granular) becomes totally incorporated within a liquid. Generally, hot liquids will melt down or liquify another ingredient better than cold but this is not always the case. For example, cornstarch must first be dissolved in a cold liquid before it's used to thicken a hot mixture.

Dock: To prick small holes in several types of pastry or certain yeast doughs to prevent the mixture from rising (bubbling) in the oven. When any dough enters a hot oven, the heat reacts with the liquid in the mixture to create steam within the dough. Since steam naturally rises, it would carry the surrounding dough upward if not docked.

Dollop: A generous spoonful of a creamy or thickened substance such as whipped cream, sour cream or preserves used to garnish or to enrich a mixture.

Drawn: Another term for "clarified" when referring to melted butter that's been skimmed of its milk solids. This term also refers to a whole fish that's been gutted.

Dredge: To coat foods with a substance (commonly flour, bread crumbs or cornmeal) before panfrying or deep-frying.

Dust: To impart a light fine coating of a powdered substance (like flour) over the surface of a food before browning or over a baking pan after greasing.

Emulsion, to emulsify: When two incompatible liquids (such as oil and water) are mixed together, they will separate from each other as soon as you stop mixing. In order to blend these substances and "emulsify" or thicken them, you'll need to add an "emulsifier," an ingredient that is compatible with each of the other substances. When you add a natural emulsifier (such as eggs or an acid like dry or prepared mustard, vinegar, lemon or wine), the ingredients become linked together in a suspended state that remains stable for a varied length of time. Egg yolks create the most stable emulsions and can last for many days (as with mayonnaise). A blender is a good choice when trying to blend a mixture that has no natural emulsifiers since a food processor tends to leave these types of mixtures thinner and more watery.

Fold: To combine gently two mixtures using a large rubber spatula. Usually one mixture is thick and highly flavored and the other is light and either plain or sweetened. The folding motion is a delicate one, used to create an ultimately lighter texture in your flavored base.

Ganache: Chocolate (usually semisweet or bittersweet) blended with heated heavy cream until smooth and then strained through a triple-mesh wire sieve. This mixture is frequently poured over cakes and rich tortes to give them an intensely shiny—almost glassy—finish.

Grate: To rub a whole food through sharp, raised holes to reduce it into small pieces or thin shreds. See also Shred.

Grease: To coat a pan with butter, shortening or oil. This also refers to the fatty, oily substance that rises to the top of a hot mixture and solidifies once chilled.

Grind: To reduce a hard or semihard substance to a fine powder. Also means to chop meat, poultry or fish to varying degrees of fineness.

Hot-water bath: A large pan of almost boiling water (also called a bain-marie) in which another pan of a delicate mixture is partially submerged so that the food cooks gently. The water cushions the mixture from direct and aggressive exposure to heat. Also used to reheat cooked foods such as rice or pasta that require gentle handling to preserve texture.

Infuse: To impart to a liquid a flavor and aroma, usually of herbs or spices through steeping or simmering. See also Steep and Simmer.

Julienne: To cut vegetables into thin sticks of equal proportion; synonymous with "matchstick."

Knead: To use your hands to work a mixture until it's smooth. When making a yeast dough, vigorous and repetitive kneading creates a glutinous network within the dough that will entrap living yeast cells. (See Notes on Baking Yeast Breads, page 373.)

Leaven: To use a substance such as baking powder, baking soda or yeast to create the formation of gases within a mixture so that it rises up, resulting in a lighter texture and increased volume when cooked.

Liaison: The addition of one substance to another (usually heated) for the purpose of thickening and enriching the texture. Some examples of mixtures used to thicken are butter and flour kneaded together until smooth (called *beurre manié*), or the combination of eggs and heavy cream, or cornstarch dissolved in a cold liquid. Another form of liaison is straining a soup or sauce, puréeing the solids (vegetables) and returning them to the liquid to thicken it. When working with a delicate egg-based liaison, it's important to add the eggs to the hot cream slowly or they can easily curdle.

Macerate: A process similar to marinating that involves steeping fruits in a liquid that usually contains alcohol, such as brandy or wine. Maceration has less to do with tenderizing and more to do with flavor absorption.

TIPS
FROM A TEACHER

How to be a Better Chopper

At the start of my cooking classes, I take aside each new student and go through the proper techniques for using a knife and the proper stance for chopping. Following are the most common problems that home cooks encounter when chopping—and their solutions. But the primary solution is a good chef's knife that's sharp and in perfect condition (see How to Keep Your Knives Sharp, page 294). A pastry scraper is a great help, too.

Don't allow your fingertips to hang over the blade and onto your work surface while chopping: Hold your fingers straight out resting on the dull side of your knife. Never, ever bend them.

Don't lift the blade completely off the board after every chop: Forget the "chop, chop, chop" method. Instead, position your knife over the pile of vegetables with the knife tip touching the board—and the handle raised. Now in a smooth, rhythmical and repetitive sequence, slide the blade down over the vegetables while pushing the tip outward (away from you). Then raise the handle only, and pull the blade back to where you originally started. While keeping the tip down at all times, repeat this motion over the pile of vegetables (moving the handle away from you and then back toward you until you run over the entire pile). The tip of the blade should never leave the work surface, allowing only the handle

Marinate: To tenderize or impart flavor to foods by coating them in a seasoned mixture (a paste of herbs and spices or a dry spice blend) or soaking them in a wet mixture that is usually acidic. When a marinade contains an acidic ingredient (vinegar, wine or citrus juice) and is applied to a tough (fibrous) type of meat for several hours or longer, the acid breaks down some of the connective tissue and renders the cooked meat more tender and flavorful. (When doing this, always use a nonreactive container or place the marinated foods into a sealed plastic bag.) Marinades are also applied to blanched vegetables, poultry and delicate types of fish, but care should be taken either to reduce the acidic ingredients or to apply the marinade for a shorter time; overmarinating these already tender foods will adversely affect their texture and in some cases (as with fish), actually cook the flesh.

Mince: To chop into very small pieces.

Mirepoix: See Soffritto.

---

to guide you as you determine in which direction to chop.

Don't use a blade that's too short for large amounts of vegetables: Although using a long blade might seem intimidating at first, in the long run it's more efficient and actually makes chopping fun instead of a chore. Generally, when chopping more than two cups of vegetables, use the larger ten-inch chef's knife.

Don't stand with your hips turned sideways when chopping: When chopping, stand with your feet spread about six to eight inches apart. Your shoulders and body should be facing straight ahead toward your work surface.

Don't chop on a counter that's too low or too high: Optimally, your counter should be just a few inches below waist level. If it's too low, you'll be forced to hunch over and risk a severe backache. If too high, you'll feel compelled to stand on your tiptoes and can easily lose your balance.

Don't chop with your body too far away from the counter, your shoulders hunched up or your elbows sticking out: At the start of my cooking courses, this is the most common chopping stance among many of my students. Before you begin to chop, make sure that your body touches the counter, that your shoulders are down and relaxed and that your elbows only slightly jut from your

sides. And your head should be tilted down with focus.

Don't scrape up your vegetables with the blade of your knife: This is a sure way to dull your blade. Instead, use a pastry scraper and put it within easy reach.

Nonreactive: A term used to describe cookware that does not react chemically with acidic foods like tomatoes, vinegar, wine and citrus juice. Nonreactive materials that can be used safely with acidic ingredients are glass, ceramic, porcelain, stainless steel, enamel-coated cast iron and anodized aluminum. Regular cast iron and aluminum and unlined copper should never be used with acidic foods.

Oxidize: A reaction that occurs when the color or texture of a specific food is adversely affected by prolonged exposure to air.

Panfry: To cook quickly vegetables, tender cuts of meat, chicken and fish in no fat or a very small amount of fat. The term is often used interchangeably with sauté.

Parboil: To precook vegetables partially and tenderize them before applying another method to cook them completely, such as sautéing. See Blanch, which is often used interchangeably.

Pare: To remove the outer peel or skin from fruits or vegetables. This also refers to the process of "paring down" a vegetable so each piece is the same size to ensure even cooking and uniform appearance; this is commonly done with root vegetables like carrots and potatoes.

Pasteurize: The commercial process of using heat to kill bacteria in milk products; the milk is then quickly cooled to protect its fresh flavor. Pasteurized dairy products are more perishable, but have a better flavor than those that have been ultrapasteurized (see Ultrapasteurize).

Pith: The undesirable bitter, white leathery substance that lies between the flesh of citrus fruits and the zest (colored outer layer). Removing the pith is best accomplished with a flexible sharp knife.

Plump: To soak a dried fruit in a warm or hot liquid to soften it. This can also be done by steaming the food over simmering water in a covered pot. Plumping is also a great way to revamp a sorry-looking vanilla bean.

Poach: To simmer or boil food in shallow liquid (stock or water) to cover. Poaching is done with the lid on and (most often) with the flame low.

Purée: To pulverize a solid (usually cooked or raw vegetables or fruits) to a smooth, liquid or pastelike consistency. This is usually done in a blender or food processor, or by cranking a mixture through a food mill.

Reduce: To concentrate flavors in a liquid by briskly boiling it uncovered until a portion of the water evaporates and the liquid thickens. Frequently, this process is applied to pan juices after roasting to intensify sauces and when making various types of stock in different strengths.

Refresh: To stop the cooking process immediately after blanching (parboiling) vegetables or fruit by quickly plunging the drained partially cooked vegetables into a bowl of ice-cold water. By doing this, the firm texture and vibrant color of the vegetable will remain. Also, this process refers to reheating briefly frozen toasted nuts or day-old (or thawed frozen) breads in order to "awaken" their fresh taste and aroma.

Ribbon: This describes the way a batter (or a creamed sugar and egg mixture) will fall back on itself when allowed to drop off of a spoon or whisk.

Roast: To cook raw foods on a shallow pan (usually in the oven) to encourage browning. Frequently both meats and poultry are placed on a wire rack within the roasting pan to enable the heat to circulate and brown the bottom of the food.

Roux: A cooked mixture of flour and butter (usually in equal proportion), used to thicken sauces and soups.

Sauté: To cook or brown foods quickly in a small amount of hot fat (usually butter or oil).

Scald: To heat a liquid to the point where tiny bubbles are visible around the edge of the liquid; this is just below the simmering point (149°F).

Score: To make overlapping shallow incisions (either in a crosshatch or diagonal lattice pattern). Frequently done to the thick layer of top fat on a ham to enable heat to penetrate the meat. Scoring also creates a decorative affect on the exterior.

Sear: To seal in juices by quickly cooking the outside of food (usually but not exclusively meat) under intense heat to induce overall browning. Meat is usually seared before braising it gently and slowly.

Shred: To rub a whole food (cheese, cabbage, lettuce) through the raised (elongated) holes of a grater to create long, thin pieces.

Shuck: To remove clams, mussels and oysters from their shells. Also to remove corn from its outer husk.

Skim: To remove any undesirable substance (such as fat or foam) that rises to the top of a mixture as it cooks or cools.

Sieve: A wire mesh container with holes of different sizes. Sieves are used to drain, sift and purée foods.

Sift: To lighten and remove lumps from flour, sugar or a combination of dry ingredients, by using a sifter, sieve or, often, a whisk.

Simmer: When a liquid is heated to the point where small bubbles are seen slowly forming under the top surface (210°F). These bubbles will burst before they reach the surface. Simmering takes place just before a mixture reaches the boiling point.

Snip: To use kitchen scissors to cut food into small pieces.

Soffritto: The Italian term for an assortment of minced aromatic vegetables, (known as *mirepoix* in French and *sofrito* in Spanish) slowly cooked as a base for various sauces and soups.

Steam: The method of cooking food above boiling liquid in a covered environment.

Steep: To submerge and soak an ingredient in liquid (usually heated) in order to infuse the liquid with flavor.

Stew: The process in which food cooks slowly within a varied amount of liquid until very tender. See Braise.

Stir-fry: To cook rapidly chunks of vegetables or strips of lean meat or poultry in a small amount of hot fat, while stirring and tossing constantly. Usually done in a wok or large skillet.

Sweat: To cook minced vegetables slowly in hot fat covered closely with greased waxed paper to prevent the loss of moisture and flavor. Vegetables are prepared this way for a soffritto and will become and stay unusually sweet.

Temper: The process of slowly adding a hot mixture to a heat-sensitive mixture (usually containing eggs or cream) to prevent the delicate ingredients from shocking and curdling. Raw eggs (alone) will begin to coagulate (curdle) at a temperature of 155°F; the addition of sugar or milk to raw eggs will raise the curdling point to 175°F (180°F maximum). The addition of flour or cornstarch to the egg, cream and sugar mixture will change the chemistry of the eggs, enabling them to be brought briefly to a boil (212°F), while stirring constantly to prevent lumps. The term "temper" is also used regarding working with melted chocolate.

Tepid: The temperature of a liquid when it touches a soft, callus-free part of the body and feels "just warm."

Ultrapasteurize: The commercial process of heating milk products to a very high temperature (300°F) and keeping them there for a certain length of time in order to retard the growth of bacteria and increase shelf life beyond the point of normal pasteurization. The flavor and whipping ability of cream, however, is adversely affected by ultrapasteurization.

Zest: The deeply colored, outer skin of citrus fruits, excluding the bitter white pith that lies just beneath it. Always scrub and dry fruit before removing the zest.

TIPS FOR THE TABLE

A beautifully set table will turn a simple, casual meal into a festive occasion. And conversely, an improperly, shoddily set table will not only detract from the food you've created but also can cause confusion for your guests. An elegant, inviting table does not require a lot of expense or family heirlooms. Just a little time, imagination and a few touches like flowers and candles will tell your guests that you really care. Whether the event is a family-style soup supper or a formal multicourse dinner, here are a few tips for your table.

I usually set my table the day before entertaining, not only for convenience —seeing the table beautifully assembled puts me in the mood for the wonderful evening to come. I also arrange fresh flowers either the evening before or early on the day of entertaining to enable the petals to open. Instead of a traditional bouquet, fill small individual bud vases with an assortment of fresh flowers and stagger them down the length of the table. Alternatively, center the table with a bowl filled with plump, deeply colored assorted vegetables, and tuck among them small bunches of fresh herbs (such as thyme) for a wonderful fragrance. Always include candles (even unlit for a luncheon), but take care with the height and position. There's nothing worse—even at the most exquisitely dressed table—than having to play peekaboo with a pot of pansies in order to see your dining companions across the table. So, don't place a tall bouquet or candelabra smack in front of a place setting.

The Proper Place Setting

When setting a table, only those utensils required by the menu should be placed on the table. And make sure there's a comfortable distance between the center of one person's plate to the center of the adjoining plate. All flatware should be lined up evenly along the bottom edge of the plate in the order of use, from the outside to the plate. The rim of the empty dinner plate (or service plate for a formal meal) should be one inch from the edge of the table. (If you will be serving a salad course to start an informal meal, place the empty salad plate in the center of the dinner plate.) Arrange the napkin to the left of the plate, either under the forks or to the left of them. (Napkins with pretty frills should be folded so the frill is facing out to the left.) At a formal dinner, place the napkin on the serving plate, using a decorative fold or a napkin ring.

Time-tested rules govern the placement of flatware and also instruct guests (without being told) which knife, fork or spoon to use for each course. Most forks go to the left of the plate in the order of use, beginning from the outside. If you are serving a salad course before the entrée, for example, the short-pronged salad fork should go to the far left, but if you plan to serve the salad after dinner, the salad fork goes between the dinner fork and the dinner plate. Most knives go to the right of the plate with the cutting edge facing the plate. If providing a fish knife or a steak knife, it goes to the right of the dinner knife. And if a salad knife is required, it goes to the far right or far left, depending on the sequence of a salad course. Teaspoons (for coffee or tea) go to the right of the dinner knife and a soup spoon, if using, or a cocktail fork goes to the far right of the knives. Dessert utensils, however, are a different matter altogether. Dessert forks and spoons should be placed (horizontally) above the top rim of the dinner plate with the prongs of the fork pointing to the right and the bowl of the spoon facing left; if using both, the fork goes above the spoon.

Other elements of a place setting include bread and butter plates and knives. These go to the upper left of the dinner plate, just over the forks; the butter knife goes across the plate with its handle on the right and its cutting edge facing the forks. If you are supplying individual salt and pepper dispensers for each guest, they go above the forks, to the left of the dessert utensils; if two guests will be sharing these, place in between them. Glasses should be placed above the knives, with the water goblet above the first knife and the wine glass to its right. If there are several glasses for multiple wines, group them in a semicircle (from left to right) in the order of use or place them in order of height, descending from the water goblet toward the right. (Only remove a wine glass when it's empty, even if a new wine has been poured.) Finally, when a hot beverage will be served with the meal, the cup and saucer should be placed to the upper right of the teaspoon. But if coffee will be served in the living room after the meal, accompany each cup with a teaspoon placed on the saucer.

Dinner is Served

Before you announce to your guests that "dinner is served," be sure to light the candles and pour ice water into the goblets—but don't pour wine until your guests are seated. Food may be served already portioned on individual dishes or from a large platter, but remember to serve from the left side and clear used plates and utensils from the right. (Of course, an informal meal can be just served family-style by placing big bowls and platters of food on the table for the guests to pass around and help themselves.)

For an informal dinner, you may place the plate or bowl containing the first course (appetizer, salad, or soup) directly on the dinner plate after the guests are seated. Then remove it, leaving the dinner plate until the entrée is ready to serve. For a very formal affair, place the appetizer plate on a service plate; then remove both plates and replace with a dinner plate immediately. There should always be a plate in front of each guest.

In addition to great food and atmosphere, memorable entertaining depends on a good mix of people. Always give as much thought to your guest list as you do to your menu. And don't stand on ceremony. Even if you have the seating all planned, you might notice that one guest is getting along especially well with someone new. Sit them together. Be flexible and remember that the more relaxed you are, the more comfortable your guests will be.

CHAPTER II

BETTER THAN STORE-BOUGHT

Those Homemade Basics

In this chapter, I have shared my recipes for those commonly pur-chased foods that taste infinitely better when made at home. Not only will these recipes provide you and your family with superior flavor and texture, but the mere presence of these homemade staples will give your kitchen a more nurturing and homey quality. This chapter is dedicated to helping even the busiest people to provide warmth and comfort to the ones they love. To those who wonder what "real" difference these recipes make, I suggest you serve your family a batch of the lightest buttermilk pancakes (made from your own dry mix) and a mug of rich hot cocoa (from a dry mix which you've mixed and stored in bulk). I think you'll be surprised at how much more nurturing these recipes will enable you to feel.

MOM'S PANCAKE AND WAFFLE MIX

YIELD: generously fills a 5-pound canister

On hectic weekday mornings, many of us substitute a "breakfast on the run" scenario for a warm meal, then feel guilty for sending our kids to school without something warm in their tummies. Even so, that box of commercial pancake mix just sat in my cupboard like a fixture for years. Then I decided to make my own mix and I was in business! The pancakes from this mix, especially when made with buttermilk, are the lightest, most tender and most delicious I've ever had, and my kids go crazy for them. Because most people don't always have buttermilk on hand, the dry mix is written for the use of whole milk. But I strongly urge that you buy some buttermilk and prepare that variation.

INGREDIENTS

14 cups plain (not self-rising) cake flour* (about two 32-ounce boxes less 1½ cups)

6 tablespoons double-acting baking powder

4 teaspoons salt

1 cup plus 2 tablespoons sugar

* See section on Staples

1) **To prepare mix:** Whisk together all the ingredients in an 8-quart mixing bowl. Sift the mixture into another large bowl and then sift back into the original bowl. Spoon into a 5-pound canister with a tight-fitting lid. Label so you don't confuse it with your regular all-purpose flour. Store in a cool dry place.

SPECIAL EQUIPMENT

Two 8-quart bowls or large pots

Sifter or large triple-mesh wire sieve

Batter whisk or wide blending fork

Nonstick griddle

Time Management Tips

Although you'll get the best texture if you mix the batter in the morning, you can combine the wet ingredients and the dry ingredients in separate covered bowls the night before. Store the wet mixture in the refrigerator and leave the dry ingredients at room temperature overnight. And the next time you have a leisurely weekend morning, try making a batch of waffles and freezing them between sheets of waxed paper in heavy-duty plastic bags for school mornings. Just pop them in the toaster straight from the freezer.

〜〜〜

Pancakes

Many cookbooks recommend leaving lots of lumps in pancake batters but I don't agree. All too often, this allows dry pockets of unincorporated dry mix to remain in the pancakes even after cooking. Because my mix is made with cake flour, which is very low in gluten, it is more forgiving of extra stirring to break up obvious lumps. Still don't go overboard; even pancakes made with cake flour will become tough if stirred too vigorously. An easy way to ladle pancake batter onto a griddle is to use a ¼-cup dry measuring scoop.

Mom's Pancakes

YIELD: eight to ten 4-inch pancakes or 3 to 4 waffles

INGREDIENTS

1 cup milk

2 tablespoons butter, melted

1 extra-large egg

2 tablespoons vegetable oil, plus more for the griddle

2 tablespoons water

1½ cups Mom's Pancake and Waffle Mix (preceding)

Fresh berries, rinsed and patted dry (optional)

Butter and warmed pure maple syrup, for accompaniments

1) *To prepare batter:* In a small bowl, combine milk, melted butter, egg, vegetable oil and the water and mix well. Measure pancake mix into a medium mixing bowl. Gently stir the wet ingredients into the pancake mix using a batter whisk or a wide blending fork. A few lumps are OK; don't overly mix the batter or your pancakes will be tough.

2) *To cook pancakes:* Heat a nonstick griddle or large skillet and, when hot, brush lightly with vegetable oil. Pour ¼ cup batter onto the hot griddle. If desired, scatter a couple of fresh berries on top. Cook over medium-high heat until bubbles appear on the surface, 1 to 2 minutes. Turn and cook on the other side until golden, about 1 minute. Remove to a platter and serve immediately with butter and warmed pure maple syrup.

Mom's Buttermilk Pancakes

These are superior in texture and taste to the version made with whole milk. Whisk 1 teaspoon baking soda into the measured dry pancake mix. Substitute 1¼ cups buttermilk for the whole milk and add an additional tablespoon water to the wet ingredients.

Mom's Waffles

It's preferable to use the batter for Mom's Buttermilk Pancakes for assured crispness! Cook in a waffle iron according to the manufacturer's instructions. Belgian waffle irons are particularly nice since the craters in the waffle are extra deep to house more warm syrup.

MOM'S HOT COCOA MIX

YIELD: enough dry mix for about 6 quarts (24 cups) hot cocoa

Have you ever met a kid who didn't welcome a hefty mug of rich hot cocoa on a chilly morning or after a day in the snow? If you have children or neighbors who have children, this recipe will undoubtedly get a lot of action! Also, if you have friends who go skiing often, this cocoa mix makes a fabulous gift.

SPECIAL EQUIPMENT
Large triple-mesh wire sieve

4- to 5-quart canister, preferably airtight

Pastry bag, preferably with a star tip (only if garnishing with whipped cream)

FOR THE COCOA MIX

3 cups Dutch-processed unsweetened cocoa powder*

4½ cups superfine sugar or vanilla sugar (following)

6½ cups dry nonfat milk

⅓ teaspoon salt

1 to 2 teaspoons ground cinnamon (optional)

FOR ONE MUG OF HOT COCOA

⅓ generous cup Mom's Hot Cocoa Mix

1 cup boiling water or ½ cup hot milk and ½ cup boiling water

½ teaspoon pure vanilla extract

SUGGESTED GARNISHES

Cinnamon sticks, for stirring

Perfect Whipped Cream (page 84)

Shaved bittersweet or semisweet chocolate (see below) or a few mini marshmallows

* See section on Staples

Vanilla Sugar

This essence is one of the easiest ways to boost the flavor of hot cocoa or iced tea, as well as to add a distinctive dimension in both flavor and appearance to many creamy desserts. Since vanilla beans can be quite costly, this recipe enables you to make use of every bit! After using the seeds to flavor ice cream, pastry cream or flan, you can quickly and easily make vanilla sugar. Simply insert the empty pod into a jar of granulated white sugar (regular or superfine) and after a good shake, cover the jar and allow it to sit undisturbed for a month or so to allow the sugar to become incredibly fragrant and infused with the sultry flavor of vanilla. To replenish your supply, simply add more granulated sugar to the jar, apply the lid and give the jar a good shake to redistribute the contents.

To start a new batch: Use 4 cups granulated white sugar or instant-dissolving superfine sugar and 1 to 3 supple vanilla beans, split lengthwise and seeds removed. (Save the shells after the seeds have been used in other recipes.) Place in a jar with tight lid and shake the sugar mixture to distribute the beans throughout. Attach a label and let the sugar sit unopened for at least 2 weeks (preferably 1 month) before using.

Lemon or orange sugar: A variation on this concept is to omit the vanilla bean and substitute the minced zest (colored part of the rind only without any white pith) of either 2 large lemons or navel oranges. Store as you would vanilla sugar.

1) *To prepare cocoa mix:* Whisk together all of the dry ingredients in a 6-quart bowl. Sift mixture through a large triple-mesh sieve into another bowl, discarding any large crystals of sugar or dry milk left in the bottom of the sieve. Sift back into the original bowl. Store in an airtight 4- to 5-quart canister.

2) *To make a cup of cocoa:* Place a generous ⅓ cup dry mix into a mug. (Use less mix for a smaller cup.) Fill mug with boiling water or hot milk and boiling water. Add vanilla and stir well (with cinnamon stick if desired) and top with any of the suggested garnishes. If serving to young children, you might want to stir in a bit of cold milk just to take the heat off.

3) *To shave chocolate, if using:* Run a regular vegetable peeler across a block of firm bittersweet or semisweet chocolate. Store extras in an airtight container.

LIP SMACKIN' LEMONADE

YIELD: about twelve 8-ounce glasses

During the summer months, even this hefty amount of lemonade is never enough since the kids seem to drink it as fast as I can make it! Always bring the lemons to room temperature before extracting the juice. I use a wooden reamer to do the job because it gives me the most control but any other juicing device will do.

INGREDIENTS

3 cups strained fresh lemon juice (from about 20 large lemons, at room temperature)

3 cups superfine sugar

12 cups cold water

2 lemons, thinly sliced into rounds

1 to 2 tablespoons grenadine syrup (optional)

Fresh mint sprigs, for garnish

Roll each lemon on your kitchen counter, cut through the middle (not through stem end) extract, measure and chill juice. Place sugar and 4 cups of the water in a medium-sized saucepan and stir to dissolve sugar. Bring mixture to a full boil over medium heat and pour into a large nonreactive mixing bowl. Stir in remaining 8 cups of cold water along with strained lemon juice. Add sliced lemons and, if desired, stir in just enough grenadine until juice becomes a subtle pinkish color. Divide between 2 large pitchers, cover well and refrigerate until thoroughly chilled. Pour into tall glasses over ice and garnish each glass with a lemon slice and a fresh mint sprig.

THE GREATEST GRANOLA

YIELD: about 6 cups

Granola is the perfect breakfast cereal. Loaded with protein and natural fiber, it's a great way to start your day or get a quick mid-morning or afternoon "pick me up." The delicious combination of tastes and textures keeps this from tasting like health food (even though it really is). Feel free to change the types of nuts, dried fruits or the kind of sweetener, so you can customize your own favorite concoction. Serve with milk for breakfast or sprinkle on yogurt for lunch. Or simply enjoy out of hand as a snack.

INGREDIENTS

2 cups regular (not quick cooking) rolled oats*

½ cup shredded unsweetened desiccated coconut*

½ cup unsweetened wheat germ*

½ cup unprocessed wheat bran*

1 cup whole nuts, toasted and chopped, below, (a combination of

TIPS
FROM A TEACHER

How to Toast Nuts and Seeds

It amazes me how many recipes use raw nuts when a toasted nut is so far superior in both taste and aroma. Eating an untoasted nut is like eating chicken stock that's been made without browned chicken bones and aromatic vegetables. The taste is flat and without dimension. The only way to bring out the full flavor in nuts is to heat them until golden. Raw seeds have a bit more character than raw nuts, but heat will always enhance their inherent flavor and better release their aroma. Nuts are usually toasted in the oven using dry heat. Or, they can be sautéed in a skillet in melted butter to give them extra richness. Seeds should be toasted dry in a skillet while stirring constantly to prevent scorching; both nuts and seeds must be toasted carefully since once they become fragrant, they are almost done. If you overtoast them they will taste bitter. The term "blanched" when referring to nuts means that the thin brown skin covering a shelled nut has been removed. When toasted, this skin becomes bitter, so it's best to use blanched nuts when toasting. And when oven-toasting nuts, avoid very dark baking sheets since they are too heat retentive and will cause the nuts to scorch on the bottom.

unsalted macadamias, blanched toasted almonds and unsalted pistachios or walnuts. Sunflower seeds, hulled pumpkin seeds, toasted pine nuts are also wonderful choices)

½ stick (4 tablespoons) unsalted butter or ¼ cup safflower or canola oil

⅓ cup mild honey or pure maple syrup or ½ cup unsweetened apple juice

1 scant teaspoon ground cinnamon

1 teaspoon pure vanilla extract

½ teaspoon pure almond extract

1 cup chopped assorted dried fruits (a combination of apricots, pitted prunes, cherries and light and dark raisins)

* See section on Staples

1) *To set up:* Preheat the oven to 350°F. In a medium-sized bowl, mix together rolled oats, coconut, wheat germ, wheat bran and toasted nuts.

To oven-toast nuts: Place nuts in a single layer on a shallow baking sheet. Place the sheet into a cold oven; then turn temperature to 350°F and bake until nuts turn golden, 8 to 12 minutes. Shake the sheet occasionally to redistribute nuts so they won't burn. Nuts can be toasted days (or weeks) in advance and stored at room temperature, well covered, for 1 week or in the freezer for longer storage.

To sauté nuts: For each 1 cup nuts, melt 3 to 4 tablespoons butter in a heavy-bottomed skillet over medium heat. When butter is hot and bubbling, add a single layer of nuts and stir to coat with butter. Reduce heat to low and cook, stirring constantly, until nuts are golden and fragrant, 3 to 4 minutes. Remove to a plate lined with paper toweling to remove excess butter. Since sautéed nuts don't store well, assemble them no more than 2 hours ahead and leave at room temperature until needed.

To toast seeds: Heat a small heavy-bottomed skillet over medium heat and, when hot, add a thin layer of seeds. Stir briskly until seeds are golden but not overly dark, 1 to 2 minutes.

Remove seeds from skillet at once to cool or use as directed in your recipe. Store as you would oven-toasted nuts.

To freeze and refresh toasted nuts: Freeze raw or toasted nuts in a doubled heavy-duty plastic bag for up to 6 months. To awaken their savory fresh flavor, place frozen seeds or nuts on a shallow baking sheet and place in a cold oven. Turn temperature to 350°F and heat nuts until warmed throughout, about 5 minutes.

2) To prepare granola: In a small saucepan, melt butter or heat the oil over low heat. Add either honey, maple syrup or apple juice and stir well to combine. Heat until just hot throughout and then stir in cinnamon. Let heat a few seconds to release the flavor of the spice. Remove from heat and stir in vanilla and almond extracts. Pour this over the dry mixture and stir well to combine.

3) To bake: Pour the granola onto a large shallow baking sheet and bake stirring every 5 minutes or so, until the mixture is golden throughout. This will take 15 to 20 minutes; if using oil and the increased amount of apple juice, bake for about 25 minutes.

4) To complete and store: Stir dried fruit into hot granola mixture. Let cool thoroughly (the granola will feel crisp when cool) and store at room temperature in an airtight container.

THE BEST DRIED BREAD CRUMBS

YIELD: 2 to 3 cups

SPECIAL EQUIPMENT
Food processor or rolling pin

Once you've tasted your own dried bread crumbs, you'll stop buying those tasteless crumbs found in the supermarket. The secret is using best-quality Italian bread that has sesame seeds on top. The seeds create a wonderful aroma and dimension in taste that truly puts these crumbs above all others. I never use stale bread, since the best crumbs are made from the freshest bread that's been perfectly toasted. Of course if you have day-old Italian bread sitting around, by all means toast it and grind away. Or if you're in a hurry and have no Italian bread, just use any white or whole wheat sandwich bread. Although the food processor will give the most uniform results, you can use a rolling pin along with your fingertips to crush the toasted slices into fine crumbs. Since these crumbs freeze perfectly, make a large batch and store them. Just scoop them straight from the freezer (no need to thaw) and use as desired. The exception to this is when using them to coat foods for deep-frying; then it's best to allow the crumbs to come to room temperature so the oil remains hot and the food will only absorb a minimum of oil.

INGREDIENTS
1 large, fresh loaf Italian bread (preferably with sesame seeds on top)

1) *To toast bread:* Preheat the oven to 375°F. Slice bread into 1-inch slices and lay in a single layer on a wire cooling rack set on a shallow baking sheet. Bake for 10 minutes. Turn off the heat and let the bread remain there until very crisp, about 15 minutes.

2) *To prepare crumbs:* When slices are cool enough to handle, crush them and drop into the bowl of a food processor fitted with the steel blade. Process bread until of fine crumb consistency. (Alternatively, crush them with a rolling pin.) Remove to a bowl and let cool. Use as directed.

3) *To store:* Place crumbs into a doubled heavy-duty plastic bag and store in the freezer until needed.

NOT-TOO-HOT CAJUN SPICE BLEND

YIELD: about 1 cup

Many people assume that foods prepared with Cajun spices will be searing hot. My blend however, is savory and mellow—my kids even love it. Although there is quite enough cayenne to liven things up, when applied to foods correctly, the intensity and individuality of these spices will meld to complement, not overpower your food. Spice blends should enhance, not overwhelm the natural flavors of fish, poultry or meat. If you wish to "boot up" my blend a bit, use rounded tablespoonfuls of ground cayenne instead of leveled ones.

SPECIAL EQUIPMENT
Wide-mouth funnel

½-pint jar with screw-top lid

INGREDIENTS

¼ cup onion powder* (not onion salt)

¼ cup garlic powder* (not garlic salt)

1 to 2 tablespoons freshly ground black pepper

1½ teaspoons ground white pepper

2 tablespoons cayenne pepper

1 teaspoon hot paprika

1 tablespoon sweet paprika

1 tablespoon salt (optional)

* See section on Staples

Combine all the ingredients in a medium-sized mixing bowl using a whisk. Insert the stem of a wide mouth funnel over the opening of a ½-pint jar and spoon in the spice mixture. Label, date and store in a cool, dark cupboard away from direct sun to preserve freshness.

There's No Churn in My Basement for . . .
HOMEMADE SWEET CREAM BUTTER

YIELD: ¾ to 1 cup butter

No, I don't have an old-fashioned churn in my basement, and it doesn't take hours or large muscles to make your own butter. With a food processor, I can make soft, delicious sweet cream butter any time I choose. The funniest part? This is one of the simplest procedures to perform and yet, it always gets the most oohs and ahhs from both my guests and students. As a rule I don't cook with my butter, but I always serve fresh homemade butter with my biscuits, homemade breads, savory muffins or as a topping for grilled meat, fish and chicken. And please make the effort to locate pasteurized cream (see Staples) since the ultrapasteurized product is not nearly as flavorful.

INGREDIENTS
2 cups heavy cream (preferably not ultrapasteurized)
½ to ¾ teaspoon salt

1) **To prepare butter:** Place cream and salt into the bowl of a food processor fitted with the steel blade (or use a blender or heavy mixer). Whip cream until the pure butterfat totally separates from the milky whey, 4 to 7 minutes (this will take longer if not using a food processor). It's finished when the mixture sounds very slushy as the liquid splashes against the sides of the bowl. When you stop the machine, the butter will be a separate mass surrounded by a shallow pool of milky liquid (this is *pure* buttermilk). Pour this mixture into a fine-mesh strainer and shake until most of the liquid has drained out. Fold a clean, strong cotton or linen kitchen towel in half and dump the butter onto the center. Gather the ends of the towel and firmly squeeze to remove any excess buttermilk.

2) *To store:* Transfer butter to an attractive 1-cup crock or ramekin and, using the towel, pat off any remaining beads of liquid. Brush the top with a decorative comb, if desired, and either use immediately or cover with plastic wrap and refrigerate. For best consistency, always bring butter close to room temperature before serving as a spread.

Variations

Transfer the finished butter into the cleaned and dried bowl of a food processor; add a few tablespoons of your favorite preserves, process until smooth and spread on fresh biscuits or plain toast. Or, add to the butter a combination of chopped fresh or crumbled dried herbs, minced garlic, minced green onion, strained fresh lemon juice and chopped drained capers; serve on top of broiled fresh fish, grilled steak or chicken.

Clarified butter (also known as "drawn" butter or as *ghee* in Indian cooking), is used both as a dipping sauce and for frying at high temperatures without burning. The clarifying process of slowly melting and straining butter removes thin, milky nonfat substances that burn easily. After melting, these nonfat substances will eventually separate from the pure, vibrant yellow butterfat. It's preferable to clarify butter before using it as a dipping sauce, because the milk solids detract from the esthetic clarity or eye appeal of melted butter when serving. Conveniently, since these milky proteins are what make whole butter more susceptible to spoilage, removing them enables clarified butter to be kept successfully for many months in the refrigerator. Despite the fact that clarified butter is very handy for certain cooking tasks, its flavor is not as rich as full butter and therefore is not recommended as a substitute when baking.

To clarify butter: Melt 1 or more sticks of butter in a heavy-bottomed saucepan (preferably with a spout) over low heat until totally liquid. Remove from heat and let butter settle for 15 minutes. Using a fine-mesh skimmer or a small spoon, remove the white foamy substance that sits on top of the butterfat. When no milky solids remain on top, pour the pure, vibrant yellow butterfat through the fine-mesh skimmer or a fine-mesh sieve into a container, leaving any milky nonfat residue behind. Store in a well-sealed container in the refrigerator for up to 6 months.

TIPS
FROM A TEACHER

Clarified Butter

LOW-FAT CREAM CHEESE OR SOUR CREAM

YIELD: about 1½ cups

SPECIAL EQUIPMENT
Food processor or blender

School lunches have always been a problem for me. My kids get into this mind-set where they'll only eat one thing for lunch every day for almost a year at a time! When my son Ben went through a "cream cheese on a bagel" period, I worried about its fat content and I began experimenting with the combination of farmer cheese, which is very low in fat, and nonfat plain yogurt as a thinner. With the help of my food processor, I was able to create a version of cream cheese that my son, who is a true connoisseur, loves. When I added a bit more yogurt, the taste and consistency became very much like sour cream. For best consistency, it's wise to chill the mixture thoroughly so it thickens properly. Don't hesitate to substitute this for cream cheese or sour cream in dips and spreads when entertaining as a good way to shave off a bit of fat without sacrificing taste. And you can really let out the stops for dessert!

INGREDIENTS

2 packages (7½ ounces each) farmer cheese (also called hoop, pot or baker's cheese), preferably salted

1 to 3 level tablespoons nonfat plain yogurt

Salt to taste (only if using unsalted farmer cheese)

Q AND **A**

Q. What is buttermilk?

A. Technically, there are two forms of buttermilk. Authentic buttermilk is the milky liquid that results from heavy cream after it has been beaten to the point where it breaks down into two separate components—pure butterfat (butter) and a thin white liquid, which tastes slightly bland yet sweet and can be used to enrich soups or sauces. Cultured buttermilk is a low-fat milk product to which specific bacteria have been added to give the milk a fermented tang and a thick texture. These products are not interchangeable. To create cultured buttermilk, stir 1 teaspoon strained fresh lemon juice into 1 cup milk and allow the liquid to stand at room temperature for 5 to 10 minutes or until slightly thickened. If stored in the refrigerator, shake or stir before using.

Pat the farmer cheese dry and place into the bowl of a food processor fitted with the steel blade or use a blender. Add 1 scant tablespoon yogurt to make cream cheese and 2 to 3 tablespoons to make sour cream. Process until very smooth, about 2 minutes, scraping down the sides occasionally. Place the contents into a container with a tight-fitting lid. Make note of the expiration date of both farmer cheese and yogurt and attach a label to the container with the expiration date. Store in the refrigerator.

Variation with Scallions

Add ⅓ to ½ cup packed minced scallions (green onions) and freshly ground black pepper to taste.

CLASSIC CRÈME FRAÎCHE

Both Savory and Sweet

YIELD: about 1¼ cups

Commercially prepared crème fraîche (unpasteurized French heavy cream), is very much like our sour cream. But the flavor of fresh, homemade crème fraîche is much more balanced with only a mildly tangy flavor and a very creamy, velvety consistency, making it more suitable for a variety of uses, sweet or savory. In most recipes, this crème fraîche can be substituted for heavy cream or sour cream. When a dessert calls for "a dollop of softly whipped heavy cream" to adorn a bowl of gorgeous fresh berries, try this topping instead, with or without the sweetener. Crème fraîche is also a superior alternative to sour cream, since the latter will quickly curdle when exposed to heat. Crème fraîche is much more stable and can be trusted not to "break," even at a boil. And check out my Skinny Crème Fraîche (following) for a version that blends low-fat cottage cheese with nonfat plain yogurt.

SPECIAL EQUIPMENT
Pint jar with screw-top lid or sturdy plastic container with tight-fitting lid

INGREDIENTS

1 cup heavy cream (*not* ultrapasteurized)

¼ cup sour cream

FOR SWEET VERSION ONLY

½ teaspoon pure vanilla extract

1 to 2 tablespoons superfine sugar

1) To prepare: Combine cream and sour cream in a small heavy-bottomed saucepan and place over very low heat until just warm (not hot) stirring constantly to prevent overheating, about 3 minutes. (Gentle heat will encourage the bacteria necessary to fermentation. Excessive heat, however, will ultrapasteurize the mixture and will prevent it from thickening properly.) Pour the crème into a jar or a plastic container with a lid. Cover securely and shake to combine well. Leave the mixture at room temperature for 12 hours or overnight.

2) To finish and store: Stir up crème and, if using sugar and vanilla, stir them in now. When well combined, replace lid and label the container with an expiration date of 10 days later. Chill thoroughly to thicken before using.

3) To serve: Serve the crème instead of whipped cream on fresh berries, fruit tarts or pies. Keep stored in the refrigerator for up to 10 days.

Skinny Crème Fraîche

YIELD: about 2 cups

For this low-fat version, choose cottage cheese and yogurt with similar expiration dates. It's low in fat, but fat on flavor!

INGREDIENTS

8 ounces low-fat small-curd cottage cheese

8 ounces nonfat plain yogurt

FOR SWEET VERSION ONLY

1 teaspoon pure vanilla extract

2 tablespoons superfine sugar

Combine all ingredients in a blender and whirl until perfectly smooth, about 2 minutes on high speed. Pour into a pint jar with a tight-fitting lid and attach a label stating the expiration date from the original containers. Refrigerate for a few hours to thicken and stir mixture before using.

SPECIAL EQUIPMENT
Blender

Pint jar with screw-top lid

For Your Next Snack Attack

For a delicious midday treat, try 1 crisp red or Golden Delicious apple, cored, cut into thin wedges and arranged like a spiral around a dollop of plain or lightly sweetened crème fraîche.

PERFECT WHIPPED CREAM

YIELD: about 4 cups

Just a spoonful of this softly whipped, lightly sweetened cream will transform a simple dessert into something extra special. And the creamy flavor and consistency turns a plain cup of hot cocoa into a magical brew. Generally, when serving whipped cream on a dessert (crème chantilly), you should whip the cream only until the mixture becomes thickened, billowy and the peaks are soft and swooping with tips that bow down slightly. On the other hand, when you intend to fold the whipped cream into other ingredients, it's necessary to whip the cream until the peaks stand straight up with only a slight sway at the tip. This stiffer consistency is also required when you want the whipped cream to maintain its shape for a decorative garnish after being pushed through a pastry tip or if you want to whip your cream hours in

SPECIAL EQUIPMENT
Electric mixer or large balloon whisk and a wide, shallow bowl

advance of using. But regardless of your chosen method of whipping, use a chilled bowl and beaters for best results. Also, it's always better to slightly underwhip your cream than to overwhip it; once you've gone too far, the cream begins to break down, clump and turn into butter. (Don't throw it out, simply use it as a spread for your morning toast.) Finally, remember that it's much easier to overwork the cream with an electric mixer, so it's wise to check the consistency frequently while whipping.

INGREDIENTS:

2 cups very cold heavy cream (preferably not ultrapasteurized)

¼ cup granulated or superfine sugar

1 teaspoon pure vanilla extract

1) **To whip cream by hand:** Add cold cream to a chilled, wide and shallow bowl. Tilt one side of the bowl upward slightly with your hand and grasp a large balloon whisk in your other hand. Apply large, sweeping, circular strokes to the cream in a continuous, repetitive motion until the cream becomes thick. Once thickened, add sugar and vanilla while continuing to beat. (To relieve some of the pressure from your mixing arm, hug the bowl in toward your body as you continue to whip until you reach the desired consistency.)

2) **To whip with an electric mixer:** Place cold cream in the chilled bowl and begin to beat with the chilled whip attachment. As cream begins to thicken, add vanilla and gradually increase the speed while adding the sugar in a steady stream. Beat until the cream is of desired consistency, checking the consistency frequently to avoid overbeating.

3) **To store:** Use the whipped cream as desired and refrigerate leftovers in a covered bowl or secured in a pastry bag (with the tip in place) standing within a tall drinking glass. (See How to Fill and Use a Pastry Bag, page 505.)

Variations

Fold 1 to 2 tablespoons melted chocolate into the already thickened cream. Or, reduce the vanilla to ½ teaspoon and, when adding to the cream, add 1 tablespoon of your favorite liqueur.

Q AND A

Q. What's the difference between pasteurized and ultrapasteurized cream?

A. During the ultrapasteurization process, the cream is brought to a high temperature (around 300°F) and kept there for a specified amount of time in order to prevent early spoilage. Although this process will considerably improve the shelf life of the cream, this excessive exposure to heat also removes most of the naturally delicious and full flavor of fresh cream as well as reducing its whipping capability. Pasteurized cream has been heated to destroy bacteria and then quickly cooled to preserve flavor; this type of cream is not available in every supermarket so be prepared to hunt around for it.

HOMEMADE MAYONNAISE

Plus Mayonnaise-Based Salad Dressings

YIELD: generous 2 cups

SPECIAL EQUIPMENT
Food processor or sturdy blender

That stout bottle of Hellmann's mayonnaise (labeled Best Foods in the West) will always have a home on my refrigerator shelf not only for the sake of convenience, but nostalgia as well. But homemade mayonnaise is far superior in both taste and texture—just one taste should convince you that it's worth the small effort required in its preparation. For best results, have all ingredients at room temperature to enable the mixture to emulsify properly. And unlike store-bought, homemade mayonnaise doesn't last forever, only one week in the refrigerator. So, it's best to make mayonnaise when needed and use it promptly. Also, any mixture containing raw eggs should not be given to babies, to the elderly or to anyone whose health is in delicate condition.

INGREDIENTS

2 extra-large egg yolks

1 whole extra-large egg

1 tablespoon Dijon mustard

2 tablespoon white wine vinegar

1 tablespoon strained fresh lemon juice

1 teaspoon sugar

1 teaspoon salt

½ teaspoon ground white pepper (optional)

¾ cup pure olive oil (not extra-virgin)

1¼ cups flavorless vegetable oil

1) **To prepare mayonnaise base:** Place all ingredients except oils in the bowl of a food processor fitted with the steel blade (or the container of a blender). Process until well combined.

2) **To emulsify:** Combine oils in a measuring cup with a spout. With the machine running, slowly add oil to the food processor through the feed tube or through the top of the blender in a very thin, but steady stream. Once you hear the mixture thickening (a chugging sound will occur), add the rest of the oil through the feed tube in a thicker, quicker stream. When all of the oil has been added, process for just a few seconds more. The mayonnaise should be creamy and nicely thickened.

3) *To store:* Scrape mixture into either a jar or a plastic container with a tight-fitting lid. Label with the date of making and refrigerate until needed. The mixture will thicken further with refrigeration.

Reduced-Fat Variation

For a mayonnaise that's lower in saturated fat, omit the whole egg and use only canola oil. Made from seeds of the rape plant, this oil is monounsaturated and also contains omega-3 fatty acids which have a reputation for lowering cholesterol. Canola is a bit bland, however, so be sure and use the white pepper to enhance the flavor.

Herb-Flavored Variation

Add ½ to 1 teaspoon crumbled dried herbs to food processor when assembling mayonnaise base. Or, add 1 to 2 tablespoons minced fresh herbs (basil, thyme or flat-leaf Italian parsley) after oil is added and mixture has emulsified. Simply pulse to combine. (If using a blender, remove the mayonnaise to a bowl and gently fold in the herbs using a rubber spatula.)

Thousand Island Dressing

Combine 1 part bottled chili sauce with 2 parts mayonnaise, some minced yellow onion and a generous amount of drained, chopped bread-and-butter pickles. Stir in freshly ground black pepper and store in the refrigerator. This is great on salads and as a spread on sandwiches or as a quick dip for raw vegetables.

Mock Caesar Dressing

Place 1 cup mayonnaise in a blender. Add 3 drained and chopped anchovy fillets, 1 tablespoon Dijon mustard, 2 chopped cloves garlic, 1 tablespoon strained fresh lemon juice, 1 tablespoon red wine vinegar, 1 teaspoon Worcestershire sauce, a generous amount of freshly ground black pepper and ½ cup freshly grated Reggiano Parmesan cheese. Whirl until smooth. Remove to a jar and use on salads (thinned with a little milk if necessary) or as a dip for raw vegetables.

Creamy Basil Vinaigrette

Place ½ cup mayonnaise in a blender. Add 3 tablespoons red wine vinegar, 2 small chopped garlic cloves, 1 tablespoon Dijon mustard, ½ teaspoon salt and a generous amount of freshly ground black pepper. Whirl until smooth. While the machine is running, add ½ cup olive oil in a slow steady stream and blend just until thickened. Remove to a bowl and stir in ¼ cup minced fresh basil leaves.

TARTAR SAUCE

YIELD: about 1½ cups

Serve this traditional condiment alongside hot grilled, broiled or fried seafood. The consistency and flavor of leftover tartar sauce (made with homemade mayonnaise) should remain fine for two to three days in the refrigerator; for one week when using store-bought mayonnaise.

INGREDIENTS

1 cup mayonnaise, preferably homemade (page 86)

¼ cup minced yellow onion

¼ cup minced drained gherkin pickles

2 tablespoons drained capers,* minced

1 generous tablespoon Dijon mustard

1 teaspoon strained fresh lemon juice

Freshly ground black pepper to taste

*See section on Staples

Combine all of the ingredients in a bowl. Cover tightly and refrigerate until needed.

CREAMY DIJON MUSTARD SAUCE

YIELD: about 1½ cups

This creamy sauce with the distinctive flavor of Dijon mustard is not only perfect with sliced corned beef or glazed ham, but also with chilled stone crabs and shrimp. If you have any left over, add some minced gherkins, yellow onions and capers, and you'll have yourself a delicious tartar sauce to serve alongside broiled, grilled or fried seafood.

INGREDIENTS

1 cup mayonnaise, preferably homemade (page 86)

4 heaping tablespoons Dijon mustard

1 to 2 teaspoons strained fresh lemon juice (only when serving with seafood)

1 teaspoon finely ground white pepper

In a small bowl, mix together all ingredients. Cover tightly and refrigerate until serving.

Q and A

Q. Is Dijon mustard named after a specific type of mustard seed?

A. No. Dijon Mustard is named after Dijon, France, where this mustard—renowned for its distinctive bite—originated. The basic ingredients are brown mustard seeds, white wine, grape juice and blended spices, which make the various brands of Dijon mustard range from somewhat mild to quite hot and sharp. Although Grey Poupon was the first Dijon mustard to become famous in the United States, this brand now must share the spotlight on the condiment shelf with many others at most supermarkets and gourmet stores.

It's A1 with Me!
STEAK SAUCE

YIELD: about ⅔ cup

SPECIAL EQUIPMENT
Small nonreactive saucepan

The taste of commercially prepared steak sauce is so assertive that no one in my family will go near it. But this easy sauce (based on my favorite chili sauce from Heinz) is just spicy enough and tastes so great that we even prefer it to ketchup on our burgers. When served just a little warm, the rich taste will enhance the most succulent cuts of steak as well as perk up the flavor of simple broiled or roast chicken. Don't hesitate to double or even triple the ingredients and refrigerate for up to two months. Also, a jar of this wonderful sauce makes a delectable house gift during barbecue season.

INGREDIENTS

⅔ cup bottled chili sauce*

1 tablespoon cider vinegar

1 tablespoon packed brown sugar

1 tablespoon unsulphured molasses*

¼ teaspoon Worcestershire sauce

Freshly ground black pepper to taste

* See section on Staples

Combine all ingredients (except fresh pepper) in a small nonreactive heavy-bottomed saucepan over medium-low heat. Bring mixture to a simmer and reduce heat to low. Simmer gently (uncovered) until flavors have combined and mixture has thickened, about 10 minutes. Remove from heat and add a generous amount of freshly ground black pepper. Let cool before serving just warm or at room temperature. Store any remaining sauce well covered in the refrigerator, but bring sauce to room temperature or warm slightly before serving.

SPICED APPLESAUCE

With Soused Raisins

YIELD: about 3 quarts

This spiced, not-too-sweet version of a comforting old-time favorite is my children's preferred accompaniment to dinner any time of the year. By far, Macintosh apples make the best applesauce so they make up the majority of this mixture. But because I prefer a textural applesauce, I add some coarsely chopped Golden Delicious apples, since they hold their shape better through cooking. If desired, Anjou or Bosc pears may be substituted for the Golden Delicious apples. Choose apples that are smooth, deeply colored and free of holes. And since they are cooked with their skins on, apples with a good amount of red will give the sauce a beautiful rosy color. Don't worry about the brandy; once it fully simmers, the alcohol will quickly evaporate so all that's left is its wonderful flavor. (If this concerns you, however, simply substitute apple juice or cider.) This recipe makes a lot of applesauce, but it will keep up to three weeks in the refrigerator—if it lasts that long!

SPECIAL EQUIPMENT

Sturdy fruit wedge cutter (optional)

8-quart nonreactive heavy-bottomed Dutch oven with lid

Medium-mesh wire strainer or food mill

Nutmeg grater

Three 1-quart jars or heavy-duty plastic containers with lids

INGREDIENTS

1 cup mixed light and dark raisins

½ cup apple brandy (imported calvados or domestic applejack) or unsweetened apple juice or apple cider

20 Macintosh apples, unpeeled, scrubbed, dried, cored and each cut into 8 wedges

5 Golden Delicious apples or Anjou or Bosc pears, peeled, cored and coarsely chopped

1⅔ cups apple cider or unsweetened apple juice

1 stick cinnamon

⅓ to ½ cup light or dark brown sugar (to taste)

1 teaspoon pure vanilla extract

1 teaspoon ground cinnamon

½ teaspoon freshly grated nutmeg

About Apple Cider

Apple cider is made from apples that are picked and stored for at least one week and up to ten days. This process is called "seating." Then, after careful scrubbing, they are ground to a pulp and strained, resulting in juice with a special woodsy taste and aroma that is far superior and more complex than commercially prepared apple juice. The brown color is not due to any added spices or sugar but from oxidation, which naturally occurs when the juice is exposed to air without the protection of a preservative. More perishable than regular apple juice, cider must remain refrigerated. An opened jug will last for about two weeks and will then begin to produce small foamy bubbles on the surface of the remaining juice. This indicates the production of alcohol (thus hard cider) and has a stronger taste with an assertive tang.

1) **To plump raisins:** Place raisins and brandy into a small saucepan and heat gently until brandy comes just to a full simmer. Remove from heat and set aside.

2) **To cook apples:** Place unpeeled apple wedges, 1⅓ cups of the apple cider and cinnamon stick in an 8-quart nonreactive heavy-bottomed pot and stir. Cover and bring the mixture to a full simmer over medium heat. Reduce heat to low and simmer apples until very tender, stirring and mashing frequently, about 15 minutes. Place coarsely chopped apples or pears and remaining ⅓ cup cider in a small nonreactive saucepan. Bring to a gentle simmer (uncovered) and cook just until tender but still textural, about 5 minutes. Remove from heat and set aside.

3) **To strain sauce:** Position a medium-mesh wire strainer or a food mill over a large bowl. Transfer the contents of the large pot in batches to strainer or food mill and force apples through, into the bowl, leaving the skins and any stray seeds behind. (A wooden spatula works perfectly when pushing apples through a strainer.) Discard skins and repeat with remaining cooked apples.

4) **To finish applesauce and serve:** Stir in sugar, cinnamon, nutmeg, vanilla and the raisins with the brandy. Fold in cooked chopped apples (along with any remaining juice). Serve applesauce warm or chilled.

5) **To store:** Cool applesauce to room temperature, divide among three 1-quart jars or plastic containers and secure with lids. The applesauce will keep perfectly for up to 3 weeks in the refrigerator.

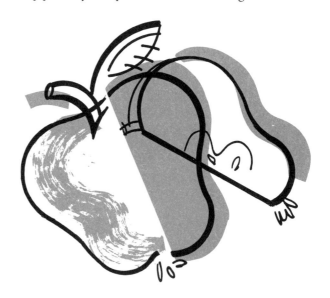

FAVORITE PIE PASTRY

For Both Sweet and Savory Purposes

YIELD: one 10-inch pie or tart shell

This recipe works perfectly whether making a pie with a savory filling for lunch or supper or making a tart with a sweet filling for dessert. Once you've learned the tricks (see following Tips from a Teacher), making perfect pastry dough is truly simple and quick (especially when using a food processor and pastry cloth). But if the very worst happens, just whirl it in the food processor with a little food coloring, give it to the kids to play with and head back to the drawing board. For best results, I suggest always giving your pastry shell a partial prebaking; this helps to ensure a crisp bottom crust even after baking a pie with a loose filling. A *totally* prebaked pastry shell is used when preparing a cold fruit tart such as the Fresh Strawberry Tart (page 464). Also see the variation instructions for deep-dish and double-crust pies and tarts. This pie dough is extra generous for a number of reasons. Since the crust is usually everyone's favorite part, I make plenty to reinforce the sides so there's more to eat. Also, since my children love to cook, I always save my scraps and keep them refrigerated wrapped in plastic (or frozen for rainy days). So, with the aid of a rolling pin and some cookie cutters, the kids have a delicious afternoon project. For the most golden crusts, I prefer to use glass pie plates and dark steel tart pans. If using these more heat-retentive materials, reduce the oven temperature in this recipe by 25°F.

SPECIAL EQUIPMENT

Food processor or sturdy hand-held pastry blender

Electric spice grinder (for savory purposes) or mortar and pestle

Wide blending fork (for the hand method)

Canvas pastry cloth (especially helpful if you are a novice at pastry making)

Tapered wooden rolling pin

10-inch pie plate or tart pan with removable bottom

Dried beans, rice or commercial pie weights

INGREDIENTS

2 cups unbleached all-purpose flour, plus more for dusting

½ teaspoon salt

2 tablespoons sugar (1 teaspoon sugar for savory version)

½ to 1 teaspoon crumbled dried thyme or oregano *or* whole or ground caraway seeds (for savory version only)

1 stick (¼ pound) very cold unsalted butter, cut into small dice

3 rounded tablespoons cold solid vegetable shortening, pulled into small bits

⅓ cup ice cold water

1) To assemble dry ingredients: Place flour, salt and sugar in the work bowl of a food processor fitted with the steel blade and process to combine and

Time Management Tips

• All variations of this pastry can be made and stored in the refrigerator for up to 3 days or wrapped in plastic wrap, then aluminum foil, sealed in a heavy-duty freezer bag and frozen for 2 months. Make sure to label and date the package before freezing.

• The pastry can be rolled and placed in the pie or tart pan 1 week ahead. Cover gently but efficiently with plastic wrap and slip pan into a jumbo freezer bag. Seal. Do not thaw before prebaking.

lighten them. Or, combine in a mixing bowl using a whisk. If making a savory pie, whisk herbs or seeds into the dry ingredients now.

2) *To cut in butter and shortening:* Drop diced cold butter and shortening bits into dry ingredients. Pulse machine until mixture resembles coarse meal. If using a hand-held pastry blender, incorporate butter and shortening until mixture reaches the desired consistency.

3) *To add liquid, if using a food processor:* While machine is running, pour in ice water in a slow steady stream, until the mixture in the bowl just starts to mass together. Stop machine and test several areas by gently pinching a piece of dough with your fingers; it should feel moist, but not wet, and should hold together. Avoid overprocessing or the pastry will be tough. If dough seems too dry or mealy, drizzle on a little more water to those dry areas. And be sure to check several areas of the dough before adding more liquid. Pulse once or twice to incorporate added liquid.

4) *To add liquid, if using hand method:* Drizzle in ice water and toss gently with a wide blending fork. As each section becomes moistened, gently shove that part to one side of the bowl as you continue to moisten the rest. (See preceding step for judging moistness of dough.)

5) *To wrap and chill dough:* Lay 2 pieces of plastic wrap in a crisscross on your work surface. Turn out dough onto the center of the plastic. Gather and lift the ends of the plastic and wrap dough. Gently flatten and shape it into a round disc and refrigerate for at least 1 hour.

6) *To roll out dough:* Remove dough from refrigerator and, if very cold, let sit at room temperature for 5 minutes. If using a pastry cloth, lay it out on your work surface and rub some all-purpose flour into the exposed surface. Lay dough on the cloth or a lightly floured cool work surface or between 2 sheets of waxed paper. Roll out dough ⅛ inch thick and 1 inch larger than the pie plate or tart pan. (For hints on rolling out pastry dough, see Tips from a Teacher, page 97.)

7) *To line pie pan:* Roll up pastry loosely on a lightly floured rolling pin and carefully unroll it onto the pie plate. Turn the overhang of dough underneath itself to reinforce the sides and crimp the rim decoratively. Lightly dock (prick) dough all over the interior including the sides and cover with plastic wrap or aluminum foil. Refrigerate or freeze for 1 hour before baking.

8) **To partially prebake pastry shell:** If using a tart pan, place a shallow baking sheet into the center of the oven (this makes it easier to remove the pan from the oven after baking). Preheat the oven to 400°F. Line the interior of the shell with aluminum foil (shiny side down). Fill foil with dried beans or pie weights and bake for 10 minutes. Carefully lift out foil and weights and lightly prick the interior again. Reduce oven temperature to 375°F and bake 8 minutes more. The crust should appear to be lightly cooked and only just starting to brown. Transfer to a wire rack to cool.

9) **To totally prebake pastry shell:** If using a tart pan, place a baking sheet into the oven as described in preceding step. Preheat the oven to 425°F (400°F if using dark steel tart pan or glass pie plate). Remove prepared tart shell from refrigerator and fill with foil and weights as described in preceding step. Bake filled tart shell for 15 minutes. Carefully remove foil and weights and reduce oven temperature to 375°F (350°F if in a dark steel or glass pan). Continue to bake shell until golden but not overly dark, 10 to 20 minutes. Remove and cool on a wire rack.

10) **To waterproof pastry shell:** To further ensure a crisp bottom crust in both sweet and savory pies, brush the interior of a cooled partially or fully baked pastry shell with a waterproofing mixture, as specified in each recipe. Once the mixture is brushed on and allowed to set, the tart shell is now further protected from moisture and ready to be filled.

Instructions for a Ten-Inch Deep-Dish Pie

When making dough: Instead of using all water, use ¼ cup ice cold water and 1 egg mixed together. (The egg will tenderize dough while helping to strengthen the higher walls of the shell.)

When rolling and filling pie pan: Roll out dough into a circle ⅛ inch thick and 2 to 2½ inches larger than the pan. Turn any excess dough behind, pressing gently to reinforce the sides. Crimp the exposed top edge decoratively by pushing it out and pinching it with your thumbs and forefingers.

Instructions for Double-Crust Pies or Tarts

When making dough: Prepare 2 separate batches of Favorite Pie Pastry and in each batch, reduce the amount of ice cold water to ¼ cup and mix in 1 egg. Wrap each batch and refrigerate.

To roll top crust: Line a plate and a shallow baking sheet with waxed paper. Roll out the remaining piece of dough in the same way as the bottom and cut out a round of dough that is 2 inches larger than the pan. Cut decorative vents out of the center of the round and place on the waxed-paper-lined plate. Carefully transfer pastry dough to the waxed-paper-lined baking sheet, cover and refrigerate. Cut out more decorative shapes from any scraps, place on plate, cover and refrigerate.

Follow both prebaking baking and waterproofing instructions for the bottom crust as prescribed in your individual recipe.

Jam-Filled Cookie Crisps from Pastry Scraps

This is a wonderful way to use leftover scraps after rolling out pastry. Line a shallow baking sheet with parchment paper and set aside. Roll out cold dough scraps on a lightly floured work surface to a thickness of ⅛ inch. Using a round or square fluted cookie cutter, cut out shapes from the dough. Make an egg wash by mixing 1 egg with 1 teaspoon water; push through a medium-mesh wire strainer into a small bowl. Place a small amount of jam on one side of each round or square and, using a pastry brush, paint the edges lightly with egg wash. Fold over the other side to enclose jam and press the ends with a fork to seal. Cut a thin slit (vent) on top with the tip of a small knife and place on the prepared baking sheet. Cover and refrigerate for 20 to 30 minutes to allow the butter to firm up.

Meanwhile preheat the oven to 375°F. Mix together as much cinnamon and sugar as needed in the proportion of 1 tablespoon cinnamon to ½ cup sugar. Paint tops of the chilled pastries with egg wash and then sprinkle with cinnamon-sugar. Bake in the preheated oven until golden and crisp, about 10 minutes. Enjoy warm for best flavor. (Take care when serving children—the jam stays hot longer than the pastry.)

Adding liquid: Be careful not to add to the dough too much water, which will create a dense crust. On the other hand, if the dough is too dry it will be difficult to roll. Only add as much (or as little) liquid as necessary to create a dough that is moist, but not wet and that holds together when gently pressed between two fingers. Test several areas of the dough before adding more liquid since one part of the dough may be a little too wet which could make up for any dry pockets.

Mixing dough: Once you add the water, the mixture should be combined rapidly, with every toss of a fork or pulse with the food processor being deliberate and focused. Overworking results in pastry that is flat, tough and chewy.

Rolling out dough: If very chilled, allow dough to sit out of the refrigerator for 5 minutes before rolling. If not using a pastry cloth, I prefer to roll pie pastry on a cool surface such as marble or a cool counter (not wood which is warm and requires more flour to prevent sticking). The best way to obtain the proper shape is to roll once, then turn dough ¼ clockwise. Roll once more using firm, even pressure on the rolling pin. To keep dough an even thickness, don't roll over the ends, but only right up to them. Keep turning dough ¼ clockwise, rolling only once until it softens slightly and the round shape is apparent. At this point, you may roll more than once in each direction until dough is the proper size. Occasionally lift dough to prevent it from sticking and lightly flour work surface only if necessary. To thin and "round" the sides, position the *center* of your tapered rolling pin on the desired area and gently roll back and forth once or twice. If the dough should break while rolling, place a piece of waxed paper over the surface and roll over the crack once or twice to mend it.

Baking shells: For a consistently crisp bottom crust, always partially prebake your pastry shell. If using a tart pan, remember to lift from the sides when removing from the oven or the pastry will pop out leaving the hot tart ring around your arm and causing the sides of the crust to fall—not to mention a bad burn.

TIPS

FROM A TEACHER

Making Perfect
Pie Pastry

CHAPTER III

JUST FOR STARTERS

Dips, Spreads and Finger Foods

I've never met anyone who didn't love hors d'oeuvres. As a matter of fact, many would like to skip dinner entirely and simply nibble and sip all evening! In this chapter I've shared my best and most requested recipes for both cold and hot starters. Whether serving these with cocktails before dinner or as a first course, the tastes are intense and the textures varied.

The most important thing to remember when serving a starter is not to stuff your guests before dinner (this isn't easy, since people usually show up ravenous for a home-cooked meal). Foods that are served before dinner are meant to stimulate the appetite, not satisfy it. Also, avoid heavy starters when the menu features wintry, braised foods that will be served with pasta, rice or potatoes since these meals require a hearty appetite. Many of these recipes can be made ahead to eliminate some of the preparation on the day of entertaining. Make sure to take advantage of my Time Management Tips.

Friends Want Me To Bottle This
SAVORY TUNA SPREAD

YIELD: about 1½ cups

This dip is so popular with my friends and students that I've been asked to manufacture it in bulk, bottle it and sell it to the public! As delicious as this is, however, it only takes a few minutes to prepare. I don't suggest using a blender in place of a food processor since the blender tends to give the dip an undesirable mousse-like texture. If a food processor is not available, use a chef's knife to mince together finely the tuna, scallions, anchovies and garlic before incorporating the remaining ingredients.

INGREDIENTS

1 can (6⅛ ounces) Italian chunk light tuna*, drained

2 heaping tablespoons Dijon mustard

½ cup mayonnaise, preferably homemade (page 86)

4 scallions (green onions), coarsely chopped (trimmed white parts and 1½ inches of the tender green)

2 teaspoons strained fresh lemon juice

4 or 5 firm anchovy fillets*, drained and torn into pieces

2 large cloves garlic, chopped

1 teaspoon ground white pepper

2 tablespoons capers*, drained and chopped

Freshly ground black pepper to taste

SUGGESTED ACCOMPANIMENTS

Assorted raw vegetables

Warmed crackers

Sliced Crusty Italian Bread (page 401)

* See section on Staples

1) **To prepare:** Put all the ingredients, except capers, black peppers and accompaniments, into the bowl of a food processor fitted with the steel blade. Process until well blended. Remove to a bowl and fold in chopped capers. Grind in some fresh black pepper. (Or finely mince together all

SPECIAL INGREDIENTS
Food processor or chef's knife

Time Management Tips

• Make this spread a day ahead and refrigerate securely covered.

• If serving this spread with assorted raw vegetables (crudités), the vegetables can be prepared a day ahead and kept well covered in the refrigerator.

To keep peeled raw carrot sticks from looking dry, wrap them in a damp paper towel, place in a sealed plastic bag and refrigerate. To refresh leftovers (for up to 5 days), soak sticks in a bowl of ice water for 10 minutes before patting dry and serving.

solid ingredients with a chef's knife and stir in mustard, mayonnaise, lemon juice and pepper.) Refrigerate (well covered) until serving time.

2) *To serve:* Surround the spread with assorted raw vegetables or warmed crackers or spread on slices of Crusty Italian Bread.

SMOKED SALMON AND SCALLION SPREAD

YIELD: about 2 cups

The forever fabulous combination of the woodsy flavor of smoked salmon and the sweet-peppery taste of minced scallions (green onions) imbedded in a mound of whipped cream cheese is just sensational. It's not only the perfect spread for sliced plain or toasted breads, warmed crackers or bread sticks, but also a savory (and substantial) dip for assorted fresh vegetables. Make this early in the day you plan to serve or as much as one day ahead for best flavor. Although choosing salmon for this recipe will depend largely on availability and personal taste, I suggest that you make every effort to purchase sliced salmon from a local delicatessen, specialty food shop or smokehouse and not use a commercially packaged, boxed type.

INGREDIENTS

12 ounces whipped cream cheese*, at room temperature or Low-Fat Cream Cheese (page 82)

2 rounded tablespoons sour cream or Low-Fat Sour Cream (page 82)

⅓ pound sliced smoked salmon, minced

½ cup packed minced scallions (green onions), trimmed white part and 1½ to 2 inches of the tender green

½ teaspoon finely ground white pepper

½ teaspoon freshly ground black pepper

SUGGESTED ACCOMPANIMENTS

Sesame Bread Sticks (page 411)

Garlic Pita Toasts or Pita Chips (page 114)

Homemade Bagels or Bagel Chips (page 407–410)

Crusty Deli Rye Bread (page 396)

Assorted raw vegetables (crudités)

* See section on Staples

1) *To prepare:* Combine cream cheese with sour cream in a medium-sized mixing bowl until well combined. Add remaining ingredients, except accompaniments, and fold together well. Spoon mixture into a serving bowl or a decorative crock and cover well. Refrigerate until ready to serve.

2) *To serve and store:* Serve as a spread on any one of the suggested accompaniments. Store leftovers in the refrigerator well covered for up to 4 days.

CREAMY CAVIAR DIP

YIELD: about 2 cups

One of my absolutely favorite hors d'oeuvres for entertaining is this dip, surrounded by fresh, hot and lightly salted homemade potato chips. However, be prepared to remind your guests to save room for dinner! Make this dip the day ahead of serving for convenience. Since the creamy ingredients laced with chopped onions ultimately predominate the overall flavors of the dip, don't waste expensive caviar. Instead, use the readily available and easily affordable black lumpfish eggs. (And read the label, since I don't suggest whitefish eggs, which usually sit right next to the jars of lumpfish. These tend to taste overly fishy and assertive.) See Tips from a Teacher: Caviar (page 102) for those special times when you might want to splurge and purchase fine caviar.

INGREDIENTS

8 ounces whipped cream cheese*, at room temperature, or Low-Fat Cream Cheese (page 82)

½ cup sour cream or Low-Fat Sour Cream (page 82)

1 tablespoon strained fresh lemon juice

2 heaping tablespoons minced yellow onion

2 to 3½ ounces black lumpfish caviar

Freshly ground black pepper to taste

SUGGESTED ACCOMPANIMENTS

Crispy Cottage-Fried Potato Chips (page 356)

Assorted raw vegetables (crudités)

Warmed crackers

* See section on Staples

1) *To prepare:* In a bowl, combine softened cream cheese, sour cream, lemon juice and minced onion. When well combined, gently but thoroughly fold in caviar, being careful not to rupture too many eggs. Add freshly ground black pepper to taste and refrigerate (well covered) until ready to serve.

2) *To serve:* Surround dip with crisp fried potato slices, raw vegetables and/or assorted warmed crackers.

TIPS
FROM A TEACHER

Caviar

Generally, it only pays to buy the "best" when caviar is allowed to shine on its own. The very best caviar (fish roe from sturgeon) is from beluga sturgeon. This also is the most expensive, but it has the smoothest and most intense flavor and the eggs are also unusually large and soft. The next two in line (in both quality and price) are osetra sturgeon roe and sevruga, which are both fine tasting but the eggs are quite a bit smaller than beluga.

Traditionally, fine caviar is served in a crystal bowl set in crushed ice. Never use a metal spoon to serve caviar since this will impart a metallic taste to the eggs. Instead, use a special nonreactive "caviar spoon" made of either silky smooth wood or mother of pearl. Ideally, it should be spooned on top of lightly buttered toast points (thin slices of white toast with the crusts removed and the slices halved diagonally after buttering) accompanied with nothing more than juicy wedges of fresh lemon. If desired, accompany the caviar additionally with small bowls of any or all of the following: minced yellow onions, sour cream, drained capers and the classic garnish of mimosa (hard-cooked egg yolks forced through a medium-mesh wire strainer). Caviar is highly perishable and should be eaten the day the tin is opened. For a special celebration, fine caviar and either a glass of fragrant Champagne or chilled vodka on the rocks is the perfect duo.

GARLICKY HERB SPREAD

YIELD: about 1½ cups

This creamy, herb-studded spread is perfect to serve with cocktails before dinner. Although I suggest using fresh herbs whenever possible, I actually prefer the intensity of dried herbs (especially oregano) in this recipe. If you want a softer consistency for a dip, just add a little more sour cream. For best flavor, assemble this spread one day ahead and enjoy leftovers for almost one week before the garlic and herbs become overly assertive. Spread lavishly on toasted bagels for lunch or use a bread stick to scoop up the spread for a quick and savory snack.

INGREDIENTS

12 ounces whipped cream cheese*, at room temperature, or Low-Fat Cream Cheese (page 82)

2 tablespoons sour cream or Low-Fat Sour Cream (page 82)

2 small cloves garlic, minced

1 tablespoon chopped fresh thyme leaves or 1 teaspoon crumbled dried thyme

1 teaspoon crumbled dried oregano

Generous amount of freshly ground black pepper

1 teaspoon salt

1 heaping tablespoon minced fresh flat-leaf Italian parsley

SUGGESTED ACCOMPANIMENTS

Fresh sugar snap peas

Garlic Pita Toasts (page 114)

Homemade Bagels or Bagel Chips (page 407–410)

Sesame Bread Sticks (page 411)

1) **To prepare:** Combine all the ingredients except accompaniments in a bowl and refrigerate overnight, so the flavors can meld.

2) **To prepare sugar snap peas, if using:** String peas and refrigerate 1 day ahead in a sealed heavy-duty plastic bag. To string a sugar snap pea, hold rinsed pod in one hand with stem facing up and seam facing you. Using the fingernails of your other hand, pinch off stem end, pulling the string down the length of the pod.

When using best quality aromatic dried herbs, they are about 3 times as potent as fresh. Use 1 teaspoon of crumbled dried leaves to 1 rounded tablespoon minced fresh herbs.

3) *To serve:* Spoon the assembled mixture into a decorative crock and surround it with fresh sugar snap peas or any of the other suggested accompaniments.

I Love This Stuff!

GUACAMOLE

YIELD: about 4½ cups

SPECIAL EQUIPMENT
Food processor or wide blending fork or *molcajete*

Tomato shark or the tip of a small sharp knife

Thin rubber gloves, for handling chili peppers

Traditionally, guacamole lends itself to warm weather entertaining. But when it's served surrounded by warmed corn tortilla chips and accompanied with a pitcher of fruit-filled white wine sangria, no one will care if there's a blizzard outside! When assembling guacamole, please don't resort to using bottled lemon or lime juice. (Both the aroma and flavor of the bottled variety have no resemblance whatsoever to that of the fresh fruit and will adversely effect the taste of any recipe.) And before serving, warm the tortilla chips to bring out a fuller, more savory corn taste. Guacamole does not keep well and should be served the same day it's assembled. For notes on handling hot chili peppers, see page 113.

INGREDIENTS

4 ripe avocados

2 tablespoons chopped fresh or drained bottled jalapeño chili peppers, stems and seeds removed (page 113)

2 cloves garlic, chopped

1½ teaspoons hot Mexican chili powder blend (or to taste)

2 heaping tablespoons minced red onion

2 heaping tablespoons minced yellow onion

1 tablespoon strained fresh lemon juice

1 tablespoon strained fresh lime juice

1 tablespoon chopped fresh cilantro

1 medium-sized tomato, unpeeled, seeded and coarsely chopped (page 151)

Kosher salt or sea salt to taste (optional)

Blue and/or yellow corn tortilla chips, for accompaniment

1) **To process avocados:** Cut 3 of the avocados in half lengthwise, remove pits, scoop out flesh and place into the bowl of a food processor fitted with the steel blade. Add chopped chili peppers, garlic, 1 teaspoon of the chili powder and minced red and yellow onions. Process using on/off turns until mixture is almost smooth, but not totally puréed. (Alternatively, place pulp in a mixing bowl and use a wide blending fork to mash avocados to the desired consistency or place in a *molcajete*—the Mexican version of a mortar and pestle—and grind to desired consistency.) Spoon the mixture immediately into a serving bowl. Stir in lemon and lime juice and chopped cilantro.

2) **To assemble:** Cut and pit remaining avocado and cut flesh into small dice. Place diced avocado along with chopped tomatoes in bowl with mashed avocados and fold together until well combined. Add coarse salt to taste and fold once more. Sprinkle the remaining ½ teaspoon chili powder on top, cover tightly and refrigerate until serving.

3) **To serve:** For best flavor, remove guacamole from refrigerator 30 minutes before serving and preheat the oven to 350°F. Ten minutes before serving, place tortilla chips on a shallow baking sheet and bake until hot, about 10 minutes. Serve guacamole slightly chilled surrounded by warm tortilla chips.

TIPS

FROM A TEACHER

Purchasing and Pitting Avocados

Purchase avocados that feel tender and give in slightly when you apply gentle pressure with your hand. Avoid soupy avocados, which will most likely have black spots and signs of rot when cut open. Store unripened avocados at room temperature for a day or two and, if necessary, refrigerate to slow the ripening process. Run the blade of a sharp knife lengthwise around the entire avocado. Twist slightly to open and split avocado in half. Hit pit with the knife blade so that it inserts just enough to keep the blade in place. Gently twist the handle of the knife to release the pit from its socket. Lift the knife away from the avocado and the pit should come away with the blade.

The Real Thing!

MEXICAN SALSA

YIELD: about 6 to 7 cups

SPECIAL EQUIPMENT
Tomato shark or the tip of
a small sharp knife

Food processor or blender or
long sharp chef's knife

Thin rubber gloves, for handling
chili peppers

Authentic and spicy, this recipe came from the owner of a local Mexican market where I was shopping for a Mexican dinner. Latin groceries were once the only places that carried fresh tomatillos, which look like small green tomatoes (although they're not) with a thin papery outer skin. But now many gourmet produce stores and upscale supermarkets are stocking them as well. Canned tomatillos are also available and, once drained, are a suitable substitute. Although this recipe yields a large amount, it keeps well in the refrigerator for up to two weeks. When entertaining, accompany the salsa and chips with White Wine Sangria (following). Also, a jar of this robust salsa makes a welcomed house gift during the summer months (include a bag of yellow or blue corn tortillas chips for a nice touch). Be sure to warm your tortilla chips before serving with salsa, since this really improves the taste of the chips. For notes on handling hot chili peppers, see page 113.

INGREDIENTS

4 or more fresh or pickled serrano or jalapeño chili peppers

5 fresh or well-drained canned tomatillos (if not available, add 5 more plum tomatoes)

3 pounds ripe plum (Roma) tomatoes

4 large cloves garlic, chopped

1 cup chopped yellow onion

½ cup chopped red onion

⅓ cup packed chopped fresh cilantro

1 tablespoon strained fresh lemon juice

1 tablespoon extra-virgin olive oil

1 tablespoon tomato paste

Freshly ground black pepper to taste

Kosher salt or sea salt to taste (optional)

Tortilla chips, for accompaniment

1) **To prepare chili peppers:** If using fresh peppers, simmer them in water to cover until tender, about 10 minutes; if using canned or pickled peppers, drain well. Remove seeds and chop them; if a spicier salsa is desired, leave in some of the seeds.

2) **To prepare fresh tomatillos:** Remove papery outer skins from tomatillos, rinse off their sticky surface, drain and dry well. Place tomatillos in a saucepan with enough simmering water to cover and simmer until softened but still firm, 5 to 10 minutes. Drain and pat dry. This step is not needed for canned tomatillos.

3) **To sear tomatoes and incorporate tomatillos:** Place a 10- to 12-inch nonreactive skillet over medium heat. When hot, add all but 5 of the plum tomatoes and sear them, turning often until softened and their skins become blistered but not blackened. Add prepared tomatillos to the skillet and cook 5 minutes, breaking up tomatoes and tomatillos with a spoon. Pour tomato mixture through a medium-mesh wire strainer placed over a bowl, shaking and stirring to remove as much liquid as possible. Reserve strained tomato mixture, pour juices back into skillet and set aside.

4) **To process salsa:** Place strained tomato mixture into the bowl of a food processor fitted with the steel blade. Add chopped garlic, yellow onions, chopped chili peppers and cilantro. Pulse mixture using on/off turns until chopped but not puréed; the mixture should retain some texture. Alternatively, use a blender for this procedure in several small batches, flipping the switch on and off. (A long sharp chef's knife can also be used, but this can get messy.) Transfer to a large mixing bowl.

5) **To prepare chopped tomatoes:** Remove seeds from the remaining 5 tomatoes as directed on page 151. Coarsely chop tomatoes and stir into processed salsa with lemon juice, olive oil and tomato paste.

6) **To reduce tomato juices:** Place the skillet with the reserved tomato juices over medium heat and bring to a full simmer. Scrape up any of the seared tomato that has clung to the bottom of the skillet and continue to cook until the juices are reduced into a thick concentrate (only a few tablespoons will remain). Stir this into the bowl of salsa.

7) **To finish and chill:** Add to the salsa a generous amount of freshly ground black pepper and, if you like, a light sprinkling of coarse salt to taste. Let mixture cool, cover and refrigerate for at least 1 hour (preferably several) before serving so the flavors have a chance to meld and ripen.

8) **To serve:** Preheat the oven to 350°F. Place tortilla chips on a shallow baking sheet and bake until hot, about 10 minutes. Serve salsa chilled surrounded by warm tortilla chips.

White Wine Sangria

This is the perfect partner for salsa and chips. In the bottom of a large pitcher, place 2 scrubbed, unpeeled, cored and sliced apples and 1 scrubbed navel orange, sliced into ¼ inch rounds and the rounds cut in half. Pour over fruit ½ cup Cognac and 1 cup Cointreau or Triple Sec. Cover and let fruit and spirits macerate for 1 hour. Then pour in 1 bottle (750 ml) dry white wine, stir gently and chill. Just before serving, stir in 2 cups cold Seven-up or Sprite. To serve, spoon some of fruit into a balloon wine glass, pour sangria over fruit, and add a few ice cubes. Serves 8.

This Jewish Mama's CHOPPED CHICKEN LIVER

YIELD: about 4 cups

SPECIAL EQUIPMENT
Food processor or long sharp chef's knife

Ethnically of Jewish origin, chopped liver maintains its rightful place in Jewish homes throughout the world as a valued part of the traditional repertoire of recipes. These are, of course, those recipes that are most trusted to comfort guests while entertaining as well as those recipes that Jewish mothers proudly hand down to their children. When you're seasoning to taste directly after assembling, remember that the warmth of the chopped liver mixture will make the seasoning seem very apparent. But not to worry. The seasoning needs to be more pronounced because chilling tends to dull flavors. In fact, for best flavor, make this one or two days ahead. Whatever your lineage, if you like chopped liver, you will adore my version of a trusted family favorite. I hope my Orthodox Jewish friends will forgive my use of butter. Obviously, I'm not kosher.

INGREDIENTS

3 heaping tablespoons rendered chicken fat (page 110),
  butter or margarine

2 extra-large yellow onions, peeled and thinly sliced

2 cloves garlic, minced

Pinch sugar (optional)

2 tablespoons butter or margarine

1 pound very fresh chicken livers rinsed, patted dry and
any connective tissue removed with a knife

Generous amount of freshly ground black pepper

3 extra-large eggs, hard-cooked and peeled (page 54)

1 teaspoon salt or to taste

FOR THE GARNISH

Kosher salt or sea salt

½ cup minced yellow onion

1 sprig of curly parsley or crisp gribenes (page 110)

SUGGESTED ACCOMPANIMENTS

Crusty Deli Rye Bread (page 396)

Bagel Chips (page 410)

Garlic Pita Toasts or Pita Chips (page 114)

Sesame Bread Sticks (page 411)

Assorted crackers

Q. What's the best way to cover a hot
mixture before it's cool?

*A. To prevent debris from falling into a
hot mixture while it cools (before refrigeration), cover the bowl with paper towel or
a clean kitchen towel. When a solid, nonporous material is used (such as a pot lid
or aluminum foil), beads of water from
rising steam, called condensation, will
form, drip into the mixture and dilute the
flavor. If you must refrigerate the mixture
before it's thoroughly cool, pull a kitchen
towel over the top of the bowl or pot and
then apply the lid.*

1) *To caramelize onions:* Melt chicken fat in a 10- to 12-inch skillet over
medium-low heat. Add onions, stir to coat with the fat and cook until
softened and fragrant, 5 to 10 minutes. Stir in minced garlic and, if you
like, a pinch of sugar. Cook, stirring occasionally, until onions are golden
brown and caramelized, about 25 minutes.

2) *To cook chicken livers:* When onions are golden, push them to the sides
of the skillet and in the center melt the 2 tablespoons butter or margarine.
When hot and bubbling, add chicken livers and cook until golden on both
sides, about 6 minutes. Stir to combine livers with onions and cover skillet. Reduce heat to very low and simmer until livers are cooked through
but retain some pink in the center, about 5 minutes. Uncover skillet, raise
heat and scrape any caramelized bits of onions and liver off the bottom of
the pan using the straight edge of a wooden spatula. Cook about 2 more
minutes over moderate heat. Grind in a generous amount of freshly
ground black pepper.

3) *To process livers:* Pour the contents of the skillet into a food processor fitted with the steel blade. Add hard-cooked eggs and 1 teaspoon salt. Process mixture using on/off pulses until finely chopped but still somewhat textural. Taste for seasoning, adding more salt and fresh pepper until well seasoned. Alternatively, mince cooked livers with onions on a large chopping board using a sharp chef's knife and mash the cooked eggs separately; combine livers, onions, eggs and seasoning, to taste.

4) *To chill:* Turn mixture into a crock or pretty bowl and cover with paper toweling until cool enough to refrigerate. Then cover with plastic wrap or aluminum foil and refrigerate at least 4 hours, preferably overnight, so the flavors can meld.

5) *To serve:* An hour or 2 before serving, remove chopped liver from refrigerator so that it's slightly chilled but not too cold for the flavors to emerge. Sprinkle the top lightly with coarse salt and fresh pepper and place the minced onion in a 1-inch border around the edge of the bowl. Place a sprig of curly parsley in the center or serve sprinkled with fresh, crisp gribenes. Surround the bowl of chopped liver with assorted crackers or any of the suggested accompaniments.

TIPS
FROM A TEACHER

*Rendered Chicken Fat
and Gribenes*

Jewish kosher cooking traditionally uses chicken fat (schmaltz) instead of butter when cooking meat, since mixing dairy and meat products is a definite no-no. Melting down (rendering) fat with minced onions gives the fat an incredible flavor and aroma that is far superior to the commercially prepared product. However, you can doctor store-bought schmaltz: Melt it down in a skillet with some chopped yellow onion, cook it slowly until the onions become golden, strain, cool and store.

Gribenes (cracklings) are bits of chicken skin that are fried until crisp during the rendering process. These small, crunchy treats add intense flavor to breads and also make a delicious garnish for Chopped Chicken Liver (page 108). To add them to yeast breads, knead some crisp gribenes into the dough after the first full rise.

To make schmaltz and gribenes from scratch, I keep a bag of chicken fat and bits of chicken skin in a heavy plastic bag in my freezer. Each time I trim my chickens, I collect portions of fat and add it to my stash. When I have accumulated at least 2 cups, I then have enough to render it down. (Before storing raw skin, I suggest snipping the skin into smallish pieces

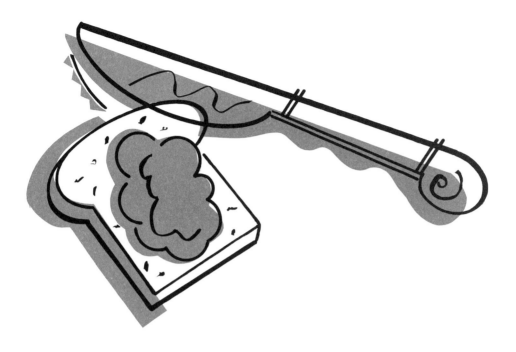

so they don't take as long to become crisp when making gribenes.)

To make schmaltz and gribenes: Place 2 to 4 cups fresh or frozen chicken fat and skin in a large skillet (preferably not nonstick) over medium heat. When fat is no longer congealed, add 1 chopped yellow onion, reduce heat to low and simmer until onions are deeply golden (but not burnt) and the skin pieces are very crisp. Using a slotted spoon, remove skin and onions to a double layer of paper towels to drain. Strain the fat through a fine-mesh sieve lined with a double thick-ness of slightly dampened cheesecloth. Pick out the gribenes to use alone or include the onions, but because they both don't store well, use within a few hours after being fried. Let the liquid fat cool to room temperature and store in a small heavy-duty freezer container. Before using frozen schmaltz, run the bottom of the container under hot tap water. Push the fat out of the container and, using a knife, chip off a piece the size you need. Return the rest to the container and place in freezer.

MARINATED ROASTED PEPPERS

With Red Onions on Garlic Pita Toasts

YIELD: serves 8 to 12

SPECIAL EQUIPMENT
Sturdy stainless steel skewers, for
roasting peppers

This combination of marinated freshly roasted peppers with a balsamic vinaigrette served over hot, crisp garlicky pita wedges has never failed to bring
sounds of delight from my guests. As a matter of fact, this recipe is so frequently requested that I always have a few typed copies ready to hand out.
It will become a trusted favorite of yours, I'm sure.

INGREDIENTS

Garlic Pita Toasts (following)

4 red bell peppers (or a combination of red pimentos and yellow bell
peppers), roasted, peeled, seeded and cut into thin strips (page 113)

4 cloves garlic, minced

Freshly ground black pepper to taste

¼ cup extra-virgin olive oil

⅓ cup kalamata olives*, pitted and cut into slivers

1 small red onion

2 tablespoons drained capers* (preferably marinated in balsamic vinegar)

2 tablespoons chopped fresh basil leaves

2 scant tablespoons balsamic vinegar

About ½ cup freshly grated Reggiano Parmesan cheese

* See section on Staples

1) *For garlic toasts:* Prepare garlic toasts as directed. Cover with plastic
wrap and refrigerate for up to 2 days before broiling.

2) *To marinate roasted peppers:* In a bowl, combine roasted pepper strips
with garlic. Add some freshly ground black pepper and drizzle with olive
oil until nicely moistened. Add olives and cover with plastic wrap. Let sit
at room temperature so the flavors can meld for a few hours.

3) *To prepare red onion:* Peel onion and cut in half through the stem end.
Cut each half into very thin wedges and separate the wedges into strips. If
a milder onion flavor is desired, soak onion strips in ice water to cover for
20 minutes. Drain, rinse and drain once more.

Time Management Tips

- The peppers can be roasted and marinated
with olive oil and garlic up to 2 days ahead
and refrigerated, well covered. Bring close
to room temperature for best flavor. The
garlic pita toasts may be totally assembled
up to 2 days ahead and refrigerated until
time to broil. Cover well with plastic wrap.

- You may broil garlic toasts up to 10 minutes
before your guests are scheduled to arrive,
then turn off the broiler and transfer the
baking sheet to the bottom shelf of the oven.
Keep in a closed oven until ready to assemble. If your oven has a separate broiling
drawer, remove once toasted and leave in a
slightly warmed oven until serving.

If you've never had freshly roasted bell peppers or pimentos, you're in for a treat! Marinated Roasted Peppers (page 112) is my favorite of the many ways to use these slightly smoky-tasting peppers to enhance a variety of menus. The list seems to go on and on. The next time you prepare your favorite tomato sauce, add roasted, peeled and sliced bell peppers or pimentos. If using only sweet bell peppers, include a variety of colors. Or for your next barbecue, roast, skin, halve and seed the peppers and layer them unsliced on a platter with slices of beefsteak tomatoes, creamy fresh mozzarella cheese and sweet red onions, topped with drained anchovy fillets. Chopped roasted bell peppers or pimentos can be added to sautéed onions and garlic and then simmered with long-grain rice. And a puréed roasted red pepper adds a fantastic dimension to the ultimate taste and color of soups and sauces.

To roast and peel peppers: This method can be used for chili peppers as well as bell peppers and pimentos. If you have a gas stove, stick a long stainless steel skewer into the stem end of a pepper and place it over direct flame. Turn the pepper as it blisters, pops and sizzles until the exterior becomes completely charred. (When you think you've gone too far, that's when it's just right!)

If your stove is electric, position the oven rack to the highest shelf and preheat the broiler until very hot. Slice the pepper in half through the stem end and remove the seeds. Lay the pepper (skin side up) on a cold broiler pan and place under broiler until the desired color is achieved. Let peppers steam in a closed paper bag or wrap in a clean kitchen towel, about 10 minutes. Then rub off the outer blackened skin, rinsing if necessary. (Don't worry if some of the skin remains since it adds a nice smoky flavor to the pepper.) Remove the seeds and pull away any flabby inner white veins. Use as directed in any recipe.

Handling hot chili peppers: Please, be careful when handling hot chili peppers. Capsaicin, an oily substance found primarily in the seeds and inner veins, can cause great discomfort to your mouth, eyes, ears or any cut or open sore. It's helpful to wear thin disposable rubber gloves (available at your local pharmacy) when doing such procedures or, after handling cut chili peppers, wash your hands with cool soapy water (as well as your work surface).

T I P S
FROM A TEACHER

How to Roast and Peel Peppers

Q. Is there any nutritional difference between the various types of hot and sweet peppers?

A. Yes. Among the mild bell peppers, the red variety has the highest amount of vitamin C—by weight three times higher than citrus fruits! But hot chili peppers have an even higher amount by weight, over 300 percent more than an orange. The different levels of capsaicin in peppers make some blazingly hot and others mild and sweet. This chemical substance is also said to act as an anticoagulant, which might help to prevent a heart attack or stroke induced by a blood clot.

4) *To finish roasted pepper mixture:* One to 2 hours before serving, add onion strips and capers to marinated peppers and leave at room temperature. Just before you broil garlic toasts, add chopped basil and balsamic vinegar to peppers and toss well to combine.

5) *To broil garlic toasts:* Preheat broiler and place garlic toasts 4 inches under broiler until golden and bubbling, about 2 minutes. Turn each wedge over and toast on the other side, about another 2 minutes. Keep a watchful eye on toasts to prevent burning.

6) *To serve:* Arrange garlic toasts on a serving platter. Using a fork, place some of the roasted pepper and onion mixture on top of each toast. Sprinkle Parmesan cheese and give a quick grind of black pepper over the top. Serve immediately.

Garlic Pita Toasts

YIELD: 1 dozen large wedges or 2 dozen small wedges

These are my very favorite crisps. In addition to serving them with marinated roasted peppers, I like to top the broiled pita toasts with Garlicky Herb Spread (page 103) or Chopped Chicken Liver (page 108). I also serve them many times alone as an accompaniment to hearty family dinners as well as lighter soup-meal lunches. For an unusually tender and more substantial (yet still very crisp) pita toast, try the pocketless variety.

INGREDIENTS

1 stick (¼ pound) butter or margarine, at room temperature

4 large cloves garlic, minced or pressed through a garlic press

Freshly ground black pepper to taste

½ teaspoon crumbled dried oregano

1 tablespoon chopped fresh flat-leaf Italian parsley or fresh basil leaves (optional)

3 large pita rounds (with or without pockets)

½ cup freshly grated Reggiano Parmesan cheese

1) **To prepare garlic butter:** In a bowl combine softened butter or margarine with minced garlic, pepper, oregano and parsley or basil, if using.

2) **To prepare garlic toasts:** If using pocketless pita rounds, spread a thin layer of garlic butter on 1 side of each round. If using regular pita bread (with pockets), cut each circle in half. Open each half so you have 4 pieces. Spread a thin layer of garlic butter on the opened inner side of each half. Regardless of the type of pita, sprinkle the buttered side lightly with freshly ground black pepper and, if desired, with grated Parmesan cheese. Cut each whole pocketless round into 4 to 8 wedges and each opened half round into 2 to 4 wedges. Place wedges on a shallow baking sheet (seasoned side up), cover with plastic wrap and refrigerate until ready to broil.

3) **To serve:** Preheat broiler. Broil garlic toast (buttered side up) until golden brown. Turn toast over and broil on the other side. Serve with roasted peppers or any of the accompaniments in the introduction to this recipe.

Pita Chips

Preheat the oven to 375°F. Cut 2 large pita rounds (with pockets) in half and open each half for a total of 8 half-moons. Press 2 cloves garlic through a garlic press directly onto your cutting board. Sprinkle ¼ teaspoon coarse salt over the garlic. Using a chef's knife, mash and scrape garlic with the salt until you create a paste. Scrape garlic paste off board into a small bowl. Add 1 generous tablespoon extra-virgin olive oil, ½ teaspoon crumbled dried oregano and a few grinds of black pepper. Mix well with a fork. Using a pastry brush, brush the mixture lightly on the outside surface of the bread. Stack pieces of pita, (seasoned side up) and cut the stack into 3 wedges for a total of 24 seasoned pita triangles and arrange (seasoned side up), on a wire rack within a shallow baking sheet. Sprinkle lightly with freshly grated Parmesan cheese and bake until golden and crisp, about 10 minutes. Let chips cool on the rack until just warm, pile them into a bowl and serve. Store leftovers in an airtight tin.

Q AND A

Q. What's the difference between a red bell pepper and a pimento?

A. Although these look very similar, sweet bell peppers have no capsaicin (heat), but fresh pimentos have varying degrees of capsaicin ranging from very low to moderate. Although fresh pimentos are not as readily available as bell peppers, they are delicious and will add extra zing to your dish. Pimentos with varying levels of capsaicin are most renowned for being dried and ground to a powder to produce sweet and hot paprika.

STUFFED FRIED ZUCCHINI SLICES

With Marinara Dipping Sauce

YIELD: 30 to 35 slices

SPECIAL EQUIPMENT

Melon ball scoop

10- to 12-inch nonstick skillet

Nonabrasive turning spatula

This recipe takes an old favorite (fried zucchini) and makes it extra special by first stuffing it with mozzarella cheese rolled with prosciutto ham. Then, the breaded zucchini slices are fried to perfection and served surrounding a bowl of fresh marinara sauce for dipping. Mozzarella cheese rolled with imported prosciutto is available in most gourmet cheese shops and some upscale super-markets. If unavailable, substitute plain mozzarella cheese or wrap a rod of string cheese with a slice of trimmed prosciutto before stuffing the zucchini.

INGREDIENTS

8 ounces mozzarella cheese rolled with prosciutto

3 medium zucchini with a hefty width

⅔ cup all-purpose flour

Salt and freshly ground black pepper to taste

3 eggs, well beaten

2 cups The Best Dried Bread Crumbs (page 78)

½ cup packed freshly grated Reggiano Parmesan cheese

Quick Marinara Sauce (page 242)

About ½ cup olive oil

2 cloves garlic, peeled and bruised

1) *To cut mozzarella:* Stand cheese roll upright so the coil of ham is exposed at one end facing up. Using a sharp knife, slice the cheese in half down the middle. Lay each half (flat side down) on your cutting surface and cut each half into strips about ½ inch wide.

2) *To prepare zucchini:* Scrub each zucchini and pat dry. Trim off the ends and discard. Take 1 cheese strip, measure it next to 1 zucchini and slice zucchini where the cheese strip ends. Set aside that strip of cheese with that chunk of zucchini together. Repeat this process with the remaining cheese strips and zucchini, so each zucchini chunk will be coupled with a cheese strip.

3) *To scoop zucchini:* Using the small side of a melon ball scoop, remove some of the interior of each zucchini chunk, creating a tunnel from one

end to the other. It's easiest to scoop alternately some from the top and then some from the bottom until you meet at the center and gently break through.

4) **To stuff and slice zucchini:** Working with 1 pair of cheese and zucchini at a time, stand the zucchini on the work surface and insert the cheese strip into the tunnel. Push gently until the cheese reaches the bottom and set aside. Using a sharp knife, slice each chunk of stuffed zucchini into ½ inch slices and lay them on a tray. (At this point the slices will resemble sushi.)

5) **To set up for breading zucchini slices:** Place flour on a plate and season with salt and pepper. Put the bowl of beaten eggs next to the flour. In a bowl, whisk bread crumbs with grated Parmesan and spread on a plate next to eggs. Line a large shallow baking sheet or tray with waxed paper and place it next to the crumb mixture.

6) **To bread zucchini:** Place zucchini, 4 rounds at a time, into the seasoned flour and dredge to coat well on all sides. Gently knock off the excess flour and dip zucchini slices into beaten eggs, turning to coat completely. With a slotted spatula lift each slice out of the eggs, turn in the crumb mixture, gently pressing to help crumbs adhere. Lift, allow excess crumbs to fall off and lay each slice on the prepared baking sheet in a single layer. (If necessary, use an additional sheet.) Fry immediately or preferably cover with plastic wrap and refrigerate for a few hours or overnight. This waiting period helps the crumbs adhere better while frying.

7) **Marinara sauce:** Prepare as directed in recipe and keep warm until ready to serve. Or prepare ahead and once cool, refrigerate until ready to reheat and serve.

8) **To panfry and drain zucchini:** Lay a long double strip of paper toweling on the work surface. Heat a nonstick skillet over medium-high heat; when hot, add enough olive oil to coat the bottom generously. When oil is hot, add garlic cloves and sear, pressing cloves occasionally with a nonabrasive spatula to release the flavor into the oil. When golden, remove garlic (either eat it or discard). Then fry zucchini in small batches in a single layer without crowding until very brown and crisp on both sides, turning once with a nonabrasive spatula. Drain briefly on the paper towels (if left too long, the cheese might ooze and stick to the paper). Once drained, either serve immediately with marinara sauce or transfer slices to a wire rack over a shallow baking sheet until it's time to reheat and serve.

Time Management Tips

- The bread crumbs can be made months ahead and kept in a heavy-duty plastic bag in the freezer. No need to thaw, just scoop them straight from the freezer.

- The stuffed zucchini can be prepared, breaded and kept in the refrigerator as much as 1 day ahead. The marinara sauce may also be made as much as 3 days ahead and stored in a tightly covered container in the refrigerator or frozen for several months.

- The slices can be fried and drained and kept at room temperature for 2 hours before reheating.

9) To reheat and serve: Preheat the oven to 375°F. Place the baking sheet with rack holding the slices in the oven and reheat until crisp and piping hot throughout, about 10 minutes. Serve the slices hot accompanied with warm marinara sauce.

Deep-Fried Variation

Alternatively, the stuffed zucchini slices can be fried in a deep-fat fryer. However, don't crowd them (fry about 4 at a time) as they might stick together while frying. If this happens, gently separate them using a wooden spoon.

MAPLE-ROASTED BACON ROLLS

YIELD: 36 to 40 rolls

SPECIAL EQUIPMENT
Food processor or blender

Shallow baking sheet and roasting rack

I don't know anyone who isn't always looking for a new finger-food recipe and this one is fabulous! These tender bacon rolls are stuffed with a savory mixture of bread crumbs, minced sautéed vegetables, herbs and chopped chicken liver. The application of pure maple syrup to the bacon before it's wrapped around the stuffing gives these rolls that extra touch that makes them a hit every time! These generous mouthfuls are perfect for a large cocktail party since they can be totally assembled one day ahead and even partially roasted an hour or two before "show time." Allow two rolls per person when accompanied with various other hot or cold finger foods. This recipe also doubles perfectly. To lower fat and cholesterol in this recipe, see following variation.

INGREDIENTS

15 to 20 slices fresh white bread or a combination of white, soft rye and whole wheat

1 stick (¼ pound) butter

¾ cup minced yellow onion

⅓ cup minced celery

2 large cloves garlic, minced

⅓ cup minced water chestnuts

2 teaspoons chopped fresh thyme leaves or ½ teaspoon crumbled dried thyme

¼ cup chopped flat-leaf Italian parsley

½ pound fresh chicken livers

1 cup Rich Chicken Stock or "Doctored" Canned Chicken Broth
(page 140 for both)

1 extra-large egg, lightly beaten

Salt and freshly ground black pepper to taste

About ½ cup pure maple syrup

2½ pounds thinly sliced bacon

Wooden toothpicks to secure bacon rolls

Time Management Tips

- The bacon rolls may be fully assembled 1 day ahead and stored in the refrigerator well covered.

- The bacon rolls may be partially roasted for 20 minutes up to 2 hours ahead and left at a comfortable room temperature until being finished off right before serving.

1) **To make bread crumbs:** Preheat the oven to 250°F. Tear bread with crusts into pieces, place in the bowl of a food processor fitted with the steel blade and process until of fine crumb consistency. Measure out 3 generous cups bread crumbs and place on a shallow baking sheet. Bake 10 minutes, then check crumbs. They should feel dry with a light golden color. If still soft, swish them around to redistribute and bake a few minutes longer, but don't allow them to scorch. Pour crumbs into a large bowl. (Alternatively, you can process several small batches of torn bread in a blender.)

2) **To sauté vegetables:** Melt 3 tablespoons of the butter in an 8-inch skillet over medium heat. When butter is hot and bubbling, stir in minced onion, celery and garlic. Sauté vegetables until softened and fragrant, about 3 minutes. Stir in minced water chestnuts and thyme. Cook gently for 1 more minute just to release the flavor of the thyme. Stir in parsley and pour contents of skillet into the bowl with the crumbs; fold together to combine. Do not wash skillet.

3) **To prepare chicken livers:** Rinse and drain livers. Cut away any connective tissue and pat dry with paper toweling. Replace skillet over medium heat and melt 2 more tablespoons butter. When hot, add chicken livers in a single layer and sear until golden, 2 to 3 minutes on each side. Reduce heat to low, cover and simmer just to cook through, about 2 minutes. Avoid overcooking; the liver should retain pinkness in the center. Uncover skillet, raise heat to medium-high and cook just a bit to caramelize the bits of vegetables and liver that cling to the bottom of the skillet, about 1 minute. Remove livers to a cutting surface and allow them to cool slightly.

4) To reduce stock and deglaze skillet: Pour butter out of skillet but do not wipe the interior. Place skillet over medium heat and pour in chicken stock. Bring to a boil and reduce by half, occasionally scraping any bits of caramelized liver and vegetables from the bottom of the pan.

5) To complete stuffing: Chop chicken livers into small but still textural pieces making sure they don't become pastelike. Fold into the bowl of crumbs. When only ½ cup of stock remains in skillet, remove from heat and swirl in the remaining 3 tablespoons butter. Pour the reduced and concentrated stock-butter mixture into the bowl of crumbs and, when just warm, stir in beaten egg. Season well with salt and pepper.

6) To assemble rolls: Lift small walnut-sized portions of the stuffing mixture and gently squeeze to help the crumbs bind together. Roll each portion into a ball and place on a tray. Cut slabs of bacon strips in half widthwise using sharp kitchen shears. Working in batches that will fit comfortably on your work surface, lay out 2 pieces of bacon in a cross pattern. Brush exposed sides of the bacon lightly with maple syrup. Place 1 ball of stuffing in the center of each bacon cross, where the 2 pieces overlap. Wrap the exposed bacon around the stuffing alternating with the bottom, side, top and side strips. Secure each roll with 1 or 2 toothpicks. If not roasting right away, cover with plastic wrap and refrigerate until needed.

7) To roast and serve: Preheat the oven to 375°F. Place stuffed bacon rolls on a roasting rack that sits over a shallow baking sheet. Bake until crisp and piping hot throughout, about 30 minutes. (Since you probably won't be able to fit all of these on 1 rack, roast in 2 batches or use 2 baking sheets and roast in the upper and lower thirds of the oven switching after half the prescribed baking time.) Serve hot or at least warm.

Reduced-Fat Variation

When sautéing vegetables, omit butter entirely and instead braise vegetables in chicken stock until tender. Substitute olive oil or canola oil for butter to sauté chicken livers. Reduce the amount of butter to 1 tablespoon when swirling into reduced chicken stock.

PEPPERED BRIE EN CROÛTE

With Sun-Dried Tomatoes and Black Forest Ham

YIELD: serves 12 to 14 as a first course and a crowd when part of a buffet

Rich, buttery brioche wrapped around a black-pepper-studded wheel of Brie cheese is an absolute show stopper! Nestled under the dough, a layer of slivered sun-dried tomatoes, ribbons of fresh basil and German Black Forest ham will bring down the house. Glazed and baked, this makes a rich and stunning addition to a cocktail party or a holiday buffet table. If using a smaller wheel of Brie, for four to six people, freeze the remaining dough or use for breakfast rolls as directed in brioche recipe or make Salami en Croûte (following). I have also outlined two different ways to use the scraps of brioche dough to decorate the top of the encased Brie round before baking, but please use your imagination. Brioche dough, when chilled, is easy and fun to work with, so enjoy it. Rounds of peppered Brie are sold at better cheese shops. If you can't find one, generously sprinkle the top of an unwrapped wheel of Brie cheese with coarsely ground black pepper. If desired, plain Brie may be substituted.

SPECIAL EQUIPMENT
Tapered rolling pin

Parchment paper

Feather brush or pastry brush with soft bristles

INGREDIENTS

1 recipe Brioche dough (page 391)

Egg glaze: 1 whole egg mixed with 1 egg yolk and 1 tablespoon water, milk or cream

Cornmeal (preferably medium-ground), for baking sheet

4 fresh basil leaves, for chiffonade

3 plump dried tomato halves, marinated (page 124), drained and cut into thin strips

1 or 2 thin slices Black Forest ham (1½ to 2 ounces), rolled lengthwise and sliced crosswise into thin slices

All-purpose flour, for dusting work surface

1 wheel (2 pounds) peppered Brie cheese

1) Brioche dough: Prepare dough as directed in recipe, allow to rise fully and chill.

2) To set up: Prepare egg glaze and push through a wire strainer into a small bowl (this removes excess coagulation from the egg, making it easier to apply with a pastry brush). Line a baking sheet with parchment paper and sprinkle paper lightly with cornmeal.

- The brioche dough may be made up to 2 days ahead and kept in the refrigerator (after the first full rise at room temperature). Make sure to cover the bowl securely and weight down the top of the bowl with a can of some sort to keep the dough from over-rising.

3) To prepare topping: Make chiffonade of fresh basil: Rinse and dry leaves, stack them and tightly roll up the stack widthwise. Slice roll crosswise into thin shreds. In a small bowl, combine basil chiffonade with slivered sun-dried tomatoes and sliced ham.

4) To roll bottom piece of dough: Turn out chilled dough onto a very lightly floured work surface. Cut dough in half and refrigerate half of the dough while you work with the other. Roll dough into a large, ¼-inch-thick circle. Place Brie (peppered side up) in the center of the round of dough. With a sharp knife, trim dough round into a circle 1½ to 2 inches larger than the Brie. Remove Brie from dough and set aside. Carefully move aside flat dough scraps and reserve for decorating the top crust. (Unrefrigerated brioche dough quickly becomes airy and difficult to roll so be sure to leave scraps flat after initial rolling.)

5) To roll top piece of dough: With the remaining piece of brioche dough, repeat step 4, except that final circle of dough should be about 3 inches larger than the Brie so that it can extend down the sides and be tucked under the round.

6) To enclose Brie in brioche dough: Place Brie in the center of the smaller round of dough. Using a soft brush, paint the exposed border of the dough with strained egg glaze. Bring dough up the sides of the cheese and press onto the sides to adhere. Scatter the tomato, ham and basil mixture on top of the Brie. Place second circle of dough over Brie, bring down the sides and tuck under neatly to secure. Remove to prepared baking sheet and continue to tuck dough under until smooth and uniform looking. Brush the exposed top and sides of dough with egg glaze.

7) To decorate top of crust: Place rolled scraps of dough onto your work surface. Cut out designs of your choice with a pretty cookie cutter with a fluted edge, or create your own designs, or use my suggestions for lattice or grape designs following this recipe. Place cutouts on top of the glazed, unbaked brioche crust and brush all exposed dough once more with egg glaze.

8) Final rising of filled dough: Let assembled Brie sit uncovered at room temperature for 20 minutes on the baking sheet. Preheat the oven to 375°F for the full 20 minutes.

9) *To bake:* Brush exposed dough once more with egg glaze and bake until a light golden brown all over, 25 to 30 minutes. Remove from baking sheet (using 2 spatulas) and let rest on a wire cooling rack for 20 minutes before cutting or serving. The dough is very insulating, so even if the brioche feels cool, the cheese will still be warm and of proper consistency. If the dough is too warm, the cheese will run out once cut and will be difficult to serve.

10) *To serve:* For a buffet serve on a platter and let guests cut their own portions. (No crackers are necessary since the cheese is wrapped in the bread.) For a formal dinner party, cut into wedges and serve on individual plates.

Dough Decorations for Brie en Croûte

Grapes on the Vine Design: Cut a thin strip of dough 4 to 5 inches long and ¼ inch wide and place it on the center of the top of the glazed dough, curving it to look like a stem. Then, take tiny portions (about half the size of a thimble) of the remaining dough and roll between the palms of your hands into smooth balls to look like grapes. Lay these balls on the stem in a cluster around and on top of the stem, leaving 1½ inches of the stem on top. As you lay each grape, brush it gently with egg glaze, so that they adhere to each other. Keep rolling more balls until the bunch seems full, putting some balls on top of each other to give depth to the bunch. Roll out any remaining scraps of dough and cut out a nice leaf shape to place at the top of the stem. Using the dull side of a small paring knife, make decorative indentations to create the veins of the leaf. Brush the decorative shapes and any exposed areas of dough once more with egg glaze.

Lattice Design: Cut thin strips of dough and lay them in a diamond lattice pattern on top of the glazed dough tucking the ends of the strips underneath. To give dimension to the lattice design, gently apply pressure (using your index fingers) to the top strips just where they surround the bottom strips. Gently brush the lattice with egg glaze.

Q. Is the home-drying procedure the same for all fruits?

A. Once the dynamics of drying tomatoes is understood, you can apply the procedure to many fruits. The secret to dry fruit successfully is to provide balanced exposure to gentle heat. The heat must be adequate enough to do the job but mild enough not to cook the food. Because all fruits start out with varying degrees of moisture, each will require a different time to dry sufficiently. Some fruits must also be treated with an acidic ingredient to prevent them from turning brown.

When a salami is initially exposed to heat, it will naturally swell up and then shrink down soon after being removed from the oven. If the salami is not given a chance to preswell before being wrapped in the brioche dough, the salami will shrink away from the walls of the brioche, causing each slice to show a gaping space between the bread and the salami.

Salami en Croûte

For a delicious addition to a hearty "soup meal" lunch or light supper, serve a savory sizzling whole salami surrounded by rich and tender baked brioche. Preheat the oven to 350°F. Place an unwrapped salami on a baking sheet and bake until the salami is swollen but not brown, 15 to 20 minutes. Remove from oven and let sit at room temperature covered loosely with aluminum foil until just warm, about 15 minutes. Meanwhile, raise the temperature to 375°F. Roll out a piece of chilled brioche dough (depending on the size of your salami) and brush it lightly with some Dijon mustard. Place the swollen lukewarm whole salami in the center and wrap it in the dough pinching to seal. Line a baking sheet with parchment paper and sprinkle with cornmeal or sesame seeds or caraway seeds or poppy seeds. Place dough-encased salami (seam side down) on baking sheet. Glaze, decorate and glaze again, as directed in Peppered Brie en Croûte recipe. Bake at 375°F until golden brown, 25 to 30 minutes. Let settle a bit. Then using a sharp serrated knife, slice and serve while still warm. This may be made a few hours ahead and kept at room temperature. Reheat gently before serving (10 to 15 minutes at 350°F).

TIPS

FROM A TEACHER

All About Dried Tomatoes

Imported sun-dried tomatoes marinated in olive oil are quite costly. To lessen the price dramatically, either purchase the tomatoes dried and packaged in cellophane bags (available in most gourmet food stores) or, if your garden is overflowing with plump, gorgeous tomatoes, dry them at home. Several types of heat are used to dry tomatoes. Nature's own sunshine unfortunately is not a viable alternative for most of us, but home cooks can use an electric dehydrator, a conventional oven or a convection oven (which I prefer to a conventional oven for this procedure). All of these methods take anywhere from twenty-four to thirty-six hours. Nevertheless, I prefer home-dried tomatoes to the store-bought versions, which are usually harder and tougher. Those dried at home are easier to reconstitute and have a more supple texture.

To prepare tomatoes for drying: Thoroughly wash and dry tomatoes. Cut each in half lengthwise and, using a tomato shark or the tip of a 3-inch paring knife, remove the stem spot and the central core of each tomato. Leave seeds intact and spread tomatoes on a nonreactive baking sheet (cut sides up). Sprinkle with 1 teaspoon canning salt or sea salt for each pound tomatoes. Cover salted tomatoes with another baking sheet and apply weights (heavy cans) to the top to flatten and help draw out moisture from tomatoes. Let sit at room temperature for 1 hour.

To steam tomatoes before drying: Uncover salted tomatoes and place on a steamer rack (in batches if necessary—avoid overcrowding). Place rack over boiling water (but not touching it) and cover the pot. Steam tomatoes for 2 minutes and check for texture: Each tomato half should appear wilted and the texture should have softened. They will probably need 1 or 2 more minutes to enable the steam to reach the interior of each tomato half.

To dry tomatoes in a conventional oven: Preheat the oven to its lowest setting (preferably 140°F) and turn on the vent (or leave the door ajar if your electric oven doesn't come vented). For best results, don't overload the oven; smaller batches do better and dry quicker. Lightly oil a stainless steel cooling rack. Place a single thickness of well-rinsed and thoroughly dried cheesecloth over rack and arrange prepared tomatoes (cut sides up) on rack. Place the rack of tomatoes directly on the oven rack on the center shelf of the oven and let tomatoes dry (turning them occasionally) until the correct texture is achieved, 24 to 36 hours. (If the oven door is ajar, they take longer to dry sufficiently.) Check texture occasionally, especially toward the end of drying. Let cool thoroughly. Remove individual tomatoes when they become dry but still pliable. When first removed from the dryer, they will feel a bit softer than desired but will firm up once cool. The overall texture should be "leathery" but not at all hard.

To dry tomatoes using an electric dehydrator or convection oven: Prepare and steam tomatoes as directed above and place on the trays of the dehydrator according to the manufacturer's instructions, making sure not to overload the trays; switch the positions of the trays often, even more often than suggested. Convection ovens come with a specific setting for drying; follow the manufacturer's instructions.

To store home-dried and commercially dried tomatoes: Store dried tomatoes in a plastic bag and twist shut. Place bag into a jar, tightly secure with the lid and keep in the refrigerator. Or, place freshly dried tomatoes directly into a jar, marinate in olive oil (see below) and refrigerate tightly covered. Dried tomatoes will keep perfectly for at least 6 months whether marinated or left dry.

To reconstitute and marinate dried tomatoes: Dried tomatoes that have been stored for any length of time must be reconstituted before marinating them. Soak in boiling water to cover for 20 to 30 minutes or until supple; drain well and pat dry. To marinate, place tomatoes in a jar and cover completely with olive oil. (Avoid overfilling jar since tomatoes will swell in the oil causing messy leakage.) Let jar sit undisturbed for 12 hours (or overnight) at room temperature. Uncover jar and add more oil if necessary to cover any exposed tomatoes. Secure the cover and store in the refrigerator. Before using, since oil will have solidified, run jar under hot tap water to loosen and liquify the oil.

CRISP POTATO BOATS

With Scallion Cream Cheese and Caviar

YIELD: 3 dozen potato boats; serves 18

SPECIAL EQUIPMENT

8-quart blanching pot with built-in strainer (optional)

Melon ball scoop

Electric deep-fat fryer or good-quality deep-fat thermometer

Pastry bag with ½-inch plain or star tip (optional)

1 small wooden or mother-of-pearl spoon, for scooping caviar

Although these luxurious mouthfuls are fantastic for a cocktail party, I could eat them for breakfast, lunch or dinner! Be sure to save the scooped-out potato balls to fry or roast and serve, lightly salted, alongside the potato boats. Usually, when caviar is served with creamy accompaniments, you can get by with inexpensive black or red lumpfish with wonderful results. But, since in this recipe the caviar is "exposed" on top of the filled potato boats, it's justifiable to purchase maybe not the best but close to it. For more information on caviar, see Tips from a Teacher (page 102). For this recipe, I would suggest either osetra or sevruga, since their taste will stand up to the rest of the ingredients without the added extravagance. (Don't get me wrong, these eggs are pricey too!) And if these are not in the budget, use the medium-sized deep orange salmon eggs (called red caviar) or black lumpfish eggs. The potato boats may be either deep-fried or roasted (see variation).

INGREDIENTS

Salt for boiling potatoes

36 small (no bigger than a mouthful) red or white potatoes, unpeeled and scrubbed

8 ounces whipped cream cheese*, at room temperature or 1 cup Low-Fat Cream Cheese (page 82)

1½ teaspoons strained fresh lemon juice

1 tablespoon sour cream or Low-Fat Sour Cream (page 82)

½ cup firmly packed finely minced scallions (green onions), trimmed white parts and 1½ to 2 inches of the tender green

Freshly ground black pepper to taste

White pepper to taste

2 quarts mild peanut oil*

About 3 ounces caviar

Kosher or sea salt

* See section on Staples

1) To boil potatoes: Bring a large pot of water to boil. Add some salt and the potatoes. Cover pot and boil potatoes until just tender but not at all soft, about 10 minutes. Drain potatoes and let cool.

2) To scoop out potatoes: When cool enough to handle, cup each potato snugly in one hand and with a melon ball scoop gently but firmly scoop out and set aside a ball of potato flesh from the center. (Use the small side of the scoop for the very tiny potatoes and the larger side for the slightly larger ones.) Leave a nice wall of potato all around. Slice a very thin layer off the bottom of each potato to help them sit upright once fried and filled. Set aside until ready to fry.

3) To make filling: In a bowl, use a rubber spatula to combine cream cheese, lemon juice, sour cream and minced scallions. Add freshly ground black and white pepper to taste. Cover and refrigerate until assembling.

4) To fry potato boats: Lay a long sheet of double paper toweling on your counter. Attach thermometer to the side of a 4-quart pot. Pour in peanut oil to half fill pot and heat to 375°F. (Or fill an electric deep-fryer following the manufacturer's instructions and turn the machine to the highest setting.) Add prepared potato boats to the hot oil in 3 separate batches and fry each batch until golden, about 5 minutes. Drain well (upside down) on the paper towels. In the same manner, fry the reserved scooped-out potato balls.

5) To assemble: Fill a pastry bag, if using, with filling as directed on page 505. Lift one potato at a time and pipe some filling into each hole swirling to the top of the potato. If not using a pastry bag, carefully use a teaspoon to fill each potato. Using a very small mother-of-pearl or wooden spoon place a dab of caviar on top of the filling.

6) To serve: Place the assembled potato boats around the edge of an attractive platter lined with a pretty paper doily. In the center, mound fried potato balls and lightly sprinkle balls with coarse salt. Serve while potatoes are warm.

Time Management Tips

- The filling may be made up to 2 days ahead and kept well covered in the refrigerator.

- The potatoes may be scrubbed, boiled and scooped early in the day that you plan to serve, then place potato boats and balls in separate bowls. Leave them at room temperature for up to 4 hours or refrigerate for a longer period. Bring close to room temperature before frying.

- The cream cheese filling may be placed in the pastry bag and kept refrigerated (standing upright in a tall drinking glass) the day before serving. Seal the top of the bag shut with a "twisty" from a box of plastic bags.

- Once the potatoes are fried, they should be assembled and served as soon as possible. However, if necessary, the fried potatoes and potato balls can be kept hot on a wire rack over a shallow baking sheet in a 375°F oven for up to 30 minutes before filling.

Q. What does the word "malossol" on the label of a container of caviar mean?

A. *Malossol is the Russian term for "a little salt." Caviar is very perishable and when a small amount of salt is used as a preservative in Russian caviar, you will see this word on the container.*

Variation: Roasted Potato Boats

Preheat the oven to 425°F. Place a wire rack inside a shallow baking sheet and line the rack with aluminum foil (shiny side up) to reflect heat up toward potatoes. Brush the foil lightly with extra-virgin olive oil and use a long 2-pronged fork to punch lots of random holes in the foil. Brush the scooped potatoes and the potato balls with more olive oil and place them (scooped side down) on the foil. Scatter potato balls to the sides of the boats. Roast for 20 minutes. Turn potato boats so they finish roasting (scooped side up) and continue to roast until golden and crisp, 10 to 20 minutes.

SPINACH-STUFFED MUSHROOMS

Baked with Bread Crumbs

YIELD: serves 8 as first course or side dish

These tender mushrooms filled with a creamy spinach-mushroom filling and topped with savory buttered bread crumbs and minced Jarlsberg cheese make a delectable first course or side dish when entertaining. In order to protect the spinach filling while being baked uncovered, I give the mushrooms a head start in the oven before filling them and then baking them assembled at a slightly lower temperature. To reduce substantially the amount of saturated fats in this recipe, see the following low-fat variation. At a dinner party, I like to serve these mushrooms as an appetizer before a main course of Honey Mustard Roast Rack of Lamb (page 300) and Garlic Sautéed Cherry Tomatoes (page 324).

INGREDIENTS

24 large fresh button mushrooms

4 bunches fresh spinach, trimmed, rinsed thoroughly and drained, or 2 packages thawed frozen chopped spinach, squeezed of all its excess liquid

½ stick (4 tablespoons) butter

½ cup packed minced yellow onion

2 cloves garlic, minced

3 ounces cream cheese, at room temperature

½ cup sour cream

½ cup packed freshly grated Reggiano Parmesan cheese

Lots of freshly ground black pepper

Salt to taste

Melted butter or olive oil for baking sheet

FOR THE TOPPING

1 cup The Best Dried Bread Crumbs (page 78)

1 stick (¼ pound) butter, melted

½ cup freshly grated Reggiano Parmesan cheese

⅓ cup minced Jarlsberg cheese (optional)

Freshly ground black pepper to taste

1) *To prepare mushrooms:* Wipe clean and carefully remove stems as directed on page 131. Set aside caps and mince 12 of the stems, using a sharp knife or a food processor fitted with the steel blade. Remove them to a clean kitchen towel and firmly squeeze out any excess liquid. (You won't believe how much liquid comes out!)

2) *To cook fresh spinach:* Place fresh spinach leaves into a heavy-bottomed pot with a tight-fitting lid. Do not add any additional liquid since the water that clings to the leaves after draining is more than sufficient. Cook leaves over medium heat until steam escapes from under the lid. Reduce heat to low and cook until spinach is totally wilted, about 4 minutes. Pour spinach into a wire strainer and place another bowl directly on top of the spinach. Press firmly on the bowl to force any remaining moisture out through the strainer. If using thawed frozen spinach, do not cook; just squeeze it in a clean kitchen towel to remove excess moisture.

3) *To prepare filling:* Melt butter in a skillet over medium heat until hot and bubbling. Add minced onions and garlic and sauté until they are softened and very fragrant, about 3 minutes. Add minced mushrooms, stir and cook until they are soft and lose their raw look, 3 to 4 minutes. Add prepared spinach and stir well to incorporate fully. Remove from heat and stir in cream cheese and sour cream, combining well. Add grated Parmesan, lots of freshly ground black pepper and salt to taste.

4) *To prebake mushrooms:* Preheat the oven to 375°F. Place mushrooms in a single layer on a greased large shallow baking sheet and bake until they just begin to exude their liquid, 5 to 10 minutes. Set aside until cool enough to handle. Reduce oven temperature to 350°F.

Time Management Tips

• The mushrooms may be fully assembled as much as 2 days ahead and refrigerated. Bring close to room temperature before baking or adjust baking time to heat through sufficiently.

5) *To prepare topping:* Place bread crumbs in a medium bowl, pour melted butter over them and stir to combine. Add grated Parmesan, minced Jarlsberg cheese, if using, and black pepper.

6) *To assemble stuffed mushrooms:* Lift each mushroom from baking dish, pour out any liquid that has accumulated in the center and place on a tray. Dry the bottom of the baking dish and brush once more with a little melted butter or olive oil. Using a spoon, fill mushrooms generously with spinach stuffing, mounding in the center. Press some of the topping mixture onto the top of each mushroom and lay them side by side in the baking dish. Grind on some additional pepper.

7) *To bake:* Bake stuffed mushrooms uncovered in a 350°F oven until crumbs are golden brown and filling is piping hot, 25 to 30 minutes. Serve hot.

Low-Fat Variation

To reduce the overall saturated-fat content of the filling:

Substitute ⅓ cup Rich Chicken Stock (page 140) for the butter when sautéeing onions and garlic. Substitute ¼ cup Low-Fat Cream Cheese for the cream cheese and ½ cup Low-Fat Sour Cream for the regular sour cream (both recipes on page 82).

The most familiar and readily available mushrooms in the United States are those cultivated here—the white button and brown cremini varieties. But since the 1980s, many varieties of wild mushrooms are being imported, and other varieties of specialty mushrooms have been developed or cultivated and are now widely available fresh or dried in our vegetable markets. Some of my favorites include shiitakes, portobellos and porcinis (cèpes). The latter (when fresh) are incredibly delicious—and pricey—and only make a brief appearance in our specialty produce markets in early autumn. Fortunately dried porcinis, once reconstituted, are also delicious and much more readily available.

To buy and store fresh mushrooms:
When selecting white button mushrooms to be stored for several days, avoid those with open caps (turn mushroom stem side up and, if the dark brown gills are visible, choose another). Button mushrooms should be firm, smooth and blemish free and, when stored properly at home, will last for about one week. If purchasing packaged mushrooms, leave them in their original container, but poke several holes in the plastic. Store on the shelf of your refrigerator. (Don't store them in the crisper, which is too humid and will provoke the mushrooms to sweat.) If purchasing unpackaged mushrooms, store them in a shallow dish draped loosely with a double thickness of slightly moistened paper towel.

To clean fresh mushrooms: Since fresh mushrooms are very absorptive and naturally loaded with liquid, it's not a good idea to run them under water to clean them. When mushrooms become wet before cooking, they will immediately release excess liquid into the hot sauté pan and lose their ability to sear and become golden. Instead, they will quickly steam within their own juice and become gray and limp. To clean fresh mushrooms properly, dampen a piece of paper toweling and wipe the cap and stem of the mushroom to remove all traces of dirt. Although it's not necessary to peel the outer skin, which will naturally begin to fall away as you wipe, I usually remove it to make the surface of each mushroom look cleaner and whiter. (Some foodies, however, are quite passionate about not peeling mushrooms; this is strictly a matter of personal preference.)

To remove stems from fresh mushrooms: Although the stems on many mushrooms are edible, some are not palatable since their texture is quite tough and the flavor sometimes gamey. To remove the stems of shiitakes or portobellos, simply slice off the stems flush with the caps. The stems of button mushrooms are as delicious as the caps so there is no need to remove the stems unless you plan to stuff the mushrooms. To release the stem from a button mushroom, simply snap it out with your thumb, using pressure from both sides alternately.

To reconstitute dried mushrooms: While excess liquid is detrimental to the texture of fresh mushrooms, dried "wild" mushrooms need excess moisture to become clean as well as supple and edible. To clean dried mushrooms, place them in a wire strainer and rinse briefly under cool running tap water. Then immediately place them in a bowl, pour in very hot water to cover and soak until fully reconstituted, 20 to 30 minutes. Strain the flavor-packed soaking liquid through a paper filter or dampened cheesecloth to remove debris and use the mushroom liquid to enhance whatever you are cooking— whether it be a sauce, soup, rice, stew; the list goes on.

To use and cook fresh mushrooms: Although fresh mushrooms may be eaten raw, it's best not to make a habit of it. Raw mushrooms contain small levels of toxins (called hydrazines), which are a natural protective substance produced in fungi to deter predators. Fortunately, most of these toxins are destroyed during cooking or after drying. To cook fresh mushrooms properly so they become golden and savory, they should be sautéed quickly over intense heat in hot butter (full or clarified) or a full-bodied oil (such as extra-virgin olive oil). Remove from heat just as they begin to exude their natural moisture. Mushrooms make wonderful containers for savory fillings for an appetizer or first course. Or they can be sliced, chopped or quartered and sautéed with garlic and fresh herbs to add to sauces, soups, rice, stews, omelets, soufflés or to top crisp hot garlic toasts. Again, the list goes on.

To use dried mushrooms: Add reconstituted dried mushrooms to sauces and stews in much the same way as fresh, but use less since their flavor is quite intense and concentrated and their price tag is high. A little goes a long way. To make up for the lack of texture in dried mushrooms, add additional fresh sliced or chopped mild cultivated mushrooms to the more powerful reconstituted fungi.

BROILED CROSTINI

With Prosciutto, Portobellos and Cheese

YIELD: 8 crostini

Crostini is a generic Italian term for garlic toast topped with "something or other" and it's the perfect choice to serve alongside the salad course as part of an Italian meal, or as a hearty accompaniment to a robust lunch or light soup-supper meal. The number of crostini creations is limited only by your imagination. One of my favorite toppings is this combination of prosciutto ham and portobello mushrooms. If I was asked to plan my last meal, it would most definitely include the incredible portobello. Another fabulous topping is prosciutto and sun-dried tomatoes, which I have included as a variation. And finally, serve crostini with Whole Garlic Roasted with Olive Oil and Herbs (page 135).

INGREDIENTS

8 slices (½-inch thick) crusty Italian bread with sesame seeds

About 5 tablespoons (⅓ cup) softened butter or margarine

3 large cloves garlic, minced

1 tablespoon chopped fresh basil or a combination of
  1 tablespoon chopped, fresh flat-leaf Italian parsley and
  ½ teaspoon crumbled dried oregano

Freshly ground black pepper to taste

1 large yellow onion

1 pound portobello mushrooms

¼ to ⅓ cup extra-virgin olive oil

4 large cloves garlic, peeled and cut into very thin slices

2 teaspoons chopped fresh thyme leaves or
  1 teaspoon crumbled dried thyme

8 to 10 thin slices imported prosciutto ham (about ¼ pound),
  trimmed to fit bread slices

1 cup grated Jarlsberg cheese

1 cup grated Gruyère cheese

Time Management Tips

- The garlic butter can be applied to the bread 1 day ahead and kept covered in the refrigerator. The cheese can be grated 1 day ahead as well and kept covered and refrigerated.

- The slices of garlic bread can be toasted 3 hours ahead and left on a wire rack at room temperature until fully assembling just before broiling.

- The vegetables for the topping may be sliced 1 day ahead and kept in separate well-covered bowls in the refrigerator.

- The vegetables for the topping may be sautéed 1½ hours ahead before broiling and left in the skillet until ready to rewarm and assemble.

- Fully assemble the crostini no more than 10 minutes ahead of broiling.

1) **To prepare garlic toasts:** In a small bowl, combine softened butter, minced garlic, chopped basil and some black pepper. Spread butter mixture lightly on both sides of bread slices. Heat a 10- to 12-inch skillet over medium-high heat. When hot, sauté the bread in batches until light brown and toasted on both sides. Let cool on a wire rack.

2) **To prepare onion:** Peel and slice onion in half through the stem end. Slice each half into thin wedges. Separate wedges into strips.

3) **To prepare mushrooms:** Wipe mushrooms clean, remove stems and discard them. Slice caps in half and then cut each half crosswise into thin slices.

4) **To prepare vegetable topping:** Reheat skillet over medium heat and when hot, add 2 generous tablespoons of olive oil. When oil is hot, add onion strips, stir and cook until softened and very fragrant, about 5 minutes. Add garlic slices and cook until onions begin to turn golden, about 10 minutes. Stir in thyme. Cook for another minute or so just to release the flavor of the herb. Remove onions and garlic to a bowl but don't wipe out the pan. Return skillet to high heat. Add 3 more tablespoons oil and when hot, stir in mushroom slices and sauté until softened, golden and cooked through, 3 to 4 minutes. Return onion mixture to the skillet and toss well to combine.

5) **To assemble and broil:** Preheat the broiler for 10 to 15 minutes before you plan to serve. Cover each slice of garlic toast with a slice of ham. If the mushroom-onion mixture has been prepared in advance, rewarm briefly just until tepid (warm to the touch) and divide among the slices. Combine grated cheeses in a bowl and mound cheese on top of each slice. Grind some fresh black pepper over the top. Broil crostini until the cheese is melted, bubbling and starting to turn golden. Serve at once.

Crostini Topped with Prosciutto, Sun-Dried Tomatoes and Fresh Basil

Prepare garlic toasts and trim proscuitto as directed in master recipe. Rinse and pat dry about 6 large basil leaves. To create a chiffonade, stack leaves and roll them up lengthwise into a snug roll. Slice the roll into very thin slices and unravel the slices. To assemble, arrange ham on top of garlic toasts as directed. Drain 6 or 7 sun-dried tomato halves that have been marinated in olive oil (page 124) and slice them into thin slivers. Scatter them over top of the crostini. Combine 8 ounces shredded fresh mozzarella cheese and ½ cup grated Reggiano Parmesan cheese in a bowl and mound cheese on top of crostini. Grind on some fresh pepper. Broil as directed just before serving. These can be fully assembled up to 1½ hours ahead of broiling. Keep loosely covered at room temperature.

Whole Garlic Roasted with Olive Oil and Herbs

When roasted, garlic becomes both incredibly succulent and perfectly sweet. These tender cloves are delicious when spread on slices of toasted or grilled crusty bread and served as part of an antipasto as a first course.

Allow 1 (whole) medium-sized head per person. Slice ⅓ inch off the pointed top of the head so the raw garlic is exposed and place each head (trimmed side up) on a square of aluminum foil (shiny side up) large enough to enclose head. Drizzle each head with 1½ teaspoons extra-virgin olive oil and sprinkle with 1 teaspoon chopped fresh thyme leaves and a grind or 2 of fresh black pepper. Wrap up each head loosely and poke a few holes in the upper portion of the foil. Place garlic packets on a shallow baking sheet and roast in a preheated 400°F oven until garlic is absolutely tender and the outer skin is light golden, glistening and sizzling, 45 minutes to 1 hour. Unwrap heads and serve hot.

Serve 1 head of roasted garlic to each person and instruct your guests to cut through the bottom (root end) of the head to release the cloves. To eat, either pull off a clove and press the bottom to push the tender and buttery clove out the top. Or insert the tines of a small seafood fork into the top of each clove and retrieve the soft nugget of garlic. Pass a basket of grilled bread and, if desired, a plate of freshly shaved Reggiano Parmesan cheese.

CHAPTER IV

HEFTY STOCKS AND HEARTY SOUPS

Nurturing Scents from the Kitchen

Whether preparing a robust lunch or an informal supper, one of the most satisfying menus to me consists of nothing more than a deep bowl of piping hot soup and a basket of light, freshly baked biscuits, savory muffins or crisps. In this chapter you'll learn how to prepare rich, fat-free homemade stocks. In addition to being the base of my hearty and satisfying soups, these stocks are the preferred choice of liquid to simmer your rice and other grains. And stock (never water) should always serve as the heart and soul of the sauces that bathe your braised dishes. Since most soups and all stocks are notoriously freezer friendly, most of the recipes in this chapter are extra "chubby" to make the most of the time that you've assigned to the kitchen. And in several recipes, such as Chicken in the Pot (page 154), I'll show you how to make soup and to replenish your stock supply at the same time.

FISH STOCK

YIELD: about 4 quarts

Fish stock (fish fumet) is quick to prepare and freezes perfectly. Avoid using the trimmings from oily or fatty fish such as bluefish, mackerel, herring or black sea bass since their flavor is too strong and fishy for stock. The most delicate, full-bodied fish stock is made from the bones, skin and tails of mild white fish such as flounder, striped bass, halibut, catfish or red snapper. To this, I add equal amounts of chicken or vegetable stock and water along with aromatic vegetables. The optional wine and crumbled thyme lend a distinctive flavor and aroma. To obtain fish trimmings easily, go to your local fish market which will most likely give them to you for free. Unlike most other stocks, fish stock needn't be simmered endlessly. To the contrary, if cooked too long, the broth will take on a bitter flavor. Also, it's important to rinse your fish frames (intact or broken skeletons) and heads thoroughly before adding them to the stockpot. Snip off any remnants of fish organs or gills (the thin, red, fan-shaped matter that's attached to both sides of the throat), which cause a bitter taste.

SPECIAL EQUIPMENT
8-quart nonreactive stockpot

Skimmer

Sturdy colander, preferably stainless steel

Fine-mesh sieve

INGREDIENTS

2 to 3 pounds fish trimmings from mild white fish including
  heads, tails, frames and skin

2 large leeks, cleaned and sliced (page 160)

1 large yellow onion, unpeeled, scrubbed, root end removed,
  and thinly sliced or chopped

3 stalks celery, cleaned and thinly sliced or chopped

3 carrots, scrubbed and thinly sliced or chopped

½ cup dry white wine (optional)

1 generous teaspoon whole black peppercorns

1 scant teaspoon salt

1 generous pinch crumbled dried thyme leaves (optional)

2 quarts Rich Chicken Stock or "Doctored" Canned Chicken Broth
  (page 140 for both)

2 quarts cold water

Q and A

Q. What's the difference between fish stock and court bouillon?

A. *Court bouillon is the light, slightly acidic poaching liquid in which fish is gently simmered until just tender. It begins with cold water and either a bit of red or white wine vinegar or lemon juice along with aromatic vegetables and (if desired) herbs. If you use your court bouillon to poach several batches of fish, it will then be considered rich enough to serve as a base for your fish stock, instead of using chicken stock. Think of court bouillon as soup that starts with water, and fish stock as soup that begins with the goodness of rich stock.*

1) **To prepare stock:** Combine all ingredients in a tall nonreactive 8-quart stockpot and bring to a brisk simmer. In the beginning, scum will rise to the surface of the stock. Skim this off and continue to cook over low heat with the cover ajar for 30 minutes, occasionally pressing hard on the solids to extract as much flavor from them as possible.

2) **To cool, strain and store stock:** Remove pot from heat and allow the broth to cool with the solids at room temperature for 30 minutes. Position a sturdy colander in a large bowl and ladle both the solids and stock into the colander. As stock goes through the colander, press hard on the solids. Discard solids and strain stock once more through a fine-mesh sieve to remove any small particles of solids. Either use stock immediately or divide among labeled freezer containers. The fresh stock can be refrigerated for 1 or (at the most) 2 days before using. Fish stock freezes perfectly for 3 months in a freezer with little temperature fluctuation. Always bring thawed stock to a rolling boil before eating.

Fish Stock Substitute

If necessary, as a substitute for homemade fish stock, use a combination of bottled clam juice and mild chicken stock by diluting Rich Chicken Stock (page 140) with an equal amount of cold water. Avoid using canned clam juice as it has a metallic taste.

SHRIMP STOCK

YIELD: about 1 quart

Here's one more example to support the concept that in the kitchen every-thing is good for something! The next time you purchase shrimp, instead of throwing the shells in the garbage, throw them into a pot with some fresh vegetables, whole black peppercorns and cold water (or even chicken stock for extra depth of flavor). After about an hour of simmering, you'll be left with a pot filled with gorgeous amber colored broth that's loaded with deli-cious flavor.

If you don't have time to shell the shrimp, ask the fishmonger to do it (but be prepared to pay for his help). However, you might have to remind him (more than once) to save the shells for you, since usually they are discarded. Don't hesitate to remind him though; the shrimp were weighed with the shells *on* before tallying the price, so they are truly yours to do with what you wish.

INGREDIENTS

Shells from 2 to 3 pounds large or jumbo shrimp

1 large yellow onion, unpeeled, scrubbed, root end removed, and chopped

2 stalks celery, cleaned and chopped with leaves

2 teaspoons whole black peppercorns

Salt to taste

Cold water or 1½ quarts diluted Rich Chicken Stock or "Doctored" Canned Chicken Broth (page 140 for both)

1) **To prepare stock:** Place all ingredients except the water into a 2½-quart saucepan. Add enough cold water to cover the solids by 2 inches. Bring to a boil, reduce heat to low and continue to simmer for 1 hour, pressing hard on the solids to extract as much flavor and amber color as possible.

2) **To strain and store:** Strain broth into a bowl and discard the solids. You can use the stock immediately or freeze it in a labeled heavy-duty freezer container for 3 months in a freezer with little temperature fluctuation.

Time Management Tips

- If time is scarce, freeze shrimp shells for up to 2 months in a doubled heavy-duty freezer bag before making stock.

Q AND A

Q. Sometimes my shrimp tastes like iodine. Does that mean the shrimp have been treated with chemicals?

A. No. Any strong, medicinal taste in "wild" shrimp is the result of their diet soon before being caught. A natural by-product of aquatic plants called "bro-mophenol" is what you're tasting. Many times, wild shrimp will feed on dead plants which is what gives them this bit-ter flavor. Although the taste is disap-pointing, this substance is harmless and is not the result of either contamination or poor handling. The shrimp found in the Gulf of Mexico are most likely to have this flavor but it's also been detected in wild shrimp as well.

RICH CHICKEN STOCK

YIELD: about 7 quarts

SPECIAL EQUIPMENT

16-quart tall stockpot

Skimmer

Large sturdy colander, preferably stainless steel

2-cup ladle

8-quart mixing bowl

Fine-mesh sieve

Assorted sizes of heavy-duty freezer containers with tight-fitting lids

The only "musts" for a good chicken stock are browned chicken parts for both deepened color and savory flavor, an assortment of best-quality aromatic vegetables and fresh cold water. Conveniently, the most valuable and flavorful parts of the chicken for stock are those that don't make for great eating. These are the bony pieces, especially the feet. Because stock needs long, slow exposure to heat to render maximum flavor and body from the bones, the flesh of the older, larger and tougher soup hen is recommended for making stock. These older birds not only need to be cooked longer, but their flesh has deepened in flavor giving added character to the overall taste of stock. I strongly suggest cutting up your own chickens (page 233) when making any recipe that calls for chicken pieces and removing the backs to store in the freezer until you're ready to make stock again. Or, instead of buying cut-up chickens, ask your butcher to custom cut your chickens, removing the backs and wrapping them separately. Another way to increase your stock supply easily is to simmer your carcass from a roast chicken or turkey (with or without the addition of raw chicken) until your broth is golden and rich. But since life isn't perfect and we don't always have the time, see my instructions for "doctoring" canned chicken broth.

INGREDIENTS

4 to 6 pounds assorted bony chicken parts with skin left intact (backs, necks, wing tips, feet etc.) and, if available, a broken-up cooked chicken or turkey carcass with meat removed

Salt as needed

3 large yellow onions, unpeeled, scrubbed, root end removed, and coarsely chopped

2 to 3 cups boiling water

Cold water to cover

1 large stewing hen (optional) with neck and gizzard (no liver), well rinsed

4 large carrots, scrubbed and sliced

4 stalks celery, cleaned and cut up with leaves

3 large leeks, trimmed, cleaned and coarsely cut up (page 160)

3 cloves garlic, unpeeled

1 tablespoon whole black peppercorns

A few sprigs parsley

Generous pinch crumbled dried thyme (optional)

1) *To roast chicken parts:* Preheat the oven to 450°F. Sprinkle dry chicken parts lightly with salt and toss with 2 onions. Scatter chicken (skin side up) and onions on 2 shallow baking sheets. Roast in the hot oven until both onions and chicken are deeply golden and caramelized, about 30 minutes. (If you're roasting on 2 racks, position the racks to the upper and lower thirds of the oven and switch the baking sheets after half of the prescribed baking time.)

2) *To prepare stock:* Remove baking sheets from oven and scrape all the browned ingredients into a 16-quart stockpot. Place baking sheet directly on the stove burner and pour in some boiling water to release any caramelized bits of chicken and onions from the bottom of the sheet. If necessary, bring the water to a simmer over low heat while you scrape the bottom with the flat edge of a wooden spatula. Pour this liquid into stockpot. Add remaining ingredients with enough cold water to generously cover solids by at least 2 inches and bring mixture to a boil. Reduce heat to very low and simmer with the cover ajar for 2 hours, occasionally skimming off any scum that rises to the surface. Carefully remove the hen (if using) and, when cool enough to handle, remove the meat for another use. Return the skin and bones of hen to the simmering broth. Continue to simmer with the cover ajar for 1 hour. Uncover and continue to simmer for another 1 to 3 hours to reduce and concentrate the flavors. During this time, occasionally press down on the solids to extract any remaining goodness.

3) *To cool and strain stock:* Remove pot from heat and allow stock to cool with the solids. Place a large sturdy colander over an 8-quart bowl and strain stock into the bowl while you discard the solids from the colander. Clean stockpot and strain stock through a fine-mesh sieve back into the pot to remove any small particles of solids. Pour strained stock back into the cleaned bowl and cover with plastic wrap. Refrigerate stock for 24 to 48 hours to allow the fat to solidify and rise to the top of the bowl.

4) *To defat and store stock:* Scoop off the thick yellow layer of congealed fat on top of the chilled gelatinous stock. At this point you can either use the

pure stock for a given recipe, reduce it further to concentrate the flavors (see next step) or divide it among labeled heavy freezer containers to store in the freezer for future use. Chicken stock will freeze perfectly for at least 6 months in a freezer with little temperature fluctuation. The stock can also be refrigerated for 2 days before using. Always bring thawed stock to a rolling boil before eating.

5) *To make an ultraconcentrated stock:* Return defatted stock to a clean stockpot and bring to a boil. Reduce heat to low and simmer briskly uncovered until the volume is reduced by at least ½ and the color becomes very rich with a thicker, more syrupy consistency. The longer you simmer the stock, the more reduced the mixture will become, resulting in a chicken concentrate with intense flavor. Allow concentrate to cool, then pour into ice cube trays and freeze. When frozen, pop each section out of the tray and pile in heavy-duty freezer bags. Use to perk up the flavor of rice, gravy and soups. This is too intense, however, to use as the only liquid in sauces so you should dilute it with stock of regular strength or some water.

TIPS

FROM A TEACHER

About Stocks

Having a supply of homemade stock on hand is truly a comfort. It's best to make a large batch when convenient and, after chilling and removing the fat, divide it among heavy freezer containers of different sizes. This way, you can easily make nourishing soups, enrich sauces and enhance rice and stews without resorting to canned or powdered versions, which are usually high in sodium and offer little if any resemblance to the real thing. Always begin your stock with cold fresh water. The amount necessary will largely depend on the amount of solids used. Since solids take up a lot of room, in order to maximize the amount of stock after straining, use an extra-large pot to accommodate more water. For best results, use a tall narrow stockpot, as opposed to a wide one, since the latter will encourage excessive evaporation. After straining and removing the congealed fat, if the stock looks lighter or thinner than desired, return stock to a boil and simmer uncovered until reduced and concentrated to suit your cooking purposes.

When shopping for ingredients, remember that stock is the base for all of your soups, sauces and rice dishes. The more aromatic and rich the stock, the less outside help your dishes will need from salt and other flavor or color enhancers. So, don't skimp on the quality of your ingredients. Although I've provided an ingredients list with specific amounts, it's not necessary to have exact dimensions when

"Doctored" Canned Chicken Broth

When you choose to prepare a recipe that requires chicken stock and you don't have a reserve in the freezer, "doctor" canned chicken broth by simmering some sliced aromatic vegetables such as carrots, celery, onion, and parsley in the broth for 1 to 2 hours. Strain, discard the solids and use as directed in your recipe. Doing this will substantially perk up both the flavor and color of canned broth. Cambell's Healthy Request line includes a better-than-average chicken broth with no MSG.

making any stock. It's best to think of making stock as a concept and not a recipe. The specified amounts I've listed are by no means etched in stone and should be used only as a guide. If your pot is smaller than suggested, simply use less solids. You can add cleaned leeks, parsnips, turnips, more carrots, less celery and the list goes on. When making any stock, avoid the use of "cruciferous" vegetables such as broccoli, cabbage, Brussels sprouts and cauliflower as they add a strong and overwhelming taste, as well as an offensive odor. Also, don't include the liver in chicken stock as it imparts a bitter flavor and clouds the color. As for seasoning, if making stock to freeze for various uses, it's best to add only a minimum of seasoning (such as herbs, spices, salt and pepper) when making the stock and season further according to your given recipe after thawing. This will allow your stock to stay as versatile as possible.

Lastly, for the most delicious and health-conscious chicken or beef stock, always allow time for the thick layer of fat to rise, so you can discard it before using it in your recipes. Since many recipes call for the addition of another fat such as butter or oil, the large inherent amount of pure chicken or beef fat is both unhealthy and unappetizing. Remember that if this excess fat doesn't end up in the garbage, it could end up in your arteries!

Q. What if I thaw more stock than I need? Is it safe to refreeze stock?

A. Yes, if certain precautions are taken. After stock has been frozen, to remove the threat of possible bacteria, you must always bring it to a full and rolling boil before using it in a recipe. Once you've done so, you may refreeze any extra stock to be used at a later date.

VEGETABLE STOCK

YIELD: about 4 quarts

SPECIAL EQUIPMENT
8-quart tall stockpot

Large sturdy colander, preferably stainless steel

Fine-mesh strainer

Assorted sizes of heavy freezer containers with tight-fitting lids

For vegetarians, this stock is the perfect answer to any recipe that calls for either chicken or beef stock. For a stock that's rich in both flavor and color, use an abundance of the freshest, most aromatic vegetables that you can find. Although browning the vegetables before simmering is not necessary, it is the secret to creating additional color as well as increasing the intensity of flavor of vegetable stock—or any stock for that matter—making it look and taste more like beef stock. I do suggest, however, always adding at least some raw vegetables to the pot. It seems that their "untouched" flavor is essential to obtaining the freshest taste.

INGREDIENTS

½ stick (4 tablespoons) butter, melted, or flavorless vegetable oil
  (only if preparing a browned vegetable stock)

3 large yellow onions, unpeeled, scrubbed, root end removed, and sliced

5 large carrots, scrubbed and sliced

4 stalks celery, cleaned and cut up with leaves

3 large leeks, trimmed, cleaned and coarsely cut up (page 160)

1 large whole head garlic, with skin left on and the entire head cut
  in half through the middle, not through the root end

1 to 2 teaspoons salt or 1 tablespoon soy sauce*

2 teaspoons whole black peppercorns

2 bay leaves (preferably Turkish*)

4 sprigs parsley

Generous pinch crumbled dried thyme (optional)

Cold water to cover

* See section on Staples

1) To prepare a light vegetable stock: Combine all of the ingredients except butter or oil in a tall 8-quart stockpot and add enough cold water to cover the solids by 2 inches. Bring mixture to a boil and reduce heat to low. Simmer stock with the cover ajar for 2 hours, occasionally pressing hard on the solids to extract as much flavor as possible.

2) ***To prepare a browned vegetable stock:*** Preheat the oven to 375°F. In a large bowl, toss about ⅔ of the prepared vegetables (with both halves of garlic) with melted butter or vegetable oil and place on a greased shallow baking sheet. Roast vegetables until tender and deeply caramelized, about 1 hour. Place in a stockpot along with the remaining raw vegetables and other ingredients, except water. Deglaze baking sheet with a thin layer of water over direct heat and as water simmers, use the flat edge of a wooden spatula to scrape up any browned bits of caramelized vegetables from the bottom of the pan. Add this liquid to stockpot along with cold water to cover the solids by 2 inches. Bring to a boil, reduce heat and simmer as directed in step 1.

3) ***To cool and strain:*** Allow stock to cool with the solids. Then strain stock through a sturdy colander, pressing on the solids, and discard them. Pour stock through a fine-mesh sieve to remove any remaining bits of solids. Either use stock immediately or allow to cool and divide among labeled heavy freezer containers and store in the freezer for future use.

4) ***To make an ultraconcentrated stock:*** Bring strained stock back to a brisk simmer and continue to cook over medium heat uncovered until the liquid is reduced and the flavors have concentrated, 30 minutes to 1 hour.

RICH BEEF STOCK

YIELD: 4 to 7 quarts of stock

The darkest, richest beef stock—one that's loaded with body—begins with an abundance of gelatine-rich beef bones and aromatic vegetables that are roasted in the oven until deeply caramelized and savory. Then the mixture is simmered for ten to twelve hours. Oxtails, short ribs, slices from the shank as well as knuckle bones are the best for beef stock. Any browned miscellaneous beef bones with small scraps of beef attached will further enhance the texture. I suggest collecting a hearty stash of beef bones and storing them in the freezer so you're always equipped to make a fresh batch of stock. If starting a supply, ask your butcher for bones (he probably has plenty). For a lighter beef stock (in both flavor and color), use veal bones, which come from a younger animal.

SPECIAL EQUIPMENT

Meat cleaver to hack up large beef bones

Large roasting pan

Cheesecloth and kitchen twine

8- to 16-quart tall nonreactive stockpot with lid

Skimmer

Large sturdy colander, preferably stainless steel

8-quart mixing bowl

2-cup ladle

Fine-mesh sieve

Assorted sizes of heavy-duty freezer containers with tight-fitting lids

INGREDIENTS

4 to 8 pounds beef short ribs, oxtails, meaty slices from the shank, beef knuckles, and/or meaty beef bones hacked into medium-sized pieces

3 large yellow onions, unpeeled, scrubbed, root end removed and coarsely chopped

4 large carrots, scrubbed and cut up

3 stalks celery, cleaned and cut up with leaves

2 to 3 cups boiling water

Bouquet garni: 4 sprigs fresh thyme or 1 teaspoon crumbled dried thyme, 1 small bunch parsley with stems intact and 1 imported Turkish bay leaf,* all wrapped in a double thickness of dampened cheesecloth and tied with kitchen twine

3 large leeks, trimmed, cleaned and coarsely cut up (page 160)

1 or 2 tomatoes, coarsely cut up

½ to 1 cup dry red wine (optional)

1 to 2 teaspoons salt

1 tablespoon whole black peppercorns

Cold water to cover

* See section on Staples

1) ***To brown bones and vegetables:*** Preheat the oven to 450°F. Place beef and bones along with onions, half the carrots and half the celery on a shallow baking sheet. Toss to combine and roast until deeply caramelized, 30 to 35 minutes. Spoon browned mixture into a nonreactive 8- to 16-quart stockpot and discard any rendered fat.

2) ***To deglaze roasting pan:*** Pour a thin layer of boiling water onto the bottom of the roasting pan and place pan over direct heat. Bring water to a simmer while using the flat edge of a wooden spatula to scrape up and dislodge any browned bits of caramelized beef and vegetables from the pan. Pour this beefy liquid into the stockpot.

3) ***To prepare stock:*** Add the remaining ingredients with enough cold water to cover the contents by 2 inches. Bring mixture to a full simmer and reduce heat to very low. Simmer with the cover ajar, occasionally skimming off any gray or brown scum that rises to the surface, for 10 to 12 hours. During this time, occasionally press on the solids to extract as much flavor from them as possible. If evaporation occurs while simmering, add enough boiling water to keep the solids submerged. Allow stock to cool with the solids before straining.

4) ***To strain stock:*** Place a large sturdy colander into an 8-quart bowl and ladle the solids and stock into the colander in batches, pressing on the solids and discarding them. Cover the bowl of strained stock with plastic wrap and refrigerate for at least 24 hours (preferably 48) to allow the thick layer of fat to rise to the surface and congeal.

5) ***To defat and strain:*** Scoop off and discard the thick white layer of hardened fat that lays on top of the chilled gelatinized stock. Return stock to stockpot and heat until totally liquified. Pour through a fine-mesh sieve to remove small particles of solids. Let cool, divide stock among labeled heavy freezer containers and securely cover before storing in the freezer. Beef stock keeps perfectly for at least 6 months in a freezer with little temperature fluctuation. Always bring thawed stock to a full rolling boil before eating. The stock can also be refrigerated for 2 days before using.

6) ***To make an ultraconcentrated stock:*** Pour defatted, strained stock into a clean stockpot and bring to a boil. Reduce heat to low and simmer briskly uncovered until the volume is reduced by at least ½ and the color becomes very dark with a thicker, more syrupy consistency and an intense beefy flavor and aroma. The longer you simmer, the more reduced, concentrated and intense the stock will become. Allow the beef concentrate

Q AND A

Q. Are oxtails from an ox?

A. Not anymore. Nowadays these bony, gelatine-rich slices are from the tails of both young and mature cows. Although quite tough at the onset (especially the tails of the older animal), this is an exceptionally succulent cut after long, slow braising. So, in addition to enhancing beef stock, oxtails are a perfect addition to stews and hearty soups.

to cool, then pour into ice cube trays and freeze. Once frozen, pop each section out of the tray and pile into heavy-duty freezer bags. Use to perk up the flavor of rice, gravy and soups. This concentrate, however, is too intense to use as the only liquid in sauces so you should dilute it with stock of regular strength or some water.

CREAM OF TOMATO SOUP

With Aromatic Rice and Sautéed Mushrooms

YIELD: 6½ quarts; serves 12

SPECIAL EQUIPMENT
8-quart blanching pot with built-in strainer (optional)

8-quart nonreactive heavy-bottomed stockpot or heavy-bottomed Dutch oven with a tight-fitting lid

8-quart mixing bowl

Food processor or heavy-duty blender

Thick and rich, this soup has a consistency that's closer to a hearty, chunky sauce than the thinner, more common versions of cream of tomato soup. It's filled with an abundance of herb-scented chopped vegetables, chunks of fresh tomatoes and a generous amount of perfectly cooked long-grain white rice that's studded with sautéed mushrooms and onions. This recipe makes a large quantity, but it freezes well. So, make it in summer when tomatoes are at their peak. Although this soup is perfect autumn or winter fare, on many occasions I've thawed a hefty container during the warmer months as well, especially when I or a family member felt in need of nurturing in a hurry. When this soup is served piping hot with a basket filled with freshly baked bread or biscuits, you've got yourself a robust lunch or a fabulous light supper! For something unusual, try my Triple-Corn and Pepper Muffins (page 427) with Homemade Sweet Cream Butter (page 80).

FOR THE SOUP

4 pounds ripe plum (Roma) tomatoes

½ stick (4 tablespoons) butter or ¼ cup extra-virgin olive oil

2 large yellow onions, chopped

2 stalks celery, cleaned, trimmed and chopped

4 large cloves garlic, chopped

1 green bell pepper, seeded and chopped

8 cups of any or a combination of Rich Beef Stock, Rich Chicken Stock or browned Vegetable Stock (pages 140 to 146)

1 teaspoon crumbled dried thyme

½ teaspoon crumbled dried oregano

3 tablespoons chopped fresh basil leaves

1 can (6 ounces) tomato paste

½ cup heavy cream (preferably not ultrapasteurized)

FOR THE RICE

2 tablespoons extra-virgin olive oil

¼ cup minced yellow onion

2 tablespoons minced celery

2 cloves garlic, minced

8 ounces fresh button mushrooms, wiped clean (page 131) and
chopped with a knife (not a food processor)

1 cup aromatic rice* (such as basmati or jasmine), thoroughly rinsed if
imported, or regular converted long-grain white rice

1½ cups beef, chicken or vegetable stock, heated

½ teaspoon Tabasco sauce

1 imported Turkish bay leaf*

10 ripe plum (Roma) tomatoes, peeled, seeded and coarsely chopped
(page 151)

¼ cup chopped fresh basil leaves

Freshly ground black pepper and salt to taste

* See section on Staples

Time Management Tips

- All the vegetables for both the soup and the rice may be assembled 1 day ahead of cooking. Store them in the refrigerator in separate well-covered bowls.

- Although tomatoes ideally should be skinned the day of cooking, (in a pinch) they may be skinned, seeded and chopped 1 day ahead and kept well covered in the refrigerator.

- The soup may be fully assembled as much as 2 days ahead, cooled and stored in the refrigerator. Before refrigerating, pull a clean kitchen towel tightly over the top of the pot and then apply the lid. The towel will prevent any accumulated condensation from falling into the soup and diluting the flavor.

- This soup also freezes perfectly for several months in a freezer with little temperature fluctuation.

1) **To prepare tomatoes:** Peel the 4 pounds tomatoes as directed on page 151. Cut each tomato in half through the middle (not through the stem end) and gently squeeze seeds out of only half of them, leaving the remaining with seeds intact. Coarsely chop all the tomatoes and set them aside in a bowl.

2) **To sweat vegetables:** Melt butter or heat olive oil over low heat in a non-reactive 8-quart stockpot or heavy Dutch oven. Brush some of the butter or oil on 1 side of a piece of waxed paper cut large enough to cover the bottom interior of the pot. Stir in onions, celery, garlic and green pepper. Place the greased side of the waxed paper directly on top of the vegetables and let sweat for 20 minutes over very low heat.

3) **To prepare soup:** In a large saucepan, heat the 8 cups stock until hot. Meanwhile, discard paper from vegetables and stir into stockpot thyme, oregano and basil, heating through to awaken the spices. Add the simmering stock with the reserved chopped tomatoes and tomato paste. Raise

heat to medium and stir well to combine ingredients as they come to a full simmer. Reduce heat to low and cook covered for 30 minutes.

4) *To strain soup and purée solids:* (See page 170 for an important safety tip when puréeing hot mixtures.) Stir into soup a generous amount of freshly ground black pepper, then carefully ladle the mixture in batches into a medium-mesh wire sieve over an 8-quart bowl. Place the solids into the bowl of a food processor fitted with the steel blade or in a blender (in several batches) and purée until smooth. Return all of the strained broth to the stockpot, adding the blended solids as each batch is finished. Stir in cream and set aside.

5) *To prepare rice:* Heat a 2½-quart saucepan over medium heat. When hot, add olive oil and, when oil is hot, stir in minced onion, celery and garlic. Reduce heat to medium-low and cook until vegetables are softened and fragrant, about 3 minutes. Stir in chopped mushrooms and raise heat to medium-high. Cook until mushrooms are golden and tender, stirring frequently, about 3 minutes. Add raw rice and cook over medium heat, stirring constantly, until rice is well incorporated with vegetables and the grains are lightly toasted. Add the 1½ cups heated stock, Tabasco and bay leaf and bring mixture to a boil. Place the 10 peeled and coarsely chopped tomatoes on top of the broth-rice mixture but do not stir. Cover pot securely and turn heat down very low. (Or move to a burner set on low, if using an electric stove.) Simmer mixture without disturbing for exactly 14 minutes for aromatic rice and 17 minutes for converted rice. Then, remove bay leaf and stir in chopped basil, adding a generous amount of freshly ground black pepper and some salt to taste.

6) *To finish soup and serve:* Stir the rice mixture into the pot with the soup and adjust the taste by adding more salt and freshly ground black pepper. Serve hot.

Peeling tomatoes is quite simple if you blanch them first in boiling water. But remember that you're not *cooking* the tomato, only exposing it to enough heat to release the skin from the flesh. If left in the water too long, the flesh just beneath the skin will appear powdery and will lack any shine. The degree of ripeness, not the size of the fruit, determines how long each tomato needs to be boiled. The best pot for blanching successive batches of tomatoes is an eight-quart blanching pot with a built-in strainer (sometimes referred to as an "everything pot"). With it you can lift each batch of tomatoes out of the boiling water and ease them into an ice-cold water bath to stop the cooking process. If you don't have one of these pots, use a perforated skimmer to retrieve the tomatoes, but keep each batch small since chasing stray tomatoes can overcook them.

To blanch and peel tomatoes: Bring a large pot of water to a boil and place a large bowl of ice water near the stove. Ease some tomatoes into the rapidly boiling water for 10 seconds for perfectly ripe tomatoes and up to 30 seconds for very firm tomatoes. Remove tomatoes from boiling water and immediately plunge them into the bowl of ice water. Using your hands, swish them about until cool, then remove tomatoes to drain on paper towels. Once dry, the skins should slip right off; use your fingernails to help pick off any stubborn spots. If the skins won't release, simply return tomatoes to the boiling water for 5 to 10 more seconds. After tomatoes are peeled, remove the stem end with the pointed spikes of a tomato shark or the sharp tip of a short knife.

To remove the seeds: Using a serrated knife, cut each tomato in half through the middle (not through the stem end) and gently but firmly squeeze the seeds out of each tomato half. If necessary, use your free hand to help release the seeds as they protrude from the flesh.

TIPS
FROM A TEACHER

How to Peel and Seed Fresh Tomatoes

CHINESE EGG-DROP SOUP

With Mushrooms and Peas

YIELD: serves 10 to 12

With a silky texture and soothing taste, egg-drop soup has always been one of my family's favorites. It's equally satisfying served as a light first course or as a more substantial lunch by ladling the soup over freshly cooked white rice. I like to accompany this soup with Fried Chinese Sesame Noodles (page 204).

INGREDIENTS

4 extra-large eggs

2 teaspoons flavorless vegetable oil

¼ cup cornstarch

3½ quarts cold Rich Chicken Stock or "Doctored" Canned Chicken Broth (page 140 for both)

1 tablespoon plus 1 teaspoon toasted sesame oil*

8 ounces fresh shiitake mushrooms or button mushrooms

About 7 scallions (green onions), trimmed white parts and 1½ to 2 inches of the tender green

2 teaspoons aromatic peanut oil*

2 cups fresh sweet green peas or thawed frozen peas

Salt and freshly ground black pepper to taste

* See section on Staples

1) **To set up:** Lightly beat eggs in a small measuring cup with a spout and add vegetable oil; mix well and set aside. In another measuring cup with a spout, dissolve cornstarch in ½ cup of the cold stock with toasted sesame oil; stir mixture briskly until cornstarch is totally smooth and set aside. Heat the rest of the stock over medium-low heat in a 4-quart heavy-bottomed saucepan until it comes just to a simmer.

2) **To prepare mushrooms:** If using shiitakes, slice off hard stems flush with the caps. Wipe caps clean and slice into thin strips. If using button mushrooms, clean and slice the entire mushroom, including the trimmed stem.

3) **To prepare scallions:** After trimming, slice scallions in half lengthwise. Lay each half (flat side down) on your work surface and cut each half into several thin lengthwise strips. Then slice strips into ½-inch pieces.

4) **To cook scallions and mushrooms:** Heat an 8-inch skillet over medium-high heat and, when hot, add peanut oil. When oil is hot, add scallions and mushrooms, toss together and cook until scallions are softened and mushrooms are golden, 2 to 3 minutes. Remove skillet from heat and set aside.

5) **To assemble soup:** Just as the stock comes to a simmer, add fresh peas, if using (you'll add thawed peas later). Stir the cornstarch mixture and pour it into the barely simmering soup in a slow steady stream, stirring as it

---

Buy peas from a market that keeps their peas refrigerated. Warm temperatures will encourage the peas to become starchy and lose valuable nutrients. Each pod should be firm with a glossy sheen, and feel like it's bursting with peas. Avoid pods in which the peas skip around. Extra-large pods won't house peas as tender or sweet as medium-sized pods and leave behind any that are speckled or yellowed with signs of pitting (little holes). It's best to cook and serve fresh peas the day you bring them home from the market. Rinse the pods before shelling them. If the pods are clean, there's no need to rinse the peas themselves.

To shell green peas: Hold the pod in one hand with the stem facing up. Using the fingernails of your other hand, pinch off the stem end pulling the string down the length of the pod. Once the string is removed, the pod should burst open exposing the peas. Push the peas into a bowl using your thumb.

To steam cook fresh peas: It's best to cook peas in as little liquid as possible in order to retain most of their natural vitamin C content. Place approximately ½ inch of cold water into a heavy-bottomed saucepan and bring it to a strong simmer. Add the shelled peas and any fresh or crumbled dried herbs (mint, rosemary, thyme, oregano, basil, Italian parsley, curry) and simmer (covered) until just tender. Avoid adding salt while cooking as it tends to dry and toughen the peas. Instead, when tender, drain and add freshly ground black pepper, salt to taste and a bit of softened butter, if desired. Serve immediately.

How to Buy, Shell and Cook Fresh Peas

thickens. When the consistency of the stock has thickened slightly, remove from heat. Hold the cup with the beaten egg mixture about 6 inches above the top of the soup pot and slowly pour eggs onto the surface of the soup, stirring constantly. (The eggs will immediately firm up and form delicate ribbons within the thickened stock.) Stir in cooked mushrooms, scallions and thawed peas, if using. Add salt and pepper to taste along with the remaining teaspoon of toasted sesame oil. Reheat very gently without letting the soup boil. Serve piping hot.

CHICKEN IN THE POT

With My Best Matzo Balls

YIELD: serves 8 to 10 generously

SPECIAL EQUIPMENT
8-quart Dutch oven or heavy-bottomed pot with tight-fitting lid

12- to 16-quart heavy-bottomed stockpot with tight-fitting lid

8-quart blanching pot with built-in strainer (optional), for matzo balls

Medium-sized ice cream scoop, for matzo balls

Here lies my recipe for perfectly delicious chicken soup, filled with vegetables and tender poached chicken. And, of course, let's not forget the renowned fluffy, pudgy dumplings affectionately called "matzo balls." Over the years, my rendition of chicken soup has soothed more colds than I can count and warmed many winter weekends. This recipe also highlights the incredible benefit of always having a supply of chicken stock in your freezer. My students often ask me, "Why is your soup richer in flavor and color than mine?" Well, the secret is simple. When making chicken soup, I poach my chicken separately and begin my soup with a base of already prepared and defatted rich chicken stock from my freezer. If you start your soup with plain water, a big raw hen and vegetables, you will undoubtedly end up serving dry chicken in pale-colored greasy broth, loaded with soggy vegetables and excess fat. But the biggest bonus of this recipe is that, at the same time you are making the fresh soup, you are also replenishing your supply of stock. I hope my kosher friends will forgive me for loving butter in this classic Jewish soup; they can always use schmaltz (page 110) or follow my low-fat (nondairy) variation and accompany with some freshly baked Crusty Deli Rye Bread (page 396).

3 whole chickens (3 to 3½ pounds each), halved down the back
   with the necks and gizzards (no liver)

1 tablespoon whole black peppercorns

1 large yellow onion, unpeeled, scrubbed, root end removed,
   and quartered

2 stalks celery, cleaned and sliced with leaves

2 carrots, scrubbed and sliced

1 parsnip, scrubbed and sliced

3 sprigs parsley

Cold water to cover

FOR THE SOUP

½ stick (4 tablespoons) unsalted butter or 3 tablespoons rendered
chicken fat (page 110)

About 3 leeks, trimmed, cleaned and thinly sliced (page 160), to measure
   3 cups

3 stalks celery, cleaned, trimmed and diagonally sliced into ⅓-inch slices

4 large carrots, scrubbed and diagonally sliced into ⅓-inch slices

1 or 2 peeled parsnips, scrubbed and diagonally sliced, or 1 turnip,
   peeled and sliced into wedges

6 quarts Rich Chicken Stock or "Doctored" Canned Chicken Broth
   (page 140 for both)

3 ripe tomatoes, peeled, seeded and coarsely chopped (page 151)

1 cup sweet fresh green peas or thawed frozen peas

2 cups firmly packed, well-rinsed, trimmed and shredded spinach leaves
   (optional)

¼ cup chopped flat-leaf Italian parsley

Salt and freshly ground black pepper to taste

My Best Matzo Balls (following)

1) *To poach chicken:* Rinse and dry chicken pieces and gizzards (reserve
   livers for another use). Place chicken and all of the remaining poaching
   ingredients in an 8-quart Dutch oven or heavy-bottomed pot and cover
   the solids with cold water. Cover pot and bring mixture to a full simmer
   over medium-high heat. Reduce heat to very low and simmer chicken

until tender but not dry, about 30 minutes. Using a slotted spoon, remove chicken to a large bowl to allow the pieces to become cool enough to handle. Remove meat from chicken, tear into chunks and set aside for soup. Return chicken carcasses, including skin and all other parts, to the pot of poaching ingredients and use to replenish your supply of stock for use at a later date (see note following recipe).

2) *To sweat soup vegetables:* Melt butter (or schmaltz) in a 10-inch deep-sided skillet over medium heat. While it melts, tear off a sheet of waxed paper (large enough to cover the bottom of the pot) and brush some butter on one side of the paper. Stir leeks, carrots, celery and parsnips or turnips into melted butter. Toss to combine and lightly coat with butter, then place the greased side of the waxed paper directly on top of the vegetables. Reduce heat to very low and let vegetables sweat until wilted and only slightly tender, 8 to 10 minutes.

3) *To simmer vegetables:* In a 12- to 16-quart stockpot, bring stock to a boil and reduce heat so stock just simmers. Add sweated vegetables to stock and simmer (covered) over very low heat until crisp tender, about 15 minutes. Remove from heat.

4) *To assemble soup:* Stir chicken chunks into stockpot along with chopped tomatoes, peas, shredded spinach, if using, and chopped parsley. Add salt and freshly ground pepper to taste. Cook matzo balls and place them in soup until ready to reheat and serve.

5) *To serve:* Reheat soup gently but thoroughly until very hot. Taste for seasoning and adjust before serving. Place a matzo ball in the center of each warmed soup bowl and ladle a generous amount of soup and vegetables over and around the dumpling. Serve piping hot.

6) *To replenish your stock supply:* Return the poaching mixture with the chicken bones to a full simmer. Reduce heat to low and simmer uncovered until the stock is rich with a golden color, 1 to 2 hours. As stock simmers, occasionally press hard on the solids to extract all of their goodness. Cool, strain, chill and remove fat as directed in master recipe for Rich Chicken Stock (page 140).

My Best Matzo Balls

YIELD: serves 8 to 10

Avoid trying to make matzo balls look so perfectly round. Some of their charm is a homemade look. (The dumplings sold in delicatessens look like they should be shot out of a cannon.) For the most delicate texture, mix the batter with a gentle hand and don't open the pot while simmering. Matzo meal is available in most well-stocked supermarkets.

INGREDIENTS

2 tablespoons rendered chicken fat (page 110)

3 rounded tablespoons minced scallions (green onions), trimmed white part and 1½ to 2 inches of the tender green

6 extra-large eggs

⅓ cup solid vegetable shortening, melted

1¾ cups plus 1 rounded tablespoon matzo meal

1½ teaspoons salt, plus salt for water

Freshly ground black pepper to taste

1 tablespoon minced flat-leaf Italian parsley

¾ cup seltzer water (still fizzing)

1) **To prepare matzo ball mixture:** Melt chicken fat in an 8-inch skillet over medium heat. When hot, add minced scallions, lower heat and cook until softened and fragrant, 2 to 3 minutes. Set aside to cool. Lightly beat eggs in a medium-sized mixing bowl and add all of the remaining ingredients along with sautéed scallions. Combine mixture gently but thoroughly, cover and refrigerate for at least 2 hours to thicken.

2) **To set up and shape matzo balls:** Bring an 8-quart pot of water to a boil. Line a shallow baking sheet or tray with waxed paper. Using a medium-sized ice cream scoop, scoop out the chilled matzo batter, releasing each portion into your hand. Round out the shape a bit and lay each round on the prepared sheet.

Time Management Tips

- The matzo ball mixture can be made 1 day ahead, covered and stored in the refrigerator; then form into balls before cooking.

- Matzo balls can be fully assembled and simmered up to 2 days ahead and kept submerged in chicken stock in the refrigerator.

- All of the vegetables can be prepared 1 day ahead of cooking and stored in the refrigerator in separate, well-covered bowls.

- The soup can be fully assembled 1 or 2 days ahead, cooled, covered and refrigerated. To refrigerate the soup in the pot, pull a clean kitchen towel over the top of the pot and then apply the lid. The towel will prevent any accumulated condensation from falling into the soup and diluting the flavor.

- Any leftover soup and matzo balls can be frozen together in securely covered heavy-duty freezer containers for several months. (Be sure to label the containers with both the date and contents.) Thaw overnight in the refrigerator and reheat gently (the microwave does a perfect job of gently reheating soup without cooking it).

3) To cook matzo balls: Add some salt to the boiling water, ease matzo balls into pot and immediately cover (if the lid has vents, make sure they are completely shut). Reduce heat to low and simmer very gently for 20 minutes without disturbing or peeking (no, not even once!). Then uncover pot and, if using a blanching pot, simply lift out the strainer along with the cooked matzo balls. If using a regular pot, remove balls with a slotted spoon but be careful not to sever them since they are very tender. When first cooked, the matzo balls might seem to be too soft. This is deliberate since they will firm up when they sit in the pot of hot chicken soup before serving.

Low-Fat Variation

Although the addition of butter will produce a richer tasting soup, you can omit it entirely by adding the fresh vegetables directly to the stock instead of sweating them.

POTATO LEEK SOUP

With Shredded Chicken and Vegetables

YIELD: about 6 quarts; serves 10 to 12

SPECIAL EQUIPMENT

5-quart heavy-bottomed saucepan

8-quart heavy-bottomed stockpot

Sturdy colander, preferably stainless steel

Food processor or heavy-duty blender

Since this soup is already so full of vegetables, you might think that the last-minute addition of shredded fresh spinach is gilding the lily. I add the spinach simply because my three children will only eat spinach when it's in this soup. This recipe not only produces a rich and nutritious soup, but gives you the perfect opportunity to replenish your stock supply. Serve this smooth-tasting soup as either a first course to an elegant dinner or with a basket of biscuits or fresh bread as a warm and wonderful light supper or hearty lunch. It's particularly good with Braided Challah or Challah Rolls (page 387) or Crispy Skillet Cornbread (page 417) and Homemade Sweet Cream Butter (page 80).

FOR POACHING THE CHICKEN

2 large whole chicken breasts, rinsed and patted dry

1 tablespoon whole black peppercorns

1 yellow onion, unpeeled, scrubbed, root end removed, and quartered

1 stalk celery, cleaned and sliced with leaves

1 carrot, scrubbed and sliced

1 parsnip, scrubbed and sliced

2 sprigs parsley

Cold water to cover

FOR THE SOUP

1½ sticks (¼ pound plus 4 tablespoons) butter or
  ½ cup rendered chicken fat (page 110)

1 large yellow onion, chopped

5 large leeks, trimmed, cleaned and thinly sliced (page 160)

3 large cloves garlic, minced

1 stalk celery, cleaned, trimmed and thinly sliced

5 carrots, peeled and thinly sliced

6 large potatoes, peeled and cubed

3 quarts Rich Chicken Stock or "Doctored" Canned Chicken Broth
  (page 140 for both)

Ground white pepper to taste

1½ cups heavy cream (preferably not ultrapasteurized) or half-and-half

2 medium zucchini, scrubbed, trimmed and cut into small dice

Freshly ground black pepper

1 pound fresh button mushrooms, wiped clean (page 131) and sliced

Kosher or sea salt to taste

2 bunches fresh spinach (optional), stems removed, leaves cleaned and
  shredded using a sharp knife

Time Management Tips

- All of the vegetables can be assembled and ready to cook 1 day ahead. Store them in the refrigerator in separate, well-covered bowls.

- The chicken can be poached 1 day ahead and kept in the refrigerator well covered. Although you can separate the flesh from the skin and bones to complete your mini stock, wait until the day of assembling to shred the cooked flesh.

- The chicken stock (for the soup base) can be made months in advance and stored in heavy-duty freezer containers.

- The entire soup may be totally assembled 1 day ahead and kept in the refrigerator. However, don't add the spinach until you reheat to serve.

- If planning to freeze some of the soup (before reheating), remove that portion after soup is puréed. Freeze in labeled, securely covered heavy-duty freezer containers.

1) ***To poach chicken:*** Place all of the poaching ingredients in a 4-quart heavy-bottomed saucepan. Cover the solids with cold water, cover pot and bring mixture to a full simmer over medium-high heat. Reduce heat to very low and simmer chicken gently until tender but not dry, about 30 minutes. Using a slotted spoon, remove chicken to a bowl to become cool enough to handle. Then separate the chicken meat from the skin and

How to Clean and
Chop Leeks

To clean a leek, cut off the roots and all but 1 to 2 inches of the tender pale green stalk (unless otherwise specified in your recipe). Cut the shaft of the leek in half lengthwise and run each half under cold water, using your fingers to separate the layers and remove all traces of sand and grit. Pat dry. To slice, position leeks so they sit horizontally in front of you, and thinly slice leeks. To chop or mince, slice the leeks into thin lengthwise strips. Turn the strips so they sit horizontally in front of you and cut strips into small pieces. To mince, run the blade of a sharp chef's knife over the pieces to reach desired size.

bones, shred chicken into irregular pieces and set aside. Return bones and skin to pot with poaching ingredients and use to replenish your supply of stock for use at a later date (see note following recipe).

2) *To sweat vegetables:* Melt 1 stick of the butter or ½ cup rendered chicken fat in a 10- to 12-inch deep-sided skillet over medium heat. Brush some of the butter on 1 side of a piece of waxed paper cut large enough to cover the bottom interior of the skillet. Stir in onion, leeks, garlic, celery, carrots and potatoes and, when coated well with butter, place the greased side of the waxed paper directly on top of vegetables. Let vegetables sweat for 20 minutes over very low heat, occasionally lifting the paper to stir and redistribute.

3) *To assemble soup:* In an 8-quart heavy-bottomed stockpot, bring stock to a boil. Boil 1 minute, if previously refrigerated, and reduce heat to simmer. Add sweated vegetables to stock and return to a full simmer. Cover and cook over low heat until vegetables are very tender, 25 to 30 minutes.

4) *To strain and purée soup:* In 2 batches, ladle simmered stock into a sturdy colander over a large bowl. Place the solids along with a little of the stock into the bowl of a food processor fitted with the steel blade or the container of a blender and purée them until smooth. (See page 170 for an important safety tip on puréeing hot mixtures.) Transfer puréed solids to another large bowl as you continue to strain the soup and puree the remaining batch of vegetables. Then return vegetable purée to the original stockpot and stir in cream. Finally, add just enough stock to reach the desired consistency. This soup should have "body." (I usually have about 1 quart leftover stock to refreeze.)

5) *To complete soup:* Melt 2 tablespoons of the butter in an 8-inch skillet and, when hot, add diced zucchini. Sauté until softened, about 4 minutes, stirring frequently. Grind in some fresh black pepper and add zucchini to soup. Melt the remaining 2 tablespoons butter in the same skillet and, when hot, stir in mushrooms and cook over medium-high heat until golden and tender, 4 to 5 minutes. Add mushrooms along with the reserved shredded chicken to the pot of soup. Add coarse salt and more black pepper to taste and set aside until ready to reheat and serve.

6) *To serve:* Reheat soup gently but thoroughly over low heat. When hot, add shredded spinach, if using, and cook until the leaves are completely wilted and the soup is piping hot. Taste for seasoning and serve.

7) **To replenish your stock supply:** If you want to augment further the amount of new stock, add any browned fresh or unbrowned frozen chicken backs and necks that you've been accumulating, along with additional vegetables and fresh water to the original poaching pot with the skin and bones from poached chicken. Place pot over medium-high heat and bring mixture to a full simmer. Reduce heat to low and simmer uncovered for 1 to 3 hours, occasionally pressing hard on the solids to extract as much goodness as possible. Remove from heat and allow the solids to cool in the stock. Strain cooled stock into a bowl and discard solids. Cover bowl with plastic wrap and refrigerate for 24 hours to allow the fat to congeal and rise to the top of the stock. Remove this fat with a spoon and freeze the stock in labeled heavy-duty freezer containers until needed.

Low-Fat Variations

To reduce the saturated-fat content of this recipe, omit butter or chicken fat when sweating vegetables and use ½ cup olive oil. Add an additional potato and substitute milk for cream. When sautéing zucchini and mushrooms, replace the butter with olive oil or canola oil.

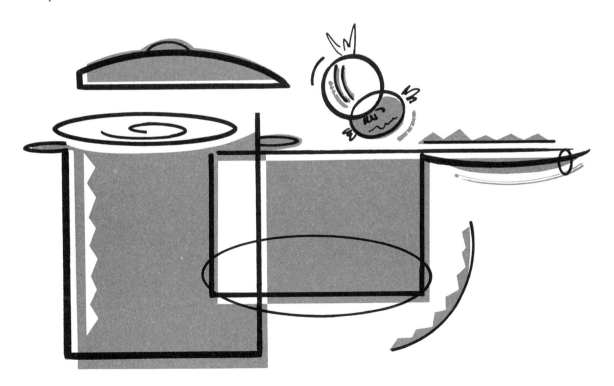

It's Better Than New England . . .

MANHATTAN CLAM CHOWDER

YIELD: about 8 quarts; serves 14 to 16

SPECIAL EQUIPMENT
Clam knife, if using clams in shells

8-quart blanching pot with built-in strainer (optional)

10-quart nonreactive heavy-bottomed Dutch oven or stockpot

Fine-mesh sieve

Although you can use canned chopped clams in this recipe, nothing comes close to the taste and texture of clam chowder made with freshly shucked clams, drenched in their naturally rich nectar—with absolutely no additives. This soup freezes perfectly, so make it, eat it, freeze it and then thaw it and eat it again! Serve with Crusty Deli Rye Bread (page 396) or Sweet Cream Biscuits (page 422) and Homemade Sweet Cream Butter (page 80).

INGREDIENTS

48 good-sized cherrystone clams in shells or 3 cups chopped fresh or canned clams

Bottled clam juice as needed

4 ounces slab bacon, cut into small dice or snipped into small pieces

1 generous cup packed cleaned and thinly sliced leeks (page 160)

1 medium-sized yellow onion, chopped

3 large cloves garlic, chopped

TIPS

FROM A TEACHER

How to Clean, Shuck and Store Hard-Shell Clams

Once you get the hang of it, it's not hard to remove clams from their shells. You must, however, have the right equipment or the process can be frustrating, if not downright dangerous. A readily available clam knife has a thin blunt blade that can easily pry the shell open. Don't improvise. A knife with a sharper blade can chip and splinter the shell and also make a nasty incision in your hand! Also, clams can be opened in the microwave.

In this country, the majority of commercially distributed hard-shell clams comes from the East Coast. They range in size, sweetness and tenderness. The smallest, sweetest and most tender clams are littlenecks with shells about one inch in diameter. Next in size are cherrystone clams with a shell that averages about two inches and then come quahogs, the largest chowder clams, with shells that are usually at least three inches through the center. (These are usually chopped or cut up with a sharp pair of kitchen shears before cooking until tender.) On the West Coast, the most common hard-shell clams are the tiny manila clams, butter clams and Pacific littlenecks, which are the same size but a different variety than their Atlantic cousins.

4 ounces fresh button mushrooms, wiped clean (page 131) and sliced

1 green bell pepper, seeded and chopped

2 medium-sized Idaho potatoes, peeled, cut into bite-sized cubes and placed in ice water until ready to use

3 large carrots, peeled and cut diagonally into ⅓-inch slices

3 large stalks celery, rinsed, trimmed and cut diagonally into ⅓-inch slices

1 teaspoon crumbled dried thyme

1 teaspoon crumbled dried oregano

2½ pounds ripe plum (Roma) tomatoes, peeled, seeded and coarsely chopped (page 151), or 2 cans (28 ounces each) tomatoes, drained

1 can (29 ounces) tomato purée

6 cups Fish Stock (page 137) and/or Rich Chicken Stock (page 140) or "Doctored" Canned Chicken Broth (page 143)

1½ cups dry white wine

½ cup water

3 generous tablespoons chopped flat-leaf Italian parsley

3 generous tablespoons chopped fresh basil leaves or an additional 2 generous tablespoons chopped parsley

Salt and freshly ground black pepper to taste

To store clams: Live clams should be refrigerated covered with a damp cloth in a colander to allow them to breathe. If very fresh, they will remain fresh for up to 4 days. Once the clams are removed from their shells, it's best to use them within 3 days and during that time they should be submerged in clam juice. If you need additional clam liquor to store the clams, mix ½ teaspoon salt for each 1 cup water and add to clams.

To clean clams: Using a stiff bristle brush, scrub each clam under cold running water. Do not leave clams submerged in water. Drain clams well and place them into the freezer on a tray for 5 (and at the very most) 10 minutes. The cold temperature relaxes the clams, making them easier to open. Then open immediately.

To open clams, using a clam knife: Lay a folded washcloth in your palm to protect your hand and grasp clam with the hinged pointed part of the shell toward the cloth facing your wrist. Working over a bowl to catch the nectar, insert the blunt blade of the knife between the shell halves near the hinge and move the blade down and around. Then twist the handle of the knife in an upward motion to pry open the shell. Use the knife to sever the muscle that attaches clam to the shell and slide clam into the bowl of nectar.

To open clams, using a microwave: After scrubbing, arrange clams in a single layer, on a microwave-safe, glass dish lined with paper toweling (a 10-inch pie plate works perfectly). Cover the top tightly with heat-resistant plastic wrap and create vents by making 1 or 2 small slits on top. Cook on high (full) power for 1 minute or until clams just open slightly. Remove dish from oven and finish opening clams by hand. Refrigerate immediately. Do this in small batches so the clams won't remain out of refrigeration too long.

Time Management Tips

- All of the vegetables (even the tomatoes) can be chopped 1 day ahead and kept refrigerated in separate, well-covered bowls.

- The soup may be fully assembled and refrigerated 1 day ahead of serving. Before refrigerating, let soup cool thoroughly (uncovered), then pull a clean kitchen towel over the top of the pot and apply the lid. The towel will catch any accumulated condensation and prevent it from falling into the soup and diluting the flavor.

- The soup also may be frozen in securely covered heavy-duty freezer containers. If planning to freeze, do so as soon as soup cools.

1) To prepare clams: Shuck clams as directed on page 162, reserving 3½ cups of the nectar. If you have less than 3½ cups or are using preshucked clams, make up the difference using bottled clam juice. Rinse and drain clams through a medium-mesh sieve and snip them into small irregular bite-sized pieces using sharp kitchen scissors. Strain clam juice through a fine sieve to remove any small pieces of shells. Refrigerate clams and juice until needed.

2) To cook bacon: Cook bacon in a 10-quart nonreactive heavy-bottomed Dutch oven or stockpot over medium heat until bacon is almost crisp and the fat is rendered. Using a slotted spoon, remove bacon to paper toweling to drain.

3) To sauté vegetables: Remove all but 2 tablespoons of bacon drippings from pot and return to medium heat. When hot, stir in leeks, onion and garlic and cook until softened and fragrant, 5 to 8 minutes, scraping up any caramelized bits of bacon into the vegetables. Add mushrooms and raise heat slightly. Cook until mushrooms lose their raw look, about 3 minutes, stirring constantly. Fold in green pepper, potatoes, carrots, celery and crumbled dried herbs and cook another 5 minutes to release the flavor of the herbs.

4) To assemble, cook and serve soup: Add to pot, tomatoes, tomato purée, stock, wine, water and reserved strained clam juice. Bring mixture to a boil, reduce heat to low and simmer for 20 minutes with the cover ajar. Add reserved cut-up clams, reserved bacon, chopped parsley and basil, if using, and simmer gently with the cover ajar until clams are tender but not rubbery, about 20 minutes. Add salt and lots of freshly ground black pepper to taste and serve very hot.

Chock Full of Vegetables
BEEF BARLEY SOUP

YIELD: about 8 quarts; serves 14

Soups don't get heartier than this one! Perfect for cold weather "soup meals," this concoction is chock full of chunks of tender vegetables, puffy soothing pearl barley and succulent braised beef—all floating within the richest of beef stock. Freeze any leftovers and on the next chilly day, heat up a batch and bathe your insides with instant warmth and goodness. Also, see the following variation with beans for a satisfying meatless version of this delicious soup. For a one-pot meal, serve with crusty bread, hot biscuits or Crispy Skillet Cornbread (page 417) and Homemade Sweet Cream Butter (page 80).

SPECIAL EQUIPMENT
8-quart blanching pot with built-in strainer (optional)

10-quart nonreactive heavy-bottomed Dutch oven or stockpot with a tight-fitting lid

INGREDIENTS

About ½ cup olive oil as needed

4 large cloves garlic, peeled and halved lengthwise

2 pounds beef stew meat (preferably chuck), cut into 1-inch cubes and patted dry

Freshly ground black pepper to taste

4 quarts Rich Beef Stock (page 146) or canned beef broth, diluted with water if too salty

½ pound medium pearl barley, rinsed with cool water through a medium-mesh sieve and drained

1 large yellow onion, chopped

1 large leek, trimmed, cleaned and thinly sliced (page 160)

2 stalks celery, cleaned, trimmed and cut diagonally into ½-inch slices

3 large carrots, peeled and cut diagonally into ½-inch slices

3 large potatoes, peeled and diced

1 small turnip, peeled, halved and sliced

1 parsnip, peeled and cut diagonally into ½-inch slices

½ teaspoon crumbled dried oregano

1 teaspoon crumbled dried thyme

½ pound fresh button mushrooms, wiped clean (page 131) and sliced

2 cups trimmed and diced zucchini

2½ pounds ripe plum (Roma) tomatoes, peeled, seeded and coarsely chopped (page 151), or 2 cans (28 ounces each) tomatoes, drained

Salt to taste

Time Management Tips

- All of the vegetables can be prepared for cooking 1 day ahead and kept refrigerated in separate, securely covered bowls. If desired, place peeled and diced potatoes in a bowl of ice water and refrigerate as well.

- Although fresh tomatoes should be peeled and seeded close to cooking, in a pinch, they can be prepared for cooking as much as 1 day ahead and kept refrigerated, well covered.

- The entire soup can be assembled fully 1 or 2 days ahead and kept refrigerated once cool. Before refrigerating, pull a clean kitchen towel over the top of the pot and apply the lid. The towel will prevent any accumulated condensation from falling into the soup and diluting the flavor.

OPTIONAL VEGETABLE

1 generous cup 2-inch pieces trimmed string beans, or 1 generous cup fresh or thawed frozen green peas, or 1 generous cup fresh corn removed from the cob with a sharp knife or unthawed frozen corn kernels

1) *To sear garlic:* Heat a 10- to 12-inch deep-sided skillet over medium-high heat and, when hot, add a thin layer of olive oil to coat the bottom of the pan. When oil is hot, toss garlic cloves in oil, pressing them into the oil as they sear and become lightly golden. Remove garlic using a slotted spoon and set aside.

2) *To brown beef:* Working in batches, add a single layer of beef cubes to the hot oil (without crowding) and sear them on all sides. Remove each batch of browned beef using a slotted spoon. Sprinkle beef with freshly ground black pepper and set aside. Leave remaining oil in the skillet and set aside.

3) *To simmer beef:* Bring stock to a simmer in a 10-quart nonreactive heavy-bottomed soup pot. Add browned meat and rinsed barley, cover and return mixture to a full simmer. Reduce heat to low and cook gently for 1½ hours.

4) *To sweat vegetables:* Return the original skillet to medium heat. While heating, cut a sheet of waxed paper large enough to fit the skillet and brush one side of paper with olive oil. If skillet seems dry, add 1 or 2 tablespoons olive oil and, when hot, stir in onion, leek, celery, carrots, diced potatoes, sliced turnip and parsnip. Stir in oregano and thyme, mix well to combine, and place the greased side of the waxed paper directly on top of the vegetables. Let them sweat over low heat until heated through and very fragrant, about 15 minutes. Discard waxed paper and transfer vegetables to a large mixing bowl.

5) *To sauté mushrooms and zucchini:* Wipe out skillet and return to medium-high heat. When hot, add 2 tablespoons olive oil and, when oil is hot, add sliced mushrooms and cook, stirring constantly, until golden, about 3 minutes. Transfer mushrooms to a separate bowl and set aside. Wipe out skillet and return to medium heat with 1 more tablespoon olive oil. When oil is hot, stir in diced zucchini and cook, stirring constantly, until crisp tender, 3 to 4 minutes. Add zucchini to mushrooms and set aside.

6) **To finish soup:** After beef has simmered for 1½ hours, add the first batch of sautéed vegetables (reserving mushrooms and zucchini). Cover pot, return soup to a simmer and cook over low heat for 15 minutes. Add chopped tomatoes, mushrooms, zucchini and reserved seared garlic and simmer covered another 30 minutes. Add one of the optional vegetables and simmer uncovered another 5 minutes. Remove pot from heat and stir in a generous amount of freshly ground black pepper and some salt to taste. Allow soup to cool to room temperature (uncovered) and spoon off any accumulated fat or grease that rises to the top.

7) **To serve:** Reheat soup gently until piping hot throughout and serve immediately. If planning to freeze some of the soup, divide it before reheating so the vegetables in the portion to be frozen won't become overcooked.

Vegetarian Bean and Barley Soup

Substitute for beef stock, an equal amount of the browned version of Vegetable Stock (page 144). Omit beef and use either 1 pound dried red kidney beans (rinsed and picked over) or 1 pound lentils. Or use 2 cans (15 ounces each) kidney beans, rinsed and drained well. If using dried (unsoaked) kidney beans, simmer them in the vegetable stock for 30 minutes before adding the rinsed barley. (If you've soaked the beans overnight, drain and add with barley.) If using canned kidney beans, add them at the end, when adding the optional vegetable and heat through. If using rinsed and drained dried lentils, add after barley has simmered for 30 minutes, before adding the remaining vegetables.

TIPS

FROM A TEACHER

How to Dice Zucchini

To dice a zucchini easily, trim off the ends and slice the zucchini lengthwise into slices, each about ¼ inch thick. Stack the slices so they lay flat on your work surface and cut again lengthwise into ¼-inch strips. Then cut the bunch of strips crosswise into small dice.

Hearty with Ham

DOUBLE SPLIT PEA SOUP

YIELD: about 8 quarts; serves 14

SPECIAL EQUIPMENT
12- to 16-quart heavy-bottomed
stockpot or Dutch oven with
tight-fitting lid

2-cup ladle (optional)

Two 8-quart bowls

Food processor or heavy-duty
blender

Here's a perfect way to use leftover baked ham. This soup is incredibly substantial and richly flavored. Served with a salad and a basket of biscuits or fresh bread, it makes a robust lunch or Sunday supper. Although this recipe can easily be halved, I purposely made it large because this soup freezes so well. The correct consistency of pea soup is strictly personal. I've seen pea soup made so thick that it almost needed a fork! I prefer a soup of medium thickness to allow the additional whole green peas, diagonally sliced carrots and chunks of smoked ham to float about on my spoon. But feel free to "fork it up," if you must. For the ham bone and diced ham, I use leftovers from my Apricot Glazed Ham (page 293). But if you're starting from scratch, you can buy ham hocks, which are the bottom portion of the hog's hind leg. Sometimes fresh hocks are available but most often they are smoked or cured and sold either whole or hacked into smaller lengths. For the smoked ham, buy a variety such as honey cured or Virginia baked.

INGREDIENTS

7 quarts Rich Chicken Stock or "Doctored" Canned Chicken Broth
  (page 140 for both)

2 pounds dried green split peas, rinsed and drained

1 pound dried yellow split peas, rinsed and drained

Meaty ham bone (shank) or 1 or 2 ham hocks, thoroughly scrubbed
  and rinsed

12 carrots, peeled

Salt as needed

1 stick (¼ pound) butter

2 large yellow onions, chopped

1½ cups trimmed, cleaned and thinly sliced leeks (page 160)

4 large cloves garlic, chopped

2 stalks celery, sliced

1½ teaspoons crumbled dried thyme

1 teaspoon crumbled dried oregano

Freshly ground black pepper to taste

4 cups diced smoked ham

1 pound frozen peas, thawed

1) *To simmer split peas:* In a 12- to 16-quart heavy-bottomed stockpot, bring chicken stock to a simmer, stir in green and yellow split peas and add ham bone or hocks. Bring back to a simmer, cover pot and cook over low heat for 1 hour.

2) *To prepare carrots:* Cut 8 of the carrots into irregular ⅓-inch slices and slice the remaining 4 carrots diagonally and keep separate. In a medium-sized saucepan, bring 2 quarts water to a boil and place a large bowl of ice water on your counter. Add a little salt and the 4 diagonally sliced carrots and boil until crisp tender, 5 to 8 minutes. Drain carrots and immediately refresh them in the bowl of ice water, swishing them around with your hand until cold. Drain slices well and set aside.

3) *To sweat vegetables:* Melt butter in a 10- to 12-inch deep-sided skillet. Tear off a piece of waxed paper large enough to cover the interior of the skillet and brush some of the butter on 1 side of the waxed paper. When butter is bubbling, stir onions, leeks, garlic, celery and the 8 sliced carrots into the skillet, coating vegetables well with butter. Add thyme and oregano and place the greased side of the waxed paper directly on top of the vegetables. Sweat vegetables over very low heat, occasionally lifting the waxed paper to stir and redistribute them, for 15 to 20 minutes.

4) *To finish cooking soup:* After split peas have simmered for 1 hour, add sweated vegetables to stockpot and cover pot securely. Simmer vegetables over low heat for 1 hour more. Remove from heat and remove ham bone or hocks from pot to become cool enough to handle.

5) *To strain and purée soup:* Ladle soup in batches into a large medium-mesh wire strainer set within an 8-quart bowl. As the strainer becomes full, place the solids into the bowl of a food processor fitted with the steel blade or a blender (see important safety tip, following). Purée each batch of solids with a little of the stock until smooth, then transfer puréed mixture to another 8-quart bowl. You will have finally 1 large bowl of stock and 1 large bowl of puréed vegetables.

Time Management Tips

- All the vegetables can be prepared and ready to cook 1 day ahead. Store them in the refrigerator in separate, well-covered bowls.

- In addition to freezing, this soup may be fully assembled up to 2 days ahead and kept refrigerated well covered. If refrigerating the soup in a pot, pull a clean kitchen towel tightly across the top of the uncovered pot and then apply the lid. The towel will prevent any accumulated condensation from the interior of the lid from falling into the soup and diluting the flavor.

When puréeing hot mixtures (especially in the blender), never fill the container more than half full or you run the risk of causing an explosive reaction when you turn on the motor. The heat creates a buildup of pressure in the container, causing the food to shoot up and over the top when blending. This can cause serious burns—not to mention the fact that you'll be cleaning pea soup off your walls and ceiling for the next week!

6) To assemble finished soup: Pour the vegetable purée into empty stockpot and add enough stock to create the desired consistency. Remove any meat from cooked ham bone or hocks; discard bone. Add to soup salt to taste and lots of freshly ground pepper along with diced ham, thawed peas and reserved blanched carrots. Cool uncovered to allow any grease to rise to the top; discard grease. Place the amount that you will be serving in a smaller pot; divide the rest among labeled heavy-duty freezer containers and place in the freezer.

7) To serve: Cover and reheat soup gently over low heat, stirring occasionally, until piping hot. Ladle into warmed, hefty wide soup mugs or deep bowls.

Reduced-Fat Variation

Although the flavor of this soup will be richest when using butter, to reduce the overall amount of saturated fat, omit butter and sweat vegetables in ¼ cup extra-virgin olive oil and ¼ cup additional chicken stock. Alternatively, use half butter and half olive oil.

You Can Feed the Whole Block . . .

PORK AND BLACK BEAN SOUP

YIELD: about 12 quarts; serves 20

Like my other soup recipes, this is on the "rotund" side, for very good reason.
It freezes perfectly, enabling you and your family to enjoy slow-cooked goodness on a rushed and crazy day when you don't have the time to shop, let
alone cook! If you choose, however, you can cut this recipe in half—and you'll
probably be able to feed only half the neighborhood! Serve a huge pot of this
thick, dark and absolutely delicious soup over a bowl of rice at your next
Super Bowl Sunday feast and invite all your favorite people to join you. When
purchasing the pork, be sure to request a meaty pork bone from your butcher
since the bone always lends so much additional body and flavor to any finished
soup. Serve with freshly made Fried Indian Bread Puffs (page 434) or Sweet
Cream Biscuits (page 422) and Homemade Sweet Cream Butter (page 80).

SPECIAL EQUIPMENT
16-quart heavy-bottomed stockpot

2-cup ladle

INGREDIENTS

5 large yellow onions

7 quarts Rich Beef Stock (page 146) or canned beef broth,
  diluted with water if too salty

4 pounds dried black beans, rinsed well and drained

¼ cup extra-virgin olive oil

4 stalks celery, cleaned, trimmed and chopped

12 large cloves garlic, minced, plus 1 tablespoon minced garlic

½ to ⅔ cup regular (not extra-virgin) olive oil as needed

4 pounds pork shoulder or pork butt, cut into 1-inch cubes and
  patted dry

1 cup dry white wine

2 teaspoons ground cumin

3 tablespoons curry powder*

Freshly ground black pepper to taste

10 carrots, peeled and cut diagonally into ½-inch slices

½ cup cornstarch

1 cup cold water or additional beef stock

Salt to taste

Freshly cooked long-grain white rice (½ to 1 cup cooked rice per person)

*See section on Staples

Time Management Tips

• All of the vegetables can be assembled
  1 day ahead and stored in the refrigerator
  in separate, well-covered bowls.

• After the initial cooling and removal of any
  accumulated fat, the fully assembled soup
  can be divided. Any soup that's not being
  served should be frozen in labeled heavy-
  duty freezer containers. The remaining
  soup can be refrigerated for up to 2
  days before reheating gently until hot
  throughout.

1) To prepare onions: After peeling, chop 3 of the onions and set aside. Cut the remaining 2 onions in half lengthwise (through the stem end), cut each half into thin wedges and separate wedges into thin strips.

2) To cook beans: Heat stock in a 16-quart stockpot until it comes to a simmer. Sort through beans to remove any small stones. Rinse and add drained beans to stock. Cover, return to a simmer and cook beans over low heat for 45 minutes.

3) To sweat vegetables: Heat a 12-inch deep-sided skillet over medium-high heat and, when hot, add ¼ cup extra-virgin olive oil. Tear off a sheet of waxed paper large enough to cover the bottom of the skillet and brush 1 side of the paper with some of the hot oil. Stir in the 3 chopped onions, celery and the 12 minced garlic cloves and reduce heat to low. Place the greased side of the waxed paper directly on top of the vegetables and sweat them slowly for 15 minutes. Occasionally lift the waxed paper to stir and redistribute the vegetables. Remove vegetables to a bowl and set aside.

4) To brown pork: Wipe out skillet and return to medium-high heat. When hot, add a thin layer of regular olive oil and, when oil is hot, brown cubed pork (in several batches) in a single layer without crowding until each batch is golden on all sides. Using a slotted spoon, remove seared pork to a platter as you continue to brown the rest. Add pork bone to skillet and brown that as well.

5) To deglaze pan: Pour out any excess oil from skillet and return to medium heat. Add white wine and as it bubbles use the flat edge of a wooden spatula to scrape up any browned bits of caramelized pork from the bottom of the skillet. Simmer until reduced by half. Add browned pork to skillet along with the sweated vegetables, cumin, 2 tablespoons of the curry powder and some freshly ground black pepper. Fold together all ingredients to combine well and set aside.

6) **To assemble soup for first phase of cooking:** After beans have simmered for 45 minutes, add the entire contents of the skillet to the pot of beans and stock. Stir, and return the mixture to a simmer. Cover and simmer gently for 1 hour and 30 minutes over low heat.

7) **To sauté remaining vegetables:** Wipe out the skillet and return it to medium heat. When hot, add 3 more tablespoons regular olive oil and, when oil is hot, stir in reserved onions strips. Sauté over medium heat until softened, about 5 minutes. Stir in reserved 1 tablespoon chopped garlic and cook until onions are just beginning to turn golden, about 10 minutes. Add carrots and cook until just warm, about 2 minutes. Then stir in the remaining 1 tablespoon curry powder and combine well. Cook an additional 2 minutes, just to release the curry flavor, and remove from heat.

8) **To finish soup:** After soup has simmered 1 hour and 45 minutes, stir in curried vegetables, cover and simmer an additional 30 minutes. Combine cornstarch and cold water or stock in a small bowl. Add cornstarch mixture to soup pot, stirring constantly until soup has thickened. Add salt to taste and lots of freshly ground black pepper. Remove from heat, uncover and cool at room temperature. While soup is cooling, remove any grease that rises to the top.

9) **To serve:** Reheat soup over low heat until piping hot throughout. Check to adjust seasoning and ladle into individual deep, warmed soup bowls over freshly cooked white rice.

CHAPTER V

PERFECT PASTA

First Course, Main Course, Side Dish

An entrée that features pasta is always soothing and often provides a quick way to whip up a substantial family meal. In this chapter, you'll find recipes for quickly assembled pasta entrées and side dishes as well as sauces that require long, slow simmering. But when preparing the latter—since my recipes are purposely on the rotund side—you can easily divide and freeze the remaining sauce to use on another occasion. If you've never made homemade egg noodles, do try my recipes for they are far superior to and have little resemblance to those noodles labeled "fresh" in the supermarket.

The easiest way to assure perfect pasta is not to overcook the noodles. "Al dente," which means firm to the teeth, is the most common term used to describe the texture of perfectly cooked pasta. Since there is a vast difference in the cooking time of fresh homemade noodles and commercially prepared dried pasta, the best way to avoid overcooking is to bite into a random strand several times during cooking. The noodle should always be firm but never crunchy.

Another secret to serving perfect pasta (whether homemade or commercially dried), is to not overdrain the noodles after cooking. Allowing some of the cooking water to adhere to the strands makes the pasta less likely to stick together. Although I always lightly dress my pasta with a little butter or oil (even when serving with an additional sauce), by not overdraining the noodles, I reduce the temptation to overdress the pasta before serving. This way both the delicate taste and texture of the pasta can shine.

Light as a Feather . . .
HOMEMADE EGG NOODLES

YIELD: about 19 ounces fresh pasta; serves 6 to 8 as a main course
or 10 as a side dish

These delicate strands of pasta are just right when you want light, fluffy egg noodles simply dressed in butter, bathed in rich, piping-hot chicken stock or nested beneath your favorite stew. My noodles are made simply from all-purpose flour, eggs, a bit of extra-virgin olive oil and, if desired, fresh herbs—along with the help of a hand-cranked pasta machine. Making pasta, whether rolling or cutting the dough into strands, is similar to handling a yeast dough. Let your hands be your guide, since any sign of stickiness means you must dust the sheet with flour before continuing to roll and cut. Once you become comfortable with making pasta dough, you can have fun by experimenting with the addition of different herbs or puréed cooked vegetables (see variation for spinach noodles). For best texture, allow the strands to hang dry on a pasta rack for a few hours before cooking. Then, after only a very brief encounter with boiling water, they will just about melt in your mouth! For a firmer, more substantial pasta, see the variation with semolina flour.

SPECIAL EQUIPMENT
Pastry scraper

Manually cranked pasta machine

Tapered rolling pin, if finishing the rolling by hand

Wooden pasta rack

8-quart blanching pot with built-in strainer (optional)

Food processor or blender, for spinach variation

Nutmeg grater (optional) for spinach variation

INGREDIENTS

3 cups unbleached all-purpose flour, plus additional flour for dusting

4 extra-large eggs, plus 1 extra-large egg yolk, at room temperature

1 scant teaspoon salt

2 generous tablespoons extra-virgin olive oil

1 tablespoon warm water

OPTIONAL ADDITIONS

2 tablespoons minced fresh herbs (flat-leaf Italian parsley, basil, thyme)
Freshly ground black pepper to taste

1) **To assemble dough:** Place flour in a medium-sized mixing bowl (preferably wide rather than tall). Make a large, wide well in the center by pushing a smaller bowl into the center of the mound and moving it in a circular motion. (This gently deepens and widens the well while keeping the walls of flour intact.) Remove the smaller bowl and crack 1 egg into

it. If there are no blemishes, add egg to the well. If a blood spot is present, either scoop it out with a piece of eggshell or discard the egg and try again. Continue until all the eggs are added. Add to the well, salt, olive oil, the water and herbs or black pepper, if using.

2) *To mix dough:* Use your nonworking hand to secure the bowl as you use the fingers of your other hand to break up the eggs. Slowly incorporate the eggs with flour by pulling in flour from inside the well. Continue to bring small amounts of flour into the eggs and, when absorbed, pull in more flour. When you reach the sides of the bowl and when the mixture sticks together in a large shaggy mass, turn it out onto a lightly floured work surface. Then knead dough with a firm and repetitive push-fold-and-turn motion. Use your pastry scraper if necessary to prevent dough from sticking. When dough is ready to rest, it will be soft, smooth and have a texture that's similar to your earlobe. Cover dough with plastic wrap for at least 30 minutes before rolling. (This relaxes the bands of elasticity developed while kneading and makes the dough less likely to "fight back" when rolling.)

3) *To roll dough with a hand-cranked pasta machine:* Unwrap dough and cut into 8 equal pieces using the blade on a pastry scraper. Keep all the pieces covered with plastic wrap while working with 1 piece at a time. Flatten a piece of dough on your floured work surface, dusting flour lightly on both sides. Starting at the largest setting, insert flattened dough into the machine and crank it through. Fold the dough into thirds and roll through this setting again. (The first setting is the only one that you will repeat.) As you proceed to roll through the remaining settings, flour the dough as needed to prevent sticking. Turn setting to #2 and feed dough through the machine. Continue this until you complete setting #5. Then flour the sheet of dough before cranking it through setting #6; for pasta with the lightest (almost see-through) texture, crank the sheet through setting #7. (It's important to flour the sheet before #6 to prevent dough from sticking and tearing when it goes through the final settings.) When completed, you will have a very long, thin and extremely light sheet of pasta. (For a slightly thicker egg noodle or for sheets of lasagna noodles, stop after setting #6.)

4) To dry dough before cutting: After rolling each piece of dough, hang on a pasta rack to dry only slightly, 2 to 3 minutes, before cutting the sheet into strands either by hand or by machine. So, after rolling out 2 or 3 pieces of dough, you should be ready to cut your first sheet. (The amount of time required to dry the sheets to the right consistency before cutting will depend largely on local weather conditions and the moisture content of your flour. On a damp and humid day, the sheet can take a few more minutes.) When ready, the sheet should still be supple enough to bend without breaking but should not be sticky. It's always best to work with a softer sheet than a drier one because once the dough becomes brittle, it's almost impossible to cut into strands. Keep track of which sheets were rolled first.

5) To cut noodles by hand: Lay the still supple sheet of pasta on a lightly floured work surface and lightly rub a very thin layer of flour onto both sides, smoothing to remove much of the excess. Roll up dough lengthwise from one end to the other in a snug (not too tight) coil. Using a sharp serrated knife, slice the coil of dough into thin slices in a sawing motion. Cut into strips ½ to 1 inch wide for wide egg noodles, ¼ inch wide for fettuccine noodles and ⅛ inch wide for tagliatelle noodles. When the roll is completely cut, gently unravel each slice and hang over one hand as you continue to unravel with the other. Lay the strands on a pasta rack to dry further while you cut the remaining sheets of dough.

6) To cut noodles using a hand-cranked machine: For soft noodle dough rolled through setting #7, use only the fettuccine or pappardella blade. If you're new at this, cut the long pasta sheet in half before feeding it into the machine. (This will make it easier for you to control and is also helpful when separating the strands.) Insert the crank to the hole controlling the cutting device and run a bit of flour through it to lubricate the blade. Hold the sheet up with your nonworking hand, position one end of the sheet so it sits right on top of the cutting blade and push in the edge gently to encourage the dough to "catch" as you turn the crank with your other hand. Continue to turn the crank until you see the pasta strands extrude from the bottom. Lay the remaining sheet over the top of the machine so you can use that hand to help "steer" the sheet (on top) as it's being fed through. Just before the last inches of cut pasta come through, place your hand underneath to catch the strands as if grasping a "pony tail." Gently separate the strands and hang on a pasta rack to dry.

7) ***To dry and store fresh noodles:*** Ideally, the noodles should dry on the rack for 2 to 4 hours before cooking. You can, however, cut them as much as 1 day ahead and, after drying, slide noodles off the rack into a large roasting pan or deep tray, cover and leave at room temperature until it's time to cook. Additionally, since this dough handles very well when chilled, it may be made a day in advance of cutting and stored in the refrigerator well wrapped in plastic. Freeze any leftover dried strands in a heavy-duty plastic bag and add directly from the freezer to boiling water.

8) ***To cook pasta:*** Cook pasta in a large pot in a generous amount of boiling water into which salt has been added just prior to adding the pasta. Although the cooking time will vary, the average time for cooking freshly made pasta that has dried for 2 to 8 hours will be only 1 to 3 minutes. And fresher pasta will cook in literally seconds. To avoid overcooking, test frequently while cooking by biting into a strand of pasta.

Firm Egg Noodles (Fettuccine) with Semolina Flour

Prepare dough as directed for Homemade Egg Noodles. But instead of all-purpose flour, use finely ground semolina flour or a mixture of 1½ cups all-purpose and 1½ cups coarse semolina combined with a whisk—or better yet—in a food processor fitted with the steel blade. Mix, knead and roll out dough as directed through step 3, only rolling through setting #6. Hang each sheet on a rack to dry and cut as directed in recipe.

Fresh Spinach Noodles

YIELD: about 17 ounces fresh pasta; serves 6 as a main course
          or 8 generously as a side dish

Can you believe that three cups of tightly packed fresh spinach leaves will only yield one-half cup cooked spinach? When purchasing fresh spinach, it's always best to buy a little more than needed to allow for some blemished leaves. And don't use frozen spinach here since it doesn't purée as smoothly and won't give the dough the same vibrant, uniformly green color that fresh spinach does. This dough is extremely easy to work with.

INGREDIENTS

3 generous cups firmly packed, stemmed fresh spinach leaves

3 cups finely ground semolina flour or 1½ cups coarse semolina lightened with 1½ cups all-purpose flour, using a food processor or whisk

3 extra-large eggs, at room temperature

1 tablespoon extra-virgin olive oil

¾ teaspoon salt

⅛ teaspoon freshly grated nutmeg (optional)

1) **To prepare spinach:** Rinse and drain spinach leaves and place in a heavy-bottomed pot with only the water that has clung to the leaves. Cover pot and cook spinach over medium-low heat until steam starts escaping from the lid. Lower heat and simmer leaves until totally wilted and tender, 3 to 4 minutes. Drain spinach *extremely* well by pouring cooked spinach into a wire strainer and placing another bowl directly on top of the spinach. Press hard on the bowl to force as much liquid as possible away from the leaves and out through the strainer. Place drained spinach onto the center of a strong, clean kitchen towel and wring out any remaining moisture. Measure ½ cup firmly packed cooked spinach and purée with 1 of the eggs in the bowl of a food processor fitted with the steel blade or in a blender until totally smooth, about 2 minutes of continual processing.

2) **To make noodles:** Follow directions for Homemade Egg Noodles, adding puréed spinach and nutmeg at the same time you add remaining 2 eggs, olive oil and salt to the well of flour. Mix, knead and roll out, rolling through setting #6 or #7, depending on desired texture. Dry on racks and cut into ¼-inch strands by hand or using the fettuccine blade of a pasta machine. If a thinner strand is desired, only roll dough through setting #6 and cut sheets using the linguine or spaghetti blade.

Q. Can I use egg whites instead of yolks to lower the cholesterol content in my pasta?

A. *Yes! Although the richest, strongest and most tender pasta is made with whole eggs, you can use fewer egg yolks and compensate by using more whites or even water in your dough. For an "all egg white" noodle dough, substitute 7 extra-large egg whites (1 cup) for the whole eggs, reduce the amount of olive oil to 1 tablespoon and omit water. Only roll the dough through setting #6 on your pasta maker.*

TIPS

FROM A TEACHER

~~~~~~

Making Homemade Noodles

Experience is the best teacher for making homemade pasta, but here are a few tips to help.

Hand-cranked pasta machines: I have found that Atlas makes one of the most durable and reliable models. These machines have seven settings for rolling dough; these start with setting #1 (the widest) and get progressively narrower until you reach #7. These machines may be used both for rolling out sheets of pasta dough and for cutting the sheets into noodles and strands. Noodles made with all-purpose flour should either be cut by hand or run through only the fettuccine or pappardella attachment on your machine. Although a dough made with a semolina flour (or a blend) will produce a nice spaghetti or linguine strand, I've never had very good results when attempting to obtain very thin strands of angel hair pasta using the blade provided with the machine.

Kneading pasta dough: At first this dough is sticky and then becomes very stiff. Hang in there when kneading! Dust dough lightly with flour only when necessary, but don't go over-board since you need traction to work the dough. (Adding too much flour will make the dough slip and slide on your work surface, making it difficult to knead.) For best leverage when kneading, stand with one foot in front of the other with your knees slightly bent and your weight toward the balls of your feet to keep steady.

Semolina flour: Made from hard durum wheat, semolina usually can be found in specialty gourmet food shops and some upscale kitchenware stores. It makes a more durable pasta to stand up to certain sauces such as the recipe for Fettuccine and Lamb Scaloppine (page 200). Frequently, semolina is sold very coarse, which produces noodles that are overly firm and heavy. If finely ground semolina is not available, try using a blend of half semolina and half all-purpose flour; whisk to lighten, or, preferably, whirl it in a food processor fitted with the steel blade. You might need to experiment with amounts here to find a blend that suits you best. Williams-Sonoma sells finely ground semolina (see Mail Order Sources).

MY FAVORITE PESTO

With Spinach and Toasted Pine Nuts

YIELD: about 3 cups sauce, when diluted with chicken stock;
serves 12 to 14 as a side dish

Basil is my favorite fresh herb and the only herb that I won't use if I can't get it fresh. Dried basil leaves don't even resemble the powerful fragrance and seductive taste of the fresh herb. So, only in a pinch, will I sometimes crumble a small amount of dried basil and use chopped flat-leaf Italian parsley for added texture, color and fresh taste. In this recipe for pesto, I incorporate the added taste of fresh spinach and Italian parsley along with a generous amount of the traditional basil, toasted pine nuts and the king of Parmesan cheese, Reggiano. This sauce is very easy to prepare and freezes perfectly if each portion is covered with a thin layer of olive oil before freezing. And since fresh basil is most abundant during the summer, it's wise to make this delicious pesto sauce in bulk and freeze it to enjoy at your leisure. So, although this amount of sauce will feed more than you might need now, since it freezes so well, it's wise to make this recipe in its entirety and freeze leftovers.

SPECIAL EQUIPMENT
Food processor or large mortar and pestle

INGREDIENTS

3 cups packed rinsed, dried and trimmed fresh basil leaves

½ cup packed trimmed, thoroughly rinsed and dried spinach leaves

¼ cup packed trimmed flat-leaf Italian parsley

6 large cloves garlic, coarsely cut up

½ cup toasted pine nuts (page 76), for sauce and optional garnish

¾ cup extra-virgin olive oil

¾ cup regular olive oil

1 cup freshly grated Reggiano Parmesan cheese

Freshly ground black pepper to taste

Salt as needed

1) To prepare pesto: Place basil, spinach and parsley in the bowl of a food processor fitted with the steel blade. Pulse to chop the greens. Then add garlic, toasted nuts and both olive oils. Process until well blended and smooth. (It's fine if little bits of toasted nuts remain distinguishable.) If you do not have a food processor, use a large mortar and pestle for this step (this takes some muscle). Add grated Parmesan cheese and a generous amount of freshly ground black pepper. Pulse until well combined. Taste and add salt only if you feel it's necessary. Do not chill if using within a few hours; if previously made, allow to come to room temperature before serving.

2) *To serve pesto with pasta:* For each pound of cooked pasta, toss in 1½ cups pesto and ½ to 1 cup hot chicken stock or vegetable stock just before serving.

3) *To store and freeze pesto:* When storing leftover pesto in the refrigerator or freezer, pour a thin layer of olive oil on top and cover well. Pesto will keep in the refrigerator for 2 weeks or freeze in a heavy-duty plastic container for up to 6 months.

TIPS
FROM A TEACHER

Fresh Basil

In the summertime, when markets and gardens are full of fresh basil, take advantage of this wonderful herb. Here are some tips for using it. When purchasing fresh basil, look for bright green leaves (unless it's the less familiar opal basil with purple leaves). Each leaf should look vibrant and have no signs of wilting or discoloration. Since fresh basil is sold with intact roots (which can be quite dirty), either wrap the roots in damp paper towels or store the bunch standing straight up with the roots submerged in cool water. This not only keeps your refrigerator clean but, if you change the water every two days, your basil will keep supple and nourished so it can last almost one week. Keep the leaves loosely covered in a perforated plastic bag.

Chock Full of Basil Vinaigrette

Place 1 tablespoon Dijon mustard, 2 cloves minced garlic, ½ teaspoon salt and ¼ cup red wine vinegar in a shallow, wide bowl and combine well with a whisk. Add ⅔ cup extra-virgin olive oil in a slow steady stream, whisking constantly. When oil is thoroughly combined, add ¼ cup packed chopped fresh basil leaves and a generous amount of freshly ground black pepper, mixing well. Cover and let mixture sit at room temperature for a while to meld the flavors. Or refrigerate for a few hours and bring close to room temperature before using. Serve over any combination of the following: thick sliced tomatoes; sliced Vadalia onions or sweet red onions; sliced fresh mozzarella cheese; drained, firm anchovy fillets or sardines; roasted, peeled and seeded red or yellow bell peppers (page 113). Yield: about 1 cup dressing; serves 4 to 6.

Pasta with Pesto and Plum Tomatoes

YIELD: serves 8 as a side dish or first course

The addition of the ripest tomatoes, toasted pine nuts and shaved Reggiano Parmesan cheese gives this pasta dish a wonderful dimension in texture as well as flavor. And the rich taste of homemade chicken stock is preferable to stand up to the robust pesto mixture.

INGREDIENTS

1 pound fresh or dried pasta of choice, cooked al dente and drained

About 1½ cups My Favorite Pesto (preceding), at room temperature

½ to 1 cup Rich Chicken Stock or Vegetable Stock (pages 140 to 144)

6 to 8 ripe plum (Roma) tomatoes, seeded (page 151), skins intact and coarsely chopped

1 cup toasted pine nuts (page 76), optional

Shaved strips of Reggiano Parmesan cheese, for garnish

Sprigs of fresh basil, for garnish

Pour cooked and drained pasta of choice into a large serving bowl. Add pesto and enough hot chicken stock to reach desired consistency. Gently mix with fork to coat noodles. Add tomatoes and, if desired, toasted pine nuts. Top each serving with a few thin shaved pieces of Parmesan and garnish with fresh basil.

TOMATO BASIL SAUCE

For Pasta and Even Pizza!

YIELD: about 8½ cups sauce; serves 10 to 12 over
cooked pasta as a side dish

SPECIAL EQUIPMENT
Nonreactive colander

Tomato shark (optional)

5-quart heavy-bottomed
nonreactive pot or Dutch oven

This vibrant and chunky tomato sauce is loaded with garlic and the most romantic herb of all—fresh basil. And this sauce is as versatile as it is delicious. Not only is it a perfect partner to hot tubes of penne—or just about any other pasta—but it's fabulous on homemade pizzas. The small, oblong Italian-style tomatoes (called plum or Roma) are best for making sauce. They have more flavor and less water than the regular round variety. For a spectacular fish dish, submerge an entire gutted striped bass or red snapper in this sauce and simmer until piping hot and tender throughout. (Slash each fish on both sides at the thickest mid-section going ¼ to ⅓ inch deep to help whole fish cook evenly.) And when you have some time, make a double batch of sauce and divide it among several freezer containers for quick and impromptu stews (see variation). If you want your sauce to be less textural, just pulse the tomatoes in the food processor after draining but before cooking.

FOR THE SAUCE

6 pounds ripe plum (Roma) tomatoes

About ⅓ cup extra-virgin olive oil

8 large cloves garlic, minced

1 can (29 ounces) tomato purée

2 heaping tablespoons tomato paste

1 cup chopped fresh basil leaves (chopped as needed so basil
  won't turn black)

Freshly ground black pepper to taste

½ teaspoon crushed red pepper flakes (optional)

TO SERVE

1½ pounds dried pasta of choice,* cooked and drained

Basil sprigs and/or shaved Reggiano Parmesan cheese (optional),
  for garnish

* See section on Staples

1) ***To prepare tomatoes:*** Peel, and seed tomatoes as directed on page 151. Coarsely chop and let drain in a nonreactive colander for 30 minutes.

2) ***To assemble sauce:*** Heat a nonreactive heavy-bottomed 5-quart Dutch oven over medium heat. When hot, add a thin layer of olive oil. When oil is hot, stir in drained tomatoes and 4 of the minced garlic cloves. Sauté for 3 minutes, then stir in tomato purée, tomato paste and ½ cup of the chopped basil. Bring to a brisk simmer over medium heat. Reduce heat to low and simmer gently with the cover ajar until the liquid reduces and the sauce thickens, 45 minutes to 1 hour.

3) ***To finish sauce:*** Stir in a generous amount of freshly ground black pepper along with the remaining ½ cup chopped basil, minced garlic and red pepper flakes, if using. Serve immediately over hot noodles and garnish with basil and shaved Parmesan, if desired. Or use sauce in other recipes as directed.

4) ***To store or freeze:*** Before storing cooked sauce, cool completely and pull a clean kitchen towel over the top of the pot before applying the lid. (The towel will prevent any accumulated condensation from falling into the pot and diluting the flavor of the sauce.) Store up to 3 days in the refrigerator. To freeze, place in well-sealed heavy freezer containers.

Stews with Tomato Basil Sauce

Use the fresh or thawed sauce for simmering pieces of browned chicken, sweet or hot Italian sausage or cubed veal leg or shoulder. (Chicken parts and lean meat from the leg of veal cook quickly whereas muscular shoulder meat requires substantially more cooking to become tender.) Strips of roasted peppers, sautéed onions and/or mushrooms make wonderful additions: Add to sauce when adding browned chicken or lean meat or after half the cooking has elapsed when simmering tougher cuts of meat. After browning meat in olive oil, empty any remaining oil and deglaze the empty skillet with some red or white wine. As wine bubbles, use the flat edge of a wooden spatula to scrape off the caramelized bits of meat from the bottom of pan and allow wine to reduce slightly. Add the sauce, browned meat and bring the whole mixture to a brisk simmer. Reduce heat to very low and simmer covered until tender. Serve stew with cooked pasta or rice.

Time Management Tips

- Although it's preferable for tomatoes to be peeled, seeded and chopped on the day of cooking, (in a pinch) they can be prepared 1 day ahead and left in a colander over a bowl to drain overnight in the refrigerator; cover the top securely with plastic wrap.

FETTUCCINE WITH ASPARAGUS AND SWEET PEPPERS

In a Tomato Cream Sauce

YIELD: serves 6 as a main course or 8 to 10 as a side dish

SPECIAL EQUIPMENT
8-quart blanching pot with built-in strainer (optional)

This creamy pasta sauce—richly textured with blanched asparagus, sweet peppers, leeks and toasted pine nuts—is substantial enough to make a meal in itself. This, however, is rich stuff (not exactly for calorie counters, but sometimes it's fun to cheat). This dish is also perfect for entertaining! All of the ingredients can be prepared in advance and the entire sauce can be assembled fully up to two hours ahead and simply reheated while you cook your fettuccine. Unless it's summer and your tomatoes are ruby red and perfectly ripe, use canned crushed tomatoes for they have an intense color and flavor that helps cut the richness of the cream.

INGREDIENTS

2 pounds fresh young asparagus

½ cup extra-virgin olive oil

About 2 large leeks, trimmed, cleaned and thinly sliced (page 160), to measure 4 cups

8 large cloves garlic, peeled and thinly sliced

2 large bell peppers (1 red and 1 yellow), roasted, peeled and seeded (page 113) and sliced into thin strips

Freshly ground black pepper to taste

1½ cups heavy cream (preferably not ultrapasteurized)

1 stick (¼ pound) butter

1 cup freshly grated Reggiano Parmesan cheese

1 generous cup peeled and puréed very ripe plum (Roma) tomatoes (page 151) or canned crushed tomatoes

Salt as needed

1 recipe Homemade Egg Noodles dough (page 175), cut ¼ inch wide or with the fettuccine blade, or 1 pound dried fettuccine*

½ cup toasted pine nuts (page 76), for garnish

* See section on Staples

1) To prepare asparagus: Trim, blanch, refresh and dry asparagus as directed on page 210. Slice stalks into 2-inch lengths.

2) To sweat vegetables: Heat a 12-inch skillet over medium-high heat. While heating, tear off a sheet of waxed paper large enough to fit within the interior of the skillet and brush some olive oil on 1 side of the paper. Add olive oil to skillet. When hot, stir in sliced leeks and garlic and lay the oiled side of the paper directly on top of the vegetables. Reduce heat to low and sweat vegetables until softened and very fragrant but not brown, 10 to 15 minutes. Fold in roasted pepper slices and sliced asparagus. Grind in some black pepper and remove from heat.

3) To complete sauce: Place cream and butter in a 2-quart heavy-bottomed saucepan over medium-low heat. When cream begins to simmer and butter has melted, stir in grated Parmesan until melted. Add tomatoes and stir well to combine. Heat through until mixture just returns to a simmer, then pour tomato cream sauce over the vegetables in the skillet and gently fold together. Set aside until ready to serve.

4) To cook pasta: Bring a large pot of water to a full boil, add some salt and then the pasta. Cook until pasta is al dente, 1 to 3 minutes for fresh, or follow the cooking instructions on your packaged dried pasta, checking frequently to avoid overcooking.

5) To assemble and serve: While pasta cooks, heat sauce and vegetables until piping hot, adding salt and freshly ground black pepper to taste. Drain pasta, allowing some of the cooking water to cling to the strands, and pour noodles into the sauce. Toss gently but thoroughly with 2 large serving forks; then pour into a large warmed serving bowl. Place individual servings on wide, shallow pasta plates and sprinkle each portion lightly with toasted pine nuts. Serve immediately.

Time Management Tips

- The asparagus can be blanched, refreshed and kept (uncut) wrapped in paper towels and stored a heavy-duty plastic bag up to 2 days ahead. It's best to slice them the day of assembling.

- The leeks and garlic can be sliced 1 day ahead and kept separately in securely covered bowls in the refrigerator. Also, the bell peppers can be roasted, peeled, seeded and sliced 1 day ahead and refrigerated, securely covered.

- Although it's best to prepare fresh tomatoes the day of serving, if necessary, they can be peeled and chopped 1 day ahead and stored in the refrigerator.

- The sauce can be completed and mixed with vegetables about 2 hours ahead and kept at room temperature before reheating to serve.

- The nuts can be toasted days ahead and kept securely covered at room temperature or frozen and refreshed briefly in a warm oven to awaken their flavor (page 76).

RIGATONI WITH GARLIC-SEARED BROCCOLI RABE

YIELD: serves 6 as a main course

SPECIAL EQUIPMENT
8-quart blanching pot with built-in strainer (optional)

If you've never tried this intensely flavored vegetable, sometimes labeled "bitter broccoli," you're in for a treat! Broccoli rabe (or *brocoletti di rape* as it's called in Italy) was once scarce in the United States. But it is now much more readily available and has become very popular in our finest Italian restaurants. In addition to being more flavorful than regular broccoli, Italian broccoli needs little trimming before being cooked. When seared in hot garlic-laced olive oil, simmered in rich chicken stock and served over piping-hot rigatoni noodles, broccoli rabe provides a nutritious entrée that's quick, easy and very delicious. I must admit that I've found it hard to eat regular broccoli ever since I took my first bite of this wonderful vegetable.

INGREDIENTS

2 large bunches broccoli rabe (2½ pounds before trimming)

3 cups Rich Chicken Stock or "Doctored" Canned Chicken Broth (page 140 for both)

½ cup extra-virgin olive oil

6 cloves garlic, very thinly sliced

2 teaspoons salt, for pasta water

1 pound dried rigatoni pasta*

Kosher salt or sea salt to taste

½ cup freshly grated Pecorino Romano cheese or Reggiano Parmesan cheese

Freshly ground black pepper to taste

* See section on Staples

1) ***To set up:*** Bring an 8-quart pot of water to a boil. Reduce to a simmer until ready to cook pasta. Thoroughly rinse broccoli and dry well. Do not remove the leaves and trim off only the very bottom of the stalks; everything else is to be cooked and eaten.

2) *To prepare sauce:* Bring stock to a boil in a small saucepan and concentrate the flavor by reducing (uncovered) to 2 cups. Heat a 12-inch, deep-sided skillet over medium heat. Add olive oil and, when hot, add garlic slices. Stir garlic constantly until it turns light brown, being careful not to burn. Add broccoli all at once and toss with garlic and oil using 2 wooden spoons or spatulas. Cook, tossing the mixture until broccoli is hot and slightly softened, 4 to 5 minutes. Add boiling chicken stock and reduce heat to low. Cover and simmer until broccoli is tender and the leaves are wilted, but the vegetable retains an al dente texture, 5 to 7 minutes.

3) *To cook pasta:* Return pot of water back to a rapid boil. Add salt and rigatoni. Stir and cook until al dente according to the package directions, checking pasta frequently to avoid overcooking. Drain, allowing some of the cooking water to adhere to the tubes.

4) *To serve:* Put individual portions of pasta on the bottom of shallow wide soup plates and ladle the hot broccoli mixture over top. Lightly sprinkle with coarse salt and serve immediately, passing grated or shaved Pecorino Romano or Parmesan at the table along with a peppermill that works.

SPINACH FETTUCCINE
WITH BAKED SCALLOPS

In Roasted Red Pepper Cream Sauce

YIELD: serves 6 to 8 as a main course

If you like scallops, you'll flip over this dish! The scallops are bathed in a delicious rosy colored sauce that begins with an intensely flavored browned roux base enhanced with the robust flavor of a puréed roasted red bell pepper. The addition of sautéed chopped onions, garlic, diced portobello mushrooms and spinach fettuccine makes this dish taste truly complex and extra special. Although this entrée tastes intricate, in reality it's quite simple to prepare. The entire dish can be fully assembled and refrigerated one day ahead of baking. Serve as a main course preceded by thickly sliced beefsteak tomatoes layered with slices of fresh mozzarella and sweet red or yellow onions.

SPECIAL EQUIPMENT
8-quart blanching pot with built-in strainer (optional)

Electric mini chopper or blender

3-quart baking dish, preferably a shallow au gratin type

Time Management Tips

- The toasted bread crumbs can be assembled (not buttered) 2 days ahead and left at room temperature securely covered; or frozen for months, stored in a doubled heavy-duty plastic bag.

- The pepper can be roasted, peeled and seeded (not puréed) 1 day ahead and kept covered in the refrigerator. All of the vegetables can also be prepared for cooking 1 day ahead and kept refrigerated in separate well-covered bowls.

- The entire scallop casserole can be fully assembled 1 day ahead of baking and kept refrigerated well covered.

INGREDIENTS

½ cup The Best Dried Bread Crumbs (page 78)

½ cup Fish Stock (page 137) or bottled clam juice

½ cup dry white wine

1 large red bell pepper, roasted, peeled and seeded (page 113)

¼ cup extra-virgin olive oil

½ cup chopped yellow onion

4 cloves garlic, minced

2 large portobello mushrooms, wiped clean, stems removed and caps diced, or 2 cups sliced fresh button mushrooms with stems intact (see directions for preparing mushrooms, page 131)

1 stick (¼ pound) butter or margarine

2 tablespoons all-purpose flour

1 cup heavy cream (preferably not ultrapasteurized) or half-and-half

Salt and freshly ground black pepper to taste

2½ pounds bay or small sea scallops

1 recipe Fresh Spinach Noodles (page 178) or 1 pound dried spinach fettuccine*

*See section on Staples

1) *To set up:* Prepare bread crumbs as directed in recipe. Bring an 8-quart pot of water to a boil and turn to a simmer until needed for pasta. Place stock and wine in a small saucepan and reduce by ½. Purée roasted pepper in a blender or an electric mini chopper until smooth. (Don't purée pepper in a full-sized food processor since pepper won't become smooth.) Position rack in upper ⅓ of oven and preheat oven to 400°F.

2) *To sauté vegetables:* Heat olive oil in a 10-inch skillet over medium heat and, when hot, stir in chopped onion. When onion is softened and very fragrant, 3 minutes, lower heat and stir in minced garlic. Reduce heat to low and cook 3 minutes more. Add diced mushrooms and raise heat to medium-high. Cook until mushrooms are golden and tender, about 3 minutes, then remove from heat and set aside.

3) *To make sauce:* Melt ½ of the butter (4 tablespoons) in a saucepan over medium heat. When hot and bubbling, stir in flour and cook, stirring constantly, until the mixture reaches the color of peanut butter. Add cream and the reduced stock mixture and cook until the mixture comes to a

simmer, stirring frequently. Simmer until thickened, then stir in puréed red pepper and cook a minute or 2 longer just to blend the flavors. Remove from heat and stir in sautéed vegetables, adding salt and pepper to taste. If not baking right away, let the mixture cool to room temperature before combining sauce with scallops. (If you plan to bake right away, proceed to step 4.)

4) *To assemble:* Rinse and drain scallops well. If using large sea scallops, slice into halves or quarters; otherwise leave whole. In a small saucepan, melt remaining ½ stick butter. Brush a 3-quart baking dish with a bit of the melted butter and place scallops in dish. Pour sauce over scallops and shake dish gently to distribute sauce throughout. Pour remaining melted butter into the toasted bread crumbs and stir to combine. Season with salt and freshly ground black pepper and sprinkle crumbs evenly over the top of the scallop mixture.

5) *To bake:* Place in the preheated oven and bake until piping hot throughout and the crumbs are golden, 25 to 30 minutes; about 10 minutes longer if the mixture has been refrigerated.

6) *To cook fettuccine:* Return pot of water to a rapid boil, add some salt and the fettuccine. Cook pasta until al dente, 1 to 3 minutes for fresh, or according to the package directions, checking pasta frequently to avoid overcooking. Drain, allowing some of the cooking water to adhere to the noodles.

7) *To serve:* Serve scallops hot over fettuccine.

LINGUINE WITH WHITE CLAM SAUCE

YIELD: serves 12 as a main course

This garlicky sauce is savory yet very fresh tasting. It's simple to prepare and it's always appreciated when served as an entrée to company. I prefer to use dried pasta for this sauce because the hard-shell clams sever the softer home-made noodles when combining. And although this recipe is large, you can easily halve it to serve a smaller group. The most pivotal time when making a clam sauce comes after the addition of the shucked raw clams. The heat must be adjusted quickly in order to prevent them from stiffening and becoming tough and rubbery. So only add the raw chopped clams after the clams in their shells are almost done. Shucking raw clams can be a tricky business the first time around, so read my directions on page 162 (twice) before getting started. Or, ask your fishmonger to shuck them for you. When entertaining, round out the menu with a first course of Baked Artichokes (page 328) or Green Bean and Roasted Pepper Salad (page 219), omitting the chicken. And if time allows, a loaf of Crusty Italian Bread (page 401) would be perfect to soak up the delicious sauce of this robust pasta dish.

SPECIAL EQUIPMENT

6- to 8-quart heavy-bottomed pot with lid

Clam brush (optional)

Clam knife

16-quart blanching pot with built-in strainer (optional)

INGREDIENTS

½ cup extra-virgin olive oil

1 stick (¼ pound) lightly salted butter

½ cup minced scallions (green onions), trimmed white parts and 1½ to 2 inches of the tender green

1 cup chopped yellow onion

12 cloves garlic, minced

2 stalks celery, cleaned, trimmed and minced

1 generous teaspoon crumbled dried oregano

1½ cups dry white wine

1½ cups Rich Chicken Stock or "Doctored" Canned Chicken Broth (page 140 for both)

Freshly ground black pepper to taste

4 dozen littleneck clams in shells, well rinsed and scrubbed

Salt, for cooking pasta

2 pounds dried linguine or spaghetti*

2 cups additional chopped raw clams with their nectar (from 2 to 2½ dozen shucked cherrystone clams) or 2 cans (7½ ounces each) minced clams with juice

¼ cup minced flat-leaf Italian parsley

Kosher or sea salt to taste

Sprigs of fresh oregano (optional)

* See section on Staples

1) *To heat water for pasta:* Bring a 16-quart pot of water to a boil, lower heat and simmer until needed for pasta.

2) *To prepare sauce:* Heat a 6- to 8-quart heavy-bottomed pot over medium heat and, when hot, add olive oil and butter. When oil is hot and butter is melted and bubbling, stir in minced scallions, onion, garlic and celery. Sauté over medium heat until softened and fragrant, about 5 minutes. Crumble in oregano and stir. Add white wine and chicken stock and bring mixture to a boil. Reduce heat and simmer uncovered until reduced by about ¼ its original volume, 8 to 10 minutes.

3) *To cook whole clams:* Add some freshly ground black pepper and little-neck clams in their shells to the sauce. Stir to coat clams with the hot liquid and vegetables, raise heat to high and cover pot tightly. Bring mixture to a boil and cook clams in the sauce, shaking the pot by its handles occasionally to redistribute clams so they cook evenly. Cook until clams just open and exude their juices, about 5 minutes.

4) *To cook pasta:* Return the pot of water to a boil, add some salt and the pasta. Cook until al dente according to the package directions. Check texture of pasta frequently to avoid overcooking.

5) *To finish sauce:* When most of the clams have opened, stir in chopped raw clams with their juices and reduce heat to low. Cover pot and cook gently until the clams with shells are wide open and the chopped clams are tender, about 4 minutes. Remove and discard any unopened clams (this means they are not edible). Stir in minced parsley, a light sprinkling of coarse salt and a generous amount of freshly ground black pepper into the clam sauce.

6) *To serve:* Drain pasta, allowing some of the cooking water to cling to the strands. Place pasta in a large deep serving bowl or divide individual servings among wide soup plates or pasta bowls. Ladle clams and sauce over pasta and fork through to combine. Garnish each plate with a sprig of fresh oregano, if available, and serve immediately.

Time Management Tips

- The vegetables for the sauce can be chopped as much as 1 day ahead and stored separately in the refrigerator, well covered.

- The clams may be shucked and chopped 3 to 4 days ahead and kept refrigerated in a well-covered container, totally submerged in clam liquor.

- The sauce (up to adding the clams) can be prepared up to to 2 hours ahead and kept at room temperature until ready to reheat and add the clams.

Low-Fat Variation

To reduce the overall saturated-fat content of this sauce, omit butter and use an additional ¼ cup extra-virgin olive oil and an additional ¼ cup chicken stock.

THE ULTIMATE MACARONI AND CHEESE

But, Where's the Macaroni?

YIELD: serves 10 as a side dish or 6 to 8 as a main course

SPECIAL EQUIPMENT

8-quart blanching pot with built-in strainer (optional)

Food processor (optional)

4-quart heavy-bottomed saucepan

6-quart oven-to-table casserole dish with lid

This pasta dish is exactly what the title implies: the ultimate macaroni and cheese. But let me stress from the beginning that this is not low in fat—as a matter of fact, it's loaded with cheese! Although this recipe is certainly not a dish for frequent consumption, when you want to splurge on the creamiest, most soothing and delicious pasta and cheese dish ever—look no further! Please don't be aghast that I use processed cheese in this sauce. There's a good reason: Authentic Cheddar cheese becomes oily and clumpy when melted, so instead I use Kraft's Sharp Old English cheese for its superior melting quality and, actually, quite distinctive flavor. Then I use a high-quality aged Cheddar for sprinkling over the top of the assembled dish. Oh, and I don't use macaroni. Instead I use spinach penne noodles because of the unique way that these large tubes of pasta catch the sauce. When you serve this as a side dish to any grilled or roasted meat, chicken or fish, along with a crisp mixed green salad, you've turned an ordinary meal into a memorable one.

INGREDIENTS

Melted butter, for greasing baking dish

4 packages (8 ounces each) Sharp Old English cheese

Flavorless vegetable oil, for food processor blade

1 stick (¼ pound) butter

3 tablespoons plus 1 ½ teaspoons all-purpose flour

4 cups milk

1 teaspoon ground white pepper

½ teaspoon cayenne pepper

Salt, for cooking pasta

1 pound dried spinach penne pasta* or plain penne or a combination

1 to 1½ cups freshly shredded best-quality mild or sharp aged
   Cheddar cheese

* See section on Staples

1) **To set up:** Bring an 8-quart pot of water to a boil and reduce to a simmer until needed for pasta. Brush the interior of a 6-quart baking dish with melted butter and brush either the interior of the lid or the shiny side of a long piece of aluminum foil; set aside.

2) **To shred cheese:** Lightly oil the steel blade of a food processor (to prevent cheese from clumping). Break up Old English cheese into chunks and place them in the work bowl. Using on/off pulses, chop cheese into small pieces and empty into a bowl. Alternatively, use a hand-held grater to shred cheese.

3) **To make cheese sauce:** Melt the stick of butter in a 4-quart saucepan over medium heat and, when hot and bubbling, stir in flour. Cook for 1 to 2 minutes, stirring constantly to cook the flour without browning. Add milk in a steady stream, whisking to combine. Stir in white pepper and cayenne and bring mixture to a full simmer whisking constantly. Once mixture begins to bubble, switch to a wooden spoon and cook, stirring constantly, until slightly thickened, 3 to 5 minutes. Add shredded Old English cheese (all at once) to the simmering sauce and stir over low heat until cheese is totally melted and sauce has thickened.

4) **To cook pasta:** Return the pot of water to a rapid boil, add some salt, then stir in the dried penne. Partially cook pasta for only ½ the lowest cooking time recommended on the package. Drain pasta well and place in a large mixing bowl.

5) **To assemble:** Pour cheese sauce over pasta and stir to combine. (The mixture will seem overly sauced at this point, but pasta will swell during baking.) Pour pasta mixture into buttered baking dish and sprinkle with grated Cheddar. Either cover and bake immediately now or allow to cool (uncovered) and bake later.

6) **To bake:** Preheat the oven to 375°F. Bake casserole (covered) for 30 minutes; then remove cover and continue to bake until the mixture is piping hot throughout and the top is golden brown, about 30 minutes. If at any time during the second half of baking, the cheese begins to overbrown, cover the top with the lid or loosely with greased aluminum foil (shiny side up).

Time Management Tips

- The cheese can be grated 1 day ahead and kept refrigerated in a securely covered bowl or sealed heavy plastic bag.

- The entire dish can be assembled as much as 1 day ahead and once cool, covered and refrigerated. If possible, bring close to room temperature before baking or adjust baking time accordingly.

Delectable Additions to Macaroni and Cheese

With tomatoes: Place ½ of the pasta and cheese sauce mixture in buttered baking dish. Top with a layer of thickly sliced ripe, juicy beefsteak tomatoes. Apply the rest of the pasta mixture on top, sprinkle with grated Cheddar cheese and bake as directed.

With broccoli: Blanch 2 to 4 cups trimmed and sliced fresh broccoli in boiling lightly salted water (with a slice of celery to kill the aroma) until softened but not cooked through, 3 or 4 minutes. Drain and immediately refresh in ice cold water to stop the cooking process. Drain, pat dry and add broccoli to the pasta and cheese mixture when assembling.

With bacon: Add 8 ounces crumbled, crisply fried bacon when combining the pasta with the cheese sauce.

BOLOGNESE SAUCE (MY WAY)

For Any Pasta, but Preferably Pappardelle

YIELD: about 16 cups sauce; for each main-course serving, use 1 scant cup sauce and 2 to 3 ounces dried pasta

SPECIAL EQUIPMENT
Food processor or chef's knife

8-quart nonreactive heavy-bottomed Dutch oven with tight-fitting lid

10- to 12-inch nonreactive skillet

8-quart blanching pot (or larger) with built-in strainer (optional)

This famous meat sauce, which originated in the northern Italian city of Bologna, is a hearty topping for any pasta. But I prefer it with pappardelle noodles, which look like thin lasagna noodles or long ribbons with curly edges —the perfect strand to stand up to such a substantial sauce. Since this sauce freezes so perfectly, I purposely wrote a large recipe to provide you with an extra batch or two tucked away in your freezer for easy and perhaps unexpected entertaining. Although it's traditional to use white wine in this sauce, I prefer the taste of red. But feel free to substitute. If desired, fold cooked green peas into the lightly buttered pasta before ladling the sauce on top. Or plant tiny fresh mozzarella balls on top of each serving and garnish with fresh basil. And be sure to pass a bowl of freshly grated Reggiano at the table.

FOR THE SAUCE

4 cups cleaned, thinly sliced leeks (page 160), trimmed whites and
   1 inch of the tender green

10 cloves garlic, chopped

2 stalks celery, cleaned, trimmed and sliced

2 carrots, peeled and sliced

1 stick (¼ pound) butter

2 pounds ground veal

4 thin slices prosciutto (preferably imported from Parma), chopped

1 cup Rich Beef Stock (page 146) or canned beef broth, diluted with
   water if too salty

¼ cup extra-virgin olive oil

1½ pounds sweet Italian sausage (casing removed)

Freshly ground black pepper to taste

1 cup dry red or white wine

3 pounds ripe plum (Roma) tomatoes, peeled, seeded (page 151)
   and coarsely chopped, or 2 cans (28 ounces each) whole tomatoes,
   drained and coarsely chopped

1 can (29 ounces) tomato purée

1 cup chopped fresh basil leaves (chopped as needed to prevent basil
   from turning black)

1 can (6 ounces) tomato paste

1 pound fresh button mushrooms, wiped clean (page 131) and sliced

½ cup heavy cream (preferably not ultrapasteurized)

½ cup freshly grated Reggiano Parmesan cheese

Salt to taste

TO SERVE

Homemade Egg Noodles (page 175), cut with the pappardelle or
   fettuccine attachment, or dried pappardelle,* freshly cooked,
   drained and lightly buttered (allow 2 to 3 ounces per person)

Sprigs of basil, for garnish

Fresh mozzarella balls* (optional), for garnish

* See section on Staples

Time Management Tips

- All of the vegetables for the sauce base can
  be sliced 1 day ahead and kept in separate
  securely covered bowls in the refrigerator.

- Although it's best to peel and chop tomatoes the day of assembling, you can if necessary, do this 1 day ahead and keep
  refrigerated well covered.

- The entire sauce can be fully assembled,
  cooled and stored in the refrigerator for 2
  days before reheating. Before refrigerating,
  pull a clean kitchen towel over the top of the
  pot and then apply the lid. The towel will
  prevent any accumulation of condensation
  (water) from falling into the sauce and diluting the flavor.

- Alternatively, the sauce can be divided and
  frozen in labeled heavy-duty freezer containers. When reheating (after thawing),
  add additional freshly ground black pepper
  and a few tablespoons chopped fresh basil
  to refresh the taste.

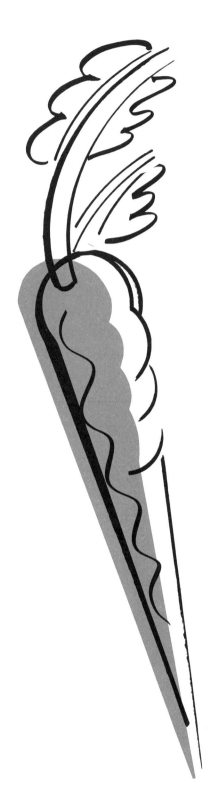

1) *To process vegetables:* Combine leeks, garlic, celery and carrots (in batches if necessary) in the bowl of a food processor fitted with the steel blade. Process using on/off turns until chopped very small but not puréed. The vegetables should remain distinguishable. If you don't have a food processor, mince vegetables individually, using a chef's knife, and then combine.

2) *To sweat vegetables:* Melt butter in a nonreactive heavy-bottomed 8-quart Dutch oven over medium heat. While it melts, tear off a sheet of waxed paper, large enough to cover the bottom interior of the pot. Brush 1 side of the paper with some of the butter. When butter is hot and bubbling, stir in vegetable mixture and lay the greased side of the waxed paper directly on top of the vegetables. Reduce heat to very low and let vegetables sweat for 15 to 20 minutes, lifting the paper occasionally to stir and redistribute.

3) *To brown veal with prosciutto:* Meanwhile, heat a 10- to 12-inch nonreactive skillet over medium-high heat. When hot, add ground veal and break it up with a fork or a wooden spoon. Stir in chopped prosciutto and cook until veal is no longer pink, 3 to 4 minutes. Using a slotted spoon, remove veal and prosciutto to a bowl. Pour out any liquid that remains in the skillet, but do not wipe out the interior.

4) *To deglaze pan:* Return skillet to high heat and add beef stock. Bring to a brisk simmer and deglaze pan by scraping up any stray browned bits of caramelized veal. Reduce stock to about ½ its original volume and pour into the bowl with the browned veal.

5) *To brown sausage and deglaze pan:* Wipe out pan and return to medium-high heat. Add 2 tablespoons olive oil and, when hot, add sausage and break it up with a fork. Season sausage with black pepper and cook until no longer pink, 3 to 4 minutes. Remove with a slotted spoon and combine with veal. Pour out any fat from skillet and deglaze once more, but this time with red wine. When wine is reduced by ½, add to meat mixture and set aside.

6) *To combine sauce:* Remove waxed paper from vegetables and stir in 2 cups of the chopped tomatoes, tomato purée and ½ cup of the freshly chopped basil. Add meat mixture along with deglazing liquids and stir in tomato paste and a good amount of black pepper. Bring mixture to a simmer, reduce heat to low and cook with the cover ajar for 30 minutes.

7) *To cook mushrooms:* Heat a 10-inch skillet over medium-high heat and, when hot, add remaining 2 tablespoons olive oil. When oil is hot, add sliced mushrooms and cook, stirring constantly, until mushrooms are golden and tender, about 3 minutes. Remove from heat.

8) *To finish sauce:* To simmered sauce, add cooked mushrooms, the remaining 3 cups chopped tomatoes and cream; simmer another 10 minutes. Stir in another ½ cup chopped basil and remove from heat. Stir in grated Parmesan cheese, season with salt if necessary and some additional pepper. Serve immediately, or store or freeze as directed in Time Management Tips.

9) *To serve:* Ladle hot sauce over freshly cooked pasta and garnish each plate with a sprig of fresh basil and, if desired, gently press 2 tiny mozzarella balls on top of each serving so the bottom of each ball melts while the top keeps its shape.

Low-Fat Variations

To reduce the amount of saturated-fat in this recipe, omit butter for sweating vegetables and simmer them in ½ cup additional beef stock. Or stir minced vegetables into 3 tablespoons hot extra-virgin olive oil and, when just softened, add ⅓ cup beef stock; cook as you would when using butter. Substitute ground turkey for the veal. Substitute Skinny Crème Fraîche (page 84) for the cream.

FETTUCCINE AND LAMB SCALOPPINE

With Onions, Wild Mushrooms and Peas

YIELD: serves 6 as a main course

SPECIAL EQUIPMENT

Heavy meat mallet

12-inch nonreactive deep-sided skillet

8-quart blanching pot with built-in strainer (optional)

Although many people associate the word "scaloppine" only with veal or chicken, in this recipe we use the lean meat from loin lamb chops. After removing the meat, the bones are browned with aromatic vegetables and then simmered to make a mini lamb stock. This is used along with reduced red wine in the sauce for the pasta. Lean lamb scallops, like veal, cook very quickly, so avoid overcooking. When choosing your pasta, this topping really deserves a substantial strand like fettuccine or even pappardelle. And don't hesitate to use reconstituted dried mushrooms since the intense flavor derived from the soaking liquid gives added dimension to the sauce. Ultimately, the combination of the lamb, sautéed wild mushrooms, onions, garlic and the vibrant color and taste of sweet green peas gives this dish both an intense flavor and a distinctive appearance.

INGREDIENTS

2 pounds loin lamb chops with bone (sliced 1½ inches thick)

FOR THE MARINADE

¼ cup extra-virgin olive oil

8 cloves garlic, minced

3 tablespoons chopped fresh basil leaves

Freshly ground black pepper to taste

FOR THE LAMB STOCK

1 medium-sized yellow onion, unpeeled, scrubbed, root end removed, and coarsely chopped

2 carrots, scrubbed and sliced

1 stalk celery, cleaned and sliced

About 5 cups colds water

1 generous teaspoon whole black peppercorns

REMAINING INGREDIENTS

1 pound assorted fresh wild mushrooms (such as portobello, chanterelle
   and shiitake) *or* 6 ounces fresh button mushrooms plus generous ½ cup
   (⅔ ounce) assorted dried wild mushrooms (such as porcini and shiitake)

8 ounces fresh or frozen peas

1 large yellow onion

¼ cup extra-virgin olive oil

3 tablespoons chopped fresh basil leaves

4 large cloves garlic, thinly sliced and slices cut into fine julienne

1 generous tablespoon balsamic vinegar

Freshly ground black pepper to taste

½ to 1 cup dry red wine

1 pound dried fettuccine noodles* or 1 recipe Firm Egg Noodles
   with Semolina Flour (page 178), cut into ¼-inch strips or with
   fettuccine blade

½ to 1 cup freshly grated Reggiano Parmesan cheese

Kosher or sea salt to taste

* See section on Staples

1) **To prepare lamb:** Using a sharp boning knife, remove the eye of the loin
   of each chop and slice the round in half crosswise (so you have 2 rounds
   of lamb). Remove meaty section from behind the bone as well. (Reserve
   lamb bones to make the stock.) Cut away and discard any excess fat or
   tough connective tissue from the meat. Lay a long sheet of waxed paper
   on the counter. Place lamb rounds (including the meat from the back of
   the bone) on the paper with about 2½ inches between each piece. Cover
   lamb with another sheet of waxed paper, and, using a heavy meat mallet,
   pound lamb until thin (¼ to ⅛ inch thick). Remove waxed paper and slice
   lamb into thin strips, as for stir-fry. Place strips in a bowl.

2) **To marinate lamb:** In a measuring cup, combine marinade ingredients,
   pour over lamb and toss to coat meat well. Cover and leave at a comfortable room temperature for 2 hours. If desired, you may refrigerate lamb
   and marinate overnight, but don't add basil until you remove lamb from
   refrigerator to come to room temperature before cooking.

Time Management Tips

- All of the vegetables for the lamb stock as
  well as the onions, garlic and fresh mushrooms can be prepared 1 day ahead and
  stored in the refrigerator (separately) in
  well-covered bowls. If using dried mushrooms, don't reconstitute them until the day
  of assembling the finished dish.

- The lamb can be cut and marinated 1 day
  ahead and refrigerated. If so, prepare your
  stock 1 day ahead as well so your preparation when assembling will be minimal.

Q AND A

Q. Are some wild mushrooms
poisonous?

A. Yes. Some varieties of mushrooms can
be deadly. Inexperienced "mushroom col-
lectors" should never eat any mushroom
that has not been positively identified as
being edible. To be safe, buy wild mushrooms from a reputable produce dealer.

3) To roast bones for lamb stock: Preheat the oven to 450°F. Cut away as much fat as possible from reserved bones and place them and chopped onion on a shallow baking sheet. Grind on some freshly ground black pepper and toss to combine. Roast until both bones and onions are very brown and beginning to caramelize, about 30 minutes.

4) To prepare lamb stock: Transfer contents of baking sheet into a 2½-quart saucepan. Add carrots, celery and just enough cold water to cover ingredients. Add peppercorns, place pan over high heat and bring mixture to a boil. Reduce heat to low and simmer stock with the cover ajar for 1 to 2 hours, occasionally pressing hard on the solids to extract as much flavor as possible. Remove from heat and allow the stock to cool with the solids. Strain stock into a bowl, pressing hard on the solids, then discard them. Measure 2 cups stock into the saucepan, bring it to a brisk simmer and cook uncovered until reduced to 1 cup. (Any remaining stock should be refrigerated and used within 3 days or frozen for up to 6 months in a freezer with little temperature fluctuation.) If time is scarce, simmer bones for as long as you can and then immediately strain and proceed.

5) To prepare mushrooms: If using fresh mushrooms, wipe them clean, remove and discard stems, and slice caps into strips as directed on page 131. If using dried mushrooms, reconstitute as directed on page 131, reserving ½ cup of the strained mushroom liquid to add to sauce, and combine with the 6 ounces button mushrooms.

6) To boil water for pasta: Bring an 8-quart pot of water to a boil and reduce heat so water simmers until ready to cook pasta.

7) To prepare peas: Place a bowl of ice water on the counter. In a saucepan, simmer fresh peas in 1 inch of boiling water for 3 minutes, drain and refresh them in ice water to stop the cooking process; drain and set aside. To quick-thaw frozen peas, place them in a colander under a gentle stream of hot tap water until softened, then drain well.

8) To sauté onions: Peel and cut in half through the stem end. Cut each half into thin wedges and separate into thin strips. Heat a 12-inch nonreactive deep-sided skillet over medium heat. When hot, add 2 tablespoons of the olive oil. When oil is hot, stir in onion strips and cook until softened, very fragrant and beginning to turn golden, about 12 minutes. Stir in chopped basil and heat through for only 1 more minute. Remove onions to a bowl but don't wipe out skillet.

9) *To sauté mushrooms and garlic:* Return skillet to medium heat and, when hot, add 2 tablespoon olive oil. When oil is hot, add sliced mushrooms (both fresh and drained reconstituted) along with garlic and toss in oil. Cook until both mushrooms and garlic are golden and tender, 3 to 4 minutes. Scrape mushrooms into the bowl with onions but don't wipe out skillet.

10) *To brown lamb:* Return skillet to high heat and, when pan is very hot, toss in a small handful of marinated lamb strips (you don't need additional oil since lamb is already lubricated). Stir-fry small batches of lamb very quickly until lamb is medium rare. As each batch browns, transfer with a slotted spoon to the bowl of sautéed vegetables. Stir balsamic vinegar into lamb-vegetable mixture along with some freshly ground black pepper and set aside.

11) *To deglaze pan:* Pour out any remaining oil from skillet and return it to medium-high heat. Deglaze pan with 1 cup wine or ½ cup wine and ½ cup strained liquid from reconstituted mushrooms. As wine comes to a boil, scrape up any browned bits of lamb, onions and mushrooms remaining on the bottom of the skillet. Reduce heat to medium-low and reduce the liquid by ½. Pour the reduction into the bowl with the lamb and vegetables. Return skillet (no need to wash it yet) to the stove but don't turn on heat.

12) *To cook pasta:* Bring the water back to a rapid boil, add some salt to the water, then the pasta. Cook until al dente, 1 to 3 minutes if fresh, or according to the package directions. Check texture of pasta frequently while cooking to avoid overcooking.

13) *To assemble and serve:* While pasta is cooking, pour reduced lamb stock into the skillet and bring to a simmer over medium heat. Add peas, along with all of the browned lamb and vegetables. Fold together as mixture heats through. (Be careful not to overcook lamb or peas.) Taste for seasoning, adding more freshly ground black pepper. Drain pasta, allowing some of the cooking water to cling to the strands and pour into a large warmed serving bowl. Pour the contents of the skillet over pasta and sprinkle with grated Parmesan cheese. Gently toss to combine, being careful not to rupture peas. Adjust seasoning with coarse salt and more pepper, if needed.

FRIED CHINESE SESAME NOODLES

With Duck Sauce

YIELD: about 10 cups cooked noodles; serves 10

SPECIAL EQUIPMENT

Wooden surface for kneading

Pastry scraper

Tapered rolling pin

Electric deep-fat fryer (optional)

Deep-fry thermometer and frying basket, only if not using an electric deep-fryer. (A slotted spoon can be used in place of the basket but it's not as safe or efficient.)

The kids won't be the only ones who'll go crazy when you present a basket that's bursting with these long crispy squiggles at the table. These blistered noodles are aesthetically authentic, and the addition of sesame seeds to the dough makes them far superior in taste to those found in even the finest Chinese restaurants! The sesame seeds not only add a savory flavor, but they actually help when rolling the dough. (The edges of the seeds sever the tight bands of elasticity developed during kneading, so you won't have to work so hard to roll the dough thin.) Although an electric deep-fat fryer is not essential, it does make the job of frying easier and safer, with results that are always dependable. Serve these fabulous noodles warm or at room temperature with Chinese Egg Drop Soup (page 152), Asian Chicken (page 235) or Whole Red Snapper (page 229). Or simply fry up a batch and serve them with cocktails accompanied with a bowl of Duck Sauce and reconstituted dry Chinese mustard.

INGREDIENTS

2 cups unbleached all-purpose flour, plus more for dusting

1 rounded teaspoon salt

¼ cup raw sesame seeds

About ⅔ cup cold water

About 1¾ quarts light peanut oil,* for deep-frying

Duck Sauce (following), optional for dipping

* See section on Staples

1) To prepare dough: Whisk together flour, salt and sesame seeds in a medium-sized mixing bowl and add the water a little at a time while mixing with your other hand. Add only enough water to create a moist (not wet) shaggy mass of dough. Turn out dough onto a lightly floured board and knead with a firm, brisk and deliberate push-fold-and-turn motion until dough is firm, smooth and elastic. Add small amounts of additional flour as needed to prevent dough from sticking to the board. Cover dough with a kitchen towel and let it relax 30 minutes for easier rolling.

2) *To set up to fry and drain:* Lay a double thickness of paper toweling on your counter and also line a baking sheet with paper towels. If using an electric deep-fryer, pour in oil to the designated line and heat to its highest setting (or follow the manufacturer's instructions). Alternatively, half fill a 2½-quart heavy-bottomed saucepan with oil. Attach a deep-frying thermometer securely to the side of the pan (without allowing the tip of the stem to touch the bottom) and heat to 365°F to 375°F. As the oil heats, insert a frying basket as well.

3) *To roll dough:* Using the blade of a pastry scraper, cut dough into 4 equal pieces. Keep covered as you as you work with 1 piece at a time. On a lightly floured board, roll out 1 piece of dough into a very thin (about 1/16-inch) rectangle. As you roll, occasionally turn over dough and dust both board and dough with additional flour.

4) *To cut noodles:* Lay the thin sheet of dough in front of you with one short end closest to you. Dust the top lightly with flour and roll up the dough away from you into a loose jelly-roll shape. Using a sharp serrated knife and a sawing motion, slice roll into 1/3-inch slices. Lift each slice and let it unroll and drape over the inside of your other hand. Lay the batch of noodles in a loose pile on a lightly floured surface and cover with a clean kitchen towel. Continue rolling and cutting the remaining pieces of dough.

5) *To deep-fry and drain noodles:* When the oil reaches the desired temperature, carefully ease a single pile of raw noodles into the hot oil and immediately separate them gently with a long 2-pronged fork. As they quickly "balloon up," little blisters will appear on their surface. Fry noodles for 5 minutes and carefully turn them over to fry the other side until noodles are golden brown, light textured and very crisp, about another 4 minutes. Lift noodles out of hot oil, shake to remove excess oil and drain on paper toweling. Then transfer noodles to the paper-lined baking sheet. Replace the oily towels with clean ones and continue to fry and drain the remaining batches of noodles. Pile each batch on top of each other on the baking sheet. (If not using an electric fryer, keep a watchful eye on the pot and regulate the heat as necessary to maintain the correct frying temperature.)

6) *To serve and store:* Serve noodles warm or at room temperature with Duck Sauce for dipping. Store any leftover noodles at room temperature in a plastic bag (they won't fit in a tin without breaking).

Time Management Tips

- Although these noodles should be made on the day of serving, their texture will remain crisp for days. For best flavor, make them early in the day and reheat them on a shallow baking sheet at 350°F for 10 minutes just before serving.

Duck Sauce

YIELD: about 1½ cups

SPECIAL EQUIPMENT
Food processor or blender

The taste of most store-bought duck sauce is just awful! This homemade version is quick and easy to assemble and so much more delicious.

INGREDIENTS

½ cup apricot conserve or preserves

½ cup peach conserve or preserves

3 tablespoons distilled, unseasoned rice wine vinegar

1 generous tablespoon minced, peeled fresh ginger root

¼ cup water

1) To prepare sauce: Combine all ingredients in a small saucepan and bring to a simmer. Gently cook uncovered for 10 minutes. Scrape mixture into the bowl of a food processor fitted with the steel blade or a blender. Process until smooth, empty into a bowl and let cool. The mixture will seem very watery when hot. As the sauce cools, the consistency will thicken.

2) To store: Cover sauce tightly and refrigerate for up to 2 weeks. Bring close to room temperature before serving; if you need to hasten this, just rewarm briefly.

CHAPTER VI

QUICK, LIGHT AND SO RIGHT

When You're Tired and Hungry

A ll of the recipes in this chapter require minimal effort and yet promise comfort and great taste. Here you'll find entrées that (without compromising on wholesome ingredients) you'll be able to prepare on days when you're tired, hungry and time is practically nonexistent. I have concentrated on the use of the freshest fish, chicken and produce that don't require lengthy cooking. Also, when appropriate, my Time Management Tips will teach you to use little bits of available time to make even your quickest meals taste slow-cooked delicious. For example, whenever lengthy marinating is suggested, by beginning the night before, you can virtually eliminate almost all the preparation time just before serving. And although the suggestion to chop your vegetables the day before might seem only minimally beneficial, when you arrive home from work and your family looks to you for a warm and nurturing meal, you'll be grateful that you have completed these steps in advance; and you'll be less likely to sacrifice these healthy and flavor-enhancing ingredients altogether.

CHILLED ASPARAGUS WITH SWEET PEPPERS AND TUNA

Dressed in My Favorite Scallion Vinaigrette

YIELD: serves 6 to 8 for lunch or a light supper; more as part of a buffet

This salad meal is fabulous and just perfect either when having guests for a weekend lunch or when you want to provide your family with a light and refreshing supper during the week. The combination of chilled asparagus, savory garlic-studded roasted peppers, garbanzo beans and tuna—all lightly dressed in my favorite scallion vinaigrette—is very delicious and always appreciated. Although I've listed canned tuna for convenience, Crusty Cajun Tuna (page 227) would also be incredible. Also, feel free to add slivered red onions, kalamata or Nicoişe olives and slivered fresh basil leaves to the roasted pepper mixture. Although roasting the peppers will greatly enhance the flavor of this recipe, it is an optional step. If time or energy is an issue, substitute drained roasted peppers from a jar.

SPECIAL EQUIPMENT

8-quart blanching pot with built-in strainer (optional)

Kitchen twine for asparagus

INGREDIENTS

2 red bell peppers *and* 2 yellow bell peppers

¼ to ⅓ cup extra-virgin olive oil

2 cloves garlic, minced

Freshly ground black pepper to taste

2½ to 3 pounds tender young asparagus, blanched and chilled (page 210)

My Favorite Scallion Vinaigrette (following)

1 can (10½ ounces) garbanzo beans (chickpeas), rinsed and well drained

2 cans (12¼ ounces each) solid white tuna (water-packed) or 4 cans (6⅛ ounces each) Italian chunk light tuna* (packed in olive oil), drained and flaked with a fork (not mashed)

⅓ cup drained capers* (optional)

 Balsamic vinegar to taste

* See section on Staples

1) **To prepare peppers:** If time allows, roast and peel peppers as directed on page 113. Seed and slice each pepper into thin strips and place in a small bowl. Add olive oil to coat well along with garlic and a generous amount of freshly ground black pepper. Set aside.

2) *To assemble and serve:* Lay 9 thin or 6 thick blanched asparagus spears on individual serving plates with the tips facing in the same direction. Stir vinaigrette and ladle some over the asparagus. Lay some of the pepper strips on top along with a few garbanzo beans. Ladle on a bit more dressing, top with some flaked tuna and, if desired, scatter some capers over top. Serve and pass additional dressing at the table along with some balsamic vinegar to drizzle on top. Be sure to have a reliable peppermill at the table.

My Favorite Scallion Vinaigrette

YIELD: about 2½ cups

Because this is my favorite vinaigrette (for all types of salads), I've provided a recipe that yields a generous amount. Keep any leftovers refrigerated in a tightly covered jar to be used for up to 3 days.

TIPS

FROM A TEACHER

How to Prepare, Blanch and Fully Cook Asparagus

In order to retain its firm texture and bright green color, asparagus should be cooked quickly and served immediately or blanched (briefly boiled and then quickly refreshed in ice water to stop the cooking process). An eight-quart blanching pot with a built-in strainer is extremely useful but not essential. Blanched asparagus may be served chilled or finished up to three days later by baking or sautéing (see the following mini recipes).

To prepare asparagus for cooking: Wash asparagus and trim off the woody ends using a sharp knife or snap off the tough fibrous bottom. Although unnecessary, you may use a vegetable peeler to remove the outer skin of each asparagus starting 2 inches below the floret in a firm but gentle downward motion. Peeling is not advised in young, delicate asparagus. Separate asparagus into 2 or 3 bunches and tie each bunch twice, 2 inches apart, with kitchen twine.

To blanch asparagus: Bring a large pot of water to boil and set a large bowl of ice water on the counter. Lightly salt boiling water and lower asparagus bundles into pot. The cooking time will be determined by the age, thickness and ultimate use of the asparagus. To serve chilled, cook until tender but al dente (slightly firm to the teeth), 4 to 8 minutes, checking after 4 minutes. If blanching to finish later, cook until stalks are softened but not yet tender, 3 to 6 minutes, checking after 3 min-

⅔ cup regular olive oil and ⅓ cup extra virgin olive oil

½ cup red wine vinegar

1 rounded tablespoon Dijon mustard

1 teaspoon salt (or less)

Generous twist freshly ground black pepper

½ cup minced scallions (green onions), trimmed white parts and
 1½ to 2 inches of the tender green

2 cloves garlic, minced

1 teaspoon crumbled dried oregano (optional)

Combine all of the ingredients in a jar or a bowl and shake well or whisk to combine. Refrigerate until ready to serve. If made in advance and very chilled, let the dressing sit out of the refrigerator to release its full flavor, before serving.

utes. In either case, immediately lift asparagus out of the boiling water and plunge into the bowl of ice water. (To lift bundles if not using a blanching pot, insert one of the prongs of a long kitchen fork under one of the strings that secure each bunch.) When asparagus is cold to the touch, remove from the ice water, lay on paper toweling and snip off the strings in order to drain properly. Gently pat dry and either use now or roll up carefully in a paper towel and place into a heavy plastic bag. Seal and keep refrigerated for up to 3 days. Enjoy cold or cook further as directed in given recipe.

To cook asparagus fully: Place prepared asparagus in a large pot of boiling water as for blanching. Check after 4 minutes; the larger, thicker stalks might require as much as 10 minutes. Fully cooked asparagus should be tender but never overly soft or they will become limp and stringy. Lift from water, drain well and serve immediately drizzled with melted butter and seasoned with salt and freshly ground black pepper to taste.

**Asparagus Baked with
Bread Crumbs**
Take asparagus that need further cooking and place in a greased baking dish. Brush spears lightly with melted butter or extra-virgin olive oil. Top with dried bread crumbs mixed with sesame seeds or chopped toasted pine nuts and a small handful of freshly grated Reggiano Parmesan cheese. Add a generous amount of freshly ground black pepper and a bit of salt to taste. Cover well and store in the refrigerator for up to 3 days, then bake the asparagus on a night when you want to embellish beautifully a simple meal.

Asparagus Sautéed in Butter
Another way to use preblanched asparagus is to dredge the spears in seasoned flour, dip the stalks in some beaten egg and sauté the coated asparagus in hot clarified butter (page 81) or olive oil in a nonstick skillet until golden on all sides. Sprinkle spears lightly with coarse salt and freshly ground black pepper and serve immediately with seedless lemon wedges (page 228).

Traditional and Not So Traditional
CAESAR SALAD

YIELD: serves 6 to 8 as first course; 4 to 6 as main course for lunch

SPECIAL EQUIPMENT
Large wooden salad bowl

Wide blending fork or large
serving fork

10- to 12-inch nonstick skillet

Many of my friends and students, who adore Caesar salad and request it often in restaurants, are intimidated by the thought of making it at home. Most feel as though theirs can't possibly taste as good, so why bother? Well, get ready for the best Caesar salad ever! Loaded with the finest ingredients you can buy, this dressing is so delicious that you will never feel hesitant to make this Caesar salad for anyone—friends, family or business associates. For a fabulous lunch or light supper, all that's needed to accompany the salad is a crusty loaf of bread lavished with some herb-infused fruity olive oil and a glass of wine. Juicy fresh fruit is always a quick and refreshing conclusion to a light meal. If using the soft-cooked (coddled) egg in this traditional dressing concerns you, see my variation without eggs.

INGREDIENTS

2 large cloves garlic, peeled and left whole

5 firm anchovy fillets,* drained and patted dry

1 rounded tablespoon Dijon mustard

1½ teaspoons Worcestershire sauce

2 tablespoons strained fresh lemon juice

2½ tablespoons red wine vinegar

1 extra-large egg, cooked in water that's just below the boiling point
  for 1 minute

½ cup olive oil (combine regular and extra-virgin)

1 cup freshly grated Reggiano Parmesan cheese

Freshly ground black pepper to taste

2 large heads very fresh, crisp romaine lettuce, rinsed, patted dry
  and torn into generous pieces

2 medium-sized red bell peppers (optional), roasted and peeled
  (page 113), seeded and sliced into thin strips

2 cups freshly made Garlic Croutons (following)

¼ cup well-drained capers* (optional), for garnish

* See section on Staples

1) **To prepare dressing:** Using a blending fork or serving fork, mash garlic in the bottom of a large wooden salad bowl until the cloves become like a coarsely textured paste. Add anchovies and mash them with the garlic until the mixture is smoother and still pastelike. Stir in mustard and Worcestershire sauce, mixing well with the fork and bringing the mixture up the sides of the bowl to further season the wood. Add lemon juice and vinegar and continue to blend in the same way. Crack the briefly cooked egg into the bowl. (If necessary, use a teaspoon to scoop any coagulated egg white from the shell and add it to the dressing.) Blend thoroughly, then add olive oil in a slow steady stream while mixing the dressing briskly. Stir in ½ cup of the grated Parmesan along with a generous amount of freshly ground black pepper.

2) **To assemble and serve salad:** Add torn romaine lettuce leaves to the bowl on top of the dressing. Sprinkle lettuce with the remaining ½ cup Parmesan, roasted red peppers strips, if using, and croutons. Toss salad gently, but thoroughly. If desired, after dividing the salad onto individual plates, sprinkle a teaspoon of drained capers over each serving. Serve immediately with a reliable peppermill passed at the table.

Garlic Croutons

YIELD: about 2 cups

INGREDIENTS

Crusty French or Italian bread, cut into ½-inch cubes to measure 2 cups, or skinny baguettes, thinly sliced and each round cut in half

½ cup extra-virgin olive oil

3 cloves garlic, peeled and sliced into thin slivers

Freshly ground black pepper to taste

¼ teaspoon crumbled dried oregano

¼ cup freshly grated Reggiano Parmesan cheese (optional)

1) **To toast bread cubes:** Preheat the oven to 375°F. Place bread cubes on a shallow baking sheet in a single layer and bake until the cubes are dry and turning golden, about 10 minutes. (The cubes should feel dry and hard, which will keep them from absorbing too much oil.)

Q. Why is the egg briefly boiled before using it in a Caesar dressing?

A. The reason for "coddling" the egg is to warm the yolk. This will enable it to hold more oil in suspension when being incorporated with the other ingredients, thus creating a better emulsion.

2) *To cook garlic:* Line a plate and a shallow baking sheet with paper toweling. Heat a 10- to 12-inch nonstick skillet over medium-high heat. When pan is hot, add olive oil and, when oil is hot, reduce heat to medium and add garlic slivers. Toss garlic in hot oil, pressing on the garlic with the back of a wooden spoon to release fully the flavor into the oil. Reduce heat to low and cook slowly, until the slivers turn golden brown and crisp (be careful not to allow the garlic to burn). Using a slotted spoon, remove garlic slices to the towel-lined plate and set aside.

3) *To sauté bread cubes:* Raise heat under skillet to medium-high and add toasted bread cubes all at once. Toss cubes in the hot oil and cook until crisp and golden brown on all sides, tossing frequently, 2 to 3 minutes. Remove croutons to the paper-lined baking sheet to remove any excess oil. Place croutons in a bowl.

4) *To assemble and store:* Chop fried garlic slices and combine with croutons. Sprinkle on some ground pepper and crumbled oregano. Let croutons cool in the bowl. If serving the same day, toss croutons with grated Parmesan cheese, if using, and let them cool further before covering and storing at room temperature. If making in bulk, omit cheese and store in an airtight tin for up to 2 weeks at room temperature.

Caesar Salad Variation without Egg

There is a real controversy regarding the safety of using raw or soft-cooked eggs in foods. If this concerns you, simply omit egg and place mustard, vinegar, lemon juice, Worcestershire sauce and olive oil into a blender. Add 1 generous tablespoon store-bought mayonnaise and blend until smooth. Prepare garlic and anchovies in a wooden bowl as described in the recipe. Add the blended dressing with ½ cup freshly grated Parmesan and fresh ground pepper to the salad bowl and use a large fork to rub the dressing in and season the bowl before adding lettuce.

FRESH CORN AND PASTA SALAD

Topped with Jumbo Shrimp

YIELD: serves 8

This textural salad is filled with blanched fresh corn kernels, small shell-shaped pasta, minced onions, sweet bell peppers, ripe olives and the distinctive taste of cilantro. The assembled salad is topped (just before serving) with tender poached jumbo shrimp that are lightly dressed in a delicious scallion and garlic-laced vinaigrette. The flavors are light and refreshing and the texture is both soothing and substantial. This is the perfect recipe to pull out when entertaining weekend guests for lunch. If you choose, simply omit the shrimp and you've got yourself a great accompaniment to a summer barbecue.

SPECIAL EQUIPMENT
8-quart blanching pot with built-in strainer (optional)

INGREDIENTS

Marinated Jumbo Shrimp (following)

Salt as needed

6 ears fresh corn, all outer husks and silk removed

8 ounces small shell pasta

1 small green bell pepper, seeded and minced

1 red bell pepper, preferably roasted (page 113), seeded and minced

⅓ cup packed minced yellow onion

⅓ cup packed minced red onion

¼ cup chopped fresh cilantro

¼ cup chopped pitted black ripe olives

My Favorite Scallion Vinaigrette (page 210), preferably with optional oregano

Freshly ground black pepper to taste

1) ***Marinated Jumbo Shrimp:*** Cook and marinate as directed in recipe.

2) ***To cook corn:*** Bring an 8-quart pot of water to a boil. Place a large bowl of ice water next to the stove. Add some salt to the boiling water, then add corn, cover and cook at a strong simmer for 5 minutes. Remove corn from water (but keep pot over heat) and dunk corn in the ice water; when cool, drain and set aside.

Time Management Tips

- Fill the blanching pot early in the day and leave turned off on the stove. As soon as you come home from work, turn on the pot so it will be heating as you prepare the vegetables. (Doing little things like this in advance makes a big difference when you come home tired and hungry.)

- The shrimp as well as the corn and pasta salad may be prepared totally a day ahead. Keep shrimp and salad separate until just before serving and, if possible, bring the corn and pasta salad close to room temperature to enjoy best flavor.

- If you don't have time to make the shrimp stock this time, place the shells in a heavy-duty plastic bag and freeze for up to 1 month. Make the stock at your leisure and freeze. This way, the next time you make this recipe, you'll have the stock ready to thaw and use as desired.

- If you don't have time to roast the pepper, chop the pepper raw or use a drained roasted pepper from a jar.

3) *To cook pasta:* Return water to a boil, add pasta and cook until tender but still firm (al dente). Transfer pasta to a colander under cold running water to stop the cooking process. Drain well and place in a large mixing bowl.

4) *To assemble salad:* Remove corn kernels from cobs with a sharp knife and place kernels in the bowl with the pasta. One at a time, hold dekerneled cobs over the bowl and briskly scrape with a knife in a downward motion to extract the natural corn cream from the cobs into the bowl. Add minced green and red bell peppers, yellow and red onions, cilantro and olives. Prepare vinaigrette, adding oregano, and pour some over the vegetable and pasta mixture to just coat nicely (avoid overdressing). Add a generous amount of fresh black pepper and fold the ingredients together. Add salt to taste and either serve immediately or cover the bowl and refrigerate.

5) *To serve:* Place corn and pasta mixture on a decorative serving platter. Stir shrimp to coat well with the marinade then pour shrimp into a wire strainer to remove any excess. Mound the shrimp on top of the salad. Add more fresh pepper, if desired, and serve.

Marinated Jumbo Shrimp

YIELD: serves 8

These shrimp are great to top or toss with just about any salad. They also make an excellent appetizer (especially in summer) served alone with toothpicks. Another warm-weather favorite is to poach the shrimp in stock or water, chill and serve them surrounding a bowl of Creamy Dijon Mustard Sauce (page 89) or bottled chili sauce doctored with a little fresh lemon juice and a generous amount of prepared white horseradish.

INGREDIENTS

1 recipe Shrimp Stock (page 139) or 4 cups cold water

2 pounds jumbo shrimp, peeled, deveined, rinsed well and drained (page 218), shells optimally reserved for stock

2 tablespoons extra-virgin olive oil

2 tablespoons mayonnaise

1½ tablespoons white wine vinegar

2 tablespoons minced scallions (green onions), trimmed white parts and 1½ to 2 inches of the tender green

Salt and freshly ground black pepper to taste

1) To cook shrimp: In a large saucepan, bring shrimp stock or the water to a simmer and add shrimp. Cook shrimp uncovered over low heat for 3 minutes. Drain immediately and place in a bowl. (If using shrimp stock, drain shrimp over another bowl and once the stock cools, refrigerate it for up to 2 days or freeze for 2 months.)

2) To marinate shrimp: In a small bowl, combine olive oil, mayonnaise, white wine vinegar, minced scallions, a generous amount of freshly ground black pepper and some salt to taste. Stir well and toss with cooked shrimp while still warm to encourage the flavors of the dressing to penetrate the shrimp. Let cool slightly, cover with plastic wrap and refrigerate at least 15 minutes or overnight in the refrigerator.

All shrimp have a black vein that runs down the length of its back. When working with a large amount of small shrimp, the tedious chore of removing the tiny vein is hardly worth the bother; simply rinse the shrimp and peel off the shells with your fingers. With larger shrimp, however, this vein (although edible) can be quite large, making it both unsightly and unappetizing. To remove both the shells and the veins, you can use either a regular serrated knife as directed below or a specifically designed deveining knife with a curved serrated edge. The tails can be left on or removed as you wish.

Butterflied shrimp are cut slightly deeper when removing the vein so they then can be spread open and sit flat with their tails sticking up. If time is scarce, your fishmonger will shell and devein the shrimp for you (be prepared to pay for his help), but be sure to ask for your shells to make Shrimp Stock (page 139).

To devein shrimp: Thoroughly rinse and drain shrimp. Using a regular serrated knife, make a slit down the outer curved portion of the shell going about $\frac{1}{8}$ to $\frac{1}{4}$ inch deep (depending on the size of the shrimp). This will split the shell and expose the greenish black intestinal vein. Peel the shell off with your fingers under cold running water to rinse away the vein. If desired, peel off the tail. Pat shells dry and either make stock or store them in a heavy-duty plastic bag and freeze for up to 2 months.

To butterfly shrimp: While severing the shell from the outside with a serrated knife, drive the blade a little deeper (about $\frac{1}{3}$ inch) into the shrimp. The incision should enable the opened section of each shrimp to lay flat with the tails standing up. If the tails fall to one side, simply cut a little deeper and try again.

GREEN BEAN AND ROASTED PEPPER SALAD

Topped with Fresh Mozzarella Balls and Grilled Chicken

YIELD: serves 6

Although the grilled chicken perfectly complements this vibrant and robust green bean salad, each can be served separately. This chilled vegetable salad, made of blanched green beans, smoky roasted peppers, meaty kalamata olives, thin strips of red onions and tiny tender white balls of fresh mozzarella cheese is quite substantial and filling without the chicken. If your time and energy are really scarce, don't roast the peppers; simply slice them into thin strips or use drained roasted peppers from a jar. Although the garbanzo beans are optional, I love their unique texture so I usually throw them in. Whenever possible, use fresh mozzarella balls for the creamiest texture and freshest flavor. Balls of different sizes can usually be found in Italian markets, specialty cheese shops and some upscale supermarkets. (If you can't find the one-ounce balls for this recipe, use a melon scoop to scoop them out of larger balls.) This gorgeous green bean salad (without the chicken) also makes a terrific first course when serving either Linguine with White Clam Sauce (page 192) or Osso Buco (page 265) as an entrée.

SPECIAL EQUIPMENT

8-quart blanching pot with built-in strainer (optional)

Strong stainless steel skewers

Indoor or outdoor grilling device or broiler pan, for chicken

INGREDIENTS

Marinated Grilled Chicken Breasts (following), optional

FOR THE DRESSING

¾ cup olive oil (mix regular and extra-virgin)

⅓ cup red wine vinegar

1 rounded teaspoon Dijon mustard

Freshly ground black pepper

¾ teaspoon salt

1 teaspoon crumbled dried oregano

FOR THE VEGETABLE MIXTURE

3 red bell peppers, roasted and peeled (page 113) and
  sliced into thin strips

½ cup extra-virgin olive oil

3 cloves garlic, minced

Freshly ground black pepper to taste

Salt, for cooking water

2 pounds green beans, ends snapped off and rinsed

1 small red onion

½ cup kalamata olives,* drained

8 to 10 tiny fresh mozzarella balls* (about 1 ounce each), halved

1 small can (10.5 ounces) garbanzo beans (chickpeas), drained, rinsed and drained again

½ cup freshly grated Reggiano Parmesan cheese

Balsamic vinegar to taste

* See section on Staples

1) *To set up:* Bring to a boil an 8-quart pot of water for the beans. While water heats, marinate chicken, if using, as directed in the following recipe.

2) *To prepare dressing:* Combine all the dressing ingredients in a bowl using a whisk. Cover and chill slightly.

3) *To dress peppers:* In a bowl, combine roasted pepper strips with olive oil, garlic and freshly ground black pepper. Toss with a fork to combine.

4) *To blanch and refresh green beans:* When the pot of water comes to a vigorous boil, set a large bowl of ice water near it. Add some salt to the boiling water and stir in the green beans. Cook until just crisp-tender, about 5 minutes. Drain and immediately plunge the beans into the ice water. Use your hands to swish the beans about to help them quickly cool so they can retain their bright green color. When cold, drain and dry on paper toweling. Refrigerate until ready to assemble.

5) *To prepare red onion:* Peel onion and cut in half through stem end. Cut each half into thin wedges and separate each wedge into thin strips. If a milder onion flavor is desired, soak onion strips in ice water to cover for 20 minutes. Drain, rinse and drain once more.

6) To assemble salad and serve: About 30 minutes before serving, combine blanched beans, red peppers (including the olive oil and garlic) and red onion strips in a large nonreactive bowl. Add olives, halved mozzarella balls, garbanzo beans, if using, and just enough dressing to coat the vegetables without drowning them. Add grated Parmesan and more fresh pepper, tossing gently to combine well. Serve salad by itself on individual plates. Or grill chicken as directed in following recipe and arrange strips of grilled chicken decoratively on top. Regardless, pass the reserved dressing at the table along with a small carafe of balsamic vinegar for drizzling on top. Always have a reliable peppermill at the table.

Marinated Grilled Chicken Breasts

YIELD: serves 6 to 8

In addition to being perfect for the green bean salad, these chicken breasts make a terrific entrée in their own right. Serve with warmed flour tortillas, cooked white rice, South-of-the-Border Beans (page 370), and Guacamole (page 104).

INGREDIENTS

4 large whole chicken breasts, skinned, boned, halved and butterflied (page 233)

Freshly ground black pepper to taste

6 tablespoons extra-virgin olive oil combined with 6 tablespoons regular olive oil

2 tablespoons balsamic vinegar

2 tablespoons red wine vinegar

¼ cup Dijon mustard

5 large cloves garlic, minced

1 teaspoon salt

3 tablespoons chopped fresh basil leaves

1 teaspoon crumbled dried oregano

Lots of freshly ground black pepper

Peanut oil or olive oil, for brushing grill

Time Management Tips

• The following steps can be done 1 or 2 days ahead and refrigerated (securely covered): Marinate chicken; roast, seed, slice and marinate peppers (bring close to room temperature before serving for best flavor); make dressing; blanch, refresh and drain string beans.

1) *To marinate chicken:* Rinse and pat dry each butterflied chicken piece and place in a glass dish. In a small bowl combine the remaining ingredients (except peanut oil) and pour over chicken, tossing with your hands to coat chicken thoroughly. Cover and marinate at least 30 minutes or overnight in the refrigerator.

2) *To grill or broil chicken:* Preheat an outdoor or indoor grill until hot and lightly brush the grid with peanut oil or olive oil. Lift each piece of chicken out of marinade, allowing any excess marinade to drip off, but don't dry them. Place on the hot grill and cook until golden and cooked through but not dry, 3 to 4 minutes per side. Alternatively, broil chicken very close to heat source until golden but not dry, 4 to 5 minutes per side.

3) *To serve:* Using a sharp knife, slice each grilled chicken piece into diagonal strips and arrange on salad as directed; or roll in tortillas or use in other recipes.

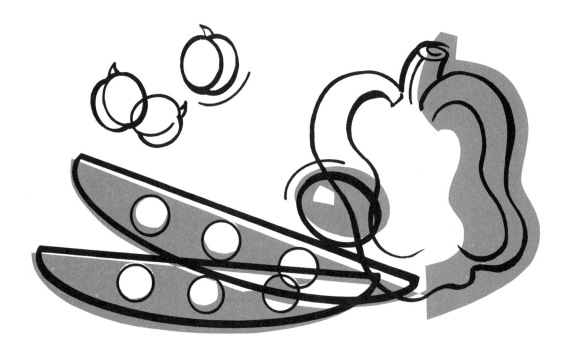

BROILED SWORDFISH

Marinated with Fresh Plum Tomatoes, Cilantro and Garlic

YIELD: serves 6

To most people, the word "marinated" means a procedure that takes hours to accomplish. This may be true for certain cuts of meat, but with delicate fish, the heightened flavors of most marinades are absorbed almost instantly. Although this marinade may be applied to the fish up to two or three hours ahead and kept in the refrigerator, only ten minutes is actually required. This recipe is not only delicious but versatile. The tomato topping is fabulous on other broiled or grilled fish as well as chicken cutlets. Serve it on garlic toasts with cocktails when entertaining, or as a simple room-temperature topping for freshly cooked pasta. As always, fresh fish is the perfect answer to both a hectic schedule and a hungry family.

SPECIAL EQUIPMENT
9x13-inch glass dish

INGREDIENTS

⅓ cup each extra-virgin olive oil and ⅓ cup regular olive oil

Strained juice from 2 juicy lemons

2 tablespoons red wine vinegar

½ to 1 teaspoon salt

4 cloves garlic, minced

2 generous teaspoons Dijon mustard

¼ cup packed chopped fresh basil leaves

2 tablespoons packed chopped fresh cilantro

Lots of freshly ground black pepper

12 ripe plum (Roma) tomatoes

6 swordfish steaks, sliced ¾ to 1 inch thick (allow 8 ounces
  for each adult and 4 to 6 ounces for children)

6 sprigs fresh basil, for garnish

1) **To prepare marinade:** Combine in a nonreactive bowl all ingredients except plum tomatoes, swordfish and garnish.

2) **To prepare tomatoes:** Cut tomatoes in half through the middle (not the stem end) gently squeeze out seeds and coarsely chop with skins on. Place them into another nonreactive bowl with about ⅓ of the marinade. Fold together to combine well, cover bowl with plastic wrap and leave at room temperature, unless preparing in advance; then refrigerate.

Time Management Tips

• The tomatoes may be assembled 1 day ahead and refrigerated. Bring close to room temperature before serving for best flavor.

• Prepare the marinade in the morning (or the day before) and pour half over the tomatoes. Reserve the remaining marinade in the refrigerator and apply the marinade to the fish when you come home from work.

3) To prepare swordfish: Rinse steaks and pat them dry. Lay them on a large glass baking dish and sprinkle liberally with freshly ground black pepper. Brush on the remaining marinade and allow to sit at room temperature for 10 minutes or cover well with plastic wrap and refrigerate for several hours.

4) To broil: Preheat broiler to very hot. Place fish on a cold broiler pan and broil close to the heat source, turning once until the fish steaks are golden but not dry, about 5 minutes per side.

5) To serve: Place fish on warmed serving plates and, using a slotted spoon, place some of marinated tomatoes on top. Serve immediately garnished with sprigs of fresh basil.

GINGER SCENTED GRILLED SALMON

YIELD: serves 6 to 8

SPECIAL EQUIPMENT
Indoor or outdoor grilling device or broiler pan

When busy, tired and hungry, the first place to head is your fish market, since with little effort, you can reward your family and friends with maximum taste and freshness. Although this recipe features salmon, this marinade would be equally enhancing to swordfish, tuna or halibut steaks. This recipe is written to serve six, but the marinade can easily be stretched to accommodate an additional pound of fish or enough for eight servings. Before you decide on a method for cooking the fish, there are a few things you should know about indoor grilling (see page 225).

And if you can't grill the fish indoors or out, simply broil it until golden on the outside and still succulent within. The perfect partners for this dish are Deliciously Simple White Rice (page 361) and Asparagus Baked with Bread Crumbs (page 211), substituting sesame seeds for the Parmesan cheese.

Time Management Tips

• The marinade can be assembled a day ahead and kept covered in the refrigerator.

INGREDIENTS
½ cup aromatic peanut oil*

3 tablespoon soy sauce*

1 tablespoon toasted sesame oil*

4 large cloves garlic, minced or pressed through a garlic press

1 tablespoon Dijon mustard

1½ teaspoons minced peeled fresh ginger root

⅓ cup minced scallions (green onions) trimmed white part and
1½ to 2 inches of the tender green

3 to 4 pounds salmon fillet, cut into 6 to 8 individual servings,
or 6 to 8 salmon steaks (allow 8 or 9 ounces of fish per adult
and 4 to 6 ounces per child)

Peanut oil or cooking spray, for grill (not needed when broiling)

* See section on Staples

1) **To prepare marinade:** In a small bowl, combine all ingredients except
salmon and oil for grill and mix thoroughly.

2) **To prepare fish:** Gently rinse fish fillets under cold water and pat dry.
Choose a glass dish that is large enough to fit fillets in a single layer. Brush
the skin side of each fillet with some of the marinade and place in the dish
(skin side down). Pour the remaining marinade over fish using a basting
brush to cover fish well. Allow to sit at room temperature for 10 minutes
or cover well with plastic wrap and refrigerate no longer than 12 hours.

3) **To grill:** (To broil, see following step.) Before heating grill, brush it well
with oil or spray with cooking spray. Heat grill or coals to hot and place
salmon (with marinade left on) on the hot grill. Cook salmon a total of
7 to 10 minutes per inch of thickness, turning once. When done, salmon
will be beautifully seared on the outside. For medium-rare, it should
retain a deeper orange tinge at the very center. If desired, cook until pink
throughout but avoid overcooking or the fish will be dry.

4) **To broil:** Preheat the broiler until very hot. Lay each fillet (with marinade
left on) on a cold broiler pan (skin side up). Broil close to heat source
turning once, until crispy and the fish flakes easily but is not at all dry, 4
to 5 minutes per side.

Variation: Oven Roasted Whole Fish

To prepare and marinate fish: To serve 6, ask the fishmonger to gut and
scale 3 whole striped bass or red snappers (1½ to 1¾ pounds each) leaving
the heads and tails intact. When you get home, thoroughly rinse and dry the
fish. Double ginger marinade ingredients in preceding recipe. Lay fish in a
9x13-inch glass dish and brush the insides of the fish liberally with marinade.
Using a sharp knife, make several slashes (⅓ inch deep) in the thickest sections of each side to promote even cooking. Insert a few whole trimmed scal-

TIPS

FROM A TEACHER

Indoor Grilling

A word to the wise about indoor
grilling: Check out your ventilation
system! Believe me—it's easier than
you think to set off your smoke alarm
while cooking. (After more than a few
episodes with my local fire department
I finally had that noisy fan fixed!) I don't
recommend grilling indoors unless
your kitchen has exhaust fans (that
work) to remove excess smoke and any
cooking smells that would tend to
linger for days in a home without
proper ventilation. When a recipe sug-
gests that you use a grill, if necessary,
you can almost duplicate the intensity
of the grill by broiling the food very
close to the heat source. However,
when doing so, it's wise to broil with
the oven door ajar to keep an eye on
things.

The general rule for cooking fish is 10
minutes of cooking per each inch of flesh.
However, when grilling, if your coals are
too hot, delicate fish flesh can take much less
time to cook.

lions (green onions) into each cavity and pour the rest of the marinade over the fish, turning to coat well. Let marinate as directed in recipe.

To roast fish: Position oven rack to the upper third and preheat the oven to 475°F for 30 minutes. Meanwhile, line the bottom of a large shallow baking sheet with aluminum foil (shiny side up to reflect heat toward fish) and brush foil with some of the marinade. Place fish on the foil, side by side, and roast until the skin is golden and blistered and the flesh flakes easily with a fork but is not dry, 20 to 25 minutes. If the flesh is finished before the outside is crisp, briefly run the fish under the broiler.

To serve: Divide each fish in half by driving a sharp knife straight down through the waist. If you want to remove the head, simply cut it off, but first pull the sweet nugget of "cheek meat" out and place on one (lucky person's) plate. Serve hot. You might remind your guests that after eating the top fillet, they should turn over the fish so the bones face the plate to enjoy the remaining flesh.

TIPS

FROM A TEACHER

〜〜〜

If Something's Fishy

I'm very picky when it comes to fresh fish. Although most of us remember holding our noses when entering the neighborhood fish market as children, fresh fish itself should not smell fishy. Each fish has its individual scent, but in all fresh fish, the aroma should be sweet, clean and barely discernable. If the fish is whole, the eyes should be perfectly clear. Lift the flaps that cover the gills on each side of the head. The gills should be a deep, bright red (cloudy eyes and brownish gills indicate that the fish has been hanging around the docks or the fish market too long). Although cold storage can help prevent spoilage, once the fish leaves the water, every hour means a loss of fresh flavor.

A general rule is: Never take fresh fish home from the market without smelling it first. Doing this will save you the trip when returning it in a huff, and you will be letting your fishmonger know loud and clear that you're a discriminating consumer who expects quality. As a result, the next time, he or she won't be as likely to give you yesterday's fish that didn't sell. Also, if the fish tastes great, let your fishmonger know! Shopkeepers (like everyone) enjoy receiving a show of appreciation regarding the quality of their work. This will encourage them to seek your approval again and again by keeping the quality high.

CRUSTY CAJUN TUNA

YIELD: serves 6

When creating this recipe for my family, I worried that the combination of seafood and Cajun wouldn't appeal to my children. But I took a chance. As the fish was cooking, each of my three kids strolled into the kitchen with their nostrils quivering to ask "What smells so good?" At dinner that night, my ten-year-old Ben (for the first time) ate an entire eight ounces of fish. Needless to say, dinner was a big hit with everyone. Although this recipe is written with tuna in mind, don't hesitate to substitute another firm fish such as swordfish, salmon, halibut or bluefish. In addition, jumbo shrimp (either in or out of their shells), seasoned this way and skewered through the body and tail before either grilling or broiling, are terrific. Although this recipe features fish, my Cajun Spice Blend is equally enhancing to chicken (see variation following). Before grilling indoors, see page 225.

SPECIAL EQUIPMENT

Indoor or outdoor grilling device or broiler pan

Long perforated metal spatula with wooden handle, for turning fish on the grill

INGREDIENTS

⅔ cup aromatic peanut oil* or extra-virgin olive oil

4 or 5 large cloves garlic, minced or pressed through a garlic press

6 tuna steaks (about 8 ounces each for adults or 4 to 6 ounces per child), sliced ¾ to 1 inch thick

Not-Too-Hot Cajun Spice Blend (page 79), for seasoning fish

Freshly ground black pepper to taste

Peanut oil or cooking spray*, for grill

1 to 2 juicy lemons, at room temperature, cut into wedges (see following tip), for garnish

* See section on Staples

*Perfectly Intact Seedless
Lemon Wedges*

If you've ever been shot in the eye by a stray squirt of fresh lemon juice, you'll appreciate this little tidbit of information. After slicing a lemon into wedges, you will notice a tough white membrane attached to the peak of some of the wedges. This membrane makes it difficult to locate and extract the seeds and causes the lemon to squirt when squeezed. The trick is to remove the membrane: First, roll each lemon on the kitchen counter to centralize both the juice and pits.

Using a sharp paring knife, cut each lemon (through stem end) into 4 to 6 wedges. Slice off the tough membrane located at the peak of each wedge and, using the tip of the knife, carefully pick out the pits before serving as a garnish or squeezing.

1) To prepare garlic oil: Heat ⅔ cup oil in a small saucepan over medium heat. When just hot, reduce heat to low, add minced garlic and sauté until just softened and fragrant, 30 seconds to 1 minute. Set aside to cool.

2) To prepare fish: Line a large baking sheet with waxed paper. Rinse steaks, pat dry and lay in a single layer on the prepared sheet. Sprinkle steaks liberally with Cajun Spice Blend and, using a pastry brush, paint each side of steaks generously with some of the garlic oil. Grind on some fresh black pepper and let sit at room temperature for 10 minutes or cover well with plastic wrap and refrigerate for up to 12 hours.

3) To grill or broil: Before heating grill, brush it well with peanut oil or spray with cooking spray. Heat grill or coals to hot and place the seasoned fish on the hot grill. Cook each steak 8 to 10 minutes per inch of thickness, turning once, basting with remaining garlic mixture. When done (for medium-rare), the fish will be beautifully seared on the outside, and the flesh will still retain some deep pink color. Avoid overcooking or the fish will be dry. To broil, preheat broiler to very hot, place fish on a cold broiler pan and broil very close to the heat source, 4 to 5 minutes. Then baste, turn and continue broiling until golden, crisp but not dry, another 4 to 5 minutes.

Variation with Chicken

For the fish, substitute 6 halved, skinless, boneless chicken breasts that have been butterflied and flattened between sheets of waxed paper (page 233). Season as directed in tuna recipe and grill as described, reducing the cooking time if necessary so the chicken remains succulent. To broil chicken breasts that are split, with bones and skin intact, you might need a bit more oil for basting. Place them on a cold broiler pan under a preheated broiler 4 to 5 inches from the heat source, and cook turning once until golden, blistered and cooked throughout. Baste occasionally and be careful not to overcook which leaves chicken dry.

WHOLE RED SNAPPER

Simmered in Black Bean Sauce

YIELD: serves 6

Presenting a gorgeous whole fish on a platter bathed in this outrageous mahogany-colored sauce gives new meaning to the term "fast food." Although this meal is quick to prepare, it tastes slow-cooked good. Chinese fermented black beans (available in Asian markets and also called "salty" black beans) are tiny soybeans that have been packed, fermented and preserved in salt. Although some cooks recommend soaking them in warm water before using, I feel no need for this provided the beans are in good supple condition. Simply rinse the beans thoroughly through a sieve and then pat the them dry. Once the jar or bag is opened, store beans in the refrigerator to best preserve flavor and texture. If the beans should become dry, soak them in warm water (after rinsing) for fifteen minutes or so, until softened but not mushy. Serve the snapper with cooked white rice and Fried Chinese Sesame Noodles with Duck Sauce (page 204).

SPECIAL EQUIPMENT

12- to 14-inch nonstick skillet with a lid

Long perforated fish spatula or 2 regular spatulas to turn fish

Large deep platter

INGREDIENTS

2 whole red snappers or striped bass (2½ to 3 pounds each
  prior to gutting)

2 scallions (green onions), trimmed of roots and dry ends of greens

2 slices unpeeled fresh ginger root (each about the size of a quarter)

½ cup cornstarch

About ½ cup aromatic peanut oil,* for searing and sautéing

FOR THE SAUCE

6 large cloves garlic, minced

2 tablespoons minced peeled fresh ginger root

½ cup fermented black beans,* rinsed, patted dry and chopped

1 cup minced scallions (green onions), trimmed white part
  with 1½ to 2 inches of the tender green (3 or 4 bunches)

½ cup soy sauce*

½ cup dry sherry

1 cup water

1½ teaspoons sugar

Time Management Tips

• All vegetables for the sauce can be assembled 1 day ahead and stored separately in well-covered bowls in the refrigerator.

1 tablespoon cornstarch dissolved with 3 tablespoons cold water

1½ tablespoons toasted sesame oil*

* See section on Staples

1) ***To prepare fish:*** Have your fishmonger gut and scale fish leaving the heads and tails intact. Rinse fish and pat dry inside and out. Using a sharp knife, slash each fish on both sides at the thickest midsection going ⅓ inch deep. This will help the fish cook evenly. Place 1 whole scallion with 1 slice ginger in the cavity of each fish.

2) ***To dredge and sear fish:*** Spread out cornstarch on a shallow baking sheet. Heat a 12- to 14-inch nonstick skillet over medium-high heat. When hot, add a thin layer of peanut oil to coat the bottom of the skillet. While oil heats, dredge 1 whole fish from the nose to the tail in the cornstarch. Lift fish and allow any excess cornstarch to fall off without shaking. Sear fish in hot oil on each side until golden but not cooked through, about 3 minutes per side. Using two spatulas, lift browned fish from skillet and lay on a platter. Repeat the procedure with the second fish adding more oil if necessary.

3) ***To prepare sauce:*** Wipe out skillet and return to medium-high heat. When hot, add a few tablespoons peanut oil. When oil is hot, add minced garlic, ginger and prepared black beans. Stir to coat with oil and stir-fry until very fragrant and just softened, about 2 minutes. Add minced scallions and stir-fry until scallions are softened, about 2 minutes. Then add soy sauce, sherry, water and sugar to skillet and bring to a simmer.

4) ***To simmer fish:*** Carefully lower both seared fish into the sauce (side by side) and spoon some sauce over fish. (If either fish is too long, cut off the tail with a pair of kitchen scissors.) Cover and simmer over low heat until cooked through, 15 to 20 minutes. Using either a long perforated fish spatula or 2 spatulas, carefully lift fish from sauce onto a long, deep heated serving platter.

5) ***To finish sauce:*** Stir dissolved cornstarch and pour into hot sauce along with toasted sesame oil. Bring to a brisk simmer while stirring to thicken. Ladle sauce over fish and serve immediately with white rice.

CHICKEN KABOBS

With Crunchy Peanut Sauce

YIELD: serves 6

This skewered chicken dish is a peanut lover's dream come true. Half of the garlicky peanut butter sauce is used to coat the chicken; the rest is embellished with crunchy chopped peanuts and minced scallions to become the dipping sauce. Although you can make this sauce in the food processor, I prefer the emulsifying capability of a blender. This recipe is the perfect quick meal that sacrifices nothing in the taste department. In fact, you can save even more time by asking your butcher to debone and butterfly your chicken (but ask him for the bones to save for stock!). Serve these golden kabobs with a crisp green salad and cooked aromatic white rice (for information see page 363).

SPECIAL EQUIPMENT
Blender

4 sturdy stainless steel skewers
(16 inches long)

INGREDIENTS

2½ pounds skinless, boneless chicken breasts, butterflied but
   not flattened (page 233)

3 tablespoons strained fresh lemon juice

¼ cup soy sauce*

⅓ cup aromatic peanut oil*

1 teaspoon toasted sesame oil*

⅔ cup smooth peanut butter (commercially prepared)

½ cup mild flavored honey

6 cloves garlic, chopped

½ cup plus ⅓ cup packed chopped scallions (green onions),
   trimmed white parts and 1½ to 2 inches of the tender green

⅓ cup chopped salted cocktail peanuts

Cooked white rice (preferably an aromatic rice such as basmati*),
   for accompaniment

* See section on Staples

Time Management Tips

• The chicken can be coated in sauce and skewered 1 day ahead and refrigerated. However, this may lengthen broiling time a bit so adjust this accordingly.

• If sauce has been prepared ahead and refrigerated, bring to room temperature before serving or heat in the microwave on low power until no longer chilled, but not hot. Under these circumstances, don't garnish the sauce with the additional minced scallions until just before serving.

*1) **To prepare chicken:*** Rinse butterflied chicken breasts, pat dry and cut them into chunks using sharp kitchen scissors. In the container of a blender combine remaining ingredients except the ⅓ cup minced scallions and salted peanuts. Blend until smooth, shaking the blender a bit to encourage the mixture to catch in the blades and purée uniformly. Pour ½ cup of the mixture over the chicken and use your hands to coat the pieces thoroughly. Transfer the remaining mixture to a bowl for the dipping sauce.

*2) **To finish sauce:*** Stir chopped peanuts and all but 1 tablespoon of the ⅓ cup minced scallions into the reserved peanut sauce. Sprinkle the remaining tablespoon scallions on top of the sauce and set aside.

*3) **To set up to broil:*** Preheat the broiler for 15 minutes with the oven rack positioned to the highest shelf. Meanwhile, skewer coated chicken chunks on 4 long stainless steel skewers, allowing ¼ inch between each piece. Place filled skewers on a cold broiler pan.

*4) **To broil:*** Broil skewered chicken very close to the heat source until cooked through, golden and blistered (but not dry), turning once, 5 to 7 minutes per side. If the pieces become golden outside before the insides are cooked sufficiently (or if the sauced chicken should "pop" from the flame), transfer pan to the next lowest shelf and continue broiling until cooked through.

*5) **To serve:*** Using the tines of a fork, push chicken from skewers onto a warmed serving platter. Serve chicken hot with rice and pass the peanut sauce at the table.

Boneless and butterflied chicken breasts are expensive, as are those thinly pounded for cutlets. You pay for labor but you don't even get your bones for stock. With a little practice and patience, you can prepare the breasts at home. The first tip is to buy whole breasts, which are easier to bone than halved breasts. And when butterflying boned chicken breasts, make sure to keep the blade of your knife parallel to the work surface and not tilted down. This is the best way to avoid cutting too deep. For the job of boning, butterflying and flattening the flesh, you will need a sharp 4- to 6-inch boning knife, an 8-inch carving knife and a heavy meat mallet.

To remove skin and fat: Pull off skin and any excess fat or translucent material and discard. If desired, snip fat and skin into small pieces and freeze in a heavy- duty plastic bag for making rendered chicken fat (page 110); otherwise discard.

To remove breastbone: Place whole chicken breast (skin side down) on work surface with the tip of the breast facing away from you. On the center of the bottom rim near you, you'll see a whitish piece of cartilage, laying directly over the breastbone. Place the blade of a knife on the cartilage and with a firm (but not hard) blow, knock your hand against the dull side of the blade so it will penetrate the cartilage without splintering the breastbone. Bend both sides of the breast down and away from each other to open the cartilage and expose the thin, curved breastbone. Use your thumb to pry under and around the bone to release it (this sometimes takes a bit of muscle). Lift out bone and run your thumb down the center of the breast under the remaining pieces of cartilage as well as the translucent skin to release both from the flesh. Remove and discard cartilage.

To remove wishbone: Move your fingers along the flesh at the base of the breast and feel around to locate the severed wishbone. Once located, pull and twist it out.

To remove rib cage: With the breast in the same position (ribs up), run the thin blade of your sharp boning knife under the left ribs (cutting toward the bone, not into the flesh). Remove rib cage on the left breast. To remove ribs on the right breast, insert the tip of the boning knife under the thin bone that stands alone (it will be pointing away from you toward your left). Run the blade from that point, all the way under the rib cage (bringing the blade toward you), releasing the bones in one single piece. Freeze bones (including the

How to Skin, Bone and Butterfly Chicken Breasts

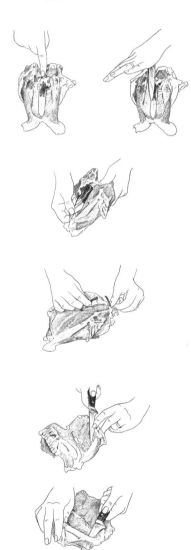

breastbone) for stock. Use the blade of your knife to cut down the center seam, dividing the breast into two halves.

To butterfly and flatten a boned chicken breast half: "Butterfly" means to open and lay flat a chicken breast (as well as steaks, shrimp and so forth), resulting in a shape that looks like a butterfly. Turn the breast half, boned side up. You will notice that one side is thicker than the other. This thicker portion is the tenderloin of breast meat. Position the breast so that the tenderloin is opposite your working hand (on the left if you're right handed). Place your other hand on top of the breast to keep it in place. Using your working hand, position the blade of a sharp carving knife parallel to your work surface, at the lower long thin side of the flesh (not at the fatter tenderloin). Carefully, while keeping the blade absolutely parallel, drive the blade through the flesh, in a smooth up, down and out stroke leaving about ½ inch of flesh attached at the opposite end. Open the breast at the split and lay it flat (don't worry that one side is thicker than the other). If after opening you feel that you didn't go in far enough, simply use the blade to slice a bit deeper.

To pound a butterflied chicken breast: Tear off a sheet of waxed paper, large enough to fold over and enclose the breast half with a generous amount of space all around. Lay the opened breast half (boned side up) 1½ inches off the center of the waxed paper and fold the remaining paper over it, allowing 1½ inches to be empty at the fold. Using your meat mallet, give the chicken flesh several whacks starting at the center or thicker portion and going out toward the edge of the flesh. As you get to the thinner sections, you should no longer "whack" but only "tap" with the mallet. Run your hand over the top layer of paper and, if not level, give those higher areas several more soft taps with the mallet (always going from the center toward the outer edge). Open the package and carefully peel off your butterflied chicken breast half. Repeat with the remaining half using a new sheet of waxed paper. Use prepared chicken breasts as directed in your recipe.

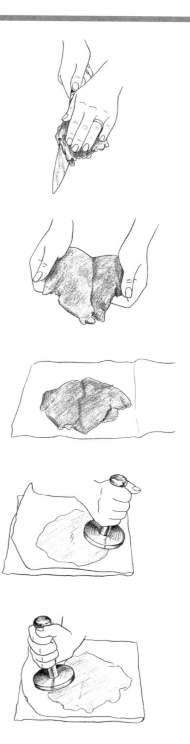

ASIAN CHICKEN

In Scallion Sauce with Shiitakes

YIELD: serves 8 to 10

A perfect dish for easy entertaining or a delicious family meal. The chicken is simmered in an incredible sauce that's loaded with ginger, garlic and scallions. When the sauced chicken is served simply over cooked white rice, you'll find it hard to finish your dinner—you'll be so busy giving everyone second helpings! If you don't have time to chop the scallions, just cut them up coarsely and pulse in a food processor fitted with the steel blade. For a variation, try this sauce with fillets of sole, instead of chicken. Even cleaned and butterflied shrimp (page 218) would be fantastic. In these cases, however, the cooking time will be slightly shorter since fish cooks so quickly. The ideal accompaniment for this Asian dish is Fried Chinese Sesame Noodles with Duck Sauce (page 204).

SPECIAL EQUIPMENT

12- to 14-inch nonstick skillet (preferably with a lid)

Nonabrasive turning spatula (preferably 2)

INGREDIENTS

About ½ cup aromatic peanut oil* as needed

5 large cloves garlic, minced

1½ tablespoons minced, peeled ginger root

2 cups chopped scallions (green onions), trimmed white parts with 1½ to 2 inches of the tender green (6 or 7 bunches)

½ to ¾ pounds fresh shiitake mushrooms, stems removed, caps wiped and thinly sliced, *or* generous ½ cup (⅔ ounce) reconstituted dried shiitake mushrooms (page 131) and ½ pound sliced fresh button mushrooms

¾ cup medium dry sherry

1 cup soy sauce*

¾ cup water

5 whole chicken breasts, skinned, boned, halved, butterflied and flattened slightly (page 233)

About 1 cup cornstarch, spread on a plate

1 tablespoon toasted sesame oil*

Cooked white rice, for accompaniment

* See section on Staples

Time Management Tips

- All of the vegetables for the sauce can be cleaned, sliced or chopped 1 day ahead and kept well covered in separate bowls in the refrigerator.

- The dish may be prepared and assembled (but not simmered) 2 hours in advance and kept at room temperature until ready to simmer and serve. If necessary, the dish may be completed totally 1 day ahead and once cool, covered and refrigerated. Reheat very gently and be careful not overcook the chicken. Always garnish just before serving.

Q AND A

Q. What's the difference between scallions and green onions ?

A. Nothing. It depends on where you live. In the East, they're called scallions and in the West, green onions. If you live in England, they're "spring onions."

1) To prepare scallion-mushroom sauce: Heat a 12- to 14-inch nonstick skillet over medium-high heat and, when hot, add 2 tablespoons of the peanut oil. When oil is hot, add garlic, ginger, 1⅔ cups of the scallions and all the mushrooms. Cook, stirring constantly, until softened, 3 to 5 minutes. Scrape mushroom mixture into a medium bowl. Deglaze pan with a little of the sherry to release any bits that cling to the skillet and pour this into mushroom mixture. Add soy sauce, water and remaining sherry mushroom mixture and set aside.

2) To dredge and brown chicken: Return skillet to medium-high heat and add more peanut oil. While oil heats, dredge in the cornstarch only as many chicken pieces as can be browned at one time and shake off excess. When oil is hot, add chicken pieces in a single layer without crowding and brown on both sides but don't cook through. Remove to a plate as you continue to brown the remaining chicken, adding more peanut oil as necessary.

3) To assemble and finish cooking: Pour out any excess oil from skillet and return to low heat. Add browned chicken and pour reserved scallion-mushroom sauce over chicken, covering the pieces well. Bring to a simmer over low heat, cover securely with lid or aluminum foil and continue to cook very gently until sauce has thickened nicely and chicken is cooked through, about 10 minutes. Uncover and drizzle with toasted sesame oil.

4) To serve: Place chicken and sauce in a warmed serving bowl (preferably one that's shaped low and wide). Garnish with the reserved ⅓ cup chopped scallions. Serve piping hot with cooked white rice.

Garlic comes in several sizes and colors. "Elephant" garlic, actually a form of leek, has huge cloves in comparison to regular all-purpose garlic, but the taste is much less assertive; try it raw with dip. The regular garlic is best for cooking, and the pure white variety is easier to peel than the heads with a purplish tinge. But whatever you buy make sure the cloves are firm and throw them out when they soften.

If you cook with loads of garlic (as I do), peel a few heads at the beginning of each week and refrigerate the cloves in a screw-top jar. This is a real time-saver. Remove any cloves that begin to "sprout" at the center and use them right away. If the sprout is light green, small and thin, it won't interfere with flavor. But if the sprout is long and a darker shade of green, it tends to impart a bitter flavor; to remove it, cut the peeled clove in half lengthwise and pull the sprout down and out.

To crack and peel garlic: Pull the desired amount of cloves away from the head. Lay clove on one of its flat sides, and apply pressure to the clove with the widest section of a chef's knife until you hear a "crack." Lift blade and remove skin. If this doesn't work the first time, try once more. If you plan to chop or mince the garlic, it doesn't matter how hard you smash it, but if your recipe calls for a whole, slivered or bruised clove, or if you plan on refrigerating peeled cloves for future use, take care to press gently.

To bruise garlic: When you want a garlic flavor to penetrate a shallow layer of cooking oil when panfrying, it's necessary to bruise the whole clove so its robust flavor can be released. To do this, apply a bit more pressure on the flat side of the knife while cracking the clove. Remove skin and hopefully you will have cracked open a small slit in the clove without actually crushing it. A crushed clove is more likely to burn in the hot oil.

To flatten, chop or mince garlic: After peeling cloves, slice off the tough root ends. Press down on each clove with a chef's knife, as you did before peeling and smash so it lays perfectly flat. Then use the sharp blade of the chef's knife to go back and forth rhythmically over the garlic until it is chopped or minced to the desired consistency. (See page 62, How to be a Better Chopper.)

MEDITERRANEAN GARLIC CHICKEN

Simmered with Cognac and Tomatoes

YIELD: serves 8

SPECIAL EQUIPMENT

Heavy meat cleaver or sharp pair of kitchen shears

5- or 6-quart heavy-bottomed Dutch oven with a tight-fitting lid

Spatter shield (optional)

Long fireplace matches

Of all my chicken recipes, this one is truly my favorite. Loaded with garlic, this dish is robust in taste, light in texture and simple to prepare. (When pressed for time, ask your butcher to cut up the chickens, but remind him to reserve the backs separately for stock.) And when you omit the optional crushed tomatoes, the chicken takes on an entirely different personality. I prefer canned crushed tomatoes because they give a more intense color to the sauce. If you're concerned with the hefty amount of garlic in this recipe, remember that garlic is both delicious and incredibly good for you! (For tips on peeling and chopping, see page 237; a food processor will also simplify the job.) And if you've never torched a dish before, don't be afraid. Just be sure not to have your face or hair over the pot when igniting and use a long wooden matchstick. The flame will die out within a minute or so, leaving only fabulous flavor (no alcohol) from the Cognac. Serve the chicken ladled over hot pasta strands or over Deliciously Simple White Rice (page 361).

INGREDIENTS

3 frying chickens (3 pounds each)

Salt and freshly ground black pepper

½ cup olive oil

18 to 20 garlic cloves, finely chopped

⅓ cup brandy (preferably Cognac)

⅓ cup Rich Chicken Stock or "Doctored" Canned Chicken Broth (page 140 for both)

2 generous cups canned crushed tomatoes (optional)

Kosher salt or sea salt to taste

⅓ cup chopped fresh basil leaves

3 tablespoons chopped flat-leaf Italian parsley

Cooked pasta or rice, for accompaniment

Time Management Tips

- Using an extra skillet to brown the chicken pieces is a real time-saver. Use additional oil as necessary.

- This dish can be fully assembled a couple of hours ahead and left at room temperature until it's time to reheat and serve.

1) **To cut up chicken:** Cut up each chicken into 8 pieces as directed on page 233. Rinse chicken pieces and dry completely. Using a heavy cleaver or sharp kitchen shears, cut each breast half widthwise in half and cut each thigh into 2 pieces. Remove the wing tips and hack off the tips of the leg bone as well. Remove the skin, if desired, and sprinkle chicken pieces lightly with salt and pepper. Store wing and leg tips with chicken backs in the freezer for stock.

2) **To brown chicken:** Heat a 5- or 6-quart Dutch oven over medium heat with olive oil. When oil is hot, add chicken pieces in a single layer (without crowding) and brown well on both sides in batches. (Use a spatter shield to prevent the oil from popping out!) As each batch browns, remove the pieces to a platter. When completed, pour oil out of pot but don't wipe out the interior.

3) **To assemble and flambé:** Return chicken to Dutch oven, along with any juices that have accumulated on the platter. Place over medium heat and sprinkle with about ¾ of the chopped garlic cloves. Stir gently to incorporate the garlic throughout. Pour brandy over chicken and carefully ignite with a long-handled match. (Stand back as the mixture flames, subsides and dies out completely, about 1 minute.) Stir in chicken stock with crushed tomatoes, if using, and cover pot. Bring mixture to a simmer, reduce heat to very low and cook until tender, about 20 minutes (avoid overcooking).

4) **To finish and serve:** Scatter the remaining chopped garlic into chicken mixture. Grind in additional black pepper and add a light sprinkling of coarse salt. Carefully stir in chopped basil and parsley and remove from heat. Ladle chicken into a deep, warmed serving bowl and serve piping hot over cooked pasta or rice.

Q AND A

Q. Is garlic really good for you?

A. Although garlic has for centuries enjoyed a reputation for having "magical" healing powers, recent medical studies (done by American, European and Asian health professionals) have recognized and documented these most incredible healing powers of garlic. The most valued property of garlic is a substance known as "allicin," which is an effective antibacterial-antifungal agent that helps ward off strep throat, dysentery, some staph infections and even typhoid! In addition, the cleansing power of allicin is equally impressive on the blood and cardiovascular system.

GOLDEN HERB-RUBBED CORNISH HENS

YIELD: *serves 6*

SPECIAL EQUIPMENT
Strong pair of kitchen scissors or
poultry shears

9x13-inch glass baking dish

1 or 2 shallow baking sheets and
roasting racks

These small, tender and fragrant Cornish hens are elegant enough for enter-taining yet simple enough for a weeknight after work. By marinating the birds the night before, you will virtually eliminate all the preparation time. But the specialness of this dish really does depend on the use of fresh herbs, which fortunately are now readily available in upscale produce markets as well as at most Asian groceries. Whenever possible, purchase fresh hens for they taste fresher and are much chubbier than the frozen ones. Most of the tiny fowl sold as Rock Cornish hens are frozen. Perdue Farms, however, markets a wonderful fresh Cornish hen that weighs in at less than two pounds, but it's not available nationally. Another option is a baby chicken (*poussin*) that weighs about a pound, but these are quite expensive. For accompani-ments, I suggest Garlic-Sautéed Cherry Tomatoes (page 324) and Deliciously Simple Long Grain White Rice (page 361).

INGREDIENTS

¼ cup strained fresh lemon juice (from about 2 juicy lemons)

6 tablespoons *each* extra-virgin olive oil and regular olive oil

1½ tablespoons *each* chopped fresh tarragon, rosemary and thyme leaves

6 large cloves garlic, minced

1 teaspoon salt

Lots of freshly ground black pepper

6 Cornish hens or baby chickens (1 to 1⅓ pounds each), preferably fresh

Kosher or sea salt to taste

1) To prepare marinade: In a small bowl, combine all ingredients (except hens and salt) and set aside.

2) To prepare hens: Wash hens and pat dry. Turn each hen (back up) and use sharp kitchen scissors to cut down each side of backbone and remove it. Release breastbone as directed in How to Bone Chicken Breasts, page 233 and spread chicken so it lays flat (shape will resemble a butterfly). Store backbones with breastbones in a heavy-duty plastic bag in the freezer for stock. Then carefully insert 2 fingers all the way down the breast (between the skin and the flesh) of each bird to loosen it, being careful not to tear the skin. Place hens in a large glass dish (it's OK to stack them if necessary).

3) To apply marinade: Give reserved herb mixture a good stir and pour it over hens. Using your hands, turn each hen and rub in the marinade to coat well. Then gently lift the loosened skin and using your other hand, scoop up some of the surrounding marinade and spread it between the skin and flesh. Let hens marinate at room temperature for 10 minutes or cover with plastic wrap and refrigerate overnight. (Let sit out of the refrigerator to "temp up" a bit before roasting.)

4) To roast: Preheat the oven to 400°F and place a wire rack over a large shallow baking sheet or roasting pan (use 2 sheets and racks if needed). Place hens (skin side up) on rack(s) and sprinkle skin lightly with coarse salt. Roast until golden, crisp and tender (but not dry), 35 to 45 minutes. If using 2 sheets, roast in the upper and lower thirds of the oven switching shelf positions after half the roasting time.

Q. What's the difference between a Rock Cornish hen and a baby chicken?

A. The little Rock Cornish hens are a crossbreed of the English Cornish sire and the American Plymouth Rock hen. (Purdue Farms dropped the name "rock" because of the frozen connotation.) Baby chickens (poussins *in French*) are just very young fattened chickens, although in France the term poussin *is sometimes used for a small German breed as well.*

QUICK MARINARA SAUCE

For Seafood, Chicken or Whatever

YIELD: about 8 cups sauce; serves 6

SPECIAL EQUIPMENT
2½-quart heavy-bottomed saucepan

4-quart heavy-bottomed saucepan, Dutch oven or deep-sided skillet with a tight-fitting lid, for seafood and chicken variations

Spatter shield (optional), for chicken variation

This sauce is not only quick, it's also hearty, robust and very satisfying on those nights when you're truly too busy to cook but have a hungry gang to feed. Each of the following trio of dishes can be tossed together in about thirty minutes—much less time, if you've made your sauce ahead. Open a few more cans to make a double or triple batch of sauce; divide and refrigerate for other meals during the week. The sauce can be prepared with seafood one night, with chicken on another and with chopped onions, crisp bacon and peas on yet another; each lends its own distinctive flavors to the sauce. Or you can just toss it, as is, over freshly cooked pasta. Any of the following variations should be served over cooked pasta or rice to catch the sauce and make the meal even more substantial.

INGREDIENTS

2 tablespoons extra-virgin olive oil

6 large cloves garlic, minced

1 can (28 ounces) crushed tomatoes

1 can (29 ounces) tomato purée

1 can (28 ounces) whole plum (Roma) tomatoes drained and coarsely cut up

½ cup chopped fresh basil leaves

⅛ teaspoon crushed red pepper flakes (optional)

Freshly ground black pepper

Heat a heavy-bottomed 2½-quart saucepan over medium heat. When hot, add olive oil. When oil is hot but not smoking, add ⅔ of the minced garlic, stir and *immediately* stir in both crushed and puréed tomatoes; combine well. Bring to a brisk simmer, reduce heat to low and simmer 15 minutes with lid ajar. Add cut-up plum tomatoes, chopped basil, the remaining cloves minced garlic, crushed red pepper flakes, if using, and a generous amount of freshly ground black pepper. Bring back to a full simmer, reduce heat and cook gently, 5 minutes more. Serve over pasta or as directed in recipes following.

Quick Seafood Marinara

YIELD: serves 6

If you're really busy, purchase the shrimp already shelled and deveined, but remind your fishmonger to reserve the shells for you. Freeze them, and when time allows, make shrimp stock.

INGREDIENTS

1 recipe Quick Marinara Sauce (preceding)

18 littleneck clams in shells, rinsed well and drained

1½ pounds large shrimp, shelled and deveined with the tails intact (page 218)

Freshly ground black pepper

Cooked pasta of choice or cooked white rice, for accompaniment

Prepare marinara sauce and, if made in advance, return to a full simmer over low heat. Add clams and raise heat to high until mixture comes to a boil. Cover, reduce heat slightly and cook briskly until clams begin to open and exude their juices into sauce, about 5 minutes. (Shake pot occasionally to redistribute clams.) Reduce heat to low and stir in shrimp. Cook uncovered until shrimp are just pink and lose their opaque look, about 3 minutes. (Avoid overcooking for best texture, since the shrimp will continue to cook in the hot sauce.) Remove and discard any unopened clams. Serve hot over cooked pasta or rice.

Quick Chicken Marinara

YIELD: serves 6

It won't take you much time to cut up two chickens (and you could do it a day ahead for convenience). If you ask your butcher to do it, however, specifically request that he remove and reserve the backs separately for you to freeze for stock.

INGREDIENTS

1 recipe Quick Marinara Sauce (preceding)

2 chickens (3 to 3½ pounds each), cut into 8 pieces (page 233), rinsed, patted very dry and skinned, if desired

Salt and freshly ground black pepper to taste

About ¼ cup olive oil as needed

½ cup dry white or red wine

½ to 1 teaspoon crumbled dried oregano

Cooked pasta of choice or cooked white rice, for accompaniment

1) *To prepare sauce:* Prepare marinara sauce and set aside or, if sauce was made in advance, return to a simmer over low heat. Remove from heat.

2) *To prepare chicken:* Sprinkle chicken lightly with salt and freshly ground black pepper. In a 10-inch deep-sided skillet, heat a thin layer of olive oil over medium heat. Brown chicken pieces in batches on all sides and remove to a platter as you continue to brown the rest. (Use a spatter shield to help prevent hot oil from popping!) Pour out any oil left in skillet and return skillet to medium heat. Add wine and, as it bubbles, scrape up any browned bits of caramelized chicken from the bottom of the skillet and pour this into the sauce.

3) *To assemble and serve:* Bring sauce to a full simmer over low heat. Add oregano and browned chicken along with any accumulated juices from the platter. Return to a full simmer, cover skillet and turn heat to low. Simmer chicken until tender, about 20 minutes. Grind in additional black pepper and serve hot over rice or pasta.

Quick Amatriciana Sauce

YIELD: serves 6

This savory tomato sauce is named after Amatrice, Italy, where it originated. It traditionally includes pancetta (salt-cured, unsmoked Italian bacon), but I usually use regular bacon since it's always in my refrigerator. The addition of sautéed onions and green peas makes this sauce extra delicious and since you're likely to have all the ingredients on hand, it's great for unexpected company. Freshly cooked rigatoni noodles are the best choice to catch this sauce perfectly. Also, when this version is merged with the preceding Chicken Marinara, you will have yet another delicious flavor combination.

INGREDIENTS

1 recipe Quick Marinara Sauce (preceding)

4 or 5 thick slices bacon (4 to 6 ounces), cut into ¼-inch dice or snipped into small pieces using kitchen shears

1 cup minced yellow onion

10 ounces frozen peas, thawed under hot running water and drained

⅓ cup freshly grated Reggiano Parmesan cheese, plus more for garnish

Freshly ground black pepper to taste

Cooked rigatoni or other pasta of choice, for accompaniment

1) *To prepare sauce:* Prepare marinara sauce and set aside or, if sauce was made in advance, return to a simmer over low heat. Remove from heat. Cook diced bacon in a medium skillet over medium heat until almost crisp, about 7 minutes; drain on paper towels. Pour out all but 1 tablespoon of the drippings and return skillet to medium heat. Add onions and sauté, scraping skillet to dislodge and incorporate any clinging pieces of bacon, until onions are softened and fragrant, about 5 minutes.

2) *To assemble and serve:* Add onions and cooked bacon to marinara sauce. Return sauce to a full simmer and cook with the lid ajar for 15 minutes over low heat. Stir in thawed peas, ⅓ cup Parmesan cheese and a generous amount of freshly ground black pepper. When hot throughout, serve immediately over freshly cooked rigatoni noodles. Pass additional Parmesan cheese at the table.

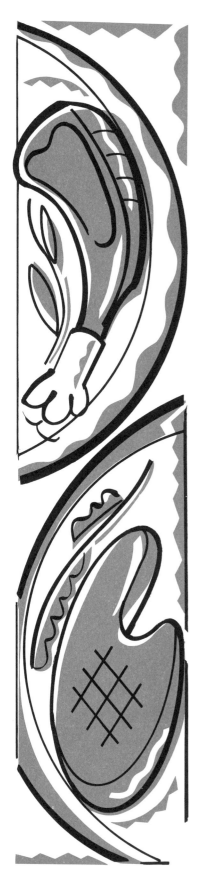

CHAPTER VII

THE MAIN EVENT

Classic Comfort from Cooking Big

A day with time to spare gives you the opportunity to prepare those dishes that provide the most comfort and fill your home with the most intoxicating aromas. I always suggest "cooking big" (whenever possible) since as both a teacher and a mother, I know that the mess created when preparing one meal is all too close to the mess created when preparing three. In this chapter you'll find many high-yield recipes that stress skills to enable you to get maximum benefits from designated "cooking days." Once these techniques are mastered, succulent braised dishes and hearty stews never need be farther away than a trip to the freezer.

These recipes, many of which appear lengthy, are highly detailed in order to assure your success. Please use my important Time Management Tips, which will eliminate many steps when you begin to assemble and cook. By breaking down a recipe into smaller steps, you'll prevent even the most classically prepared dish from over-whelming you. And try not to shy away from a recipe with many ingredients. Instead, break down the list and determine the level of ease or difficulty required to get your shopping done. Most often, the ingredients can be purchased from either your local supermarket or produce market. And since you have to go there anyway, choosing some additional items for a braised dish is a simple step to make your meal ultimately healthier and better tasting. In addition to braised dishes, I've also included my favorite "comfort food" recipes, many of which reflect classic American cuisine.

What's That Incredible Smell?
PERFECT ROAST TURKEY

YIELD: serves 8 generously

Roasting a turkey to perfection can sometimes be difficult and often causes much anxiety to home cooks—especially at holiday time when so many things are going on in the kitchen! The hope is always that the darker thigh area will be cooked thoroughly without leaving the delicate breast meat overcooked and dry. To ensure a juicy turkey, I carefully turn the bird as it roasts. This way one side of the bird is never overexposed to excessive periods of dry heat. Also, stuffing a turkey lengthens the cooking time by about forty-five minutes. So, by not stuffing the cavity, the white meat has less chance of becoming dry. I recommend that you bake the stuffing in a separate covered casserole. Purchase a fresh turkey if possible for best flavor and texture. If serving a crowd, I suggest using two twelve-pound birds instead of one enormous turkey; the younger (smaller) bird is not only more tender and cooks quicker, but the extra bird provides more legs and wings to go around. Whether or not I stuff my turkey, I usually truss (sew) the cavity shut, secure the legs together and fold the wing tips down and under the bird. This not only helps to maintain the best appearance through roasting, but the compact position of the bird makes it easier to turn over while roasting. In this recipe, the poultry is sprinkled liberally with a mixture of dry spices, which are "rubbed" into the bird using vegetable oil as a lubricant—a method of cooking that has been used for many years in the West Indies. Lawry's seasoned salt is a spice blend that has no MSG and (when used sparingly) is particularly complementary to poultry. In addition to stuffing, accompany the turkey with Sweet Sautéed Carrots (page 320) and Triple-Corn and Pepper Muffins (page 427).

INGREDIENTS

1 large carrot, scrubbed and thinly sliced

1 large yellow onion, thinly sliced

1 stalk celery, cleaned and thinly sliced

About 6 whole black peppercorns

Vegetable spray or oil, for roasting rack

1 turkey (about 12 pounds)

Onion powder* (not onion salt)

Freshly ground black pepper to taste

SPECIAL EQUIPMENT

Large stainless steel roasting pan with sturdy roasting rack

Trussing needle

Kitchen twine

Blender

Bulb baster

Flat gravy whisk

Fine-mesh wire sieve

Time Management Tips

- The turkey or chicken may be fully cleaned and seasoned 1 day ahead and refrigerated overnight in a bowl (covered with plastic wrap or aluminum foil). **Do not stuff turkey until just before roasting.**

- All of the vegetables that are placed underneath the bird while it roasts may be prepared 1 day ahead and kept covered in the refrigerator. The mushrooms and shallots for the gravy may be chopped 1 day ahead and kept in separate well-covered bowls in the refrigerator.

Seasoned salt* or kosher salt

Sweet Hungarian paprika*

FOR THE CAVITY

1 recipe Everything but the Kitchen Sink Stuffing (page 340) *or* large yellow onion, 1 stalk celery, and 2 sprigs parsley

Flavorless vegetable oil, for rubbing turkey

1½ sticks (¼ pound plus 4 tablespoons) lightly salted butter or margarine

5 cloves garlic, minced or pressed through a garlic press

FOR THE GRAVY

3½ cups Rich Chicken Stock or "Doctored" Canned Chicken Broth (page 140 for both)

½ cup dry white wine (optional)

2 tablespoons butter

1 shallot, minced

2 medium-sized fresh button mushrooms (optional), wiped clean (page 131) and finely minced or coarsely chopped

3 to 4 tablespoons all-purpose flour

2 tablespoons cream or milk (optional)

* See section on Staples

1) *To set up to roast:* Preheat the oven to 450°F. Place carrot, onion, celery and peppercorns into the bottom of a large nonreactive roasting pan. Place a metal roasting rack over the vegetables to raise up the turkey as it roasts, giving it full heat exposure (that's the secret to successful roasting). Spray rack with vegetable spray or brush with oil.

2) *To clean and season turkey:* Remove neck, liver and gizzards from turkey, reserving all but the liver for the stock. Thoroughly rinse and dry turkey, trimming away any excess fat from the cavity opening. Sprinkle the inside of the cavity with onion powder and freshly ground black pepper. Turn turkey (breast side down) and generously sprinkle its back with onion powder, then with freshly ground pepper, then lightly with seasoned salt and finally with sweet paprika. Turn turkey over and season breast, legs and wings in the same order as the back. Using your hands, rub vegetable oil generously over the backs, sides and top of turkey.

3) To stuff turkey: If planning to stuff turkey, prepare stuffing as directed and spoon it loosely into the cavity (don't overfill since stuffing will expand as turkey roasts). If not using stuffing, peel and quarter onion, clean and halve celery and and place in cavity with parsley.

4) To truss turkey: Thread a 12- to 14-inch piece of kitchen twine through a trussing needle and tie a knot at the bottom end of the string. Starting at the top of the cavity (in front of the breast bone), sew through both side flaps of fleshy skin until you reach the bottom of the cavity. Pull to secure closed and use the remaining twine to wind around the knobby ends of the drumsticks (while pulling) to bring them together. Tie in a knot to secure the legs in place and clip off loose ends of twine. The bony tips of the wings should be bent downward to sit underneath the turkey. Place turkey (breast side down) on the prepared roasting rack.

5) To prepare garlic butter: Melt butter in a saucepan over medium heat. When bubbling, reduce heat to low, add garlic and sauté until garlic is soft and fragrant, about 3 minutes. Pour garlic butter into a blender and whirl until smooth. Spoon half the melted garlic butter over seasoned turkey.

6) To roast turkey: Roast turkey in the preheated oven for 20 minutes. Reduce oven temperature to 325°F and roast 1½ hours longer. Then remove roasting pan from oven and carefully turn turkey (breast side up) using the knobs of the drumsticks to move the bird. Pour on the remaining garlic butter and roast 45 minutes, basting occasionally with pan juices using a bulb baster. Turn again and roast (breast side down) for 30 minutes basting frequently; then turn once more to finish roasting (breast side up) for the last 15 to 30 minutes, basting every 10 minutes. As the skin becomes crisp and golden, check turkey frequently for signs of doneness (see Tips from a Teacher) and remember, an unstuffed turkey roasts quicker than a stuffed one. When fully cooked, remove turkey from oven and let it rest on the roasting rack (loosely tented with aluminum foil) over a platter or carving surface for 10 to 20 minutes so the juices settle.

7) To prepare neck and gizzard: While turkey is roasting, simmer neck and gizzard (never the liver which makes the stock bitter) in chicken stock until tender, about 30 minutes for the neck and 1 hour for the tougher gizzard. Pull meat off neck and shred or chop it; remove and discard any gristle from gizzard and chop it as well. Set aside stock, chopped neck and gizzard for the gravy.

8) To deglaze roasting pan: While roasted turkey rests, pour off all but 2 tablespoons of drippings from the roasting pan. (Keep all those browned bits clinging to the bottom of the pan along with the vegetables.) Set roasting pan over medium-high heat. Pour in wine, if using, and ½ cup of the reserved chicken stock (or 1 cup stock) and, using a gravy whisk or a wooden spatula, move the ingredients around the bottom of the pan to combine the caramelized browned bits of vegetables, drippings and wine. Simmer until liquid is reduced by ½, occasionally pressing on the vegetables to extract any remaining flavor.

9) To make gravy: Melt butter in a 2-quart heavy-bottomed saucepan over medium heat. When bubbling, add minced shallot and chopped mushrooms, if using. Sauté until softened and fragrant, about 2 minutes, then sprinkle on flour, stirring to combine. Cook mixture over medium heat another 2 minutes, stirring constantly. Pour in remaining chicken stock and stir with a whisk to break up flour. Bring to a simmer, reduce heat to low and cook until thickened, 2 to 3 minutes. Place a fine-meshed sieve over the saucepan and carefully pour the deglazing mixture from the roasting pan into the sieve. Press hard on the solids as you force the

TIPS
FROM A TEACHER

Roasting Poultry

Choosing poultry: Purchase free-range chickens when possible. Not only are they more delicate and flavorful but they were bred and raised under conditions that are more natural and humane, making them less likely to present a health risk. And *please* (after carving), instead of throwing the poultry carcass in the garbage, throw it into a pot with some aromatic vegetables, a few whole black peppercorns, the giblets (if they weren't used for the gravy) and cold water to cover. Bring it to a boil, then turn it down to simmer. There—you've just replenished your stock supply! See page 140 for further instructions on defatting stock.

To check poultry for doneness: Occasionally (using an oven mitt), grasp and rotate the bony tip of the drumstick. When it wiggles freely without tugging back at the joint, that's a good indication of readiness. Or, insert the sharp tip of a needle in the thickest part of the thigh while a spoon is positioned just underneath the puncture. If the exuded juices are tinged with red (or even pink), the bird needs more time in the oven. If, however, the juices run clear yellow, it's ready. Don't always trust pop-up timers since they don't always work! If the bird shows signs of doneness, remove from the oven and tent loosely with aluminum foil for 10 to 20 min-

enriched stock/wine mixture through and into the pot; discard the solids. Stir in reserved chopped neck meat and gizzards, and simmer over low heat until hot and well combined. Season to taste with salt and freshly ground black pepper and keep the gravy warm over low heat until the turkey is carved and ready to serve.

Perfect Roast Chicken

A 6- to 8-pound roasting chicken or 2 smaller birds can be perfectly roasted with very few changes to the preceding turkey recipe. Stuffing the bird, whether with stuffing or aromatic vegetables, as well as trussing, is an optional step. Use only 5 tablespoons butter and 4 garlic cloves and pour *all* the garlic butter over chicken before roasting. Roast chicken(s) (breast side up), in a preheated 375°F without turning, basting occasionally with pan juices (frequently once chicken begins to become crisp). Roasting time will vary from 1 hour and 15 minutes to 2½ hours, depending on size of chicken(s). (For criteria on doneness, see Tips from a Teacher.) When making the gravy, the neck, gizzards, shallot and mushrooms are all optional additions. The chicken need only rest about 10 minutes before carving.

utes. If working, the timer should pop up during this resting period.

To skin or not to skin poultry?: There's no need to skin poultry before roasting. Contrary to popular belief, removing the skin before roasting does nothing to reduce fat. The skin serves to lubricate and self-baste the flesh as it roasts and helps to ensure supple tender meat. To reduce the fat content of cooked poultry (or to flavor the flesh directly in order to remove the cooked skin from your portion), simply loosen the skin from the flesh by inserting the fingers of one hand under the skin covering the breast, being careful not to tear skin. Make a mixture of olive oil and a liberal amount of the listed seasonings and rub this under the skin, flavoring the flesh. Rub the outside of the bird as directed and, remove the skin from your portion after carving. Also, to further reduce fat, omit the garlic butter and baste more frequently with some additional spiced oil.

General Timing Guidelines for Roast Turkey

For a 12-pound bird: 15 to 20 minutes per pound.

For a larger turkey (16 pounds and over): 13 to 15 minutes per pound. For a larger bird, after intitial searing and roasting for 1½ hours (back side up), keep turning every 30 minutes having the bird breast side up for the last 30 minutes of roasting. Baste frequently with pan drippings to keep moist.

Regardless of the size: An internal temperature of 170°F should be reached before removing turkey from the oven (180°F after settling).

For a stuffed bird: Once the stuffing is stored in the cavity of raw poultry, it must reach 165°F before being consumed.

HONEY-ROAST CHICKEN

YIELD: serves 6

SPECIAL EQUIPMENT
1 or 2 shallow baking sheets with
1-inch rims

One of my favorite reasons for making this dish over and over again (other than its delicious taste) is to watch how it always converts confirmed "curry haters." Unfortunately, curry seems to be one of the most misunderstood spice blends around. But this recipe performs miracles as the cooking aromas from the curried honey sauce drive people crazy with anticipation! When curry haters see the chicken glistening on a platter and taste its wonderful blend of flavors, they happily accept a flavoring that they had previously thought too strong and overly ethnic. Without exception, I've never met anyone who didn't love this chicken recipe. The key to success is using a shallow baking sheet with one-inch sides, so the chicken pieces can become crisp as they self-baste. Since the pieces are liberally coated with sauce, if you use a pan that's deeper than suggested, the chicken will bake instead of roast. The low-sided pan enables the exterior of the chicken to gain better exposure to heat, allowing the top to become gloriously brown (almost mahogany). The result is one of the best and most versatile chicken dishes that I prepare. The recipe also doubles easily. Serve this chicken with Deliciously Simple White Rice (try the variation with corn and bell peppers on page 362), Sweet Sautéed Carrots (page 320) and if time allows, fry up a batch of Fried Indian Bread Puffs (page 434).

INGREDIENTS

1 stick (¼ pound) butter or margarine

½ cup minced yellow onion

2 large cloves garlic, minced

¼ cup Dijon mustard

½ cup mild honey

1 teaspoon salt

1 rounded teaspoon curry powder*

2 tablespoons peach or mango chutney*

Small handful dried currants or chopped dark raisins

2 roasting chickens (3½ pounds each)

* See section on Staples

1) **To make sauce:** Melt butter in a heavy 1½- to 2-quart saucepan over medium heat. When bubbling, sauté onion and garlic until softened, 3 to 5 minutes. Add remaining ingredients except chicken and stir until combined. Heat until warm throughout and set aside to cool slightly.

2) **To prepare chicken:** Rinse and pat each chicken dry. Cut each chicken into 8 serving pieces as directed on page 256. (Reserve and freeze backs for stock.) Dip each piece in honey mixture, coating chicken completely. Lay chicken pieces (skin side up) on 1 or 2 shallow baking pans. Spoon any remaining sauce over chicken.

3) **To bake:** Place chicken in a cold oven, turn heat to 400°F and bake 1 hour. If you are using 2 baking sheets, roast in the upper and lower thirds of the oven and switch shelf positions after half the baking time.

4) **To serve:** Transfer chicken to a warmed serving platter and serve hot, at room temperature or slightly chilled.

Curried Chicken Salad

A good reason to double this recipe is the leftovers. They not only reheat well, but they also make fabulous chicken salad! Just remove any thick pieces of skin and tear flesh into bite-sized pieces, add some coarsely chopped, unpeeled Golden Delicious apples, coarsely chopped toasted almonds, dried currants and minced scallions. Make a dressing with mayonnaise, curry powder, some Dijon mustard and a touch of honey. Toss chicken salad with just enough dressing to bind, adding salt and freshly ground black pepper to taste. Serve with salad greens and some crusty rolls and you've got a yourself great lunch or a light supper!

CRISPY CHICKEN CUTLETS

With Lemon Twists

YIELD: serves 6

SPECIAL EQUIPMENT
Meat mallet

12-inch nonstick skillet

Nonabrasive turning spatula,
preferably 2

This basic technique for breading cutlets can be applied to thinly sliced leg of veal, pounded veal rib chops, different types of fish fillets and shrimp, as well as various vegetables. In order to do this procedure quickly, efficiently and enjoyably, you must first set up your ingredients in an assembly-line fashion. The combination of The Best Dried Bread Crumbs (page 78), made from pulverized toasted slices of crusty Italian bread, and nutty Reggiano Parmesan cheese makes these cutlets taste so savory and smell so enticing. They may be served hot, at room temperature or cold for sandwiches. When served at room temperature, the cutlets make an easy and delicious meal when entertaining. Present them on a large platter, each adorned with a beautiful twist of lemon. If you don't have time to debone and butterfly the chicken breasts, ask your butcher to do this for you.

INGREDIENTS

3 large whole chicken breasts

2 cups all-purpose flour

Salt and freshly ground black pepper to taste

2½ cups The Best Dried Bread Crumbs (page 78)

1½ cups freshly grated Reggiano Parmesan cheese

3 cloves garlic (optional)

4 eggs, lightly beaten

⅔ cup to 1 cup olive as needed

2 tablespoons butter or additional olive oil

2 large lemons, scrubbed and dried, for twists

3 tablespoons chopped flat-leaf Italian parsley, for garnish

1) *To turn whole chicken breasts into cutlets:* Rinse chicken and pat dry. Split each breast in half, skin, debone and butterfly each half as directed on page 233. Using a meat mallet, pound each breast to ¼-inch thickness.

2) *To set up to bread cutlets:* Place flour on a plate and season lightly with salt and pepper. Combine bread crumbs with Parmesan cheese on a shallow baking sheet. If desired, press 1 clove of the garlic through a garlic

press into the beaten egg; mix with a fork. Position eggs in between the flour and crumbs.

3) **To bread cutlets:** Sprinkle prepared cutlets lightly with salt and pepper. Dredge each one in the seasoned flour to coat well and shake off the excess. Dip chicken into beaten eggs to coat thoroughly. Working with 1 cutlet at a time, lay the egg-coated cutlet on top of the crumb mixture and turn to coat each side, pressing gently to help the crumbs adhere. Lay the heavily breaded cutlet on a large tray or baking sheet.

4) **To set up to panfry cutlets:** Arrange a long double thickness of paper toweling on your kitchen counter, as close to the stove as safely possible. Heat a 12-inch nonstick skillet over medium-high heat and, when hot, add enough olive oil to generously coat the bottom of the pan. If desired, bruise 2 of the garlic cloves (page 237) and add to hot oil. Sear garlic, pressing to release its flavor into the oil. When just golden, remove garlic and discard (or enjoy).

5) **To panfry cutlets:** Add butter to hot oil and when bubbling, fry 2 cutlets at a time until golden brown and crisp on both sides, about 4 minutes per side. (Use a turning spatula occasionally to press gently on the center of the cutlet to avoid uneven cooking. Use 2 nonabrasive spatulas to turn cutlets safely.) When cooked through, drain each cutlet on paper toweling. Place on a hot serving tray and, if desired, keep warm in the oven until all the cutlets are cooked. If butter becomes overly dark while frying or if there is an accumulation of dark crumbs on the bottom of the pan, dump out the oil, wipe out the skillet and add more oil, garlic and butter before frying the next batch.

6) **To make lemon twists:** If desired, use a vegetable peeler to remove any stamped letters from rind. Slice lemons into ¼ inch rounds and lay on a flat surface in pairs of 2 slices. Using a sharp knife, slit 1 slice from each pair, from the center of the slice through 1 side of the rind. Slit the remaining slices from just below the top rind through the bottom rind. To form decorative twists, lift the slice with the smaller cut, twist the cut portion in opposite directions and place twisted slice on the counter. Then lift a slice with the large slit and twist the slit open as you lay it over the bottom twist. The design will look like a flower or spoke pattern.

7) **To serve:** If serving individual portions, lay each cutlet on a plate and position a lemon twist on top. Sprinkle lightly with freshly chopped Italian parsley. Alternatively, serve the cutlets on a warmed platter as suggested in the introduction to this recipe.

Time Management Tips

- The cutlets may be breaded and placed on a shallow baking sheet up to 2 days ahead. Cover well with plastic wrap and refrigerate. Assembling them several hours ahead and chilling will encourage the crumbs to adhere better through frying.

Chickenalla Parmigiana

With the addition of marinara sauce and a topping of three cheeses, chicken cutlets become Chickenalla Parmigiana. Prepare Quick Marinara Sauce (page 242). Prepare Crispy Fried Chicken Cutlets through frying and draining on paper towels. Brush the inside of a rectangular baking dish with olive oil and add a bit of marinara sauce to the bottom. Lay cutlets in a single layer on the bottom of the dish and spoon more sauce generously over top. Scatter a combination of freshly grated mozzarella, Muenster and Parmesan cheeses over top. Crush a bit of dried oregano between your fingers to give a light dusting over the top of the cheese. Bake at 375°F until piping hot throughout and the cheese is bubbling and beginning to turn golden, 35 to 45 minutes. Serve hot with Garlic Bread (page 405).

TIPS
FROM A TEACHER

How to Cut a Raw Chicken into Eight Serving Pieces

Why do I ask you to do something that can easily be done by a butcher? I'm not suggesting this to make your life more difficult. But I do want to give you a valuable skill that will make you a more effective and accomplished cook and also enable you to feel more connected to the craft of cooking. It's time we all learned to master a culinary procedure that was second nature to our grandmothers. Other than the sense of accomplishment from per-

forming this earthy task, there are several other reasons to acquire this skill. First, when you purchase a precut chicken or chicken parts, you're not able to view the original condition of the bird. The only way to have more control over the quality of your poultry is to see the bird whole. Also, when chickens are precut, the bony chicken backs often are split up and attached to other parts. Since the backs aren't great for eating but make wonderful stock, why cook them with the rest of the chicken? It makes more sense to remove the backs yourself and store them in your freezer until you develop a substantial stash; then use them to enrich a hefty pot of chicken stock. Finally, when you learn to cut up a raw chicken you also learn how to locate the "points of interference" (hard bone); this makes you more proficient at carving cooked poultry instead of simply "winging it" (no pun intended) and hoping for the best.

Necessary equipment: You will need a well-sharpened 10-inch carving knife, a strong pair of kitchen scissors and preferably a *wooden* (not plastic) cutting surface. Recent research has reversed the long-held opinion that wood encourages the growth of bacteria; it is now believed to be safer than plastic, but be sure to wash it well with a mild disinfectant after cutting up poultry (see The Cutting-Surface Controversy, page 23).

To prepare chicken to be cut up: Thoroughly rinse and dry chicken. Pull out any excess fat from the opening of the cavity and trim away excess skin. If desired, cut both fat and skin into small pieces and store them together in the freezer until you accumulate enough to make rendered chicken fat (page 110); otherwise discard them.

To remove legs: Lay chicken (breast up) on your work surface. Grasp a drumstick and gently pull it away from the body to stretch the piece of skin in between the leg and body. Using a sharp carving knife, make a slit in the skin only without severing the meat.

Firmly grab the top of the leg and bend it all the way back, down and away from the body to release the thigh (hip) bone from its socket. Bend leg still further until the tip of the bone has broken away from the body and is sticking straight up. (This is the hard

bone or the "point of interference.") Now all that's connecting the leg to the body is the flesh from the bottom side of the back. Grasp chicken by the leg and simply cut off the leg going under and around the thigh bone. Repeat with the remaining leg.

  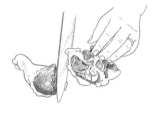

To separate drumstick from thigh: Place the leg with thigh attached (thigh skin side down) on your work surface and use your finger-

tips to locate the small empty space between the top of the meaty drumstick and the beginning of the thigh. Remove your finger as you place the

blade of your knife in this space. In one down-away-from-you and back-toward-you stroke, cut and separate the drumstick from the thigh.

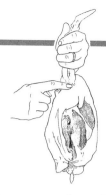

To remove wings: First locate the spot under the wings (the armpit) as if you were going to "tickle" the chicken. To do this, lift up the chicken by the wing to stretch the skin that connects the wing to the body. This will expose the "ticklish spot." With your knife make an incision (about ⅓ inch) into this spot and, while holding the wing, bend it back and down while twisting to release the wing bone from its socket. Bend back further to expose totally the round white bone tip and, using your knife, cut down, under and around the bone; this will release the wing into your hand.

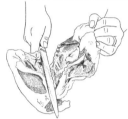

To remove backbone: Using your knife or sharp kitchen scissors, cut along each side of the backbone, removing any thin, flimsy, fleshy side areas along with the back. This will leave you with one whole chicken breast. (Place the back into a heavy-duty plastic bag and store in the freezer for making stock.)

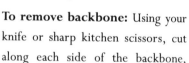

To split breast: Place breast (skin side down) on work surface with the tip of the breast facing away from you. On the center of the bottom rim near you, you'll see a whitish, translucent piece of cartilage, laying directly over the breastbone (your point of interference). Place the blade of your knife on the cartilage and with a firm (but not hard) blow, knock your hand against the dull side of the blade so it will penetrate the cartilage only without splintering the breastbone. Bend both sides of the breast down and away from each other to open the cartilage and expose the thin, curved breastbone. Use your thumb to pry under and around the bone to release it (this sometimes takes a bit of muscle). Lift out the bone (add it to the bag with the back in the freezer) and run your thumb down the center of the breast under the remaining pieces of cartilage as well as the translucent skin to release both from the flesh. Remove and discard cartilage. Cut directly down the center of the breast separating it into two equal halves. See, you did it!

To clean up: When finished, wash your cutting surface as well as all utensils (and your hands) thoroughly before using them to prepare other foods that might be eaten raw.

SOUTHERN FRIED CHICKEN

With or without the Skin and Mushroom Gravy

YIELD: serves 6 to 8

These crisp and tender pieces of crunchy fried chicken retain a distinctive and tangy garlicky-peppery flavor from the marinade. The secret ingredients are the buttermilk (which is also a natural tenderizer) and the bite of cayenne pepper along with a generous amount of freshly ground black pepper. If you choose, remove the skin before marinating. And if you don't have time to make fresh stock for the gravy, use previously made and frozen Rich Chicken Stock or "Doctored" Canned Chicken Broth (page 140 for both). Oh, and leftovers from this down-home dish make a great brown-bag-it lunch for work the next day. Accompany the chicken with Mashed New Potato Casserole (page 344), and Sautéed Baby Green Beans (page 318). And in my house, this meal wouldn't be the same without a bowl of Spiced Applesauce (page 91) and a basket of Sweet Cream Biscuits (page 422).

SPECIAL EQUIPMENT

Strong pair of kitchen shears

Garlic press

6- to 8-quart mixing bowl

12-inch heavy-bottomed skillet with a lid

Frying thermometer

Spatter shields (optional)

Fine-mesh wire sieve for straining the gravy

INGREDIENTS

3 frying chickens (3 to 3½ pounds each)

FOR THE MARINADE

4 cups (1 quart) buttermilk

1 generous tablespoon cayenne pepper

2 large cloves garlic, pressed through a garlic press

2 teaspoons ground white pepper

1½ teaspoons salt

Freshly ground black pepper to taste

2 to 3 teaspoons Tabasco sauce

FOR THE STOCK

1 large yellow onion, scrubbed, unpeeled, root end removed and coarsely chopped

2 carrots, scrubbed and sliced

1 stalk celery, cleaned and sliced, including leaves

3 sprigs parsley

1 teaspoon whole black peppercorns

Pinch crumbled dried thyme

Time Management Tips

- The chicken can be marinated 1 day ahead and kept well covered in the refrigerator.

- The vegetables for making stock as well as the shallot and chopped mushrooms can be prepared for cooking 1 day ahead and kept refrigerated in separate, well-covered bowls.

- The stock should be made 1 day ahead and refrigerated (so the fat can be removed). If you don't have time to do this, use 2½ cups Rich Chicken Stock (page 140) from your freezer and freeze the wing tips, backs and giblets for future stock-making. Or use "Doctored" Canned Chicken Broth (page 143).

- The chicken can be fried 2 hours ahead and left at a comfortable room temperature or reheated before serving.

FOR THE FLOUR MIXTURE

5 cups all-purpose flour

1 tablespoon seasoned salt* or regular salt

2 teaspoons sweet Hungarian paprika*

About 2 teaspoons freshly ground black pepper

1 teaspoon ground white pepper

About 2 cups flavorless vegetable oil or mild peanut oil, for frying

FOR THE GRAVY

2 tablespoons butter

2 tablespoons all-purpose flour

1 shallot, peeled and chopped

3 medium-sized fresh button mushrooms, wiped clean (page 131) and minced

2 to 3 tablespoons cream or milk (optional)

* See section on Staples

1) **To prepare chicken:** Cut each chicken into 8 serving pieces as directed on page 256 and reserve backs, along with neck, gizzards and heart for stock. Rinse chicken pieces and dry well with paper towels. Using kitchen shears, snip off the wing tips and, if desired, remove skin.

2) **To marinate chicken:** Pour buttermilk into a 6- to 8-quart bowl, add marinade ingredients and adjust seasoning to taste. Add chicken pieces and, using your hands, toss the mixture to coat each piece well with marinade. Cover bowl with plastic wrap and refrigerate for at least 4 hours or preferably overnight.

3) **To make chicken stock:** Preheat the oven to 450°F. Place chicken backs, wing tips and chopped onions on a shallow baking sheet and sprinkle with a little salt and some black pepper. Roast until turning golden and caramelized about 20 minutes. Transfer browned chicken parts and onions to a 2½-quart saucepan. Add reserved chicken neck, gizzard, heart (but not the liver) along with remaining stock ingredients except thyme. Add cold water to cover and bring mixture to a boil. Reduce heat to low, add thyme and simmer stock with the cover ajar for 2 hours, occasionally pressing hard on the solids. Then remove the lid and cook 1 hour more to reduce and concentrate the flavor. Strain stock into a bowl, pressing

hard on the solids. Discard solids and let stock cool, preferably overnight. Spoon off and discard any accumulated grease or congealed fat from stock before using.

4) *To set up to fry chicken:* If possible, remove marinated chicken from the refrigerator an hour or so before frying. Line 2 wire cooling racks with a double thickness of paper toweling or rip open a brown paper bag and line the rack with the paper. Place all ingredients for flour mixture in a large mixing bowl and combine well with a whisk. Place a heavy-bottomed 12-inch skillet on the stove and pour about 1 inch of oil into the pan. (If available, use 2 skillets to fry the chicken as a substantial time-saver. Also, the safest way to fry chicken is to use a spatter shield which prevents the hot oil from popping up and out.)

5) *To fry chicken:* Heat oil over medium-high heat to 365°F. (The oil should have a rippling sheen on top but should not be smoking.) Remove some of the chicken pieces from the marinade, pat them almost dry with paper towels and toss them in flour mixture with your hands to coat each piece well. Lift chicken pieces 1 at a time from mixture and gently shake off a little of the excess (the chicken should remain well coated). Without crowding, lay chicken pieces (skin side down) in the hot oil in a single layer and fry on the first side until a light golden brown, about 5 minutes. Turn chicken, using 2 stainless steel spatulas, and fry another 5 minutes. Turn chicken once more so skin side is down and cover skillet. Reduce heat to low and simmer until cooked through, 4 to 5 minutes. Uncover skillet, raise heat to medium-high and turn over chicken pieces once more. Cook another 1 or 2 minutes, just to crisp up the under side. Remove cooked pieces to the prepared wire racks and continue frying all the pieces of chicken.

6) *To complete stock:* Heat the defatted chicken stock. Pour oil out of the skillet(s), reserving the browned flour mixture that lies on the bottom. (If using 2 skillets, combine the browned flour in one of them, using some of the hot chicken stock to deglaze and loosen any browned flour from the other skillet.) Place skillet with browned flour over medium heat and stir in hot chicken stock. Bring mixture to a simmer and cook until thickened.

7) *To finish gravy:* Melt butter in a medium-sized saucepan over medium heat. When hot and bubbling, add shallot and mushrooms, stirring to coat vegetables with butter, and cook until tender, 2 to 3 minutes. Stir the 2 tablespoons flour into mushroom mixture and cook, stirring constantly, for 2 minutes. Place a fine strainer over the pan with the mushrooms and

carefully pour the thickened stock from the skillet into the strainer. Use a wooden spatula to stir and help the gravy pass through the mesh into the pan. Press hard on any solids that remain in the strainer and discard. Add cream, if using, to gravy and adjust seasoning, if needed, with salt and freshly ground black pepper. Set aside to allow any excess oil to rise to the top. Spoon off and discard any grease before reheating to serve.

8) *To serve:* Serve chicken either at room temperature or reheat on a wire rack over a shallow baking sheet in a 350°F oven for 10 to 15 minutes. Just before serving, reheat gravy until piping hot and pass it in a gravy boat at the table.

Variation with Cornish Hens

Substitute for the chicken, 6 to 8 Cornish hens or baby chickens (1 to 1⅓ pounds each) that have been butterflied (see Golden Herb-Rubbed Cornish Hens, page 240). Marinate whole and fry as directed for Southern Fried Chicken. Just before serving (after reheating), split each hen in half through the breast. Serve each guest 1 whole hen, arranged decoratively on the plate surrounding a serving of Mashed New Potato Casserole (page 344).

BRAISED CHICKEN AND SWEET ITALIAN SAUSAGE

With Fresh Tomatoes and Roasted Peppers

YIELD: serves 10

SPECIAL EQUIPMENT
8- to 10-quart nonreactive Dutch oven with tight-fitting lid

8-quart blanching pot with built-in strainer (optional)

10- to 12-inch nonreactive skillet

Sturdy stainless steel skewers

Spatter shield (optional)

When this tomato-rich, flavor-packed chicken and sausage stew is simmering on the stove, you can expect family and friends to make frequent trips to the kitchen to peek into the pot. For a robust meal serve this stew over hot linguine, simply dressed with garlic and melted butter or fruity olive oil. Garnish with slivered fresh basil and tiny fresh mozzarella balls—and pass a sliced loaf of Crusty Italian Bread (page 401). Shallow soup plates with rims that slope upward are perfect for serving this or any robust stew over pasta or rice (although any plate will do the job). This chicken dish also makes a fabulous presentation as part of a buffet when served from a large bowl, garnished as above; serve the pasta in a separate warmed bowl. This recipe may be doubled easily and frozen.

INGREDIENTS

About ½ cup *each* extra-virgin olive oil and regular olive oil

1 large yellow onion, peeled and chopped

1 large green bell pepper, seeded and chopped

6 large cloves garlic, minced, plus an optional addition
  of 2 minced cloves

1 cup packed chopped fresh basil leaves (chopped just before using so
  basil won't turn black)

Freshly ground black pepper to taste

2 cans (28 ounces each) crushed tomatoes

3 pounds fresh ripe plum (Roma) tomatoes, peeled and seeded
  (page 151) and coarsely chopped, or 2 cans (28 ounces each)
  whole plum tomatoes, drained, seeded and coarsely chopped

2 cups tomato purée

2 rounded tablespoons tomato paste

1 *each* red, green and yellow bell peppers, roasted, peeled,
  seeded and sliced into thin strips (page 113)

2 roasting chickens (4 to 4½ pounds each), each cut into 8 parts
  (page 256)

Salt and freshly ground black pepper to taste

¾ cup Rich Chicken Stock or "Doctored" Canned Chicken Broth
  (page 140 for both)

2½ pounds sweet Italian sausage

¾ cup dry red wine

¾ pound fresh button mushrooms, wiped clean (page 131) and sliced

FOR GARNISH AND ACCOMPANIMENTS

Fresh basil sprigs

Tiny fresh mozzarella balls*

Freshly grated Reggiano Parmesan Cheese

Hot cooked linguine or white rice

* See section on Staples

Time Management Tips

- This recipe can be totally assembled (through step 5) up to 2 days ahead and refrigerated. The flavors even benefit from this. To prevent an accumulation of condensation (rising steam) from falling into the stew and diluting the flavor, pull a clean kitchen towel over the pot and place the cover on top of the towel. Bring to room temperature before reheating gently.

- To freeze: After completing step 5, place the amount that you will be serving into a smaller pot and divide the remaining mixture among several heavy-duty freezer containers. Apply the lid securely and attach a label and the date before placing in the freezer. To thaw, place in the refrigerator overnight and reheat in the microwave (page 289) or over low heat as directed. After reheating, this dish benefits by being refreshed with a few tablespoons of freshly chopped basil and a sprinkling of freshly ground black pepper.

TIPS
FROM A TEACHER

〜〜〜

Fresh Mozzarella Balls

Tiny fresh mozzarella balls *(bocconcini)* can sometimes be found in the super-market (marketed as "petite" mozzarella balls by Polly-O). If not, try a local Italian delicatessen. As an alternative, you can scoop miniature rounds out of mozzarella from a larger ball of cheese using a small melon-ball scoop. Since these are perishable, purchase them in small quantities and use as soon as possible. But if you find yourself with leftovers, keep them refrigerated covered in lightly salted water which will help keep them supple and white. (If not purchased from a dated container, be sure to ask the shopkeeper for the expiration date.)

1) To make sauce base: Heat ⅓ cup extra-virgin olive oil in an 8- to 10-quart nonreactive Dutch oven over medium heat. Tear off a piece of waxed paper large enough to cover the bottom interior of the pot and brush one side lightly with additional extra-virgin olive oil. When oil is hot, reduce heat to low, add onions, chopped green bell pepper and 3 cloves of the minced garlic. Stir to coat with olive oil, then lay the greased side of the paper directly on top of vegetables. Cook gently until softened and very fragrant, about 15 minutes. Remove and discard waxed paper, add ½ cup of the chopped basil, some freshly ground black pepper, crushed tomatoes, chopped plum tomatoes, tomato purée and tomato paste. Stir and bring to a simmer. Reduce heat to low, place cover ajar and simmer, stirring occasionally, for 30 minutes. Remove from heat and stir roasted pepper strips into sauce.

2) To brown chicken: Rinse and thoroughly dry chicken pieces. Heat a 10- to 12-inch nonreactive skillet over medium heat and, when hot, add a thin layer of regular olive oil. When oil is hot, brown chicken pieces a few at a time on both sides without crowding. Transfer chicken to Dutch oven with the sauce. Drain excess oil from skillet but do not wipe out the interior. Return skillet to medium-high heat and add chicken stock, swirling and prying loose any browned bits of chicken using a wooden spatula. Simmer briskly until syrupy, 2 to 4 minutes. Add this syrupy mixture to the sauce.

3) To brown sausage: Using sharp kitchen scissors or a serrated knife, cut sausage into 1½-inch chunks. Wipe out skillet and reheat over medium heat. Add a thin layer of regular olive oil to the skillet and, when hot, add sausage, a few pieces at a time, and brown on all sides. Transfer pieces with a slotted spoon to sauce. Pour out excess oil from skillet and deglaze with red wine over medium-high heat. Reduce as with chicken stock and add the syrupy reduction to the sauce. (Because of the alcohol, wine will reduce quicker than stock.)

4) To braise stew: Gently fold together ingredients in Dutch oven to combine well and bring to a full simmer over medium heat. Reduce heat to very low, cover and simmer slowly until chicken is tender, 30 to 40 minutes, stirring occasionally. Avoid overcooking or the chicken will be dry.

5) **To prepare mushrooms and finish stew:** Heat an 8- to 10-inch skillet over medium heat and add 2 tablespoons extra-virgin olive oil. When hot, add sliced mushrooms with the remaining 3 cloves of minced garlic and stir. Cook mushrooms until golden and set aside. Ten minutes before the stew has finished cooking, add cooked mushrooms to the Dutch oven with the remaining ½ cup chopped basil and lots of freshly ground black pepper. Fold together gently to combine. If desired, stir in an additional 2 minced garlic cloves. Remove from heat to cool.

6) **To serve:** Using a spoon, remove any accumulated grease from the top of stew. Reheat gently and serve piping hot over hot cooked linguine or rice. Decorate each serving with a pretty basil sprig and then drop 3 small fresh mozzarella balls on top of the hot sauce. Pass grated Reggiano Parmesan cheese at the table.

The use of a spatter shield is very helpful to prevent the hot oil from popping onto your skin while browning chicken. I recommend having a few of them since the diameter of certain pots exceeds the diameter of the shield. Just overlap on top of the pot.

OSSO BUCO

With Traditional Gremolata Garnish

YIELD: serves 8 to 10

The delicate and savory marrow bone of the veal shank (*osso buco* in Italian), braised until meltingly tender, lends its name to this distinctive and famous Milanese dish. The sauce begins with a *soffritto,* a generous mixture of finely chopped vegetables that are cooked slowly in melted butter to intensify their inherent sweetness. Conveniently, this dish (as do most braised dishes) benefits from one or two days in the refrigerator. During this time the flavors will marry, concentrate and intensify. Since this freezes so perfectly, (even if you aren't planning to serve a large group), I suggest preparing the full amount and freezing half for another occasion. Serve each slice of veal alongside individual servings of fettuccine and, at the table, pass a small bowl of the traditional parsley-garlic garnish called *gremolata* to be spooned sparingly on top of the veal.

SPECIAL EQUIPMENT
Food processor or chef's knife

10-quart nonreactive heavy-bottomed Dutch oven with tight-fitting lid

12-inch nonreactive skillet

Time Management Tips

- All of the vegetables can be assembled 1 day ahead and kept well covered in separate bowls in the refrigerator. Don't combine the vegetables to be chopped in the food processor until you are ready to cook them. Prepare chopped tomatoes 1 day in advance only if necessary.

- The entire dish can be cooked fully and refrigerated for 2 days before serving. To refrigerate once cooled, pull a clean kitchen towel over the top of the pot and apply the lid. The towel will prevent any accumulation of condensation from falling into the pot and diluting the flavor. Bring close to room temperature before slowly reheating over a low flame with the cover ajar.

- Alternatively, this can also be divided and frozen for another meal. When placing veal in a freezer container, lay shanks side by side in a single layer with the bone sticking up to avoid losing the marrow. Coat each slice generously with sauce before applying the cover and remember to label the container with the contents as well as the date for easy identification.

- If desired, all the ingredients (with the exception of the chopped parsley) for the gremolata can be prepared but kept in separate bowls a few hours ahead and kept at room temperature. Chop parsley and combine ingredients just before serving.

INGREDIENTS

1 large yellow onion, chopped

5 large cloves garlic

4 carrots, peeled and thinly sliced

4 stalks celery, cleaned, trimmed and thinly sliced

4 large leeks, cleaned (page 160) and sliced

1 stick (¼ pound) butter

8 large ripe tomatoes, peeled and seeded (page 151), coarsely chopped and drained

1 cup chopped fresh basil leaves

1 can (28 ounces) crushed tomatoes

1 can (6 ounces) tomato paste

8 to 10 slices veal shank (each 1 to 1½ inches thick)

About 1½ cups all-purpose flour

Salt and freshly ground black pepper to taste

About ½ cup olive oil

1 cup dry red wine

1 cup Rich Beef Stock (page 146) or canned beef broth, diluted with water if too salty

FOR THE GREMOLATA GARNISH

2 tablespoons chopped flat-leaf Italian parsley

1 tablespoon minced garlic

1 teaspoon minced lemon zest

GARNISH AND ACCOMPANIMENT

8 to 10 beautiful fresh basil sprigs

Cooked and buttered Homemade Egg Noodles (page 175) or fettuccine

1) *To prepare soffritto:* Combine onion, garlic, carrots and leeks in a mixing bowl. Place in batches in the bowl of a food processor fitted with the steel blade and pulse until the vegetables are chopped very small but still remain distinguishable. Alternatively, finely mince each vegetable individually, then combine.

2) *To sweat soffritto:* Melt butter in a 10-quart nonreactive Dutch oven. Tear off a piece of waxed paper large enough to cover the bottom interior

of the pot and brush 1 side of the paper with some of the meltedbutter. Stir chopped vegetables into butter and place the greased side of the waxed paper directly on top of the vegetables. Sweat them over very low heat for 20 to 30 minutes, occasionally lifting the paper to stir and redistribute. Remove and discard waxed paper and stir in chopped tomatoes, basil, crushed tomatoes and tomato paste. Bring to a simmer, reduce heat to low and cook for 15 minutes with the cover ajar.

3) *To dredge and brown veal shanks:* Place flour on a plate and season with salt and freshly ground black pepper. Heat a 12-inch nonreactive skillet over medium-high heat and, when hot, pour in a thin layer of olive oil to coat the bottom of the pan. Dredge in flour to coat well only as many slices of veal shank as can be browned at 1 time without crowding. Shake off any excess flour and, when oil is hot, sear shanks on both sides until golden. Remove to a tray as you continue to flour and brown the remaining pieces of veal.

4) *To deglaze skillet:* Pour out oil from skillet but don't wipe out the interior. Return to medium-high heat, add wine and stock and bring to a brisk simmer. Continue to simmer, scraping up any browned bits of caramelized veal that may have adhered to the bottom of the skillet, until the liquid is reduced to about ¼ its original volume.

5) *To braise veal:* Stir reduced liquid into the simmering sauce in the Dutch oven, along with some freshly ground black pepper. Lay veal shanks in the sauce side by side so the marrow that runs down the center of the shank bone is facing up. Cover pot, bring to a full simmer, then reduce heat to low and simmer until veal is very tender but not dry, about 2 hours. Remove lid and let cool.

6) *To prepare gremolata:* In a very small serving bowl combine all of the *gremolata* ingredients.

7) *To reheat and serve:* With a spoon, remove any grease that has risen to the top of the stew. Reheat covered over low heat or in a 350°F oven until piping hot throughout. Place a veal shank slice on each individual serving plate next to a serving of hot freshly cooked, lightly buttered fettuccine noodles. Taste sauce for seasoning, adding salt and freshly ground black pepper to taste and spoon some sauce on top of the veal and, if desired, on the pasta as well. Garnish each plate with a basil sprig and serve hot. Pass the bowl of *gremolata* at the table. (If the marrow bones should become dislodged from the eye of the shank, simply retrieve from pot and serve alongside meat.)

Variation with Veal Shoulder

Substitute for the veal shanks, 4 pounds veal shoulder cut into 1½ inch cubes. Flour and brown as described, but reduce cooking time slightly.

Reduced-Fat Variation

To lower the overall saturated-fat content of this dish, omit the butter and use ½ cup additional beef or chicken stock to simmer the soffritto. Brush the waxed paper with extra-virgin olive oil.

AROMATIC VEAL STEW

With Peas and Baby Artichokes

YIELD: serves 6 to 8

SPECIAL EQUIPMENT
Food processor or chef's knife

6-quart nonreactive heavy-bottomed Dutch oven with tight-fitting lid

12-inch nonreactive skillet

This dish combines the flavors of succulent braised veal and finely chopped aromatic vegetables with the earthy taste of fresh oregano. It's punctuated with the textures of pan-seared baby artichokes and sweet green peas and smells as heavenly while cooking as it is delicious to eat. And here's a bit of trivia to tantalize your dinner guests. "Baby" artichokes are not "young" artichokes. They are those grown on the bottom of the stalk and weigh in at about two ounces each. Typically, the largest artichokes are found growing on the center of the stalk. Although this stew can be totally assembled one day ahead, I would refrain from adding the peas until just before serving so they don't become overly soft and lose their vibrant green color. Serve this stew accompanied with a gorgeous loaf of Crusty Italian Bread (page 401) and Deliciously Simple White Rice (page 361).

INGREDIENTS

2 large yellow onions, chopped

5 cloves garlic, chopped

2 stalks celery, cleaned, trimmed and chopped

About ⅓ cup olive oil as needed

2 tablespoons chopped fresh oregano or 2 teaspoons crumbled dried oregano

1 can (6 ounces) tomato paste

1½ cups Rich Chicken Stock or "Doctored" Canned Chicken Broth
  (page 140 for both)

1½ cups Rich Beef Stock (page 146) or canned beef broth,
  diluted with water if too salty

Freshly ground black pepper to taste

1½ cups all-purpose flour

Salt to taste

3½ pounds veal shoulder, cut into 1½-inch cubes

1 cup dry white wine

2 tablespoons butter

1 tablespoon extra-virgin olive oil

4 cups (about 2 pounds) whole fresh baby artichokes or 2 packages
  (10 ounces each) frozen baby artichokes, thawed and dried

10 ounces frozen peas, thawed, or 2 cups fresh peas
  (about 2 pounds peas in pods)

FOR ACCOMPANIMENTS AND GARNISH

Deliciously Simple White Rice (page 361)

Sprigs of fresh oregano (optional)

Shaved Reggiano Parmesan cheese (optional)

1) *To process vegetables:* Combine chopped onion, garlic and celery in
   the bowl of a food processor fitted with the steel blade and pulse until
   they are finely chopped but not puréed; the vegetables should remain
   distinguishable. Alternatively, finely chop each vegetable separately, then
   combine.

2) *To sweat vegetables:* Heat 3 tablespoons of the olive oil in a nonreactive
   6-quart heavy-bottomed Dutch oven. Tear off a piece of waxed paper
   large enough to fit within the bottom interior of the pot and brush 1 side
   of the paper with olive oil. When oil is hot, add minced vegetables along
   with the dried oregano, if using (fresh oregano should be added later).
   Place the greased side of the waxed paper directly on top of the vegetables
   and reduce heat to low. Cook slowly and gently until the vegetables are
   softened and very fragrant, 10 to 15 minutes. Occasionally lift the paper
   and stir to redistribute and prevent scorching.

Time Management Tips

- The aromatic vegetables for the sauce base can be sliced 1 day ahead and kept refrigerated in separate well-covered bowls; do not pulse in the food processor until ready to cook.

- If preparing stew 1 day ahead, prepare through step 6 and refrigerate after cooling and removing any accumulated grease. Before refrigerating, to prevent condensation (water droplets) from falling into the stew and diluting the flavor, pull a clean kitchen towel over the top and cover the towel with the lid. Bring to room temperature before reheating gently and completing steps 7 through 10.

For an easy way to remove excess flour from dredged meat, place the flour-coated pieces into a medium-mesh wire strainer and bounce them around allowing the excess flour to come out through the mesh. Do this over the tray of remaining flour.

3) **To complete sauce base:** Remove and discard waxed paper from sweated vegetables and stir in tomato paste, chicken stock and beef stock. Bring mixture to a slow boil, reduce heat to low and add freshly ground black pepper. Simmer sauce base with the cover ajar while you continue to assemble stew.

4) **To dredge and brown veal:** Place flour on a plate and season with salt and freshly ground black pepper. Heat a 12-inch nonreactive skillet over medium-high heat. When hot, add a thin layer of olive oil. Dredge some of the veal in the seasoned flour to coat well, shaking off excess flour. (Only coat as many pieces of veal as can be browned at 1 time in a single layer without crowding.) When oil is hot, add floured veal and brown on all sides. As each batch of veal is browned, use a slotted spoon to remove to a platter and continue with remaining veal.

5) **To deglaze skillet:** Pour out any excess oil from skillet, but do not wipe out the interior. Return skillet to medium-high heat and add white wine. As wine comes to a brisk simmer, scrape up any browned bits of caramelized veal that cling to the bottom of the pan. Continue to simmer until wine is reduced by almost half.

6) **To assemble and braise stew:** Pour reduced wine into the sauce with browned veal. Bring the mixture to a full simmer, reduce heat to low and simmer covered until meltingly tender, about 1½ hours. (If using fresh oregano, add it for the last 30 minutes of cooking.) Then, remove from heat, uncover and let cool.

7) **To prepare artichokes for cooking:** If using fresh artichokes, bring 4 quarts of water to a boil. Cut off each stem end as well as the top ¼ inch of the leaves. Remove the tough outer leaves toward the bottom. Snap off the top portion of the darker green leaves leaving meatier bottoms attached; leave paler interior leaves intact. Slice each artichoke in half lengthwise and scoop out the soft, thin petals at the center. If the artichokes halves seem a bit large, slice them further into lengthwise strips. Blanch in lightly salted boiling water for 5 minutes, drain well and set aside. If using thawed frozen baby artichoke halves, don't cut up or blanch; just dry them on paper toweling.

8) **To sauté artichokes:** In an 8- to 10-inch skillet, heat butter with extra-virgin olive oil over medium-high heat. When hot, add prepared artichokes and cook quickly tossing frequently until tender and a light golden brown, 5 to 7 minutes.

9) *To finish stew:* Using a spoon, remove any grease that has risen to the top of stew and reheat gently but thoroughly over low heat. Add the sautéed artichokes and peas and simmer until the peas are tender and the entire mixture is piping hot. Season to taste with salt and freshly ground black pepper.

10) *To serve:* Serve the veal and vegetables with freshly cooked rice and garnish each plate, if desired, with a few sprigs of fresh oregano and a few strips of shaved Reggiano Parmesan cheese.

CHOPPED STEAKS AL PORTOBELLO

With Sauteed Onions, Mushrooms and Slivered Garlic

YIELD: serves 6

This, the most elegant of hamburgers, is special enough for company, especially when each chopped steak is served topped with tender caramelized onion strips, garlic slices and portobello mushrooms with their incredible taste and meaty texture. Accompany these beautiful burgers with Crusty Garlic Bread (page 405) and a large platter of hot Crispy Cottage-Fried Potato Chips (page 356) and my A1 version of steak sauce (page 90). Garlic Sautéed Cherry Tomatoes (page 324) will round out the menu.

FOR THE GROUND MEAT MIXTURE

2 tablespoons extra-virgin olive oil

½ cup packed minced yellow onion

2 large cloves garlic, minced

1 tablespoon chopped fresh basil leaves or flat-leaf Italian parsley

2¼ pounds ground beef (sirloin, round, chuck or a combination) or ground turkey (a combination of light and dark meat)

1 extra-large egg, lightly beaten

1 egg yolk

½ cup bottled chili sauce*

2 teaspoons Worcestershire sauce

1 tablespoon Dijon mustard

½ teaspoon salt

Freshly ground black pepper to taste

SPECIAL EQUIPMENT
Wide blending fork or large serving fork

12-inch nonreactive skillet with a lid

Time Management Tips

- The chopped steaks can be assembled totally early in the day or as much as 1 day ahead and refrigerated well covered.

- The onions and garlic can be sliced and the mushrooms cleaned and diced 1 day ahead and kept refrigerated in separate, well-covered bowls.

- The onion and mushroom topping can be assembled fully 2 hours ahead and kept in the skillet removed from heat. (This will also leave your home smelling fabulous for your guests to enjoy upon their arrival.) Reheat before serving.

FOR THE TOPPING AND COOKING STEAKS

1 large yellow onion

Extra-virgin olive oil, for sautéeing

3 large cloves garlic, peeled and thinly sliced

4 cups cleaned and coarsely chopped fresh portobello mushrooms (page 131) or button mushrooms with stems intact

Freshly ground black pepper to taste

Kosher or sea salt to taste

⅓ cup dry red wine

⅓ cup Rich Beef Stock (page 146) or canned beef broth, diluted with water if too salty

* See section on Staples

1) **To prepare ground meat mixture:** Heat an 8-inch skillet over medium heat. When hot, add olive oil. When oil is hot, stir in minced onions and garlic and cook over medium heat until softened and very fragrant, about 5 minutes. Then stir in chopped basil and remove from heat to cool. Place ground beef in a large mixing bowl. Add remaining ingredients for meat mixture and the cooled sauteed onions and garlic. Using a blending fork or a large serving fork, gently but thoroughly combine mixture. Don't overwork the ingredients or the chopped steaks will be tough.

2) **To assemble chopped steaks:** Divide meat mixture into 6 generous portions and shape each into an oval pattie at least 1 inch thick. Wrap each pattie in waxed paper and place on a platter. Cover the entire plate with plastic wrap and refrigerate.

3) **To prepare onion strips:** Peel the large onion, cut in half through the stem end and slice each half into very thin wedges. Separate each wedge into thin strips.

4) **To assemble topping:** Heat a 12-inch nonreactive skillet over medium heat and when hot, add a few tablespoons olive oil. When oil is hot, add onion strips and cook, stirring frequently, until softened and very fragrant, 5 to 8 minutes. Stir in sliced garlic and cook until mixture becomes golden, about 8 minutes more. Transfer onions and garlic to a bowl and return skillet to medium-high heat. When hot, add 2 to 3 tablespoons

olive oil. When oil is hot, add chopped mushrooms and cook, stirring constantly, until tender and golden, 3 to 4 minutes. Mix sautéed mushrooms into onion mixture and add a generous amount of freshly ground black pepper.

5) *To cook chopped steaks:* Wipe out skillet and place over medium-high heat. When very hot, brush generously with olive oil. When oil is very hot, lightly sprinkle with coarse salt, then add chopped steaks in a single layer without crowding. Sear meat uncovered until well browned, 4 to 5 minutes, then turn with a thin stainless steel spatula and brown the other side. Cover, then reduce heat to very low. Cook for only a few minutes more or until they are done to your liking. Remove steaks to a warmed serving platter and drape aluminum foil loosely over them.

6) *To deglaze pan:* Pour out any accumulated fat from the skillet but don't wipe out the interior. Return skillet to medium heat and add wine and stock. Bring liquid to a strong simmer and, as the mixture bubbles, use the flat edge of a wooden spatula to scrape the bottom of the skillet to dislodge any pieces of caramelized meat. Reduce liquid by ½ and remove from heat.

7) *To serve:* Top each chopped steak with a generous tablespoon of the reduced wine and stock. Then spoon on the vegetable topping or pass it separately at the table. Serve at once.

Are the Chopped Steaks Ready?

Instead of cutting into the chopped steak and releasing valuable flavor-packed juices, use your finger to determine "doneness." When the chopped steaks appear almost done, check for texture by gently pressing your forefinger on the top center of each steak.

Rare: a soft, springy feeling.

Medium rare: slightly firmer but still quite bouncy at the center. Your finger will meet only slight resistance when pressing.

Medium: Moderately firm but still yielding slightly to pressure from your finger.

Well done: Firm with little movement. Your finger will meet real resistance when pressing.

I'd Walk More than a Mile for . . .
MY MEATLOAF

YIELD: serves 8

SPECIAL EQUIPMENT
Wide blending fork or
large serving fork

9x13-inch glass baking dish

Until recently, meatloaf was often viewed as being ordinary by food professionals and "gourmet" home cooks. Although meatloaf is now touted as "chic" in trendy restaurants focusing on American cuisine, many home cooks still hesitate to serve this truly comforting entrée when entertaining. What a shame! This meatloaf recipe will fill your home with a sensational aroma and fill your mouth with extraordinary flavor, whether you're one of those secret admirers or an out-of-the-closet meatloaf fan. Although I specify a combination of ground beef and veal, feel free to substitute all ground turkey (mix dark and light meat), only ground beef (round, chuck or top sirloin), beef and pork—or a combination of all four. For best results, ask the butcher to grind the meats together for the best balance of flavors and try to assemble the meatloaf early in the day (or as much as one day ahead) so the mixture binds together well. To complete a comforting menu, serve Mashed New Potato Casserole (page 344), omitting the Swiss cheese in either the meatloaf or the potatoes, and Sautéed Fresh Corn (page 321). And leftover meatloaf makes the most fabulous sandwiches when thinly sliced and piled high on toasted slices of Crusty Deli Rye Bread (page 396).

INGREDIENTS

2 tablespoons extra-virgin olive oil

1 cup minced yellow onion

2 large cloves garlic, minced

1 green bell pepper, seeded and minced

3 slices homemade-type white bread, crusts removed and
   the bread cut into very small cubes

¼ cup milk

2 pounds ground beef and 1 pound ground veal
   (preferably ground together)

½ cup prepared chili sauce* plus 1 bottle (12 ounces), for topping

1 tablespoon Dijon mustard

1 cup chopped Swiss cheese (optional)

3 extra-large eggs, lightly beaten

Salt and freshly ground pepper

* See section on Staples

1) **To sauté vegetables:** Heat a 10-inch skillet over medium heat and, when hot, add olive oil. When oil is hot, add chopped onion and garlic and sauté, 3 to 5 minutes. Add green pepper and saute until softened and fragrant, about 3 minutes more. Remove from heat and let cool.

2) **To assemble meatloaf:** In a small bowl, soak bread cubes in milk. Place ground meat in a large mixing bowl and add the ½ cup chili sauce and all the remaining ingredients (except chili sauce for the topping). Gently squeeze bread cubes to remove excess milk and add bread to the bowl along with the cooled vegetables. Combine ingredients gently using a wide blending fork or a large serving fork. Avoid mashing or squeezing the mixture, which tends to result in a tough meatloaf. Transfer mixture to a 9x13-inch baking dish and, using your hands, gently shape into a free-form loaf. Smooth the top with your hands and sprinkle generously with more freshly ground black pepper.

3) **To top and bake:** Pour and spread the entire bottle of chili sauce over the loaf, covering the top and sides completely. Place loaf into a cold oven, turn on heat and bake at 350°F for 1 hour (375°F if not using a glass dish). Remove from oven, cover loosely with aluminum foil and let meatloaf sit undisturbed for 5 minutes. Meanwhile, warm a serving platter.

4) **To serve:** Insert 2 turning spatulas under opposite ends of meatloaf, so that they meet close to the center. Carefully lift and transfer the loaf to the warmed platter. Slice and serve hot or at room temperature. Or enjoy chilled directly from the refrigerator.

Time Management Tips

- The listed vegetables may be chopped or minced 1 day ahead and kept refrigerated in separate, well-covered bowls.

- The meatloaf can be assembled totally, but not topped or baked, 1 day ahead and kept refrigerated well covered. Bake straight from the refrigerator following the prescribed baking time.

A Blast from the Past, Only Better!
SLOPPY JOES

YIELD: serves 6 to 8

SPECIAL EQUIPMENT
10-inch nonreactive deep-sided skillet

My husband is frequently asked, "What's your absolutely favorite meal at home?" Most people are quite surprised by his answer, which is always the same: "Lauren's Sloppy Joes." This combination of ground meat simmered in an intensely flavored sauce, served atop toasted, homemade hamburger buns seems to send my husband back to his childhood. (Of course the sauce we all had back then was from a can, the buns were always store bought and the eating place was usually the school cafeteria.) Since this sauce freezes so perfectly, I recommend that you make a large batch and freeze it in separate small containers. Then on nights when you're exhausted, simply purchase some fresh ground beef and go to your freezer for the sauce. Within minutes, you'll have a delicious, quick and truly comforting meal. Also, don't hesitate to use ground turkey in place of beef. It's one way to make something lower in fat when no one knows the difference!

INGREDIENTS

2 cups Sloppy Joe Sauce (following)

2 generous pounds freshly ground beef (chuck, round, sirloin or a combination) or ground veal and/or turkey

Freshly ground black pepper to taste

6 to 8 hamburger buns, preferably homemade (page 389)

Butter or margarine, for buns

1) *Sloppy Joe Sauce:* Prepare as directed in following recipe, measure out 2 cups and freeze the rest.

2) *To brown ground meat:* Heat a 10-inch nonreactive deep-sided skillet over medium heat. When hot, add ground meat and break up with a wooden spatula. Cook meat until separated and no longer pink, about 4 minutes. Then remove from heat and drain out any excess fat from skillet. Return skillet to low heat, add sauce and stir to incorporate. Bring mixture to a gentle simmer and cook uncovered until the flavors mingle and the mixture is piping hot throughout, about 10 minutes. Add some more freshly ground black pepper and serve immediately.

3) To assemble Sloppy Joes and serve: While sauce is simmering, split hamburger buns, spread lightly with butter or margarine and toast the cut and buttered sides only. Spoon ground beef mixture over buns and serve hot.

Sloppy Joe Sauce

YIELD: about 4 cups; serves 12 to 16

This makes twice as much sauce as called for in the preceding recipe. You can cut it in half or double it so you will have plenty on hand in your freezer. (Plan on using one cup sauce for each pound meat to serve three or four.) The sauce is enhanced with Bovril, a beef-flavored concentrate, available in most supermarkets.

SPECIAL EQUIPMENT
2½-quart nonreactive saucepan

INGREDIENTS

3 tablespoons olive oil

1 cup packed minced yellow onion

½ cup packed seeded and minced green bell pepper

¼ cup seeded and minced red bell pepper

2 tablespoons minced celery

6 cloves garlic, minced

2 cups canned tomato purée

2 rounded tablespoons tomato paste

1 cup prepared ketchup*

2 tablespoons cider vinegar

¼ cup unsulphured molasses*

2 teaspoons Worcestershire sauce

1 tablespoon extra-virgin olive oil

1 cup chopped cleaned fresh button mushrooms or
  portobello mushroom caps only (page 131)

1½ cups peeled, seeded and coarsely chopped ripe plum (Roma)
  tomatoes (page 151) or drained and seeded canned plum tomatoes

1 teaspoon crumbled dried oregano

1 teaspoon Bovril seasoning*

Freshly ground black pepper to taste

* See section on Staples

1) To start sauce: Heat a 2½-quart nonreactive saucepan over medium heat and, when hot, add oil. When oil is hot, stir in minced onion, green and red pepper, celery and garlic. Cook until vegetables are softened and fragrant, 4 to 5 minutes. Stir in tomato purée, tomato paste, ketchup, vinegar, molasses and Worcestershire sauce. Bring the mixture to a simmer, reduce heat to very low and simmer with the cover ajar for 1 hour.

2) To sauté mushrooms: Heat an 8-inch skillet over high heat and, when hot, add olive oil. When oil is hot, add chopped mushrooms and cook, stirring, until mushrooms are golden, 2 to 3 minutes. Remove from heat and set aside.

3) To finish sauce: After sauce has simmered 1 hour, add sautéed mushrooms, chopped plum tomatoes, oregano, Bovril seasoning and some freshly ground black pepper. Return to a simmer and cook with the cover ajar 30 minutes more. If you plan on using right away, measure out as much sauce as needed. Let the remaining sauce cool and freeze in tightly sealed containers.

Serving Variations

The assembled Sloppy Joe mixture (including meat) is not only great on buns, it's fabulous over hot, lightly buttered pasta; toss in some cooked peas for a hearty and delicious meal. Alternatively, stir some into a bowl of Deliciously Simple White Rice (page 361) for a change of texture. And don't throw out any leftovers. Reheat Sloppy Joe mixture on the next night and spoon it onto baked potatoes; if desired, sprinkle the tops lightly with grated Cheddar cheese and bake or broil until the cheese is melted and bubbling.

MY FAVORITE RIB-EYE STEAKS

With a Choice of Three Marinades

YIELD: serves 6

The next time you want to treat yourself and your guests to an all-American meal to knock their socks off, these incredibly flavorful steaks are just the thing! When this thick (almost pastelike) garlicky-oniony-mustardy-peppery marinade is applied liberally all over the meat and then broiled under an intense flame, you are left with the most savory steaks imaginable. Rib-eye steaks (also called club steaks) are from the rib section, just between the chuck and short loin of cattle and are exceptionally tender and succulent— although pricey. Other appropriate cuts of beef are porterhouse or T-bone (also from the loin section), London broil (top sirloin is best and top round is acceptable but drier) and strip or New York steaks (porterhouse steaks without the fillet). Following this recipe, you'll also find two other wonderful marinades and instructions for grilling steaks over hot coals. An accompaniment worthy of these gorgeous steaks is Spinach, Leek and Potato Casserole with Crisp Potato Skins (page 346) with a steaming hot loaf of Garlic Bread (page 405). And don't forget my Steak Sauce (page 90)—I'm sure it will be A1 with you, too.

FOR THE MUSTARD MARINADE

¾ cup Dijon mustard

9 large cloves garlic, minced

1 cup minced scallions (green onions), trimmed white parts and 1½ to 2 inches of the tender green

¼ cup red wine vinegar

¼ cup extra-virgin olive oil

Freshly ground black pepper to taste

FOR THE STEAKS

6 rib-eye steaks, cut 1½ inches thick and trimmed of most external fat

6 Hand-Carved Mushroom Caps (optional), page 337

SPECIAL EQUIPMENT

9x13-inch glass baking dish

Sharp steak knives

Time Management Tips

- Marinating beef for more than 24 hours in a mixture with an acidic ingredient could adversely affect the ultimate texture when cooked. On the other hand, when choosing to marinate for only 30 minutes to 2 hours, the ultimate flavor of the cooked beef will benefit but any tenderizing potential is minimized. Fortunately, this particular cut of beef is naturally tender, so do what's most convenient without exceeding 24 hours. Whatever your choice, however, while marinating always use a nonreactive container such as glass. If you only have an aluminum pan, place steaks in a heavy-duty plastic bag, apply marinade as directed and place sealed bag in pan.

1) *To prepare marinade:* In a medium nonreactive bowl, combine all marinade ingredients and stir well, using lots and lots of freshly ground black pepper—grind until it hurts, then do two more!

2) *To marinate steaks:* Lay steaks in a 9x13-inch glass baking dish in a single layer and coat each steak generously on both sides with the marinade mixture. Grind a generous amount of additional black pepper on each side. Cover and leave at a comfortable room temperature for 3 hours or refrigerate overnight and bring to room temperature before cooking.

3) *To broil:* Position the rack to the upper ⅓ of the oven and preheat the broiler for 15 minutes. Lay steaks on a cold broiler pan (with the marinade left on meat) and place under preheated broiler. For medium rare, broil 5 inches from the heat source (with the door ajar, if applicable to your oven), about 8 minutes on the first side. Turn steaks and broil 5 minutes or until the exterior of steaks is deeply sizzling, golden and incredibly savory looking. If the meat was taken from the refrigerator just before broiling, steaks will take about 2 minutes more per side.

4) *To serve:* Serve steaks hot, accompanied with sharp steak knives. For a festive touch, top with sautéed Hand-Carved Mushroom Caps (page 337).

Peanut-Scented Asian Marinade with Fresh Ginger

YIELD: about 1¾ cups; serves 6

INGREDIENTS

½ cup soy sauce*

½ cup aromatic peanut oil*

4 large cloves garlic, minced

2 teaspoons minced peeled fresh ginger root

⅓ cup dry sherry

½ cup packed minced scallions (green onions), trimmed white part and 1½ to 2 inches of the tender green

1 generous teaspoon toasted sesame oil*

* See section on Staples

Combine all ingredients in a small nonreactive bowl or jar and marinate beef as directed in preceding recipe.

Simple Vinaigrette Marinade

YIELD: about 1⅔ cups; serves 6

INGREDIENTS

½ cup regular olive oil and ½ cup extra-virgin olive oil

⅓ cup red wine vinegar

1 tablespoon Dijon mustard

8 large cloves garlic, minced

1 teaspoon salt

Fresh ground black pepper to taste

1 teaspoon crumbled dried oregano or 1 tablespoon
  chopped fresh oregano

Combine all ingredients in a small nonreactive bowl and marinate beef as
directed in preceding recipe.

Grilling Variations for Steaks

Instead of rib-eye steaks, use more economical London broil and serve thinly
sliced. Skirt steaks are wonderful on the grill. Each weighs 1½ to 2 pounds;
slice on the diagonal (with knife blade at 45 degree angle) for best texture.
For all individual steaks on the bone, allow 8 ounces per person to compensate for shrinkage during grilling. Marinate steaks as directed in preceding
recipe. Then lift meat from marinade and let the excess drip off. (Save the
remaining marinade to baste while grilling). Grill over hot coals until done
to your liking, basting occasionally with reserved marinade.

MAPLE-BRAISED BRISKET

With Chunks of Fresh Carrots and New Potatoes

YIELD: serves 12

SPECIAL EQUIPMENT
10- to 12-quart heavy-bottomed
Dutch oven with tight-fitting lid

Food processor or blender

1 or 2 oven-to-table baking dishes,
for reheating and serving

When you want to make someone feel truly special and cared for, prepare this maple-braised brisket surrounded by tender and glistening chunks of fresh carrots and creamy new potatoes. It's both soothing and simple to prepare. Brisket comes from the forequarters of cattle and is extremely juicy and flavorful, primarily due to the savory fat and tissue interspersed among the muscles within the meat. Although considered a tough cut of beef, properly cooked and sliced brisket is one of the most succulent cuts of meat available. The most important facet of cooking a brisket is moist, slow, even and uninterrupted heat exposure. The bottom of the Dutch oven should be heavy to prevent scorching and the lid must fit perfectly to prevent steam from escaping. Brisket can be pricey, but you can substitute any well-trimmed large cut from the middle chuck section. Complete this "meal in a pot" with Spiced Applesauce (page 91) and golden freshly baked Braided Challah (page 387).

INGREDIENTS

About 5 tablespoons flavorless vegetable oil or mild olive oil as needed

2 large yellow onions, chopped

3 large cloves garlic, minced

1 well-trimmed beef brisket, (7 to 8 pounds) or 2 lean first-cut, well-trimmed briskets (about 4½ pounds each), with a thin layer of fat on the top for best flavor

Freshly ground black pepper to taste

Kitchen Bouquet seasoning* to taste

1 cup pure maple syrup

½ cup Dijon mustard

1 cup Rich Beef Stock (page 146) or canned beef broth, diluted with water if too salty

Instant dissolving flour,* for thickening gravy

8 generous cups large carrot chunks (3½ pounds after removing tops)

12 large new potatoes, peeled, halved if very large and soaked in ice water to prevent discoloring

* See section on Staples

1) **To sauté onions and garlic:** Heat a 10- to 12-quart heavy-bottomed Dutch oven over medium-high heat. When hot, add 2 tablespoons of the vegetable oil and, when oil is hot, stir in chopped onions and garlic. Reduce heat and cook vegetables until softened and fragrant, 5 to 8 minutes. Transfer onions and garlic to a bowl and set aside.

2) **To sear brisket(s):** Sprinkle brisket on both sides with freshly ground black pepper and rub both sides generously with Kitchen Bouquet. Heat 3 more tablespoons of oil in the Dutch oven and, when very hot, add seasoned meat (fat side down) and sear until golden, about 5 minutes. Use 2 sturdy turning spatulas to turn meat over and brown on the other side. Remove to a platter. If using 2 first-cut briskets, brown the remaining piece in the same way.

3) **To assemble:** Pour out any remaining oil from the Dutch oven and spoon half of the sautéed onion-garlic mixture onto the bottom of the pot. Lay meat (fat side up) on top of onions. In a small bowl, combine maple syrup and mustard and pour over meat. Spoon remaining onions on top of meat and sprinkle with more pepper. Pour beef stock over and around meat and strew carrots and potatoes around the sides.

4) **To braise:** Place lid on securely, place in a cold oven and turn on heat to 325°F. Cook brisket for 4 hours without disturbing. (Alternatively, this may be simmered on top of the stove for the same amount of time. Begin timing as soon as you turn on the heat but cook over medium heat at first and, when the pot feels hot, reduce heat to low.) When cooked, carefully remove meat to a large platter and allow to cool slightly. Transfer carrots and potatoes to another platter and cover with aluminum foil (or to a long heatproof dish, if preparing in advance).

5) **To finish gravy:** Pour beefy liquid and minced onions from roaster through a medium-mesh wire strainer into a bowl and place the solids into the bowl of a food processor fitted with the steel blade or a blender. Purée solids and pour them back into the bowl of liquids. Pour contents of bowl into a 2-quart heavy-bottomed saucepan and place over low heat. Bring gravy to a simmer and sprinkle in a little instant dissolving flour while stirring constantly with a whisk. Continue to simmer gently, adding more flour (a little at a time) until the desired consistency is achieved. Taste for seasoning, adding salt and freshly ground black pepper to taste and remove from heat.

Q AND A

Q. What does it mean to cut "against the grain?" And why is my sliced brisket stringy?

A. Even the most perfectly cooked brisket will be a disappointment if not sliced properly. You'll know immediately if you're doing it wrong as the meat will fall apart and become stringy as you slice. In order to obtain tender, intact slices, the cooked meat must be cut across or against the grain (lines of connection within the meat). Letting the meat cool for a while after cooking also encourages it to settle down and behave.

6) To slice, reheat and serve: Using a sharp carving knife, slice meat against the grain into thin slices. Lift slices carefully, using 2 spatulas, onto a long platter (or, if preparing in advance, a long heatproof dish). Pour some of the gravy on top and around the slices, saving some to ladle over the vegetables. To reheat, place the meat and vegetables on separate shelves in a preheated 350°F oven until piping hot, about 30 minutes, switching shelf positions after 15 minutes.

Time Management Tips

• The onions can be chopped 1 day ahead and kept refrigerated, securely covered. Also, the carrots can be peeled and sliced 1 day ahead, wrapped in damp paper towels and stored in a large heavy-duty plastic bag in the refrigerator.

• Although the meat would benefit from being cooked 1 day ahead, the vegetables really taste best when served on the day of cooking. So, make this early in the day and simply reheat sliced meat on one platter and vegetables in another dish. Make sure that both reheat in ample gravy and serve any remaining gravy in a gravy boat at the table or on a buffet.

• If time is scarce, simply prepare the meat 1 or 2 days ahead (omitting the carrots and potatoes) and refrigerate. The day before serving, blanch the same amount of diagonally sliced fresh carrots in lightly salted boiling water until almost tender, refresh in ice water and, once cold, drain and refrigerate as described above. To serve, sauté carrots in a little melted butter until nicely caramelized just before serving. And instead of new potatoes, serve Oh-So-Good Latkes (page 359).

• Or, if holiday season is on its way and you're planning a large menu, braise the brisket a month in advance. Once the meat becomes cool, slice it and layer slices with ample gravy and freeze in a labeled heavy-duty freezer container; then the day before "show-time," bring it out and thaw in the refrigerator. Reheat as directed.

To Soothe What Ails You . . .

BEEF STEW AT ITS BEST

YIELD: serves 12 to 16

What could be more soothing on a frigid winter night than a home filled with the nurturing scent of a simmering stew? Since stews are notorious for being freezer friendly, I have provided an extra-large recipe to enable you to enjoy slow-cooked goodness on days when you just don't have the time. This is another of those fabulous meals to whip up from your freezer for unexpected guests. If desired, halve the recipe and serve six to eight. Serve the stew ladled over hot lightly buttered Homemade Egg Noodles (page 175) and accompany the meal with tender Sweet Cream Biscuits (page 422).

SPECIAL EQUIPMENT
12-quart nonreactive heavy-bottomed Dutch oven with tight-fitting lid

8-quart blanching pot with built-in strainer (optional)

INGREDIENTS

8 ounces bacon (preferably slab), cut into small cubes

Butter and/or olive oil, for sautéing

3 large onions, chopped

8 cloves garlic, minced

6 pounds beef chuck, cut into 1½-inch cubes

1½ cups all-purpose flour, seasoned with salt and freshly ground black pepper

1½ cups dry red wine

About 2½ cups Rich Beef Stock (page 146) or canned beef broth, diluted with water if too salty

1 can (12 ounces) tomato paste

2½ pounds carrots, peeled and sliced diagonally ½ inch thick

6 stalks celery, cleaned and sliced diagonally ½ inch thick

12 large new potatoes, peeled and cut into quarters

4 pounds ripe tomatoes, peeled, seeded and coarsely chopped (page 151), or 2 cans (28 ounces each) whole peeled tomatoes, drained, seeded and coarsely chopped

1 pound medium-sized fresh button mushrooms, wiped clean and quartered (page 131)

1¼ pounds fresh pearl onions or 2 boxes (10 ounces each) frozen pearl onions, thawed

Time Management Tips

- Chop and slice all the vegetables (except potatoes) 1 day ahead and refrigerate in separate, well-covered bowls.

- The flavor of all stews is enhanced if made a day ahead so the flavors can intensify. When stew is cooled and grease removed, pull a clean kitchen towel over the top of the pot and place the lid over the towel. The towel will prevent any accumulation of condensation (rising steam) from falling into the stew and diluting the flavors. Refrigerate and bring to room temperature before reheating gently.

Salt and freshly ground black pepper to taste

1 pound frozen peas, thawed under hot running water

Cooked and lightly buttered Homemade Egg Noodles (page 175), for accompaniment

1) To cook bacon: Lay a double thickness of paper toweling on a plate. Heat a 12- inch deep-sided skillet over medium heat. Fry bacon until crisp and the fat is rendered, then drain on paper towels. (If using sliced bacon, crumble after draining.) Remove half the drippings from skillet and reserve separately. (Alternatively, remove all drippings from skillet and substitute olive oil and/or butter.)

2) To sauté onions and garlic: Heat skillet with drippings or olive oil over medium heat and add onions. Cook onions, stirring frequently, until softened and very fragrant, about 10 minutes. Add minced garlic, reduce heat and cook vegetables until softened and a light golden brown throughout. Transfer with a slotted spoon to a 12-quart nonreactive heavy-bottomed pot.

3) To dredge and brown meat: Add some more drippings or olive oil to the skillet and return to medium-high heat. (Using 2 skillets to brown meat saves time.) While drippings are heating, dredge some of the meat in seasoned flour (only coat as many pieces as will brown at one time in a single layer without crowding). Sear meat on all sides and, as each batch becomes golden, transfer using a slotted spoon to the pot with the sautéed onions and garlic. Continue to sear all the meat, adding additional drippings or olive oil to the skillet to prevent meat from sticking. (While searing, if burnt-looking flour accumulates on the bottom of skillet, dump out oil, wipe out the interior, add fresh oil and continue browning meat.) Fold meat with vegetables to combine and stir in cooked bacon.

4) To deglaze skillet(s): Pour out any excess oil from skillet and return to medium-high heat. Add red wine and 1½ cups of the beef stock and bring to a boil. As liquid bubbles, scrape up brown bits of caramelized meat and onions from the bottom of skillet. Let mixture continue to reduce for about 6 minutes and pour the reduction into stew pot. (If using 2 skillets, divide deglazing liquids between them and reduce by half.)

5) *To simmer beef:* Stir tomato paste into stew and, if necessary, add more beef stock to almost cover the mixture. Bring to a full simmer and fold together to redistribute. Reduce heat to very low, cover and simmer gently for 1½ hours, stirring occasionally to prevent sticking or scorching on the bottom. If at any time the mixture seems overly thick, add a little more beef stock. (Remember, however, that tomatoes will be added later and will exude their own liquid.)

6) *To add vegetables to stew:* After stew has simmered for 1½ hours, fold in carrots, celery, potatoes and tomatoes. Raise heat to medium so stew returns to a good simmer, then reduce heat to very low, cover and simmer slowly for 40 minutes.

7) *To peel and blanch pearl onions:* Bring a large pot of water to a rapid boil. Meanwhile, cut an X into the trimmed root end of each onion and place a large bowl of ice water on the counter. Blanch onions in boiling water for 3 minutes. Drain and plunge onions into the ice water, swishing them around with your hands to immediately stop the cooking process. Drain onions and slip off their outer peels.

8) *To sauté mushrooms and finish stew:* Heat an 8-inch skillet over medium-high heat and, when hot, add 2 tablespoons butter or olive oil. Sauté mushrooms until golden and tender, about 3 minutes, stirring constantly. Add sautéed mushrooms and blanched pearl onions to stew and simmer with the cover ajar until meat is very tender but vegetables are not at all mushy, about 10 minutes. Add salt to taste with lots of freshly ground black pepper and remove pot from heat to cool. As stew cools, use a spoon to remove any grease that rises to the top.

9) *To reheat, add peas and serve:* Reheat stew, covered, on the stove top over low heat or in a preheated 350°F oven until piping hot throughout. While reheating, occasionally stir up stew from the bottom. When hot, add thawed frozen peas and when stew returns to a simmer, serve immediately over lightly buttered egg noodles.

10) *To freeze:* Once cool, divide stew among heavy freezer containers and attach a label and date before storing in the freezer. To thaw, allow the container to sit in the refrigerator overnight and reheat gently as directed or by using a microwave (page 288).

*How to Defrost or
Reheat Prepared Foods
in a Microwave*

Although I rarely use a microwave to cook (with the exception of fresh artichokes), I find this appliance perfect for defrosting soups, stocks and stews and for gently reheating cooked pasta, rice, vegetables, seafood and poultry. I do not, however, use it to thaw breads or rolls, which should be allowed to come back to room temperature naturally. You should know a few things about the microwave before using it to thaw or reheat prepared foods. Both microwaves and conventional ovens cook foods from the outside in, but they differ in their speed of doing the job. Conventional ovens must heat the food before actual cooking takes place, whereas microwave energy zaps directly into foods with no preliminary heating time. This zapping causes the molecules within the food to vibrate and create instant heat.

Microwave containers: Only certain materials are suitable for microwave heat. These are heat-resistant glass, porcelain, ceramic (not mugs with glued-on handles), heavy-duty plastic wrap, certain types of paper toweling and microwave-safe plastic containers. To check if a container is microwave safe, fill a glass measuring cup with water and place it inside the container. Place both into the microwave and cook on high

power for 1 minute. The water in the cup will be hot, but the plastic container should feel cool to the touch (or just slightly warm). If the container feels hot, it should not be used in the microwave. Don't use metal in the microwave or you run the risk of causing sparks (arcing). The only exception to this is using small pieces of aluminum foil to shield particular areas of foods to prevent them from overcooking; place the foil flat (without crimping) over those areas (crimps or wrinkles in the foil can cause sparks). Also, any paper towel that's made with synthetics (such as nylon) can cause the towel to burn. Your best bet is to look for toweling labeled microwave, like Bounty microwave. Don't use a sheet of toweling more than once in the microwave since this has been known to spark microwave fires. And beware that the lids to many of the microwave-safe plastic containers are not heat resistant. It's best to reheat foods covered with vented heavy-duty plastic wrap (I prefer Reynolds Plastic Wrap). Also, round dishes seem to encourage the most even distribution of microwave heat. And a microwave turntable is very helpful (though not essential) to help the food reheat evenly; after you wind up the movable tray, the turntable continually rotates the food being reheated. Alternatively, rotate the dish a quarter turn after every few minutes in the microwave.

To prepare food for the microwave: If your frozen food is in a dish that is not microwave safe, place the bottom of the container under hot tap water to release the frozen block of food; then transfer it to an appropriate material. Cover the dish with heavy-duty plastic wrap and vent the top. To create vents, either cut several small slits in the top of the plastic, or vent only one corner of the dish by folding back one corner of plastic so that corner remains open. Venting is important, not only to prevent the plastic from ballooning up, but also to reduce the buildup of steam, which can cause a bad burn when uncovering the dish. Wind up a microwave turntable, if using, and place in the center of the microwave.

To reheat a frozen mixture evenly in the microwave: Place the dish on the turntable and using medium power, thaw the mixture, stopping the microwave every few minutes to check the progress. Remember, the object here is to reheat only, not to cook the mixture. When the sides become liquified, pour the liquid into another pot or bowl and continue to zap the remaining mixture, removing the liquid and softened ingredients as they thaw. Once the container no longer holds large pieces of frozen food, pour the entire mixture back into the container, cover with a new piece of plastic, cut vents in the top, rewind your turntable, if using, and reheat on medium-low power, checking and stirring every 2 or 3 minutes, until hot throughout.

To reheat cooked (not frozen) prepared foods in the microwave: If reheating rice, pasta, vegetables or prepared casseroles, add additional water or stock to the mixture (2 to 3 tablespoons per cup of food) before placing into the microwave. Using the same equipment and venting procedure as described above, reheat mixture on medium-low power, checking every 2 minutes. Each time you check, stir the foods from the sides of the dish (which will reheat first) in toward the center and bring the center out to the sides. Remove when piping hot throughout but not overcooked.

Foods not to prepare or reheat in the microwave: Fried (crisp) foods, eggs in their shells, home-canned items, crêpes or pancakes, large roasts and breads.

BROWN SUGAR–GLAZED CORNED BEEF

With Boiled New Potatoes

YIELD: serves 6 to 8

SPECIAL EQUIPMENT
8-quart blanching pot with built-in strainer (optional)

You don't need to be Irish to appreciate this traditional St. Patricks Day meal. A generous application of a mustard and brown sugar glaze makes the surface of this corned beef almost candied. When purchasing the cured brisket, remember that cooking a corned beef is a little like cooking fresh spinach. Although initially you put a substantial amount into the pot, after cooking due to shrinkage, you'll swear that someone absconded with your food! So, it's always best to prepare more than you think necessary since leftovers are easily made into hash or a fabulous Reuben Pie (recipe follows). And when possible, purchase lean first-cut corned beef since less fat at the beginning means more meat after the initial simmering. For best flavor, the corned beef should be cured in a salt and water solution only; avoid beef that's pickled in heavy brine. Mosey's is the brand that's never let me down. To enhance your menu, add a side dish of Braised Cabbage with Caraway (page 335) and serve the sliced corned beef with Creamy Dijon Mustard Sauce (page 89).

INGREDIENTS

2 first-cut corned beef briskets (about 4 pounds each)

1 cup orange juice or unsweetened pineapple juice (optional)

FOR THE BROWN SUGAR GLAZE

½ cup dark brown sugar

¼ cup Dijon mustard

¼ cup pineapple or peach preserves (optional)

FOR THE BOILED NEW POTATOES

12 to 16 medium-sized new potatoes

½ to ¾ stick (4 to 6 tablespoons) butter, melted

2 tablespoons chopped flat-leaf Italian parsley

Kosher or sea salt to taste

Freshly ground black pepper to taste

ACCOMPANIMENT

Creamy Dijon Mustard Sauce (page 89)

1) *To poach corned beef:* Bring an 8-quart pot of water to a simmer. (If using a blanching pot, remove strainer for now.) If the brisket has a heavy layer of fat on top, trim it so only a thin layer remains. Carefully lower meat into simmering water, cover and return to a full simmer over medium heat. Reduce heat to low and simmer meat for 3 hours. Turn off heat, but keep pot covered and let meat sit in the water for an additional 30 minutes.

2) *To glaze corned beef:* Ladle out 1 cup of the poaching liquid from pot (or substitute orange or pineapple juice) and pour onto the bottom of a shallow baking sheet (nonreactive if using juice). Carefully remove beef from water and place (fat side up) on baking sheet. (Reserve remaining poaching liquid to cook potatoes.) In a small bowl, combine brown sugar with mustard and, if desired, preserves. Brush mixture liberally over the exposed areas of meat.

3) *To roast:* Meanwhile, preheat oven to 325°F. Roast corned beef until hot and the glaze has caramelized and is becoming crisp, about 45 minutes.

4) *To boil potatoes:* While corned beef roasts, bring poaching liquid back to a boil and, if using a blanching pot, insert strainer. Add potatoes to boiling water and cook (covered) until tender, but not mushy, 15 to 20 minutes at a strong boil.

5) *To carve corned beef:* Transfer glazed meat to a carving board and let settle (loosely covered with aluminum foil) for 10 minutes. Slice each brisket into ⅓-inch slices, going against the grain with a sharp knife. Cover meat with foil while you finish potatoes.

6) *To finish potatoes and serve:* Melt butter in a 10- to 12-inch deep-sided skillet. Just before serving, drain potatoes, add to skillet and shake the handle gently to swirl each potato in melted butter. Sprinkle with chopped parsley, freshly ground black pepper and a light application of coarse salt. Swirl once more. Carefully spoon each potato into a warmed serving bowl. Serve potatoes while hot with the sliced corned beef. Pass mustard sauce at the table.

Time Management Tips

• The corned beef can be simmered hours in advance and left at room temperature on the prepared baking sheet (with the glaze applied) until ready to roast. If necessary, place glazed beef on the sheet, cover with waxed paper, then plastic wrap and refrigerate overnight. Bring close to room temperature before roasting.

• The potatoes can be peeled early in the day and left in a bowl of ice water to prevent them from discoloring.

REUBEN PIE FROM LEFTOVER CORNED BEEF

YIELD: one 10-inch quiche

Whenever I serve corned beef I use the leftovers to prepare this fabulous pie and serve it with a green salad for lunch or a light supper. I usually bake this earlier in the day and fully reheat it (in a preheated 350°F oven) just before serving. I find that this initial settling period helps the pie to hold its shape better after being cut into wedges.

SUGGESTED EQUIPMENT

10-inch pie plate

8- or 10-inch nonstick skillet

Spice grinder (only if adding ground caraway seeds to pastry dough)

INGREDIENTS

1 recipe *savory version* of Favorite Pie Pastry (page 93)

1 teaspoon ground caraway seeds (optional)

3 tablespoons clarified butter (page 81) or flavorless vegetable oil

3 medium-sized leftover boiled potatoes, chilled and diced

1 scant tablespoon Dijon mustard

1½ cups shredded Swiss or Jarlsberg cheese

2½ cups diced leftover glazed corned beef or plain boiled corned beef

1 cup leftover Braised Cabbage with Caraway (page 335)
  or steamed shredded green cabbage

4 extra-large eggs

2 cups heavy cream (preferably not ultrapasteurized)

¾ teaspoon salt

Freshly ground black pepper to taste

1) **Favorite Pie Pastry:** Prepare pastry dough as directed, adding ground caraway seeds, if desired. *Partially* prebake pastry shell and let cool.

2) **To sear potatoes:** Heat an 8- to 10-inch nonstick skillet over medium heat and, when hot, add clarified butter or oil. Add diced potatoes to hot butter and sear until golden on all sides, stirring often. Transfer to a plate using a slotted spoon.

3) **To assemble:** Preheat the oven to 375°F. Brush interior of the cooled partially prebaked pie shell with mustard. Sprinkle 1 cup of the shredded cheese on bottom of shell. In a bowl, mix together diced corned beef, braised cabbage and seared potatoes and spoon on top of cheese. In another bowl, lightly beat eggs and stir in cream, salt and a generous amount of freshly ground black pepper. Pour all but ¾ cup over the filling and scatter the remaining ½ cup cheese on top. Pour the remaining egg mixture over cheese and grind on some more fresh pepper.

4) **To bake and serve:** Bake until golden and egg mixture has set, 45 to 50 minutes. Place on a wire rack to settle before slicing into wedges and serving.

APRICOT-GLAZED HAM

For a Holiday Buffet

YIELD: serves 12 to 20 as part of a buffet

The mere sight of a glistening, freshly roasted, glazed ham on a holiday table will undoubtedly bring back to your guests memories of holidays past. When buying a ham, you will have choices to make. Will you start with a fully cooked, partially cooked or uncooked ham? Which brand is the best? Should you choose a smoked ham or simply a cured ham? Do you want leftovers? What will you do with the leftovers? This recipe produces a ham that is savory and rich using the method that I prefer most for ease of preparation. It probably would be chic to say that my favorite type of ham wore the renowned name of Smithfield, but truthfully I prefer a ham that's processed with moisture and my favorite is manufactured by a company called Esky. Not only are these hams delicious, but I don't find them overly salty or smoky-tasting. I usually opt to leave the bone in since it creates a deeper dimension in flavor, but having the butcher saw off the oyster bone (sometimes called the aitch-bone) will help to facilitate carving. For a cocktail party, however, I suggest having most of the bone removed (leaving only the tip of the shank for appearance). This will make carving uniform slices much easier when entertaining a large number of guests. And regarding leftovers, plan to make a huge pot of Double Split Pea Soup (page 168).

SPECIAL EQUIPMENT

Sturdy roasting rack
Sturdy nonreactive roasting pan

Meat thermometer that will register a temperature as low as 120°F.

INGREDIENTS

1 whole cooked, cured ham on the bone (about 14 pounds),
  trimmed of leatherlike skin and oyster bone removed

¾ cup packed dark brown sugar

¾ cup Dijon mustard

¾ cup apricot jam or preserves

1 cup unsweetened pineapple juice

SUGGESTED ACCOMPANIMENTS

Assorted mustards and/or Creamy Dijon Mustard Sauce (page 89)

Sliced Crusty Deli Rye Bread (page 396)

1) To sear ham: Preheat the oven to 350°F. Score ham's exposed top fat
in a diamond pattern and place (fat side up) on a sturdy wire rack inside
a sturdy, nonreactive roasting pan. Roast until ham just starts to turn
golden, about 1 hour.

TIPS

FROM A TEACHER

Secrets of Sharp Knives

The majority of kitchen accidents are caused by using dull knives or by grasping an improperly stored knife. When the blade is dull, cooks overcompensate by using hard, forceful, sawing motions from a knife that should only require relaxed rhythmical movement. Keeping your blades sharp will not only help keep you safe but will make the whole procedure of chopping, slicing, carving and trimming more productive and enjoyable.

Always store your knives in a specifically designed knife block. This will protect your blades as well as your fingers from being cut when hunting around your utility drawer for the right tool.

Most professionals still rely on a 12-inch rod called a "sharpening steel" (or butcher's steel) to keep their blades meticulously sharp. The rod has a rough texture to create the necessary friction for sharpening a blade until almost razor sharp. Although there are ceramic rods available, they are more fragile and therefore less durable. And using a thick rod is preferable to a thin one since the thicker rod presents more surface friction to the blade. Rods should not be washed, but when necessary brush off with a brass bristle brush.

Proper technique is imperative to sharpen your blades and best results are achieved when the blade is sharp-

2) **To glaze ham:** In a small bowl, mix together brown sugar, mustard and apricot jam. Remove ham from oven (leave oven on and remove from rack. Pour out any accumulated fat from bottom of pan. Pour pineapple juice onto bottom of pan and place ham directly on top of juice (again fat side up). Using a rubber spatula, spread ⅔ of the prepared glaze mixture over the entire exposed surface of the ham.

3) **To roast ham:** Insert a meat thermometer *deeply* into ham in its thickest spot on top (but don't allow stem to touch bone). Return ham to oven and roast until the thermometer reaches 120°F, about 2 hours for a boneless ham and 1½ hours for a ham with bone. Spread on the remaining glaze, covering completely. Return ham to oven and continue to roast until ham is piping hot throughout and the outside is crusty and deeply caramelized. The meat thermometer should read 137°F. A 14-pound ham (with bone) will take approximately 3 hours in a regular conventional oven, including the initial searing time. The glaze on the finished ham will become very shiny with a deep, intensely dark color, but it should not be black.

ened frequently rather than allowing it to become very dull before each sharpening session. Seriously dull knives should be taken to a professional for a more intensive sharpening session.

To sharpen knives with a sharpening steel: Hold the rod by the handle in your nonworking hand with the rod pointing away from you but tilted up. Position the knife blade at a shallow 15- to 20-degree angle and run the blade up and down, back and forth and across the textured rod 7 to 12 times in a smooth and rhythmical motion. It's important to always keep the blade at the same angle while sharpening. Always thoroughly rinse and dry your blade after sharpening and never sharpen your knives directly over food or your work surface to prevent carbon dust from being ingested.

Q. I thought the internal temperature of pork should be between 150°F and 155°F in order to kill trichina (a parasite found in raw pork). Why do you remove the ham from the oven at 137°F?

A. *When cooking a raw pork leg, the higher internal temperature is required to ensure a bacteria free ham. However, when cooking a smoked and/or cured ham that's already been fully or partially cooked, all that's required is a thorough reheating to the bone or center of the ham; 137°F is perfect.*

4) *To remove from oven:* When ham is almost done, bring a kettle of water up to boil and let simmer until needed. Carefully transfer ham from oven to your carving board to settle for 15 minutes or longer before slicing and serving. Immediately pour boiling water over the interior of the baking pan to facilitate cleaning by loosening fallen candied glaze.

5) *To slice and serve:* Don't worry about slicing with or against the grain. Slice thinly in the direction that gives you the largest slice with the least interference from the bone. Serve hot, warm or chilled (not cold) with assorted mustards or mustard sauce.

Variations for Cooking a Larger or Smaller Ham

For a larger ham that weighs 17 to 22 pounds, increase the glaze ingredients to 1 cup brown sugar, mustard and jam. If baking a 16- to 18-pound ham (before trimming), the initial searing time will be 1½ hours. For a 19- to 22-pound ham, sear 2 hours, covering loosely with aluminum foil (shiny side up) for the last 30 minutes if the ham is becoming overly brown. For a smaller ¾ shank ham that weighs only 10 to 11 pounds before trimming, only 35 to 40 minutes of searing is needed. Once the glaze is applied, the cooking times will remain the same. Because a larger ham will need more time to cook through, if the glaze is applied too early, the exterior will burn.

GLAZED LOIN OF PORK

With Apple Cider and Mustard Gravy

YIELD: serves 8 to 10

You'll be proud to serve this tender glistening pork roast with its apple-mustard-shallot gravy at either an elegant dinner party or a cozy dinner for the extended family. Because most pork sold today comes from swine that only are six to nine months old, the resulting meat is one-third leaner than in the past, and it requires proper cooking for maximum taste and succulence. Unfortunately, people are so spooked about ingesting trichina (a parasite found in raw pork) that they end up cooking the poor thing to death! But don't worry. Trichinae are killed when an internal temperature of 137°F is reached. By cooking pork until it reaches 150°F to 155°F, you can be sure the meat is safe to eat. When purchasing fresh pork, choose meat that is pale pink in color. Flesh with a deeper tone indicates that it comes from an older

SPECIAL EQUIPMENT

12-inch nonreactive skillet

Sturdy roasting rack

Sturdy nonreactive roasting pan

Meat thermometer, preferably not instant

Flat gravy whisk or sauce whisk

Fine-mesh wire strainer

animal. The external fat should be pure white (as opposed to yellow) with only a small amount of marbling within the meat. Serve these tender slices of roast pork with the luscious gravy passed separately at the table. Perfect accompaniments are Braised Cabbage with Caraway (page 335), Sautéed Spiced Golden Delicious Apples (page 339) and Maple-Basted Delicata Squash (page 336).

INGREDIENTS

⅓ cup Dijon mustard

⅓ cup packed dark brown sugar

2 tablespoons soy sauce*

2 tablespoons apple juice or apple cider

5 large cloves garlic, minced or pressed through a garlic press

1 loin of pork (4 to 4½ pounds), trimmed and tied with twine
 at 2-inch intervals

Freshly ground black pepper to taste

3 tablespoons clarified butter (page 81) or olive oil or
 aromatic peanut oil*

FOR THE GRAVY

3 tablespoons butter

1 large shallot, minced

1 cup apple juice or cider

2 cups Rich Chicken Stock (page 140) or a combination of
 chicken stock and Rich Beef Stock (page 146)

3 tablespoon all-purpose flour

2 tablespoon apple cider vinegar

1 teaspoon Dijon mustard

Salt and freshly ground black pepper to taste

* See section on Staples

1) *To set up:* Preheat the oven to 475°F. For the glaze, combine in a small bowl, mustard, brown sugar, soy sauce, apple juice and garlic; set aside.

2) *To sear pork:* Sprinkle pork with freshly ground black pepper. Heat butter or oil in a 12-inch nonreactive skillet. When hot, add pork, fat side down, and sear on all sides until golden, about 10 minutes. Remove from skillet and discard any remaining fat from skillet but do not wipe out the interior; set aside.

3) *To glaze and roast pork:* Place pork (fat side up) on a rack that sits over a roasting pan. Rub the entire exterior of pork generously with ¾ of the glaze. Insert a meat thermometer into the thickest part (through the top) of the loin so the tip of the stem reaches the center of the eye. Roast in hot oven for 30 minutes. Reduce temperature to 325°F and pour the remaining glaze over pork. Continue roasting until the internal temperature is between 150°F and 155°F (check after 20 to 30 minutes). Remove from oven and let roast sit on its rack, tented loosely with aluminum foil, over a platter to catch the juices for 10 to 15 minutes. (This waiting period enables the inner juices to centralize.) Meanwhile, warm your serving platter.

4) *To deglaze skillet:* Heat the original searing skillet over medium heat and, when hot, add 1 tablespoon of the butter. When butter is bubbling, add minced shallot and cook until tender and fragrant, about 2 minutes. Add apple juice and bring to a brisk simmer, stirring to release any browned bits of pork from bottom of skillet. Continue to cook until reduced by almost ½.

5) *To make gravy:* Tip roasting pan so only the fat drains out leaving the thick accumulated glaze on the bottom. Place pan directly over medium-low heat and add the remaining 2 tablespoons butter. When melted and hot, sprinkle bottom of pan with flour and stir well to combine using a wooden spatula. Raise heat to medium and cook flour, stirring constantly, for 1 to 2 minutes. Add stock and bring to a brisk simmer, stirring as the mixture becomes thoroughly incorporated. Continue to cook, stirring constantly, until thickened and smooth, using a flat gravy whisk or a regular sauce whisk. Pour thickened stock mixture into skillet with the reduced apple juice. Then add cider vinegar and mustard. Stir and simmer until the mixture is well combined and slightly reduced.

6) *To strain gravy:* Position a fine-mesh wire strainer over a 1-quart saucepan and carefully pour gravy into the strainer. Use a wooden spatula to stir and push gravy through the mesh and discard whatever remains in the strainer. Season to taste with salt and pepper and keep warm until ready to serve.

7) *To serve:* Slice roast into ⅓-inch slices and arrange on a large warmed serving platter. Pour any reserved juices from from your carving board over the pork and serve hot. Pass a bowl of hot gravy separately at the table.

MEDITERRANEAN LAMB CHOPS

Marinated with Olive Oil, Garlic and Fresh Mint

YIELD: serves 4

Preparing lamb chops bathed with this garlicky-minty mixture is not only delicious but quick and simple to prepare. Applying melted mint jelly to the broiled chops gives them a wonderful flavor and a caramelized sheen. Use fresh mint whenever possible and don't skimp on the garlic—or the fresh pepper!

SPECIAL EQUIPMENT
Sharp steak knives

INGREDIENTS

⅓ cup *each* extra-virgin olive oil and regular olive oil

6 cloves garlic, minced or pressed through a garlic press

2 tablespoons chopped fresh mint leaves or 2 teaspoons crumbled dried mint leaves

Freshly ground black pepper to taste

8 loin lamb chops (1 to 1½ inches thick)

Generous ½ cup mint jelly or apple-mint jelly, melted

1) *To marinate chops:* In a small bowl, mix olive oils, garlic, mint and lots of freshly ground pepper. Lay chops in a single layer in a large shallow glass dish and sprinkle them liberally with fresh pepper. Spoon marinade over chops, turning each over to coat on all sides. Pour any remaining marinade over all. Cover with plastic wrap and allow to sit at room temperature from 30 minutes to 2 hours or refrigerate overnight.

Time Management Tips

• The lamb chops can be marinated as long as 2 days ahead and kept well covered in the refrigerator.

2) *To broil chops:* Position oven rack to upper ⅓ and preheat the broiler until very hot. Melt jelly in a small saucepan over low heat. Place chops on a cold broiler pan and broil 5 inches from heat source, turning once until almost medium-rare, 4 to 5 minutes per side. Remove from broiler and spoon about 1½ teaspoons melted jelly on top of each chop. Place back under broiler for 1 to 2 minutes to caramelize jelly.

3) *To serve:* Place chops on a heated serving platter and garnish with fresh mint leaves. Serve hot with sharp steak knives.

HONEY MUSTARD ROAST RACK OF LAMB

YIELD: serves 4 generously and 6 adequately

This elegant and easy roast rack of lamb is the perfect entrée when you want to serve something special without a lot of preparation. The gentle sweetness of the honey combined with the spiciness of the Dijon mustard gives the lamb a wonderful barbecue flavor without having to use the grill. And since this marinade is also great on both pork and beef ribs, I suggest doubling it and storing half in the refrigerator to use on another occasion. Although the lamb is delicious enough to be served without an embellishing sauce, the traditional accompaniment of mint jelly is always appreciated. The degree to which a rack of lamb is trimmed can vary dramatically: Some people like the rib bones to be trimmed totally with only the eye of meat remaining; others prefer that only 1½ inches of the rib tips be trimmed. In either case, be sure to remind your butcher to saw through the spinal column behind the eye of meat for easy carving. And always request that a thin layer of fat be left on top to keep the lean meat moist during roasting. Before you purchase a rack of lamb or if your racks needs some additional sprucing up when you get home, see my Tips from a Teacher.

SPECIAL EQUIPMENT
Blender

9x13-inch glass baking dish

Sharp steak knives

INGREDIENTS

2 racks of lamb (8 ribs each), well trimmed

½ cup bottled chili sauce or ketchup*

¼ cup mild honey

2 tablespoons soy sauce*

2 tablespoons Dijon mustard

4 large cloves garlic, minced

1 tablespoon red wine vinegar

Freshly ground black pepper to taste

Mint jelly, for accompaniment

* See section on Staples

1) **To prepare lamb:** If necessary, finish trimming racks of lamb as directed in Tips from a Teacher (following). Score the layer of top fat in a diamond pattern using a sharp knife, being careful not to sever the meat.

2) **To prepare marinade:** Place all remaining ingredients except black pepper and mint jelly into a blender and blend until smooth. Pour mixture into a small heavy-bottomed saucepan and bring to a simmer uncovered. Simmer over low heat for 10 minutes. Remove from heat and add a generous amount of freshly ground black pepper. Let cool.

Time Management Tips

• To marinate the lamb 1 day ahead, cover and reserve the remaining 1/4 cup of marinade in the refrigerator and bring to room temperature along with the lamb before roasting.

Before purchasing a rack of lamb, examine the color. Top-quality young lamb should be bright-bright cherry red. So should any tinges on the back of the ribs as well as any exuded droplets of moisture on the surface of the meat. Before trimming, the top layer of fat shouldn't be overly thick—1/8 to 1/4 inch is just about perfect. The scent should be identifiably "lamblike" without being overly gamey and strong. If your lamb needs some extra trimming before roasting, it's easy to accomplish as long as your knives are sharp.

To finish trimming a rack of lamb before seasoning: To thin the layer of top fat so it's no more than 1/4 inch thick, position the blade of a sharp carving knife parallel to top of the fat. Tilt blade down (ever so slightly) and run down the fat in a steady sawing motion. Be careful not to sever the meat. If the ribs have small scraps of meat or sinew attached, use a sharp paring knife to scrape the bones clean. When perfectly bare, use a paper towel to wipe each rib clean and, if desired, to remove the white, creamy substance that runs down the length of the spinal column. And be sure that the spinal column is completely severed between each rib for easier carving. If not, use a heavy meat mallet to drive the tip of a meat cleaver through any pieces of bone.

TIPS

FROM A TEACHER

*Choosing and Trimming
a Rack of Lamb*

3) To marinate lamb: Place trimmed racks of lamb in a 9x13-inch glass baking dish. Pour all but ¼ cup of marinade over lamb, spreading to coat well on all sides. Cover and marinate at a comfortable room temperature up to 3 hours or overnight in the refrigerator.

4) To set up for roasting: If chilled, remove lamb and reserved marinade from the refrigerator 2 to 3 hours before cooking to bring almost to room temperature (keep lamb covered). Line the bottom of a shallow baking sheet with aluminum foil (shiny side up) and place a wire rack on top of the foil. Position the oven rack to the center shelf and preheat oven to 500°F until very hot.

5) To roast: Uncover lamb and spoon some of the surrounding marinade from the dish over the meat. Place lamb (bone side down) on the rack in the prepared baking sheet and grind some fresh black pepper over the top. Wrap a sheet of aluminum foil (dull side up) around the exposed rib bones to keep them from charring. Roast in the hot oven for 10 minutes. Baste with reserved marinade and reduce temperature to 400°F. Roast an additional 25 minutes for medium rare. If desired, remove foil surrounding rib bones for the last 10 minutes of roasting and baste ribs with a bit of marinade. Remove from oven and let lamb sit undisturbed for 10 minutes loosely tented with aluminum foil. Meanwhile, warm your serving platter.

6) To carve and serve: Remove each rack to a carving board and separate rack into individual chops by driving a sharp knife down through the top of the eye of meat until you completely sever the remaining connective cartilage that surrounds the spinal cord. Arrange chops on a warmed serving platter and serve hot. Accompany with sharp steak knives and pass mint jelly at the table.

LAMB CURRY

Simmered with Dried Currants and Scallions

YIELD: serves 8

The distinctive scent of a curried stew simmering on the stove makes it hard to wait for dinner! The currants and sautéed onions add a subtle sweetness to balance the peppery taste of the scallions. And don't hesitate to make this one or two days ahead since the flavors only get more complex and wonderful. Lamb shoulder is relatively inexpensive compared to the rest of the animal and, to get the most meat for your money, purchase young lamb (between the months of May through November); the meat of the younger lamb has a lower fat content than its older buddies. Shoulder meat is also preferred for its generous marbling, giving superb flavor and rendering it incredibly succulent after braising. However, meat from the shank is also quite good and even less expensive. Serve with Deliciously Simple White Rice (page 361) and, to scoop up the delicious sauce, a basket of Fried Indian Bread Puffs (page 434).

SPECIAL EQUIPMENT
6-quart nonreactive Dutch oven with tight-fitting lid

10- to 12-inch nonreactive deep-sided skillet

INGREDIENTS

4 pounds lamb shoulder, cut into 1½-inch cubes

Salt and freshly ground black pepper to taste

3 tablespoons regular olive oil, or more as needed

3 tablespoons extra-virgin olive oil

3 large yellow onions, peeled and thinly sliced

8 cloves garlic, minced

½ cup dry white wine

3 to 4 cups Rich Chicken Stock or "Doctored" Canned Chicken Broth (page 140 for both), heated

3 tablespoons curry powder*

¾ cup dried currants

3 tablespoons cornstarch

½ cup cold water

2 bunches scallions (green onions), chopped (trimmed white parts and 1½ to 2 inches of the tender green)

Deliciously Simple White Rice (page 361), for accompaniment

* See section on Staples

Time Management Tips

- The vegetables can be chopped 1 day ahead and kept refrigerated in separate, well-covered bowls.

- The stew can be assembled fully 2 days ahead. Once cool, pull a clean kitchen towel over the top of the pot and place the lid on top. The towel will prevent any accumulation of condensation (rising steam) from falling into the stew and diluting the flavors. Refrigerate and bring to room temperature before reheating gently.

Q. When I attempt to brown meat, the pieces turn gray instead of brown. Why?

A. Avoid crowding meat when browning. When the pieces are too close, they give off steam which results in meat with a gray, sometimes gluey quality. To sear meat properly so it turns golden, each piece should have at least one inch empty space all around. Although this requires cooking it in several smaller batches, the resulting savory flavor is worth it.

1) **To brown lamb:** Sprinkle lamb lightly with salt and pepper. Heat a 6-quart nonreactive Dutch oven over medium-high heat and, when hot, add the 3 tablespoons regular olive oi!. When oil is hot, add some of the cubed lamb in a single layer without crowding and brown pieces on all sides. Using a slotted spoon, remove browned lamb to a plate and continue to brown the rest in batches, adding more olive oil if necessary to prevent sticking. Pour out any remaining oil from pot but don't wipe out the interior; set aside.

2) **To sauté and simmer onions and garlic:** Heat a separate 10- to 12-inch nonreactive deep-sided skillet over medium-high heat and, when hot, add the 3 tablespoons extra-virgin olive oil. When oil is hot, sauté onions with 2 cloves of the minced garlic until softened and beginning to turn golden. Add wine and simmer onions and garlic until wine is reduced by ½. Scrape onion mixture into a bowl including any browned bits of onion and garlic clinging to the bottom and sides of the skillet.

3) **To deglaze Dutch oven:** Heat the Dutch oven used to brown lamb over medium heat and, when hot, add ½ cup of the hot chicken stock. As the stock begins to bubble, scrape up all the browned bits of caramelized lamb.

4) **To assemble and simmer stew:** Add to deglazed pot, browned lamb, sautéed onions, remaining 6 cloves of minced garlic, remaining chicken stock and curry powder, stirring to incorporate all the ingredients. Bring mixture to a brisk simmer and reduce heat to very low. Simmer covered for 1½ hours, occasionally stirring mixture up from the bottom to prevent scorching. Add currants and simmer another ½ hour.

5) **To finish sauce:** Meanwhile, mix cornstarch and the cold water, stirring until thoroughly combined. After the last ½ hour of cooking, give cornstarch mixture a good stir and add to stew. Raise heat slightly and cook uncovered, stirring constantly, until mixture thickens. Fold in chopped scallions, lots of freshly ground black pepper and some salt to taste. Remove from heat to cool and spoon off any grease that rises to the top.

6) **To serve:** Reheat stew, covered, on the stovetop over low heat or in a preheated 350°F oven until piping hot throughout. While reheating, occasionally stir up stew from the bottom. Serve hot with cooked rice.

Chicken Curry Variation

For the lamb, substitute 3 frying chickens (3½ to 4 pounds each), each cut into 8 pieces (page 256). Either remove the skin or leave intact and season each piece lightly with salt and freshly ground black pepper. Brown chicken in olive oil as directed for lamb (use a spatter shield to prevent popping) and follow the remaining directions, adding the currants when you first assemble stew. Reduce cooking time to about 25 minutes after the mixture comes to a simmer. When done, chicken should be tender but not dry.

LET'S HAVE A PIZZA PARTY!

YIELD: two 15-inch pizzas

At my house, homemade pizza is far better than anything made at a pizza par-lor. The sauce is not canned, but mostly made from ripe fresh plum tomatoes, loads of garlic and chopped fresh basil. It's topped, not with one cheese, but two or three different types, including my favorite Reggiano. The olive oil is always extra-virgin and there's no end to the variety of toppings. And for the crispiest of crusts, I prebake my empty pizza crusts on quarry tiles (page 400) or on a large pizza stone, although this is not absolutely necessary. When experimenting with the concept of partially prebaking my crust, I not only found a way to ensure crispness in my assembled pizza, but in the process I stumbled on a way to provide successive batches of hot, delicious personalized pizzas to a hoard of hungry kids or adults without even having to touch flour when entertaining! How can you do this? It's simple—see Game Plan for a Pizza Party (following). And for those of you on diets, salad pizzas are fabulous! Just forget any toppings and bake the crust until crisp with a very thin layer of grated Parmesan and some sauce. After baking, pile on a lightly dressed salad, slice and serve. If you are new to bread making, please read through Notes on Baking Yeast Breads (page 373) before beginning.

SPECIAL EQUIPMENT

5-quart mixing bowl, for rising dough

Wooden surface, for kneading

Pastry scraper

Set of quarry tiles or a large pizza stone

Two perforated 15-inch pizza pans, for baking pizza

Docker or the tines of a large serving fork

Food processor (optional), for grating cheese

Baker's peel, to remove baked pizzas from oven

Two nonperforated 15-inch pizza pans, for serving baked pizzas to prevent sauce and cheese from running through holes

Pizza wheel, the larger the better!

INGREDIENTS

About 3 tablespoons extra-virgin olive oil as needed

1 package active dry yeast

½ cup lukewarm water for yeast, plus 2 cups lukewarm water for dough

Pinch, plus 2 teaspoons sugar

1 scant tablespoon salt

1 to 2 teaspoons freshly ground black pepper (optional)

Up to 6½ cups high-gluten (high-protein) bread flour, including flour for dusting

Cornmeal, (preferably medium-ground) for pizza pans

Glaze (optional): 1 egg white, at room temperature, mixed with 1 teaspoon water

Sesame seeds (optional), for topping rim of pizza

Freshly ground black pepper

About 6 cups freshly grated cheese (preferably a combination
of fresh mozzarella, Muenster and Parmesan)

1½ to 2 cups Tomato Basil Sauce (page 184)

About ½ cup chopped or slivered fresh basil leaves

ADDITIONAL TOPPING SUGGESTIONS

Sliced and sautéed mushrooms

Thinly sliced pepperoni

Fresh chopped garlic

Thinly sliced onions or leeks, sautéed in extra-virgin olive oil

Drained and coarsely chopped firm anchovy fillets

Small cubes of eggplant, lightly tossed in seasoned flour and
panfried in olive oil

Diced potatoes, boiled 5 minutes, drained and panfried

Pitted and sliced kalamata olives

Red and/or yellow bell peppers, roasted and seeded (page 113)
and sliced into thin strips

Fresh Italian sausage, removed from casings and sautéed in
extra-virgin olive oil with minced onion and garlic

Crushed red pepper flakes (be careful)

1) *To set up:* Brush the interior of a 5-quart mixing bowl generously with
olive oil and set aside for rising dough.

2) *To assemble liquid mixture:* Dissolve yeast in ½ cup lukewarm water
with a pinch of sugar. In a large mixing bowl, combine the 2 cups lukewarm water, 1 generous tablespoon of the olive oil, salt, the 2 teaspoons
sugar, and pepper, if using. When yeast mixture is creamy and starting to
bubble, add to mixing bowl and briskly stir in just enough bread flour, a
little at a time, to create a mass that is not easily stirred in the bowl. Turn
out dough onto a lightly flour wooden board. Using floured hands, knead
dough in a brisk push-fold-and-turn motion, until perfectly smooth and
elastic, about 5 minutes. Add only as much additional flour as necessary
to keep dough from sticking to your hands and work surface. Use a pastry
scraper while kneading to scrape dough off board cleanly as you continue
to knead in a sufficient amount of flour.

Time Management Tips

- After the dough completes the first rise at room temperature, it can remain in the refrigerator for up to 2 days before shaping.

- The sauce can be made well in advance and frozen in small heavy-duty freezer containers.

- The crusts can be partially prebaked early in the day and left at room temperature.

- The toppings can be gathered a couple of hours before assembling pizzas.

- After prebaking and cooling the crust, you can either freeze the empty crust or a fully assemble pizza. Wrap both well in aluminum foil. Let an empty crust thaw (wrapped) before topping it and baking. Bake a fully assembled frozen pizza directly from the freezer (unwrapped) on a perforated pizza pan in a preheated 400°F oven until crisp and hot throughout.

3) *To rise dough twice:* Place dough in the prepared rising bowl and turn to coat it with olive oil. Cover bowl with a piece of oiled plastic wrap and then with a clean kitchen towel. Let rise in a warm, draft-free spot until doubled, about 2 hours. Punch down dough with several swift swats with the back of your hand until dough is totally deflated. Although dough can be used right away, it's preferable to refrigerate it for at least 1 hour and as long as 2 days before shaping crusts. (This chilling relaxes this high-gluten dough so it won't fight back so much when being stretched into shape and the extra time allows the dough to develop a deeper, more satisfying flavor.)

4) *To set up to prebake crusts:* Position the oven rack in the lower third of the oven and, if using, place a sheet of quarry tiles or a large pizza stone onto rack. Preheat the oven to 450°F for at least 30 minutes before baking. Lightly brush both perforated pizza pans with olive oil and sprinkle with cornmeal; tilt to coat pans and tap out excess meal. If using, set egg-white glaze and sesame seeds next to your work surface.

5) *To shape pizza dough:* Turn out dough onto a lightly floured board and gently knead just to release air pockets. Using the blade of a pastry scraper, divide dough into 2 equal pieces. If dough is not chilled, cover and let rest for 10 minutes to relax dough. If not working with a double oven and thus can only bake 1 crust at a time, return half the dough to the bowl, cover and refrigerate until the first pizza crust goes into the oven. Pat the remaining half dough into a low round on the floured work surface.

6) *To stretch dough:* Spread the fingers of your hand and smack dough several times until visibly flattened but still round. Flour your fists, lift up dough and drape it (centered) over your floured fists. Stretch dough by pointing your fists upward and gently pulling them away from each other. Take care to stretch evenly; if dough starts to feel bottom heavy and is becoming too thin, lay it on your work surface, rearrange it, then lift and continue to stretch. Use as much flour as necessary to keep dough from sticking to your hands, which can cause it to tear.

7) **To place dough in pan:** Lay stretched dough in the prepared pan, arranging it so the edges of dough meet the rim. Press and pat out dough until it totally covers the pan, building up the rim of dough so it's a little thicker and higher than the interior of the circle. It doesn't have to be perfect, just not overly thick in one spot and paper thin in another. If dough resists at any point, just throw a towel over it for 5 minutes. If dough should tear, just pinch it together with floured fingertips. And if the rim seems too thin, simply fold 1 inch of the edge over onto itself and press to adhere.

8) **To prepare crust for prebaking:** Brush the interior of the circle (excluding the 1-inch rim) with some olive oil and prick the oiled section of the dough deeply all over with a docker or the prongs of a large fork. Sprinkle oiled dough with freshly ground black pepper. If desired, brush the raised rim of dough with egg white glaze and sprinkle rim generously with sesame seeds.

9) **To prebake crust:** Place 4 ice cubes into a 1-cup measuring cup and add enough cold water to measure ¼ cup. Prick the interior surface of crust once more and place pizza pan directly on hot tiles, stone or oven rack. Immediately toss ice water onto the oven floor, underneath the tiles, and shut the oven door. Bake until lightly golden, about 15 minutes. Remove pan from oven using a baker's peel and place it on a wire rack to cool. Meanwhile, as crust is baking, remove the reserved half of dough from refrigerator and prepare the second crust completely through the preceding step. As soon as you remove the first crust from the oven, prick the second crust again, place in oven and administer ice water as directed above.

Q. Why do you dock a dough?

A. *Docking a dough before baking by pricking holes in it with a docker or fork tines helps to prevent dough from rising or forming bubbles in the oven. The concept is the same as docking a pie crust shell before prebaking.*

10) *To set up for baking topped pizza:* After prebaking, the crust is sealed, so if you like, you may remove quarry tiles or pizza stone from oven. If baking 2 pizzas in the same oven, position oven racks to the upper and lower thirds; if using a double oven, use the center rack for each pizza. Preheat oven to 450°F until very hot.

11) *To prepare topping:* Scatter some grated cheese over the interior of the prebaked crust. Spoon or ladle about 1 cup tomato sauce on top of cheese (not too much or your pizza will be soupy). Spread sauce over crust, stopping just before the rim. Scatter one or more of the suggested toppings over sauce, along with chopped basil leaves. Scatter half of the grated cheese over the top, allowing some of the toppings to be visible through cheese. Drizzle 1 teaspoon fruity olive oil over pizza and then finally top with some sliced pepperoni, if desired. Grind on some fresh black pepper. Repeat with the remaining pizza.

12) *To bake and serve completed pizza:* Bake in the hot oven until crust is deeply golden, toppings are piping hot and cheese is bubbling, about 20 minutes. If using the same oven for both pizzas, switch positions of pies after half the baking time for even heat exposure. To serve, insert a baker's peel under the pizza pan and place the pie on a solid (nonperforated) pizza pan. Slice into wedges using a pizza wheel and serve immediately.

Free-Form Pizzas Baked Directly on Quarry Tiles or a Pizza Stone

You do not need a pizza pan for this method and you do not need to prebake the crust before assembling and baking. Position the rack and quarry tiles or pizza stone as directed for prebaking crusts. When preheating, increase the oven temperature to 500°F. Sprinkle a baker's peel generously with cornmeal. Prepare and stretch dough as directed and place it directly on the peel. Rearrange the thin round, to correct the shape. Brush the interior of dough with olive oil and sprinkle with fresh pepper. Docking is not necessary since the weight of the toppings will prevent dough from swelling underneath. (If applying seeds to the rim, try not to let the egg white drip onto the baker's peel since this will cause dough to stick to the peel.)

Top dough as you would a prebaked crust and assemble ice cubes and water as directed. Lift the loaded baker's peel and give it a gentle shake to make sure that the pizza is not stuck. Open oven door and insert peel all the way to the back of the oven. With one swift jerk, remove peel, leaving pizza on the hot tiles. Immediately, toss ice water onto the oven floor and shut the door. Bake until golden and bubbling, 18 to 20 minutes. Remove pizza by sliding the peel underneath it and place on a nonperforated pizza pan. Cut into wedges and serve immediately.

Game Plan for a Pizza Party

The day before serving, prepare a double batch of dough and allow it to have a second cool rise in the refrigerator overnight. Make your sauce and grate your cheese. Early the next day, prebake 4 crusts and once cool, let them sit "stacked" at room temperature. A few hours before "show time," remove sauce from refrigerator and gather your assorted toppings. About 30 minutes before "chow time," preheat oven and ask your guests "who wants what" on their pizza. Then, assemble and bake away!

Grating Cheese in a Food Processor

Before adding cheese to the work bowl of a food processor, brush the steel blade lightly with vegetable oil. Cut cheese into small pieces and use the pulsing button to maintain best control. If grating in batches, remove the first batch of grated cheese before adding the next batch. Also, when emptying the work bowl (between batches), check the inside of the steel blade shaft for any stray pieces of cheese (especially the softer types of cheese) and remove them. Otherwise, when you reinsert the blade onto the shaft, the cheese acts like glue and it might be difficult to remove the blade.

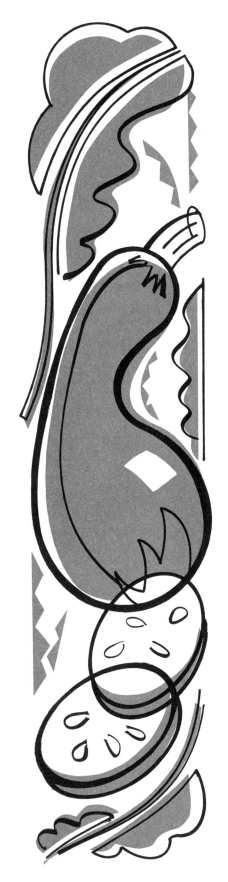

CHAPTER VIII

ON THE SIDE

Ideal Partners to Share the Spotlight

In this chapter you'll find a wide variety of my favorite recipes for delicious, colorful and textural side dishes to accompany the entrées in this book; you'll also find perfectly cooked rice to serve under some of my soups. These have all passed the "great taste test" many times over and I trust that they will find a permanent place in your repertoire. When deciding on a dish to accompany your entrée, think of color as well as taste. Creating vibrant contrasts in color on one plate will not only be stimulating to the eye, but will also heighten your guests' anticipation of flavor.

When it comes to texture, don't be timid about mixing starches; the combination of rice and beans, or corn, pasta and rice is not only soothing but a great way to make your meal more nutritious, while keeping it economical. And by serving a combination of starches along with sautéed vegetables in one dish, you can easily omit a heavier entrée since these side dishes not only boost the meal nutritionally but also provide quite a bit of substance to your stomach.

Whether serving a soothing starch and/or a vegetable dish, always buy the freshest and the best ingredients you can find. By doing so, you'll be able to accomplish more "do-ahead" shopping, since only the freshest produce will be able to withstand several days of storage, when necessary. And use my Time Management Tips to use small increments of available time in advance of your meals to blanch or peel and/or chop your vegetables and to roast, seed and slice your peppers. These aromatic additions will make your overall meal much healthier and, needless to say, more satisfying to eat.

In Celebration of Summer . . .
RATATOUILLE

YIELD: serves 10 to 12

When your garden is bursting with gorgeous specimens of ripe tomatoes, eggplant, zucchini and sweet bell peppers, or when low market prices reflect the abundance of summer, prepare this renowned vegetable sauté from the south of France. In little time you can easily whip up a large batch, then fire up the barbecue and invite the neighborhood to join you! Conveniently, ratatouille tastes even better if the flavors have a chance to marry for a few hours or overnight. And whether you serve it hot, cold or at room temperature, the stewed texture feels soothing and the taste is always wonderfully fresh. Store leftovers in the refrigerator to use throughout the week. Use as a delicious filling for omelets or spooned on top of hot slices of Garlic Toast (page 133) or even in a quiche (recipe follows).

SPECIAL EQUIPMENT
Nonreactive colander

12-inch nonreactive deep-sided skillet

INGREDIENTS

3 pounds fresh plum (Roma) tomatoes

2 medium-large eggplant

12 large cloves garlic

About ⅔ cup extra-virgin olive oil

4 cups coarsely chopped yellow onions

1 green bell pepper, seeded and coarsely chopped

1 red bell pepper, seeded and coarsely chopped

2 cups coarsely chopped zucchini (2 medium zucchini scrubbed and trimmed)

1 can (6 ounces) tomato paste

2 teaspoons crumbled dried oregano

1 cup chopped fresh basil leaves (chop just before needed to prevent basil from turning black)

Lots of freshly ground black pepper to taste

Kosher or sea salt to taste

1) *To prepare tomatoes and eggplant:* Peel, seed and coarsely chop tomatoes (page 151) and set them in a nonreactive colander to drain for at least 30 minutes. Shortly before cooking (to avoid excessive discoloration),

Time Management Tips

- Although it's best to peel tomatoes the day of cooking, (in a pinch) they may be peeled, seeded and chopped 1 day ahead and refrigerated well covered in a colander.

- The onions, peppers and zucchini may be cut 1 day ahead and refrigerated in separate well-covered bowls.

- Both the chopped garlic and the blanched garlic can be prepared early in the day of cooking and kept covered at a comfortable room temperature until ready to assemble.

dice eggplant. Trim off stem end and slice eggplant lengthwise into ⅓-inch slices. Stack and slice into ½-inch strips. Then cut strips into ½-inch cubes to measure 9 cups.

2) *To prepare garlic:* Chop 6 cloves of the garlic. Peel and blanch the remaining 6 cloves in boiling water for 2 minutes. Drain, blanch and drain again, then cut each whole clove in half lengthwise.

3) *To sauté vegetables:* Heat a 12-inch nonreactive deep-sided skillet over medium heat and, when hot, add ¼ cup of the olive oil. When oil is hot, stir in chopped onions and chopped garlic. Cook vegetables until softened, very fragrant and beginning to turn golden, about 10 minutes. Add chopped bell peppers and zucchini and cook until fragrant and slightly softened, about 4 minutes. Transfer to a large mixing bowl. Return skillet to medium heat and, when hot, add another ⅓ cup olive oil. When oil is hot, stir in diced eggplant and cook until softened slightly and just beginning to turn golden, about 4 minutes.

4) *To assemble and simmer:* Add to skillet the drained tomatoes, sautéed vegetable mixture, tomato paste, oregano and ½ cup of the chopped basil. Fold together gently but thoroughly, bring mixture to a brisk simmer, reduce heat to low and cook gently with the cover ajar for 30 minutes.

5) *To sauté blanched garlic:* Meanwhile, heat a 6- to 8-inch skillet over medium heat and, when hot, add 2 tablespoons olive oil. When oil is hot, add halved and blanched garlic cloves and sear them in the hot oil until cloves are golden but not overly dark. Remove garlic with a slotted spoon and set aside.

6) *To finish assembly and to serve:* After the vegetable mixture has simmered 30 minutes, gently stir in seared garlic and the remaining ½ cup of chopped basil. Cook uncovered another 10 minutes. Add a generous amount of freshly ground black pepper and remove from heat. Let cool, if desired, and taste for seasoning, adding coarse salt to taste. Serve hot, warm or at room temperature.

RATATOUILLE QUICHE

YIELD: One 10-inch quiche; serves 8

INGREDIENTS

1 recipe *savory version* of Favorite Tart Pastry (page 93)

1 egg yolk (optional)

1 to 1½ cups cubed or grated cheese, preferably a combination of
   Muenster, fresh mozzarella (pat dry before cubing) and freshly
   grated Reggiano Parmesan cheese

2 cups leftover Ratatouille (preceding)

¼ cup toasted pine nuts (page 76), optional

3 extra-large eggs, lightly beaten

1½ cups heavy cream (preferably not ultrapasteurized)

Salt and freshly ground black pepper to taste

1) Favorite Tart Pastry: Prepare pastry, line a 10-inch pie plate, *partially*
prebake and cool as directed in recipe. If desired, brush some egg yolk
on the bottom and sides of the cooled pastry to waterproof it and set
aside. Preheat the oven to 375°F.

2) To assemble quiche: Arrange 1 cup of the cheese on the bottom of the
prepared pie crust. Using a slotted spoon, spread ratatouille over cheese.
Sprinkle toasted nuts, if using, over vegetable mixture. In a small bowl,
combine eggs with cream. Season well with salt and pepper and pour over
the filling. If desired, scatter the remaining ½ cup cheese over the top.

3) To bake and serve: Bake quiche until the filling is puffed and set, 50 to
55 minutes. Let sit and settle before slicing into individual wedges. Serve
hot, warm or at room temperature.

TIPS

FROM A TEACHER

How to Buy, Store and Chop Onions

Other than tasting distinctively delicious, onions are high in vitamin A and have been documented to inhibit the formation of blood clots and to lower blood pressure and cholesterol levels. Interestingly, the scent of whole, unpeeled onions is rather benign but as soon as the flesh is severed, amino acids react with other enzymes to produce a sulfuric acid that gives the onion its pungent scent and robust flavor. And the older the onion, the stronger and more assertive these compounds become. But pungent doesn't mean "foul"; a bad smell indicates a bad onion that should be bypassed in the market or discarded at home. Fortunately, during cooking, onions go through a chemical change that leaves them incredibly sweet and savory.

To buy onions: Look for those with a thin outer skin that feels like dry crackly paper. The neck of the onion should be closed tightly with no signs of sprouting, mold or soft brown spots. As a general rule (but this will vary with area), white onions tend to be stronger than yellow or red onions. Reds are usually eaten raw, and yellows are the best choice for an all-purpose onion. The huge Spanish onions are my personal favorite for their consistently sweet taste, especially after cooking. And now, a slew of spring and summer hybrids are being bred primarily for sweetness. These varieties (Vadalia, Walla Walla, Maui Sweet and Italian Sweet) should be eaten raw to enjoy fully their intense flavor.

To store onions: Store onions loose in a dark, dry bin with plenty of space around each to prevent them from sweating. And although onions and potatoes are a match made in heaven when cooked, don't store them raw in the same bin since both emanate moisture and gas that cause each other to spoil. If you have leftover cut onions,

store them in the refrigerator tightly wrapped in plastic wrap and use them as soon as possible to prevent drying and an "off" scent and flavor. Chopped onions can be frozen, if desired, but they tend to become somewhat wet and translucent after thawing; they're fine for sauces, but won't brown well.

To stop those tears: Regarding those handed-down secret tricks to keep you from crying elephant tears when chopping onions, I inevitably just squint and whimper through the entire process. Chilling the onion before cutting helps somewhat. Although many suggest running them under water, I have found that it adversely affects the color and texture of the cooked onions unless you squeeze the onions in a towel after chopping to remove excess moisture. (I don't chop onions in the food processor for the same reason unless their ultimate use will be as one component of a minced vegetable base for

certain sauces.) The best remedy is to learn to chop more efficiently so that your crying time will be reduced. Sorry, it's the best trick I have.

To chop onions: The secret to chopping an onion is to keep each half intact at the root end until you complete the final (third) slicing. Using a well-sharpened 8- to 10-inch chef's knife, trim off the pointed top and remove the outer papery skin, but leave the root end intact. Cut onion in half lengthwise through the root end (not through the round middle). Working with one half at a time, lay it (flat side down) on your work surface. Hold onion in place with one hand and position your knife so it's parallel to the cutting board, about ¼ inch above the bottom. Starting at the bottom, drive the knife through the onion in a sawing motion until you reach ½ inch from the root end. Ease out the blade, reinsert it ¼ inch up from the preceding cut, and follow the same proce-

dure. Repeat until you reach ¼ inch from the top. Next (with the onion in the same position) point the knife blade down and make vertical lengthwise slices ¼ inch apart from the top to within ½ inch of the root end (grasp the onion with your other hand as you do this so that it stays intact.) Finally, starting at the top, slice crosswise at ¼ inch intervals until you reach the uncut root end, releasing small diced pieces onto your work surface. Turn the uncut portion flat-side down, slice off and discard the root end and make horizontal, then vertical cuts as described above. If a finer texture is desired, use the knife to go back and forth over the onions in a smooth rhythmical motion.

To mince onions: Follow the preceding procedure for chopping onions, but make incisions ⅛ inch apart.

SAUTÉED BABY GREEN BEANS

With Onions, Garlic and Sweet Red Peppers

YIELD: serves 4 to 6

SPECIAL EQUIPMENT
8-quart blanching pot with built-in strainer (optional)

Frencher, if baby beans are not available

Today, young, thin green beans (or *haricots verts* as the chic refer to them in the culinary world) are readily available (although "pricey") in fancy produce markets. These beans are either called French or American baby beans. Those labeled "French" (where they originated) are not actually from France these days, but are usually imported from South America. They are darker and thinner than the American baby beans, which look similar to regular green beans, only shorter and thinner. Either variety is delicious and only requires minimal preparation. If only fully grown beans are available, choose the youngest looking ones that you can find. They should be short in length, bright and firm with no brown spots, pitting or wrinkles, which are sure signs of age. If using the mature (longer and thicker) green beans, use a "frencher," a gadget that slices beans into thin strips.

INGREDIENTS

1½ pounds baby green beans

Salt for boiling beans

1 large yellow onion

½ stick (4 tablespoons) butter or ¼ cup extra-virgin olive oil or a combination

3 large cloves garlic, cut into thin lengthwise slices

1 large red bell pepper, seeded and cut into thin strips or roasted and peeled (page 113) before slicing

⅓ cup freshly grated Reggiano Parmesan cheese (optional)

Freshly ground black pepper and kosher or sea salt to taste

1) To prepare and blanch beans: Bring an 8-quart pot of water to a boil. Rinse and drain beans and pick off dry ends with your thumbnail. When water boils, place a large bowl of ice water on your counter, add some salt to the pot and stir in beans. Boil until just crisp tender, about 3 minutes (avoid overcooking). Drain beans and immediately plunge them into ice water. (This completely stops the cooking process so the bright green color and crisp texture is retained.)

2) To prepare onion: Cut peeled onion in half through the stem end and slice each half into very thin wedges. Separate each wedge into strips.

3) To sauté vegetables: Melt butter or heat olive oil in a 10- to 12-inch deep-sided skillet over medium-high heat. When hot, add onions and cook until softened and fragrant, about 5 minutes. Add garlic, reduce heat to medium-low and cook until onions are very tender and lightly brown, about 8 minutes, stirring often. Add red pepper strips and cook 3 to 5 minutes more. Raise heat to medium-high, add blanched beans and toss to combine. Cook until tender (but not soft), about 4 minutes, stirring and tossing frequently.

4) To serve: Turn beans into a serving bowl and add grated Parmesan cheese, if using. Grind on some fresh pepper and sprinkle lightly with coarse salt, if desired. Serve hot.

Variations for Green Beans

Here are some easy additions and combinations to try with sautéed green beans:

With pine nuts: Blanch and refresh the beans as directed before sautéing. Sauté beans in hot butter or olive oil and, when hot throughout and tender, add ½ cup toasted pine nuts (page 76) and ½ cup freshly grated Parmesan cheese or (for a sharper flavor) grated pecorino cheese.

With garlic butter: Thinly slice 5 cloves garlic. Sauté very slowly in 4 tablespoons melted butter until tender and lightly golden, 3 to 5 minutes. Remove garlic, add blanched beans and cook until tender. Toss with the sautéed garlic adding freshly ground black pepper to taste.

With ginger: Heat ¼ to ⅓ cup very fragrant peanut oil* over medium-high heat and sauté 2 teaspoons peeled, minced fresh ginger root, 2 cloves minced garlic and baby beans. When hot throughout, stir in ¼ cup toasted sesame seeds (page 76). Cook 1 minute over high heat then drizzle on 1 tablespoon dark (toasted) sesame oil*.

* See section on Staples.

SWEET SAUTÉED CARROTS

With Toasted Walnuts and Calimyrna Figs

YIELD: serves 8

SPECIAL EQUIPMENT

8-quart blanching pot with built-in strainer (optional)

On that brisk autumn day when I created this carrot dish, I was roaming through the supermarket (as usual) and the combination of ingredients seemed to jump out at me! At dinner that night, I absolutely flipped over the taste and texture contrasts of the vibrant orange carrots, the crisp toasted walnuts and the tender sweet Calimyrna figs. The name "Calimyrna" is derived from California, (where they are now grown) and the ancient Turkish seaport of Smyrna (now Izmir), where they originated. Calimyrna figs are available in some supermarkets and many gourmet food shops. If unavailable, substitute dried mission figs. Although this is delicious any time of the year, I think it's just perfect for Thanksgiving.

INGREDIENTS

2½ pounds carrots, peeled and sliced diagonally ½ inch thick

Salt, for boiling carrots

1 stick (¼ pound) butter

1 cup walnut halves

About 9 ounces dried Calimyrna figs (2 cups whole figs)

1½ to 2 tablespoons chopped flat-leaf Italian parsley

Time Management Tips

• The carrots can be blanched 1 day ahead. After drying, line a bowl with paper toweling and add the carrots. Cover bowl well with plastic wrap and refrigerate.

• The figs can be cut days ahead and kept covered at room temperature.

1) *To blanch carrots:* Bring a large pot of water to a rapid boil and place a large bowl of ice water on the counter. Add some salt to boiling water, then stir in sliced carrots. Boil until softened, but not cooked through, about 8 minutes. Drain carrots and immediately plunge into ice water, swishing carrots around with your hands to help stop the cooking process. When carrots are cold, drain them and pat dry. Set aside or refrigerate until needed.

2) *To slice figs:* Remove the hard stems from figs and slice fruit lengthwise into ¼-inch-wide slices. Cut each slice in half widthwise. You should net 1 rounded cup sliced figs.

3) *To pan toast the walnuts:* Melt 3 tablespoons of the butter over medium heat in a 10- to 12-inch deep-sided skillet. When bubbling, add walnuts and cook, stirring constantly, until toasted and fragrant, about 5 minutes. Remove nuts with a slotted spoon and drain on paper towels. Wipe skillet clean.

4) *To sauté carrots:* Return skillet to medium heat and add remaining 5 tablespoons butter. When melted and hot, add carrots and cook, stirring and tossing, until almost tender and beginning to caramelize, about 8 minutes. Reduce heat to low, stir in sliced figs and cook with carrots uncovered, for 3 minutes. Add toasted walnuts and cook until hot and the flavors mingle, about 3 minutes.

5) *To serve:* Pour into a warmed serving bowl and toss with chopped parsley. Serve hot.

The time required to blanch a given vegetable to reach the desired consistency depends largely on the width, age and overall condition of the vegetable before cooking. Generally, the older the vegetable, the more cooking time it will need. So, a young carrot will require far less cooking than a more mature (wider) carrot, which has a thick internal core.

SAUTÉED FRESH CORN

With Onions, Sweet Peppers and Natural Corn Cream

YIELD: serves 10 to 12

This recipe features my favorite way to prepare fresh corn. The corn kernels are sliced off their cobs and the creamy, delicate substance that I call "corn cream" is scraped from each cob into the kernels. Until recently, fresh corn was only available in the summer months. Now, thanks to Florida growers, the taste of "summer sweet" corn is available all year long. Through experimentation, they have come up with a variety of corn called "Florida Sweets," which has twice the sugar content of regular corn, and the natural sugar converts to starch at a much slower rate. This allows the corn to stay crisp and sweet longer after being picked and shipped. Serve this crisp and colorful side dish with any grilled, broiled or roasted meat, poultry or fish (it's especially wonderful with lamb or chicken). And even if you're not serving a crowd, prepare the entire amount of the recipe and save the leftovers to throw into salad or soup. Or prepare the following recipe of Corn Cakes.

SPECIAL EQUIPMENT
Pastry scraper to scoop corn off work surface (optional)

Time Management Tips

- The vegetables can be chopped 1 day ahead and refrigerated separately in well-covered bowls.

- Although corn should remain in its husks as long as possible, in a pinch, you can clean the corn and remove the kernels and corn cream early in the day of serving (especially if using a super-sweet variety). Keep the bowl of corn well covered and refrigerated since warmth encourages the natural sugar in corn to convert into starch.

INGREDIENTS

12 ears fresh corn, outer husks and all silk removed, or 1 pound frozen corn, unthawed

½ stick (4 tablespoons) butter or margarine

2 cloves garlic, chopped

1 large yellow onion, chopped

1 red bell pepper, seeded and chopped

Freshly ground black pepper and kosher or sea salt to taste

3 tablespoons chopped flat-leaf Italian parsley

½ cup heavy cream (preferably not ultrapasteurized) or half-and-half (only if using frozen corn)

1) *To remove corn kernels from cobs:* Stand the cob on its flat end and, beginning at the pointed top, run the blade of a sharp knife down the cob in a sawing motion. This will release the kernels so they fall onto your work surface. Avoid cutting into the cob with the knife. Instead, allow a small portion of the bottom of each kernel to remain attached to the cob. Scoop up the kernels using a pastry scraper and place them into a bowl.

2) *To extract corn cream:* Scrape the milk from each cob by holding the cob so it rests horizontally over the edge of the bowl of corn. Position the blade of the knife on the cob so that the top (dull side) is tilted away from you and the sharp edge is toward you. Pull the blade (going away from you) down over the cob in a brisk, firm and repetitive motion. As the corn cream is released from the cob, it will fall into the bowl of corn. Discard empty cobs.

3) *To sauté vegetables and serve:* Heat butter in a 10- to 12-inch deep-sided skillet over medium heat and, when bubbling, add chopped onions. Sauté until softened and very fragrant, about 5 minutes. Reduce heat to low, add garlic and cook until onions are starting to turn golden, about 5 minutes. Stir in chopped red pepper and cook for another 3 minutes. Stir corn with corn cream (or frozen corn with heavy cream) in the skillet and cook uncovered over low heat until the corn is crisp tender and very hot, about 10 minutes.

4) *To serve:* Add freshly ground black pepper and some coarse salt to taste along with the chopped parsley.

CORN CAKES

Or Crab Cakes

YIELD: serves 6 to 8

With the addition of crab meat, this is a substantial main dish. But you can leave out the crab to create an interesting side dish that tastes like corn fritters with the shape of potato pancakes. If making crab cakes, serve with Tartar Sauce (page 88).

INGREDIENTS

2 extra-large eggs, lightly beaten

½ cup buttermilk

1 generous tablespoon pure maple syrup

3 cups leftover Sautéed Fresh Corn (preceding)

2 packed cups (1 pound) lump crab meat (optional), picked over to remove any cartilage

Freshly ground black pepper to taste

¾ cup all-purpose flour

1½ teaspoons double-acting baking powder

1 teaspoon baking soda

1 teaspoon salt

Mild peanut oil or flavorless vegetable oil, for frying

Kosher or sea salt to taste

SPECIAL EQUIPMENT

Sifter or triple-mesh wire sieve

Batter whisk or wide blending fork or large serving fork

Deep-frying thermometer

Small gravy ladle or ¼-cup dry measuring cup

1) **To assemble batter:** In a mixing bowl, combine eggs, buttermilk, maple syrup, corn mixture, crab meat, if using, and a generous amount of freshly ground black pepper. In a separate bowl, combine flour, baking powder, baking soda and salt, using a whisk. Sift the dry ingredients into the bowl with the vegetable mixture and fold together until thoroughly combined. Set aside to rest for 10 minutes to 1 hour at room temperature or up to 2 hours, covered, in the refrigerator.

2) **To fry corn cakes:** Line a large wire cooling rack with a triple thickness of paper toweling. Pour ½ inch of peanut or vegetable oil into a 10- to 12-inch skillet and heat until oil reaches 365°F or until a small cube of bread instantly sizzles and quickly becomes golden. Using a small gravy ladle or a ¼-cup dry measuring cup, scoop a portion of the batter and ease it into

the hot oil. Add several more (without crowding) and fry until golden on both sides, turning once. Watch that the temperature of the oil doesn't become overly hot or the next batch of pancakes may burn.

3) *To serve:* Drain well on paper toweling, gently blotting the tops to remove excess oil. Serve hot. Alternatively, these may be made 30 minutes ahead and reheated on a wire rack within a shallow baking sheet in a preheated 350°F oven until hot and crisp but not overly dark, about 10 minutes. Blot once more before serving.

GARLIC-SAUTÉED CHERRY TOMATOES
With Ribbons of Fresh Basil

YIELD: serves 8

This quick and simple accompaniment is the perfect way to perk up a menu easily with vibrant color and fresh taste. And for added eye appeal, combine both yellow and red cherry tomatoes. For best results these should be sautéed just before serving, but because the tiny tomatoes cook so quickly, those at the table will hardly know that you're gone. If the tomatoes are chilled, bring them to room temperature for an hour or so before cooking so they require less cooking to become hot throughout. Otherwise, the outsides of the tomatoes may burst before the interior becomes hot. Among the many entrées that pair well with this pretty side dish are Mediterranean Lamb Chops (page 299) Golden Herb-Rubbed Cornish Hens (page 240) or Crusty Grilled Cajun Tuna (page 227).

INGREDIENTS

1 medium-sized bunch fresh basil leaves

2 pint boxes (about 1 pound each) red cherry tomatoes
   or mixed red and yellow cherry tomatoes

3 tablespoons extra-virgin olive oil

3 cloves garlic, minced

Freshly ground black pepper

⅓ cup freshly grated Reggiano Parmesan cheese

1) **To prepare basil and tomatoes:** Remove stems from tomatoes, rinse, drain well and gently roll them on a clean kitchen towel to remove excess water droplets. Rinse and dry basil leaves. To cut them into chiffonade, stack leaves and, beginning on one long side, roll stack up in a tight roll. Using a sharp chef's knife, slice roll into thin slices then unravel the slices; measure out ½ cup and set aside.

2) **To sauté tomatoes:** Heat a 10- to 12-inch deep-sided skillet over medium-high heat and, when hot, add olive oil. When oil is hot, add cherry tomatoes in a single layer. By maneuvering the handle of the skillet, swirl tomatoes in the hot oil and then sprinkle in minced garlic. Continue to cook, continually swirling tomatoes for 2 minutes, or until just hot throughout but not long enough to have their outer skins burst. Add slivered basil leaves to the skillet along with some freshly ground black pepper and swirl to incorporate well.

3) **To serve:** Pour tomato mixture into a warmed dish and serve immediately, passing a bowl of grated Parmesan at the table.

Q AND A

Q. Are yellow tomatoes really low in acid?

A. No. Yellow tomatoes are said to be lower in acid because of their noticeably sweeter taste. These vibrant yellow tomatoes, which range in size from large beefsteaks to the tiniest cherry tomatoes, are higher in sugar, not lower in acid. Their natural sweetness counteracts the acidity.

CREAMED SPINACH PORTOBELLO

Baked with Bread Crumbs

YIELD: serves 6 to 8

Before you write me off as crazy for specifying such a hefty amount of spinach, see how much nine bunches shrink after cooking—to only about three cups! Spinach is available in three basic varieties (sold by the bunch or the bag), which taste the same but look different. Savoy, the most textural type, is also the most difficult to clean; the leaves are crunched with curls and deep crevices. I prefer flat-leaf spinach, which has long, smooth spade-shaped leaves. Not only are they easier to examine for signs of spoilage, but any sand or grit is easily rinsed away. The third variety is a combination of savoy and flat-leaf (referred to as semisavoy) and is now becoming more readily available throughout the country. This soothing, old-time side dish (enhanced with sautéed onions, garlic and chopped portobello mushrooms) is special enough to embellish the most elegant menu. A nice twist in the presentation is to spoon the creamed spinach into hollowed-out, well-drained tomato cups, instead of a baking dish. Since this is one of those once-in-a-while recipes, I feel that it should not be altered to lower the fat. But if

SPECIAL EQUIPMENT
2-quart oven-to-table baking dish

8-quart heavy-bottomed pot with tight-fitting lid

Large medium-mesh wire strainer

Food processor or rolling pin for bread crumbs

Nutmeg grater (optional)

Time Management Tips

- If using fresh spinach, the leaves can be cleaned 1 day ahead and refrigerated in sealed heavy-duty plastic bags.

- The entire dish can be assembled totally 1 day ahead and kept well covered in the refrigerator. Adjust baking time accordingly.

- Dry bread crumbs can (and should) be made months in advance and kept in the freezer. No need to thaw.

you are counting calories, see my variation for a low-fat spinach side dish. Serve with My Favorite Rib-Eye Steaks (page 279) or Honey Mustard Roast Rack of Lamb (page 300).

INGREDIENTS

8 or 9 bunches (4 to 5 bags) fresh spinach or 4 boxes (10 ounces each) frozen chopped spinach

About 1 stick (¼ pound) butter

1 cup packed minced yellow onion

3 cloves garlic, minced

1 cup packed cleaned and chopped portobello mushrooms caps (page 131) or fresh button mushrooms with stems

3 tablespoons all-purpose flour

1½ cups half-and-half or light cream

Freshly ground black pepper to taste

¼ teaspoon ground nutmeg (preferably freshly grated)

Salt to taste

¼ cup The Best Dried Bread Crumbs (page 78)

1) **To clean and cook spinach:** Remove stems and thoroughly clean spinach leaves in several changes of fresh water. Drain well but do not attempt to dry leaves. Measure out 20 firmly packed cups into an 8-quart heavy-bottomed pot with only the water that clings to the leaves after draining. Cover pot and place over medium heat. When steam starts escaping from the lid, reduce heat to very low and simmer spinach until wilted and tender, 4 to 5 minutes. If using frozen spinach, cook according to package directions.

2) **To drain and chop spinach:** Transfer cooked spinach into a large medium-mesh wire strainer and place another, smaller bowl into the sieve directly on top of the cooked spinach. Firmly press down on the inside bowl to squeeze all excess liquid from spinach. Wrap drained spinach in a strong, clean kitchen towel and squeeze out any remaining moisture. Then chop spinach into small pieces but don't overdo it; allow spinach to retain some texture. Place in a large mixing bowl and set aside.

3) **To sauté remaining vegetables:** Melt 4 tablespoons of the butter in an
   8-inch skillet over medium heat. When bubbling, stir in minced onions
   and cook until softened, about 2 minutes. Reduce heat to low, add minced
   garlic and cook gently until onions and garlic are tender and very fragrant,
   about 3 minutes. Raise heat to medium high and stir in chopped mushrooms. Cook until mushrooms are golden and tender, 3 to 4 minutes.

4) **To make cream sauce:** Stir flour directly into sautéed vegetables over
   medium-high heat, stirring constantly, for 2 minutes. Stir in half-and-half
   and bring mixture to a simmer, stirring constantly. Cook at a constant
   simmer, while stirring, until thickened, about 3 minutes. Add some freshly
   ground black pepper, freshly grated nutmeg and salt to taste. The mixture
   should taste well seasoned, but go easy on the nutmeg.

5) **To assemble casserole:** In a small saucepan, melt 2 to 4 tablespoons butter. Brush a 2-quart baking dish with some of the butter. Pour vegetables
   with cream sauce over chopped spinach; fold together to combine well and,
   if desired, stir in 2 tablespoons of the melted butter. Pour spinach mixture
   into the prepared baking dish, smoothing the top. Combine bread crumbs
   with 1 tablespoon melted butter and sprinkle over spinach. Sprinkle the
   top with a bit of salt and grind on some additional black pepper.

6) **To bake and serve:** Preheat the oven to 375°F. Cover baking dish loosely
   with aluminum foil (dull side up) and bake until piping hot throughout
   and the bread crumbs are golden brown, about 30 minutes. Serve immediately from the baking dish at the table.

Low-Fat Spinach

Simmer spinach as directed in this recipe. After draining well, toss wilted
leaves briefly in a hot skillet with only a few tablespoons extra-virgin olive oil
and 1 or 2 cloves minced garlic. Add freshly ground black pepper and a light
sprinkling of coarse salt. Serve hot.

BAKED ARTICHOKES

With Bread Crumbs and Parmesan

YIELD: serves 8

SPECIAL EQUIPMENT

12- to 16-quart nonreactive pot and/or steamer rack, or microwave turntable, for cooking artichokes

9x13-inch glass baking dish (2 inches deep)

Sharp kitchen scissors

Shallow-rim soup plates (optional)

These regal artichokes are topped with an incredible bread crumb mixture spiked with minced garlic, chopped fresh parsley and Reggiano Parmesan cheese and intensified with the toasted sesame seeds in The Best Dried Bread Crumbs. The artichokes are then baked in a shallow bath of rich chicken stock and served in rimmed soup bowls within a generous puddle of the hot stock. These are magnificent served as a first course followed by Osso Buco (page 265) for an earthy but elegant dinner. These would be equally appropriate as an unusual side dish to spark up a simple meal of grilled beef, chicken or fish.

INGREDIENTS

8 large globe artichokes

2 or 3 lemons, for cleaning and cooking artichokes

½ stick (4 tablespoons) butter or margarine, plus more for greasing

2 large garlic cloves, minced

1 generous cup The Best Dried Bread Crumbs (page 78)

½ cup freshly grated Reggiano Parmesan cheese

1 generous tablespoon minced flat-leaf Italian parsley

Freshly ground black pepper and salt to taste

About 8 cups Rich Chicken Stock or "Doctored" Canned Chicken Broth (page 140 for both), for baking

1) To prepare artichokes: As directed on page 330, clean, trim, cook and drain artichokes, using lemons and their juice. But, since the artichokes will also be baked in this recipe, reduce the cooking time to 35 to 45 minutes for steaming and 25 to 30 minutes for simmering. When using a microwave, cook for 12 or 13 minutes on high power. (If your artichokes are medium sized or smaller, adjust cooking time as needed.) The heart should be almost tender when pierced with the tip of a sharp knife.

2) **To prepare topping:** Melt butter in a small saucepan over low heat and, when bubbling, add minced garlic. Cook briefly until garlic is softened and very fragrant but not brown, 30 seconds to 1 minute. Place bread crumbs into a medium-sized bowl and pour melted garlic butter over them. Mix in Parmesan cheese, chopped parsley, freshly ground black pepper and, if needed, salt to taste.

3) **To assemble:** Lay cooled artichokes (stem side down) in a 9x13-inch baking dish. Sprinkle prepared bread crumb mixture generously over each artichoke, spreading the leaves slightly to let some of the crumbs fall in. Pour stock to a depth of 1½ to 2 inches around artichokes. Drizzle tops of each artichoke with a teaspoon or so of additional stock and grind some fresh black pepper over the tops. Butter the shiny side of a sheet of aluminum foil large enough to cover the dish and cover dish (buttered side down). Bake now or later.

4) **To bake and serve:** Preheat the oven to 375°F. Bake artichokes covered for 15 to 20 minutes. Uncover and bake until the crumbs are golden brown and the stock and artichokes are pipping hot and tender throughout, another 10 to 15 minutes. Remove from the oven. Serve hot in individual shallow-rimmed soup plates with some of the hot stock ladled around and underneath.

Time Management Tips

- The dish can be assembled fully early in the day that you plan to serve and, if necessary, as much as 1 day ahead. Cooking time will be longer after refrigeration.

Globe artichokes are cultivated in California throughout the year, but are most abundant in spring and briefly appear in October. When purchasing artichokes, look for bright green specimens with tight, unblemished leaves. Artichokes with leaves that spread outward and look woody are over the hill. Also, hold each artichoke stem side up and check the bottoms for small holes, a sign of worms. Purchase them no more than three days before you plan to use them; place in plastic bags and store in the refrigerator. The methods used most often to cook fresh artichokes are either boiling (actually brisk simmering), steaming or using the microwave; the cooking time, however, varies dramatically with each method. I prefer to cook artichokes in the microwave since it leaves them considerably less waterlogged than simmering; steaming takes too long. Regardless of how you cook your artichokes, it's very important to drain them properly after cooking in order to enjoy fully their unique taste and texture.

Special equipment: You will need a microwave turntable, if using the microwave method; an 8- to 16-quart nonreactive pot, if boiling artichokes and a steaming rack, if steaming artichokes.

To clean artichokes: Fill a large nonreactive mixing bowl with cold water and add the juice of 1 lemon. Working with 1 artichoke at a time, hold artichoke by the stem and dunk it into the bowl, swishing to remove any dust, debris or insects.

To trim artichokes: Using a sharp stainless steel knife, cut off the top inch of each artichoke as well as the stem end and about ¼ inch of the artichoke bottom (this helps them to sit flat while cooking). Rub cut surfaces with a cut lemon half to prevent discoloration. Pull off any short, coarse leaves from the base of the artichoke and, using sharp kitchen shears, cut the pointed tips off all of the leaves. Rub the cut edges with lemon as well.

To cook artichokes using a microwave: Add ¼ cup water to the bottom of a shallow nonreactive microwavable dish that's large enough to hold the artichokes in a single layer. Squeeze some lemon juice into the dish and sit artichokes (stem end up) in dish. Cover securely with heatproof plastic wrap and make 2 small slits (vents) on top with the tip of a sharp knife. Place dish on a microwave turntable and cook on high power for 16 minutes for large artichokes, 13 minutes for smaller ones. Let dish of artichokes settle (still covered) on a wire cooling rack for 10 to 20 minutes. (If you don't have a turntable, turn the dish a quarter turn every couple of minutes so artichokes cook evenly.)

To simmer or steam artichokes: Half fill an 8- to 16-quart nonreactive pot with water and bring to a rapid boil. Add the juice of 1 lemon and 2 teaspoons salt. Carefully lower artichokes into boiling water, cover pot and, when steam escapes from the lid, reduce heat to low, cover and briskly simmer for 30 to 40 minutes. Check for doneness and drain as directed below. Alternatively, you may steam artichokes on a rack above briskly simmering water for 45 minutes to 1 hour. Replenish with *boiling water* as needed due to evaporation.

To test for doneness: Test artichoke by pulling out a center leaf and, if it comes out easily, that's a good indication that the heart will be tender. Pull the inner lining of leaf between your teeth; the flesh should come off easily and be tender to chew. To check further, insert the sharp point of a knife into the stem end. It should go in easily but the heart should not be overly soft.

To drain cooked artichokes: In order not to wind up with soggy artichokes, you must drain them properly. Grasp each artichoke with a clean kitchen towel (they will be quite hot) and hold (bottom up) over the sink. Gently but firmly, squeeze each artichoke to release excess moisture. Serve immediately or place on a wire rack (again, bottom up) until cool enough to handle.

To remove choke (optional): After cooking, draining and cooling, gently but firmly open the center leaves of artichoke and pull out the flowery petals, exposing the hairlike choke. Using a teaspoon, scrape the choke off the bottom heart, leaving the heart clean. Discard the choke. (Always remove the choke when serving whole artichokes to children.)

To serve: Serve artichokes hot with clarified ("drawn") butter (page 81) or chilled with a dressing made with Homemade Mayonnaise (page 86) or use as directed in recipe.

CARAMELIZED BRUSSELS SPROUTS

With Sautéed Onions, Toasted Chestnuts and Bacon

YIELD: serves 8

SPECIAL EQUIPMENT
8-quart blanching pot with built-in strainer (optional)

Brussels sprouts, which look like tiny heads of cabbage, have a delicious and intriguing flavor. When caramelized and combined with sautéed onions, fresh chestnuts and bacon, the sprouts are transformed into a dish of incredible taste, interesting eye appeal and earthy elegance. Although we consumers rarely are allowed to hand pick our sprouts in the market, the specimens that are visible through the cellophane-wrapped containers should be bright green, tight and compact. Brown spots or wilted outer leaves indicate old age. And for the most delicate flavor, use Brussels sprouts within three days of purchase since the longer they sit, the more pungent and strong they become.

TIPS
FROM A TEACHER

How to Roast and Peel Fresh Chestnuts

Chestnuts—the only nuts with vitamin C—are only available fresh from September through February, making them a traditional ingredient in many dishes associated with Thanksgiving and Christmas. Although chestnuts can be purchased dried, I don't find them appealing (even after reconstituting) and rarely use them this way. In a pinch, I buy jars of whole, peeled chestnuts, but even those don't compare to the taste and texture of fresh. Before cooking chestnuts, you must remove their hard mahogany-colored shells by roasting, blanching or boiling them; then peel off the thin inner bitter skin that covers the meat. The cooked flesh has a potatolike consistency, a sweet and nutty taste and can be puréed or sautéed to greatly enhance an otherwise ordinary side dish. When purchasing fresh chestnuts, choose those with smooth, firm shells that have no signs of "buckling," pitting (small holes) or other distinct blemishes. Store them in a cool, dry place; once peeled, they must be refrigerated in a covered container.

To roast or blanch chestnuts: Cut an X on the flat side of each chestnut, using a sharp knife, and place them on a shallow baking sheet (X side up) in a single layer. Roast in a preheated

2½ pounds Brussels sprouts

Salt as needed

1 stalk celery, cleaned and halved with leaves

16 fresh chestnuts, toasted, peeled and cut into quarters (page 332),
   or 2 cups pecan halves, coarsely chopped

2 tablespoons butter, plus ½ stick (4 tablespoons) butter
   or ¼ cup extra-virgin olive oil

6 slices bacon

1 large yellow onion

½ cup Rich Chicken Stock or "Doctored" Canned Chicken Broth
   (page 140 for both)

Freshly ground black pepper to taste

Kosher or sea salt to taste

375°F oven until the shell bursts open at the X, about 15 minutes. Shake pan occasionally during roasting to redistribute. Alternatively, to remove shells by blanching, slit nuts in the same way and boil in water to cover until shell opens, for 3 to 5 minutes. Drain and peel as soon as nuts are cool enough to handle.

To peel roasted or blanched chestnuts: While nuts are still warm, peel off the hard outer shell and thin brown inner skin. If you have trouble removing the skin, drop chestnuts into a saucepan of boiling water and remove pan from stove. Let nuts steep for 4 to 5 minutes, then drain and (when still warm but cool enough to handle) gently rub off the skins with a clean kitchen towel. Use the sharp tip of a small paring knife to pick out any deeply embedded pieces of skin from the crevices. Pat nuts dry and use as directed in recipe.

To boil fresh chestnuts: Lay chestnuts on your work surface (flat side down) and, using a heavy cleaver, whack each nut to divide in half. Place nuts in a saucepan with enough water to cover by 1 inch, and bring water to a boil. Cook nuts (uncovered) for 3 to 4 minutes. Drain and, using the tines of a small seafood fork, pry nuts out of their shells. (If chestnuts are large, cut each half in half.) Usually, the brown skins will be left behind in the shell. Use the tip of a sharp knife to pick out any stubborn spots. Return peeled chestnuts to saucepan with fresh water to cover and bring to a boil. Reduce heat to low and simmer (uncovered) until tender, 30 to 45 minutes. (Use the lesser time if planning to cook nuts further as part of another recipe.) Drain nuts and pat dry.

- The sprouts can be blanched 1 day ahead. Place them (well dried) in a bowl lined with paper towels. Cover bowl securely with plastic wrap and refrigerate. Don't halve sprouts until the day of assembling.

- The onion can be sliced 1 day ahead and refrigerated securely covered with plastic wrap.

A stalk of celery in the cooking pot will help keep the pungent aroma of cooked Brussels sprouts, cabbage or broccoli to a minimum.

1) *To trim and blanch Brussels sprouts:* Bring an 8-quart pot of water to a rapid boil. Trim off the hard stem end of sprouts, remove all loose outer leaves and cut an X on the stem end. When water boils, set a large bowl of ice water on the counter. To boiling water, add 2 teaspoons salt, sprouts and celery. Blanch sprouts until just tender but still firm, about 4 minutes. Drain vegetables and immediately plunge them into the ice water. Swish them around until totally cold, then drain and pat dry. Discard celery, cut each sprout in half through the core end and set aside.

2) *To pan sauté diced chestnuts:* Heat an 8-inch skillet over medium heat with the 2 tablespoons butter. When hot and bubbling, add diced chestnuts and cook, stirring constantly until chestnuts are golden with a savory aroma, about 3 minutes. Remove with a slotted spoon to a plate and set aside.

3) *To prepare bacon:* Slowly fry bacon in a 10- to 12-inch deep-sided skillet over low heat until crisp and drain on paper toweling. Either reserve 1 tablespoon of the drippings in the skillet, or discard and add 1 tablespoon of the butter or olive oil to the skillet. Slice bacon into ⅓-inch pieces and set aside.

4) *To prepare and cook onion strips:* Peel onion and slice in half through the stem end. Cut each half into 2 equal wedges. Slice each wedge into very thin wedges and separate each wedge into thin strips. Measure out 1 generous cup of strips. Return skillet to medium heat with reserved bacon drippings, butter or olive oil. When hot, add onion strips and sauté until softened and turning golden, 5 to 7 minutes. Add chicken stock and simmer until the stock is reduced to about ½, about 5 minutes. Pour onions and reduced stock into a mixing bowl and set aside.

5) *To assemble and serve:* Return skillet to medium heat and, when hot, add remaining 3 tablespoons butter or olive oil. When oil is hot, add blanched sprouts and cook, tossing frequently until sprouts are tender, turning golden and caramelized on the outside, 5 to 7 minutes. Stir in sautéed onions with any reduced stock along with cooked bacon pieces and sautéed chestnuts. Cook until piping hot throughout. Season with freshly ground black pepper and coarse salt to taste. Serve at once.

BRAISED CABBAGE WITH CARAWAY

And a Touch of Cider Vinegar

YIELD: serves 8 to 10

Unfortunately, many people only associate cabbage with coleslaw or stuffed cabbage. Here, thinly sliced green cabbage is wilted until crisp tender with rich chicken stock, whole caraway seeds and the distinctive bite of a small amount of apple cider vinegar. When completed, you have a delicious and fiber-rich side dish, which is a perfect partner for any roasted, broiled or grilled beef, chicken or pork—not to mention the classic marriage of corned beef and cabbage. And save any leftover cabbage to make a hearty Reuben Pie (page 292). Serve the cabbage alongside Brown Sugar-Glazed Corned Beef (page 290), Apricot-Glazed Ham (page 293) or Glazed Loin of Pork (page 296).

INGREDIENTS

1 medium to large head green cabbage, trimmed of any discolored or wilted outer leaves

½ stick (4 tablespoons) butter or margarine

1 cup Rich Chicken Stock or "Doctored" Canned Chicken Broth (page 140 for both)

¼ cup cider vinegar (optional but highly suggested)

1 tablespoon whole caraway seeds

Freshly ground black pepper

Kosher or sea salt to taste

1) **To prepare cabbage:** Using a sharp chef's knife, slice the head of cabbage in half (through the core end). Cut each half into wedges and cut out the bottom tough core from each wedge. Slice wedges into very thin lengthwise slices. Separate slices and place them in a large bowl.

2) **To braise and serve:** Heat a 12-inch nonreactive deep-sided skillet over medium heat. Add butter and, when bubbling, add shredded cabbage. Toss to coat cabbage with butter and raise heat to sear the shreds until lightly wilted and well moistened. Add chicken stock, vinegar, if using, and caraway seeds. Cover, reduce heat to low and simmer cabbage until tender, 5 to 10 minutes. Uncover and season to taste with freshly ground black pepper and coarse salt to taste. Serve at once.

SPECIAL EQUIPMENT
12-inch nonreactive deep-sided skillet

TIPS
FROM A TEACHER

Cabbage

For the sake of convenience, cabbage can be sliced days in advance and kept refrigerated in a securely sealed, heavy-duty plastic bag, but the vegetable will lose vitamin C soon after being sliced or torn. So, buying half of a head (even if it's well wrapped) is not a great idea. If left whole and wrapped tightly and refrigerated, cabbage will remain fresh and in good condition for two weeks. Since slicing cabbage by hand is not hard to do and makes little mess, it's better to slice it shortly before cooking. If you don't need to slice an entire head, only wash the parts that you intend to use right away. Keep the remainder in the refrigerator tightly wrapped with plastic and use within one or two days.

Variation with Sautéed Onions and Pasta

You could make this dish even more substantial by adding 1 large chopped yellow onion, sautéed in a bit of melted butter or olive oil until golden. Just before serving, stir sautéed onions into braised cabbage along with 8 ounces of freshly cooked bow-tie pasta and a tablespoon or so of chopped flat-leaf Italian parsley. Season to taste with freshly ground black pepper and coarse salt.

MAPLE-BASTED DELICATA SQUASH

The Best Squash in the Whole World!

YIELD: serves 6

SPECIAL EQUIPMENT
Large roasting pan that will hold 6 squash halves in a single layer

These capsule-shaped gourdlike squash boast beautiful orange skins, which are usually streaked with yellow or green stripes, and have a unique texture and flavor that's a cross between acorn squash and a creamy sweet potato. Although Delicata has a limited season (late September through December), it's by far my favorite variety. When basted (outside and in) with melted butter and pure maple syrup and baked until meltingly tender, the skin (unlike most winter squashes) is totally edible and delectable. This recipe can be used with both acorn or sweet dumpling squash, but I'm always saddened when the brief Delicata season comes to an end. When purchasing these gems, look for squash that are deeply colored. The stem end should be completely dry and the size should be about nine inches long with a diameter of three inches. If you plan to store them, they should be blemish free and feel quite firm. Store them in a cool, dry place.

INGREDIENTS

3 Delicata squash or acorn or sweet dumpling squash

6 tablespoons butter or margarine, melted

⅓ cup pure maple syrup

1) **To prepare squash:** Scrub each squash and slice in half lengthwise using a sharp chef's knife. Scoop out seeds and strings using a spoon. Brush all sides of squash first with melted butter and then with syrup. Arrange (cut side down) in a large roasting pan in a single layer and cover the pan (dull side up) with aluminum foil.

2) **To bake:** Preheat the oven to 375°F. Poke a few holes in the foil and bake squash for 30 minutes. Uncover, baste with more syrup and turn over squash. Baste the exposed, cut sides of squash with more maple syrup and melted butter. Continue to bake until the flesh is very tender and creamy, about 30 minutes. Since sweet dumpling squash are smaller, they will need a bit less cooking time; check after 45 minutes in the oven. On the other hand, the thick-skinned acorn squash might need a bit longer.

3) **To serve:** Slice each half of cooked squash in half widthwise and serve on a platter. Allow a full half (2 pieces) per adult and 1 piece for a small child. Remember, the skins are edible and a good source of fiber!

HAND-CARVED MUSHROOM CAPS

It's Easy to be Impressive!

YIELD: serves 6

These decorative mushrooms, sitting atop sizzling steaks and even hamburgers, are always incredibly impressive to guests. But actually, it's a simple skill to master. Regular button mushrooms work best since their white-white color makes it easy for you to monitor your design. It's important to keep the mushroom resting on your work surface while creating your design to provide bottom support when applying moderate pressure on top of the cap. Also, when sautéing the mushrooms, avoid overcooking since once the caps become floppy and overly dark, the design almost fades out of sight. I suggest that you always purchase at least two additional mushrooms to allow for some breakage. And don't worry if you do make a mistake. You can always pretend it was part of the design or just sauté the messed-up mushroom along with the others and eat it before serving.

SPECIAL EQUIPMENT
3-inch or smaller paring knife

INGREDIENTS

8 fresh large, white button mushrooms, wiped clean (page 131)

2 to 3 tablespoons butter or extra-virgin olive oil

Freshly ground black pepper to taste

Kosher or sea salt to taste

Chopped flat-leaf Italian parsley (optional), for garnish

1) *To carve mushrooms:* Slice off stem end of each mushroom so it's flush with the cap and lay mushrooms flat on your work surface. Grasp the handle of a small paring knife and extend your index finger down the full length of the blade toward the tip. Securing the mushroom with your other hand, press down the knife tip on the mushroom cap to make small pointed indentations (⅛ inch deep) that resemble tiny tepees. Continue around the surface of the mushroom cap until the entire cap is filled with decorative depressions.

2) *To sauté:* A few minutes before serving, heat an 8- to 10-inch skillet over medium heat. When hot, add butter or olive oil and, when hot, add carved mushroom caps and raise heat to high. Sauté mushrooms quickly until golden on both sides and tender throughout, about 2 minutes on each side. Avoid overcooking or they'll turn limp and quite wet.

3) *To serve:* Place 1 or 2 mushroom caps on the center of each steak. Add a light sprinkling of coarse salt over all and, if desired, a bit of chopped parsley. Serve immediately.

SAUTÉED SPICED GOLDEN DELICIOUS APPLES

YIELD: serves 6 to 8

As these spiced apples sauté until just tender, the delicious aromas wafting throughout your home will make it hard to wait for dinner—or breakfast, for that matter! I use my favorite Golden Delicious apples for their pearlike flavor and for their ability to hold their shape well through cooking. Although treating the apples with lemon juice will prevent them from quickly turning brown, after thirty minutes the color will be affected. But since the spices will change the ultimate color of the apples anyway, in a pinch you can slice them one hour ahead, but cover them well to help prevent oxidation. Serve as a condiment with roast chicken or pork or as part of a soothing breakfast simply topped with a tablespoon or so of light cream. These apples are also terrific layered inside a fluffy omelet with or without some cubed Brie cheese (remove the rind before cubing cheese).

SPECIAL EQUIPMENT

Large nonreactive mixing bowl

Sturdy fruit wedge cutter and corer (optional)

10- to 12-inch nonreactive deep-sided skillet

Nutmeg grater (optional)

Small nonreactive saucepan

INGREDIENTS

2 tablespoons strained fresh lemon juice

6 large Golden Delicious apples

3 tablespoons unsalted butter

½ teaspoon ground cinnamon

½ teaspoon ground nutmeg (preferably freshly grated)

2 tablespoons sugar

½ cup mixed light and dark raisins (optional)

2 tablespoons Calvados or unsweetened apple juice or apple cider (optional)

1) **To prepare apples:** Pour lemon juice into a large nonreactive mixing bowl. Peel, core and slice each apple into 8 wedges. Immediately, drop slices into the bowl and toss to coat with lemon juice.

2) **To sauté apples:** Melt butter in a 10- to 12-inch nonreactive deep-sided skillet over medium heat. When hot and bubbling, add sliced apples, cinnamon, nutmeg and sugar and fold together to combine well. Cook until apples are crisp tender and the spices are fully awakened, about 10 minutes. Using the handle, shake the skillet frequently to redistribute apples without rupturing them.

Golden Delicious apples range in color from greenish yellow to pure yellow with tiny brownish freckles. The latter are the sweetest and have the most pronounced pearlike flavor. Before selecting Golden Delicious apples, carefully inspect the skin. An apple with even tiny wrinkles indicates old age and poor (mealy) texture.

3) To plump and add raisins, if using: Meanwhile, place raisins and apple brandy or juice into a small nonreactive saucepan over very low heat and stir so raisins are lightly coated with brandy. Heat just until liquid begins to bubble and remove from heat. When apples have almost finished cooking, stir in raisins and brandy and cook just a minute more to combine the flavors thoroughly.

4) To serve: Serve hot or just warm as suggested.

EVERYTHING BUT THE KITCHEN SINK STUFFING

YIELD: serves 14 to 18

SPECIAL EQUIPMENT

8-quart mixing bowl or pot to combine stuffing

8-quart oven-to-table baking dish

This stuffing is not just my very own favorite, it was the hit of the day when I was teaching a Thanksgiving class to a group of Japanese women for the CBS "This Morning" show. Although most recipes recommend the use of stale bread for stuffing, I've never agreed with this concept. Stale bread just tastes stale, so instead I cut a variety of fresh breads into cubes and dry them in the oven to obtain the proper consistency. The bread cubes are then combined with loads of sautéed vegetables and chestnuts, selected herbs and even sausage and cranberries, if you like. If you're concerned about the generous amount of butter, see my reduced-fat variation. But if you're celebrating an annual holiday, to enjoy the stuffing's fullest flavor, I would leave it as it stands. Naturally, this stuffing is also wonderful baked inside a turkey. A note on that process follows this recipe.

INGREDIENTS

20 cups bread cubes (assorted breads such as homemade-type white, whole wheat, soft rye, and Italian with sesame seeds, with crusts)

8 ounces *each* fresh button mushrooms and fresh shiitake mushrooms *or* mostly button mushrooms and ⅔ ounce (rounded ½ cup) dried shiitakes or porcini mushrooms

2 sticks (½ pound) lightly salted butter, plus butter for baking dish

¾ pound fresh chestnuts toasted, peeled and cut into small cubes (page 332) or 1½ to 2 cups coarsely chopped shelled pecans

1 tablespoon olive oil

1 pound lean chicken-veal sausage or sweet Italian sausage (both optional, but highly suggested), removed from casings

2 to 2½ cups Rich Chicken Stock or (only if necessary) "Doctored" Canned Chicken Broth (page 140 for both)

2 large yellow onions, chopped

2 stalks celery, cleaned, trimmed and minced

5 large cloves garlic, minced

1 small red bell pepper, seeded and minced

½ cup chopped fresh flat-leaf Italian parsley

2 teaspoons crumbled dried thyme

2 teaspoons crumbled dried oregano

1½ tablespoons chopped fresh sage leaves or 1 rounded teaspoon crumbled dried sage

1½ cups fresh cranberries (optional), rinsed, picked over, drained and chopped, or thawed frozen cranberries

3 extra-large eggs, lightly beaten

Kosher or sea salt and freshly ground black pepper to taste

Time Management Tips

- The stuffing can be assembled totally 1 day ahead, cooled, covered and refrigerated. Bring close to room temperature before baking or adjust baking time to achieve the desired results. Do not stuff a turkey until just before roasting.

1) **To toast bread cubes:** Preheat the oven to 350°F. Toast bread cubes in batches on a shallow baking sheet in a single layer until light golden, about 15 minutes. (If using dark baking sheets, the bread will toast faster.) Turn off oven and let the cubes sit there until dry, 20 to 30 minutes. Then transfer them into an 8-quart mixing bowl or a large pot.

2) **To prepare mushrooms:** Clean fresh mushrooms; trim stems of button mushrooms and remove stems from shiitakes (page 131). Then slice thinly. If using dried mushrooms, reconstitute them as directed on page 131; strain and reserve ½ cup soaking liquid.

3) **To toast peeled chestnuts:** Heat an 8- to 10-inch skillet over medium heat and, when hot, melt 3 tablespoons of the butter. When hot and bubbling, stir in diced chestnuts or pecans and sauté, stirring constantly until chestnuts are golden brown and toasted, 3 to 5 minutes. Remove to a plate and set aside.

4) **To cook sausage, if using:** Heat a 10-to 12-inch deep-sided skillet over medium heat. When hot, add 1 tablespoon olive oil and, when oil is hot, add sausage, stirring to break up the meat using a fork or wooden spatula. Fry sausage until the exterior becomes brown but the inside is still pink.

Preparing a Stuffed Turkey

Some of this stuffing, of course, may be baked inside a Perfect Roast Turkey (page 247). Prepare stuffing as directed through its assembly and stuff the bird just before placing it into the oven. Don't overstuff the cavity since the mixture will expand in the oven and, if packed too tightly, the stuffing will be heavy and overly dense. To estimate accurately the amount of stuffing that will fit comfortably within the cavity, figure on ½ cup of stuffing for each pound of turkey. And make sure to allow for a longer roasting time since stuffed poultry takes longer to reach the desired internal temperature of 170°F for the breast meat, 180°F for the thigh and 160°F for the stuffing. (Insert an instant reading thermometer directly into stuffing to check the temperature.) Bake any remaining stuffing in a buttered casserole as described in this recipe. Make sure to remove any leftover stuffing from within the cooked turkey carcass before refrigerating to eliminate the possibility of bacterial contamination to the stuffing.

Add ½ cup of the chicken stock to sausage and simmer until no longer pink and the stock is just about absorbed. Pour sausage into the bowl with bread cubes.

5) *To sauté vegetables:* Wipe out the interior of the skillet and return to medium heat. Melt 1 stick of the butter and, when hot and bubbling, stir in chopped onions, celery and garlic. Reduce heat and cook gently until vegetables are softened and very fragrant, about 10 minutes. Raise heat, stir in chopped red pepper and sliced mushrooms. (If using reconstituted dried mushrooms, add them when red peppers are almost tender.) Cook vegetables until all are tender, about 5 minutes more. Just as they finish cooking, stir in parsley, thyme, oregano and sage. Heat for just a few seconds to release the flavor of the herbs. Remove from heat and pour vegetable-herb mixture into the bowl with the bread cubes and cooked sausage. Then add chopped cranberries, if using, and chestnuts.

6) *To assemble fully:* In a small saucepan, heat only 1 cup of the remaining stock (or ½ cup reserved mushroom liquid and ½ cup stock) with the remaining 5 tablespoons butter until stock is hot and butter is melted. Add to the stuffing, along with eggs. Fold all ingredients together to combine thoroughly. If you desire a moister stuffing, add the remaining ½ cup of stock. Season to taste with coarse salt and lots and lots of freshly ground black pepper—grind until it hurts and then give it 2 more grinds!

7) *To prepare casserole:* Butter the interior of an 8-quart casserole dish and also butter the interior of the lid or the shiny side of a sheet of aluminum foil. Spoon stuffing mixture into the prepared dish. Sprinkle the top with a little more coarse salt and grind on a bit more pepper; when cool, cover the dish. (If planning to stuff a turkey, see directions left.)

8) *To bake and serve:* Preheat the oven to 375°F. Bake the covered stuffing for 45 minutes. Uncover and continue to bake until stuffing is piping hot throughout and the top is crusty and golden brown, about 15 minutes. Serve hot from the casserole at the table.

Reduced-Fat Variation

To reduce the overall saturated-fat content of the stuffing, omit butter when sautéing vegetables and stir the chopped vegetables into ¼ cup hot extra-virgin olive oil or canola oil; when they are just beginning to soften, add ¼ cup additional chicken stock and simmer until tender. You can also omit the 5 tablespoons of butter when assembling the stuffing or reduce to 1 or 2 tablespoons. Finally, you can use 1 whole egg and 3 extra-large egg whites and adjust the amount of stock to achieve correct consistency. If making these variations, I suggest using some extra dried mushrooms and including at least ½ cup of the strained reconstituting liquid. This will heighten the overall flavor of the stuffing so you'll be less likely to miss the richness of the butter. No need to reduce the amount of fresh mushrooms.

Truly Soothing . . .
MASHED NEW POTATO CASSEROLE

YIELD: serves 6

Mashed potatoes don't get any better than this casserole—creamy, soothing and simply delicious. While the ingredients are quite rich, you can easily alter them to make this lower in saturated fat (see following variation). Potatoes are often differentiated according to age and only those that are freshly harvested can be called "new" potatoes. The size of new potatoes ranges from quite tiny to as large as a full-sized mature potato. Because they have a high moisture content, new potatoes will cook more quickly and their naturally high sugar content gives them (once cooked) a distinctively sweet and delicate flavor. They are, however, more perishable than most other potatoes and should be used within one week of purchase. And remember not to store your potatoes in the same bin with onions since, when together, they produce a chemical reaction that encourages each to spoil more quickly.

SPECIAL EQUIPMENT

8-quart blanching pot with built-in strainer (optional)

Potato masher, preferably with perforated disc on the bottom

2-quart oven-to-table casserole dish, preferably with lid

Decorating comb or the tines of a large serving fork

INGREDIENTS

3½ pounds red new potatoes (about 9 large potatoes),
  peeled and cut in half

Salt to taste

About 1 stick (¼ pound) butter or margarine

1 cup minced scallions (green onions), trimmed white part
  and 1½ to 2 inches of the tender green

½ cup sour cream

½ cup milk, heated

3 ounces cream cheese, at room temperature

3 ounces Swiss cheese (optional), chopped

½ teaspoon white pepper

Freshly ground black pepper to taste

Kosher or sea salt to taste

Sweet Hungarian paprika to taste

1) **To cook potatoes:** Bring an 8-quart pot of water to a rapid boil. Add some salt to boiling water, then potatoes and boil (covered) until tender, about 30 minutes for medium chunks, more for larger ones.

2) **To sauté scallions:** While potatoes cook, heat an 8- to 10-inch skillet over medium heat and melt 2 tablespoons of the butter. When hot and bubbling, reduce heat to low, add minced scallions and sauté until softened and fragrant, about 4 minutes.

3) **To assemble:** Drain potatoes and place them in a large mixing bowl. Add sour cream, hot milk, remaining 3 tablespoons of the butter and cream cheese. Mash with an old-fashioned potato masher, combining well until mixture is very smooth and fluffy. (For extra smoothness, whip mixture with a hand-held electric mixer once you've mashed down any large chunks of potatoes; don't use a food processor which makes them gluey—and awful.) Add sautéed scallions and chopped Swiss cheese, if using, to potato mixture and combine well. Stir in ground white pepper, salt to taste and a generous amount of freshly ground black pepper. (Potato mixtures taste best when well seasoned.)

4) **To prepare casserole:** Butter a 2-quart casserole and the interior of the lid or the shiny side of a piece of aluminum foil. Spoon potato mixture into the buttered baking dish and smooth the top with a spatula. Using either a decorating comb or a large serving fork, create a design starting at the rim of the dish and going around and around until you reach the center. Sprinkle the top lightly with coarse salt, black pepper and paprika. Dot with a few bits of additional butter or margarine, if desired.

5) **To bake and serve:** Preheat the oven to 375°F. Cover casserole and bake 30 minutes. Remove cover or foil and continue to bake until piping hot and crusty brown on top, about 30 minutes.

Reduced-Fat and Low Cholesterol Variations

Substitute hot well-seasoned chicken stock for the milk (or simply use potato water). Blend 1 generous cup low-fat cottage cheese in the blender or food processor until smooth; substitute this for the 3 tablespoons butter, cream cheese and sour cream when assembling. Use olive oil instead of butter to sauté scallions.

Time Management Tips

- Peel potatoes early in the day (or as long as 1 day ahead) and keep totally submerged in cold water until you boil them. The water is essential to prevent the potatoes from oxidizing and turning brown once peeled. If peeled a day ahead, keep submerged and refrigerated.

- The entire casserole can be assembled fully a few hours before you plan to bake it. Cool and keep covered at a comfortable room temperature. Although refrigeration will adversely affect the texture of the mixture somewhat, (in a pinch) leave covered in the refrigerator overnight and bring close to room temperature before baking.

SPINACH, LEEK AND POTATO CASSEROLE

With Crisp Potato Skins

YIELD: serves 10 to 12

Crusty on top, creamy on the inside, this side dish combines freshly cooked spinach and creamy mashed potatoes with the gentle sweetness of tender leeks. And the crisp potato skins are the perfect vessel to scoop and eat the potato mixture! If not planning to prepare the skins, boil new potatoes instead of baking the Idahos, since new potatoes have the creamiest texture for mashing. And for nights when you feel the need to cut back on calories, see my low-fat variations. Serve this soothing side dish with Golden Herb-Rubbed Cornish Hens (page 240), Mediterranean Lamb Chops (page 299) or My Meatloaf (page 274), omitting the Jarlsberg cheese in either the meatloaf or the potatoes.

SPECIAL EQUIPMENT

8-quart blanching pot with built-in strainer, only if boiling new potatoes

5-quart heavy-bottomed saucepan with tight-fitting lid

Potato masher, preferably with perforated disc on the bottom

6-quart oven-to-table casserole dish with lid

INGREDIENTS

8 large or 10 medium-sized Idaho baking potatoes or, if not using potato skins, 12 large new potatoes

4 bunches (2 bags) fresh spinach or 2 packages (10 ounces each) frozen chopped spinach

½ stick (4 tablespoons) butter, melted, plus more for the baking dish

½ to 1 cup Rich Chicken Stock or "Doctored" Canned Chicken Broth (page 140 for both)

2 cups minced cleaned leeks (page 160)

2 cups minced prosciutto ham (optional), preferably imported from Parma

½ cup freshly grated Reggiano Parmesan cheese

¾ cup milk, heated

1 cup sour cream

Salt to taste

1 teaspoon ground white pepper

Freshly ground black pepper to taste

Kosher or sea salt to taste

1 cup grated Jarlsberg cheese (optional)

FOR THE POTATO SKINS (OPTIONAL)

½ stick (4 tablespoons) butter, melted

2 cloves garlic, minced

Empty (scooped out) skins from 8 large baking potatoes

Freshly ground black pepper to taste

Kosher or sea salt

¼ cup freshly grated Reggiano Parmesan cheese (optional)

1) *To bake potatoes:* Preheat the oven to 375°F. Scrub potatoes and dry well. Bake on a shallow baking sheet until the pulp is very tender and the skins crisp, about 1½ hours. If not planning on making potato skins, peel, halve and boil 12 large new potatoes in a generous amount of lightly salted water until tender, about 35 to 45 minutes.

2) *To prepare spinach:* Remove stems and thoroughly clean spinach leaves in several changes of fresh water. Drain well but do not dry leaves. Measure out 10 packed cups into a 5-quart heavy-bottomed pot with only the water that clings to the leaves after draining. Place over medium heat until steam starts escaping from the lid. Reduce heat to low and cook spinach until tender and totally wilted, 4 to 5 minutes. Pour spinach into a large medium-mesh wire strainer and place another smaller bowl into the strainer directly on top of spinach. Using firm pressure, press down on the inside bowl to squeeze all excess liquid from spinach. Chop spinach and set aside. If using frozen chopped spinach, cook according to the package directions and drain in the same way as described above.

3) *To sweat leeks:* Melt the ½ stick butter in a 10-inch deep-sided skillet over medium heat. Tear off a sheet of waxed paper large enough to cover the bottom interior of the pan and brush 1 side of the paper with some of the melted butter. When butter is bubbling, stir in minced leeks along with only ½ cup of the chicken stock. Bring mixture to a simmer, place the buttered side of the waxed paper directly on top of the leeks and reduce heat to very low. Sweat leeks until softened and very fragrant, about 10 minutes.

4) *To add ham and cheese:* Remove and discard waxed paper from leeks and stir in minced prosciutto, if using, and cook gently for 5 minutes more. Remove from heat and stir in chopped spinach and grated Parmesan cheese. Stir well to combine and set aside.

Time Management Tips

- The spinach can be cleaned 1 day ahead and refrigerated in sealed heavy-duty plastic bags. The leeks can also be cleaned and minced 1 day ahead and kept well covered in the refrigerator.

- The potato mixture can be assembled totally earlier in the day, cooled, covered and left at a comfortable room temperature. If very warm, refrigerate the mixture but bring it to room temperature before baking.

- The potato skins can be fully assembled 2 to 3 hours ahead and kept at room temperature covered with plastic wrap.

5) *To scoop and mash potatoes:* Remove potatoes from oven and allow to cool only slightly. (Potatoes absorb other ingredients more efficiently when warm.) Cut potatoes in half lengthwise and scoop out the pulp into a mixing bowl allowing a very thin layer of potato to remain on the walls of the skin. If using boiled potatoes, drain, peel and place them into a mixing bowl. Using an old-fashioned potato masher, mash potato pulp in the bowl with hot milk and sour cream until smooth, adding additional hot chicken stock if potatoes seem at all dry. Fold in spinach-leek-ham mixture and combine well adding salt, white pepper and freshly ground black pepper to taste.

6) *To prepare casserole and bake:* Preheat the oven to 375°F. Butter the interior of a 6-quart baking dish and the interior of the lid or the shiny side of a piece of aluminum foil. Pour potato mixture into baking dish and smooth the top with a rubber spatula. Season the top lightly with coarse salt and more freshly ground black pepper and, if desired, scatter grated Jarlsberg on top. Cover casserole and bake for 30 minutes. Uncover and bake until piping hot throughout and the top is golden, about 30 minutes.

7) *To prepare potato skins, if using:* Melt butter over medium heat and, when bubbling, add minced garlic. Reduce heat to very low and sauté garlic until just softened and fragrant, about 30 seconds (avoid browning). Cut each potato skin in half lengthwise and brush both sides with the garlic butter. Lay each piece (scooped side up) on a shallow baking sheet and sprinkle generously with freshly ground pepper and lightly with coarse salt.

8) *To bake potato skins:* Bake skins in the upper third of the preheated 375°F oven for 30 to 40 minutes or until hot, crisp and golden. For the last 10 minutes of baking, if desired, scatter grated cheese lightly over the tops of the seasoned skins. If the rest of the meal is ready and the skins are not quite as crisp as desired, run them briefly under the broiler.

9) *To serve:* Spoon individual portions of the potato mixture on a plate and arrange 4 crisp wedges of potato skins in a spoke pattern around it. Serve hot.

Low-Fat Variations

To sweat leeks and prepare potato skins use extra-virgin olive oil instead of butter. Substitute Low-Fat Sour Cream (page 82) for the regular sour cream and use low-fat milk or substitute more chicken stock for the whole milk. Omit ham and Jarlsberg cheese.

SWEET POTATO CASSEROLE WITH MARSHMALLOWS

The Only Way to Go

YIELD: serves 12

This is the answer to kid-heaven—of course the kid can be anywhere from two to ninety-two! This sweet and mildly spiced traditional dream of a dish is a must for the holidays. Although mashed white potatoes seem to lose something when made a day ahead, sweet potatoes do just fine. Conveniently, this will give you more time to do other things when making a holiday feast. And do use the mini marshmallows whenever possible since the bigger ones have a tendency to rise as they bake and fall off the edge of the baking dish. Regarding the low-fat, no-fat, high-fat issue, this recipe is holiday stuff, so enjoy yourself within moderation. However, on other nights you might consider my low-fat variation for a lighter, but still delicious alternative. And for just the two of you, I have an answer for that also.

SPECIAL EQUIPMENT

6-quart oven-to-table casserole with lid

8-quart blanching pot with built-in strainer (optional)

Potato masher, preferably with perforated disc on the bottom

Nutmeg grater (optional)

INGREDIENTS

1 stick butter (¼ pound) butter or margarine, melted

Salt as needed

11 large sweet potatoes (about 7½ pounds) scrubbed, peeled and cut into medium-sized chunks

About 1 cup milk, heated

¾ cup pure maple syrup or maple-flavored syrup

1 teaspoon ground cinnamon

½ teaspoon ground nutmeg (preferably freshly grated)

1 bag (10½ ounces) mini marshmallows

1) To set up: Using some of the melted butter, grease a 6-quart baking dish and the lid or the shiny side of a piece of aluminum foil.

2) To cook and mash potatoes: Bring a large pot of water to a rapid boil; add 2 teaspoons salt and then potatoes. Cover and boil until very tender, about 30 minutes. Drain well and put potatoes into a large mixing bowl. Add remaining melted butter and mash well with an old-fashioned potato masher. Add enough of the hot milk to give potatoes a very soft and creamy texture. Add ½ cup of the maple syrup along with cinnamon and nutmeg. Stir well and taste for seasoning, adding a little salt if needed.

Time Management Tips

- The potatoes may be assembled fully, but not baked, 1 day ahead. When mashed and potato mixture is cool, cover and refrigerate. Bring close to room temperature before baking or adjust baking time accordingly.

3) ***To assemble and bake:*** Preheat the oven to 375°F. Spoon potato mixture into the prepared casserole and smooth the top with a spatula. (The top of the potatoes should be an inch or so below the top of the dish to allow for the marshmallows.) With a long 2-pronged fork, poke holes into the top of the potato mixture going half way down to the center. Drizzle the remaining ¼ cup maple syrup over potatoes and smooth with a spatula. Cover and bake for 30 minutes. Uncover casserole, reduce oven temperature to 350°F and bake until very hot throughout, about 30 minutes.

4) ***To finish and serve:*** Lay mini marshmallows over the top of the potatoes pressing them in slightly. Raise heat to 375°F and bake casserole until marshmallows are melted and golden brown, 5 to 8 minutes. Serve piping hot from the casserole at the table. (If using larger marshmallows, place a shallow baking sheet underneath the casserole dish to catch any marshmallows that swell and fall off the sides during baking.)

Low-Fat Variations

To reduce the overall saturated-fat content as well as some of the sugar in this recipe, do the following: Omit milk and substitute potato cooking water or instead use half low-fat milk and half potato water. Instead of butter or margarine, use 1 cup nonfat cottage cheese, puréed in a food processor or blender until smooth. Omit the ½ cup maple syrup and substitute 1 cup apple cider that's been simmered down and reduced to ½ cup. And don't worry, marshmallows have no fat or cholesterol (hooray!).

Sweet Potatoes for Two

If your "holiday crowd" consists of just the two of you, bake 2 plump sweet potatoes and when tender, split the tops and gently fork in a teaspoon *each* softened butter and maple syrup with a dash of ground cinnamon and freshly grated nutmeg. Carefully stir the pulp (staying within the confines of the skin) and top with a few mini marshmallows. Bake in a preheated 375°F oven on a shallow baking sheet until marshmallows swell and turn golden, 5 to 8 minutes.

Sweet potatoes are not true yams, which are usually very large (some incredibly so) and are mostly grown in Asia and Africa. Because yams are not usually available in this country but are used in the same ways as sweet potatoes, the terms "yam" and "sweet potato" are sometimes used interchangeably, and the darker variety of sweet potato is often marketed as yam. Sweet potatoes are quite perishable and should be used as soon as possible after purchase. Don't refrigerate them, but store them in a dry, well-ventilated bin for up to one week. (A cool basement is a perfect place for storage.) Avoid buying sweet potatoes with pitting, holes, wrinkles or soft spots; they should feel hard, dense and "weighty" with very smooth, thin skins.

The majority of our sweet potatoes are grown in Louisiana, California and New Jersey. The two most common varieties are those with vibrant orange flesh, which are very sweet and moist (often called yams), or those with a pale yellow pulp and a much drier texture. The moist variety takes longer to cook and, although both varieties are interchangeable, they should not be used together in the same recipe. Since sweet potatoes taste so rich, they have a reputation for being a food to avoid while watching one's waistline. In reality, a medium-sized sweet potato has only about 120 calories (no more than a white potato). And although most traditional recipes use lots of butter and the like, sweet potatoes really need no embellishments to be fully enjoyed.

GARLIC ROAST POTATOES

With Rosemary and Thyme

YIELD: serves 6

SPECIAL EQUIPMENT
Shallow oven-to-table baking dish

These aromatic potatoes are baked—almost braised—with fresh garlic and herbs, adding a touch of simple elegance to many different types of menus. Whether embellishing an elegant rack of lamb or a simple piece of broiled fish, these tender potatoes are easy to prepare and always appreciated by family and friends. For another version of this recipe, peel the potatoes and roast uncovered for the last thirty minutes, or until golden brown and crisp. They are also terrific roasted (under the rack) with a whole chicken or roast beef.

INGREDIENTS

½ stick (4 tablespoons) lightly salted butter or
  ¼ cup extra-virgin olive oil

4 large cloves garlic, minced

1 tablespoon chopped fresh rosemary or 1 generous teaspoon chopped
  dried rosemary

1 tablespoon chopped fresh thyme leaves or 1 generous teaspoon
  crumbled dried thyme

12 medium-sized new potatoes, unpeeled, scrubbed and dried

Freshly ground black pepper to taste

Kosher or sea salt to taste

1) *To set up:* Preheat the oven to 375°F. Place a long piece of aluminum foil in a shallow baking dish (dull side up), extending the foil 1½ inches beyond rim.

2) *To prepare garlic butter or oil:* Melt butter or heat oil over low heat in a small saucepan. When hot, sauté garlic very slowly until softened and fragrant, but not brown, 1 to 2 minutes. Stir in rosemary and thyme and remove from heat.

3) **To assemble:** Pour garlic-herb mixture into the prepared baking dish and place potatoes in a single layer on top of herb mixture. Roll each potato in herb mixture and sprinkle on a generous amount of freshly ground black pepper. Place another piece of aluminum foil over the top (dull side up) and pinch the foil at the sides to secure shut.

4) **To bake and serve:** Using either a skewer or the tip of a sharp knife, poke several holes in the top foil. Bake potatoes 1½ hours. When done, they will be very soft and creamy inside and sizzling and glistening outside. Remove bottom foil by lifting up side so that potatoes slide back into baking dish; scrape the crisped savory herbs onto the potatoes. Add a light sprinkling of coarse salt and serve immediately.

TIPS
FROM A TEACHER

Buying and Storing Potatoes

When possible, hand pick your potatoes instead of purchasing a whole bag. Each potato should be smooth, well shaped and free from cracks, bruises and black spots. Each potato also should feel very firm and the skins should be dry and wrinkle free. Avoid any potatoes with sprouts; although they are technically edible, sprouting, which indicates age, means that the potato might have begun to produce a toxin called solanine. Also, skin with a greenish tinge indicates the presence of solanine as well as improper storage.

Don't wash potatoes before storing and keep them in a cool, dark and very dry place since both warmth and light encourage sprouting. Avoid refrigerating uncooked potatoes (or storing below 45°F). Generally, excessively cold temperatures will encourage a desirably starchy potato to become undesirably sweet. On the other hand, warm temperatures will encourage the natural sugar content in potatoes to covert to starch, causing them to become mealy. Avoid storing onions and potatoes together in the same bin since both give off gases that hasten spoilage of each other.

POTATOES ANNA À LA LAUREN

With a Pocket of Caramelized Onions and Herbs

YIELD: serves 8

SPECIAL EQUIPMENT
Mandolin or food processor, for slicing potatoes (optional)

10-inch lined round copper pan with side handles or cast iron skillet

The traditional version of this classic French dish is simply made with potatoes, butter, salt and pepper. But I have added caramelized onions and herbs for extra texture and savory flavor. This recipe does call for a lot of butter (to baste potatoes and prevent sticking), but much of it is drained off before serving. For best results, I recommend using a lined 10-inch round copper pan with side handles and sloping sides. Copper is preferred for its excellent heat conduction qualities and for its ability to go from the stove to the oven and then back to the stove. A seasoned cast iron skillet (page 29) is another (although heavier) alternative. A mandolin or a food processor helps to slice the potatoes uniformly. This classic potato dish makes a beautiful presentation and a perfect accompaniment to My Favorite Rib-Eye Steaks (page 279) or Honey Mustard Roast Rack of Lamb (page 300)

INGREDIENTS

6 medium-sized Idaho baking potatoes

1 large yellow onion

2 tablespoons extra-virgin olive oil

1 tablespoon chopped fresh thyme leaves or 1 generous teaspoon crumbled dried thyme

Scant 1½ teaspoons chopped fresh rosemary or ½ teaspoon chopped dried rosemary

Freshly ground black pepper to taste

1⅔ sticks (¼ pound plus 5 tablespoons) unsalted butter, melted

Kosher or sea salt

3 tablespoons chopped flat-leaf Italian parsley

1) To prepare potatoes: Fill a large bowl with ice water. Scrub potatoes and either peel them or thoroughly dry the skins. Slice into ⅛-inch slices and place immediately into the bowl of ice water to prevent slices from turning brown.

2) *To prepare and sauté onion strips:* Peel onion and cut in half through the stem end. Cut each half into 2 wedges and cut each wedge into very thin wedges. Separate into thin strips. Heat olive oil in an 8- to 10-inch skillet over medium heat. When hot, add onion strips and stir to coat with oil. Cook until onions are golden and caramelized, 10 to 20 minutes, stirring occasionally. Add thyme and rosemary and heat just to release their flavor. Grind on some fresh black pepper and remove from heat.

3) *To set up to assemble:* Preheat the oven to 400°F. Brush the bottom and sides of a 10-inch round lined copper pan or seasoned cast iron skillet with a generous amount of melted butter. Line your work surface with a very long strip of double-thickness paper toweling. Drain potatoes and line them up on the towels. Cover with another long sheet of paper toweling and pat slices dry.

4) *To assemble:* Arrange a decorative layer of potato slices on the bottom of the buttered pan. Sprinkle lightly with a little salt, freshly ground black pepper and some of the chopped parsley. Spoon on a generous layer of melted butter. Place another layer of potatoes on top and add, as with the preceding layer, more salt, pepper, parsley and butter. Then, place some of the potatoes around the edges of the dish, tucking them in so they stand up like a border covering the entire slope on the sides of the dish. Pour caramelized onions on top, spreading to cover potatoes. Sprinkle lightly with coarse salt and place another layer of potato slices on top of onions, adding seasoning and parsley as before. Continue until you use all of the potatoes, but don't season the last layer.

5) *To sear potatoes:* Brush a piece of waxed paper with melted butter and place (buttered side down) over potatoes. Place a heavy skillet or heat-proof pot on top to weigh down potatoes. Cook over medium heat for 10 minutes, pressing down on the rim of the upper pan occasionally. (If not using copper or cast iron, sear potatoes over medium-high heat.)

6) *To bake:* Remove waxed paper and pour all the remaining melted butter over potatoes. Season the top generously with salt and freshly ground black pepper. Bake in hot oven until potatoes are golden brown, sizzling and very crisp on top, about 1½ hours.

Time Management Tips

- The onion can be sliced 1 day ahead and kept refrigerated in a well-covered bowl.

- The potatoes can be peeled and sliced early in the day and kept totally submerged in cold water to prevent discoloration.

7) *To finish cooking:* Warm a flat round serving platter, slightly larger than the skillet. Remove potatoes from oven. Using a thin, nonabrasive spatula, gently ease it around the edge and down to the bottom of the pan to make sure potatoes aren't stuck. Return pan to direct medium heat for 5 to 10 minutes to make sure that the bottom layer (which will be the top) is golden. Run the spatula once more around and under potatoes. Then carefully (using a pot lid to secure potatoes in place) tip the pan over the sink and drain off all excess butter.

8) *To invert and serve:* To invert safely and easily, wear an oven mitt on each hand. Place warmed serving platter over the pan. Carefully invert potatoes onto platter and remove the pan. If any of potatoes became dislodged, just place them back on top (crisped sides up). Sprinkle the top lightly with coarse salt and a grind or 2 of black pepper. Serve immediately from platter at the table, cutting into individual wedges with a sharp knife.

CRISPY COTTAGE-FRIED POTATO CHIPS

YIELD: allow 1 large potato per person

SPECIAL EQUIPMENT
Electric deep-fat fryer (optional) or deep-frying thermometer and frying basket or slotted spoon

Crinkle slicer, food processor or chef's knife

These gloriously golden potato slices are not only perfectly crisp but absolutely addicting! My secret is frying them twice. To peel or not to peel? I rarely peel potatoes since the skins lend a contrast of taste and color and are also richer in fiber and vitamins than the flesh of the potato. If you do choose to peel the potatoes, remove as little of the flesh as possible because most of the nutrients of the potato are found just beneath the skin. Finally, use only Idaho (Russet) potatoes because their high starch content makes them superior for frying. And be sure the potato slices are well drained before frying so the hot oil will be less likely to spatter when they are added. For other hints on deep-frying, see Tips from a Teacher (page 358). As a side dish, hot potato chips are a tradition to everything from casual burgers to elegant steaks. But I also frequently serve these crisp slices with drinks before dinner surrounding a bowl of Caviar Dip (page 101).

INGREDIENTS

1 large Idaho potato per person

About 2 quarts flavorless cooking oil

Kosher or sea salt to taste

1) **To prepare potatoes:** Fill a large bowl with ice water. Scrub potatoes and either peel them or dry skins thoroughly. Slice potatoes into ⅛-inch slices and immediately place into the bowl of ice water to prevent discoloration and to remove some of the excess surface starch.

2) **To heat oil for deep-frying:** If using an electric deep-fat fryer, pour in oil to the designated line and turn to the highest setting (or follow the manufacturer's instructions). Otherwise use a 2½- to 4-quart heavy-bottomed saucepan and half fill with oil. Attach a deep-frying thermometer securely onto the side of the pan (don't allow the tip to touch the pan's bottom). Insert frying basket into the oil and heat oil to between 365°F and 375°F.

3) **To deep-fry potatoes:** Lay long sheets of double-thickness paper toweling on your work surface and also line a baking sheet or deep platter with paper toweling. When oil is approaching the desired temperature, drain thoroughly a generous handful of potato slices and dry on the paper towels. Lift basket from oil, carefully add well-dried slices and lower basket into the hot oil. Using a long fork, give potatoes an immediate and careful stir to help distribute them throughout the oil and separate the slices. Fry until potatoes just begin to turn golden, 4 to 6 minutes.

4) **To drain potatoes:** Lift basket from oil and carefully shake off any excess oil into the pot. Drain potato slices on paper toweling then transfer them to the towel-lined platter. Continue to dry and fry the remaining slices, replacing paper towels when they become oily. Reserve oil in fryer or saucepan. Don't be alarmed at the soggy, limp and pale appearance of the potatoes at this point. Remember, this is only a preliminary frying and they will be perfect later (trust me).

5) **To set up for refrying potatoes:** Soon before serving, replace frying basket in oil and reheat to 375°F. Lay long sheets of double-thickness paper toweling on a wire cooling rack. Place a heatproof serving platter lined with paper toweling into the oven at its lowest setting (preferably 140°F).

6) **To refry and serve:** When oil reaches the desired temperature, take 1 or 2 handfuls of limp potato slices and place into hot oil, swishing gently with a long fork to separate. Fry until deeply golden and crisp, about 4 minutes. Drain potatoes as before on paper towels and transfer them to the warmed serving platter in the oven while you fry the rest. Remove platter from oven and sprinkle potatoes lightly with coarse salt. (Applying salt to crisp foods too early encourages them to become soggy.)

Q AND A

Q. What's the difference between coarse salt and regular table salt (other than the obvious size of the grains)?

A. Generally, since regular table salt dissolves easily, it's added to a dish to lend a seasoned flavor throughout (during or after cooking). Coarse salt (whether Kosher or sea salt), which doesn't dissolve as readily, is used on "crisped" foods such as potato chips. When table salt is used here, it tends to render crisp foods soggy. Coarse salt is also preferred to give the outer surface of roast meats an intensely savory flavor. Although coarse salt can be used as you would table salt, you'll need more of the coarse grains to achieve the same flavor as finely ground table salt. As far as the flavor is concerned, I prefer the flavor of kosher salt to sea salt when garnishing, but this is individual.

Time Management Tips

- The potatoes can be sliced early in the day and kept submerged in ice water at room temperature. Occasionally, throw in a few ice cubes to keep the water cold.

- The first preliminary frying can be done as much as 4 hours ahead; keep potatoes piled on top of each other on a platter at room temperature.

Oven Roasted Variation

Although deep-frying twice will ensure the crispest potatoes, they also can be oven roasted. To do this, brush the dried slices lightly with oil and sprinkle lightly with freshly ground black pepper. Place slices in a single layer on an oiled shallow baking sheet and roast them in a preheated 450°F oven until golden, about 30 minutes, turning the slices halfway through roasting. Reduce oven temperature to 350°F and cook until crisp, 15 to 20 minutes. (Try to slice uniformly for best results.)

TIPS
FROM A TEACHER

Deep Frying

For healthiest results when deep frying, choose an oil that's high in polyunsaturated fat with a high smoke point (approximately 450°F). Your choices include canola, sunflower, safflower and mild peanut oil. Don't use extra-virgin or "pure" olive oil or any other first-pressed aromatic oil; these are too flavorful and smoke at a lower temperature.

Avoid frying large amounts of food at once. It's better to fry in a series of smaller batches to keep the absorption of oil by the food to a minimum. And although you'll need to start out with quite a bit of oil to deep-fry properly, the oil can be cooled, strained and stored in its original bottle to use several more times before discarding. (Always allow the oil to cool in the pot before you attempt to strain it.) The color of the oil will deepen with each use, but this will have no affect on performance or taste. The only exception to this is when frying aromatic foods like fish or broccoli that would flavor the oil, making it unsuitable for reuse.

If you plan on deep-frying often, I highly recommend purchasing an electric, thermostatically controlled deep-fat fryer. Not only are they safer (especially when kids are around), but they eliminate the guesswork in regulating the temperature of the oil. If frying in a pot with a handle, make sure to always have pot turned around so the handle can't be accidentally hit or caught on clothing, causing the pot of hot oil to spill. Also make sure to have plenty of good-quality paper towels on hand for absorbing the excess oil.

OH-SO-GOOD LATKES

Otherwise Known as Potato Pancakes

YIELD: about 12 pancakes; serves 6

Crisp on the outside and well seasoned on the inside, these oil-fried potato pancakes are served during the Jewish holiday of Hanukkah. Latkes, like most other traditional Jewish foods, represent much more than just something wonderful to eat. Hanukkah commemorates the Jews' defeat of the Syrians some two thousand years ago and the relighting of the eternal oil in the temple of Jerusalem. Thus during the eight nights of celebration, Jewish people all over the world light their menorahs (using candles instead of oil) and deliberately use oil to fry various foods. In this way, the Jewish heritage is kept alive through this annual re-enactment of events that symbolize the struggle, perseverance and ultimate survival of the Jewish people. However, this is one of those traditional recipes that tastes so great that anyone of any heritage will adore and enjoy serving it throughout the year. Serve these potato pancakes hot, accompanied with Spiced Applesauce (page 91) and Maple-Braised Brisket (page 282), omitting the braised potatoes.

SPECIAL EQUIPMENT
Food processor or hand-held grater

Triple-mesh strainer

10- to 12-inch heavy-bottomed skillet, preferably seasoned cast iron (page 29)

Deep-fry thermometer (optional)

Small gravy ladle or ¼ cup dry measuring cup

INGREDIENTS

4 large Idaho baking potatoes

1 medium-sized yellow onion, peeled and cut into wedges

1 extra-large egg

2 tablespoons matzo meal

2 tablespoons chopped flat-leaf Italian parsley

Kosher salt as needed

Freshly ground black pepper to taste

About 1 cup flavorless vegetable oil or mild peanut oil

1) *To prepare and grate potatoes:* Scrub and peel potatoes and place them in a bowl of ice water to prevent discoloration and to remove some of the excess surface starch. When ready to fry, remove potatoes from water, rub dry and cut into chunks. Place them with onion wedges and egg in the bowl of a food processor fitted with the steel blade. Process until puréed and fairly smooth. (Avoid using a blender or your potato pancakes will be

Time Management Tips

- The potatoes can be peeled early in the day and kept totally submerged in water. Leave them at room temperature for a few hours or refrigerate for longer storage.

- Although best when eaten right away, the latkes can be cooked up to 4 hours in advance and left at a comfortable room temperature. To reheat, place them on a wire rack that sits within a large shallow baking sheet in a preheated 350°F oven until hot and crisp, about 15 minutes.

- Cooked latkes also can be frozen in a heavy freezer container separated by sheets of waxed paper. (If planning to freeze them, remove from hot oil when lightly golden but not a deep brown.) To reheat, don't thaw but heat on a wire rack within a shallow baking sheet in a preheated 400°F oven until hot throughout, brown and very crisp, about 20 minutes. Cover pancakes loosely with aluminium foil (shiny side up to deflect heat), if the latkes start to become overly brown.

gluey.) Pour mixture into a triple-mesh strainer that sits over another bowl and gently lay a doubled sheet of paper toweling directly on top of the puréed mixture to keep it from turning brown. Allow to drain for 3 to 5 minutes. Alternatively, rub potatoes and onion against the raised holes on a hand-held grater over a bowl.

2) *To heat oil:* Cover a few wire cooling racks with a double thickness of paper toweling. Pour vegetable oil into a 10- to 12-inch skillet (preferably cast iron) to measure ½ inch. Heat until the top looks shimmering but not smoking (365°F).

3) *To assemble batter:* Pour drained potato mixture into a large mixing bowl. Add matzo meal to puréed potato mixture with chopped parsley. Season generously with salt and freshly ground black pepper.

4) *To fry pancakes:* Using a small gravy ladle or a ¼ cup dry measuring cup, scoop portions of potato mixture and ease it into the hot oil. Use the bottom of a turning spatula (not a spoon) to flatten slightly. Fry until golden brown on both sides (turning once) and, using 2 spatulas to help press out excess oil, carefully remove each cooked pancake from the hot oil to drain on the prepared wire racks. Continue frying until you've finished the batter.

5) *To serve:* Serve hot on a warmed serving tray and, if desired, just before serving, sprinkle the top lightly with coarse salt. (Don't salt the latkes until just before serving since applying salt in advance will cause the potatoes to lose some of their crispness.)

DELICIOUSLY SIMPLE WHITE RICE

Simmered in Rich Stock

YIELD: serves 6 to 8

Technically a "pilaf," this method is the best and most simple way to cook white rice and lends itself to unlimited variations. The rice is stirred into the hot butter or oil and toasted so the outer starch layer that surrounds each grain becomes sealed—the most effective way to ensure separate grains of rice after cooking. Then you add a liquid, which may range from a light fish stock to a deeply flavored and colored poultry or beef stock. Into this, you may incorporate a favorite fruit juice or some fresh or canned tomatoes. However, the higher the concentration of acid in the liquid used (such as tomatoes, fruit juice, vinegar or wine), the longer the cooking time will be. So, if including these ingredients, it's best to dilute them with stock or (when necessary) water. Then comes the fun part—experimenting. It's easy to change this recipe to suit your mood and seasonal availability or to enhance a particular entrée by adding various sautéed vegetables and/or complementary spices, herbs and simmering liquids or by trying some of the other long-grain aromatic white rice now available. For more information on cooking rice, see All About Rice (page 363).

SPECIAL EQUIPMENT
2½-quart heavy-bottomed saucepan with tight-fitting lid

INGREDIENTS

2 tablespoons extra-virgin olive oil or butter

2 cups enriched long-grain converted white rice*

1 to 2 teaspoons curry powder* *or* several dashes Tabasco and/or a bay leaf (preferably Turkish*) and/or ½ teaspoon crumbled dried herbs (such as oregano or thyme)

4 cups rich chicken, beef, shrimp, fish or vegetable stock, preferably homemade (pages 140 to 146)

Salt and freshly ground black pepper to taste

1 tablespoon additional butter (optional)

*See section on Staples

1) **To toast rice:** Heat a 2½-quart heavy-bottomed saucepan over medium heat. When hot, add olive oil or butter and, when hot and bubbling, stir in rice. (If using a spice blend like curry, stir it in now to awaken the flavor.) Stir rice over medium heat to toast the grains, 2 to 3 minutes.

2) To simmer: Pour in stock, adding any additional flavorings (Tabasco, bay leaf or dried herbs) and stir. Bring stock just to boiling, immediately cover pot and reduce heat to low. (If using an electric stove, move pot to another burner preheated to low.) Simmer rice for exactly 17 minutes without disturbing—don't peek.

3) To finish and serve: When rice is cooked, remove pan from heat and stir in a generous amount of freshly ground black pepper, salt to taste and 1 tablespoon additional butter, if desired. Cover tightly and let sit until rice fluffs, butter melts and rice absorbs any remaining moisture, 3 to 5 minutes. If using a bay leaf, remove before serving. Serve rice hot.

Variation with Corn and Bell Peppers

In the oil or butter, sauté 1 cup minced yellow onion and, when softened, add 2 minced cloves garlic and 1 minced green or red bell pepper. Sauté until softened and fragrant, about 2 minutes. Then sauté rice with vegetables until toasted, add chicken stock and, just before it comes to a boil, add 1½ to 2 cups corn kernels— either removed from 2 large fresh cobs, or 1 large can (12 to 16 ounces) drained, or 1 box (10 ounces) frozen corn (do not thaw before using). Bring to to a boil, cover and simmer over low heat as directed in recipe.

Variation with Tomatoes, Mushrooms and Onions

In the oil or butter, sauté ¾ cup minced yellow onion and ½ cup minced celery until softened. Add 2 cloves minced garlic and 1 cup cleaned and sliced fresh button mushrooms. Raise heat to medium-high and sauté vegetables until mushrooms are golden, about 2 minutes. Stir in rice and, when toasted, add only 2 cups beef, chicken, shrimp or vegetable stock and 8 peeled, seeded and coarsely chopped plum (Roma) tomatoes; or 1 can (28 ounces) peeled tomatoes, drained, and 1 cup canned crushed tomatoes. Season with 1 teaspoon crumbled dried oregano and ¼ teaspoon crushed red pepper flakes. Bring to a boil, cover, reduce heat to very low and simmer 19 minutes. Uncover and stir in 3 tablespoons chopped fresh basil leaves. Season with salt and freshly ground pepper, cover, allow to fluff, and serve.

Other Suggestions for Variations

Vegetables to sauté and simmer with uncooked rice: diced carrots, thinly sliced leeks, diced zucchini or yellow squash.

Additions to stir into cooked rice: cooked fresh peas or thawed frozen peas; blanched asparagus sliced into 1-inch pieces and briefly sautéed to rewarm; broccoli florets, treated the same as asparagus; cleaned and sliced wild mushrooms sautéed in hot olive oil with minced garlic; toasted nuts such as pine nuts or coarsely chopped blanched almonds; pan sautéed fresh chestnuts or toasted pumpkin seeds; assorted dried fruit cut into small pieces.

TIPS

FROM A TEACHER

All About Rice

What's converted rice? Not only is converted white rice relatively quick to prepare and easy to embellish, but contrary to popular belief, it's also nutritious. Although white rice has, during milling, lost its fiber-rich bran layer, converted white rice is enriched before being milled with a generous dose of niacin, thiamin and iron. So much so, that white rice is said to actually exceed brown rice in these nutrients. When white rice (not converted) is processed in the mill, the outer oily germ and bran layers are polished and scrubbed away with a wire-brush machine. This allows for a longer shelf life, but many nutrients are lost. Converted rice is parboiled before being processed in the mill. The entire grain is then soaked in water, steamed and dried before milling. This soaking process enables the nutritional qualities of converted rice to exceed those of regular rice and does not adversely affect the ultimate shelf life. Although all domestic white rice is now somewhat enriched, converted rice ranks highest nutritionally among them. Converted rice needs to be simmered about 3 minutes longer than regular enriched rice.

What about basmati and other exotic rice? Basmati rice (once grown only in Pakistan and India), is now also grown in the United States. This type of aromatic, long-grain rice (although pricey) is notable for its nutty, butter-like, seductive flavor and its distinctive texture due to the grains swelling more in length than in width during cooking. Basmati rice is also lower in starch; this encourages the grains to remain separate. Jasmine rice, another long-grain white rice once grown exclusively in Thailand, is now also grown here. The flavor is similar to basmati although the texture is somewhat softer when cooked. The other readily available types of aromatic rice are grown in the United States and come in white, tan and brown varieties. These new domestic breeds are an attempt to duplicate the flavor and aroma of basmati, at a more affordable price. Among them are Texmati, Wehani and Popcorn rice (also called Wild Pecan rice). Aromatic rice needs to be simmered about 3 minutes less than converted rice.

Should I rinse rice before using? Domestically milled rice is usually very clean and since the outer surface of converted rice has been enriched to replenish lost nutrients, if you rinse the rice, many of those nutrients will go literally down the drain. However, the (nonenriched) imported aromatic rice, such as jasmine or basmati, or any rice scooped from open bins should be rinsed to remove dust and any bits of debris.

What's the secret for cooking rice? The general rule is to use twice as much liquid as rice. The pot used should have a tight-fitting lid to prevent steam from escaping, which would alter both the ultimate texture as well as the overall cooking time. And as soon as the liquid comes to a boil, it's important to turn down the heat to low and simmer the rice very gently while covered to avoid scorching or a mushy texture. Cooked long-grain rice, like pasta, should be served al dente or firm to the teeth.

What's the best white rice? I prefer converted long-grain rice to the shorter and stubbier grains commonly available. Not only is the texture of the longer grain more satisfying but the converted grains keep their shape better through cooking. I don't recommend quick or instant rice since they lack much of the texture and nutritional value of converted rice.

CURRIED RICE AND ZUCCHINI

With Dried Currants and Toasted Almonds

YIELD: serves 10

This rice dish is the perfect companion to just about any lamb dish—and chicken as well. But feel free to change both the type of stock and the herbs to complement another menu. For instance, you may omit the curry, chutney and currants and instead add 1 tablespoon chopped fresh thyme leaves and a bit of crumbled dried oregano. Or you may substitute a mixture of dark and golden raisins in place of the currants. And instead of almonds, you can use toasted pine nuts, shelled unsalted pistachios or hulled pumpkin seeds sautéed in a bit of butter. Once you understand the concept of seasoning and simmering rice, you can do what you wish, depending on what's available or your mood.

INGREDIENTS

½ stick (4 tablespoons) butter or ¼ cup aromatic peanut oil* or
  extra-virgin olive oil

1 cup finely chopped scallions (green onion), all trimmed white
  part and 1½-to 2-inches of the tender green

2 cloves garlic, minced

6 small zucchini, scrubbed, trimmed and cut into small cubes
  to measure about 4 cups

2 teaspoons curry powder*

3 tablespoons peach or mango chutney*

½ cup dried currants

3 cups converted long-grain white rice*

4½ cups Rich Chicken Stock or "Doctored" Canned Chicken Broth
  (page 140 for both), heated

½ cup toasted, sliced almonds, sautéed in butter or toasted dry
  in the oven (page 76 for both)

Freshly ground black pepper and salt to taste

* See section on Staples

Time Management Tips

- All of the vegetables can be prepared 1 day ahead and refrigerated in separate, well-covered bowls.

1) *To sauté vegetables:* Heat a 4-quart heavy-bottomed saucepan (with a tight-fitting lid) over medium heat and, when hot, add butter or oil. When melted and bubbling, add scallions and garlic and lower heat. Cook until softened and fragrant, stirring frequently, for about 3 minutes. Add diced zucchini and sauté until slightly softened, about 2 minutes. Stir in curry powder, chutney and currants and stir and cook until heated through and well combined, about 2 minutes.

2) *To add rice and simmer:* Stir in rice and cook over medium heat until rice is toasted and turning golden, 3 to 5 minutes. Add hot stock and bring to a boil. Reduce heat to very low, cover pot and simmer slowly for exactly 17 minutes. (Don't peek!)

3) *To add nuts and serve:* When rice is cooked, stir in sautéed almonds along with some freshly ground black pepper and salt to taste. Serve hot.

HERBED BROWN RICE

With Aromatic Vegetables and Parmesan

YIELD: serves 8 to 10

The nuttier taste and chewier texture of brown rice is a nice change from the more usual white rice. Brown rice is also full of natural fiber and important nutrients since, unlike white rice, the grains retain their outer layer of bran. In this dish, before the grains are simmered with sautéed vegetables in rich stock, the hard external layer of the rice must be softened by parboiling. But you may also use partially cooked brown rice, which is now readily available and cooks in about half the time of the raw rice. To simmer the rice, choose the stock that best complements your menu.

INGREDIENTS

1 stick (¼ pound) butter or 4 tablespoons *each* extra-virgin olive oil
  and butter

2 cups minced yellow onion

3 large cloves garlic, minced

½ cup minced celery

1 tablespoon chopped fresh thyme leaves or 1 teaspoon crumbled
  dried thyme

8 ounces fresh button mushrooms, cleaned (page 131) and chopped to
  measure 2 cups

2 cups long-grain brown rice (either raw or the quick-cooking variety)

3½ cups rich chicken, beef or vegetable stock, preferably homemade
  (pages 140 to 146)

½ cup freshly grated Reggiano Parmesan cheese

Salt and freshly ground black pepper to taste

1) *To sauté vegetables:* Melt butter in a 2½-quart heavy-bottomed saucepan with a tight-fitting lid over medium heat. When hot and bubbling, stir in onions, garlic, celery and thyme. Lower heat and cook vegetables until softened and fragrant, 5 to 7 minutes. Raise heat, stir in chopped mushrooms and cook until mushrooms turn light brown. Remove from heat and set aside.

2) *To parboil raw brown rice, if using:* Bring 3 quarts water to a boil in a 4-quart heavy-bottomed saucepan. Add rice and boil 5 minutes to soften the hard outer bran layer that covers each kernel. Drain rice and stir into the sautéed vegetables. Cook over medium heat until grains are lightly toasted, about 3 minutes, stirring constantly.

3) *To toast quick-cooking brown rice, if using:* Since rice has been partially cooked, there is no need to parboil. Instead, stir rice directly into sautéed vegetables and cook over medium heat until the grains are lightly toasted, about 3 minutes, stirring constantly.

4) *To simmer:* Add hot stock to rice mixture and bring to a boil. Cover pan, reduce heat to very low and simmer rice undisturbed 30 minutes for raw rice and 15 minutes for quick-cooking rice. The liquid should be absorbed and rice tender, but not at all mushy. (If your stove is electric, after rice comes to a boil, move it immediately to another burner preheated to low.)

5) *To serve:* When rice is cooked, stir in grated Parmesan cheese and a generous amount of freshly ground black pepper. Place cover on and let sit undisturbed for 5 minutes. Taste, adding salt only if necessary, and serve very hot.

TIPS
FROM A TEACHER

Buying, Cooking and Storing Brown Rice

A natural coating of bran gives brown rice its distinctive tan color and the browner the better. The darker hue is a good indication that more of the nutritious bran layer has been left intact after milling. Even though brown rice needs to be cooked longer than white rice, it's important to avoid overcooking brown rice since, to enjoy fully the unique texture and flavor, each grain should retain a slight bite, similar to al dente pasta. And because the oily bran layer makes brown rice more susceptible to rancidity, its shelf life is normally only six months. To extend this considerably, the rice should be refrigerated.

Time Management Tips

- All of the vegetables can be chopped as much as 1 day ahead and refrigerated in separate, well-covered bowls.

THIS MAMA'S KASHA VARNISHKES

YIELD: serves 8

SPECIAL EQUIPMENT

8-quart blanching pot with built-in strainer (optional)

5-quart heavy-bottomed Dutch oven or saucepan with tight-fitting lid

Although kasha (buckwheat groats) is usually regarded as a grain, in reality, these stubby triangular seeds come from an herb plant. Of Russian descent, these nutty-tasting kernels are prepared in many ways: ground and used as flour, simmered and served as a porridge, or to make the famous Russian blini. But of all the ways to cook groats, this recipe for kasha varnishkes is, for me, the most savory and soothing of all. Here, coarsely crushed buckwheat groats are simmered in hot chicken stock and combined with freshly cooked bow-tie pasta (*varnishke* to the Russians, *farfalle* to the Italians). Finally chopped onions and mushrooms, sautéed in rendered chicken fat (affectionately known as schmaltz), are folded throughout. When seasoned well with salt and freshly ground black pepper, this is truly comforting and well worth the occasional splurge in the fat department. Buckwheat groats are available in many supermarkets and most health food stores.

INGREDIENTS

3 cups Rich Chicken Stock or "Doctored" Canned Chicken Broth (page 140 for both)

2 extra-large eggs

1½ cups coarsely ground or whole toasted buckwheat groats

2 rounded tablespoons rendered chicken fat (page 110) or an equal amount of butter, margarine or mild olive oil

1 large yellow onion, chopped

¾ pound fresh mushrooms, wiped clean and thinly sliced (page 131)

Salt as needed

Freshly ground black pepper

8 ounces dried bow-tie pasta*

½ stick (4 tablespoons) butter or margarine, melted

*See section on Staples

1) **To set up:** Bring a large pot of water to a boil and turn to a simmer until ready to cook pasta. Heat stock in a 1½-quart saucepan until boiling, reduce heat to low and keep hot.

2) **To coat and dry groats:** Lightly beat eggs in a medium-sized mixing bowl. Stir in buckwheat groats, making sure that each kernel is coated with beaten eggs. Heat a 5-quart heavy-bottomed Dutch oven or sauce-pan over medium-high heat. When hot, add groat-egg mixture and cook stirring constantly with a wooden spatula until eggs are no longer at all wet and the kernels are completely separate from each other, about 4 minutes.

3) **To simmer groats:** Return stock to a boil. Pour boiling stock onto groats and stir (be careful, this might spatter). Cover pot and simmer over low heat until the grains are swollen and tender but not mushy, and the stock is absorbed, about 20 minutes. (Groats should retain texture; avoid overcooking.)

4) **To sauté onions and mushrooms:** While groats are cooking, heat a 10-inch deep-sided skillet over medium-high heat. When hot, add chicken fat and, when melted and hot, stir in chopped onions and lower heat to medium-low. Sauté onions until softened, very fragrant and beginning to turn golden, about 10 minutes. Raise heat to medium-high and add sliced mushrooms. Cook until mushrooms are tender and golden, about 3 minutes. Remove from heat and set aside.

5) **To cook pasta:** Return the pot of water to a rapid boil and add some salt. Add pasta, give it a good swish with a long fork and cook until just tender or according to the directions on the box. Check the texture frequently toward the end to avoid overcooking. Drain pasta and toss with 4 tablespoons melted butter or margarine.

6) **To assemble and serve:** When groats are cooked, stir in sautéed vegetables and buttered pasta. Add salt and lots of freshly ground black pepper. Serve hot.

Time Management Tips

- The onions can be chopped and the mushrooms can be cleaned and sliced 1 day ahead. Refrigerate in separate, securely covered bowls.

- This recipe can be assembled fully hours in advance and reheated. Either reheat in the microwave until hot throughout (page 288) or (if a more crusty and savory texture is desired) reheat in a heavy-bottomed pot over medium heat with 2 tablespoons melted butter. Stir frequently as the kasha reheats to redistribute the mixture when it develops crisp pockets of kasha and pasta throughout. Taste for seasoning and serve very hot.

SOUTH-OF-THE-BORDER BEANS

With Jalapeños and Sweet Peppers

YIELD: serves 6 to 8

To soak or not to soak—that is the question! To be honest (because I frequently forget) I usually don't soak my beans and just cook them an extra hour. It is said, however, that soaking dry legumes aids in digesting beans. Pinto beans are definitely the most ethnically correct legume to use in this recipe, but I often use the mild, large white Great Northern beans with delicious results. Regardless of the type, simmering the beans in rich chicken stock with jalapeños and tricolored bell peppers, provides the ideal accompaniment for a Mexican meal. Serve individual bowls of this light bean soup alongside Marinated Grilled Chicken Breasts (page 221) wrapped inside fresh flour tortillas. Pass a bowl of Guacamole (page 104) at the table. And remember to be careful when handling the hot chili peppers (see page 113).

INGREDIENTS

1 pound dried pinto beans or Great Northern beans

2 to 2½ quarts Rich Chicken Stock or "Doctored" Canned Broth (page 140 for both)

6 slices bacon

1 medium-sized yellow onion, chopped

½ cup chopped red onion

3 large cloves garlic, chopped

3 small bell peppers (red, green and yellow), seeded and chopped

1 stalk celery, cleaned, trimmed and chopped

2 or 3 fresh or jarred jalapeño chili peppers, seeded and chopped (for additional heat, leave in a few seeds)

3 tablespoons chopped fresh cilantro

Freshly ground black pepper

Kosher or sea salt to taste

Time Management Tips

• All of the vegetables can be chopped 1 day ahead and refrigerated in separate, well-covered bowls.

• The beans can be prepared early in the day that you plan to serve them. Leave the cooked bean mixture uncovered at room temperature until it cools. I've also doubled this recipe and frozen half with good results.

1) **To clean beans:** Spread out beans out on a plain (preferably white) kitchen towel and carefully pick through them to remove any small stones or damaged beans. Rinse beans well in a colander, then drain well.

2) **To soak beans:** If you choose to soak beans, place them in a large bowl with enough cold water to cover and soak 8 hours or overnight at a comfortable room temperature (or refrigerate if the room is very warm). After soaking, discard any beans that are floating on top of the water and drain beans well. Rinse and drain once more and set aside.

3) **To precook unsoaked beans:** If beans have not been soaked, add them to a 4-quart heavy-bottomed saucepan with simmering stock, bring to a boil, reduce heat to low and simmer (covered) for 1 hour.

4) **To cook bacon:** Fry bacon in a 10-inch skillet over medium heat until semicrisp and drain on a double layer of paper toweling. Pour out all but 1 tablespoon of the bacon drippings from the skillet and slice bacon into ½-inch slices. Set bacon aside.

5) **To sauté vegetables:** Heat the skillet with the tablespoon of drippings over medium heat and, when hot, stir in chopped yellow and red onions, garlic, bell peppers, celery and jalapeños. Reduce heat to low and simmer vegetables until they become very fragrant, about 5 minutes, stirring occasionally to redistribute vegetables and release any caramelized particles of bacon from the bottom of the skillet.

6) **To simmer beans with vegetables:** In the pot of stock, combine presoaked or precooked beans with sautéed vegetables, sliced bacon and chopped cilantro. Raise heat to medium until stock begins to bubble; then reduce heat to low, cover and simmer gently until beans are just tender when pierced with the tip of a knife, 45 minutes to 1 hour. Check frequently to avoid overcooking, which yields beans with broken skins and a mushy texture.

7) **To serve:** Ladle beans, broth and vegetable mixture into individual bowls and serve piping hot.

TIPS
FROM A TEACHER

About Beans

Store dried beans on a cool pantry shelf in well-sealed containers. They should remain in good condition for at least 1 year. When cooking, avoid mixing older beans with newly purchased ones since the cooking times for each will differ. If your beans become shriveled looking, don't throw them away; instead, store them in a jar and use them for pie weights when prebaking your pie crusts.

CHAPTER IX

A PASSION FOR BREADS

From Bagels and Biscuits to Crusty Loaves

I'm always happy in my kitchen, but baking brings me pure joy, especially when my hands are aggressively working to create a yeast dough. This chapter covers many types of breads from easy-to-make biscuits and muffins to bagels and brioche. But my primary goal is to remove the mystique from working with yeast and to delve deeply into proper kneading technique. Without intimidating equipment—simply by using a wooden spoon, pastry scraper, a flour scoop, my hands and a conventional home oven—I am able to create voluptuous Old World breads with incredible taste, texture and aroma.

Never would I advocate using those so-called bread machines and for very good reason. Not only do these machines create stubby loaves that resemble doorstops, but using a machine to make bread blatantly robs the cook of the true fulfillment that comes from real bread making. No machine can tell me when my dough has been worked sufficiently; that's strictly between me and my dough.

The crustiness of some of my favorite breads, however, is enhanced by the use of quarry tiles or a pizza stone. But these are not difficult to use or purchase (see page 400) and ensure the texture of a true hearth bread from your home oven. For your assured success, please read my important Notes on Baking Yeast Breads before beginning any of the following recipes for yeast doughs and refer back to them whenever necessary.

NOTES ON BAKING YEAST BREADS

The only way to become an accomplished baker is to understand the roles of the major players (yeast, liquid, sugar, salt and flour) and how they ultimately affect the finished bread through the processes of kneading, rising and baking.

Yeast bread is initially leavened by a tiny single-cell organism that multiplies when given its favorite food (sugar or starch) within a warm and moist environment. As these yeast cells consume sugar or starch, their enzymes convert to glucose (simple sugar), which ferments over time converting the yeast into alcohol and carbon dioxide, the substance that forces the dough to rise. Yeast breads all begin in a totally liquid state. Liquid is the vital component that enables yeast to flourish and flour to release its inherent protein that enables the dough to trap the yeast and rise evenly.

Meanwhile, salt plays an important role in the development of the dough. Just as sugar and warm liquid encourage the yeast to "rise and shine," salt tells the yeast to "slow down and smell the roses." If you omit the salt, the yeast cells will multiply so quickly that they won't have time to ferment throughout the dough, which is what deepens both both the flavor and texture in your baked bread. In addition, the quicker the dough rises, the more likely it is to overrise and exhaust itself, limiting its ultimate leavening capability. Undersalted dough also tends to lack depth of color when baked. For superior bread—although you might be tempted—*don't alter the amount of salt in any recipe.*

Finally flour, which initially helped feed the yeast, adds gluten (structure) to the dough. Through the process of kneading, the gluten makes the dough elastic and creates a network of passageways that permit the dough to rise and ferment evenly throughout. Once the fermented risen dough hits the hot oven, the initial burst of warmth will encourage the yeast to make a final rise before the organisms are completely killed off. The remaining rise is accomplished by the upward movement of trapped air (steam) within the glutinous network, producing a light, billowy texture in the baked bread.

Types of Yeast

Several types of baking yeast are available. My recipes are written for active dry yeast, sold in ¼-ounce packets of dry granules (a bit less than 1 tablespoon)—the type preferred by most home cooks. Another type comes in a square block known as "cake" or "compressed" yeast, which is much more perishable than active dry yeast. You may, however substitute ½-ounce compressed yeast for 1 packet dry yeast (these blocks are in the refrigerated section of most supermarkets). Use a wooden spoon to cream cake yeast into warm water with a bit of sugar and when visibly active, add it to the remaining ingredients. Store your yeast (whether dry or cake) in the refrigerator. Although quick-rising yeast is also readily available, I never use it. Most serious bakers will agree that both the flavor and texture-developing power of this product are inferior to the old-fashioned slower-moving yeasts.

Proofing—How to Tell if Your Yeast Is Alive

"Proofing" is the process of making sure that your yeast has not died from poor storage or old age. To prove the yeast worthy of your muscle, you must first reconstitute the granules in a small amount of lukewarm (not hot) water. To give further incentive to the yeast to "wake up and smell the coffee," you add a pinch of its favorite food—sugar. After only a few minutes, the yeast granules will begin to swell and take on a light beige color and creamy texture. If left alone, the yeast would produce many bubbles that would rise to the top of the cup. After the first creamy reaction, proceed to create your dough so the powerful yeast action is saved for your assembled dough and not wasted in the cup.

Although yeast can be killed in liquid that's too hot, I have never used a thermometer to measure the temperature of the proofing water. This is both unnecessary and intimidating to someone who is embarking on the art of bread making for the first time. The water used to proof yeast should feel like tepid bath water. If it stings when you put your wrist under the faucet, it's too hot. And if it feels like you want to jump in and soak, it's just right. Other liquids used should be about the same temperature.

About Flours and What They Do

Unbleached all-purpose white flour (a blend of hard and soft wheat) is my choice for the majority of everyday cooking procedures. "Unbleached" means that the flour has been allowed to mature naturally and develop both flavor and strength. Millers chemically bleach flour so they can quickly whiten, strengthen and sell it. Unfortunately, this process also removes much of the vitamins and reduces the overall protein (gluten) level, which builds texture in bread. Conversely, naturally matured flour increases the protein content and produces a dough with better rising potential for an ultimately lighter loaf of bread. Be sure to use the unbleached variety in all recipes that call for all-purpose flour.

When making certain types of bread, the specific amount of protein in the flour, (which is listed on the package) is crucial for the correct textural results. In bread terms, protein or gluten refers to the elastic properties that are present in varying degrees in all types of wheat flour. These properties are released, with or without yeast, when the flour is stirred briskly with any liquid. The components of gluten give the dough plasticity (enabling it to spring back into shape when kneaded) and elasticity (the capacity to be stretched and pulled to varying degrees without breaking).

When making soft breads that will rise and bake within a loaf pan and whenever a chewy texture is not desirable, the softer, less glutinous all-purpose flour is preferable. When using coarser, flavorful flours (like whole wheat or coarse rye meal), their rough texture actually inhibits kneading. As you work the dough, the sharper edges of the coarse grains actually cut the very glutinous strands that you are attempting to create. So you need to beef up the dough by adding a stronger (harder) and smoother white flour. This is also true of a dough with a high-fat content from using a hefty amount of butter and/or eggs. These ingredients make the dough more tender, but they also make it more difficult for the yeast to travel. Bread flour (high-protein flour) is necessary to compensate for these factors and it's becoming readily available in many supermarkets. For a dough made almost exclusively from a coarser grain, you can add 1 tablespoon of 100 percent pure-gluten flour for every cup of whole wheat flour in your recipe. Pure-gluten flour, however, is only available through specialty baker's catalogs. See Mail Order Sources.

To know the protein content of flour, check the side of the bag. All-purpose flour usually has between 11 percent and 15 percent protein (perfect for biscuits, quick breads and muffins). For soft yeast breads (sandwich loaves) made exclusively with white flour (without eggs), choose an all-purpose flour with a minimum of 15 percent protein. And for chewy breads or free-form, decoratively shaped or egg-enriched doughs, use a minimum of 20 percent protein for the best rise, authentic texture and shape retention.

How Much Flour to Add?

Although many bread recipes give a precise amount of flour, I rarely do for several reasons. Not only does the moisture content of flour vary with each bag and with each brand, but local weather conditions on that bread-baking day also can determine the amount of flour needed. My strongest reason for only specifying a general amount of flour is that in order to become truly

Time Management Tips

- When making yeast breads, there's no need to be chained to your kitchen throughout all the rising times. The following tips apply to most yeast breads.

- Although the first rise should take place at room temperature, the second rise may be completed in the refrigerator overnight (or for as long as 48 hours), if desired. Afterwards, let the bowl of dough sit out at room temperature for 1 to 2 hours before shaping the loaves. Alternatively, the loaves can be shaped and allowed to rise overnight in the refrigerator (covered with well-greased plastic wrap and a towel). Either way, you should try to allow the dough to come close to room temperature (or until soft, billowy and no longer cold to the touch) to obtain maximum size and best texture.

- If time is scarce and you can't wait for the dough to "temp up," be aware of certain pitfalls when baking cold dough. When a dense, cold loaf goes into a hot oven, the top will inevitably rise up quickly leaving the heavier middle and bottom behind. This results in a baked loaf with a deep crack on the sides. To remedy this, place the chilled loaves into a cold oven and bake at the lower temperature of 325°F. Although baking time will be a bit longer, your overall waiting time will be substantially reduced. This concept is not applicable when baking free-form ethnic breads on quarry tiles. It works best with soft sandwich breads baked in loaf pans.

proficient in making bread, you need to feel your way through the process. This is how I learned to become an accomplished baker and this is how I teach others. Ultimately, the amount of flour that your dough requires is between you and your dough. Your hands are your best indicator to perceive a properly kneaded dough. Learn to trust them and alter the amounts of flour to suit the conditions.

That brings me to the next step: how to add flour to a yeast dough. Don't dump in large amounts of flour and quickly turn out a large heavy mass of unstructured dough onto your work surface. Instead, stir in flour by the cupful and don't add any more until it's absorbed. Remember that gluten is released in flour simply by coming in brisk contact with liquid. So, if you stir flour into your dough in small amounts, you will ultimately develop more elasticity earlier in the kneading process. Following is a guide to take you from a total liquid state (which is how all dough starts out) to a fully kneaded dough that's ready to rise.

When you need more flour, never, never put your hand into the canister: Use a flour scoop to avoid transfering loose particles of dough from your hand into your fresh flour to prevent the growth of bacteria.

When dough is totally liquid: Add 2 cups flour and stir briskly with a wooden spoon until combined. If dough is still almost totally liquid, only slightly thicker, stir in another 2 cups.

When dough is "pasty": Stir in flour 1 cup at a time and only add more when mixture is totally smooth. Make sure the spoon hits the bottom of the bowl as you briskly stir in one direction.

When dough leaves the sides of bowl: Stir in ½ cup flour at a time.

When dough has formed a mass that attaches to the spoon and is no longer easily stirred: Flour your wooden board and use a rubber spatula to scrape the dough out of the bowl. Scrape dough off your wooden spoon and add to the shapeless mass of dough. Place 1 heaping cup of flour next to your board and take handfuls as needed to sprinkle on dough, your hands and work surface as you knead dough until sufficient texture has been developed. Refill cup with flour as necessary.

Important Notes on Kneading

For best traction when working the dough, use a wooden surface. Since wood is porous and will retain flavors and odors from other foods, avoid kneading dough on a board that's used to chop aromatic vegetables. For best results, use a separate board for each purpose. Don't attempt to make bread without the aid of a pastry scraper. This vital tool will act as your right hand during the beginning of the kneading process, when the dough is at its stickiest. Finally, remember that you are the boss! (Although, sometimes you might not be sure.) Don't be afraid to be pushy and aggressive when kneading. The most important thing to remember is to knead quickly. The longer your hands remain on any one spot of dough, the more likely that your dough will stick to your hands—and tear the very structure that you are trying to create.

Push-pull-fold: After turning out dough onto a floured board, sprinkle some flour on top of the dough mass. Use the blade of your pastry scraper to scrape up cleanly the corners of the dough from the board back onto itself. This way you can start to work the dough without allowing your hands to get stuck in the initially sticky mixture. Sprinkle flour on top of the dough, flour your hands and (without grabbing the dough) firmly *push* the palms of your hands toward the center of the shapeless mass. Quickly remove your hands and (using your fingertips) *pull* the dough from the side farthest from you in toward the center. Push in your palms toward the center once more and then *fold* the dough. (If at any time, the dough looks "wet," sprinkle *that section* with flour before continuing to work the dough with floured hands.) Try to make each movement deliberate, focused and productive. And *never* make your dough tell you twice that it needs more flour. This is very important since the first indication of stickiness is usually minimal but just one more push or turn of the dough can leave it a tacky, sticky mess.

At the first sign of stickiness: Using a pastry scraper in one hand, scrape the dough completely and cleanly off the board. While holding the dough in one hand, use the other to spread a fine layer of white flour on your board and dump the dough back onto the floured surface. Lightly flour your hands and begin to knead again until the next indication of stickiness. Although once the dough is kneadable, the addition of flour should be minimal, this flour is vital to enable you to work the dough sufficiently in order to develop optimal texture. If the dough continually sticks and tears while kneading, your efforts will be self-defeating since this will sever the very elastic structure that you are trying to build.

Knowing when to stop kneading: As the dough becomes more stable, continue this push, pull and folding motion until the texture is perfectly smooth, supple and bounces back when gently squeezed and then released. You will know that the dough has been kneaded sufficiently when you push your palms into the dough and meet noticeable resistance at the center. If the dough is at all tacky, keep kneading, adding small amounts of flour as necessary until the desired texture is achieved.

Where Should Your Dough Rise?

Often times the term "warm draft-free spot," sends the novice bread baker into a panic. No, you don't have to place the bowl in a closet under a blanket. With the exception of extreme heat (when the yeast is quickly killed) or the freezer (where the yeast becomes suspended in time) your dough will surely rise any place you put it. Basically, the temperature that surrounds the bowl of dough as it rises will largely determine how long the dough will take to double and sometimes even triple its original bulk state. Since yeast cells love gentle warmth, they will multiply faster in this environment. So, if your kitchen is chilly, your dough will rise more slowly and, if the day is very warm and humid, your dough could take less time than specified in a recipe.

My recipes assume that the dough will be rising in a room that's at a comfortable room temperature with little fluctuation. The most effective way to keep the temperature constant (in order to estimate accurately the length of time required for rising) is to avoid placing the dough near a door that's continually being opened and shut or in an area that gets a lot of foot traffic. Be assured, however, that if your dough is placed in a greased bowl, covered with greased plastic wrap and covered again with a clean kitchen towel, the dough will be moist, cozy and happy to perform for you.

YUMMY HONEY WHEAT BREAD

YIELD: three 9x5-inch loaves or four 8x4-inch loaves

If you wonder why I don't call this "whole wheat" bread, it's because a true whole wheat dough must not contain any white flour. Unfortunately, loaves made exclusively with whole wheat flour tend to be heavy and not to rise as much because the coarser wheat flour cuts into the beneficial glutinous strands created during kneading and reduces the elasticity of the dough. Thus it also won't rise to be as billowy and light textured as a dough made exclusively with white flour. In order to compensate for this, I use a combination of whole wheat and stronger white (bread) flour. If determined to make a "whole" whole wheat bread (with good texture), however, you will need to purchase 100 percent pure-gluten flour, which is available through specialty bakers' catalogs. (See Mail Order Sources.) Whenever possible, purchase stone-ground whole wheat flour since it's more nutritious than regular steel-ground flour. Although my honey wheat bread is perfect for wrapping around your favorite luncheon salad or making toasted triple-decker BLT, I think it tastes best when sliced fresh and topped with good-old peanut butter and jelly. If you are new to bread making, please read through Notes on Baking Yeast Breads (page 373), including the Time Management Tips, before beginning. Also, I recommend that you halve this recipe the first few times, so you have an easier time controlling the dough.

INGREDIENTS

½ stick (4 tablespoons) unsalted butter, melted

4 cups milk

4 tablespoons solid vegetable shortening

⅔ cup mild honey

2½ teaspoons salt

2 packages active dry yeast

½ cup lukewarm water

Pinch sugar

5 cups whole wheat flour

Up to 6 cups high-gluten (high-protein) bread flour, including flour for dusting

SPECIAL EQUIPMENT

8-quart mixing bowl, for rising dough

Wooden work surface, for kneading

Pastry scraper

Tapered rolling pin

Three 9x5-inch or four 8x4-inch loaf pans

1) **To set up:** Brush the interior of an 8-quart mixing bowl with melted butter and set aside for rising dough.

Q. How can I give a thawed loaf of bread that "just baked" flavor and aroma?

A. *Place thawed, unwrapped bread on a shallow baking sheet in a preheated 400°F oven. Turn off the oven and allow the bread to remain there for 10 minutes. Remove to a wire rack and allow to settle and cool slightly before slicing.*

Since it's easy to loose track of time when rising bread dough, label the bowl with a sticker stating your "punch down" times.

2) **To assemble liquid mixture:** In a medium-sized saucepan, heat milk with the shortening until just warm (no need to melt shortening) and pour into a large mixing bowl. Stir in honey and salt. Dissolve yeast in the lukewarm water with sugar. When creamy and starting to bubble, stir yeast mixture into milk mixture. Then stir in all the whole wheat flour, about 2 cups at a time. Beat briskly with a wooden spoon in 1 direction.

3) **To complete and knead dough:** Stir in enough bread flour, 1 cup at a time, to create a mass that leaves the sides of the bowl and is not easily stirred. Turn out the mass onto a lightly floured wooden surface. Knead, using a brisk push, fold and turning motion until dough is smooth and elastic, adding only as much all-purpose flour as needed to keep dough from sticking to your hands and work surface. Knead about 5 minutes. Because this dough is large, the beginning of the kneading process may seem a bit frustrating. Hang in there and don't be afraid to sprinkle on flour as needed—and use your pastry scraper.

4) **To rise dough twice:** Place dough into the greased rising bowl and brush the top of dough with melted butter. Cover bowl with buttered plastic wrap and then again with a clean kitchen towel. Place in a warm, draft-free spot to rise until doubled in bulk, about 2 hours. Uncover dough and punch it down with several swift blows so it is totally deflated. Turn dough over in the bowl and knead briefly just to redistribute the yeast. Re-cover the bowl and allow the dough to rise again for 1½ hours.

5) **To shape loaves:** Brush your loaf pans with melted butter. Uncover dough and punch down once more. Turn out dough onto a lightly floured wooden board and massage gently to let trapped air escape. Using the blade of a pastry scraper, cut dough into 3 or 4 equal pieces. Shape dough as directed on page 381 and place in prepared pans.

6) **To rise finally, bake and cool:** Cover loaves with a clean kitchen towel and let rise for 45 minutes. Preheat the oven to 375°F for metal pans and 350°F if using glass pans. For an extra-soft crust, brush tops of loaves with melted butter. Bake loaves, with 1½ to 2 inches between them, until golden and the bottom of the loaves sound hollow when tapped, 35 to 40 minutes. Remove from oven and brush tops with more melted butter. Turn loaves out of their pans and allow to cool thoroughly on wire racks before slicing or storing. (Omit last application of butter on those loaves that you plan on freezing since this tends to make them look shriveled after thawing.)

Prepare dough, let rise, punch down and cut into pieces as directed in recipe. Keep dough covered while shaping 1 piece at a time. Lay a piece of dough on lightly floured board and flatten gently with your hand. Using gentle, deliberate and even pressure with a rolling pin, roll out dough into a 8x10-inch rectangle. (To ensure an even thickness, don't roll over the ends but just up to them. If dough loses its shape while rolling, simply knock the sides back in place with the long side of the pin.)

Starting with the short end of the rectangle, roll dough in jelly-roll style into a snug log, pinching after each revolution to remove any air pockets. When you get to the bottom of the rectangle, pull up the last lip of dough and pinch well to seal.

Lift up one end of the log of dough to expose the coil created by rolling. With your fingers, gently push in the coil towards the center. Pinch the outer rim of dough together, pulling to elongate it slightly. Fold down elongated section to attach to the seam. Repeat on the other end of the rolled dough. Rotate loaf gently back and forth on your floured board to plump the shape and lay loaf (seam side down) in a buttered loaf pan. Let loaf rise and bake as directed in your recipe.

Baking and rising tips for four loaves: If baking 4 loaves, use the upper and lower thirds of the oven and switch shelf position of pans after half the baking time. Or, after shaping, place 2 loaves in the refrigerator to slow down the rise. After the first batch goes into the oven, remove the refrigerated loaves and allow them to complete the rise at room temperature.

TIPS

FROM A TEACHER

How to Shape Yeast Dough for a Loaf Pan

SWEET CORNMEAL AND MOLASSES ANADAMA BREAD

YIELD: two 9x5-inch loaves

SPECIAL EQUIPMENT

6-quart bowl, for rising dough

Wooden surface, for kneading

Pastry scraper

Tapered rolling pin

Two 9x5-inch loaf pans

What kind of name is Anadama for a loaf of bread? The story goes that years ago, a fisherman's wife named Anna would send her husband to work every day with cornmeal porridge for lunch—to his dismay. One day, this hard-working soul got so exasperated seeing the same old mush that he threw it on the floor and bellowed "Anna, damn 'er!" That night he demanded that she make him bread instead. Well—using cornmeal and molasses—she did and this is what he called it. (Personally, I would have told him to make his own lunch.) Anyway, this bread is not at all mushy or predictable. To the contrary, this tawny-colored tender loaf is such a wonderful change from the regular slice, that my son frequently asks "Mommy, where's that brown bread—you know the sweet one?" Thanks Anna. If you are new to bread making, please read through Notes on Baking Yeasts Breads (page 373), including the Time Management Tips, before beginning.

INGREDIENTS

1½ cups cold water

1½ cups milk

1 cup unsulphured molasses*

1 stick (¼ pound) unsalted butter, cut into pieces, plus 3 to 4 tablespoons melted butter for brushing

1 cup medium or finely ground white or yellow cornmeal

1 tablespoon salt

2 packages active dry yeast

½ cup lukewarm water

Pinch sugar

Up to 7 cups high-gluten (high-protein) bread flour, including flour for dusting

* See section on Staples

1) **To prepare cornmeal mixture:** Combine the 1½ cups cold water and milk in a 2½-quart heavy-bottomed saucepan. Add molasses and butter pieces. Bring the mixture just to a boil and reduce heat to low. Sprinkle in cornmeal, a little at a time, whisking constantly to prevent lumps. (Add more cornmeal only after the preceding amount has been fully incorporated.) Then continue to simmer mixture, stirring occasionally for 15 minutes. Pour mixture into a large mixing bowl. Stir in salt and let cool (covered with a clean kitchen towel), stirring occasionally, until just warm, 20 to 30 minutes. (The lengthy cooling process is important; if you add yeast to the hot mixture, you run the risk of killing it and preventing the dough from rising.)

2) **To complete and knead dough:** Brush a 6-quart bowl with melted butter for rising dough. When cornmeal mixture is just warm to the touch, dissolve yeast in the ½ cup lukewarm water with sugar. When yeast is creamy and starting to bubble, add to cornmeal mixture and stir until smooth. Stir in enough bread flour, a cup at a time, to create a mass that leaves the sides of the bowl and is no longer easy to stir. Turn out the mass onto a lightly floured wooden board and knead, using a brisk push, fold and turning motion until it forms a smooth and elastic dough. Continue adding only as much flour as needed to keep dough from sticking to your hands and work surface. And hang in there with this dense and "tacky" dough! When kneading, if you feel tacky pockets of the cornmeal mixture, the dough needs more flour and you're not finished kneading. Continue to work dough, adding more flour as necessary, until your palms meet resistance at the center of the dough. Ultimately, you will knead this dough a bit longer than most other soft doughs, 8 to 10 minutes.

3) **To rise dough twice:** Place dough in greased rising bowl and brush top of dough with a bit more melted butter. Cover bowl with buttered plastic wrap and a clean kitchen towel and place in a warm draft-free spot to rise until doubled in bulk, about 2½ hours. Uncover dough and punch down with several swift swats, using the back of your hand, until dough is totally deflated. Turn dough over in bowl and knead briefly just to redistribute the yeast. Re-cover bowl and let rise for 1 hour more.

4) **To shape dough:** Brush the interiors of two 9x5-inch loaf pans with melted butter. Uncover dough and punch down again. Turn out onto a lightly floured wooden board and, using the blade of your pastry scraper, divide dough into 2 equal pieces. Shape into loaves as directed on page 381.

Shape into loaves as directed on page 381.

Q AND A

Q. Why do you ask that bread be allowed to cool thoroughly before slicing?

A. Although it might be appealing to tear off a hunk of fresh bread soon after it leaves the oven, it's not a great idea, for several reasons. First, hot cooked dough is bad for your digestion and can give you quite a stomach ache. You'll notice that hot bread is very doughy and heavy. That's because it hasn't fully expanded— that can only take place once the loaf has come out of the oven. When bread is cut before it's cool, the cooking process is interrupted and the quality of texture in the entire loaf is sacrificed. So, it's best to think of the cooling process as part of the cooking process and allow the bread to cool fully before slicing. Once the loaf is cool, if desired, you can reheat it and enjoy it warm.

5) *To rise dough finally and bake:* Cover loaves with a clean kitchen towel and allow to rise for 45 minutes. Preheat the oven to 400°F for metal pans or 375°F if using glass loaf pans. For an extra-soft crust, brush tops of loaves with melted butter. Place loaves in oven with 1½ to 2 inches between and immediately reduce oven temperature by 25°F. Bake until golden and the bottom of the loaves sound hollow when tapped, about 45 minutes. Cover loosely with aluminum foil, (shiny side up) if loaves become overly brown. Remove from oven and brush tops with more melted butter, if desired. Turn loaves out of their pans and allow to cool thoroughly on wire racks before slicing or storing.

RAISIN BREAD WITH A CINNAMON SWIRL

YIELD: four 9x5-inch loaves

SPECIAL EQUIPMENT

8-quart mixing bowl, for rising dough

Wooden surface, for kneading

Pastry scraper

Tapered rolling pin

Four 9x5-inch loaf pans

Because this is my son's absolutely favorite bread (and I never seem to have enough in my house), I purposely devised a hefty recipe so I'll always have a loaf or two in my freezer. Although nothing compares to the taste of the first slice of a fresh loaf, this bread is very forgiving and will be equally delicious days later when toasted for breakfast. If desired, the cinnamon sugar can be rolled into any soft sandwich bread such as Yummy Honey Wheat Bread (page 379). The richer egg-based doughs such as Brioche (page 391) and Challah loaves (page 387) are equally wonderful with both cinnamon sugar and raisins. If you are new to bread making, please read through Notes on Baking Yeast Breads (page 373), including the Time Management Tips, before beginning. Also, I recommend that you halve this recipe the first few times, so you have an easier time controlling the dough.

INGREDIENTS

1 stick (¼ pound) unsalted butter

4 cups milk

½ cup solid vegetable shortening, pulled into small bits

2½ teaspoons salt

2 cups mixed dark and golden raisins

1 cup sugar, plus pinch sugar for dissolving yeast

2 packages active dry yeast

½ cup lukewarm water

Up to 12 cups unbleached all-purpose flour, including flour for dusting
1 cup sugar whisked with 2 tablespoons ground cinnamon

1) **To set up:** Melt ½ stick of the butter and brush the interior of an 8-quart
bowl with butter. Set bowl aside for rising dough.

2) **To assemble liquid mixture:** Cut remaining ½ stick of butter into small
bits and place in a 2-quart saucepan. Add milk and shortening and heat
gently over medium-low heat until warm to the touch, stirring occasionally. Pour into a large mixing bowl and stir in salt, raisins and 1 cup sugar.
While milk mixture cools to just warm, dissolve yeast in ½ cup lukewarm
water with the pinch of sugar.

3) **To complete dough and knead:** When yeast mixture is creamy and starting to bubble, add to milk mixture and, using a wooden spoon, stir in
enough all-purpose flour to create a mass that leaves the sides of the bowl
and is not easily stirred. Turn out the mass onto a lightly floured wooden
board and knead this mixture using a brisk push, fold and turning motion
until it forms a smooth and elastic dough, adding only as much flour as
needed to keep dough from sticking to your hands and work surface.
Because this dough is large, the beginning of the kneading process may
seem a bit frustrating. Hang in there and don't be afraid to sprinkle on
flour as needed—and use your pastry scraper.

Q AND A

Q. What if I can't be home to punch
down my dough through two rises?

A. The second rise may be completed in
the refrigerator for 4 hours or up to 48
hours, if desired. Allow dough to come to
(or close to) room temperature before
shaping into loaves. Alternatively, after
dough has risen twice, the loaves can be
shaped and allowed to rise overnight in
the refrigerator (covered with buttered
plastic wrap and a towel). To obtain maximum size and best texture in your baked
loaves, allow unbaked loaves to become
soft, billowy and no longer chilled when
touched. Or, if time is scarce, place
chilled loaves into a cold oven and reduce
oven temperature called for in your recipe
by 25°F. Although baking time will be a
bit longer, your overall waiting time will
be substantially reduced.

4) To rise dough twice: Place dough into the buttered rising bowl and brush top of dough with melted butter. Cover bowl with buttered plastic wrap and a clean kitchen towel and set in a warm, draft-free spot to rise until double in bulk, about 2½ hours. Punch down dough with several swift blows so it's totally deflated. Knead gently and briefly in the bowl. Turn dough over, re-cover and let rise again for 1 hour. Punch down once more.

5) To shape loaves: Brush your loaf pans with melted butter. Turn out dough onto a lightly floured wooden board and divide into 4 equal sections using the blade of your pastry scraper. Cover all pieces as you work with 1 at a time. Follow the directions for shaping dough into loaves on page 381 with the following exceptions. After rolling out 1 piece of dough, sprinkle with ¼ cup cinnamon-sugar mixture, spreading it out to cover the entire surface of the rectangle. After rolling dough into a snug log, be careful when pushing the coil ends in toward the center. If you push in too far, you will lose some of the spiral design created by the cinnamon sugar. (The cinnamon sugar makes it impossible to pinch and seal after each revolution; to compensate for this, roll dough into a tighter log.)

6) To rise dough finally, bake and cool: Cover loaves with a clean kitchen towel and let rise 45 minutes. Preheat the oven to 375°F for metal pans or 350°F for glass loaf pans. Brush tops of 4 risen loaves lightly with melted butter and bake until golden and the bottom of the loaves sound hollow when tapped, 35 to 40 minutes. Cover loaves loosely with aluminum foil (shiny side up) for the last 10 to 15 minutes if loaves are becoming overly brown. Remove loaves and for an extra-soft top crust (unless you are planning to freeze loaves) lightly brush tops again with more melted butter. Turn loaves onto wire racks to cool thoroughly before slicing or storing.

7) To freeze and thaw: Wrap loaves securely in aluminum foil and place in large heavy-duty plastic bags. (Be sure to label with date and contents.) They will freeze perfectly for up to 1 month. To thaw, let the loaf come to room temperature completely wrapped overnight. In the morning, preheat the oven to 400°F. Unwrap loaf and place it on a wire rack that sits within a shallow baking sheet. Place baking sheet in oven, turn off heat and keep there for 10 minutes. Let cool slightly before slicing. Then, wrap the remaining bread in pliable plastic wrap and store in the original plastic bag.

BRAIDED CHALLAH

Plus Challah Loaves and Burger Buns

YIELD: 2 braided loaves; variations yield three 8x4-inch loaves and
10 hamburger buns

The spectacular taste and texture of this egg-enriched yeast dough lends itself
to a wide variety of shapes and sizes. Among them are the following recipes
for free-form braids, loaves for an extraordinary sandwich bread and tender
hamburger buns. I suggest reading this recipe in its entirety (including the
variations and tips), to fully familiarize yourself with your shaping and glazing options before you begin. If you are new to bread making, please read
through Notes on Baking Yeast Breads (page 373) before beginning.

SPECIAL EQUIPMENT

8-quart mixing bowl, for rising
dough

Wooden surface, for kneading

Pastry scraper

INGREDIENTS

1 stick (¼ pound) plus 3 tablespoons unsalted butter, at room
  temperature

1 cup milk

⅓ cup sugar, plus pinch sugar for yeast

1 tablespoon mild flavored honey

2½ teaspoons salt

2 packages active dry yeast

½ cup lukewarm water

4 extra-large eggs, at room temperature

Up to 6 cups high-gluten (high-protein) bread flour, including flour
  for dusting

Cornmeal (preferably medium-ground), for baking sheet

Glaze: 1 egg beaten with 1 egg yolk and 1 tablespoon cream or water

OPTIONAL TOPPINGS

Sesame and/or poppy and/or whole caraway seeds

Kosher or sea salt

1) To set up: Melt 3 tablespoons of the butter and brush the interior of an
8-quart mixing bowl with some of the butter. Set bowl aside for rising
dough.

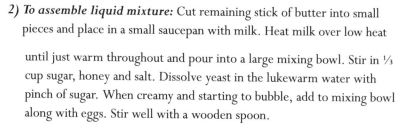

2) *To assemble liquid mixture:* Cut remaining stick of butter into small pieces and place in a small saucepan with milk. Heat milk over low heat

until just warm throughout and pour into a large mixing bowl. Stir in ⅓ cup sugar, honey and salt. Dissolve yeast in the lukewarm water with pinch of sugar. When creamy and starting to bubble, add to mixing bowl along with eggs. Stir well with a wooden spoon.

3) *To complete and knead dough:* Stir in just enough flour, a little at a time, to create a mass that leaves the sides of the bowl and is not easily stirred. Knead dough in a brisk push, fold and turning motion, until perfectly smooth and elastic, adding only as much additional flour as necessary to keep the dough from sticking to your hands and work surface.

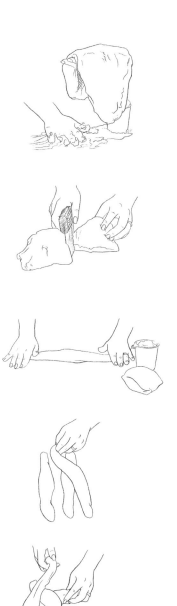

4) *To rise dough twice:* When dough is of proper consistency, place it in the buttered rising bowl and brush top of dough with more melted butter. Cover bowl with buttered plastic wrap and a clean kitchen towel and let rise in a warm, draft-free spot until double in bulk, about 2 hours. Uncover bowl and punch down dough with several swift swats with the back of your hand, totally deflating dough. Re-cover bowl and let rise until doubled, about 1 hour and 15 minutes.

5) *To form braided loaves:* Line 2 large shallow baking sheets with parchment paper and sprinkle the paper with cornmeal. On a lightly floured work surface, use the blade of your pastry scraper to divide dough in half. Cover one half as you work with the other. Divide 1 section of dough into 3 equal pieces. Roll each piece into a strand about 10 inches long with tapered ends and slightly chubby centers. (Use extra flour only as necessary to keep dough from sticking to your hands and work surface; too much flour will prevent traction necessary for rolling strands.) Align strands and beginning from the center (going down) braid as you would braid hair, alternately bringing outside strands over center strand. Turn the braided portion up so the unbraided strands point down and continue to braid—but this time bring the center strand alternately over the outside left strand and then the right strand until you reach the bottom. Pinch to seal and tuck all pinched ends underneath. Place each loaf on prepared baking sheet, gently "plump" the loaf and realign the shape. Cover with a kitchen towel and let rise 40 minutes. Preheat the oven to 375°F. (If not working with a double oven, you can bake both loaves at the same time in the upper and lower third shelves of the oven by switching positions after half the baking time; or allow 1 braided loaf to rise in the refrigerator until the first loaf enters the oven.)

6) *To glaze loaves:* Push egg glaze through a medium-mesh wire strainer into a small bowl. Remove braided loaves from the refrigerator and, using a pastry brush, paint exposed surface gently but thoroughly with glaze. Let glaze set for 5 minutes and reapply. (Reserve any remaining glaze to use if necessary during baking.) If desired, sprinkle tops and sides of loaves generously with sesame, poppy and/or caraway seeds. Even if you don't add seeds, I suggest that you lightly sprinkle the tops of the loaves with coarse salt.

7) *To bake:* Place loaves in a preheated 375°F oven until loaves are golden and sound hollow when tapped on the bottom, 35 to 45 minutes. (If applicable, remove chilled braid from refrigerator as soon as first loaf enters the oven to continue rising at room temperature.) Check braided loaves after baking for 20 minutes; as the dough expands in the oven, new dough will become exposed. Brush these white spots with a little of the reserved glaze and continue to bake. Cover top loosely with aluminum foil (shiny side up) if loaves begin to become overly brown.

8) *To cool:* Remove from oven and cool thoroughly on a rack to allow the interior to relax and expand before slicing or reheating. If applicable, glaze, bake and top remaining braided loaf as directed.

Challah Baked in Loaf Pans

Prepare challah dough as directed in recipe through 2 risings. Generously grease three 8x4-inch loaf pans with melted butter and sprinkle the interiors lightly with cornmeal. Shake out excess. Uncover fully risen dough and punch down once more. Turn out dough onto a lightly floured board and, using the blade of your pastry scraper, divide the dough into 3 equal sections. Shape dough into loaves as directed on page 381. Or braid loaves as directed in step 5 of Braided Challah recipe and place (plump side up) in prepared loaf pans. Cover and let rise 45 minutes, glaze, top and bake in a preheated 375°F oven for metal pans and 350°F for glass loaf pans until golden and loaves sound hollow when tapped on the bottom, 30 to 35 minutes.

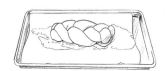

Hamburger Buns from Challah Dough

Prepare challah dough as directed through 2 risings. Line 2 shallow baking sheets with parchment paper and sprinkle paper with cornmeal. Turn out fully risen dough onto a lightly floured board and knead briefly and gently. Using the blade of your pastry scraper, divide dough into 10 equal pieces.

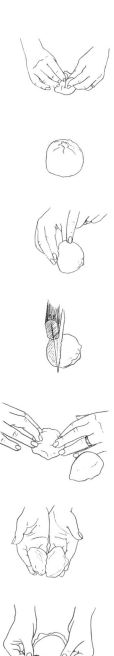

Work with 1 piece of dough at a time, covering remaining pieces with a towel. Shape each piece of dough into a round. Then pull up the sides of the round, pinching at the top of the dough ball. (The round should be taut and perfectly smooth on all sides except at the pinched top.) Turn ball on its side and drive the blade of your pastry scraper down through the waist of the ball (not through the pinched end), cutting the ball in half. Lay both halves (cut side up) and gently open them to lay flat. Sandwich both cut sides together and pinch around the circumference of the circle of dough to seal. Flatten the circle gently, but firmly and use your fingers to shove the pinched seam gently under the bun as you flatten. Lay buns (smoothest side up) on the prepared baking sheets and cover them with a clean, dry kitchen towel. Let rise for 30 minutes, starting after the last bun has been shaped.

If a topping is desired, follow directions for a soft crust with a topping (following). Bake as directed in Braided Challah recipe, but reduce baking time to 25 to 30 minutes. Cool on wire racks and store in a large heavy-duty plastic bag. To freeze buns, place in a doubled heavy-duty freezer bag. To serve, remove outer bag and thaw buns in the remaining sealed bag at room temperature. Refresh in a warm oven or split and toast cut sides before serving.

Glazes and Toppings for Challah

Egg glazes: When making an egg glaze, water gives a shinier finish to the bread and cream (or milk) gives a more golden matte finish.

For the softest crusts: Omit egg glaze and brush the fully risen loaves just before and immediately after baking with melted butter. This is better suited for loaves baked in loaf pans and buns since the soft crust is preferable in sandwiches.

For a soft crust with a topping: Omit egg glaze and as soon as the last loaf or bun is shaped, brush the tops with 1 room temperature egg white mixed with 1 teaspoon water. Sprinkle on one or more of the suggested toppings for Braided Challah. Cover with a towel and rise as directed. Brush fully risen loaves or buns just before and immediately after baking with melted butter (over the seeds). This topping is best suited for loaves baked in loaf pans or for hamburger buns.

A Dough for All Occasions
BRIOCHE

YIELD: 2 large or 12 individual fluted rolls

This rich classic French yeast dough has both a silky texture and eggy, buttery flavor. Traditionally shaped with a round knob on top and baked in round fluted pans, the bread is know as *brioche à tête*; a smaller individual version, *petite brioche à tête* is served plain as a breakfast roll. This dough is also perfect to encase savory ingredients such as cheese, sausage or seared fillet of beef (Beef Wellington), and one of my own favorite appetizers, Brie Baked en Croûte (page 121). When preparing this dough, please take your time to cream the butter and eggs, since this (along with not overloading the dough with flour) is the key to creating a baked brioche with a truly light and velvety texture. For convenience, the dough can be assembled two days ahead and kept refrigerated or frozen for as long as two weeks. Also, see variations for a sweeter version of brioche or for ways to give the plain version an even more savory flavor. If you are new to bread making, please read through Notes on Baking Yeast Breads (page 373), including the Time Management Tips, before beginning.

SPECIAL EQUIPMENT
Heavy-duty electric mixer

5-quart mixing bowl, for rising dough

Wooden surface, for kneading

Pastry scraper

2 large fluted brioche molds or 12 small individual molds (not necessary if planning to use the dough for another purpose)

1 cup milk, heated to lukewarm

2 packages active dry yeast

⅓ cup lukewarm water

Pinch sugar

2 cups unbleached all-purpose flour

FOR THE DOUGH

1½ sticks (¼ pound plus 4 tablespoons) unsalted butter, at room
   temperature, plus 2 or 3 tablespoons melted butter for brushing

3 tablespoons sugar or 2 generous tablespoons mild honey

2 teaspoons salt

3 extra-large eggs, at room temperature

1 extra-large egg yolk, at room temperature

2 cups high-gluten (high-protein) bread flour

Up to 1½ cups unbleached all-purpose flour, including flour for dusting

Glaze: 1 egg mixed with 1 egg yolk and 1 tablespoon of water, milk or
   cream

OPTIONAL TOPPINGS

Sesame seeds, poppy seeds, whole caraway seeds, coarse kosher
   or sea salt

1) **To prepare sponge:** Pour warm milk into a 2½-quart mixing bowl.
   Dissolve yeast in the lukewarm water with sugar. When the yeast mixture
   is creamy and starting to bubble, add to warm milk along with 2 cups all-
   purpose flour. Beat briskly until thoroughly combined and smooth. Scrape
   down the sides of the bowl, cover with plastic wrap and let sit at room
   temperature for 1½ hours.

2) **To set up:** Melt 3 tablespoons butter in a small saucepan and brush some
   of the melted butter on the interior of a 5-quart mixing bowl. Set aside
   for rising dough.

3) **To assemble liquid mixture:** In the bowl of a heavy-duty electric mixer
   thoroughly cream 1½ sticks butter with sugar (or honey) and salt. The
   mixture should be creamy and pale lemon yellow. Meanwhile, beat eggs

and egg yolk with a fork in a measuring cup with a spout and drizzle a small amount of the beaten eggs into the whipped butter. When *fully* incorporated, add a bit more eggs. Continue adding eggs, bit by bit, until mixture is light and fluffy and eggs are totally homogenized with the butter. (You'll need patience—this could take 10 minutes.)

4) ***To complete and knead dough:*** Turn off electric mixer and scrape in the fully risen sponge. (If you don't stop mixer when adding sponge, the glutinous mixture will actually climb up the paddle attachment.) Turn mixer on again at a medium-low setting and mix until well combined. Turn down mixer to low, add 2 cups bread flour and mix well. Remove bowl from mixer and clean off beaters, scraping mixture back into the bowl. Using a wooden spoon, stir in only enough all-purpose flour to make a dough that leaves the sides of the bowl and is no longer easily stirred. Turn out dough onto a lightly floured wooden board and knead with floured hands until smooth and elastic. Add only enough additional flour to keep dough from sticking to your hands and work surface and use your pastry scraper to remove dough from the board as you work.

5) ***To rise dough and refrigerate:*** Place dough in the buttered rising bowl and brush more butter on top of dough. Cover bowl with buttered plastic wrap and a clean kitchen towel and let rise in a warm draft-free spot for 2 hours. Punch down dough with several swift swats from the back of your hand and turn dough over in the bowl. Cover with plastic wrap and refrigerate for 4 to 48 hours.

6) ***To shape brioches:*** Brush with melted butter the insides of 2 large or 12 individual brioche molds. Turn out well-chilled dough onto a lightly floured work surface. Use the blade of your pastry scraper to divide the dough in half for 2 large brioches or into 12 equal pieces for individual molds. Working with 1 piece of dough at a time, cover the remaining pieces with a towel. Use the blade of a pastry scraper to cut off ¼ of the piece of dough. With floured fingertips, shape the larger piece into a round ball and continue to pull the walls of dough up to pinch at the top of the ball creating a tight, firm round of dough. Place round (pinched side down) into the prepared mold. For the top knob, shape the smaller piece of dough the same way but once tight, shape the bottom half of the round into a point. Using your index finger, poke a deep depression in the top of the larger round and insert the pointed section of the knob into the hole. Reshape with your hands until the top knob sits snugly within the

Q AND A

Q. What is the purpose of a yeast-risen sponge?

A. *Although a sponge can be used to enhance and lighten the texture of any yeast dough, it's particularly helpful in a dough, such as brioche, that is extremely rich in both butter and eggs. Here we allow the yeast to ferment and grow in order to develop both depth of flavor and lightness in texture, unencumbered by the eventual addition of the richer, heavier ingredients. The ultimate purpose of a sponge is to lighten the fully assembled dough so the yeast won't have to work as hard to travel throughout when rising.*

larger round. (If making individual brioches, work quickly since dough must remain chilled to handle properly. If new to working with dough, refrigerate half of the dough while you shape the first half.)

7) **To glaze and rise brioche:** Push glaze ingredients through a medium-mesh wire strainer into another small bowl. Using a pastry brush, paint the exposed surface of dough with glaze, being careful not to let any drip into the mold, which makes the dough stick during baking. (Reserve unused glaze.) Cover molds loosely with clean kitchen towels and let rise in a warm draft-free spot until almost doubled in volume, 45 minutes for smaller molds and 1 hour for the larger ones (begin timing after you shape your last brioche).

8) **To reglaze, top and bake:** While brioches are rising, preheat the oven to 375°F. Reapply glaze to brioches and wait 5 minutes before applying once more for an intensely colored crust. Top with seeds, if desired, and lightly sprinkle tops with coarse salt. Bake individual brioches 20 to 25 minutes and bake larger brioches 35 to 45 minutes. Cover loosely with aluminum foil (shiny side up) if the tops begin to become overly brown. To check for doneness, turn 1 brioche out of its pan and if it feels light and sounds hollow when tapped on the bottom, it's done. If heavy with a thud sound when tapped, replace into the pan, bake for a few more minutes and test again.

9) **To cool:** Turn brioches out of their pans and (for best texture) allow the larger ones to cool thoroughly before slicing. The small brioche can be eaten after cooling to just warm.

To Freeze Brioche Dough

This dough may be frozen up to 2 weeks with very good results. However, I don't recommend freezing any unbaked yeast dough for longer than 2 weeks. After that time, the yeast converts to alcohol, which adversely affects the flavor of the baked bread. After the dough has completed the first full rise at room temperature (before refrigerating), punch down as directed. Brush a long piece of waxed paper with melted butter and turn out dough onto buttered side. Wrap dough snugly and place into a plastic bag. Remove all air from bag and twist bag shut just at the top of dough to prevent dough from rising before it has a chance to freeze. Place the bag of dough into a heavy-duty freezer bag and seal well after removing excess air. Deep-freeze in a freezer with little temperature fluctuation. The day before planning to bake, let thaw and soften in the refrigerator for a few hours before carefully peeling off the waxed paper. Place dough in a buttered 5-quart bowl, cover with buttered plastic wrap and allow it to thaw and rise completely overnight in the refrigerator. Shape and bake brioches as directed in this recipe or use to encase various foods or fillings as directed in other recipes.

Savory and Sweet Variations

For a savory brioche: When incorporating the sponge into the dough, stir in ½ cup freshly grated Reggiano Parmesan cheese and/or 1 tablespoon chopped fresh herbs, such as basil, thyme or flat-leaf Italian parsley. If planning to freeze, use crumbled dried herbs and reduce the amount to 1½ teaspoons (thyme, rosemary and oregano are particularly nice).

For a sweet brioche: Increase the amount of sugar to ½ cup and when incorporating the sponge into the dough, stir in 1 cup chopped candied fruits or 1 cup mixed light and dark raisins that have been plumped in hot water, tea or apple juice and drained.

CRUSTY DELI RYE BREAD

YIELD: 2 loaves

SPECIAL EQUIPMENT

6- or 8-quart bowl, for rising dough

Wooden surface, for kneading

Pastry scraper

Electric spice grinder or mortar and pestle to grind caraway seeds

Tapered rolling pin

Set of quarry tiles or large pizza stone

Dark shallow baking sheet, only if not using quarry tiles or a pizza stone

Baker's peel or flat cookie sheet, only if using quarry tiles or a pizza stone

Plastic spray bottle (optional)

This extraordinary—and authentic—rye bread has a crusty golden exterior that's topped with a generous amount of whole caraway seeds and a light dusting of coarse salt. The interior is soft and tender, yet perfectly chewy and rich with the distinctive taste of caraway seeds. Through much experimentation, I've found that the key to creating the most robust flavor in rye bread is to add a generous amount of powdered caraway seeds along with the whole caraway seeds for texture. To do this, I use a small electric spice grinder, although a mortar and pestle can be used as a less expensive substitute. The traditional oblong loaf, baked on hot quarry tiles or a pizza stone, will unquestionably produce the most earthy and seductive looking bread (see page 400). But I have also included instructions for baking these loaves without the tiles. And a variation follows for baking these loaves in cornmeal-coated loaf pans, which yield a softer, more billowy slice preferred by children. Before tossing out any leftover bread, see the following recipe for Deli Rye Croutons. If you are new to bread making, please read through Notes on Baking Yeast Breads (page 373), including the Time Management Tips, before beginning.

INGREDIENTS

2 to 4 tablespoons unsalted butter, melted

2 packages active dry yeast

2¾ cups lukewarm water

About 1 rounded tablespoon sugar

1 scant tablespoon salt

¼ cup solid vegetable shortening

3 cups medium rye flour

1½ rounded tablespoons whole caraway seeds

2 rounded tablespoons finely ground caraway seeds

Up to 3½ cups high-gluten (high-protein) bread flour, including flour for dusting

Cornmeal, for baker's peel or baking sheets (preferably medium-ground)

Flavorless vegetable oil or spray for baking sheets (if not using quarry tiles)

Glaze: 1 room temperature egg white mixed with 1 teaspoon water

Whole caraway seeds and kosher or sea salt (optional but highly suggested), for topping

4 ice cubes and ice water, for baking

1) **To set up:** Brush the interior of a 6- or 8-quart mixing bowl with melted butter and set aside for rising dough.

2) **To assemble dough:** Dissolve yeast in ½ cup of the lukewarm water with a pinch of sugar and set aside until creamy and starting to bubble. In a large mixing bowl, combine remaining 2¼ cups lukewarm water, 1 rounded tablespoon sugar, salt, shortening and the dissolved yeast mixture. Briskly stir in rye flour, whole and ground caraway seeds and, when smooth, stir in enough bread flour, ½ to 1 cup at a time, to create a mass that's not easily stirred in the bowl, but not dry. Turn the mass out onto a floured wooden board and knead until smooth and elastic, adding only as much flour as necessary to prevent dough from sticking to your work surface and hands. In the beginning of the kneading process, this dough will feel quite "pasty" because of the rye flour. As always, use a pastry scraper while kneading to scrape dough off the board cleanly as you continue to knead in a sufficient amount of flour.

3) **To rise dough twice:** When dough is smooth and elastic, place it in the buttered rising bowl. Cover bowl with buttered plastic wrap and a clean kitchen towel. Let rise in a draft-free spot until doubled in bulk, about 2 hours. Punch down dough with several swift swats from the back of your hand to deflate dough totally. Turn over dough, cover and let rise again for 1 hour.

4) **To shape oblong loaves:** Turn out fully risen dough onto a lightly floured board and use the blade of your pastry scraper to divide dough in half. Work with half the dough at a time, keeping the other half covered. Lay 2 clean kitchen towels on your counter and sprinkle them lightly with bread flour. Roll dough half into a 7x10-inch rectangle. Starting at the short end farthest from you, roll dough toward you, pinching to seal as you go. Pinch to seal the ends and tuck under to attach to the bottom seam. Rotate and plump dough to finish shaping and place shaped loaf (seam side up) diagonally on a prepared towel. Form a sling by joining the corners of the towel farthest from the loaf. Secure the joined towel points within a closed drawer (in a quiet area) so the loaves hang undisturbed in their slings for 45 minutes.

Q AND A

Q. The pilot light on my gas oven seems to extinguish easily. How can I create steam without using ice water?

A. Omit the additional water and just use the ice cubes. Also, after the loaf has been baking for 2 minutes, open the oven and spray loaf with a light mist of ice water (two quick shots).

5) *To set up for baking loaves:* While bread is rising, position the rack in the lower third of the oven. If using quarry tiles or a pizza stone, place on rack and sprinkle a baker's peel or a flat cookie sheet with cornmeal. Preheat oven to 450°F as soon as the tiles are in place. If not using tiles or a stone, brush or spray 1 or 2 large (preferably dark steel) shallow baking sheets with vegetable oil and sprinkle interior with cornmeal. Place egg white and water glaze next to your work surface. Just before baking, place 4 ice cubes into a 1-cup measuring cup and add enough cold water to reach the ¼ cup mark. As an optional step to ensure a crisp crust, pour some ice cold water into a spray bottle.

6) *To slash and glaze loaves:* Working with 1 loaf at a time, carefully release slings and gently turn out loaves from towels (smooth side up) onto the prepared baker's peel or baking sheet at least 2 inches apart. Use your hands gently to plump loaf into shape. Using a sharp knife or a razor, slash tops of each loaf 3 times horizontally, going ⅓ inch deep into the dough. Using a pastry brush, paint tops and sides of loaves (excluding slashes) with egg white glaze and sprinkle tops with whole caraway seeds, if using, and then with a sprinkling of coarse salt.

7) *To bake loaves:* If baking with tiles, lift baker's peel and shake gently to make sure that the loaves will not stick to the surface. Insert the peel all the way to the back of the oven and with one swift jerk pull out the peel, leaving loaves on the hot tiles (preferably not touching). Immediately toss the cup of ice water onto the oven floor and close the door. If not using tiles, place loaves into the hot oven and toss ice water underneath the baking sheets as directed. Whether or not you're using tiles, if desired, 2 minutes after inserting the loaves, spray a fine mist of ice water into the oven (2 quick shots) and immediately close the door. Bake loaves at 450°F for 30 minutes (including initial 2 minutes). Reduce heat to 400°F and bake for 10 minutes. Reduce heat to 375°F and bake for 5 minutes more. Turn off oven and let the loaves sit there for 5 minutes. Remove from the oven and place on wire racks to cool thoroughly before slicing.

Deli Rye Bread Baked in Loaf Pans

Butter two 9x5-inch loaf pans and sprinkle generously with cornmeal. Shake pan to distribute meal and shake out the excess. Shape loaves as directed for oblong loaves, omitting floured towels, and place loaves (seam side down) in the prepared pans. Cover with towels and let rise 45 minutes. While loaves rise, preheat the oven to 450°F for metal pans and 425°F for glass loaf pans. Slash tops using a short knife with a very sharp blade. Glaze and top loaves as directed for loaves baked on tiles and bake for 20 minutes. Reduce temperature by 50°F and bake for 25 minutes more. Remove loaves and turn out of their pans onto wire racks to cool.

Deli Rye Croutons

Don't throw away leftover rye bread since it makes the most delicious croutons! Cut Deli Rye Bread into ½-inch cubes, including crusts, and melt ½ cup clarified butter (page 81) for each 2 rounded cups cubes. Place cubes in a single layer on a shallow baking sheet and bake in a preheated 375°F oven until light golden, about 10 minutes. Turn off oven and allow cubes to remain there until hard and dry, 10 to 15 minutes. Remove from oven and let cool. Heat butter in a 10-inch skillet over medium heat, add dried cubes and toast them further, tossing constantly. When golden, drain croutons on paper towels and place in a bowl. Sprinkle on some freshly ground black pepper and, if desired, give them a light sprinkling of coarse salt. Toss to mix well. Once cool, store in an airtight tin at room temperature.

TIPS

FROM A TEACHER

About Quarry Tiles

Quarry tiles—terra-cotta colored clay tiles especially made for baking—are now easily obtainable in many specialty kitchen shops or from cookware mail order catalogs. These tiles provide the best way to simulate the intense dry heat of the brick ovens originally used in the Old World and by some professional bakers today. They produce breads with a tender and chewy interior and a very crisp crust. After preheating these tiles to very hot, the fully risen dough—whether rolls, free-form loaves or baguettes—is slid from a cornmeal-dusted wooden baker's peel directly onto the tiles. Immediately a small amount of ice cubes and water are tossed onto the oven floor (underneath the tiles). When the oven door is closed, the cold water hitting the hot oven causes a burst of steam to rise to the top of the oven. The tiles then draw the mist down over the dough and the steam quickly evaporates from the intense dry heat in the oven. The combination of extreme heat, steam and the tiles creates the ideal atmosphere to ensure a crisp, crackly, authentic exterior while retaining the tender interior. (If you are worried about the water extinguishing the pilot light of your gas oven, omit the water and just toss ice cubes into the hot oven.)

The tiles I use are called "Hot Bricks" and fit within their own baking sheet. They are the best way to produce authentic ethnic breads using conventional heat in a home oven. Always allow tiles to cool thoroughly before rinsing and dry each individual tile before replacing them back on their sheet for storing.

If choosing between quarry tiles or a pizza stone, opt for the tiles since the darker terra-cotta color is more heat retentive than the lighter stone, thus producing breads with a deeper, darker crust. I've also found that most pizza stones are smaller than my sheet of tiles and are thus less able to accommodate my lengthy loaves of Italian bread. If tiles or stones are not available, use dark, steel, shallow baking sheets.

Expect the tiles to darken with use—but this only makes them better. For best results, make sure your oven is *very hot* before inserting the dough onto the tiles (preheat for at least thirty minutes). Try not to allow loaves or rolls to bake too close to one another or they will become attached during baking and won't brown evenly. If you're planning to bake successive batches of crusty loaves, rolls, or bagels, the easiest way to prevent smoking from excessive cornmeal is to sweep it away in between each batch with a short-handled broom called a cornmeal sweeper.

CRUSTY ITALIAN BREAD

YIELD: 1 extra-large loaf, 2 medium-sized loaves or 12 rolls

When this dough is shaped into one loaf, it's enormous and simply gorgeous! It's perfect Italian bread: soft and tender on the inside yet firm and crusty on the outside with a generous amount of savory sesame seeds covering the exterior. Adding some whole wheat flour and freshly ground black pepper to the dough changes both the color and character of the finished bread. Although a pizza stone or cookie sheet may be used, I suggest baking this extra-long loaf on quarry tiles (page 400) which cover more of the oven rack. Because the terra-cotta color of the tiles is more heat retentive, they will produce a more deeply colored loaf. I usually recommend a baker's peel to transfer unbaked loaves to the hot tiles but since this loaf is longer than most, I suggest you instead position the loaf diagonally across a rectangular cookie sheet (without sides) to place it in the oven. And although I prefer to have my loaf rise (seam side up) on a towel before inverting onto a baker's peel, if not using the tiles or a stone, it's easiest to simply rise the loaf seam side down and bake it directly on the cookie sheet. If you are new to bread making, please read through Notes on Baking Yeast Breads (page 373), including Time Management Tips, before beginning.

SPECIAL EQUIPMENT

5-quart mixing bowl, for rising dough

Wooden surface, for kneading

Pastry scraper

Set of quarry tiles or extra-large pizza stone

Plastic spray bottle (optional)

Flat cookie sheet

INGREDIENTS

3 tablespoons extra-virgin olive oil or unsalted butter, melted, for brushing

½ cup milk

2 tablespoons solid vegetable shortening

1¼ cups lukewarm water

2 teaspoons sugar, plus a pinch

1 scant tablespoon salt

1 teaspoon freshly ground black pepper (optional)

1 package active dry yeast

⅓ cup whole wheat flour (optional)

3 cups high-gluten (high-protein) bread flour

Up to 2 cups unbleached all-purpose flour, including flour for dusting

Cornmeal (preferably medium-ground), for cookie sheet

Glaze: 1 egg white mixed with 1 teaspoon water

¼ cup sesame seeds

4 ice cubes and ice water, for baking

1) **To set up:** Brush a 5-quart mixing bowl with olive oil or melted butter and set aside for rising dough.

2) **To assemble liquid mixture:** Heat milk and shortening in a small saucepan over low heat until warm throughout and shortening is almost melted. Pour into a large mixing bowl. Stir in 1 cup of the lukewarm water, 2 teaspoons sugar, salt and freshly ground black pepper, if using. Dissolve yeast in the remaining ¼ cup lukewarm water with a pinch of sugar. When yeast is creamy and starts to bubble, add it to the ingredients in the mixing bowl.

3) **To complete and knead dough:** Briskly stir in whole wheat flour, if using, along with bread flour, 1½ cups at a time. When well combined and smooth, stir in enough all-purpose flour, a little at a time, to create a mass that's not easily stirred in the bowl. Turn mass onto a lightly floured wooden board and knead dough using a brisk push, fold and turning motion until smooth and elastic, about 5 minutes. Add only as much all-purpose flour as needed to keep the dough from sticking to your hands and work surface. As always, use a pastry scraper while kneading to scrape dough off the board cleanly as you continue to knead in a sufficient amount of flour.

4) **To rise dough twice:** When dough has been kneaded sufficiently, place it in the greased rising bowl. Brush top of dough with olive oil or melted butter and cover bowl with greased plastic wrap and then with a clean kitchen towel. Set bowl in a warm, draft-free spot to rise until dough is doubled in bulk, about 2 hours. Punch down dough with several swift swats with the back of your hand to deflate dough totally. Turn dough over in the bowl and knead briefly just to redistribute the yeast. Re-cover bowl and let dough rise again for 1 hour.

5) **To set up before shaping loaves:** Sprinkle a flat cookie sheet with corn-meal and some sesame seeds. If baking on quarry tiles, lay 1 or 2 clean kitchen towels on the kitchen counter and sprinkle them lightly with all-purpose flour. (If shaping 2 loaves, each should rise on its own towel. The cookie sheet will be used to transfer the loaf to the hot tiles or, if not using tiles, to bake the loaves.)

6) **To shape loaves:** Punch down dough again and turn out onto a lightly floured board. Knead gently and briefly to release trapped air. Then, if making 2 loaves, use the blade of a pastry scraper to divide dough in half; cover 1 piece while you work with the other. Roll and rotate dough under

the palms of your hands so that it resembles a very big sausage. Flatten dough by pressing lightly with your fingertips and taper the ends slightly, so that the shape now looks like a flat cigar and sits horizontally in front of you. Roll the long side (farthest from you) down toward you until you reach the middle, pinching to seal, after each revolution. Then, roll up from the opposite long side (closest to you) to meet at the middle, pinching to seal as before. When both sides reach the middle, use your fingertips to pull up the outsides of each long side and pinch together at the top to seal and create a tight seam. The loaf at this point will be too long for your oven, so lift and turn in about 2 inches of dough from each tapered end and pinch to seal this to the seam. To enclose the folded ends, pull and pinch together the outer sides of dough (as before) so there is 1 long straight seam. (When shaping, if the sides of the loaf seems uneven, continue pulling and pinching until you're satisfied with the shape.)

7) **To transfer loaf to towel or cookie sheet:** Lift each end of the loaf, covering with your hands as much of the bottom of the loaf as possible. To avoid overstretching the loaf as you lift, move your hands in toward the center of the loaf. If using tiles, place loaf (seam side up) on the prepared towel; otherwise place (seam side down) on the prepared cookie sheet. Using floured fingertips, gently correct the shape with your hands. Cover with another towel and allow loaf to rise for 45 minutes. If applicable, repeat this shaping procedure with the remaining piece of dough. If not using tiles and baking 2 loaves on the same cookie sheet, position each loaf lengthwise on sheet with 2 inches between them.

8) **To set up for baking:** While loaf is rising, position the rack in the lower third of the oven and, if using them, cover rack with the sheet of quarry tiles or an extra-large pizza stone. Preheat oven to 450°F. Place egg white glaze next to your work surface. Just before baking, put 4 ice cubes into a 1-cup measuring cup and add enough cold water to reach the ¼-cup mark. As an optional step to ensure a crisp crust, pour some ice cold water into a spray bottle.

9) **To slash and glaze loaf for baking:** If using quarry tiles, position the long side of the prepared cookie sheet alongside the loaf. Carefully, using a long side of the towel, invert loaf (seam side down) onto the sheet. Gently position loaf diagonally across the sheet to accommodate its full length. If transfering 2 loaves, position them, 1 at a time, as directed in step 7. If not using tiles, simply uncover the risen loaf or loaves. Using a razor or a sharp knife, make 3 or 4 diagonal slashes ⅓ inch deep on top of

Q AND A

Q. Why are certain loaves and rolls "slashed" before they enter the oven?

A. When a loaf of unbaked bread enters a hot oven, the liquid component of the dough interacts with the surrounding heat and forms steam which naturally rises upward. Because ethnic hearth breads are usually baked initially at an extremely high temperature (450°F), the outer crust tends to seal shut before the steam has had a chance to escape fully. If these breads are not deliberately slashed to enable this steam to exit easily, the pressure from within will cause both loaves and crusty rolls to burst during baking. To slash correctly, position the blade of a very sharp knife so it's parallel to the surface of the dough. Tilt the cutting edge of the blade down only slightly—the blade should be almost horizontal to the surface of the dough—and with one clean, deliberate stroke, make a 2- to 5-inch slash (depending on the type and size of the loaf) going ⅓ inch into the dough. Remove the blade and the slashes should immediately lift upward revealing some interior dough. This takes some practice, but in time becomes easy.

loaf. Using a pastry brush, paint egg white glaze around the slashes and on the sides of the loaf. (If using tiles, don't allow any glaze to fall on the cookie sheet which will cause the loaf to stick.) Sprinkle sesame seeds generously on top, trying to exclude slashes.

10) *To bake 1 large loaf:* If using tiles, lift cookie sheet, insert loaf into the hot oven and give the sheet several swift jerks to release loaf onto the hot tiles. If not using tiles, place cookie sheet directly on hot oven rack. In either case, immediately toss the ice water onto the oven floor, underneath tiles or cookie sheet and shut the door. If desired, 2 minutes after inserting the loaf, spray a fine mist of ice water into the oven (2 quick shots) and immediately close the door. Bake at 450°F for 30 minutes (including initial 2 minutes). Reduce oven temperature to 400°F and bake for 10 minutes. Reduce temperature to 375°F and bake for 5 minutes. Turn off oven and allow loaf to sit there for 10 minutes. Remove immediately to a wire rack and let cool completely before slicing or storing.

11) *To bake 2 smaller loaves:* Bake at 450°F for 25 minutes. Reduce oven temperature to 400°F and bake 5 minutes. Turn off heat and allow loaves to sit there for 5 minutes. Remove and cool as described above.

12) *To store:* If planning to use bread on the day of baking, keep at room temperature, either fully exposed or stored in a paper bag (once cool). To store loaf to serve the next day, wrap in pliable plastic and store at room temperature. To refresh before serving, place unwrapped loaf on a wire rack over a shallow baking sheet and place in a preheated 400°F oven. Turn off oven and let loaf remain there for 10 minutes.

Crusty Italian Rolls

Except for shaping, slashing tops and cooking time, the method for making these rolls is almost identical to making crusty Italian loaves. They also may be baked either on quarry tiles or a cookie sheet. After the second rising, punch down dough again and shape into a long rope. Use the blade of your pastry scraper to cut the dough into 12 equal pieces. (To divide evenly, cut dough into quarters, then cut each quarter into thirds). Work with 1 piece of dough at a time, covering the remaining pieces with a towel.

Take 1 piece of dough and roll it in your hand to smooth the outer surface. Sit the ball on your lightly floured board and use floured fingertips to pull the sides up to form a small knot on top. Continue to pull and pinch at the top until you have formed a tight, round, ball with a small "pinched" area on top.

Lay the roll (pinched side up) on the floured towel. Cover with another towel and continue shaping the remaining pieces. Let rolls rise 45 minutes; begin timing after you have shaped your last roll.

Meanwhile, prepare oven as described in bread recipe and preheat to 450°F. To bake, turn fully risen rolls (smooth side up) on the prepared peel or cookie sheet. Using a razor or a very sharp knife, make 1 slash going from 1 end of the top to the other or cut an X in the top of each ball with sharp kitchen scissors. Glaze, apply seeds, insert into oven and toss in ice water as directed for loaves. Bake in the preheated 450°F oven for 25 minutes. Reduce temperature to 400°F and bake for 5 minutes. Turn off heat and let rolls sit there for 10 minutes more. Remove rolls from oven and let them cool on a wire rack (to just warm) before eating and cool thoroughly before storing.

Garlic Bread

YIELD: 1 standard loaf

My daughter Jessie has loved this bread since she was younger than two. Although I usually serve Crusty Italian Bread (preceding) only with a little fruity olive oil or fresh butter, garlic is another alternative that always makes people happy. Or you can purchase best-quality Italian bread with sesame seeds to make garlic bread. If using an extra-large loaf of homemade Italian bread, you will need more butter or margarine to accommodate the hefty size. So, up the ingredients by one half.

INGREDIENTS

1 stick (¼ pound) butter or margarine, at room temperature, or
   ⅓ cup fruity olive oil

4 to 5 large cloves garlic, minced or pressed through a garlic press

1 tablespoon chopped flat-leaf Italian parsley

½ teaspoon crumbled dried oregano

1 medium-sized loaf crusty Italian bread topped with sesame seeds

⅓ cup freshly grated Reggiano Parmesan cheese (optional but highly
   suggested)

Freshly ground black pepper to taste

Time Management Tips

• The loaf of garlic bread may be totally assembled and securely wrapped 2 days in advance and kept refrigerated.

1) **To prepare bread:** In a small bowl, combine butter, margarine or oil with garlic, parsley and oregano. Cut bread in half lengthwise (going in from the side, not the top) but don't cut all the way through. Open up bread and lay it flat. Spread garlic mixture generously over bread using a rubber spatula (or a pastry brush for olive oil). Sprinkle grated Parmesan, if using, and fresh pepper on top. Close bread and secure it shut (with cut side up). Using a sharp serrated knife make a cut crosswise every 1½ inches down the entire length of the loaf, being careful not to slice through the uncut side of the crust. Wrap loaf in a double thickness of aluminum foil (dull side out), positioning the opening slit of foil along the sliced side of the loaf. Place on a shallow baking sheet.

2) **To bake:** Position the oven rack to the upper third shelf and preheat oven to 375°F. Open foil a little at the top and bake bread until hot throughout, 15 to 20 minutes. Turn on the broiler. Open foil and spread open the loaf so it lays flat and the seasoning is fully exposed. Broil until golden, 2 to 3 minutes. If some edges of the loaf are becoming overly brown before the rest, pull up foil to cover those edges.

3) **To serve:** Line a long Italian bread basket with a cloth napkin or towel and transfer the loaf into the basket. Serve hot. Your guests will break off their own pieces at the table.

You Haven't Lived 'til You've Tasted . . .
HOMEMADE BAGELS

YIELD: 12 large bagels

Homemade bagels are very different from store-bought bagels, which are too doughy for my taste; I always end up scooping out the center. My bagels are lighter and crisper with infinitely more flavor. I'm really quite prejudiced because I have truly labored over this recipe for several years, perfecting the shaping process. The secret to creating and keeping the correct bagel shape through rising, boiling and baking is to make the hole disproportionately large when shaping. Because the bands of elasticity are so strong, the shaped dough has a tendency to rise up, not out. This will cause the hole to disappear if too "appropriate" looking at the onset. As for texture, the choice is yours. The chewiest bagels are made with just water, but the taste is richer with milk; a combination of the two will also produce a fine bagel. Using liquid barley malt extract instead of sugar in the dough also makes bagels chewier (look for it in gourmet or health food stores). And for best results, I bake my bagels on quarry tiles (page 400), but you can use a pizza stone or a dark steel baking sheet instead. Please don't be afraid to try this recipe; I've already made all the mistakes for you. If you are new to bread making, please read through Notes on Baking Yeast Breads (page 373), including Time Management Tips, before beginning.

INGREDIENTS

3 to 4 tablespoons unsalted butter, melted, for brushing

2 cups lukewarm water or any combination of milk and water to equal 2 cups, plus ¼ cup lukewarm water, for yeast

3 tablespoons solid vegetable shortening

1 package active dry yeast

2 tablespoons sugar or liquid (not dry) barley malt extract, plus 3 tablespoons sugar, for boiling bagels

1 tablespoon salt

1 to 2 teaspoons freshly ground black pepper

Up to 6 cups high-gluten (high-protein) bread flour, including flour for dusting

Cornmeal (preferably medium-ground) or a combination of cornmeal and sesame seeds, for baker's peel

Vegetable oil or spray, for baking sheet (if not using quarry tiles)

SPECIAL EQUIPMENT
5-quart mixing bowl, for rising dough

Wooden surface, for kneading

Pastry scraper

Set of quarry tiles or large pizza stone or shallow dark steel baking sheet

Stainless steel skimmer or large slotted spoon

Wooden baker's peel or a flat cookie sheet, only if using quarry tiles or a stone

Cornmeal sweeper, only if making successive batches of bagels using tiles or a stone

Plastic spray bottle (optional)

Q and A

Q. Why are bagels boiled before being baked?

A. *When bagels (or any dough) are boiled, the overall starch content in the dough is lowered resulting in a chewier texture after baking.*

Glaze: 2 egg whites, at room temperature, lightly beaten with
   1 teaspoon water

4 ice cubes and cold water, for baking

OPTIONAL TOPPINGS

Sesame seeds, poppy seeds, caraway seeds

Kosher or sea salt

Minced onions sautéed in a little vegetable oil

Dried garlic chips or toasted onions reconstituted in some hot water
   until softened

1) **To set up:** Brush the interior of a 5-quart mixing bowl with melted butter and set aside for rising dough.

2) **To assemble liquid mixture:** If using milk, heat in a medium-sized saucepan over medium-low heat until just warm throughout. Pour milk into a large mixing bowl and add shortening and ½ cup lukewarm water. (If milk became too hot, cool to just warm.) If not using milk, pour the 2 cups lukewarm water into a mixing bowl and add shortening (no need to melt). Dissolve yeast in ¼ cup lukewarm water with a pinch of the sugar. When yeast is creamy and starts to bubble, add to mixing bowl with 2 tablespoons of the sugar or the barley malt extract, salt and black pepper, if using.

3) **To complete and knead dough:** Briskly stir enough bread flour, a little at a time, to make a dough that is not easily stirred in the bowl. Turn out dough onto a floured wooden board and knead in a brisk push, fold and turning motion, until smooth and elastic, about 5 minutes. Add only as much additional flour as necessary to keep dough from sticking to your hands and work surface. As always, use a pastry scraper while kneading to scrape dough off the board cleanly as you continue to knead in a sufficient amount of flour.

4) **To rise dough:** Place dough in the buttered rising bowl. Brush top of dough with more melted butter, cover with buttered plastic wrap and a clean kitchen towel. Let rise in a warm, draft-free spot for 1 hour (or up to 2½ hours for an extremely light and flavorful bagel).

5) **To prepare dough for shaping:** Punch down risen dough with several swift blows until totally deflated and turn out dough onto a lightly floured

board. Use the blade of your pastry scraper to divide dough into 12 equal pieces (to divide dough equally, cut into quarters and then each quarter into thirds). Work with 1 piece at a time, covering the remaining pieces with a towel.

6) ***To shape and give bagels a cool rise before boiling:*** Lay a clean kitchen towel on each of 2 shallow trays or baking sheets and sprinkle towels lightly with flour. Shape a piece of dough into a very tight, round ball by drawing dough up and pinching it at the top. Keep pinching and pulling upward, keeping ball on a lightly floured board. The ball should be perfectly round with the exception of a little knot of pinched dough on top. Turn ball (knot side down) and flatten gently. Lift dough pattie and push your index finger through the center of the circle where the knot was. Gently stretch the hole, being careful not to tear the rim, until hole measures about 2 to 2½ inches in diameter (the hole will shrink after rising and baking). Place shaped bagels on the prepared towel-lined trays spaced 2 inches apart. Cover bagels with another towel and refrigerate for 1 to 4 hours.

7) ***To set up for boiling and baking:*** Bring a large pot of water to a boil and let simmer until ready to cook bagels. Position the rack to the lower third of the oven. If using quarry tiles or a large pizza stone, place them on the oven rack and sprinkle a baker's peel *generously* with cornmeal or sesame seeds. Otherwise, brush or spray a large dark steel shallow baking sheet with vegetable oil and sprinkle the interior as described above. Preheat oven to 500°F at least 30 minutes before you plan to boil and bake bagels. Place the prepared egg white glaze next to your work surface.

8) ***To boil:*** Bring the pot of water back to a rolling boil and add the remaining 3 tablespoons sugar. Remove 1 tray of risen bagels from refrigerator and carefully lower 2 to 4 bagels into the water. (Bagels should be able to sit freely in the water without touching. They will expand in the water.) Once bagels rise to the top, boil for 1½ minutes on each side, turning with a round slotted skimmer or a large slotted spoon. Remove with a slotted spatula to drain on a kitchen towel. Repeat with the remaining bagels.

9) ***To glaze and top bagels:*** Gently pat excess water off bagels with paper toweling and place (smoothest side up) on the prepared baker's peel or baking sheet. Using a pastry brush, paint boiled bagels with egg-white glaze. Don't worry if the glazed bagels seem wrinkled; this will smooth in the oven. When all bagels have been boiled and positioned on the peel or

baking sheet, brush tops and sides of bagels once more with glaze. Sprinkle desired toppings on each bagel or just glaze and leave plain. (Try not to let the glaze fall in puddles around bagels as this makes bagel dough stick to the peel. Having the egg whites of the glaze at room temperature helps remove their clumsy gelatinous quality.)

10) **To bake bagels:** Just before baking, put 4 ice cubes into a 1-cup measuring cup and add enough cold water to reach the ¼-cup mark. As an optional step to ensure a crisp crust, pour some ice cold water into a spray bottle. If using tiles, place baker's peel all the way to the back of the hot oven and with a swift jerk, remove the peel, leaving the bagels on the hot tiles (or place baking sheet on hot oven rack). Immediately toss the ice water on to the oven floor, underneath the tiles or baking sheet, and shut the door. If desired, 2 minutes after inserting bagels, spray a fine mist of ice water into the oven (2 quick shots) and immediately close the door. Bake at 500°F for 10 minutes (including initial 2 minutes); reduce temperature to 350°F and bake until uniformly golden and crisp, about 5 minutes. Remove with a spatula onto wire racks to cool before storing.

11) **To prepare oven for remaining batch of bagels:** Before reheating oven to 500°F, allow oven to become cool enough so you can sweep any excess cornmeal and seeds from the tiles using a cornmeal sweeper. (This is to prevent smoking.) Preheat oven, boil, glaze, top and bake remaining bagels as described above.

12) **To store:** Store cooled bagels to be served on the day of baking in a paper bag. Store remaining bagels in heavy-duty plastic bags at room temperature. Bagels also freeze perfectly in well-sealed freezer bags. To thaw, remove from the freezer the night before and allow bagels to thaw overnight in the sealed bag.

Bagel Chips

Don't throw away your day old-bagels! Instead, slice, butter and bake them for a delicious cracker! Cut bagels into ¼-inch slices, lightly spread them with softened butter mixed with herbs of your choice, and sprinkle lightly with coarse salt. Place on a wire rack set inside a shallow baking sheet. Bake in a preheated 375°F oven until crisp throughout and golden brown, 10 to 20 minutes. Cool on a wire rack and store in an airtight tin.

SESAME BREAD STICKS

YIELD: 40 to 42 bread sticks

The perfect bread stick, in my opinion, must be thin, uniformly golden brown, loaded with sesame seeds and make an audible snap when broken in half. This recipe produces a bread stick with all those qualities. For best results, use a set of quarry tiles (page 400) or a pizza stone for baking these, but it's not absolutely necessary. Nevertheless, when choosing the baking sheet for this recipe, please remember that the darker the pan the more heat retentive, and thus the browner your bread sticks. When I make these, I use a black steel pan with low sides to get the results I want. But if your oven is overly hot, you might want to use a shinier pan to deflect some of the heat away or simply reduce the baking time. By the same token, if you only have shiny pans and your oven is perfectly calibrated, you might want to leave the bread sticks in the oven a bit longer to reach a deep brown color. Of course, all of this is personal; if you like lighter, chewier bread sticks, by all means, suit your own taste. If you are new to bread making, please read through Notes on Baking Yeast Breads (page 373), before beginning. When entertaining, it's whimsical to serve these bread sticks standing straight up in a tall glass accompanied with one of my savory spreads from Just for Starters or simply at a cozy family dinner with a crock of Sweet Cream Butter (page 80)

SPECIAL EQUIPMENT

3-quart mixing bowl, for rising dough

Wooden surface, for kneading

Pastry scraper

Set of quarry tiles or large pizza stone (optional)

2 large shallow baking sheets

Parchment paper

Plastic spray bottle (optional)

INGREDIENTS

Olive oil or melted butter, for brushing

½ package active dry yeast

¼ cup lukewarm water, for yeast

Pinch plus 1½ teaspoons sugar

¼ cup milk, heated to just warm

⅔ cup lukewarm water, for dough

1½ teaspoons salt

2 tablespoons melted butter

2 tablespoons whole wheat flour

Freshly ground black pepper (optional)

Up to 4 cups unbleached all-purpose flour, including flour for dusting

Glaze: 2 egg whites, at room temperature, mixed with 1 tablespoon water

1 cup sesame seeds

4 ice cubes and cold water, for baking

Time Management Tips

• The dough can be fully assembled and left in the refrigerator for 2 days before shaping and baking. So, if you like, you can shape and bake the second batch a couple of days after the first.

Q and A

Q. What's the purpose of a lengthy rise for bread dough when creating a light texture is not an issue?

A. *Texture isn't the only reason that yeast is allowed to grow throughout a given dough. As the yeast cells multiply, they also ferment, which increases the overall flavor potential in your baked dough.*

1) ***To set up:*** Brush a 3-quart mixing bowl with olive oil or melted butter and set aside for rising dough.

2) ***To assemble liquid mixture:*** In a 1-cup liquid measuring cup, dissolve yeast in ¼ cup lukewarm water with a pinch of sugar. In a large mixing bowl, combine warm milk, the ⅔ cup warm water, the 1½ teaspoons sugar, salt and the 2 tablespoons melted butter. When yeast is creamy and starting to bubble, add to mixing bowl. Stir in whole wheat flour and black pepper, if using.

3) ***To complete and knead dough:*** Briskly stir in enough all-purpose flour, a little at a time, to make a dough that leaves the sides of the bowl and is no longer as easy to stir. Turn out mass onto a lightly floured wooden board and knead dough until smooth and elastic, about 5 minutes. Add only as much flour as needed to keep dough from sticking to your hands and work surface. As always, use a pastry scraper while kneading to scrape dough off the board cleanly as you continue to knead in a sufficient amount of flour.

4) ***To rise dough twice:*** Place dough into the prepared rising bowl and grease top of dough as well. Cover with greased plastic wrap and then with a clean kitchen towel and let rise in a warm draft-free spot until doubled in bulk, about 2 hours. Punch down dough with several swift swats from the back of your hand until dough is totally deflated. Turn over dough in the bowl, cover as before and let rise in the refrigerator for 2 hours or overnight.

5) ***To set up to bake:*** Position the oven rack to the lower third of the oven and, if using, place the sheet of quarry tiles or a pizza stone on the rack. Line 2 shallow baking sheets with parchment paper. Set the prepared egg-white glaze next to your work surface and place sesame seeds on a shallow tray.

6) ***To shape bread sticks:*** Punch down chilled dough and turn out onto a lightly floured board. Knead gently and briefly, then use the blade of your pastry scraper to divide dough in half. Return ½ to bowl, cover, and refrigerate while you work with the first half. Divide remaining dough in half and then divide each half into 10 or 11 small pieces. Work with 1 piece at a time, keeping the rest covered. Roll each piece into a very thin rope,

7 to 9 inches long, dusting lightly with flour if necessary to prevent sticking. Roll out the remaining pieces and place side by side on your counter, covered with a towel. These pieces might seem too skinny at first, but they will swell considerably.

7) *To glaze, coat and rise bread sticks:* Brush some of the egg-white glaze in a strip (about as long as the bread sticks) on your counter and place each strand of dough (1 at a time) on this wet spot. Brush top and sides of the strand with glaze, then lay it in the sesame seeds. Use your hands to scatter seeds on top of the strand to coat completely. Place coated strand on the prepared baking sheet. Continue until completed, laying each seeded strand side by side without touching (it will seem crowded). Cover bread sticks with a kitchen towel and let rise 15 minutes.

8) *To bake bread sticks:* While bread sticks rise, preheat the oven to 450°F. Just before baking, place 4 ice cubes in a 1-cup measuring cup and add enough cold water to measure ¼ cup. As an optional step to ensure a crisp exterior, pour some ice cold water into a spray bottle. When bread sticks have risen for 15 minutes, place the filled baking sheet onto the hot tiles (or oven rack). Toss ice water onto the oven floor underneath the tiles and shut the door. If desired, 2 minutes after inserting baking sheet into the oven, spray a fine mist of ice water into the oven (2 quick shots) and immediately close the door. Bake for 10 minutes (including initial 2 minutes), reduce oven temperature to 375°F and bake for 15 more minutes. Then turn off heat and allow bread sticks to sit there until they are golden brown and very crisp, about 30 minutes. (They should not feel at all springy when pressed.) Remove baking sheets from oven and, using a thin spatula, remove bread sticks to wire racks to cool thoroughly. After the first batch of bread sticks have been removed from oven, shape, rise, preheat oven and bake the remaining batch as described above.

9) *To store:* These stay perfectly fresh and crisp for 2 weeks when stored in an airtight tin at room temperature. Longer storage will affect taste but not texture.

ENGLISH MUFFINS

With a Choice of Flavors

YIELD: 10 large muffins

SPECIAL EQUIPMENT

5-quart mixing bowl, for rising dough

Wooden surface, for kneading

Pastry scraper

Tapered rolling pin

3-inch round cutters with a plain, nonfluted edge

Nonstick skillet or griddle (2 will speed the cooking process)

My family eats these rather voluptuous English muffins as fast as I can make them! Since these freeze perfectly, taste so much better than the store-bought variety and are relatively quick to prepare, I suggest making them in bulk and freezing them. Use my following variations to create several types of muffins so you can fill each bag with an assortment before freezing. And if looking for the perfect house gift for a friend, these rather rotund muffins (wrapped in a clear bag and tied with ribbon) along with a jar of preserves will be truly appreciated. Slicing an English muffin with a knife will remove much of the unique character and texture of the toasted muffin. It's traditional to "fork split" the muffin before pulling the two sides apart. After opening, you should see both deep and shallow crevices, which when toasted will form dark crisp peaks while the bottom stays light and tender. If you are new to bread making, please read through Notes on Baking Yeast Breads (page 373), before beginning.

INGREDIENTS

1½ cups milk, heated to lukewarm

2 tablespoons unsalted butter, at room temperature, plus 3 to 4 tablespoons melted butter, for brushing

1 generous tablespoon mild honey

1 package active dry yeast

¼ cup lukewarm water

Pinch sugar

1 cup whole wheat flour (optional)

Up to 3 cups unbleached all-purpose flour (if using whole wheat flour) or up to 4 cups (without whole wheat), including flour for dusting

1¼ teaspoons salt

½ to 1 cup yellow cornmeal (preferably medium-ground)

Flavorless vegetable oil, for griddle

1) **To assemble sponge:** Pour warm milk into a medium-sized mixing bowl. Stir in 2 tablespoons softened butter and honey. Dissolve yeast in ¼ cup lukewarm water with sugar and, when creamy and starting to bubble, pour into the warm milk mixture. Using a wooden spoon, briskly stir in 1 cup whole wheat flour, if using, with 1½ cups all-purpose flour (or 2½ cups all-purpose flour, if not using whole wheat). When mixture is well combined, smooth and glutinous, cover bowl with plastic wrap and then a clean kitchen towel and let ferment for 1 hour. (This sponge will give your finished English muffins a very light texture.)

2) **To complete and knead dough:** Brush a 5-quart bowl with some of the melted butter and set aside for rising dough. When sponge has fermented, stir in salt and enough remaining all-purpose flour, by the handful, to make a dough that leaves the sides of the bowl. Turn out dough onto a lightly floured wooden board. With floured hands, knead dough in a brisk push, fold and turning motion until perfectly smooth and elastic, about 5 minutes. Add only as much flour as necessary to keep dough from sticking to your hands and work surface. As always, use a pastry scraper while kneading to scrape dough off the board cleanly as you continue to knead in a sufficient amount of flour.

3) **To rise dough:** Place dough into the buttered rising bowl and brush top of dough with more butter. Cover bowl with greased plastic wrap. Let rise in a warm draft-free spot until doubled in bulk, about 1 hour.

4) **To shape and rise muffins:** Flour your fist and punch down risen dough with several swift swats from the back of your floured hand until dough is totally deflated (this dough is sticky). Sprinkle a 12x8-inch section of your work surface generously with cornmeal. Turn out dough onto the cornmeal and sprinkle more cornmeal on top. Pat or gently roll out dough ½ to ¾ inch thick. Sprinkle dough lightly with more cornmeal and cut into as many 3-inch rounds as possible, using a floured cutter. After each cut, using a thin spatula, lift up the round and place it on another section of cornmeal. Cover cut muffins with a clean kitchen towel. Then gently knead the scraps of dough until the outer surface is smooth. Roll and cut out more rounds as directed above. Let rise for 30 minutes. (Don't be concerned if extra cornmeal goes into the dough when recombining scraps. The meal will enhance the overall flavor of your cooked muffin.)

5) **To cook muffins:** Heat a nonstick griddle or skillet over medium heat and, when hot, lightly grease with vegetable oil. Using a spatula, carefully transfer muffins in batches to the hot griddle. Cook for about 2 minutes

on each side to sear the outsides until light brown (don't scorch). Reduce heat to low and continue to cook, turning every few minutes, for a total cooking time of 17 minutes. (If using an electric stove, preheat a second burner to low so you can quickly transfer the griddle to the lower temperature.) Continue to cook remaining muffins, but do not add more vegetable oil to griddle.

6) *To cool and serve:* Remove muffins to wire racks to cool thoroughly. With a fork, split muffins in half before toasting. Serve hot.

7) *To store:* Store in a heavy-duty plastic bag at room temperature. Or freeze some in a double thickness of the same type of bag. To thaw, remove bag from the freezer the night before and let sit in the original storage bag at room temperature. In the morning they'll be just right for splitting and toasting.

Freshly Baked English Muffins for Breakfast or Brunch

After the fully assembled dough completes the first rise at room temperature, cover the bowl and refrigerate it overnight. For best texture, allow dough to sit out of the refrigerator for an hour or so before shaping or allow cut muffins to rise longer so that the dough can become soft and billowy. Cook on the griddle, cool, split and toast as directed.

Rye English Muffins

Substitute 1 cup medium rye flour for the whole wheat flour and add 1 rounded tablespoon finely ground caraway seeds (use a spice grinder) and 2 teaspoons whole caraway seeds to the sponge.

Cinnamon-Raisin English Muffins

In the sponge, substitute ¼ cup light brown sugar for the honey and add 1 teaspoon ground cinnamon. Omit whole wheat flour and use only all-purpose flour. After the sponge has fermented, add ¾ cup mixed light and dark raisins that have been plumped for 10 minutes in warmed apple juice, tea or hot water and drained.

CRISPY SKILLET CORNBREAD

YIELD: one 10½-inch round; serves 8

Even as a child I loved corn, but I didn't become a devout fan of cornbread until I was an adult. Once I began experimenting with cornmeal, however, I realized that it does more than contribute a rich nutty taste to mixtures. Ground dried corn adds a unique texture, not only to the inside but also the outside of both baked and fried foods. This recipe is pretty basic, except for the addition of sautéed chopped onions. But to this, you may add a myriad of other ingredients, depending on your mood and who you are feeding (see variations). For the most interesting texture, use medium-ground (not fine) cornmeal. And cultured buttermilk is the secret ingredient to making the best-tasting, crispest, (yet incredibly tender) cornbread. (Buttermilk is the secret to so many different recipes that I've lost count!) Using a well-seasoned cast iron skillet ensures the crispest results but in a pinch, a heavy round cake pan will do.

INGREDIENTS

Flavorless vegetable oil, for brushing cake pan (if using)

1 tablespoon butter or margarine

½ cup minced yellow onion

Freshly ground black pepper to taste

1½ cups medium-ground yellow or white cornmeal

1 cup unbleached all-purpose flour

2 teaspoons baking soda

1½ teaspoons salt

2½ tablespoons sugar

2 cups cultured buttermilk, at room temperature

2 extra-large eggs, lightly beaten

½ stick (4 tablespoons) butter, melted

3 tablespoons clarified butter (page 81) or solid vegetable shortening

Homemade Sweet Cream Butter (page 80), for accompaniment

1) **To set up:** Place a 10½-inch cast iron skillet or heavy cake pan on the center shelf of the oven. (If using a cake pan, brush the sides with flavorless vegetable oil.) Preheat the oven to 425°F.

SPECIAL EQUIPMENT

Wide blending fork or batter whisk

Sifter or triple-mesh wire strainer

10½-inch (1½ inches deep) well-seasoned cast iron skillet (page 29) or heavy 10-inch round cake pan (2 inches deep)

Time Management Tips

- The dry ingredients can be mixed, sifted and left in a covered bowl days before needed. Just give a good swish with a whisk to combine and lighten before assembling.

- Although batters leavened only with baking soda should be baked soon after being assembled, this batter can be fully combined, covered and left at a comfortable room temperature for up to 1 hour before pouring into the preheated skillet. Or, for best results, simply combine the dry ingredients in one bowl and the wet ingredients in another and refrigerate the latter—hours ahead. Add the sautéed onions to the wet ingredients and allow them to sit out at room temperature for 1 hour before combining wet and dry ingredients (along with melted butter) just before baking.

2) *To sauté onions:* Heat a small skillet over medium heat with 1 tablespoon butter. When melted and bubbling, add minced onion and sauté until softened and fragrant, 2 to 3 minutes. Add some freshly ground black pepper, remove from heat and set aside.

3) *To assemble batter:* Place cornmeal, flour, baking soda, salt and sugar in a medium-sized mixing bowl. Using a whisk, combine well and then sift into another bowl. Pour buttermilk into a separate bowl, add lightly beaten eggs and mix well. Pour buttermilk mixture and sautéed onions into the bowl with the dry mixture and add melted butter with another grind or 2 of fresh black pepper. Using a wide blending fork or a batter whisk, gently combine mixture until there are no dry pockets.

4) *To bake:* Place clarified butter or solid shortening into the preheated pan while it remains in oven. Close oven door and allow the fat to liquify and become hot (1 minute). Open the oven door and carefully (using oven mitts!) pull the rack holding the skillet toward you. Using a rubber spatula, quickly (so the oven doesn't cool) pour cornmeal mixture into the hot skillet (the batter should sizzle furiously). Push the pan back into the oven and close the door. Bake until firm but not overly dry and a toothpick comes out clean when inserted into the center of the bread, about 20 minutes. Meanwhile warm your serving plate.

5) *To invert and serve:* Carefully remove pan from oven and run a knife around its circumference. Place a wire rack over the top and invert bread onto rack. Immediately invert once more onto a warmed serving plate so bread is right side up. Cut into wedges and serve hot with Sweet Cream Butter.

Cornbread Variations

The sautéed onions can be omitted. Or, while sautéeing the onions, add 1 or more of the following: ⅓ cup minced red or green bell pepper; 1 chopped, stemmed and seeded jalapeño chili pepper and/or ⅓ cup chopped hard sausage (andouille, or pepperoni, or chorizo, with the casing removed); you can also sauté 3 pieces bacon until crisp, drain and coarsely chop. Then sauté the onion in 1 tablespoon of bacon drippings instead of the butter and add chopped bacon when assembling batter. Another variation is to sauté ⅓ cup crumbled fresh sweet or hot Italian sausage in a bit of olive oil until golden; pour out any accumulated fat and add onions and 1 clove of minced garlic.

MY MOST LUXURIOUS BANANA BREAD

YIELD: two 9x5-inch loaves

Ripe bananas are one of my favorite foods and the irresistible aromas that emanate from the kitchen when these loaves are baking make this my favorite recipe for banana bread. Topped with a sugar, nut and spice mixture, this brings the flavor of a typical banana bread to new heights. And although I know it's hard not to "dig in" to a hot, freshly baked loaf of bread, it's important to allow this loaf to cool completely before slicing. Actually, it improves both in flavor and texture if it's allowed to sit undisturbed for twenty-four hours before slicing. This is a "quick" bread, so handle the batter gently, not vigorously as you would a yeast bread.

FOR THE TOPPING

1 rounded tablespoon granulated white sugar or vanilla sugar (page 74)

2 rounded tablespoons coarsely chopped walnuts

½ teaspoon ground cinnamon

FOR THE BREAD

Vegetable spray or softened butter, for greasing pans

1 cup golden raisins or a combination of light and dark raisins

2 cups plus 1 tablespoon unbleached all-purpose flour

2½ cups sifted cake flour, measured after sifting

1 tablespoon double-acting baking powder

½ teaspoon baking soda

¾ teaspoon salt

2 teaspoons ground cinnamon

1 teaspoon ground nutmeg (preferably freshly grated)

3 extra-large eggs

1 cup packed light brown sugar

1 cup granulated white sugar

½ cup sour cream or Classic Crème Fraîche (page 83)

½ cup milk

1½ teaspoons pure vanilla extract

3 cups puréed bananas (5 or 6 large very ripe bananas)

1½ sticks (¼ pound plus 4 tablespoons) unsalted butter, melted

SPECIAL EQUIPMENT

1-quart (or smaller) saucepan, preferably with a spout

Two 9x5-inch loaf pans, preferably nonstick

Sifter or triple-mesh wire sieve

Nutmeg grater (optional)

Food processor or mortar and pestle

Blender, for puréeing bananas

Electric mixer

Batter whisk or wide blending fork

How to Sift Flour Before Measuring

Place a spoutless measuring cup for dry ingredients on a sheet of waxed paper. Place either a sifter or a triple-mesh wire sieve over the cup and pour flour directly into the sifter or sieve. Sift flour over the cup (or shake the sieve) mounding the flour so it extends over the top of the cup. Level the top with the straight edge of a knife, allowing the excess to fall on the paper. Lift both sides of waxed paper to transfer excess flour back to your canister. (For easy clean-up, measure all dry ingredients over waxed paper.)

Grated Nutmeg

In most recipes, the readily available, pre-ground nutmeg can be used as a substitute for fresh, but both the peppery flavor and intoxicating aroma of freshly grated nutmeg are really quite special. If possible, purchase an inexpensive hand-held grater (available at most hardware stores) and experience the superior taste of this freshly grated seed of the fruit from a tropical evergreen tree.

1) *To prepare topping:* Combine all of the topping ingredients in the bowl of a food processor fitted with the steel blade and process until mixture is ground small but still textural. Transfer to a bowl and set aside. Alternatively, grind together ingredients with a mortar and pestle.

2) *To prepare raisins:* Toss raisins with the 1 tablespoon all-purpose flour (which prevents them from sinking to the bottom of the batter). Place raisins in a small wire strainer and bounce around to remove any excess flour.

3) *To set up for baking:* Preheat the oven to 350°F. Grease two 9x5-inch loaf pans with vegetable spray or butter and set them aside.

4) *To prepare dry ingredients:* Place sifted cake flour, the 2 cups all-purpose flour, baking powder, baking soda, salt, cinnamon and nutmeg into a large bowl and combine well using a whisk. Sift mixture into another large bowl and set aside.

5) *To mix batter:* In the bowl of an electric mixer, beat eggs with brown and white sugars until well combined and lightened. Add sour cream, milk and vanilla. Then add banana purée and combine well. With mixer on low, add sifted dry ingredients, alternating with melted butter. Mix only until just combined. Turn off mixer and, using a rubber spatula, gently fold in flour-dusted raisins. With the spatula, scrape down to the bottom of the bowl to incorporate the mixture fully. Avoid overworking the batter for the best and most delicate texture.

6) *To bake:* Pour mixture into the prepared loaf pans, dividing equally, and smooth the tops with a rubber spatula. Sprinkle the top of each loaf with half of the prepared topping and place loaves about 2 inches apart on center shelf of preheated oven. Bake until a toothpick comes out clean when inserted into the center of loaf and tops are golden, 55 to 60 minutes.

7) *To invert, cool and serve:* Remove loaves from oven and sit them (in their pans) on a wire rack for 10 minutes. Run the dull side of a knife or a spatula around the sides of the pans. To invert, place a piece of waxed paper on top of the loaf and turn out onto a rectangular platter or a wire rack. Remove pan and invert loaf (right side up) onto the wire rack and remove the waxed paper. Allow loaves to cool thoroughly before slicing and serving.

8) *To store:* When thoroughly cool, wrap loaves securely in pliable plastic wrap and store in a heavy-duty plastic bag at room temperature. Alternatively, the loaves may be frozen: Wrap securely in aluminum foil and place into labeled heavy-duty plastic freezer bags.

It always surprises me that many experienced cooks are unaware of the difference between obtaining an accurate dry measurement and a liquid one. Of course, liquids are easy to measure in a glass cup since they pour and settle at the correct measurement line. But measuring dry ingredients is quite different. In order to have real success with most baking recipes, it is essential to measure ingredients like flour, sugar, baking powder and spices with the "dip, scoop and sweep" method using specifically designed dry measuring cups. Nested in sets, these cups are made of either plastic or stainless steel, which I prefer since they are more durable. The standard set consists of cups with capacities of ⅛, ¼, ⅓, ½ and 1 cup; there is also a very handy 2-cup measure, which usually must be purchased separately. Although measuring spoons are used to measure accurately small amounts of sugar, spices and leavenings, the technique is the same.

For measuring flour or sugar, make sure that your canisters have a mouth that's wide enough to allow you easy access with a loaded 2-cup dry measuring cup. Also, before dipping your cup into flour, it's best to give the flour a good swish with a whisk to lighten it and break up any lumps. Dip the cup or measuring spoon into your dry ingredient and scoop it up so it mounds at the top. Don't shake off any excess; this condenses the ingredient and creates an inaccurate measurement. Instead, slide the straight blunt edge of a knife twice across the top of the cup or spoon so the excess falls back into the cannister and the ingredient is perfectly level with the rim. This procedure is applicable to *all* dry ingredients when a specific measurement is required in a recipe.

SWEET CREAM BISCUITS

YIELD: about eleven 2½-inch biscuits

SPECIAL EQUIPMENT

Hand-held pastry blender or food processor

Wide blending fork or large serving fork

2½-inch biscuit cutter, preferably fluted

Tapered rolling pin

Flat cookie sheet, preferably not cushioned and without sides, or shallow baking sheets with 1-inch sides

These are my family's favorite biscuits, so I make them more than any others. Sometimes, for added flakiness I cut in the optional diced cold butter and sometimes not. Either way, these biscuits come out tender, moist and absolutely wonderful. These fluffy rounds are equally appropriate when served at breakfast to accompany scrambled eggs, at dinner alongside Perfect Roast Chicken (page 251) or to embellish an informal menu of soup and salad. Serve by themselves or with fresh butter and preserves.

INGREDIENTS

Flavorless vegetable oil or parchment paper, for baking sheet

2 cups unbleached all-purpose flour, plus more for dusting

1 tablespoon double-acting baking powder

1 tablespoon sugar

1 generous teaspoon salt

½ teaspoon freshly ground black pepper (optional)

3 tablespoons cold unsalted butter (optional), cut into small dice

Up to 1½ cups heavy cream (preferably not ultrapasteurized)

2 tablespoons melted unsalted butter, for glaze

1) *To set up:* Preheat the oven to 400°F. Brush a flat cookie sheet or a shallow baking sheet very lightly with vegetable oil or line with ungreased parchment paper.

2) *To assemble dry ingredients:* Combine flour, baking powder, sugar, salt and pepper, if using, in a 2½- to 3-quart mixing bowl using a whisk. If using diced cold butter, cut it into the flour mixture using your fingertips, a pastry cutter or the bowl of a food processor fitted with the steel blade. To use a food processor, process dry ingredients until well combined and lightened. Then add diced butter and continue to process until the mixture is well incorporated and the whole mixture looks like coarse meal; then pour the flour-butter mixture into another bowl.

3) ***To mix and knead dough:*** Pour 1⅓ cups heavy cream into the bowl of dry ingredients. Using a wide blending fork, combine the wet and dry ingredients gently but thoroughly without overworking the mixture. As some of the flour is moistened by the cream, push that section of dough to the side of the bowl. Continue until mixture resembles a moist, shapeless mass. If dry, add up to 2 more tablespoons cream. Turn the mass out onto a lightly floured surface and knead the dough gently and superficially, about 8 or 9 times.

4) ***To cut biscuits:*** Pat or roll dough out to a thickness of a scant 1 inch. Using a floured 2½-inch biscuit cutter, cut out as many rounds as possible, using a straight down, up and out motion. Lay biscuits on the prepared baking sheet. Gather the scraps and gently knead them to smooth the surface. Pat or roll again and cut out more rounds.

5) ***To glaze, bake and serve:*** Brush tops of biscuits with melted butter and bake on the center shelf until they are high and light golden brown, 18 to 20 minutes. Remove and serve hot.

Variation with Egg Wash Glaze and Seed Topping

This will give a shiny, golden finish to your baked biscuits. Mix 1 egg with 1 teaspoon water or milk or cream. Pour through a strainer into a small cup (this removes any coagulation from the egg, making it easier to apply with a pastry brush). Brush on the tops of biscuits before baking. If desired, sesame seeds, poppy seeds (or a combination) can be sprinkled over the glaze before baking for a delicious taste variation.

Time Management Tips

• These biscuits can be assembled totally, placed on a baking sheet, covered loosely with plastic wrap and left at room temperature for an hour or so before baking. However, when including the optional cold butter, the flakiest texture will be achieved if you bake the biscuits immediately after assembling.

• You also can prepare the dough 1 day ahead of baking, cover well and refrigerate. However, if you bake them straight from the refrigerator, you will sacrifice some height and overall texture. For best results, bring close to room temperature before baking.

Although it's usually common practice to sift the dry ingredients in biscuits before assembling the dough, I find this unnecessary. The all-purpose flour available today is already sifted many times before packaging. When making biscuits, whisking the ingredients together does a fine job of thoroughly combining and lightening the mixture at the same time.

Kneading dough: When assembling biscuit dough, it's important to remember that you are not working with a yeast dough that needs to be worked aggressively in order to achieve proper texture. To the contrary, being rough and bossy will result in tough, chewy biscuits. To create the lightest, most tender biscuits, both the kneading and rolling process should be gentle and superficial at best. Actually, the kneading is just to smooth the outside of the dough without actually entering into the center.

Rolling dough: Each time you reroll biscuit dough, the potential for tough biscuits increases; so cut as many rounds as you can at first. Also, try not to twist the cutter as you drive the blade down into the dough since usually this results in lopsided biscuits. Another option is to cut the biscuits into squares using a sharp knife. Doing so will not only eliminate the need for rerolling, but you won't be left with any stray scraps of dough.

Baking sheets: Overgreasing the baking sheet will encourage biscuits to spread out instead of rise up. For best baking results, I don't recommend "cushioned" cookie sheets for biscuits, because the padded bottom inhibits the quick penetration of heat necessary to encourage the biscuits to rise before the dough sets. If however, these are all you have, bake the biscuits on the bottom shelf of the oven for the first half of the prescribed baking time, then switch to the center shelf for the remaining time. And although these biscuits are best when cut thick so they bake high, if desired you can gently roll the dough a little thinner before cutting to yield a few more biscuits.

SAVORY CREAM BISCUITS

With Scallions, Sweet Red Peppers and Cheese

YIELD: Twelve 2½-inch biscuits

These attractive biscuits—studded with sautéed minced scallions and sweet red peppers—are both sweet and savory at the same time. Perfect with soup and salad, they are equally at home with roast, grilled or broiled meat as well as fish or poultry. Because they are so frequently requested by those closest to me, I feel confident that these biscuits will become a family favorite of yours as well. Before beginning, see my Tips from a Teacher on page 424 for information on necessary equipment and proper handling of biscuit dough.

INGREDIENTS

2 tablespoons butter, for sautéing vegetables

¼ cup minced scallions (green onions), trimmed white part and 1½ to 2 inches of the tender green

¼ cup seeded and minced red bell pepper

Freshly ground black pepper to taste

Ingredients for Sweet Cream Biscuits batter (preceding), omitting optional items

½ cup finely shredded Swiss or Jarlsberg cheese

1 to 2 tablespoons freshly grated Reggiano Parmesan cheese (optional)

1) *To set up:* Preheat the oven to 425°F. Prepare a flat cookie sheet or a shallow baking sheet, as directed in preceding recipe.

2) *To sauté vegetables:* Melt 2 tablespoons of the butter in a small skillet and, when hot and bubbling, stir in minced scallions. Cook over low heat until softened and fragrant, about 1 minute. Add minced red peppers and continue to sauté until tender, 1 to 2 minutes over low heat. Add a few grinds of fresh black pepper and remove from heat.

3) *To assemble biscuit dough:* Prepare dough for Sweet Cream Biscuits with the following exceptions: Increase salt to 1¼ teaspoons, limit cream to 1⅓ cups, and add sautéed vegetables to cream before combining wet and dry ingredients.

4) *To roll, cut, fill and assemble:* Knead, roll out and cut biscuits as directed in preceding recipe, except that dough should be rolled out ¼ to ⅓ inch

Time Management Tips

• The batter can be assembled fully early in the day, covered and refrigerated. Or assemble 2 hours ahead, cover and leave at a comfortable room temperature. If chilled, bring batter close to room temperature before baking or adjust baking time to compensate for the chilled batter.

thick. Cut out 24 rounds, place half of the rounds (1 inch apart) on the prepared cookie sheet. Top each round generously with Swiss cheese and then top with the remaining rounds of dough, pressing gently.

5) *To glaze, bake and serve:* Brush each biscuit with a little melted butter and, if desired, sprinkle lightly with grated Parmesan cheese. Bake on the center shelf of the preheated oven until golden, 16 to 17 minutes. Serve hot.

BUTTERMILK BISCUITS

YIELD: about ten 2½-inch biscuits

These down-home crisply textured biscuits are another variation on Sweet Cream Biscuits. The ingredients change slightly, but the method is almost identical, as is the required equipment. Cultured buttermilk is a low-fat product and cup for cup has only five more calories than skim milk. For best results, bake these soon after assembling.

INGREDIENTS

2 cups unbleached all-purpose flour, plus more for dusting

2 teaspoons double-acting baking powder

1 teaspoon baking soda

1 teaspoon salt

1½ teaspoons sugar

A few grinds of freshly and coarsely ground black pepper (optional)

3 tablespoons cold unsalted butter, cut into small dice

¾ cup plus 2 tablespoons cultured buttermilk

2 tablespoons melted butter, for glaze

Follow directions for Sweet Cream Biscuits (page 422) with the following changes. Preheat the oven to 425°F. Adding diced butter is not optional. Add buttermilk to dry ingredients when directed to add cream. Roll out only ¾ inch thick. Bake until golden and crisp, 12 to 15 minutes.

Q AND A

Q. What if a recipe calls for buttermilk and I don't have any in the house?

A. If you don't have buttermilk on hand, stir 1 tablespoon strained fresh lemon juice into 1 cup milk and allow it to stand until thickened, about 5 minutes.

TRIPLE-CORN AND PEPPER MUFFINS

YIELD: 12 muffins

These muffins are moist and tender with three kinds of corn and loads of contrasting textures and colors. The perfect accompaniment to a soup and salad supper, these muffins also make an annual appearance on my Thanksgiving table. Serve alone or with Sweet Cream Butter (page 80).

SPECIAL EQUIPMENT
Standard-sized 12-cup muffin tin, preferably with a nonstick finish

Sifter or triple-mesh wire strainer

Batter whisk or wide blending fork

INGREDIENTS

Melted butter or vegetable spray, for muffin tin

2 tablespoons butter

½ cup minced yellow onion

½ cup seeded and minced red bell pepper

2 tablespoons chopped fresh basil leaves and 1 tablespoon chopped flat-leaf Italian parsley *or* 1 scant teaspoon crumbled dried basil and 2 tablespoons chopped fresh parsley

1 cup medium-ground yellow cornmeal

2 cups unbleached all-purpose flour

¼ cup sugar

1½ tablespoons double-acting baking powder

½ teaspoon baking soda

1¼ teaspoons salt

Freshly ground black pepper to taste

1 cup canned creamed corn

1 can (11 ounces) whole corn kernels, drained

½ cup sour cream

½ cup milk

2 extra-large eggs, lightly beaten

1) *To set-up:* Preheat the oven to 400°F. Grease a 12-cup nonstick muffin tin with melted butter or vegetable spray. Be sure to grease the top of the tin as well as the cups—even if nonstick.

2) *To sauté vegetables:* Melt the 2 tablespoons butter in a small skillet over medium heat. When hot and bubbling, stir in minced onions and bell peppers and sauté until softened and fragrant, 3 to 4 minutes. Add basil and

parsley and cook for 1 minute more. Remove from heat and let vegetables cool slightly.

3) *To assemble batter:* In a large bowl, whisk together cornmeal, flour, sugar, baking powder, baking soda, salt and pepper. Sift into another bowl and set aside. In another bowl, combine creamed corn, whole corn, sour cream, milk and lightly beaten eggs. Then stir in cooled sautéed vegetables. Pour corn and pepper mixture over the sifted flour mixture. Using a wide blending fork or batter whisk, combine mixtures gently, but thoroughly. Be sure to go all the way to the bottom of bowl to incorporate any dry pockets.

4) *To bake:* Spoon batter into the prepared muffin tin, mounding at the top of each cup. Place tin on the middle shelf of the hot oven and bake until a toothpick comes out clean and the tops are slightly golden, about 25 minutes. Remove to a wire rack and allow the muffins to remain in the tin for 5 minutes before removing them to a wire rack to cool.

5) *To serve and store:* Serve muffins warm from the oven or reheat in a 350°F oven for 10 minutes. Refrigerate leftover muffins individually wrapped in pliable plastic wrap and stored together in a heavy-duty plastic bag.

LOADED WITH BLUEBERRIES MUFFINS

YIELD: 12 muffins

These muffins are extremely light, tender and not too sweet! And when baked within insulating paper liners and wrapped individually in pliable plastic wrap, they stay soft and tender for days after baking. To enjoy these blueberry muffins throughout the year, flash-freeze fresh blueberries at the end of July and beginning of August when they are most abundant and voluptuous —some are so large, they resemble grapes! And because there's nothing like the taste of a freshly baked blueberry muffin first thing in the morning, follow my Time Management Tips and provide yourself and family with a delectable (and aromatic) way to start your day!

SPECIAL EQUIPMENT

12-cup standard-sized muffin tin, preferably nonstick

Paper muffin liners (optional)

Nutmeg grater (optional)

Batter whisk or wide blending fork

INGREDIENTS

Melted butter or nonstick vegetable spray, for muffin tin

3 cups unbleached all-purpose flour

1½ teaspoons double-acting baking powder

2 teaspoons baking soda

½ teaspoon salt

1½ teaspoons ground cinnamon

1 teaspoon ground nutmeg (preferably freshly grated)

1¼ cups cultured buttermilk

2 extra-large eggs, lightly beaten

⅔ cup flavorless vegetable oil

½ cup firmly packed light brown sugar

½ cup granulated white sugar

1 teaspoon pure vanilla extract

2 generous cups plump fresh blueberries or unthawed frozen berries

About 1 tablespoon granulated white sugar or vanilla sugar (page 74), for topping

Rinse berries and place on shallow baking sheet lined with doubled paper toweling. Gently pat and roll berries until dry. Remove paper towel and place sheet (uncovered) in the freezer. Once frozen, pour berries into a heavy-duty plastic bag. Place into another bag for added protection against the formation of ice crystals. To retain best texture, use berries straight from the freezer without thawing.

1) To set up: Preheat the oven to 400°F. If not using paper liners, brush with melted butter or spray the interior of a 12-cup nonstick muffin tin. Even if using paper liners, butter or spray the tops of the tin, between each muffin cup.

2) To assemble batter: Place flour, baking powder, baking soda, salt, cinnamon and nutmeg in a large mixing bowl and combine thoroughly using a whisk. In a separate bowl, combine buttermilk, eggs, vegetable oil, brown and white sugars and vanilla. Mix well. Add the wet ingredients to the bowl with the dry ingredients and, using either a batter whisk or a wide blending fork, combine the mixture gently but thoroughly. Gently, fold in blueberries using a rubber spatula and take care not to overwork the batter or rupture the berries.

3) To bake: Spoon batter into muffin tin, filling each cup and mounding the top. Sprinkle tops generously with some granulated sugar. Place tin in the preheated oven and bake until a toothpick comes out clean when inserted into the center and the tops are golden and crisp, about 20 minutes. Remove from oven and place tin on a wire rack. Cut in between each muffin (where the edges merged during baking), carefully lift out muffins and stand on a rack to cool. Allow muffins to settle for 10 minutes before enjoying warm.

4) To store: Muffins to be served on the day of baking should be placed on a tray and, once cool, covered with aluminum foil. Those to be stored for the next day should be wrapped individually in pliable plastic. Either way, they should be stored at room temperature.

Freshly Baked Muffins for Breakfast

The night before, combine all of the wet ingredients, cover well and refrigerate. Whisk together all dry ingredients and leave at room temperature. Line tins with paper liners and spray tops of tins. In the morning, preheat oven, combine wet and dry ingredients and then fold in berries. Fill tin, pop into the oven and set your timer for 20 minutes.

Q. Is there one type of wrap that's better than another to keep foods fresh?

A. *Exposure to air causes loss of moisture and this is what encourages cooked foods to spoil and baked goods to become stale. When wrapping baked goods such as individual muffins and quick breads, it's important to use a strong pliable plastic that has the capacity to stretch and conform closely to the food (thus keeping air out and moisture in). In addition, a poorly made plastic wrap will allow aromas from cut aromatic vegetables to escape into the refrigerator. When choosing plastic wrap, purchase a brand that's not made with polyethylene which allows both air and moisture to pass through. The best brand that's readily available is Reynolds Plastic Wrap. This brand can also be used in the microwave.*

Q. Why do you say to grease a tin with a nonstick surface ?

A. *It seems that most baking sheets, muffin tins and cake pans made with a nonstick finish are only "nonstick" until they decide to stick. From personal experience, I say grease your pan in every place that will come in contact with your batter!*

From the Fridge to the Oven . . .
PRUNE AND RAISIN BRAN MUFFINS

YIELD: 36 muffins

These muffins are small, incredibly moist and absolutely the best-tasting bran muffins I've had yet. This recipe is purposely large so you can keep the batter in the refrigerator for at least three weeks and have fresh muffins in the morning, afternoon or anytime you choose. As a matter of fact, this batter seems to bake even better when it's cold—straight from the refrigerator. I don't suggest using nonstick paper muffin-tin liners in this recipe, since the outer texture of these muffins is better when baked without them.

INGREDIENTS
Melted butter or vegetable spray, for muffin tin

4 cups bran cereal with raisins

1½ cups unprocessed wheat bran*

1 quart cultured buttermilk

2 cups bite-sized pitted prunes, halved, or larger pitted prunes, quartered

2 cups unbleached all-purpose flour

1 tablespoon baking soda

1½ teaspoons double-acting baking powder

1¼ teaspoon salt

1 tablespoon ground cinnamon

½ cup solid vegetable shortening

2 cups packed dark brown sugar

½ cup unsulphured molasses*

2 extra-large eggs

⅓ cup flavorless vegetable oil

1 teaspoon pure vanilla extract

* See section on Staples

1) **To set up:** If planning to bake some or all of the muffins right away, preheat the oven to 400°F. (If using a black muffin tin, preheat to 375°F.) Brush the interior of one or more 6- or 12-cup nonstick muffin tins with melted butter or spray with vegetable spray.

2) **To assemble batter:** Place bran cereal, wheat bran, buttermilk and cut prunes into a large mixing bowl and stir well to combine. Set aside so the cereal has a chance to absorb the buttermilk. In another bowl, whisk together flour, baking soda, baking powder, salt and cinnamon. Set aside. In the bowl of an electric mixer, cream shortening with brown sugar and molasses. Add eggs, 1 at a time, combining well after each addition. Add vegetable oil and vanilla. Scrape down the sides and mix once more. Scrape this mixture into the bowl with the swollen bran mixture. Stir well. Pour the flour mixture on top of the wet ingredients in the large mixing bowl and, using either a batter whisk or a wide blending fork, gently but thoroughly combine the batter.

3) **To bake:** Using a medium-sized ice cream scoop or a spoon, scoop uniform portions of batter into the greased muffin tin until each cup is ¾ full (don't overfill). Place in preheated oven and bake 20 minutes; if not using a black muffin tin, reduce temperature to 350°F and bake for 5 more minutes, covering loosely with aluminum foil (shiny side up) if the tops are becoming overly brown. If your muffin tin is black, your muffins will bake faster; bake at 375°F for 20 to 25 minutes. Muffins are done when they reach the top of the tin, are a deep brown color but not overly dark, and a toothpick will come out clean when inserted into the center.

4) **To invert, cool and serve:** Remove tin to a wire rack for 2 minutes (just to settle muffins). Invert them onto a wire rack and let them cool upside down. Serve just warm or at room temperature.

5) **To store batter:** If not baking all the muffins at the same time, place the remaining batter into a heavy-duty container with a tight-fitting lid. Label and date the container and refrigerate. Spoon directly from the refrigerator into prepared muffin tins as directed. The batter should remain good for at least 3 weeks under refrigeration.

6) **To store leftover muffins:** Muffins to be served the day of baking should be placed on a tray and, once cool, covered with aluminum foil. Those to be stored for the next day should be wrapped individually in pliable plastic. Either way, they should be stored at room temperature.

About Bran

Tasteless but powerful wheat bran transforms a good recipe into one that is good for you. Most grains have been milled to remove the inedible hull, making the kernels easier to cook and digest. Unfortunately, milling removes varying amounts of the fiber-rich bran layer that covers the kernel. This is clearly the most nutritious part and supplies 86 percent of the niacin, 43 percent of the riboflavin and 66 percent of all the minerals in the grain, as well as the majority of its natural dietary fiber. As a result, bran is not present in most refined grain products. What's so great about the fiber in wheat bran? It's been scientifically documented to have a positive affect on fighting cancer of the colon. The next time you're in the supermarket or health food store, pick up a box or bag of this important ingredient and don't limit its use to muffins. Sprinkle some into your meatloaf, fresh breads, morning cereal and fresh fruit milk shakes. Since it's tasteless, no one should know the difference. Once opened, store wheat bran in a tightly sealed moisture-proof container in the refrigerator to prevent it from going rancid.

FRIED INDIAN BREAD PUFFS

YIELD: sixteen 2-inch triangles; serves 8 to 10

SPECIAL EQUIPMENT
Sifter or triple-mesh wire strainer

Wooden surface, for kneading

Pastry scraper

Tapered rolling pin

Frying thermometer (optional)

This unusual bread that originated in India was taught to me by a woman who grew up eating these triangular puffs of fried dough. Your kids won't be the only ones who instantly gobble up these chubby, slightly sweet, airy puffs of golden dough. In most cases, the first bite will expose a deep pocket, which becomes the perfect scoop for the luscious sauce of curried dishes. Now, the tricky part: The oil must be hot enough or the dough won't puff correctly, but if the oil is too hot, the dough can easily burn because the sugar makes it extra sensitive to heat. After you make these once or twice, you'll get the hang of it. Whether or not they puff, these taste great and will be most appreciated by anyone you serve. I don't use a cast iron skillet to fry these, because I find the darker heat-retentive interior makes it more likely to cause the dough to scorch. These puffs are the ideal accompaniment to Lamb Curry (page 303) or Honey-Roast Chicken (page 252).

INGREDIENTS
2 cups unbleached all-purpose flour, plus flour for dusting

⅓ cup sugar

1½ teaspoons salt

1 tablespoon double-acting baking powder

⅔ to ¾ cup very warm tap water (almost hot)

Flavorless vegetable oil or light peanut oil

1) *To assemble dough:* In a large bowl, combine all ingredients except water and oil. Whisk to lighten and thoroughly mix. Sift into another bowl and sift again back into the original bowl. Slowly pour in the water, while using the fingertips of your other hand to blend the wet and dry ingredients.

Time Management Tips

• Although these puffs must be served as soon after draining as possible, you can combine and sift your dry mixture early in the day (or days before needed). Give the mixture a good swish with a whisk before adding water.

2) To knead dough: Begin to knead dough (inside the bowl) until it forms a mass. Turn out mass onto a lightly floured wooden board and continue to knead in a push, fold and turning motion until smooth, elastic, and not sticky. If necessary, as you work dough, lightly dust board with additional flour to prevent sticking. If dough sticks during kneading, use a pastry scraper to remove it cleanly from the board. Cover dough and allow it to rest and relax for 15 to 30 minutes. If desired, dough can rest up to 1 hour but it should be covered with ungreased plastic wrap to prevent a skin from forming.

3) To cut and roll dough: Using a pastry scraper, cut dough into 4 equal sections. Shape each section into a smooth ball and cover the remaining balls while you work with 1 at a time. Flatten 1 ball of dough and roll it out on a lightly floured board until 5 to 6 inches in diameter and about $\frac{1}{4}$ inch thick. Cut the circle of dough into 4 equal wedges and cover while you roll and cut the rest. When completed, you will have 16 pieces in all. (For specific rolling instructions to obtain a uniform round of dough, see Making Perfect Pie Pastry, page 93.)

4) To set up for frying: Line a tray or shallow baking sheet with a double thickness of paper toweling. Line a serving basket with a pretty napkin. Heat $\frac{1}{2}$ inch vegetable oil in a 10- to 12-inch skillet until 365°F. If not using a thermometer, the oil should shimmer but never smoke; add a small piece of bread and, if it quickly sizzles and turns golden, the oil is ready. Adjust oil while frying to avoid burning.

5) To fry: One at a time, ease some of the triangles (in batches) into the hot oil, allowing each to sit free without touching another. Within 30 seconds, the dough should begin to puff through the center (the size of each puff will vary). Cook on the first side for 1 or 2 minutes, then turn over triangles and fry on the other side until golden on both sides but not burnt, about 1 minute.

6) To drain and serve: Remove each batch and drain on prepared paper towels. Continue to fry the remaining triangles of dough and serve hot.

CHAPTER X

SWEET ENDINGS

For the Kid Who Lurks in All of Us

In this chapter, you'll find loads of delicious ways to splurge occasionally and satisfy your "gotta have it" cravings. These desserts are also guaranteed to bring a smile to your dinner guests—even the most stoic character at the table. You'll find decadent brownies (filled with creamy peanut butter), assorted ice creams, fresh fruit sorbets, old-fashioned fruit pies, melt-in-your-mouth cookies and voluptuous cakes. When possible (and deemed practical), I've provided low-fat tips to lighten things up a bit. But most often, these buttery old-time favorites should be prepared as written and enjoyed on special occasions—in moderation, of course.

From the unanimous approval of my family, friends and students, you can trust that the taste of these desserts is well worth any effort required. But as always, when a recipe seems unusually lengthy, please look to my Time Management Tips to reduce substantially your final preparation time.

COCONUT RASPBERRY CLOUD CAKE

YIELD: one 9-inch layer cake; serves 12

This light, tender cake resembles a giant coconut-covered marshmallow. The icing is a shiny, fluffy Italian meringue, which incorporates a hot, candied sugar syrup into beaten egg whites. If you choose to add the raspberry jam to the icing, the ultimate color of the cake will become a very subtle, soft pink under a sea of shredded coconut. Serve a wedge of this cake alone on a plate. It needs only a fork to be enjoyed as the perfect homey dessert.

INGREDIENTS

1 jar (12 ounces) seedless raspberry jam

FOR THE CAKE

Melted butter, for cake pans

3½ cups sifted cake flour (sifted before measuring), plus 2 tablespoons sifted cake flour for pans

1½ tablespoons double-acting baking powder

¾ teaspoon salt

2 sticks (½ pound) plus 3 tablespoons unsalted butter, at room temperature

2¼ cups superfine sugar

5 extra-large eggs, at room temperature, lightly beaten with a fork in a cup with a spout

2½ teaspoons pure vanilla extract

1⅓ cups milk

FOR THE RASPBERRY CLOUD ICING

3 extra-large egg whites, at room temperature

1 cup superfine sugar, for syrup, plus up to ⅓ cup for egg whites

⅓ cup water

2 tablespoons light corn syrup

¼ teaspoon cream of tartar

Pinch salt

1½ teaspoon pure vanilla extract

2 to 3 cups shredded sweetened coconut

SPECIAL EQUIPMENT

Two 9-inch cake pans (2 inches deep)

Parchment paper

Sifter or triple-mesh wire sieve

Electric mixer

1-quart heavy-bottomed saucepan, preferably with a spout

Candy thermometer

Long sharp serrated knife

Cardboard cake discs

Rotating cake stand

Icing spatula

Domed cake cover (6 inches high)

- The cake layers can be baked weeks in advance and frozen. To freeze, wrap each layer securely in aluminum foil and then seal in labeled, heavy-duty plastic bags. After 1 month, the cake will become progressively drier with each passing day from loss of moisture.

1) *To strain raspberry jam:* Push raspberry jam through a medium-mesh wire strainer placed over a small bowl and set aside. If you like, 2 tablespoons of this may be added to icing and the rest used to spread on the cake layers.

2) *To set up for cake layers:* Position the rack to the center of the oven and preheat oven to 350°F. Brush the interior of two 9-inch cake pans with melted butter. Line pans with rounds of parchment paper (page 440) and after greasing paper, lightly dust with flour.

3) *To prepare cake batter:* In a large bowl, whisk together the 3½ cups sifted cake flour, baking powder and salt. Sift mixture into another bowl and set aside. In the bowl of an electric mixer, beat softened butter until smooth and light. While beating on moderate speed, very gradually add sugar, beating as much air into the mixture as possible. Fully incorporate each addition of sugar before adding more (beating longer than you think necessary). When all the sugar has been incorporated and mixture is very light, drizzle in beaten eggs (only a little at a time), beating well after each addition. Add vanilla. Turn off machine and scrape the mixture up from the bottom of the bowl using a rubber spatula. Beat again until smooth. With the machine on low, add dry ingredients, alternating with milk. When just incorporated, turn off machine and scrape batter from the bottom and sides. Turn on machine to moderate and mix for 10 seconds. Remove bowl from machine.

4) *To bake, invert and cool:* Divide the mixture between the prepared cake pans, smoothing the tops. Lift each pan and gently rap on the counter once, to remove air pockets. Bake in preheated oven until a toothpick comes out clean when inserted into the center of the cake, about 35 minutes. Transfer to a wire rack for 10 minutes. Run the dull side of a knife around the edge of the pans and carefully invert onto a flat cardboard cake disc or another wire rack. Turn one of the cakes right side up, leaving the other bottom side up. Let both cakes cool thoroughly before assembling.

5) *To prepare icing:* Place egg whites into the (well cleaned and dried) non-reactive bowl of an electric mixer and place bowl in a skillet with 1 to 1½ inches of hot, not simmering, water. Place over low heat and whisk constantly as whites become warm to the touch. (This will happen almost immediately if the whites were at room temperature; be careful not to overheat, or the whites will cook.) Remove bowl from skillet and attach it to the electric mixer.

6) *To prepare sugar syrup:* In a small heavy-bottomed saucepan, combine the 1 cup sugar, the water and corn syrup. Using the thin stem of a wooden spoon, stir just until incorporated and place over medium heat until the mixture comes to a full boil. If using, attach a candy thermometer to the side of the pot (by the clip) so that the bottom tip of the stem doesn't touch the bottom. Boil until temperature reaches between 238°F and 240°F (the very end of the soft ball stage to the beginning of the firm ball stage). To test for this, if not using a candy thermometer, place a small bowl of ice water and a teaspoon next to the stove. As the sugar mixture boils viscously, check the consistency every minute by dropping a few drops of the boiling syrup into the ice water. When the syrup forms a mass that is soft and pliable but will almost hold its shape after being rolled into a ball, the mixture is ready. If this procedure is new to you, remove the syrup from the hot burner as you check to avoid overcooking.

7) *To complete icing:* While sugar mixture is boiling, set speed of your mixer to moderate and whip warm egg whites until frothy and beginning to turn white. Add cream of tartar and salt and raise speed to high. Slowly add more sugar (⅓ cup if not using optional 2 tablespoons jam or 3 rounded tablespoons if using jam) while continuing to beat until whites thicken and hold soft peaks. When sugar syrup has reached correct temperature, carefully pour it down the side of the bowl while whipping constantly at a moderately high speed. (Take care not to pour directly into the beaters or syrup will splatter onto the sides of the bowl and immediately harden into candy.) After all the syrup has been incorporated, add vanilla, raise speed to highest setting, and continue to beat mixture until very thick and the bottom of the bowl is thoroughly cool. By this time the whites will be very shiny, firm and spreadable, with a consistency of melted marshmallows. If you wish to add jam to the icing, beat in 2 tablespoon now. Turn off machine and remove bowl.

8) *To assemble and ice layers:* When the baked cakes are very cool, cut each horizontally into 2 even layers, as directed on page 440. Working first with the cake that's bottom side up, carefully separate the layers and place the bottom half on a flat cardboard cake disc (cut side up). Brush the entire cut surface thinly and evenly with strained jam. Using an icing spatula, spread a dollop of the icing in a thin, even layer on top of the jam (the icing will become swirled with jam). Place the remaining layer from the same cake (cut side down) on top of the icing. Spread as before with jam and icing. Place the bottom half of the remaining cake (cut side up) on top, spreading with jam and icing. Finally, cover with the remaining layer (cut side down), but don't apply any jam.

9) *To ice sides and top of cake:* Lightly ice sides of cake as directed below. Spread a more generous layer of the icing on top, swirling as you go. Take handfuls of shredded coconut and very generously coat the sides and top of the cake. Carefully brush any excess coconut off the exposed rim.

10) *To store:* Cover the assembled cake with a tall domed cake cover and store at room temperature.

TIPS
FROM A TEACHER

General Directions for Making Layer Cakes

To cut a perfect round of parchment paper to fit any size cake pan: Regardless of the size of your cake pan, the technique for cutting a perfect round of parchment liner is the same. Start with a 12- to 15-inch square of parchment paper. Fold in half and then fold it in half widthwise so you have a folded square half the size of the original. Lay the square on your work surface with the enclosed folded edges along the bottom and left side and make a triangle by folding the bottom right corner to meet the upper left corner. Then fold up the long side of the triangle to meet the top. Fold up bottom side to meet top once or twice again until you have a long thin spear. (Don't worry about the edges at the wide part of the wedge not meeting exactly; you will trim them off anyway.) Lay the wedge of paper on the bottom of your cake pan so the tip is positioned at the center. Mark with your finger where the wedge of paper meets the outer rim of the pan. Using sharp scissors, cut away any paper that extends past that point. Unfold the paper and you should have a round of parchment that will fit perfectly within the bottom interior of your pan. A 12-inch piece of parchment works for any size up to 12 inches, but it's preferable to use a sheet of paper larger than the pan's diameter.

To line a cake pan with parchment paper: Line the bottom of each buttered cake pan with a round of parchment paper and brush paper with

melted butter. Sprinkle some sifted cake flour on the buttered surface and tilt to coat pan evenly. Turn pan upside down and rap firmly over the edge of the sink to remove any excess flour so only a fine dusting remains.

To cut a baked cake into horizontal layers: Place baked cake on a rotating cake stand or on a cardboard cake disc to allow the cake to rotate while slicing. Place the tip of a long serrated knife ½ up from the bottom of cake (or ⅓ up if cutting into 3 layers) and make an incision. If not using a rotating cake stand, keep the bottom side of your cutting hand resting on the work surface so your hand will remain steady. Use a sawing motion to cut all around the layer going only an

inch or so in from the sides. As you cut, use your other hand to turn the cake from the top. When you arrive at the point where you made the first incision, go around again, cutting deeper toward the center. Repeat until you've cut through the center, then withdraw the blade. If cutting into 3 layers, repeat this procedure (going ⅔ up from the bottom).

To ice between layers and on the sides of a layer cake: Place the assembled cake (on its cardboard disc) onto a rotating cake stand. Cut several strips of aluminum foil or waxed paper 2 inches wide and carefully slip them between the cake and the disc, going all around the bottom of the cake. This will keep rim of the exposed cake disc

clean while applying the icing to the sides. Using a thin icing spatula, apply a thin even layer of icing between each cake layer. (Don't apply too much or the layers will slip and slide off each other.) Apply a thin layer of icing to the sides of the cake starting from the bottom, using an upward motion. Do not put too much icing on the sides or it will sink down to the bottom of the finished cake. Ice the top (you can be more generous here) and continue decorating cake as directed in recipe. Then carefully pull out the strips of paper leaving the edges of the cake disc clean.

CLASSIC GÉNOISE

With Pastry Cream and Assorted Fresh Fruit

YIELD: one 9-inch cake; serves 8

SPECIAL EQUIPMENT

9-inch cake pan (2 inches deep)

Parchment paper

Sifter or triple-mesh wire sieve

Small butter pot with a spout (optional)

Electric mixer

Long sharp serrated knife

Cardboard cake discs

Rotating cake stand

Icing spatula

Sugar shaker, preferably with a wire mesh top

Domed cake cover (6 inches high)

These tender layers of a simple French cake—sandwiched with luscious pastry cream laced with Grand Marnier and topped with an abundance of berries and fruit—create a dessert that looks as spectacular as it tastes. Although the "classically classic" version of génoise is not made with butter, many food professionals like myself feel that the butter not only gives it a richer taste and more tender texture, but helps to protect the cake from becoming dry. Also, if you choose, you can toast the melted butter by slowly bringing the color to a light golden brown—producing a cake with a deeper and nuttier flavor. If you choose to omit the butter, be a bit more generous when applying the sugar syrup to give the cake added moistness. When choosing fruits, in addition to berries, look for the small bunches of tiny purple grapes called "champagne grapes" and include them (cut into small clusters) with the berries for a fabulous presentation!

INGREDIENTS

1 recipe Vanilla Custard Cream (page 444), flavored with 1½ teaspoons pure vanilla extract, 1 to 2 tablespoons Grand Marnier or other orange-flavored liqueur and 2 teaspoons minced orange zest

FOR THE GÉNOISE

1 stick (¼ pound) unsalted butter, melted and cooled to lukewarm in a cup with a spout, plus more for greasing pan

4 extra-large eggs, at room temperature

¼ teaspoon salt

¾ cup superfine sugar

1 teaspoon pure vanilla extract

1 cup sifted cake flour (sifted before measuring), plus more for dusting

FOR THE SUGAR SYRUP

⅔ cup water

⅓ cup sugar

1 tablespoon pure vanilla extract or fresh strained orange juice

FOR THE FRUIT TOPPING

4 to 5 cups assorted whole or cut-up berries and other fruits
(blueberries, raspberries, fresh currants, champagne grapes,
hulled and quartered strawberries, sliced ripe plums)

Confectioner's sugar, for topping

Fresh mint sprigs, for garnish

1) *To make filling:* Prepare recipe for Vanilla Custard Cream as directed,
flavoring the cream with the 1½ teaspoons vanilla, 2 tablespoons Grand
Marnier and 2 teaspoons minced orange zest.

2) *To set up:* Brush a 9-inch cake pan with melted butter. As directed on
page 440, line the pan with parchment paper, butter and lightly dust with
sifted cake flour. Position the rack to the center of the oven and preheat
oven to 350°F.

3) *To prepare eggs for batter:* Crack eggs into the bowl of an electric mixer
and sit the bottom of the bowl in a skillet with 1 to 1½ inches of hot (not
simmering) water over low heat. Whisking constantly, add salt and then
sugar in a slow steady stream. Heat mixture until just warm to the touch
(which will happen very quickly if eggs were at room temperature).

4) *To assemble batter:* Attach the bowl to mixer with the whipping attachment and, while mixing at a moderate speed, add vanilla and beat mixture
until cold and very thick, shiny and light in color. (Take your time since
developing volume and lightness at this point will determine the overall
lightness of your baked génoise.) Lower speed and add lukewarm melted
butter alternating with sifted cake flour, beginning and ending with butter.
Do not overmix. When the mixture is combined, pour into the prepared
pan. Gently tap the bottom of the pan against the counter once or twice
to release any large air bubbles that could cause tunnels or holes in your
baked génoise.

5) *To bake:* Bake in the preheated oven until light golden and a toothpick
comes out clean when inserted into the center, about 30 minutes. Transfer
cake to a wire rack to cool for 10 to 15 minutes. Run a spatula or dull
knife around the sides of cake and place another wire rack or a flat cake
plate on top. Invert cake, remove pan and peel off parchment paper. Invert
once more, so the cake sits right side up and cool thoroughly on the rack.

Time Management Tips

- The pastry cream can be fully assembled 2
days ahead and kept securely covered in
the refrigerator.

- The génoise can be baked 1 day ahead
and kept moist (at room temperature) by
covering with plastic wrap and covering
once more with a domed cake cover.

- This cake also freezes perfectly for 1 month
if wrapped securely in aluminum foil and
sealed in a labeled heavy-duty plastic bag.
After 1 month, the cake will become progressively drier with each passing day from
loss of moisture.

- The cake can be assembled up to adding
fruits early in the day that you plan to serve
and kept refrigerated. Take out of the refrigerator 30 minutes or so before serving to
take off the chill.

- Assemble your fruits early in the day of
serving and keep each type separate in the
refrigerator well covered. Just before serving, fold the fruit together, spoon onto the
cake and garnish as directed.

6) *For the sugar syrup:* Combine water and sugar in a small saucepan and swirl to help dissolve sugar. Bring mixture just to a boil, remove from heat and stir in vanilla or orange juice. Let cool.

7) *To assemble layers:* Slice cooled cake into 3 equal layers as directed on page 441. Carefully remove the top 2 layers and place on your work surface. Insert a cardboard cake disc under the bottom layer and, using a pastry brush, gently "dab" (not brush) the layer with some of the prepared sugar syrup to lightly moisten the top. Spread a thin layer of chilled pastry cream on top of the moistened cake. Top with the middle cake layer and apply sugar syrup and pastry cream. Then place the remaining layer on top (cut side down). Apply some more sugar syrup on cake and spread another (more generous) layer of pastry cream on top. Lay a sheet of waxed paper lightly over the last custard layer and cover with a domed cake cover until ready to serve.

8) *To serve:* Using a slotted spoon, pile the assorted fruits on top of the pastry cream mounding nicely. Sift a generous amount of confectioner's sugar on top of the fruit and garnish with fresh mint. Present the cake fully assembled and slice into individual wedges at the table.

Vanilla Custard Cream

YIELD: about 3 cups

SPECIAL EQUIPMENT
Electric mixer

Although many recipes use flour alone to thicken pastry cream, I feel that cornstarch gives the custard a smoother, less pasty texture on the tongue. And although some do, I don't recommend freezing pastry cream since the texture definitely loses something after thawing. If you find that you're left with some leftover cream, store it in the refrigerator and before serving, lighten it by folding in softly whipped heavy cream or crème fraîche; serve in a balloon wine glass with mixed fresh berries. The Grand Marnier is optional but lends itself beautifully to both desserts using pastry cream in this book. If you choose to omit it, however, use the larger amount of vanilla.

INGREDIENTS

¼ cup cornstarch

1½ cups milk

1 cup heavy cream (preferably not ultrapasteurized)

1 plump vanilla bean

6 extra-large egg yolks, at room temperature

1 extra-large whole egg

⅔ cup vanilla sugar (page 74) or granulated white sugar

½ stick (4 tablespoons) unsalted butter, cut into 4 pieces

¼ teaspoon salt

1½ teaspoons to 1 tablespoon pure vanilla extract

1 to 2 tablespoons Grand Marnier or other orange-flavored liqueur
  (optional)

2 teaspoons minced orange zest (optional)

1) *Set up to strain cooked custard:* Set a medium-mesh wire sieve in a
3-quart mixing bowl and place close to the stove.

2) *To prepare cornstarch and cream mixture:* Use a whisk to break up
lumps in cornstarch before measuring over a sheet of waxed paper.
Combine milk and cream in a measuring cup. Pour ⅔ cup of this mixture
into another cup, stir in cornstarch and set aside. Pour the remaining milk
mixture into a 2½-quart heavy-bottomed saucepan. Cut vanilla bean in
half (widthwise) and run the tip of a small sharp knife gently down the
length of one half, opening only 1 side of the bean. Spread bean wide open
and use the dull side of the knife to scrape down the length of the bean,
removing the seeds. Place seeds in saucepan with cream mixture and gently whisk to disperse seeds throughout. Heat milk and cream mixture over
medium-low heat until tiny bubbles form around the edge of the pot.

3) *To combine eggs with cream for filling:* Place egg yolks and whole egg
into the bowl of an electric mixer. Place bottom of bowl in a skillet with
1½ inches of hot tap water over low heat and whisk constantly to warm
yolks until just warm to the touch. (Watch out—this happens quickly.)
Place bowl of warm yolks onto the mixer with the whipping attachment.
With the machine on medium, whip yolks while gradually adding sugar
until very thick and light. Then add cornstarch mixture and combine well,
stopping occasionally to scrape down the sides and up from the bottom of
the bowl as necessary. With mixer on low, pour about ½ cup of

Q and A

Q. Why must I stir constantly while cooking a mixture with eggs?

A. *Most mixtures made with eggs are extremely sensitive to heat and if you don't stir constantly, you risk overheating the mixture and curdling the eggs. Although a recipe that includes cornstarch or flour changes the chemistry of the eggs so that they are no longer susceptible to curdling, the mixture must still be stirred continually to prevent the formation of lumps and scorching on the bottom from uneven heat exposure.*

the hot cream mixture into the whipped yolks. When the mixture is combined and warmed throughout, mix in the remaining hot cream mixture. When combined, pour contents of bowl back into the saucepan and return to medium heat. Bring the mixture to a slow boil, stirring constantly with a whisk. Then reduce heat to low and, using a wooden spoon, stir mixture constantly until thickened, 2 to 3 minutes.

4) *To complete and chill filling:* Pour hot egg-cream mixture through strainer (without scraping the mixture that clings to the bottom of the pot). Remove strainer and stir in butter, 1 tablespoon at a time, stirring to blend well before adding the next piece. Add salt, vanilla and, if using, Grand Marnier and minced zest. Place bowl on a wire rack and lay a piece of heat-resistant plastic wrap directly on top of the cream to prevent a skin from forming. Cool until just warm, then place in the refrigerator to chill thoroughly before using. (The mixture will become substantially thicker after refrigeration.)

Variations to Pastry Cream

If using pastry cream to fill a fruit tart, vary your flavorings to complement your choice of fruit. Following are some wonderful combinations. In each case, reduce the vanilla extract to 1½ teaspoons and add 1 to 2 tablespoons of: Armagnac for a plum tart; bourbon or dark rum for apples or pears; framboise for raspberries, plums, strawberries; kirsch for cherries; amaretto for apricots; Grand Marnier for any fruit, but particularly strawberries.

CARROT CAKE ICED WITH CREAM CHEESE

And Lavished with Toasted Coconut

YIELD: one 9-inch cake; serves 12

Tall and amber colored, this moist cake has a rustic, countryish look. The intense flavor of its thick, toasted coconut coating gives this dessert its extra special taste. Be careful though; coconut can easily burn while toasting. Although this cake needs to be refrigerated because of the cream cheese icing, it's best to remove it from the refrigerator at least one hour before serving to enjoy fully the flavor and texture. Leftover cake will taste great for up to one week if refrigerated well covered with a domed cake cover (you'll need a tall one for this cake.)

SPECIAL EQUIPMENT

Electric mixer

Food processor or chef's knife, for carrots

Two 9-inch cake pans (2 inches deep)

Parchment paper

Sifter or triple-mesh wire sieve

Long sharp serrated knife

Cardboard cake discs

Rotating cake stand

Icing spatula

Domed cake cover (6 inches high)

FOR THE CREAM CHEESE ICING

16 ounces cream cheese, at room temperature

1 stick (¼ pound) unsalted butter, at room temperature

3 tablespoons sour cream or Classic Crème Fraîche (page 83)

1 teaspoon pure vanilla extract

2½ cups sifted confectioner's sugar (sifted before measuring)

FOR THE CAKE

6 or 7 medium-sized carrots, peeled and thinly sliced

Salt as needed

⅔ cup mixed light and dark raisins

3 tablespoons dark rum

Melted butter, for baking pan

4 to 5 cups sweetened shredded coconut

3½ cups sifted cake flour (do not use self-rising flour; and sift before measuring), plus more flour for dusting pan

2½ teaspoons double-acting baking powder

1 teaspoon baking soda

1 tablespoon ground cinnamon

4 extra-large eggs

½ cup unsulphured molasses*

2 cups firmly packed dark brown sugar

1¼ cups flavorless vegetable oil

Time Management Tips

- Make cream cheese icing 1 or 2 days ahead, cover well and keep refrigerated.

- Toast coconut up to 3 days ahead and keep well covered at room temperature.

- The cake layers can be baked weeks in advance and frozen. To freeze, wrap each layer securely in aluminum foil and then seal in labeled heavy-duty plastic bags. After 1 month, the cake will become progressively drier with each passing day.

½ cup sour cream

1 tablespoon pure vanilla extract

1 can (8 ounces) unsweetened crushed pineapple, well drained

½ cup chopped walnuts or pecans

* See section on Staples

1) To prepare icing: In the bowl of an electric mixer, cream together cream cheese and softened butter until very smooth. Add sour cream and vanilla and mix well until totally free of lumps. Beat in confectioner's sugar, mixing until silky looking. Cover well and refrigerate.

2) To prepare carrots and raisins: In a medium-sized saucepan, cook carrots in lightly salted boiling water until tender, about 10 minutes. Drain and place in the bowl of a food processor fitted with the steel blade. Process until finely chopped but not quite puréed. Measure out 2 packed cups and set aside. Alternatively, use a chef's knife to chop cooked carrots finely. Heat raisins with rum in a small saucepan over low heat until raisins are warm and plumped and the rum is almost totally absorbed, about 2 minutes. Set aside.

3) To set up: Preheat the oven to 350°F. Butter two 9-inch cake pans (2 inches deep); as directed on page 440, line pans with parchment paper, butter and lightly dust with flour. Measure out 1 cup packed coconut and reserve for cake batter. Toast the remaining coconut as directed on page 474 and set aside for topping.

4) To assemble cake batter: In a large mixing bowl, whisk together sifted cake flour with baking powder, baking soda, cinnamon and 1 scant teaspoon of the salt until well combined and lightened. Place eggs, molasses and brown sugar into the bowl of an electric mixer and beat until well combined. Add sour cream, vanilla and vegetable oil and mix until smooth. Mix in the reserved cup of untoasted coconut and drained crushed pineapple. Scrape the bottom of the bowl to release any clinging brown sugar and mix again. Add reserved raisins (with any remaining rum), reserved chopped carrots, and walnuts. When well mixed, turn machine to its lowest setting and add reserved flour mixture, combining gently but thoroughly.

5) **To bake:** Divide batter between the prepared cake pans and smooth top with a spatula. Bake in the center of preheated oven (1½ inches apart) until a toothpick comes out clean when inserted into the center, 45 to 55 minutes. Place pans on a wire rack for 5 minutes.

6) **To invert cakes:** Run a table knife around the edge of each cake and place another wire rack or flat plate on top of one cake. Turn upside down, remove cake pan and peel off parchment. Place original rack back on top of cake and invert once more so the rounded top is facing up. Invert the other cake once, leaving the bottom side up on a wire rack. Cool thoroughly before applying icing.

7) **To assemble and ice layers:** Slice each cooled cake in half horizontally as directed on page 441. Working first with the upside-down cake, carefully separate layers. Place the top flat-bottomed layer (cut side up) on a cardboard cake disc and spread a thin even layer of icing on top. Don't apply too much icing or the layers will slip and slide off each other. Then carefully lay the other half of cake on top of the icing (cut side down) and spread with a thin layer of icing. Separate layers of the other cake and place the flat-bottomed half on top of the last layer of icing (cut side up) and apply a thin layer of icing on top. Finally, lay the top of the cake (rounded side up) on top but don't apply any icing.

8) **To ice sides and garnish cake:** Ice the sides of the cake as directed on page 441. Ice the top more generously and when the entire surface of the cake is covered with icing, firmly, but gently press toasted coconut onto the icing, covering the entire cake. The cake should be very generously coated with toasted coconut.

9) **To serve:** If not serving within a couple of hours, refrigerate cake under a high cake dome. For best texture and flavor, remove the cake from the refrigerator 1 to 2 hours before serving. When entertaining, present the cake whole and cut into individual wedges at the table.

OODLES OF BLUEBERRIES
DOUBLE-CRUST PIE

YIELD: one 9-inch double-crusted pie; serves 6

SPECIAL EQUIPMENT
9-inch pie plate or tart pan with removable bottom

Parchment paper, only if using a tart pan with a removable bottom

Food processor or blender

Fine-mesh wire sieve

Every July, my whole gang and I set out on a blueberry expedition. (One year we picked twenty-eight pounds of blueberries—that's not counting the hundreds of berries that found a home in my children's bellies.) Needless to say, I always spend the next three days making everything possible with blueberries and I inevitably prepare this blueberry filling topped and cradled within a perfectly thin and flaky pastry crust. If at all possible, go to a fruit orchard at the peak of season. It's not only fun, but truly educational for the whole family. And if you still have too many blueberries, it's easy to flash-freeze them (page 430). Serve this pie with a scoop of Old-Fashioned Vanilla Ice Cream (page 497) or a spoonful of lightly sweetened Perfect Whipped Cream (page 84).

FOR THE CRUST

Melted unsalted butter, if using pan with removable bottom

Double recipe Favorite Pie Pastry (page 93), using double-crust instructions

Waterproofing glaze: 1 tablespoon seedless raspberry jam or red currant jelly

FOR THE FILLING

6 cups blueberries, lightly rinsed, picked over and drained

1 tablespoon strained fresh lemon juice

3 tablespoons cornstarch

1⅓ to 1½ cups sugar

3 tablespoons unsalted butter, diced

Egg wash: 1 egg mixed with 1 teaspoon water

1 tablespoon sugar or vanilla sugar (page 74), for topping

1) **To prepare shell and top crust:** If using a tart pan with a removable bottom, lightly brush the fluted sides of the pan with butter and line the bottom disc with a round of parchment paper as directed on page 440. Mix and roll out dough and *partially* prebake bottom crust as directed in recipe. Roll out and chill top crust and cut out decorative shapes as directed in the variation.

2) **To waterproof pastry shell:** In a small saucepan, melt jam over low heat until liquified. When pastry is cool, paint melted jam over the interior of the shell and set aside.

3) **To set up for baking:** Place a shallow baking sheet on the center rack of the oven and preheat oven to 425°F.

4) **To prepare filling:** Combine 1 cup of the blueberries with lemon juice in a food processor fitted with the steel blade and process until puréed. (If necessary, use a blender.) Pour purée into a fine strainer placed over a mixing bowl and push through mesh using a wooden spatula. Stir in cornstarch and then fold in the remaining 5 cups of blueberries. Add sugar, adjusting the amount to the desired sweetness. Combine well and set aside.

5) **To assemble pie:** Push egg wash through a medium-mesh sieve to remove excess coagulation. Pour blueberry filling into the partially prebaked pie shell and dot with diced butter. Roll up the chilled top crust loosely on a rolling pin and carefully unroll dough on top of the filling. Press to seal the top dough to the bottom rim, crimping decoratively. Brush all exposed pastry with egg glaze. Arrange the chilled decorative cutouts on top of the pie and brush the shapes and the top once more with glaze. Sprinkle the top generously with sugar.

6) **To bake:** Place pie onto the hot baking sheet and bake 30 minutes. Reduce oven temperature to 375°F and bake an additional 30 minutes, covering pie loosely with aluminum foil (shiny side up) if the top is getting overly brown. Place pie on a wire rack to cool.

7) **To serve:** Serve pie cut into wedges, either slightly warm or at room temperature.

Q. Why are the bottom crusts of my fruit pies always soggy?

A. If you've been disappointed with the mushy quality in the bottom crust of your double-crust fruit pies, it's probably because you've used the more traditional method of filling an unbaked pastry shell. To me, a mushy crust is like eating a soggy French roll; pie crust, bottom or top, should always be crisp. To assure best results, always partially prebake your bottom crust and once cool, seal the interior by painting on a small amount of melted jelly or strained preserves.

MILE-HIGH LEMON-ORANGE MERINGUE PIE

YIELD: one 9-inch pie; serves 6

This homey-looking dessert acquires a sophisticated accent from its crisp crust painted with puréed orange marmalade and its creamy not-too-tart, not-too-sweet lemon-orange filling. When assembling the filling, it's easier to remove the citrus zest before you halve the fruit to extract the juice. Ideally, for best texture and appearance, this gorgeous pie should be assembled not more than three hours ahead and kept at room temperature until serving. Although leftovers may be refrigerated, this does tend to toughen the meringue and cause it to develop a shriveled and somewhat shrunken appearance.

SPECIAL EQUIPMENT

9-inch pie plate or tart pan with removable bottom

Mini food processor or blender, to purée marmalade

Domed cake cover (6 inches high)

FOR THE PASTRY SHELL

1½ cups all-purpose flour

1 tablespoon sugar

¼ teaspoon salt

1 stick (¼ pound) cold unsalted butter, cut into small dice

¼ to ⅓ cup ice water

Waterproofing glaze: 1 to 2 tablespoons smoothly puréed orange marmalade

FOR THE CITRUS FILLING

⅓ cup cornstarch

1¼ cups superfine sugar

1 teaspoon finely minced lemon zest

1 teaspoon finely minced orange zest

½ cup strained fresh lemon juice

½ cup strained fresh orange juice

1 cup water

3 extra-large egg yolks

3 tablespoons cold unsalted butter

FOR THE MERINGUE

6 extra-large egg whites, at room temperature

½ teaspoon cream of tartar

Pinch salt

¾ cup superfine sugar

1 teaspoon pure vanilla extract

Time Management Tips

• The filling can be made 1 day ahead and stored in the refrigerator.

1) **To prepare pastry shell:** Using the preceding ingredients, mix and roll out dough and *totally* prebake shell as directed in the recipe for Favorite Pie Pastry (page 93). While baked pie shell is cooling, prepare glaze by melting puréed marmalade with only a few droplets of water over low heat until liquified. Paint the interior of the cooled crust with the glaze and allow it to set.

2) **To prepare citrus-cornstarch mixture:** Use a whisk to break up lumps in the cornstarch before measuring over a sheet of waxed paper. In a medium-sized bowl, whisk together sugar and cornstarch until very smooth. In another bowl, combine lemon and orange zests and juices with the water. Whisk this mixture into the sugar-cornstarch until smooth.

3) **To add egg yolks to filling:** Place a medium-mesh wire sieve over a medium-sized mixing bowl and place next to the stove. In a small bowl, lightly mix egg yolks with a fork. Pour citrus-cornstarch mixture into a 2½-quart heavy-bottomed saucepan and stir constantly over medium-low heat as mixture comes to a simmer. Continue to cook and stir until thickened, 1 to 2 minutes. Whisk about ¼ of the thickened mixture into the bowl with the egg yolks. Then stir this mixture back into the saucepan and simmer over low heat, stirring constantly with a wooden spoon, for 2 minutes. When mixture is smooth and thick, pour through the sieve, pushing it through with a wooden spatula. Stir in butter 1 tablespoon at a time, stirring to blend fully before the next piece is added. Stir mixture until very smooth and place a piece of heat-resistant plastic wrap directly on the surface to prevent a skin from forming. Place the bowl on a wire rack and when no longer hot, refrigerate to chill thoroughly.

4) **To make meringue:** Ideally, not more than 3 hours before serving, prepare meringue. Preheat the oven to 425°F. Break egg whites into the non-reactive bowl of an electric mixer. Place bowl in a skillet with an inch or more of hot tap water and whisk over low heat until whites are just warm to the touch—this will happen quickly. Attach bowl of warm egg whites

onto the mixer. Beat on medium speed until whites become frothy and begin to whiten; add cream of tartar and salt, then slowly add sugar, beating continuously. When sugar is fully incorporated, increase speed to high and beat until whites triple in volume and develop a deep shine. Add vanilla just as they are about to become stiff. Turn off mixer several times while whipping to check for consistency: Remove whipping element and turn whip up. If whites form a peak that stands up straight, your texture is correct, but if peak curves down, whip a few more seconds at high speed and check again.

TIPS
FROM A TEACHER

All About Eggs

Buying and storing eggs: Although it feels homey to buy eggs from a farmers market where the cartons are sitting on a warm counter next to inviting fruits and vegetables, it's not wise to do so. Eggs kept at room temperature for one day will age as rapidly as a refrigerated egg ages in one week! Never wash or even wipe your eggs before storing since you will remove their protective waxy covering, which helps to prevent strong odors of other foods from penetrating the porous egg shells. Any eggs with cracks should be thrown out as these are more likely to have been mishandled during shipping and could be contaminated with bacteria. To maintain a constant temperature, store eggs in their original carton in the coldest part of the refrigerator (bottom shelf) and not in the "egg tray" on the refrigerator door.

The question of room temperature: Most baking recipes request that eggs be at room temperature because it's better to whip the whites and cream the yolks when they are not chilled. (Your whipped whites will be more voluminous and your cake batters will be much lighter.) But conversely, eggs are much easier to separate when they are cold. The yolk has a protective translucent skin (which keeps it separate in the shell) and the white is heavy and very gelatinous. These qualities make it easy for the weighty egg white to fall naturally away from the yolk when you separate them. But as the egg warms to room temperature, the gelatinous quality of the white becomes watery and thin (perfect for whipping) and the protective skin around the yolk melts away, encouraging it to "bleed" into the white while separating the two. So it's always best to separate eggs when chilled and then bring up their temperature for beating and creaming. Since eggs are highly perishable, it's best not to leave them out at room

5) **To assemble pie:** Using a rubber spatula, spread filling in the prepared pie shell. Using a clean rubber spatula, spread meringue around the border of the pastry and filling which will "seal" meringue to pastry. Pile remaining meringue onto the center of the filling and, using the spatula, cover the entire filling by using a dipping motion to create deep valleys and beautiful peaks in the meringue.

6) **To bake:** Place pie in preheated oven for about 5 minutes, until the tips are toasted and the rest of the meringue is a light golden color (check every 2 minutes). Place on a wire rack to cool. Cover with a domed cake cover and let sit at room temperature until serving. Cut into wedges.

temperature for hours to "temp up." Instead, after separating the yolks from the whites, bring each up to tepid (warm to the touch) by placing the bowl containing each (one at a time) in a skillet of hot, not simmering, water over very low heat while whisking constantly.

To separate eggs: Place three bowls on your counter (preferably one with a thin rim for cracking the eggs). Crack a chilled egg against the rim of a bowl to create one neat split. Cradle the egg in the fingers of both hands over one bowl, turn egg (cracked side up) and insert the tips of your thumb nails into the split. Carefully open the shell allowing some of the white to fall out and into the bowl. Then tilt egg to one side as you completely open the shell encouraging the yolk to sit inside one half of the shell. Dump any white from the other half into the bowl and carefully transfer the yolk back and forth from shell to shell, allowing any remaining white to fall into the bowl. (If the egg shell didn't split evenly and one side is too small to accommodate the yolk, pour the whole egg onto the fingers of one hand and allow the white to slip through your fingers and into the bowl.) Place the yolk into another bowl and, if the separation was successful and there are no traces of yolk in the whites, pour the pure egg white into the third (empty) bowl. If any yolk should drip into the egg white, discard that white and wipe out the bowl before trying again.

To whip egg whites: Before placing egg whites into the whipping bowl, make sure that both the bowl and the beating element are immaculate. Also, it's best to warm the whites in a shallow hot-water bath (above) to encourage them to lose all trace of coagulation before whipping. This way, the thin and watery whites are better able to incorporate the air necessary to form the millions of tiny bubbles that make up those white fluffy clouds when whipped. The sugar not only sweetens the meringue but also acts as a stabilizer, as do cream of tartar and salt. As for consistency, it's always better to underwhip your whites slightly than to overbeat them into a dull, dry, broken mass. If by chance this should happen, add another tepid white or two, and give it another go with the mixer. Cream of tartar is helpful to stabilize and build volume in egg whites while whipping. However, if you choose to use a copper bowl and whip your egg whites manually with a balloon whisk, omit the cream of tartar since the chemical reaction between it and the copper will cause the whites to take on a greenish tinge. (Since copper itself is a stabilizer, cream of tartar is not needed.) Also, aluminum bowls turn egg whites gray. So, always use a non-metallic or a stainless steel bowl when using cream of tartar.

DEEP-DISH CARAMELIZED APPLE TART

YIELD: one 10-inch tart; serves 8 to 10

SPECIAL EQUIPMENT

10-inch deep-dish fluted tart pan with removable bottom

Large nonreactive mixing bowl

Sturdy fruit wedge cutter (optional)

10- to 12-inch nonreactive deep-sided skillet

Nutmeg grater (optional)

Electric mixer

1-quart heavy-bottomed saucepan with light-colored interior (enamel-coated cast iron works best)

Domed cake cover (6 inches high)

Whether I'm teaching a class or entertaining, this gorgeous tart brings more ohs and ahs than any other. Its deep, crisp shell is filled with sautéed spiced apples studded with raisins and bathed in a sweetened cream cheese mixture. Then it's topped with a candied, caramel-nut mixture. When this tart leaves the oven, it's truly a sight to behold! As with most tarts, for best texture and flavor, this should be assembled and baked the day of serving. However, by making the pastry dough in advance (or even rolling the dough, lining the tart shell and freezing it), you can reduce substantially the overall assembly time. And feel free to use this filling (omitting the caramel topping) in a double-crust pie. Follow the directions in Oodles of Blueberries Double-Crust Pie (page 450), using a deep-dish pie plate to accommodate the entire apple filling. Serve with Perfect Whipped Cream (page 84) or a small scoop of Old-Fashioned Vanilla Ice Cream (page 497).

FOR THE TART SHELL

1 recipe Favorite Pie Pastry (page 93), using deep-dish instructions

Waterproofing glaze: ¼ cup apple jelly, melted over low heat

FOR THE FILLING

Strained juice from 1½ lemons

8 large apples (combination of Granny Smith and Golden Delicious)

½ stick (4 tablespoons) unsalted butter

1 teaspoon ground cinnamon

½ teaspoon ground nutmeg (preferably freshly grated)

8 ounces cream cheese, at room temperature

1 tablespoon sour cream or Classic Crème Fraiche (page 83)

⅓ cup firmly packed dark brown sugar

⅓ cup granulated white sugar

1 extra-large egg

1 teaspoon pure vanilla extract

½ cup unbleached all-purpose flour

½ cup mixed light and dark raisins

FOR THE CARAMEL-NUT TOPPING

¼ cup water

1 cup granulated white sugar

3 tablespoons unsalted butter

¼ cup heavy cream (preferably not ultrapasteurized)

½ teaspoon pure vanilla extract

Rounded ⅓ cup coarsely chopped walnuts

Boiling water, as needed during baking

1) *To prepare tart shell:* Mix and roll out dough as directed in recipe and deep-dish instructions; *partially* prebake shell. Push melted apple jelly through a medium-mesh wire strainer into a small bowl. Paint interior of the cooled pastry shell with jelly and allow it to set for a few minutes before assembling tart.

2) *To set up for baking:* Position the oven rack to the center shelf. Line a shallow baking sheet with aluminum foil (dull side up) and place on oven rack. Preheat the oven to 375°F.

3) *To sauté apples:* Pour strained lemon juice into a large nonreactive bowl. Peel, core and slice each apple into 8 wedges and immediately toss wedges in lemon juice. Melt butter in a 10- to 12-inch deep-sided nonreactive skillet and, when butter is bubbling, add apple slices and toss with hot butter. Stir in cinnamon and nutmeg and cook over medium heat just to soften apples and awaken spices, about 8 minutes. Remove from heat.

4) *To prepare filling:* In an electric mixer, cream the cream cheese with sour cream and brown and white sugars until light, creamy and free of lumps. Add vanilla and egg and beat until smooth. Pour sautéed apples and pan juices into the large bowl and stir in the cream cheese mixture and raisins. Add flour and fold the mixture together until well combined.

5) *To assemble and bake:* Spoon filling into prepared tart shell, mounding apples up high in the center. While filling, tilt the shell a few times so cream cheese mixture distributes evenly throughout the apples. Place filled tart pan on the baking sheet in the preheated oven and bake for 35 minutes.

Q AND A

Q. When you use aluminum foil during baking, why do you specify that the shiny side of the foil be up or down?

A. Aluminum foil helps to prevent baked foods from becoming overly dark on top before the interior is sufficiently cooked. Laying a piece of foil loosely over the top of the food with the shiny side up deflects heat from the top while the food cooks from the bottom. Using foil as a liner on a baking sheet saves some work when cleaning the sheet after cooking; place the dull side up so you don't deflect heat from the food being cooked.

Apple-Picking Time

In many parts of North America, autumn is apple season and local orchards are bursting with gorgeous specimens just waiting to be picked! An apple-picking excursion is ideal for doing something fun as a whole family. Also, picking or purchasing apples during their season of abundance enables you to acquire them in bulk at a good price.

6) **To prepare caramel-nut topping:** Halfway through the baking process, prepare caramel-nut topping. Place the ¼ cup water, then sugar in 1-quart heavy-bottomed saucepan. Boil down to form a caramel syrup as directed on page 472. (This procedure takes 5 to 10 minutes; stay close by because, once you smell the savory aroma of caramel, the syrup will color quickly.) When syrup reaches a deep amber color, remove pan from heat and add butter and cream. The mixture will bubble up furiously and then settle down. Stir in nuts and vanilla.

7) **To apply topping to tart and finish baking:** Fill a small heat-resistant bowl with some of the boiling water and place a teaspoon in the water. Remove baking sheet from oven and pour caramel-nut mixture over apples, covering as evenly as possible. Return sheet with tart to oven and reduce temperature to 350°F. Bake another 30 minutes. As the caramel drizzles down the sides of the tart pan and forms puddles on the bottom of the baking sheet, every 5 to 10 minutes, using the hot spoon, pick up the fallen syrup and baste apples. (Immediately return spoon to the cup of hot water; otherwise syrup will harden to the spoon.) Remove baking sheet from oven and carefully transfer tart (by its sides) to a wire rack to cool in tart pan for 2 hours.

8) **To release tart pan:** Carefully run the tip of a small sharp knife between the crust and the the fluted rim of the tart pan. Using both hands, lift tart and, with your fingers, gently push the removable bottom disc upwards. Keep tart on the disc and place on a rack to cool. Then cover with a domed cake cover until serving time.

9) **To serve:** Before serving, remove tart from the bottom disc by carefully inserting a very thin (completely flat) cookie sheet between the tart and the disc. Once removed, gently push tart onto your serving plate. Serve tart at room temperature or only slightly warmed. Slice into wedges with the suggested accompaniments listed in the introduction to this recipe. (If you overheat this tart before serving, the deep-dish sides can collapse.)

Reduced-Fat Variation

When sautéing apples, substitute 2 to 4 tablespoons unsweetened apple juice for half or all the butter. When making the filling, substitute ¾ cup Low-Fat Cream Cheese (page 82) for regular cream cheese and substitute 1 tablespoon Skinny Crème Fraîche (page 84) for Classic Crème Fraîche or sour cream.

EASY PUMPKIN PIE WITH CANDIED PECANS

YIELD: one 10-inch pie; serves 8

When I was teaching a group of Japanese women to prepare a traditional American Thanksgiving, this was the dessert on the menu. It was very exciting for me to expose them to the taste of pumpkin for the first time! Each one savored every bite of this sensational, but not overly sweet pie. You might have seen us cooking away that day since the class was taped and broadcast on the CBS "This Morning" show! Since this special dessert is usually saved for the holidays, I never alter the full ingredients to assure the richest flavor. The maple syrup and maple extract (usually available at specialty gourmet shops) gives it a special early American touch.

SPECIAL EQUIPMENT
10-inch pie plate

Nutmeg grater (optional)

FOR THE PIE SHELL
1 recipe Favorite Pie Pastry (page 93)
Waterproofing glaze: 1 tablespoon melted apple jelly

FOR THE FILLING
1 can (16 ounces) pure pumpkin (not pumpkin pie mix)
½ cup sour cream
½ cup packed light brown sugar
¼ cup granulated white sugar
⅓ cup pure maple syrup
5 extra-large eggs, lightly beaten with a fork
1 cup heavy cream (preferably not ultrapastuerized)
1 teaspoon ground cinnamon
1 teaspoon ground ginger
1 teaspoon ground nutmeg (preferably freshly grated)
¼ teaspoon ground cloves
Pinch salt
1 teaspoon pure vanilla extract
½ teaspoon maple extract or an additional ½ teaspoon vanilla extract

FOR THE TOPPING
¼ cup light corn syrup
6 tablespoons pure maple syrup

1 tablespoon packed light brown sugar

3 tablespoons unsalted butter

1 teaspoon pure vanilla extract

1 generous cup perfect pecan halves

FOR ACCOMPANIMENT

Perfect Whipped Cream (page 84)

1) ***To prepare pie shell:*** Mix and roll out dough and *partially* prebake as directed in recipe. Push apple jelly through a medium-mesh wire strainer into a small bowl. Paint the interior of the cooled pastry shell with jelly and allow it to set for a few minutes before assembling the pie.

2) ***To prepare filling, assemble and bake pie:*** Line a shallow baking sheet with aluminum foil (dull side up). Position the oven rack to the center shelf and place baking sheet on the rack. Preheat the oven to 350°F. To prepare filling, combine all filling ingredients (in the order given) in a large bowl and stir until very smooth. Pour filling into prepared pie shell and carefully transfer to baking sheet in the preheated oven. Bake for 40 minutes.

3) ***To prepare topping:*** While pie bakes, combine all topping ingredients (except vanilla and pecans) in a small saucepan. Bring to a gentle boil and cook over medium heat until mixture thickens slightly, 3 to 5 minutes. Remove from heat and stir in vanilla and pecans. Let become cool enough to handle.

4) ***To top with pecans:*** Remove baked pie (on baking sheet) from oven, but don't turn off. Place baking sheet on a wire rack and arrange the candied pecans in 2 rows around the edge of the pie in a decorative border. They look particularly nice when placed vertically from the rim, pointing toward the center of the pie. Reserve any unused pecans to use if necessary after baking.

5) *To finish baking:* Return pie (still on baking sheet) to the oven and bake until the center is no longer "concave" looking, about 20 minutes. (If rim of crust is becoming overly brown, pull up foil from baking sheet and loosely cover rim.) Remove to a wire rack to cool. The pie will appear puffed when leaving the oven but will settle down as it cools. If a small crack appears on top, just place some reserved candied pecans decoratively over it.

6) *To serve:* Serve this pie the same day of baking either slightly chilled or at room temperature with a dollop of lightly sweetened whipped cream. Store leftovers in the refrigerator.

PRUNE AND TOASTED ALMOND TART

YIELD: one 10-inch tart; serves 8

If you think that prunes only should be eaten stewed for breakfast, you'll change your mind with this recipe! This chewy and candied tart oozes with incredible flavor and texture. In fact, it's my favorite tart in the world! In the supermarket, prunes are packaged in several ways: in a box, a carton, a foil pouch or in a vacuum-packed can labeled "premium" prunes. These are very plump, moist and most appropriate for this recipe (I prefer the Sunsweet brand). If premium prunes are not available, the next best choice are those in foil pouches; although smaller, they are also very moist. But if only regular dried prunes are available, plump them as directed in this recipe. For best texture and flavor, this tart should be served the same day it's baked. When assembling, be sure to line the bottom of your tart pan with parchment paper and lightly butter the tart ring or you'll be in trouble when you try to release the candied tart from the pan.

SPECIAL EQUIPMENT
Parchment paper

10-inch tart pan with removable bottom

FOR THE TART SHELL

1 recipe Favorite Pie Pastry (page 93)

Melted butter, for tart pan

Waterproofing glaze: 1 tablespoon apricot jam or preserves mixed with 1 scant teaspoon water

FOR THE FILLING

3 cups extra-moist dried pitted prunes (vacuum packed or foil packed), sliced in half

3 tablespoons unsalted butter, cut into small dice

1 cup heavy cream (preferably not ultrapasteurized)

1 cup sugar

½ scant teaspoon almond extract

2 tablespoons amaretto (almond-flavored liqueur)

2 cups sliced blanched almonds, toasted (page 76)

FOR ACCOMPANIMENT

Perfect Whipped Cream (page 84)

Time Management Tips

• The almonds can be toasted in advance, covered and left at room temperature for 2 days or frozen in a heavy-duty plastic bag for a month. No need to refresh them since they will bake again in the tart.

1) **To prepare pastry shell:** Mix and chill dough as directed in recipe. Cut a round of parchment paper to fit the bottom of tart pan (page 440). Place the parchment round in tart pan and lightly brush paper and inside rim of pan with melted butter. Roll out dough and line pan as directed but only lightly prick the surface—without going completely through dough. Then *partially* bake and cool pastry shell as directed. Melt jam and water over low heat and, if using preserves, purée them or push them through a medium-mesh wire sieve. Brush the interior of the pastry shell with the glaze and allow it to set for a few minutes before assembling the tart.

2) **To plump regular prunes:** If the extra-moist prunes are not available, steep regular large pitted prunes in a bowl of simmering water (to cover) until supple, 10 to 15 minutes. Drain, pat dry, slice and proceed.

3) **To fill tart and set up for baking:** Line a shallow baking sheet with aluminum foil (dull side up). Place sheet on the center rack of the oven and preheat oven to 400°F. Place prune slices overlapping in the prepared pastry crust and dot with butter. In a medium-sized bowl, whisk cream with sugar, almond extract and amaretto until sugar dissolves. Fold in toasted almonds and pour the almond-cream mixture on top of prunes, spreading almonds to cover prunes.

4) **To bake:** Place filled tart shell on the baking sheet in the hot oven and bake 35 to 40 minutes. (Although the filling might bubble over a bit while baking, the baking sheet will catch any spills.) The filling of the baked tart should be visibly bubbling and a very rich golden brown color and the sugar and cream should have caramelized nicely. Once the correct color is achieved, even if some of the filling appears to be a bit liquid, remove tart from oven since those spots will firm once cool.

5) **To cool and remove tart ring:** Let tart cool on a wire rack for 30 minutes. When tart is just warm but no longer hot, carefully remove tart ring by first inserting the tip of a sharp knife between the rim of pastry and the fluted tart ring; this will release any candied filling from the rim. Lift tart by the sides and, using the fingers of both hands, push up gently the bottom disc of the tart pan, releasing the tart ring. Place tart on its bottom disc on the wire rack to cool thoroughly. (Immediately wash or soak the tart ring for easier cleaning. And if using a black steel pan, dry it meticulously or it will rust.)

6) **To serve:** Before serving, remove tart from the bottom disc carefully by inserting a very thin cookie sheet between the tart and the disc. Once

Nuts: Because of the fatty oils contained in nuts, improper storage can easily cause them to turn rancid. Whenever possible, purchase nuts stored in vacuum-packed cans and store them on your pantry shelf. To best preserve freshness, bags of nuts as well as opened cans should be emptied into a doubled heavy-duty plastic bag; secure the seals of each bag and place in the refrigerator for up to two weeks or freeze for longer storage.

Dried fruits: (Raisins, apricots, prunes, Calimyrna figs, pitted dates, dried currants and dried cherries) Once opened, store the bag in a doubled (securely sealed) heavy-duty plastic bag on your pantry shelf for up to two weeks. Alternatively, slip the original bag in a glass jar with a screw-top lid and refrigerate for longer storage. (If canned, keep dried fruit sealed in original container.)

removed, gently push the tart onto a serving plate. Serve sliced into wedges, adorned with a dollop of whipped cream. This tart needs no refrigeration.

Variation with Apricots

Best quality dried, pitted whole apricots (or a combination of apricots and prunes) may be substituted for prunes. To soften apricots, cover them with water, bring to a simmer and cook gently (uncovered) for 10 to 15 minutes. Drain and pat dry. If combining prunes and apricots, alternate when overlapping the fruit in the pastry shell.

FRESH STRAWBERRY TART

With Vanilla Custard Cream Filling

YIELD: one 10-inch tart

Most everyone loves fresh fruit tarts. This one—filled with a classic *crème pâtissière* (pastry cream) and then topped with red, ripe strawberries—is always a hit. One of the best things about this recipe is its flexibility. You can use a myriad of fresh fruits and flavorings (see variations). Both the custard cream and pastry crust can be prepared in advance; but to preserve the best texture in your finished dessert, avoid assembling the tart more than a couple of hours ahead of serving. Anyway, since final assembly can be done quickly, this shouldn't interfere with your entertaining schedule.

SPECIAL EQUIPMENT
Electric mixer

10-inch fluted tart pan with removable bottom

Strawberry huller (optional)

Feather brush

Domed cake cover

INGREDIENTS

1 recipe Vanilla Custard Cream (page 444), flavored with 1½ teaspoons pure vanilla extract, 1 to 2 tablespoons Grand Marnier and 1 to 2 teaspoons minced orange zest (optional)

1 recipe Favorite Pie Pastry (page 93)

½ cup red currant jelly, melted over low heat

2 baskets (12 to 16 ounces each) fresh ripe strawberries, rinsed, dried, hulled and halved through stem end

1) **To prepare custard cream:** Prepare Vanilla Custard Cream as directed, flavoring with 1½ teaspoons vanilla, 1 to 2 tablespoons Grand Marnier and, if desired, 2 teaspoons minced orange zest. Cover and chill until needed.

2) **To prepare pastry shell:** Using a 10-inch tart pan, mix, roll out and totally prebake pastry shell, as directed in Favorite Pie Pastry recipe. When cool, paint the interior with 1 tablespoon melted currant jelly and set aside so glaze can set.

3) **To assemble and serve tart:** As close to serving time as possible, rewarm red currant jelly. Spread a generous layer of the chilled pastry cream into the tart shell, smoothing the top. Lay halved strawberries decoratively on top of pastry cream and, using a delicate feather brush, paint strawberries with the remaining melted red currant jelly. Present the tart whole and slice into individual wedges (using a sharp knife) at the table.

Variations for Tarts with Vanilla Custard Cream Filling

Other berries and fruits: Any assortment of fresh fruits or berries may be substituted for the strawberries. And, in the off season, drained canned fruits like cling peaches would work perfectly. Try alternating bananas (sliced on the diagonal) with sliced strawberries. If using fresh bananas or fresh peaches, make sure to treat them with strained fresh lemon juice to prevent them from discoloring. To flavor the custard filling to complement your choice of fruit, see Variations to Pastry Cream (page 446).

Glazing alternatives: Choose your glaze to complement your choice of fruit. If using light-colored fruits—such as green grapes, kiwis, peaches or bananas—your glaze should be light in color, such as melted apple jelly or melted and strained apricot preserves. Darker fruits—like strawberries, raspberries, plums and red seedless grapes—are beautifully enhanced by the deeper color of red currant jelly. If your tart combines both light and dark fruits, use the lighter glaze. Fruits such as blueberries need no glaze at all; only a light dusting of sifted confectioner's sugar over the top of the berries just before serving will give them an enticing snowy appearance. Raspberries are equally wonderful with either confectioner's sugar or the application of a red currant glaze.

Time Management Tips

• Although the pastry cream can be made up to 3 days ahead, to enjoy freshest flavor, 1 or 2 days is preferable.

• The strawberries can be rinsed, dried and hulled early in the day of assembling the tart. Avoid slicing them however, until just before assembling. Or, slice and lay cut side down on a tray lined with absorbent paper toweling. Cover well with plastic wrap and refrigerate until needed.

• This tart ideally should be assembled no more than 2 hours ahead and kept at room temperature. But if necessary, you can assemble it 4 hours ahead and store it, covered with a domed cake cover, in the refrigerator.

BAKED MOCHA CUSTARD

With an Espresso Cream Filling and Chocolate-Nut Crust

YIELD: one 10-inch baked custard; serves 12 to 14

SPECIAL EQUIPMENT

10-inch cake pan (2 inches deep)

Parchment paper

Food processor (optional)

1-quart heavy-bottomed saucepan, preferably with a spout

Electric mixer

Large roasting pan (2 inches deep)

Cake cover (12 inches in diameter)

Stainless steel icing spatula

Decorating comb (optional)

Feather brush, only if making chocolate leaves

The word "mocha" means either a type of coffee bean or a coffee-chocolate flavoring. This luscious dessert uses both from its rich creamy baked custard and its espresso-flavored chocolate cream topping (ganache) to its garnish of mocha beans and/or decorative chocolate leaves. And all this sits on a nutty crust of crumbled chocolate cookies. If you're looking for a chocoholic's dessert that makes a fabulous presentation on your holiday table, look no further! When ingredient shopping, look for mocha beans in gourmet food stores and buy Nabisco brand (my favorite) chocolate wafers.

INGREDIENTS

Chocolate Leaves (following) and/or ½ cup mocha beans, for garnish

FOR THE COOKIE CRUST

5 tablespoons unsalted butter, melted, plus more for greasing pan

2 cups finely ground plain chocolate wafer cookies (about 8 ounces wafers)

½ cup halved walnuts, finely chopped

FOR THE CUSTARD FILLING

2 cups heavy cream (preferably not ultrapasteurized)

1 cup milk

1 rounded teaspoon instant coffee or espresso powder

½ cup boiling water

¼ cup Dutch-processed unsweetened cocoa powder*

4 ounces cream cheese, at room temperature

1 cup granulated white sugar or vanilla sugar (page 74)

5 extra-large eggs, at room temperature

2 extra-large egg yolks, at room temperature

1 teaspoon pure vanilla extract

FOR THE CHOCOLATE CREAM TOPPING

8 ounces mixed semisweet and bittersweet chocolate, chopped

½ cup heavy cream (preferably not ultrapasteurized)

1 rounded teaspoon instant coffee or espresso powder or finely ground instant coffee powder

½ teaspoon flavorless vegetable oil

* See section on Staples

Time Management Tips

- The custard can be baked 2 days ahead and kept refrigerated.

- Apply chocolate cream topping, as well as garnish, early in the day that you plan to serve and refrigerate as directed in recipe.

- The chocolate leaves can be made weeks or months ahead and stored in the freezer in an airtight container.

1) *To set up:* Prepare chocolate leaves, if using, at least 2 hours (or months) in advance and keep in freezer. Brush the interior of a 10-inch cake pan (2 inches deep) with melted butter and line bottom of pan with a round of parchment paper (page 440). Butter paper and set aside. Preheat the oven to 350°F.

2) *To prepare cookie crust:* In a food processor fitted with the steel blade, grind cookies and nuts and combine them in a medium-sized bowl. Alternatively, place cookies in a heavy-duty plastic bag and crush them with a rolling pin or wine bottle until finely ground. Mix crumbs and nuts to combine well, then stir in the 5 tablespoons melted butter. Turn out mixture into prepared cake pan and press to cover the bottom evenly (not extending up the sides). Refrigerate while you prepare the custard filling.

3) *To prepare custard filling:* Combine cream and milk in a 1-quart heavy-bottomed saucepan (preferably with a spout) and scald over low heat, but do not simmer. In a measuring cup, dissolve coffee or espresso powder in the ½ cup boiling water and stir in cocoa until smooth. Stir this into scalded cream mixture and turn off heat, but leave pan on the warm burner. Cream softened cheese in the bowl of an electric mixer, gradually adding sugar while continuing to beat until smooth. Add whole eggs, 1 at a time, beating well after each addition. Beat in egg yolks and when mixture is smooth, turn off machine and scrape any accumulated cream cheese off the bottom of the bowl. Mix once again to combine and reduce machine to its lowest setting. Slowly pour in the hot cocoa-cream mixture and vanilla and mix until smooth.

4) *To assemble and bake:* Pour 1 inch of boiling water into a large roasting pan. Pour custard filling over chilled crust in the cake pan. Carefully place cake pan into the roasting pan. With great care, transfer roasting pan to preheated oven. Bake until the blade of a sharp knife comes out clean

Q and A

Q. What does it mean to scald liquid?

A. A scalded mixture gets hot enough to form tiny bubbles along the rim of the liquid. This happens shortly before a mixture starts to form larger bubbles below the surface, called simmering. Still larger, more turbulent bubbles that continually break the surface is boiling.

when inserted into the center of the filling, about 1 hour. Remove cake pan from water and allow to cool on a wire rack. Cover the top with a piece of waxed paper and then aluminum foil and refrigerate until thoroughly chilled.

5) *To prepare chocolate cream:* Do this just before unmolding the chilled custard. Position a medium-mesh wire sieve over a mixing bowl and set aside. Place chopped chocolate in a small bowl. Heat cream in a small saucepan over low heat and when just coming to a boil, remove from heat and stir in instant coffee or espresso powder. Pour this over chopped chocolate and stir until chocolate is totally melted and the mixture is smooth. Stir in vegetable oil and pour mixture into the sieve, rubbing it through with a spatula. Set aside until just warm.

6) *To unmold custard:* When baked custard is thoroughly chilled, uncover and run the blade of a table knife around the circumference of the pan. Place another piece of waxed paper on top of the custard and invert custard onto a flat plate or cookie sheet (if stubborn, place a hot, damp towel on top and shake to help custard release); peel off parchment paper and discard. Carefully center your serving platter on top of the cookie crust and invert so the baked custard filling is facing up; peel off waxed paper. (Avoid lining your serving platter with a doily, since this moist crust tends to stick to the paper.)

7) *To apply chocolate cream topping:* If chocolate cream has stiffened, place the bowl into a skillet with some hot (not simmering) water and stir to soften. Pour mixture onto the top center of the baked custard and using an icing spatula, spread the chocolate cream right up to the edge of the custard; don't let chocolate drip down the sides—you want the custard to be visible. Using either the jagged edge of a decorating comb or the tines of a fork, encircle the entire top (starting at the outer rim) with decorative ridges or lines. Garnish with a border of mocha coffee beans or chocolate leaves or both. Cover with a cake cover and refrigerate until shortly before serving.

8) *To serve:* Remove from refrigerator 10 to 15 minutes before serving. Present at the table and slice into wedges.

Chocolate leaves are a quick and easy way to make a simple dessert stand out and shine. My favorite leaf for coating is by far the lemon leaf (easy to obtain from most flower shops), which has the perfect texture for this process and comes in a wide variety of sizes. But you can also use any shiny, firm, non-toxic leaf. Rose leaves, although suitable, are more delicate to handle. Leaves with a fuzzy coating are not recommended since they usually stick to the chocolate. To coat 20 to 30 leaves, you will need 12 ounces of chopped semisweet or bittersweet chocolate or chocolate chips and 2 generous teaspoons of solid vegetable shortening. (If using white chocolate, double the amount of shortening.)

To prepare leaves: Wipe each leaf clean with a dampened paper towel and wipe completely dry with another. Lay leaves on baking sheets lined with wax paper and refrigerate while chocolate melts. Melt chocolate with shortening in the top of a double boiler over hot (not yet simmering) water, stirring constantly until smooth. Remove chocolate from heat. Working with 1 leaf at a time, turn so the underside faces up. Using either a feather brush or a small paint brush, carefully paint only the face-up side with an ⅛-inch-thick layer of melted chocolate. Brush a slightly thicker layer of chocolate at the stem end but not over the stem. Carefully wipe the edges of the leaf so only the veined side has chocolate and lay each leaf (chocolate side up) on the baking sheet in the freezer. If your brush needs to be cleaned during this process, do not use water; simply wipe brush gently with paper toweling. Keep chocolate-coated leaves in the freezer for at least 30 minutes before unmolding.

To unmold: Work with 1 leaf at a time, keeping remaining leaves in the freezer. Hold coated leaf in one hand (chocolate side up) and using the thumb and forefinger of your other hand, lift the uncoated stem tip and gently peel the leaf away from the chocolate. Lay chocolate leaf on a paper towel and carry it immediately back to the freezer to firm up. Store in an air-tight tin, separated by sheets of waxed paper, for up to 3 months in a freezer with little temperature fluctuation.

CREAMY BANANA FLAN

With a Border of Walnuts

YIELD: serves 6 to 8

SPECIAL EQUIPMENT
9-cup soufflé dish

Blender

2-quart heavy-bottomed saucepan with light-colored interior, preferably with a spout (enamel-coated cast iron works best)

Roasting pan, for water bath

I love to throw together my favorite foods in all sorts of ways. Two of my absolutely favorite foods are perfectly ripe bananas and creamy flan with a deep caramelized exterior. So this combination was a natural! This flan should be baked in a nine-cup soufflé dish. Although the custard mixture will fit into an eight-cup dish, the smaller dish causes the top of the custard to become overly brown. If you don't have the larger dish, check the top of the flan as it bakes and, if necessary, cover loosely with aluminum foil (shiny side up). And plan to make a day before serving; the flan should chill overnight.

FOR THE CARAMEL SYRUP
½ cup water
2 cups sugar

FOR THE CUSTARD
Plenty of boiling water, kept at a simmer
About 2 large perfectly ripe bananas
2¼ cups heavy cream (preferably not ultrapasteurized)
1 tablespoon pure maple syrup
4 extra-large eggs
4 extra-large egg yolks
½ cup granulated white sugar or vanilla sugar (page 74)
1½ teaspoons pure vanilla extract
½ cup walnuts halves, for garnish

1) **To coat soufflé dish with caramelized syrup:** Combine water and sugar in a 2-quart heavy-bottomed saucepan and boil down to form a caramelized sugar syrup as directed on page 472. Immediately put on your oven mitts and pour syrup into 9-cup soufflé dish; tilt and swirl dish to coat the bottom and sides thoroughly with syrup. Continue tilting and swirling as the syrup cools, until mixture thickens and holds onto the sides. Place dish on a wire rack. Immediately pour some boiling water into saucepan to release clinging syrup; after cleaning and drying pan, return to stove but don't turn on heat. (Expect the caramelized syrup to harden in soufflé dish as it cools.)

2) **To set up for baking custard:** Preheat the oven to 350°F. Fold a washcloth or kitchen towel in half and place it in the center of a standard-sized roasting pan.

3) **To prepare custard:** Just before assembling, purée bananas in a blender and measure out 1 cup purée into the 2-quart saucepan. Stir in cream and maple syrup and scald over medium-low heat, being careful not to allow it to boil. In the bowl of an electric mixer, beat eggs with egg yolks and sugar on medium speed until light colored and thickened, about 2 minutes. Pour in scalded cream-banana mixture (a little at first, to temper the egg mixture) and stir in vanilla. Mix on low speed until just combined and warm throughout, taking care to prevent an overabundance of tiny bubbles in custard. Pour custard into the caramel-lined soufflé dish.

4) **To bake flan:** Place the dish of custard on top of the cloth in the roasting pan. Fill roasting pan with enough simmering water to come halfway up the side of the dish. Carefully transfer to the center shelf of the preheated oven. Bake until a knife comes out clean when inserted into the center, about 55 to 60 minutes. Expect the flan to jiggle slightly at this point; the custard will set further as it cools. Set on a wire rack to cool, then cover securely and refrigerate 8 hours or overnight.

5) **To unmold and serve:** Invert flan onto a serving platter. (If necessary, give the dish a good shake to help release flan.) Spoon any remaining caramel syrup over the top and sides of flan. Decorate the top with a border of walnut halves. Present the flan fully assembled and slice into individual wedges at the table.

Q AND A

Q. When making a flan, how do I get the hard candied layer off the soufflé dish after unmolding?

A. Cleaning the bottom of the baking dish can be difficult. After unmolding the flan onto your serving platter, let the flan dish soak in several changes of boiling water to dissolve the hard caramelized layer that remains on the bottom of the dish after baking.

TIPS

FROM A TEACHER

~~~~~~~~

How to Make a
Caramel Syrup

Many home cooks panic at the thought of making a caramel syrup. But actually, it's remarkably easy. In the simplest of terms, when sugar with a little water boils down, you're left with a perfectly clear sugar syrup. As the syrup continues to boil, the water evaporates away and the sugar starts to caramelize, eventually turning a deep amber color. To line a flan dish, this amber syrup is poured into a baking dish or pan and swirled around until it thickens and coats the interior of the dish. The secret to producing a never-fail caramel syrup is the right type of pot. A heavy-bottomed saucepan, specifically with a light-colored interior, lets you view the true color of the mixture as it boils, thickens and caramelizes. This type of pot not only removes the need for a candy thermometer, but the heavier pan will greatly reduce the risk of scorching the mixture from the bottom. I recommend an enamel-coated cast iron saucepan (by Le Crueset), preferably one with a spout.

To prepare caramelized sugar syrup: Bring a kettle of water to a boil; place a cup of boiling water next to the stove and insert a pastry brush into the water. Reduce heat under kettle to low and simmer until needed for clean-up. Place water and sugar (as specified in your recipe) in a heavy-bottomed saucepan with a light interior. Stir gently, using the stem of a wooden spoon, taking care to keep the sugar granules off the sides of the pan. Place pot over medium heat and dissolve sugar, gently swirling the pan occasionally. When the mixture is perfectly clear, raise heat and bring it to a boil. Let mixture boil (uncovered and without stirring or swirling) until syrup becomes a deep amber color, similar to a rich cup of tea, 5 to 10 minutes. If at any time during boiling, sugar crystals cling to the sides of the pan, use the wet pastry brush to wash them away. (This prevents the clinging sugar from burning and falling into the syrup, which would adversely affect both its flavor and consistency.) While syrup is boiling, stay close by. Once you smell the savory aroma of caramel, the syrup will color quickly. (Put on your oven mitts—the syrup is dangerously hot.) When it's ready, remove from stove and *immediately* pour it into a baking dish or use as directed in recipe. Then quickly pour simmering water into the saucepan and swirl to dissolve and release any sticky syrup before it hardens. See, you did it!

ORANGE-SCENTED COCONUT FLAN

YIELD: serves 8 to 10

I can't decide whether this or the preceding banana flan is my favorite flan. But if you like coconut, you'll love my rendition of this creamy, silky coconut-laced custard, subtly flecked with minced orange zest. And conveniently, best results are achieved when this flan is prepared one day ahead of serving. A word of caution when toasting coconut, keep your nose on top of things since the first fragrant whiff of toasted coconut usually indicates that the process is just about finished. And when cutting zest from the orange, be careful that all the white pith is removed from the zest.

SPECIAL EQUIPMENT
9-cup soufflé dish

2-quart heavy-bottomed saucepan with light-colored interior, preferably with a spout (enamel-coated cast iron works best)

Roasting pan, for water bath

FOR THE CARAMEL SYRUP

2 cups sugar

½ cup water

FOR THE CUSTARD

Plenty of boiling water, kept at a simmer

2 pieces navel orange zest (each 1 inch wide and 2 inches long)

½ cup plus 2 tablespoons sugar

2¼ cups heavy cream (preferably not ultrapasteurized)

1 cup canned coconut cream* (if not smooth, purée in a blender before measuring)

4 extra-large eggs

4 extra-large egg yolks

1 cup shredded sweetened coconut,* plus ⅓ cup for garnish

1 teaspoon almond extract

1 teaspoon pure vanilla extract

* See section on Staples

1) **To coat soufflé dish with caramelized syrup:** Combine water and sugar in a 2-quart heavy-bottomed saucepan and boil down to form a caramelized sugar syrup as directed on page 472. Immediately put on your oven mitts and pour syrup into 9-cup soufflé dish; tilt and swirl dish to coat the bottom and sides thoroughly with syrup. Continue tilting and swirling as the syrup cools, until mixture thickens and holds onto the

TIPS

FROM A TEACHER

～～～

How to Toast Coconut

Preheat the oven to 250°F. Spread out shredded coconut on a shallow (not dark) baking sheet. Toast in oven until coconut turns golden brown, 10 to 20 minutes. Check every 5 minutes at first (be careful not to burn) and stir to redistribute when you check. Remove toasted coconut from oven and let cool on the baking sheet. Store in an airtight container or well-covered bowl at room temperature for up to 3 days before using—after that, the flavor will lose potency.

Q AND A

Q. Why are custard mixtures baked in a water bath?

A. *Since eggs are extremely heat sensitive, they must be protected against aggressive, direct heat exposure or they will curdle. The hot water cushions the custard from such excessive heat (as does the folded towel) and helps the mixture to cook more gently.*

sides. Place dish on a wire rack. Immediately pour some boiling water into saucepan to release clinging syrup; after cleaning and drying pan, return to stove but don't turn on heat. (Expect the caramelized syrup to harden in soufflé dish as it cools.)

2) *To prepare sugar-blanched orange zest:* In another small saucepan, blanch strips of zest in ¾ cup boiling water for 2 minutes. Drain and repeat, but add the 2 tablespoons sugar to the water. Drain and stack slices; cut stack into slivers and then mince slivers.

3) *To set up for baking custard:* Preheat the oven to 350°F. Fold a washcloth or kitchen towel in half and place it in the center of a standard-sized roasting pan.

4) *To prepare custard:* In the 2-quart saucepan, combine heavy cream with coconut cream. Scald over medium-low heat, being careful not to boil. In the bowl of an electric mixer, beat eggs with egg yolks and the ½ cup sugar on medium speed until light colored and thickened, about 2 minutes. Stir a little of the scalded cream mixture into the egg-sugar mixture to bring up the temperature of the eggs; then stir in the remaining scalded cream. Stir in the 1 cup shredded coconut, minced orange zest, almond extract and vanilla extract. Mix gently, trying not to create too many little bubbles in the custard. Pour custard into the caramel-lined soufflé dish.

5) *To bake flan:* Carefully place the dish of custard on the cloth in the roasting pan. Fill roasting pan with enough simmering water to come halfway up the side of the dish. Carefully transfer to the center shelf of the preheated oven. Bake until a knife comes out clean when inserted into the center, 55 to 60 minutes. Expect the flan to jiggle slightly at this point; the custard will set further as it cools. Place soufflé dish on a wire rack to cool. Once cool, cover securely and refrigerate 8 hours or overnight.

6) *To unmold, garnish and serve:* At least an hour before serving, toast the remaining ⅓ cup coconut as directed at left. Invert flan onto a serving platter and spoon any remaining caramel syrup over the top and sides of the flan. (If necessary, give the dish a good shake to help release flan.) Decorate the top with a border of toasted coconut, allowing it also to coat the sides, if desired. Bring to the table and slice into individual wedges as you serve.

BREAD PUDDING

With Bananas, Spiced Apples and Brandied Raisins

YIELD: serves 8 to 10

The flavor and aroma of this comforting dessert is reminiscent of banana bread, but the consistency is chunkier and the top is crisper. The combined flavors—bananas, sautéed spiced apples and raisins plumped in apple brandy—make this bread pudding one that you will never forget. The most preferred type of bread for this recipe is challah (page 387) that's been baked in a loaf pan without a seeded top, but any high quality store-bought white or egg bread (without seeds) would also produce fine results. This dessert is particularly soothing in cold weather, served slightly warm with a dollop of Perfect Whipped Cream (page 84). And in warmer weather, layer this bread pudding slightly warmed in a parfait glass with Old-Fashioned Vanilla Ice Cream (page 497).

SPECIAL EQUIPMENT
Nutmeg grater (optional)

2-quart baking dish (2 inches deep)

Blender

FOR THE TOPPING

⅓ cup walnut halves

2 rounded tablespoons granulated white sugar

1 teaspoon ground cinnamon

¼ teaspoon ground nutmeg (preferably freshly grated)

FOR THE PUDDING

Melted butter or vegetable spray, for baking dish

4 packed cups day-old egg bread or white bread with crusts,
 cut into 1-inch cubes

⅓ cup mixed light and dark raisins

¼ cup apple brandy (Calvados or applejack)

6 tablespoons unsalted butter

2 cups packed peeled, cored and coarsely chopped Golden Delicious
 apples

1 teaspoon ground cinnamon

½ teaspoon ground nutmeg (preferably freshly grated)

1½ cup heavy cream (preferably not ultrapasteurized) or half-and-half

3 extra-large eggs, lightly beaten

1 cup banana purée (about 2 large very ripe bananas)

1½ teaspoons pure vanilla extract

½ cup packed light brown sugar

Perfect Whipped Cream (page 84), for garnish

1) **To prepare topping:** Place all topping ingredients into the bowl of a food processor fitted with the steel blade. Process, using on-off turns, until mixture is finely chopped. Set aside. (Alternatively, place topping ingredients into a heavy-duty plastic bag and roll over mixture with a rolling pin until finely ground.)

2) **To set up:** Preheat the oven to 350°F. Brush a 2-quart baking dish with melted butter or spray with vegetable spray. Place cubed bread in a large bowl. Place raisins and brandy in a small saucepan over low heat until brandy comes to a simmer. Remove from heat and let plump in brandy.

3) **To sauté apples:** Melt 3 tablespoons of the butter in an 8- to 10-inch skillet over medium heat. When bubbling, add chopped apples. Stir in cinnamon and nutmeg and, when apples are well coated with butter and spices, reduce heat to low. Cook over low heat until apples are softened and spices are fragrant, about 5 minutes. Remove from heat. (Do not overcook apples; they should remain textural.)

4) **To assemble bread pudding:** In a large mixing bowl, combine cream, eggs, banana purée, vanilla and brown sugar. Stir well to combine and pour over the bowl of bread cubes. Scrape sautéed apples onto bread mixture and fold together to combine well. Dice the remaining 3 tablespoons butter and fold into mixture. Pour mixture into the prepared baking dish and sprinkle the reserved topping evenly over the top.

5) *To bake and serve:* Bake in the preheated oven for 45 minutes. Remove from oven and let sit until just warm. Serve warm or at room temperature with a spoonful of softly whipped cream.

6) *To store and reheat:* Place leftovers covered in the refrigerator; bring to room temperature or rewarm gently before serving. The best way to reheat bread pudding is in the microwave on low since conventional heat tends to dry it out. If you desire a crisper top, after microwaving, run the pudding very briefly under the broiler. Keep a watchful eye out to avoid burning.

Reduced-Fat Variations

Although you'll lose some of the flavor, you can substantially reduce the saturated-fat content of this recipe by doing the following: When sautéing apples, omit butter and substitute 3 tablespoons unsweetened apple juice or cider, simmering until softened and fragrant. When assembling pudding, use milk instead of cream and reduce eggs from 3 to 1; increase banana purée to 1½ cups and omit the last application of diced butter to the pudding.

POACHED PEARS IN RASPBERRY SYRUP

YIELD: serves 10

SPECIAL EQUIPMENT
5-quart heavy-bottomed pot
with lid

Food processor or blender

Fine-mesh sieve

When choosing pears for poaching, I find that Anjou pears hold their shape more consistently. For best results, avoid soft pears. And if faced with the choice between a pear that's either overly ripe or underripe, always pick the latter; after poaching and macerating in the hot syrup, even underripe fruit will take on the perfect "tender but al dente" consistency. When you add the strained raspberry purée to the poaching syrup, don't be concerned if (at first) the color seems inconsistent. As the syrup cools, the color will become totally uniform, evolving into a glorious muted ruby color. Poire Williams— a crystal-clear eau-de-vie distilled from French Williams pears—is my choice of brandy for this syrup but you may substitute framboise (raspberry brandy): both are quite potent so use sparingly. These elegant pears are just right as a cool and refreshing ending to a summer meal or as a light dessert after a more substantial and robust winter meal. For added elegance and smooth flavor, drizzle the top of each pear with crème anglaise just before serving.

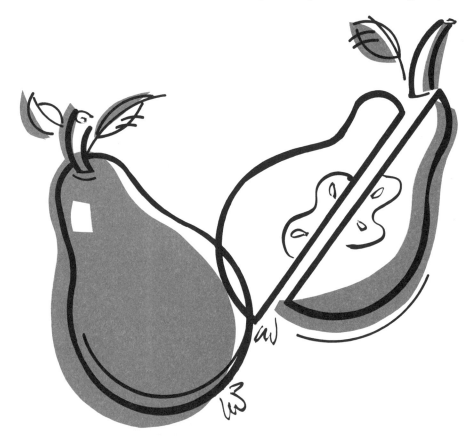

INGREDIENTS

Strained juice of 2 lemons

10 firm, ripe Anjou pears

8 cups cold water, for poaching

3 cups plus 3 tablespoons sugar

1 supple vanilla bean, split down the length and opened

2 baskets (4 ounces each) fresh raspberries

2 generous tablespoons pear eau-de-vie

Crème Anglaise (page 510), (optional) for accompaniment

1) **To prepare pears:** Pour lemon juice into a 6-quart nonreactive mixing bowl; add enough water to fill bowl halfway. Using a vegetable peeler, peel pears leaving the stem intact. Using a sharp knife, cut a thin slice off the bottom of each pear so it will stand upright when served. Immediately place pears in the bowl of acidulated water to prevent discoloration.

2) **To poach pears:** Place the 8 cups of cold water, the 3 cups sugar and the opened vanilla bean in a 5-quart heavy-bottomed pot over medium heat. Stir to dissolve sugar and bring to a boil. Reduce heat to low and simmer 5 minutes. Raise heat to high and add pears. Return quickly to a simmer, reduce heat to low and gently simmer pears with the cover ajar for only 5 minutes. Remove from heat and carefully transfer pears to a large bowl, using either a wide skimmer or a slotted spoon. Pour or ladle the hot syrup (including vanilla bean) over pears. Set aside.

3) **To prepare raspberry syrup:** Place a fine-mesh sieve over a bowl and set aside. Rinse and drain raspberries and place them in the bowl of a food processor fitted with the steel blade (or in a blender). Process until berries are puréed. Empty purée into the strainer and, using a wooden spatula, force through the strainer into the bowl extracting as much purée as possible. Stir the 3 tablespoons sugar into purée and pour into the bowl with pears. Gently fold raspberry mixture through the poaching syrup, being careful not to sever pears. Let cool to room temperature, then remove vanilla bean and stir in the pear eau-de-vie. Cover and refrigerate until serving time.

4) **To serve:** Place each pear upright in an individual shallow-rim soup plate. Spoon some of the syrup over the top and, if desired, drizzle some créme anglaise over the pears as well.

Time Management Tips

• The pears can be fully assembled 1 day ahead and kept refrigerated.

TIPS

FROM A TEACHER

How to Core a Pear

Although an apple corer does the job of coring many fruits, it doesn't work on pears. Due to the shape of a pear, an apple corer would inevitably remove much of the tapered top along with the core. The only part of a pear that's not edible is the small circular patch of seeds and a thin rope-like interior stem that goes from the seeds up to the stem end. To remove these parts quickly, easily and exclusively, first peel and halve the pear through the stem end and then use a melon ball scoop to remove the pits. If not cooking right away, immediately submerge your pears into water mixed with about two tablespoons of lemon juice to prevent them from discoloring.

SLICED STRAWBERRIES AND BANANA CREAM

With Caramelized Banana Slices

YIELD: serves 8

The title of this fabulous recipe speaks for itself! Soft, creamy banana-infused whipped cream is layered with macerated strawberries and topped with broiled banana slices coated with brown sugar. I love this dessert. Judging from the unanimous approval of my family, friends and students, I trust you will too. The key is to have all of the ingredients to be whipped very cold (bananas included). And do use a blender to purée the bananas since they become much thicker and more emulsified than when puréed in a food processor. Allow the brown sugar to dry for at least two hours before sieving it onto the banana slices. This drying time helps the sugar turn crisp under the broiler instead of becoming overly liquid.

SPECIAL EQUIPMENT

Strawberry huller (optional)

Electric mixer or a balloon whisk and shallow wide bowl

Sifter or triple-mesh wire sieve

Blender

Time Management Tips

- The berries can be fully assembled 1 day ahead and refrigerated well covered.

- The banana cream can be assembled early in the day of serving, covered and refrigerated.

- When entertaining (before serving dinner), place a shallow baking sheet (with a wire rack) on your counter. Squeeze and strain lemon juice and place dried brown sugar close by. Halfway through dinner, preheat broiler. Don't slice bananas until just before assembling.

INGREDIENTS

¼ cup firmly packed light brown sugar

3 baskets fresh strawberries (12 to 16 ounces each)

⅓ cup granulated white sugar

2 tablespoons Grand Marnier or other orange-flavored liqueur

2 cups very cold heavy cream (preferably not ultrapasteurized)

¼ cup sifted confectioner's sugar (sifted before measuring)

1½ teaspoons pure vanilla extract

1⅓ cups freshly puréed bananas (about 4 medium-sized *cold* bananas)

2 ripe bananas, for caramelized garnish

1 teaspoon strained fresh lemon juice

Fresh mint sprigs, for garnish

1) **To set up:** Chill the bowl and whipping element of an electric mixer in the refrigerator. Spread out brown sugar on a shallow baking sheet and let it dry (uncovered) at room temperature for at least 2 hours.

2) **To macerate strawberries:** Rinse and drain strawberries thoroughly. Remove stems and hulls and cut into slices through the stem end. Place strawberries in a large bowl and stir in granulated sugar and Grand Marnier. Cover and let berries macerate for at least 2 hours at room temperature or refrigerate for 4 hours or overnight.

3) **To prepare banana cream:** In the chilled bowl of the electric mixer, whip cream until thickened. Add sifted confectioner's sugar and vanilla and continue to whip until very stiff but not broken. Using a rubber spatula, fold cold banana purée into whipped cream until well blended. Cover and refrigerate until serving. (Don't purée bananas until just before assembling banana cream to prevent them from turning brown.)

4) **To set up for serving:** Position broiler rack to the highest position and preheat broiler. Slice the 2 ripe bananas on the diagonal into ½-inch slices, place on shallow tray and, using your finger or a pastry brush, gently paint both sides with lemon juice. Lay each slice on a broiler pan or on a wire

We all have purchased a prepackaged box of strawberries, only to find that the berries on the bottom were not nearly as nice as those on top. It's important to confront those situations head on by letting your shopkeeper know of your dissatisfaction. The next time you buy strawberries, call the market in the morning and ask your grocer to make a basket of beautiful berries just for you. Then (and this is the most important part of my speech), the next day make sure to call him and give him a compliment!

How to clean and hull strawberries: To prevent strawberries from retaining excess water, always rinse and thoroughly drain strawberries before removing their hulls—the white, tasteless central core of each berry. Using a strawberry huller, remove stems and hulls by inserting the ends of the tweezer-shaped tool into the stem end and twist while squeezing to lift out stems with hulls attached. If a huller isn't available, hold the strawberry in one hand with the stem up. Use your other hand to grasp and gently but firmly push down on the stem while twisting clockwise to release it from the interior of the strawberry. Discard hulls and stems.

T I P S

FROM A TEACHER

Buying and Preparing Strawberries

rack set in a shallow baking sheet and pat tops dry with a paper towel. Place brown sugar in a medium-mesh wire sieve and push sugar through directly onto banana slices. Place some berries into the bottom of a stemmed parfait glass. Place a generous spoonful of banana cream on top of berries. Top cream with more berries and top with another good dollop of cream. Broil banana slices until sugar is nicely caramelized, about 1 minute. Arrange banana slices among the glasses decoratively by standing each slice against the edge of the glass with one tip inserted into the cream. Garnish with a fresh mint sprig and serve at once.

Reduced-Fat, Full-Flavored Variation

Replace heavy cream with a double batch of very chilled Skinny Crème Fraîche (page 84), using both the vanilla and sugar. If desired, add some freshly grated nutmeg or ground cinnamon when assembling. Just before serving, for best texture, blend banana purée with the skinny crème fraîche and optional spices in a blender. Assemble as directed.

MIDNIGHT BROWNIES

With or without a Peanut Butter Pocket

YIELD: about 22 brownies

SPECIAL EQUIPMENT
9x13-inch baking pan
(2 inches deep)

Sifter or triple-mesh wire sieve

These brownies are named for their dark, fudgelike appearance and texture. Ironically, they look much sweeter than they taste. The addition of light corn syrup in the batter creates a wonderful shine on the top of the baked brownies and, although most brownies have a tendency to crack or sink in the center, these have never done either. As for the peanut butter filling—it elevates the entire brownie eating experience to new heights! But be forewarned; these brownies disappear immediately in my house. I practically have to frisk my son in the morning. Once I found wrapped brownies in each pocket of his pants—on the sides, in the back and down the legs! For best flavor, if your instant coffee is granular (not powdered), pulverize it to a fine powder using an electric spice grinder; or put the granules in a plastic bag and crush them with a rolling pin or a wine bottle. Also, if you're using the peanut butter filling, use the optional cup of chocolate chips in the batter instead of walnuts or peanut butter chips.

FOR THE PEANUT BUTTER FILLING (OPTIONAL)

1 cup creamy or chunky peanut butter

1 cup confectioner's sugar, plus more for dusting

FOR THE BROWNIES

2 sticks (½ pound) unsalted butter, plus more for baking dish

6 ounces unsweetened baking chocolate

1 teaspoon instant coffee granules, pulverized, or espresso powder

2 teaspoons pure vanilla extract

1 cup unbleached all-purpose flour

3 tablespoons unsifted cake flour

1 teaspoon double-acting baking powder

½ teaspoon salt

1½ cups granulated white sugar

3 generous tablespoons light corn syrup

3 extra-large eggs, at room temperature

1 extra-large egg yolk, at room temperature

OPTIONAL ADDITIONS:

1 cup semisweet chocolate chips *or* 1 cup chopped walnuts *or* ½ cup peanut butter chips mixed with ½ cup semisweet chocolate chips

Time Management Tips

- The peanut butter filling can be made 3 days ahead and kept in the refrigerator until needed. However, if the filling is very chilled, remove it from the refrigerator an hour before using so it won't affect the overall baking time of the brownie mixture.

- As a time-saver when assembling, sift the dry ingredients days ahead and leave in a covered bowl at room temperature. Give the mixture a good swish with the whisk before incorporating it into your batter.

1) ***To prepare peanut butter filling, if using:*** In a large bowl, thoroughly combine peanut butter with confectioner's sugar. Knead briefly with your hands until smooth. Lightly dust a 14-inch sheet of waxed paper with confectioner's sugar and place peanut butter mixture on the center of the paper. Lightly sprinkle the top of the filling with more confectioner's sugar and place another sheet of waxed paper on top. Press filling to flatten gently and, using a rolling pin, roll out filling ¼ inch thick into a 9x13-inch rectangle (or a bit smaller). Refrigerate until needed.

2) ***To set up:*** If using a glass baking dish, preheat the oven to 325°F; if using a metal pan, preheat to 350°F. Line baking dish with aluminum foil (dull side down for glass, dull side up for metal), allowing a 2-inch overhang at each end. Brush foil with melted butter and set aside.

3) *To assemble brownie batter:* In a 2-quart heavy-bottomed saucepan, melt the 2 sticks butter with chocolate over low heat. Remove from heat and stir in instant coffee and vanilla; let cool slightly. In a medium-sized mixing bowl, whisk together both flours, baking powder and salt. Sift this mixture into another bowl. Whisk sugar and corn syrup into the melted chocolate mixture until smooth. Add eggs (1 at a time) and egg yolk, whisking well after each addition. Add dry ingredients to pan with chocolate mixture and, using the whisk, gently but thoroughly combine until smooth. If desired, fold in walnuts or chips, using a rubber spatula.

4) *To assemble brownies:* If using peanut butter filling, pour ½ the brownie batter into the prepared baking dish and gently spread to each corner, using a rubber spatula. Peel off 1 sheet of waxed paper from filling and invert so filling sits directly on top of batter. Peel off the remaining piece of waxed paper and pour on remaining batter, spreading to enclose filling. If not using the filling, simply pour all of the batter into the prepared pan.

5) *To bake and cool:* Bake in preheated oven until a toothpick comes out almost clean when inserted in the center, 23 minutes (avoid overbaking). Place on a wire rack to cool thoroughly. Once cool, cover pan with aluminum foil and let sit at least 4 hours—preferably overnight. Then lift the brownie "cake" out of the pan (using the overhang of foil as a handle) and slice into 2-inch squares using a sharp knife. For easier slicing, wipe off any accumulated chocolate that clings to the knife after each cut.

6) *To store:* To best preserve moistness, store sliced brownies in an airtight tin separated by sheets of waxed paper or wrap each brownie in pliable plastic wrap. Either way, store at room temperature.

LOADED WITH GINGER SNAPS

YIELD: 30 to 32 cookies

When I was a little girl, we always had store-bought ginger snaps at home. At the time I thought they were good, but not after tasting these. Loaded with ginger and just the right amount of molasses, the flavor is truly alive. Their ultimate texture, however, depends on the baking time. When baked for only ten minutes, the cookie will be chewy (my husband and children adore them this way) and when baked for twelve minutes, they will become very crisp and will yield an audible "snap" when broken (my own preference). So, I always mix up the baking times to make everyone happy. In addition to baking time, the type of cookie sheet will also influence texture. The newer "cushioned" sheets bake a little slower than the thin old-fashioned ones and are preferable for these cookies. But if you only have the thin sheets, simply shorten the baking time to reach the desired look and texture.

SPECIAL EQUIPMENT
Sifter or triple-mesh wire sieve

Parchment paper

Cushioned cookie sheets

Electric mixer (optional)

Cookie scoop with capacity of 2 liquid tablespoons (optional)

INGREDIENTS

1 rounded tablespoon instant coffee granules

3 cups unbleached all-purpose flour

2 teaspoons baking soda

2 tablespoons ground ginger

1 teaspoon ground cinnamon

½ teaspoon ground allspice

½ teaspoon salt

Pinch ground cloves

1 cup firmly packed dark brown sugar

1 cup granulated white sugar

2 sticks (½ pound) unsalted butter, at room temperature

½ cup unsulphured molasses*

1 teaspoon pure vanilla extract

1 extra-large egg

* See section on Staples

1) **To set up:** Position both oven racks to the upper and lower levels and pre-heat oven to 375°F. Line 2 to 4 cookie sheets with parchment paper; do not grease the paper. Pulverize instant coffee granules to a fine powder in an electric spice grinder; or put granules in a plastic bag and crush them with a rolling pin or a wine bottle.

2) **To prepare cookie batter:** In a medium-sized mixing bowl, whisk together flour, pulverized coffee, baking soda, ginger, cinnamon, allspice, salt and cloves. Sift this mixture into another bowl. In a large bowl, using an electric mixer or a wooden spoon, cream brown and white sugars with softened butter, molasses and vanilla. When well combined, add egg. Once the mixture is smooth, set electric mixer to lowest setting, if using, and add sifted dry ingredients, mixing well.

3) **To shape and bake:** Place generous tablespoonfuls of batter or level cookie scoops of batter on the prepared cookie sheets. For best results, place mounds in 3 rows of 3, without crowding. Place 2 of the sheets into the preheated oven using the upper and lower third shelf positions. Bake for 10 to 12 minutes, switching the position of the sheets after half the baking time. While in the oven, these cookies will first plump as they spread. They will then deflate and become flat; once this happens, they are done. Bake remaining sheets of cookies.

4) **To cool and store:** After baking, place sheets on a wire rack for 3 to 5 minutes. Then, using a thin metal spatula, transfer cookies to wire racks to cool before storing in an airtight tin.

Ginger Snap Ice Cream Sandwiches

These cookies make fabulous ice cream sandwiches! Freeze cookies for an hour or so before spreading the flat side of 1 cookie with a layer of slightly softened Old-Fashioned Vanilla Ice Cream (page 497). Top with another cookie (flat side down). Squish a little, wrap in pliable plastic wrap, slip sandwiches into individual waxed-paper bags and freeze until firm.

CHUNKY PEANUT BUTTER CHOCOLATE CHIP SANDIES

YIELD: about 4 dozen cookies

These cookies will absolutely melt in your mouth! Typically, a cookie labeled a "sandie" is one with a seductive texture that's firm at first bite and then melts away on the tongue. Because this cookie has the added texture of chopped peanuts and chocolate chips, the dough tends to be on the crumbly side, but it's still easy to work with. This recipe is always a hit with my students, frequently requested by my friends and always gobbled up by my family. Once cool, these cookies store well and make a nutritious addition to a lunch box or an after-school snack. At holiday time, bake them in bulk, package them in decorative tins and send them off to friends and business associates.

INGREDIENTS

Melted butter, for cookie sheets

3 cups unbleached all-purpose flour

1½ teaspoon double-acting baking powder

2 sticks (½ pound) unsalted butter, at room temperature

1½ cups sugar

1 extra-large egg

1 rounded cup smooth peanut butter

1 cup salted cocktail peanuts, finely chopped

12 to 16 ounces semisweet or milk chocolate chips

1) **To set up:** Position both oven racks to the upper and lower positions and preheat oven to 375°F. Lightly butter cookie sheets and set aside.

2) **To prepare cookie batter:** In a large bowl, whisk together flour and baking powder. In another large bowl, using a wooden spoon or electric mixer, cream softened butter with sugar until light. Add egg and mix until smooth. Add peanut butter and combine well. Stir in nuts and chocolate chips. Finally, stir in flour mixture and continue to stir until batter is smooth throughout. If dough is a bit crumbly on the bottom, squeeze dry areas gently with your hand to help mixture bind together.

SPECIAL EQUIPMENT

Cookie sheets, either cushioned or thin

Food processor or sharp chef's knife to chop peanuts

Electric mixer (optional)

Cookie scoop with capacity of 2 liquid tablespoons (optional)

Q AND A

Q. Can I use homemade peanut butter in these cookies?

A. No. Only the creamy texture of commercially produced peanut butter will give this cookie the right texture. More important, shipments of fresh peanuts in their shells can easily grow a hazardous mold called aflatoxin, so using peanuts that have not been inspected by the USDA before being ground into peanut butter is not wise. Commercially packaged roasted peanuts (sold in vacuum-packed jars or cans) are likely to be safer due to this inspection. If you make or purchase freshly ground peanut butter, refrigerate it to prevent it from turning rancid and add some salt to extend shelf life. If you detect mold on top, throw away the entire batch.

3) **To shape and bake cookies:** Place rounded tablespoonfuls or level cookie scoops of dough 1½ inches apart on the prepared cookie sheets. You should be able to bake 4 rows of 4 cookies per sheet. (If using a tablespoon, shape each portion of dough into a round.) Using a fork, press each round gently in a crosshatch pattern. Bake cookies on both levels of the preheated oven until light golden, about 10 minutes, switching shelf positions of the sheets after half the baking.

4) **To cool and store cookies:** Place cookie sheets on wire racks to cool for 5 minutes. Then remove cookies using a thin metal spatula and allow to cool thoroughly on wire racks before storing in an airtight tin.

CHOCOLATE CHIP COOKIES

Toll House, My Way . . . for My Three Biggest Fans

YIELD: 40 large cookies

SPECIAL EQUIPMENT
2 to 4 cookie sheets, preferably cushioned type

Parchment paper

Electric mixer (optional)

Cookie scoop with capacity of 2 liquid tablespoons, only if not using the cylinder method described in Time Management Tips

The original chocolate chip cookie was created at the Toll House Restaurant in Massachusetts. But thanks to the promotion of Nestlé (which acquired the name), every mother in America probably has her own version of "Toll House" cookies. Well, here's mine—crisp, with just enough "give" in the center. Whenever possible, I make these thirty minutes before my kids are due home. This way—my son's idea—the cookies are cool enough to handle but the chocolate is still gooey inside. Because the texture of chocolate chip cookies never is as good the day after baking, I usually refrigerate and/or freeze the batter in cylinders so I can bake and serve fresh cookies whenever I choose. The thicker "cushioned" cookie sheets are preferable for these cookies since they allow them to bake more gently and are less likely to cause them to scorch on the bottom. If you don't own these, use an inverted shallow baking sheet to bake the cookies. This way the batter will be further from the hot oven rack during baking. Adjust baking time, if necessary.

INGREDIENTS

3 cups unbleached all-purpose flour

3 tablespoons unsweetened Dutch-processed cocoa powder*

¾ teaspoon double-acting baking powder

¾ teaspoon salt

1 scant teaspoon ground cinnamon

2 sticks (½ pound) unsalted butter, at room temperature

⅓ cup solid vegetable shortening

2 cups packed dark brown sugar

½ cup granulated white sugar

1½ teaspoons pure vanilla extract

2 extra-large eggs

36 ounces semisweet chocolate, broken into chunks, or packaged chips

* See section on Staples

Time Management Tips

- Split cookie batter into 4 equal sections and roll each into an 11- to 12-inch cylinder. Double wrap each cylinder in pliable plastic wrap and place in a heavy-duty freezer bag. Label with date and refrigerate for up to 1 week or freeze for 2 months. If frozen, thaw overnight in the refrigerator before slicing and baking.

1) **To set up:** Position the oven racks to the upper and lower levels and pre-heat oven to 375°F. Line cookie sheets with parchment paper; do not grease paper.

2) **To prepare cookie batter:** In a large mixing bowl, whisk together flour, cocoa, baking powder, salt and cinnamon. In another large bowl, use an electric mixer or a wooden spoon to cream butter and shortening until smooth. Add brown and white sugars and beat until well combined and light. Add vanilla, then eggs, beating well after each addition. Turn mixer to low and stir in dry flour mixture. Finally add chocolate pieces and stir well to distribute evenly.

3) **To shape cookies:** Using a cookie scoop or a spoon, place generous table-spoonfuls of the batter onto parchment-lined cookie sheets, in 3 rows of 3, 2 inches apart. Alternatively, use the cylinder method described in Time Management Tips, and slice log into ¾-inch slices and bake as directed.

Q and A

Q. Why should I use a thin spatula to remove cookies from the baking sheet?

A. *When removing cookies (especially thin ones) from a baking sheet, it's more difficult to slide the thicker spatulas with a nonstick coating cleanly underneath.*

Q. My day-old cookies always seem hard. Is there a way to improve their texture?

A. *Yes. Place an unwrapped apple slice on a small piece of waxed paper and place in the tin with cookies. The moisture in the fruit will help to soften the cookies. Replace with a fresh apple slice every day.*

4) *To bake and cool:* Bake in the preheated oven for 10 to 12 minutes, switching the shelf position of the sheets after half the baking time. Remove from the oven when cookies are just turning golden around the edges but still seem "a little too soft" in the center. Place each cookie sheet on a wire rack for 3 to 4 minutes, then, using a thin metal spatula, transfer cookies to a wire rack to cool. These are best served slightly warm from the oven. Store in an airtight tin or tightly covered cookie jar.

5) *To freeze the dough:* If you've formed cylinders of dough (as described in the introduction to this recipe), double wrap each log in pliable plastic wrap and seal in labeled heavy-duty plastic bags. This dough will freeze perfectly for up to 2 months. Thaw overnight in the refrigerator before slicing and baking.

Cookie Creativity

It's very easy to alter this recipe to suit your mood or personal craving, with the following variations.

With chopped nuts: Omit cocoa powder, use light brown sugar and substitute chopped toasted macadamia nuts or toasted blanched almonds for some of the chocolate.

With coconut: Use light brown sugar. Add 1½ cups packed shredded sweetened coconut, 1 cup chopped toasted macadamia nuts, 1 cup raisins and omit chocolate pieces.

With white chocolate: Using the original recipe, substitute white chocolate for semisweet or use a combination of white, semisweet and milk chocolate.

With dried fruits: Omit cocoa and substitute 1½ cups rolled oats (not quick cooking) for 1½ cups of flour. Reduce the amount of vanilla to 1 teaspoon and add ½ teaspoon pure almond extract. Add 1 cup chopped toasted nuts of your choice, 1½ cups diced dried fruit (apricots, pitted prunes, figs etc.) and omit the chocolate pieces.

BUTTERY LEMON-SCENTED SUGAR COOKIES

For the Holidays

YIELD: about 80 2½-inch cookies

These light, lemony sugar cookies are perfect for the holidays! This extra-large recipe provides you with plenty of cookies to give away and also to fill your own cookie jar. It's fun to collect a variety of cookie cutters in various sizes and shapes. When preparing the lemons, use an old-fashioned vegetable peeler to retrieve quickly the most zest with the least amount of bitter white pith. And although regular cookie sheets are fine, the newer cushioned type protects these thin and delicate cookies from becoming overly brown on the bottom. If you don't own these, use an inverted shallow baking sheet to bake the cookies; this way the batter will be further from the hot oven rack during baking. Adjust baking time, if necessary. For the tops of the cookies, choose either the raw, blond-colored turbinado sugar (available in health food stores), or, for a more festive touch, use the coarse multicolored rainbow sugar, which is available in many gourmet shops and cake decorating stores.

SPECIAL EQUIPMENT

Sifter or a medium-mesh wire sieve

Electric mixer

Tapered rolling pin

2 cookie sheets, preferably cushioned type

Parchment paper

INGREDIENTS

5 cups unbleached all-purpose flour, plus more for cookie cutters

1¼ teaspoons salt

1½ teaspoons double-acting baking powder

½ teaspoon baking soda

5 sticks (1¼ pounds) unsalted butter, at room temperature

2½ cups vanilla sugar (page 74) or granulated white sugar

3 extra-large eggs

2 tablespoons sour cream

2½ teaspoons pure vanilla extract

1 tablespoon strained fresh lemon juice

2½ teaspoons minced lemon zest

Coarse decorative sugar, for topping

1) To prepare cookie batter: In an extra-large mixing bowl, whisk together flour, salt, baking powder and baking soda. Sift into another bowl and then sift back into the original bowl. Cream butter in the bowl of an electric mixer. While mixing at medium speed, gradually add vanilla sugar and beat mixture until very light. Add eggs, 1 at a time, beating well after

Time Management Tips

• The dough can be frozen successfully for 1 week before cutting and baking.

Q and A

Q. What's the difference between citrus zest and rind?

A. Zest refers to only the colored part of the skin without any of the bitter white pith that lies just below.

each addition. Add sour cream, vanilla, lemon juice and zest. Turn off mixer and scrape the batter up from the bottom, using a rubber spatula, and turn on mixer to beat briefly. Turn mixer to its lowest setting and add the sifted dry ingredients in batches, mixing before adding the next batch. Do not overmix. Remove bowl from mixer and scrape any dough from beaters back into the bowl. This should be a very soft, pasty mixture at this point.

2) **To chill dough:** Lay a long piece of pliable plastic wrap about 14 inches long on your work surface. Spoon ⅓ of the batter on the center of the bottom third of the wrap. Cover with another long piece of plastic. Using gentle, even pressure with your rolling pin, roll out batter to an even thickness of ¼ inch. Lay covered sheet of dough in the freezer. Repeat process with each of the remaining thirds of dough and let sheets remain in freezer for at least 1 hour.

3) **To set up to cut and bake cookies:** Line 2 cookie sheets with parchment paper. Put a small amount of all-purpose flour into a bowl (for cookie cutters) near your work surface. Position oven racks to the upper and lower levels and preheat oven to 375°F.

4) **To cut and bake:** Work with 1 sheet of chilled dough at a time. Remove from freezer and, if dough has been in freezer for days, let it soften in the refrigerator for 5 to 10 minutes. Carefully unwrap the sheet of dough and lay it on your lightly floured work surface (preferably a cool counter). Dip cookie cutters into flour, cut out assorted shapes and lay cutouts on the prepared baking sheets ¾ to 1 inch apart. (Lay scraps on a piece of plastic wrap.) When you have filled both baking sheets, sprinkle each cookie generously with decorative sugar. Place each sheet on a rack in the preheated oven and bake for 9 to 11 minutes, switching the shelf position after half the baking time. The cookies are done when the edges are a light golden color, but the centers are still light. Using a thin spatula, immediately transfer to wire racks to cool before storing in airtight tins.

5) **To cut out and bake remaining cookies:** Continue cutting and baking remaining sheets of chilled batter. (The parchment paper is reusable; wipe the paper with a clean kitchen towel and allow sheets to cool thoroughly. Then fill and bake.) Combine all of the scraps on 1 or 2 sheets of plastic wrap. Roll, wrap, freeze, cut, top and bake them as directed.

ORANGE-STRAWBERRY SORBET

In Sugared Orange Boats

YIELD: 1 generous quart; serves 8

Oranges and strawberries are a fabulous combination however they're served. But when spiked with Grand Marnier, churned into a smooth sorbet and housed in sugar-coated orange shells, they make a spectacular dessert. Whenever a recipe calls for a specific amount of fruit to yield a precise amount of juice, it's wise to purchase more fruit than called for, since the amount of juice contained in fruit varies greatly. And don't go overboard with the Grand Marnier, since too much alcohol will prevent the sorbet from freezing properly. Also taste the mixture after churning since chilling tends to dull flavors. If you want to add more sugar, simply sift on a bit of confectioner's sugar and stir it in before storing in the freezer. To enjoy perfect flavor and texture in your sorbet, plan on freezing and serving the mixture on the same day. Accompany the boats with a platter of Buttery Lemon-Scented Sugar Cookies (page 491).

SPECIAL EQUIPMENT
Food processor or blender

Ice cream maker (optional)

Medium-sized ice cream scoop

INGREDIENTS

2 tablespoons granulated white sugar

½ cup water

½ cup light corn syrup

10 medium-sized juicy navel oranges

12 medium-sized ripe strawberries, rinsed, drained and hulled

About ½ cup superfine sugar, for orange boats

1 egg white

2 tablespoon chilled Grand Marnier or other orange-flavored liqueur (optional)

1) *To make sugar syrup:* In a small saucepan, combine sugar and the water and bring to a boil to dissolve sugar. Remove from heat and stir in corn syrup. Cover and chill thoroughly.

2) *To prepare orange juice:* Scrub and dry oranges and cut them in half through the middle (not the stem end). Carefully scoop out the flesh with a teaspoon (a grapefruit spoon works well), trying not to rip the outer rind. Reserve 8 of the nicest orange shells and discard the rest. Place orange pulp into the bowl of a food processor fitted with the steel blade

Time Management Tips

- The sugar syrup can be prepared and the orange shells can be sugared 1 day ahead and stored in the refrigerator.

- The fruit mixture can be assembled fully and stored in the refrigerator 2 days before freezing.

- For best texture, the sorbet should be eaten the day of freezing. The orange boats can be filled 5 hours ahead of serving.

Q. What's the difference between a sorbet and sherbert?

A. *A sorbet (sorbetto in Italian) usually is made exclusively with fruit purée and a syrup made from water, sugar and light corn syrup. Some sorbets are made from a mixture of fruit and wine and are served as a "palate cleanser" between courses. Interestingly,* sorbet *is the French term for "sherbet" but in American usage the two are quite different. Sorbets have a slightly icy texture. Sherbets are slightly creamier and usually are made from fruit and milk or cream. Cup for cup, sorbets have more fruit and less flavor-enhancing ingredients (such as extracts) than sherbets.*

or a blender and process until pulp is totally broken down. Pour this into a medium-mesh wire sieve over a large mixing bowl. Push juice through strainer extracting as much juice as possible, ideally 3 cups.

3) ***To prepare strawberries and complete mixture:*** Purée strawberries in food processor or blender, adding a bit of orange juice to help liquify; they should yield 1 cup. Combine strawberry purée with chilled sugar syrup and orange juice. Cover and chill thoroughly.

4) ***To prepare sugared orange boats:*** Place a sheet of waxed paper on a shallow baking sheet. Spread superfine sugar on a plate or shallow tray. Slice a very thin layer off the bottom (rounded) side of each orange shell to help it stand upright on a plate. Brush the outside of each shell (including the rim) with egg white and roll it in sugar until the outside rind and rim are well coated. Place coated shell (rim side down) on the waxed paper. When all the shells are coated, place them in the freezer.

5) ***To freeze sorbet:*** If using an ice cream maker, freeze orange-strawberry mixture according to the manufacturer's instructions and, when thickened but not yet frozen, add chilled Grand Marnier, if using, and continue to churn until finished. Alternatively, freeze mixture in a sturdy container and, when thickened as described above, stir in liqueur and continue to thicken further. Spoon into a sturdy freezer container, cover and place in the freezer to firm up before assembling in orange boats.

6) ***To assemble fully and serve:*** Using a medium-sized ice cream scoop, fill each frozen orange shell with sorbet. Serve immediately or sit them upright on the baking sheet, cover with plastic wrap and store in the freezer until serving time.

Pucker-Up for . . .
THE CREAMIEST LEMON SORBET

YIELD: 1½ quarts

It always amazes me how this lemony liquid, which starts out thin and watery, ends up looking like creamy whipped potatoes after churning in an ice cream maker! The addition of corn syrup is the secret to developing the extra smooth texture, and although the pucker-up taste suits me and my family, I suggest that you taste the sorbet after churning until thickened and if you feel it needs more sugar, simply stir in some sifted confectioner's sugar before freezing until firm. Depending on your ice cream maker, you might have to freeze the mixture in two batches but the liquid lemon mixture will stay fine in your refrigerator for three full days.

SPECIAL EQUIPMENT
Food processor, only if making lemon boats

Ice cream maker (optional)

Medium-sized (oblong shaped) ice cream scoop

Pastry bag fitted with plain or star tip, only if you plan on piping the sorbet into sugared lemon boats

INGREDIENTS

2 cups water

2 cups granulated white sugar

About 20 large lemons, at room temperature

½ cup light corn syrup

FOR SUGARED LEMON BOATS (OPTIONAL)

1 egg white

⅓ to ½ cup superfine sugar or regular granulated white sugar

1) *To prepare sugar syrup:* Combine the water and sugar in a saucepan and bring to a boil to dissolve sugar. Remove from heat and chill thoroughly.

2) *To extract lemon juice:* The shape of lemon boats must be oblong so, if using, you'll need to cut as many as 12 scrubbed lemons lengthwise (through stem end) instead of through the middle, only removing ¼ of one long side of each lemon. Remove pulp as directed in Orange-Strawberry Sorbet (page 493), set empty lemon shells and tops aside and place lemon pulp into the bowl of a food processor fitted with the steel blade.

Time Management Tips

- Same as Orange-Strawberry Sorbet (page 493)

3) To prepare lemon mixture: Use a wooden reamer to remove the juice from the remaining lemons and add to the food processor. Process to pulverize pulp with juice, push through a medium-mesh wire sieve and measure 3 cups. Stir chilled sugar syrup and corn syrup into lemon juice and chill thoroughly before proceeding.

4) To prepare sugared lemon boats, if using: Cut a thin slice off the bottom rounded side of each empty lemon rind which will enable it to stand upright without wobbling. Turn to page 494 and follow the instructions for sugar orange boats, only include the tops in the sugar coating procedure as well. Freeze the boats and tops on a shallow baking sheet lined with waxed paper until ready to fill with sorbet.

5) To freeze sorbet: If using an ice cream maker, freeze lemon mixture according to the manufacturer's instructions. Alternatively, freeze mixture in a sturdy container and when half frozen, give mixture a good stir and continue to freeze until scoopable. If using an ice cream maker, sorbet is finished when it looks like very creamy whipped potatoes. Spoon sorbet into a freezer container and freeze until sturdy enough to pipe or firm enough to scoop. If using lemon boats, spoon sorbet into a pastry bag fitted with a plain or star tip and pipe into prepared lemon boats following the directions on page 505. Or, use an oblong-shaped ice cream scoop to fill boats or any scoop when serving in bowls. Serve immediately or sit them upright on the baking sheet, cover with plastic wrap and store in the freezer until serving time.

6) To serve: Place a filled boat on each plate and place 1 sugared top on top of sorbet. Or serve individual scoops of sorbet in small bowls.

OLD-FASHIONED VANILLA ICE CREAM

YIELD: about 1 quart; serves 6 to 8

Whether you love—or hate—vanilla, this recipe is the answer to ice cream heaven. It is the base for an entire collection of rich and creamy ice creams made using the classic method of starting with a cooked custard base. This is the key to making great-tasting ice cream with a superior texture; the eggs enable the ice cream to maintain its smooth and creamy texture for days after churning. But since most of us feel the need for both this full and traditional ice cream and a lighter version, see my variation for Skinny Vanilla Ice Cream.

SPECIAL EQUIPMENT
Triple-mesh wire sieve

2-quart heavy-bottomed saucepan, preferably with a spout

Electric mixer or whisk

Manual or electric ice cream maker

INGREDIENTS

Ice cubes or crushed ice, for cooling custard

2 cups heavy cream (preferably not ultrapasteurized)

1 cup milk

1 large supple vanilla bean

6 extra-large egg yolks

1 cup vanilla sugar (page 74) or granulated white sugar

2 teaspoons pure vanilla extract

Pinch salt

1) **To set up for custard:** Place a shallow layer of ice cubes or crushed ice on the bottom of a 6-quart bowl. Add a little water to the ice and place a 3-quart bowl into the larger bowl, pushing its bottom into the ice. Place a triple-mesh wire sieve over the smaller bowl. The iced bowl helps to stop the cooking process to minimize the risk of curdling the custard.

2) **To scald cream and milk for custard base:** Pour cream and milk into a 2-quart heavy-bottomed saucepan (preferably with a spout). Using a sharp knife, slit vanilla bean lengthwise through the top of skin only. Open bean and (using the dull side of the knife) scrape down the length of the bean, removing the seeds. Whisk seeds into milk to disperse seeds throughout. Place the pan over medium-low heat and scald mixture, but do not let it simmer.

Q. What's the best way to crush ice?

A. Unless the instructions that come with your blender specifically state that it can be used to crush ice, don't try. Crushing with a blender can easily ruin the blades and exhaust the motor. Instead, wrap ice cubes within a strong paper towel or clean kitchen towel and, using a hammer, whack the ice into small pieces.

3) *To assemble and cook custard base:* Meanwhile beat egg yolks in the bowl of an electric mixer (or use a whisk), while gradually adding sugar until mixture is thick but light in texture and a pale lemon color. Lower speed of mixer to slow and add scalded milk mixture (a little at a time at first to temper yolks). When all of the milk is added and incorporated, pour the contents of the bowl back into the saucepan off the heat. Use a rubber spatula to scrape any remaining mixture from the bottom of the bowl into the saucepan. Place over medium-low heat and cook custard, stirring constantly with a wooden spoon, until mixture is thickened and coats the back of the spoon, about 4 minutes once mixture becomes hot throughout.

4) *To strain, flavor and chill:* Pour cooked custard into the sieve over the icedbowl setup and strain custard, discarding anything that remains in the sieve. Stir in vanilla and salt. Place a clean kitchen towel or paper towel over the top of the iced bowl and let cool to just warm, stirring occasionally before placing both bowls into the refrigerator to cool custard thoroughly. (Add more ice to the larger bowl, going up the sides, to help chilling process.)

5) *To freeze and store:* Transfer chilled custard into the bowl of an ice cream maker and follow the manufacturer's instructions. Serve at once or store in the freezer in a sealed container until serving time.

Vanilla Ice Cream with Extra Crunch

When churning the ice cream add one or a combination of the following to the base when it has thickened but is not yet hard.

Chips or nuts: 1 cup regular or mini-sized semisweet or milk chocolate chips. Or use ½ cup chips and ½ cup chopped toasted walnuts. Peanut butter chips or butterscotch chips may be substituted. Or try a combination of butterscotch chips and ½ cup chopped toasted blanched almonds.

Cookies and cream: 1 cup crushed chocolate sandwich cookies (such as Oreos)

Candy bar crunch: 1 cup crushed chocolate-covered toffee bars or crunchy peanut butter bars (such as Heath bars and Butterfinger bars)

Toasted almond: Reduce vanilla extract to 1½ teaspoons and add 1 scant teaspoon pure almond extract and 1 cup chopped toasted blanched almonds (page 76).

A custard must be cooked until it thickens properly, but this egg yolk–based mixture is extremely heat sensitive. Thus it's crucial that you never allow the sauce to come too close to a boil or you run the risk of curdling, which will produce a custard with a granular texture from little bits of cooked egg yolks. If using an electric stove, I suggest preheating two burners to different low settings. This way, as you stir the sauce while it cooks and thickens, you can frequently transfer the pot back and forth between the burners to regulate the heat more effectively. And always remove the pot from the heated burner every time you check the consistency to prevent accidental overheating.

Coconut: Reduce vanilla extract to 1½ teaspoons and add ½ teaspoon pure almond extract and 1 cup grated unsweetened (desiccated) coconut (available in health food stores). Or add a combination of ½ cup coconut and ½ cup toasted macadamia nuts (it's preferable to use unsalted nuts, but they're hard to find; rub salted nuts in a kitchen towel).

Brownies and cream: Add 1 to 1½ cubed Midnight Brownies (page 482).

Mint chocolate chips: Stir a couple of drops of green food coloring into the cooled ice cream mixture. Reduce vanilla extract to 1½ teaspoons and add 1 scant teaspoon peppermint extract. Add 1 cup regular or mint chocolate chips.

Skinny Vanilla Ice Cream

Set up iced bowls, but leave off the sieve. Prepare 1 recipe of Skinny Crème Fraîche (page 84), omitting vanilla and sugar. Place in a heavy-bottomed saucepan with 2 cups low-fat milk, the seeds from 1 plump vanilla bean and ¾ cup superfine sugar. Whisk over medium heat for just 1 minute until sugar is totally dissolved. Pour mixture into iced bowl and stir in 2 teaspoons vanilla extract. Chill thoroughly before freezing in the container of your ice cream freezer according to the manufacturer's instructions.

I'll Take Those Speckled Ones Please . . .
BANANA ICE CREAM

YIELD: about 1½ quarts; serves 10

Smooth and delicious banana ice cream is definitely one of those foods that I'd want as part of my last meal on earth. Select only the ripest bananas for the fullest flavor. If you don't have very ripe bananas, visit your local produce market. Usually, they remove the extra-ripe bananas from their stands once they appear to be over the hill. Except for the ingredients, this recipe is almost identical to Old-Fashioned Vanilla Ice Cream (page 497).

SPECIAL EQUIPMENT
Same as Old-Fashioned Vanilla Ice Cream, plus a blender for the bananas

INGREDIENTS

Ice cubes or crushed ice, for cooling custard

1½ cups heavy cream (preferably not ultrapasteurized)

1½ cups whole milk

4 extra-large egg yolks

1 cup plus 1 tablespoon sugar

1½ cups fresh banana purée (about 2 large very ripe bananas)

1 teaspoon strained fresh lemon juice

2 teaspoons pure vanilla extract

Pinch salt

1) **To prepare custard:** Using the amounts of cream, milk, eggs and sugar specified in this recipe, prepare custard base as directed for Old-Fashioned Vanilla Ice Cream (steps 1 through 3, omitting vanilla bean).

2) **To strain, flavor and freeze:** Strain custard into iced bowl, as directed for Vanilla Ice Cream. Then stir in banana purée with lemon juice, vanilla extract and salt. Freeze and store as directed for vanilla ice cream.

Peanut Butter Banana Ice Cream

Prepare preceding recipe for banana ice cream as directed. When thickened but not yet stiff, stir in teaspoonfuls of creamy or chunky peanut butter or broken up crunchy chocolate-covered peanut butter candy bars or peanut butter cups (use 1 cup total).

Q AND A

Q. I hate dealing with rock-hard ice cream, but I always forget to take out my ice cream in advance so it can soften. Any tips?

A. Early on the day of serving (or as much as one day ahead), scoop out individual portions of softened ice cream and place on a shallow baking sheet or tray lined with waxed paper. Cover scoops with plastic wrap and store in the freezer until needed.

Strawberry-Banana Ice Cream

Prepare preceding recipe for banana ice cream as directed. But increase the amount of sugar to 1¼ cups and banana purée to 1⅔ cups and add 1½ cups pureed fresh strawberries with banana purée. (Rinse, drain and hull strawberries before puréeing.)

Oh What a Buzz...
COFFEE ICE CREAM

YIELD: about 1 generous quart; serves 8

If you're a borderline insomniac, I suggest that you substitute coffee without caffeine. But if you love the taste of real coffee, this ice cream is just great! And for a drink that you could have used when studying for final exams, make a coffee float by placing a scoop of the ice cream into a tempered glass mug and filling to the top with hot, freshly brewed coffee. This is another of those wonderful recipes with different ingredients but the same method as Old-Fashioned Vanilla Ice Cream (page 497).

SPECIAL EQUIPMENT
Same as Old-Fashioned Vanilla Ice Cream

INGREDIENTS

Ice cubes or crushed ice, for cooling custard

2 cups heavy cream (preferably not ultrapasteurized)

1 rounded teaspoon instant espresso powder

4 extra-large egg yolks

2¼ cups sugar

2 cups strong brewed coffee, thoroughly chilled

1 teaspoon pure vanilla extract

Pinch salt

1) **To prepare custard:** Using ingredients for this recipe, follow directions for Old-Fashioned Vanilla Ice Cream (steps 1 through 3) with following exceptions: In step 2, scald cream with 1 cup of the sugar and espresso powder, stirring constantly with a whisk to dissolve sugar. In step 3, beat egg yolks with the remaining 1¼ cups sugar.

2) **To strain, flavor and freeze:** Strain custard into iced bowl as directed in step 4 of vanilla ice cream recipe. Then stir in chilled coffee, vanilla extract and salt. Freeze and store as directed for vanilla ice cream.

Coffee-Fudge Swirl Ice Cream

Add 1 cup cooled leftover Hot Fudge Sauce (page 507), 1 tablespoon at a time, to the thickened but not yet hard coffee ice cream.

QUICK AND EASY
ICE CREAM BIRTHDAY CAKE
For Kids from 3 to 103!

YIELD: one 9-inch cake; serves 12

SPECIAL EQUIPMENT
9-inch springform pan

Food processor (optional)

Electric mixer or a balloon whisk and wide shallow bowl

Metal icing spatula, preferably with an elbow bend

Pastry bag with star tip

Cardboard cake box (optional), for freezing

You'll probably think I'm crazy to end a book on cooking from scratch with a recipe based on commercial cookies and candy bars. But we all have our weak moments and, besides, it's fun to see a group of adults regress to child-like behavior. Believe me, they do at the sight of this decadent ice cream cake. This candy-studded cake is always requested by my children, husband, parents, brothers and friends. When their birthdays roll around, I wouldn't think of serving anything else. Although I love making homemade ice cream I usually purchase best-quality commercially prepared ice cream for this cake (Häagen-Dazs is my favorite). Throughout this recipe I've specified my favorite specialty brand names but if you're partial to another of the same sort, by all means go for it!

INGREDIENTS

1 box Nabisco thin chocolate wafers

¼ to ½ teaspoon ground cinnamon (optional)

1 stick (¼ pound) unsalted butter, melted

1½ pints *each* best-quality vanilla, chocolate and strawberry ice cream, softened to a spreadable (not soupy) consistency

4 large Butterfinger bars, crumbled (hit with a can or meat mallet while still wrapped)

1½ cups crushed Oreo cookies (regular or fudge-covered)

1 recipe Perfect Whipped Cream (page 84)

OPTIONAL TOPPINGS

Assorted colored sprinkles (also called "Jimmies")

Cake decorating gel

Chopped unsalted dry-roasted peanuts

M&Ms candies (regular or peanut-filled)

Since clean hands are your best tool, use them to help spread the ice cream over each layer. Use hot water to thaw your hands as necessary.

1) To prepare cookie crust: Put chocolate wafers in the bowl of a food processor fitted with the steel blade and grind them fine. Alternatively, place broken up cookies (in batches) in a heavy-duty plastic bag and roll over them with a rolling pin until finely crushed. Transfer crumbs to another bowl and whisk in cinnamon, if using. Add melted butter, mixing with a fork until thoroughly blended. Press a thin layer of crumbs on the bottom and up the sides of a 9-inch springform pan, using all of the crumbs. Place pan in freezer on a shallow baking sheet lined with wax paper to firm up crust while ice cream continues to soften to a spreadable consistency.

2) To assemble cake: Squeeze vanilla ice cream out of its containers onto the bottom of the chilling crust. Using a metal spatula and your hands, spread the softened ice cream evenly over the bottom of the chilling crust. (Dip your hands in the hot water as necessary but always dry them thoroughly before continuing.) Cover ice cream with crumbled Butterfinger bars, pressing gently. Spread chocolate ice cream over crumbs and cover with crushed Oreos, again pressing gently. Cover crushed cookies with strawberry ice cream and smooth the top with a metal spatula. Place into the freezer to firm for 1 hour.

3) ***To top cake:*** Prepare Perfect Whipped Cream as directed in recipe. Spread ⅔ of the whipped cream over the top of cake and reserve the rest for a decorative border. (For smoothest surface, spread only once in one direction then scrape off excess whipped cream into bowl. Continue spreading and scraping until surface is perfectly smooth.) Return cake to the freezer for 10 to 20 minutes, just to firm the whipped cream.

4) ***To decorate cake:*** Fit your pastry bag with a star tip and fill bag with remaining whipped cream. Remove cake from freezer and pipe on a simple swirled border around its circumference. If desired, sprinkle border with some colored sprinkles. Return to freezer to firm for 20 minutes. Then, if desired, write a message on top with decorating gel and/or sprinkle the inside of the piped whipped cream with another thin border of crushed unsalted peanuts or a ring of M&Ms.

5) ***To freeze and store cake:*** Freeze cake (uncovered) for up to 4 hours. For longer storage, either purchase a cardboard cake box from a bakery or stick toothpicks in the border of peanuts (to camouflage the holes) and drape aluminum foil loosely over the top. This will help prevent freezer burn.

6) ***To remove springform sides and serve:*** When cake is thoroughly frozen, dip a dish towel in very hot water and wring it out. Place the hot towel around the sides of the pan to help release it from the crust. Unlatch lock and ease off sides. Return cake to freezer. To serve, remove cake from freezer 30 to 40 minutes before serving to enable it to become softened enough to cut into wedges. Present the cake whole and cut into wedges at the table.

Although disposable pastry bags are wonderful for piping very soft mixtures, I don't recommend them for mixtures with texture (even minced vegetables), since they often clog up the tip. For the heavier and more textural mixtures, I recommend the sturdier bags made of either tightly woven cloth, nylon, plastic-lined cotton or polyester. To develop proficiency with a pastry bag, practice with mashed potatoes of different consistency.

To fill pastry bag: Insert the tip of your choice into the bag (pointed side down). (If using a professional bag, secure tip in place with the plastic screw attachment.) Place bag (tip down) into a tall drinking glass and fold top of bag over the rim of the glass to form a cuff. Fill inside of bag no more than two-thirds full using a rubber spatula. Alternatively, simply cuff the top portion of bag over one hand and scoop your filling into bag with your other hand. Gather the folded portion of bag at the top and, after pushing out any excess air at the top, twist shut. Proceed to pipe your mixture or secure bag with a "twisty" from a trash-bag box, place bag (tip down) in a tall glass and refrigerate until needed. This way, the bag can stand upright without the contents spilling out.

To use pastry bag: Grasp bag at the top where it's twisted shut and place your other hand underneath bag so you can control the tip. Remove excess air from bag by gently squeezing from the top until some filling extrudes through the bottom tip. When piping your mixture, always squeeze from the top with one hand and direct the tip with the other hand. When squeezing, adjust the pressure according to the density of the mixture being piped. Your tip should be positioned at a 45-degree angle, just above the area to be piped. For the most balance and control, hold top of bag close to your body as you bend toward the area to be piped.

To clean pastry bag: After each use, you must thoroughly clean and air-dry your pastry bag. Make sure to check the seams as you rinse to remove any filmy residue or hidden bits of food. To dry, place the large opening of the cleaned empty bag (turned inside out) over a tall wine bottle for a few hours or overnight. And, if you detect an off or sour odor, it's time to purchase another bag since they don't last forever.

To Gild the Lily
DESSERT SAUCES

In this section, you'll find five luscious dessert sauces to ladle on top of ice cream or cut-up assorted fresh fruits. For your added convenience when entertaining, all of these sauces can be prepared at least one day ahead of serving and stored in the refrigerator. If you choose not to make homemade ice cream, whenever possible purchase ice cream from an ice cream parlor instead of the supermarket for freshest flavor.

Fresh Strawberry Sauce
YIELD: serves 6 to 8

SPECIAL EQUIPMENT
Strawberry huller (optional)

This ruby red sauce that's loaded with berries is just great with a scoop of Old-Fashioned Vanilla Ice Cream (page 497) or Banana Ice Cream (page 500). Place ice cream in bowls, ladle sauce over top, add a good dollop of Perfect Whipped Cream (page 84) and sprinkle with toasted sliced almonds (page 76).

INGREDIENTS

2 baskets (12 to 16 ounces each) strawberries, cleaned, hulled and kept whole

1 jar (12 ounces) seedless raspberry jam

⅔ cup water

½ cup sugar

3 tablespoons Grand Marnier or other orange-flavored liqueur (optional)

Place strawberries in a large bowl. Combine jam, water and sugar in a 1-quart saucepan. Stir over low heat to dissolve sugar and liquify jam, stirring frequently. When mixture begins to bubble from the center, remove pan from heat and stir in Grand Marnier. Pour mixture over strawberries and cool uncovered. When cool, cover with plastic wrap and refrigerate for at least 4 hours or overnight.

Hot Fudge Sauce

YIELD: about 2½ cups; serves 12 to 14

The way I see it, every so often, it's downright good for a person to indulge in a small portion of something absolutely decadent! So when it's that time for you, serve this triple-chocolate sauce over a scoop of Coffee Ice Cream (page 501) or Old-Fashioned Vanilla Ice Cream (page 497) or Banana Ice Cream (page 500).

SPECIAL EQUIPMENT
Double boiler, only for reheating sauce

INGREDIENTS

⅔ cup sugar

½ cup unsweetened Dutch-processed cocoa powder*

¾ cup light corn syrup

2 ounces unsweetened chocolate, chopped

4 ounces bittersweet chocolate, chopped

1 rounded teaspoon instant coffee powder or espresso powder

6 tablespoons unsalted butter, cut into 6 pieces

⅔ cup heavy cream (preferably not ultrapasteurized)

2 teaspoons pure vanilla extract

Pinch salt

* See section on Staples

1) *To prepare sauce:* In a medium-sized bowl, whisk together sugar and cocoa. Sift the mixture into another bowl. Bring corn syrup to a boil in a 2-quart heavy-bottomed saucepan over medium heat. Allow syrup to boil 3 minutes, then reduce heat to low and slowly whisk in the cocoa mixture combining well after each addition. When mixture is smooth, using a wooden spoon, stir in chopped chocolates and instant coffee powder. Stir until smooth, then add butter 1 piece at a time, stirring well after each addition. Stir in heavy cream, raise heat to medium and bring the mixture to a boil. Continue to cook for 1 minute, then remove sauce from heat and stir in vanilla and salt.

2) *To serve and store:* If planning to serve shortly, pour sauce into another bowl and let cool slightly and thicken before ladling over scoops of your favorite ice cream. If serving later that day, keep at room temperature; otherwise store for up to 5 days in the refrigerator. Reheat in a double boiler over hot (not simmering) water.

Butterscotch-Walnut Sauce
With or without Walnuts

YIELD: generous 2 to 3 cups; serves 8 to 12

SPECIAL EQUIPMENT
Double boiler, only for reheating sauce

There aren't any low-fat tips accompanying this recipe, because I wouldn't dare alter this sauce. It's the simplest, quickest to prepare and best butterscotch sauce I've ever had—particularly on Old-Fashioned Vanilla Ice Cream (page 497). Although the nuts are optional, I strongly suggest including them. Or for a change, substitute toasted fresh chestnuts (page 332), diced and sautéed in a little unsalted butter until golden.

INGREDIENTS

1½ cups firmly packed light brown sugar

½ cup heavy cream (preferably not ultrapasteurized)

½ cup light corn syrup

½ stick (4 tablespoons) unsalted butter

1 teaspoon pure vanilla extract

1 cup shelled walnuts (optional), coarsely chopped

1) **To prepare sauce:** Place all ingredients except vanilla and nuts into a 1½-quart heavy-bottomed saucepan over medium-low heat. Stir to combine while butter melts and mixture comes to a strong simmer. Continue to simmer briskly over medium-low heat uncovered until thickened, about 5 minutes, stirring occasionally. Remove pan from heat and stir in vanilla and walnuts, if using. Transfer sauce to a bowl or jar and let cool until just warm before serving or cool thoroughly, cover and refrigerate.

Since walnuts can easily become rancid (bitter tasting with an "off" scent), make sure to smell and taste them before using in a recipe. If purchasing walnuts out of their shells, choose those that come in vacuum-packed containers instead of cellophane bags. The clear bag allows light to filter in, increasing the likelihood of flavor loss even before they leave the market. To best maintain freshness once opened, freeze remaining nuts in a sealed heavy-duty plastic bag.

2) **To serve:** If thick and cool, place sauce in the top of a double boiler over hot but not simmering water. Warm over low heat just to soften the consistency and warm throughout. Ladle sauce over individual scoops of vanilla ice cream.

Honey Roasted Peanut Brittle Sauce

YIELD: about 2 cups; serves 8

This sauce tastes like melted peanut brittle—can you imagine? And it's a perfect partner to Banana Ice Cream (page 500) or Old-Fashioned Vanilla Ice Cream (page 497). Of course, if you're on the "barter system" diet, serve over Skinny Vanilla Ice Cream (page 499). Honey roasted peanuts are available in the supermarket with the other peanuts. Their slightly sweet yet salty taste adds an interesting dimension to the sauce. You could, however, use any salted dry roasted peanuts instead.

SPECIAL EQUIPMENT
2-quart heavy-bottomed saucepan with light-colored interior (enamel-coated cast iron works best)

Double boiler, only for reheating sauce

INGREDIENTS

¼ cup water

¾ cup sugar

¼ cup light corn syrup

⅓ cup heavy cream (preferably not ultrapasteurized)

½ stick (4 tablespoons) unsalted butter, at room temperature

1 teaspoon pure vanilla extract

1 cup honey roasted peanuts (not chopped)

1) *To prepare caramelized sugar syrup:* In a 2-quart heavy-bottomed saucepan (preferably with a light interior), combine the water, sugar and corn syrup. Boil down to a caramelized sugar syrup as directed on page 472.

2) *To finish sauce:* When the deep amber color is achieved, immediately remove syrup from heat and add cream and butter all at once. (The mixture will bubble furiously, then subside.) Stir to combine and then stir in vanilla and nuts.

3) *To serve and store:* If planning to serve shortly, pour sauce into another bowl and let cool slightly and thicken before ladling over scoops of your favorite ice cream. If serving later that day, keep at room temperature; otherwise, store for up to 5 days in the refrigerator. Reheat in a double boiler over hot (not simmering) water.

Crème Anglaise
(Vanilla Custard Sauce)

YIELD: about 3½ cups; serves 12 to 16

SPECIAL EQUIPMENT
Triple-mesh wire sieve

Electric mixer

2-quart heavy-bottomed saucepan, preferably with a spout

There's such a mystique about this classic velvety custard sauce, flecked with vanilla seeds for an exquisitely aromatic flavor. But the method and ingredients are almost identical to the custard base for Old-Fashioned Vanilla Ice Cream—only the proportions and ultimate consistency differ. For a light and elegant dessert, ladle this sauce generously over individual servings of cut-up fresh fruit served in pretty parfait glasses (or balloon wine glasses). Then, if desired, add some Fresh Strawberry Sauce (page 506) on top and garnish each serving with a beautiful sprig of fresh mint. This sauce can sit underneath a piece of chocolate cake and also serves as a delightful dip for cut-up fruits.

INGREDIENTS
1½ cups heavy cream (preferably not ultrapasteurized)

¾ cup milk

1 plump vanilla bean

6 extra-large egg yolks, at room temperature

½ cup plus 1 tablespoon sugar

Pinch salt

1 tablespoon pure vanilla extract

1) ***To prepare custard:*** Using the amounts of ingredients listed above, prepare vanilla custard according to the directions in steps 1 through 3 for making the custard base in Old-Fashioned Vanilla Ice Cream (page 497), with the following exceptions. You may use a 2-quart bowl in the iced bowl setup and the custard itself will have a thinner consistency, as follows.

2) ***To test custard sauce for proper consistency:*** When you think sauce has thickened and looks velvety, remove pan from the burner. Raise the wooden spoon from the sauce and turn it over. The custard mixture should coat the back of the spoon. Next, draw a line down the film of custard with your finger. If the sauce is thick enough, the line will remain when you remove your finger. If the sauce is too thin, the line will quickly fill up after you draw the line. If necessary, return the pot to the stove for 1 to 2 minutes before removing to retest.

3) ***To strain and cool sauce:*** When the custard is of proper consistency, immediately pour it through the wire strainer into the prepared iced bowl. Remove sieve and stir in salt and vanilla. Cover bowl with a clean kitchen towel, let cool slightly, remove cloth and cover bowl with plastic wrap. Refrigerate to chill thoroughly for up to 2 days before serving.

When using pure vanilla extract in your recipes, don't add it until your mixture has been removed from direct heat. Otherwise, both the potent flavor and seductive aroma of this essence literally will cook away, leaving only a faint resemblance to vanilla in your mixture.

Q AND A

Q. If my recipe calls for yolks only (or visa versa), can I freeze the remaining whites or yolks?

A. Yes. To freeze egg whites, pour each white into an individual ice cube cup. When frozen, pop them out and store in a heavy-duty plastic bag. Egg yolks don't freeze well by themselves and need to be mixed with a bit of salt, sugar or light corn syrup before freezing. Salt is the most versatile since it won't affect the flavor as sugar does. For every two egg yolks, mix in a pinch of salt and place in a small labeled container. Thaw yolks or whites overnight in the refrigerator and use them promptly.

MAIL ORDER SOURCES

Adriana's Bazaar

(212) 877-5757
2152 Broadway
New York, NY 10023

A fabulous source for hard-to-find ingredients, like fermented black beans, and for a vast variety of dried chili peppers, herbs, spices, beans, grains, rice, ethnic condiments and oils.

**Aux Delices des Bois
(Mushrooms by Mail)**

(212) 334-1230
4 Leonard Street
New York, NY 10013

Offers over twenty different types of cultivated mushrooms including cremini, shiitake, white trumpet, oyster and portobello. A catalog states seasonal varieties, but they ship throughout the country year round.

Balducci's

(212) 673-2600
Mail order catalog
If mailing out of state: (800) 822-1444
If mailing within New York State:
(800) 225-3822
424 Sixth Avenue
New York, NY 10011

This store carries an extraordinary variety of imported jarred items, dried pastas, specialty flours, cured meats, assorted types of fine-quality vinegars and olive oils. If the catalog doesn't list something that you want, request it; they will ship any item sold in the store.

Bridge Kitchenware

(212) 688-4220
214 East 52nd Street
New York, New York 10022

A mail order catalog is a recent feature of this New York store that focuses on supplying the professional chef. There is an incredibly extensive list of imported as well as domestic cookware, baking equipment, tools, cake decorating equipment, parchment paper and pastry bags (disposable and regular).

Chef's Catalog

(800) 338-3232
3215 Commercial Avenue
Northbrook, IL 60062

An extensive list of high-quality cooking and baking equipment as well as gadgets, tools, utensils and appliances. Every serious cook should get this catalog regularly.

The Chocolate Gallery

(212) 675-2253
34 West 22nd Street
New York, NY 10010

Supplies a line of extremely efficient equipment necessary to make home-made chocolates, whimsical cookies, decorative cakes. They sell edible toppings as well.

Culinary Parts Unlimited

Outside California: (800) 543-7549
California residents: (800) 722-7239
80 Berry Drive
Pacheco, CA 94553

Replacement parts for appliances—what a great idea! This company stocks accessories and parts for household appliances made by twenty of the most popular manufacturers. These include Cuisinart, Braun, KitchenAid, Krups, Oster, Farberware, Salton, Hamilton Beach, Proctor-Silex and many others.

Dean & Deluca

(800) 221-7714
560 Broadway
New York, NY 10012

Supplies best-quality dried fruits, nuts, exotic jams and jellies, extracts, fine chocolate and baking equipment.

J. B. Prince Company

(212) 302-8611
29 West 38th Street
New York, NY 10018

Impressive collection of fine tools and unusual hard-to-find items geared toward the professional. Extensive catalog available.

Jessica's Biscuit Cookbook Catalog

(800) 878-4264
P.O. Box 301
Newtonville, MA 02160

A wonderful catalog for learning about the latest cookbooks, as well as for buying some old-timers that are hard to find. Great prices and special offers, as well.

King Arthur Flour Baker's Catalogue

(800) 827-6836
P.O. Box 876
Norwich, VT 05055

This terrific company provides many different hard-to-locate flours, grains, extracts, tools and baking equipment. This catalog is a must for the serious baker.

Lamalle of New York

(212) 242-0750
36 West 25th Street
New York, NY 10010

Whether you are a professional chef or a dedicated home cook, this company will locate unusual hard-to-find imported French cookware and baking equipment, including a nice supply of copper items. They also sell basic hand-held tools.

Maid of Scandinavia

(800) 851-1121
3244 Raleigh Avenue
Minneapolis, MN 55416

A fabulous catalog for any serious baker! Everything you could possibly want is listed—from edibles such as extracts, chocolates and specialty colored sugars to whimsical cake pans and tools of the trade.

Paprikas Weiss

(212) 288-6117
1546 Second Avenue
New York, NY 10028

This favorite of many New Yorkers supplies a wide variety of spices and herbs in bulk. They also sell by mail fabulous candied citron for Christmas cakes, vanilla beans, coffee beans, dried fruits and nuts, jarred condiments, many different types of flour, grains and beans, as well as baking utensils and a full line of Hungarian cold cuts.

William Glen

(800) 842-3322
2651 El Paseo Lane
Town & Country Village
Sacramento, CA 95821

This store produces a wonderful catalog with an extensive list of cookware, baking equipment, kitchen appliances and culinary gadgets.

Williams-Sonoma

(800) 541-2223
Mail Order Department
100 North Point
San Francisco, CA 94133

Their stores are renowned for providing the highest-quality baking equipment, cooking utensils, small electrical appliances, new cooking gadgets, cake decorating equipment, extracts, pasta flour, cocoas, chocolates and you name it. The seasonal catalogs reflect their consistent quality and imagination.

The Wooden Spoon

(800) 431-2207
Route 145, Heritage Park
P.O. Box 931
Clinton, CT 06413

This helpful catalog is mostly devoted to cooking equipment with emphasis on hand-held tools and gadgets.

Zabar's

(212) 787-2000
2245 Broadway
New York, NY 10024

Anyone who's been to Zabar's in New York knows that this store is one of a kind! Their catalog has a huge selection of cookware, baking equipment, small electrical appliances, kitchen tools, coffee beans and specialty foods (like smoked fish and assorted jarred condiments).

BIBLIOGRAPHY

Although I've learned so much and have been inspired by many books over the course of the last eighteen years, the books mentioned below helped me immensely while writing my manuscript.

Child, Julia, and Simone Beck. *Mastering the Art of French Cooking.* Vol 2. New York: Alfred A.Knopf, 1970.

Ettlinger, Steve. *The Kitchenware Book.* New York: Macmillan,1992.

Friberg, Bo. *The Professional Pastry Chef.* 2nd ed. New York: Van Nostrand Reinhold, 1990.

Greene, Janet, Ruth Hertzberg, and Beatrice Vaughan. *Putting Food By.* 4th ed. Lexington, MA: Stephen Greene Press, 1988.

Herbst, Sharon Tyler. *Food Lover's Companion.* Hauppauge, NY: Barron's Educational Series, 1990.

Hillman, Howard. *Kitchen Science.* Rev. ed. Boston: Houghton Mifflin, 1989.

Margen, Sheldon, M.D. and the editors of the University of California at Berkeley Wellness Letter. *The Wellness Encyclopedia of Food and Nutrition.* New York: Random House, Rebus, 1992.

McGee, Harold. *On Food and Cooking.* New York: Macmillan, Collier Books, 1984.

Ortiz, Elisabeth Lambert, ed. *The Encyclopedia of Herbs, Spices & Flavorings.* Boston: Dorling Kindersley, 1992.

Ubaldi, Jack and Elizabeth Crossman. *Jack Ubaldi's Meat Cook Book.* New York: Macmillan, 1987.

INDEX

TABLE OF EQUIVALENTS

The exact equivalents in the following tables have been rounded for convenience.

US/UK

oz = ounce
lb = pound
in = inch
ft = foot
tbl = tablespoon
fl oz = fluid ounce
qt = quart

Metric

g = gram
kg = kilogram
mm = millimeter
cm = centimeter
ml = milliliter
l = liter

Weights

US/UK	Metric
1 oz	30 g
2 oz	60 g
3 oz	90 g
4 oz (¼ lb)	125 g
5 oz (⅓ lb)	155 g
6 oz	185 g
7 oz	220 g
8 oz (½ lb)	250 g
10 oz	315 g
12 oz (¾ lb)	375 g
14 oz	440 g
16 oz (1 lb)	500 g
1½ lb	750 g
2 lb	1 kg
3 lb	1.5 kg

Oven Temperatures

Fahrenheit	Celsius	Gas
250	120	½
275	140	1
300	150	2
325	160	3
350	180	4
375	190	5
400	200	6
425	220	7
450	230	8
475	240	9
500	260	10

Liquids

US	Metric	UK
2 tbl	30 ml	1 fl oz
¼ cup	60 ml	2 fl oz
⅓ cup	80 ml	3 fl oz
½ cup	125 ml	4 fl oz
⅔ cup	160 ml	5 fl oz
¾ cup	180 ml	6 fl oz
1 cup	250 ml	8 fl oz
1½ cups	375 ml	12 fl oz
2 cups	500 ml	16 fl oz
4 cups/1 qt	1 l	32 fl oz

Length Measures

⅛ in	3 mm
¼ in	6 mm
½ in	12 mm
1 in	2.5 cm
2 in	5 cm
3 in	7.5 cm
4 in	10 cm
5 in	13 cm
6 in	15 cm
7 in	18 cm
8 in	20 cm
9 in	23 cm
10 in	25 cm
11 in	28 cm
12/1 ft	30 cm

All-Purpose (Plain) Flour / Dried Bread Crumbs / Chopped Nuts

¼ cup	1 oz	30 g
⅓ cup	1½ oz	45 g
½ cup	2 oz	60 g
¾ cup	3 oz	90 g
1 cup	4 oz	125 g
1½ cups	6 oz	185 g
2 cups	8 oz	250 g

Whole-Wheat (Wholemeal) Flour

3 tbl	1 oz	30 g
½ cup	2 oz	60 g
⅔ cup	3 oz	90 g
1 cup	4 oz	125 g
1¼ cups	5 oz	155 g
1⅔ cups	7 oz	210 g
1¾ cups	8 oz	250 g

Brown Sugar

¼ cup	1½ oz	45 g
½ cup	3 oz	90 g
¾ cup	4 oz	125 g
1 cup	5½ oz	170 g
1½ cups	8 oz	250 g
2 cups	10 oz	315 g

White Sugar

¼ cup	2 oz	60 g
⅓ cup	3 oz	90 g
½ cup	4 oz	125 g
¾ cup	6 oz	185 g
1 cup	8 oz	250 g
1½ cups	12 oz	375 g
2 cups	1 lb	500 g

Raisins/Currants/Semolina

¼ cup	1 oz	30 g
⅓ cup	2 oz	60 g
½ cup	3 oz	90 g
¾ cup	4 oz	125 g
1 cup	5 oz	155 g

Long-Grain Rice/Cornmeal

⅓ cup	2 oz	60 g
½ cup	2½ oz	75 g
¾ cup	4 oz	125 g
1 cup	5 oz	155 g
1½ cups	8 oz	250 g

Dried Beans

¼ cup	1½ oz	45 g
⅓ cup	2 oz	60 g
½ cup	3 oz	90 g
¾ cup	5 oz	155 g
1 cup	6 oz	185 g
1¼ cups	8 oz	250 g
1½ cups	12 oz	375 g

Rolled Oats

⅓ cup	1 oz	30 g
⅔ cup	2 oz	60 g
1 cup	3 oz	90 g
1½ cups	4 oz	125 g
2 cups	5 oz	155 g

Jam/Honey

2 tbl	2 oz	60 g
¼ cup	3 oz	90 g
½ cup	5 oz	155 g
¾ cup	8 oz	250 g
1 cup	11 oz	345 g

Grated Parmesan / Romano Cheese

¼ cup	1 oz	30 g
½ cup	2 oz	60 g
¾ cup	3 oz	90 g
1 cup	4 oz	125 g
1⅓ cups	5 oz	155 g
2 cups	7 oz	220 g